Computers and Ethics in the Cyberage

D. Micah Hester
Mercer University School of Medicine

Paul J. Ford
Vanderbilt University

Upper Saddle River, New Jersey 07458

Library of Congress Cataloging-in-Publication Data

Computers and ethics in the cyberage / [edited by] D. Micah Hester,
  Paul J. Ford.
      p.   cm.
    Includes bibliographical references.
    ISBN 0-13-082978-1 (paper)
    1. Computers—Moral and ethical aspects.   I. Hester, D. Micah.
  II. Ford, Paul J.
  QA76.9.M65 C66 2001
  175—dc21   00-021795

Editor in Chief: Charlyce Jones Owen
Acquisitions Editor: Ross Miller
Assistant Editor: Katie Janssen
Prepress and Manufacturing Buyer: Tricia Kenny
Production Director: Barbara Kittle
Production Liaison: Fran Russello
Editorial/Production Supervision and Interior Design: Joseph Barron/
  P. M. Gordon Associates, Inc
Cover Design: Bruce Kenselaar
Copy Editor: Barbara Willette

This book was set in 10/12 ITC Trump Medieval by Pub-Set, Inc.
and was printed and bound by RR Donnelley & Sons Company.
The cover was printed by Phoenix Color Corp.

© 2001 by Prentice-Hall, Inc.
A Division of Pearson Education
Upper Saddle River, New Jersey 07458

Printed in the United States of America
10 9 8 7 6 5 4 3 2 1

ISBN 0-13-082978-1

Pearson Education Limited (UK), *London*
Pearson Education Australia Pty. Ltd., *Sydney*
Prentice Hall Canada Ltd., *Toronto*
Pearson Educación de Mexico, S.A. de C.V.
Pearson Education Japan KK, *Tokyo*
Pearson Education China Ltd.
Pearson Education Asia Pte. Ltd., *Singapore*

CONTENTS

Preface

Our Current Landscape

Computer technologies permeate our everyday lives. Even the quickest, simplest survey of daily experience proves laden with digitally based instruments and information. We find World Wide Web addresses on our cereal boxes, ATMs, magazines, cleaning detergent bottles, and evening news programs. The "Y2K bug" was not a biological entity but a political and economic concern. Not only are "Nintendo" and "Sega" a part of our common vocabulary, they are rites of passage for today's children. An estimated 55 million Americans have access to the Internet, which provides an entrée into a vast array of information and entertainment. Computers even reach into our understanding of religion and what is sacred, as evidenced by a headline from *USA Today* that reads "Cyberfaith: Teenagers expect the Internet will substitute for their current churchgoing experiences in coming years."[1] Of course, this is only a very small sampling of how computers and computer-based technologies pervade and shape aspects of our daily lives and thoughts.

With this revolution, or shift in paradigm, a great deal of hyperbole and myth making arises from a variety of sources. People in commerce and industry try to show how their computer products are necessary for our existence, as demonstrated by the bombardment of advertising showing that computers bring order to people's businesses and lives. Politicians try to ride the wave of technophilia to get the popular vote. The military produces propaganda concerning the precision and effectiveness of computers in expensive defense projects. According to these and many other sources, computers are the penicillin for the problems of life, liberty, and society. Ideas about the magic of computer technologies have been integrated into, and further supported by, the modern *ethos* of our culture: "faster, better, stronger." Of course, in reality, these claims are much too optimistic and overstated.

On the other side of the debate we see cautionary tales presented by entertainment media, among others. In the same way that novels like Mary Shelley's *Frankenstein* articulated a nineteenth-century anxiety about new technologies, films like *Terminator, War Games, Brazil, The Net,* and *The Matrix* act as heralds of the danger of computer proliferation into important aspects of our lives. Backlash movements of neo-Luddites[2] have also arisen calling for a return to simpler times where experience felt less mediated by technological apparatuses.

But no matter the perspective, all sides agree that computer technologies mean power. Computer technologies create new abilities to be exercised. But with such power comes a need for reflective thought concerning the use of these technologies. This reflection ought to be done before implementation of the new technologies. As we are inundated with images and information about computers, we need to be attentive to the possible harms and goods that the integration of computer technologies brings. If we want to implement them in the best possible way, we need to guide the current love of technology in directions that will improve our daily lives, not just for today but for tomorrow as well. One way to do so is to recognize the hyperbole, the politics, and the basic desires expressed on both sides of the debate. Once we get by this hype, then we are better able to ask the important questions concerning the impacts and underlying values associated with these technologies.

Preliminaries About the Book: The Complexity of the Issues

No one textbook can have both the breadth and depth to cover exhaustively the challenges created by the microchip, cyberspace, and related technologies. For example, in this text references to computer technologies correspond not only to the box sitting on your desk (or the microchips therein) but also to the political organizations created through the implementation and development of electronic computing, the social processes that bring these artifacts into existence, and formerly unmanageable tasks computer technologies allow to be undertaken. It is important to take all of these elements into consideration when discussing the ethical impacts of computer technologies. The computer is not simply a bundle of plastic, metal, and silicon; rather, it is a technology that arises from, and is used in, a particular social context. For the study of this text, careful reflection is necessary when reading each essay in order to best decipher how "computer technologies" are understood, as well as the social-ethical values that are implicated therein.

Our desire is to help both teachers and students begin to understand and evaluate social and ethical issues that are raised by the use of computer technologies. We hope to have included a representative sampling of issues to demonstrate the gravity of our current and future situations. Furthermore, these concerns are not found just at the local or national level. *Global* concerns are critical in considering technological issues.

Like all textbooks, this anthology is a pedagogical device. As such, a word or two should be mentioned up front about its design and features so that it may be used by teachers and students effectively both in the classroom and out.

Organization I: What We Have Included

As you can see from the table of contents, the book is divided into four sections and a set of appendices. Each section is further divided into chapters consisting of essays from the disciplines of philosophy, sociology, psychology, computer science, journalism, politics, and literature. After an initial introduction by the editors, Section 1 acts as an introduction to the philosophy of technology and the realm of values occasioned by this age of technology—in particular computer technology—in which we find ourselves. Section 2 concerns the impact computers have on our quality of life and asks serious questions about our almost blind acceptance of computers as a good. Section 3 turns to more specific challenges the uses and abuses of these technologies bring about. Finally, Section 4 explores new and future possibilities for computer development as well as the ethical issues that need to be confronted before and as these new developments take hold.

To help explain the logic of each section's organizing principles, we have included a brief introductory statement for each section that maps out the flow of the section. Also, as an aid in understanding some basic features of each essay, we provide a paragraph introduction directly preceding each individual essay. Each section concludes with a selected bibliography of material related to the topics discussed in the section.

The appendices provide further reference and resource material. These resources include professional codes of ethics, institutional statements on ethical use, and a list of library, government, and Internet resources. Teachers and students are encouraged to use these resources to augment discussions of the issues that this book is attempting to bring to light.

Organization II: What We Have NOT Included

We have left out the customary introductory chapter on normative ethics (utilitarianism, deontology, virtues, natural law, etc.). Many fine, short, and accessible books exist that provide the necessary groundwork in ethical theory. Prentice Hall alone has published several solid books in this area, ranging from the most recent, *Basic Ethics* by Michael Boylan (2000), to the classic *Ethics* by William Frankena (1973). Knowing that many instructors prefer to use such ancillary texts, we believe that the space in this text is better utilized by core articles on computers and technology. (Of course, a few of the articles included do briefly discuss ethical theories—e.g., those of Nissenbaum in Chapter 8.)

Also within these pages you will not find study questions for any essay, chapter, or section. Aside from the brief introductory material discussed above, it is not our intention to lead teachers and students by the hand through these issues. This would both stifle creative, intelligent thinking by the student and unnecessarily direct instructors. Our approach encourages the instructor to use the essays as he or she sees fit.

How to Reorganize the Volume

Having said this, though, it may be of some benefit to point out that issues raised by these essays often cross the artificial organization boundaries of chapters and sections we have established. An article in the chapter on computer professionals, for example, may relate well, directly or indirectly, to articles on hacking, value-laden technologies, or networking. This being the case, we would like to point to some related articles that are not grouped together under our organizational schematic. We hope this cross-referencing demonstrates flexibility in the use of the essays.

Here are a few suggestions, though hardly exhaustive, on how instructors might create a section of greater depth concerning several of the prominent themes running through this book:

Topic: International Perspectives on Computers

CONTENT: Articles written by individuals outside of the United States or articles explicitly written about global concerns

ESSAYS TO USE:

- All essays in Chapter 5—Computers in Developing Nations
- "Privacy, Respect for Persons, and Rick" in Chapter 7
- "The Morality of Software Piracy: A Cross-Cultural Analysis" in Chapter 8
- "*Baku:* EPICAC XIV" in Chapter 10
- "Effects of Participating in Virtual Environments" in Chapter 11

Topic: Professional/Research Concerns

CONTENT: Articles particularly relevant for students involved in the development and research of computer programs and hardware

ESSAYS TO USE:

- All essays in Chapter 6—Computer Professionals and the Professional Use of Computers
- "Computers and Reason" in Chapter 2
- "Implantable Brain Chips? Time for Debate" in Chapter 4

- "The Ethical Dilemma Caused by the Transfer of Information Technology to Developing Nations" in Chapter 5
- "Hacking and Viruses" in Chapter 9
- "Some Aspects of Ethics and Research into the Silicon Brain" in Chapter 10
- "Effects of Participating in Virtual Environments" in Chapter 11
- "The Virtual Sky Is Not the Virtual Limit: Ethics in Virtual Reality" in Chapter 11

Topic: Internet/Cyberspace

CONTENT: Articles relating to networked environments and virtual realities

ESSAYS TO USE:

- All essays in Chapter 11—Virtual Environments
- All essays in Chapter 12—Networking and the Internet
- "The Virtual Community" in Chapter 3
- "Is There a There in Cyberspace?" in Chapter 3
- "Cool Runnings: The Contradictions of Cybereality in Jamaica" in Chapter 5
- "Electronic Power to the People: Who Is Technology's Keeper on the Cyberspace Frontier?" in Chapter 7

Here are some other suggestions for supplementing existing chapters with essays from other parts of the book:

Chapter 2—Computer Technologies as Value-Laden.
Supplement with:
- "The State, Computers, and African Development: The Information Non-Revolution" in Chapter 5

Chapter 4—Alienation, Anonymity, and Embodiment.
Supplement with:
- "Assimilation of the Machine: New Cultural Values" in Chapter 1
- "The Virtual Community" in Chapter 3
- "A Rape in Cyberspace" in Chapter 12
- "Losing Our Souls in Cyberspace" in Chapter 12

Chapter 7—Freedom, Privacy and Control in an Information Age.
Supplement with:
- "On Space, Sex, and Being Stalked" in Chapter 12

- "The State, Computers, and African Development: The Information Non-Revolution" in Chapter 5

Chapter 10—Artificial Intelligence.
Supplement with:

- "Implantable Brain Chips? Time for Debate" in Chapter 4
- "EPICAC" in Chapter 4

Acknowledgments

As is true of any project of this size, we could not have done this alone. Therefore, we must take a moment to express our gratitude to the following individuals. Our strongest support came from the former editor for philosophy texts at Prentice Hall, Karita France. She promoted this anthology as part of Prentice Hall's already well-supplied catalog in computer ethics. Her assistant, Jennifer Ackerman, and marketing director Ilse Wolf have been of great help. Further, we would be remiss if we did not thank the anonymous reviewers for their comments on our proposal and initial table of contents, and copy editor Barbara Willette for painstakingly going over the entire text with her sharp red pencil and even sharper eye.

We were also fortunate to belong to a graduate department of philosophy that was supportive in these proceedings. In particular, Professors John Lachs, Michael Hodges, and Richard Zaner encouraged much of our work on this project. And department secretaries Stella Thompson and Judy Thompson both have aided us at times with the frustrating work of copying, mailing, and distributing information.

A special nod goes to Professor John J. McDermott of Texas A&M for his ready participation. John and his wife Patricia (a quite capable philosopher in her own right) sat down with us to discuss issues in computer use and the quality of life that computers create for us. Their insights helped to stimulate much discussion between us, and John's follow-up notes and calls displayed his ever warm and supportive attitude toward this project.

Finally, our friends and family deserve the most praise from us. In particular, Micah would like to thank Robert Talisse and Tom Burke, who have taken up slack on other projects also in full swing to which he has not given attention. He would also very much like to thank and give love to his wife Kelly and daughter Emily. Paul would like to pass on his love and thanks to his parents Gwen and Gary Ford for their continued support and encouragement as well as their supplying the opportunity for Paul to develop practical computer experience in their small business. Also critical in providing support and good mental health were Laura McMullen, Tim Ford, and Jenny Ford.

We dedicate this volume to those who made computers and technology interesting in their social contexts: for Micah, Professors James D. Hester, David B. Bragg, Larry Harvill, and the late Harry Mullikin; for Paul, Professors Anthony Aaby, Jim Klein, and Larry Hickman and especially Mr. Heath Spangler.

Notes

1. *USA Today*, May 14:1998, 1D.
2. Cf. Bill Henderson (ed.), *Minutes of the Lead Pencil Club* (Pushcart, 1996); and J. Brook, I. Boal (eds.), *Resisting the Virtual Life: The Culture and Politics of Information* (City Light Books, 1995); among others.

Technology, Computers, and Values

We clearly live in an "age of technology." So much of our culture depends not just on human activity and craft but on machinery and microchips. Surely, it is not wholly impossible to live without cars, conveyor belts, and (of course) computers, but face it—we do not want to do so. As a matter of fact, those few people who attempt to live without such things are often indirectly influenced by the existence of these human-designed apparatuses, since not only the economy but also the natural environment are directly affected by different forms of technology. Even Henry David Thoreau and the Unabomber employed degrees of technology. It behooves us, therefore, not only to talk about the narrower field of computer technologies but also to step back to larger questions concerning philosophy and ethics related to technology in general.

A number of fundamental questions need to be addressed. How is "technology" to be defined, and what status should be, or is it, given? Is technology only a grouping of objects for human use—that is, "value neutral"—such that any questions concerning the ethics of technology are, at best, misguided? Or instead, are there benefits and dangers inherent in technology itself—that is, is technology "value-laden"? Of course, if technology is value-laden, then questions concerning which values it portrays and enforces become extremely important. In other words, to what extent do value-laden technologies reinforce or modify our cultural values? What benefits do they supply, and why do we see them as benefits? What, if any, dangers also arise from the implementation of these technologies?

The articles in Section 1 suggest that we not take technology for granted but, instead, begin the process of questioning technology and computers in both their positive and negative contributions to society. Several of the authors also approach answers to questions about the social and ethical nature of computers by arguing that computers and computer design are in fact richly value-laden characteristics.

In particular, the first three selections in Chapter 1 survey a variety of opinions about the character and value of technology. While reading these pieces, carefully consider where computer technologies fall within these critiques. Is computer technology fundamentally a different kind of technology such that no general view of technology captures the essence of the issues at play? Or are there important similarities among all human technologies that can be addressed, at least generally, by a single critique? In particular, the last selection (Maner) in Chapter 1 answers this question by arguing that, in fact, computers do raise some unique ethical issues that should be addressed by a unique discipline called computer ethics (a discipline that this textbook both arises from and hopes to contribute to).

Chapter 2 carries the discussion further by showing that computers are value-laden not just in their implementation but also in their design and use of logic. Computers affect how we see the world and how we interact with one another. For some, this is something about which to be cautious and reticent (e.g., Roszak and Heim), while others take this as demonstrating great beneficial potential (e.g., Dertouzos and Newell). These articles give a foundation for understanding the types of important issues that are addressed throughout this volume under the rubric of "computer ethics."

CHAPTER ONE
From Ethics of Technology to Ethics of Computers

ASSIMILATION OF THE MACHINE: NEW CULTURAL VALUES

Lewis Mumford

In this selection, Lewis Mumford (a mid-twentieth century cultural critic, historian, and philosopher) explains that the shift from handicraft and manually manipulated tools to automated machinery was itself a shift in cultural values. He argues that because of the seeming "independence" of machines from human activity, it is easy to be fooled into thinking that machines are themselves nothing but the items or ends they produce. However, this is misleading, since it is the very methods and logic demanded by the machine—that is, the means that the machine enacts—that are themselves valuable and are in part responsible for changing our very desires. Ultimately, though, without human intelligence machines will not improve human experience.

The tools and utensils used during the greater part of man's history were, in the main, extensions of his own organism: they did not have—what is more important they did not *seem* to have—an independent existence. But though they were an intimate part of the worker, they reacted upon his capacities, sharpening his eye, refining his skill, teaching him to respect the nature of the material with which he was dealing. The tool brought man into closer harmony with his environment, not merely because it enabled him to re-shape it, but because it made him recognize the

Excerpt from "Assimilation of the Machine" in *Technics and Civilization* by Lewis Mumford, copyright 1934 by Harcourt, Inc. and renewed 1961 by Lewis Mumford, reprinted by permission of the publisher.

limits of his capacities. In dream, he was all powerful: in reality he had to recognize the weight of stone and cut stones no bigger than he could transport. In the book of wisdom the carpenter, the smith, the potter, the peasant wrote, if they did not sign, their several pages. And in this sense, technics has been, in every age, a constant instrument of discipline and education. A surviving primitive might, here and there, vent his anger on a cart that got stuck in the mud by breaking up its wheels, in the same fashion that he would beat a donkey that refused to move: but the mass of mankind learned, at least during the period of the written record, that certain parts of the environment can neither be intimidated nor cajoled. To control them, one must learn the laws of their behavior, instead of petulantly imposing one's own wishes. Thus the lore and tradition of technics, however empirical, tended to create the picture of an objective reality. Something of this fact remained in the Victorian definition of science as "organized common sense."

Because of their independent source of power, and their semiautomatic operation even in their cruder forms, machines have seemed to have a reality and an independent existence apart from the user. Whereas the educational values of handicraft were mainly in the process, those of the machine were largely in the preparatory design: hence the process itself was understood only by the machinists and technicians responsible for the design and operation of the actual machinery. As production became more mechanized and the discipline of the factory became more impersonal and the work itself became less rewarding, apart from such slight opportunities for social intercourse as it furthered, attention was centered more and more upon the product: people valued the machine for its external achievements, for the number of yards of cloth it wove, for the number of miles it carried them. The machine thus appeared purely as an external instrument for the conquest of the environment: the actual forms of the products, the actual collaboration and intelligence manifested in creating them, the educational possibilities of this impersonal cooperation itself—all these elements were neglected. We assimilated the objects rather than the spirit that produced them, and so far from respecting that spirit, we again and again attempted to make the objects themselves seem to be something other than a product of the machine. We did not expect beauty through the machine any more than we expected a higher standard of morality from the laboratory: yet the fact remains that if we seek an authentic sample of a new esthetic or a higher ethic during the nineteenth century it is in technics and science that we will perhaps most easily find them.

The practical men themselves were the very persons who stood in the way of our recognizing that the significance of the machine was not limited to its practical achievements. For, on the terms that the inventors and industrialists considered the machine, it did not carry over from the factory and the marketplace into any other department of human life, except as a means. The possibility that technics had become a creative force, carried on by its own momentum, that it was rapidly ordering a new kind of environment and was producing a third estate midway between nature and the humane arts, that it was not merely a quicker way of achieving old ends but an effective way of expressing new ends—the possibility in short that the machine furthered a new mode of *living* was far from the minds of those who actively promoted it. The industrialists and engineers themselves did not believe in the qualitative and cultural aspects of the machine. In their indifference to these aspects, they were just as far from appreciating the nature of the machine as were the Romantics: only what the Romantics, judging the machine from the standpoint of life, regarded as a defect the utilitarian boasted of as a virtue: for the latter the absence of art was an assurance of practicality.

If the machine had really lacked cultural values, the Romantics would have been right, and their desire to seek these values, if need be, in a dead past would have been justified by the very desperateness of the case. But the interests in the factual and the practical, which the industrialist made the sole key to intelligence, were only two in a whole series of new values that had been called into existence by the development of the new technics. Matters of fact and practice had usually in previous civilizations been treated with snobbish contempt by the leisured classes: as if the logical ordering of propositions were any nobler a technical feat than the articulation of machines. The interest in the practical was symptomatic of that wider and more intelligible world in which people had begun to live, a world in which the taboos of class and caste could no longer be considered as definitive in dealing with events and experiences. Capitalism and technics had both acted as a solvent of these clots of prejudice and intellectual confusion; and they were thus at first important liberators of life.

From the beginning, indeed, the most durable conquests of the machine lay not in the instruments themselves, which quickly became outmoded, nor in the goods produced, which quickly were consumed, but in the modes of life made possible via the machine and in the machine: the cranky mechanical slave was also a pedagogue. While the machine increased the servitude of servile personalities, it also promised the further liberation of released personalities: it challenged thought and effort as no previous system of technics had done. No part of the environment, no social conventions, could be taken for granted, once the machine had shown how far order and system and intelligence might prevail over the raw nature of things.

What remains as the permanent contribution of the machine, carried over from one generation to another, is the technique of cooperative thought and action it has fostered, the esthetic excellence of the machine forms, the delicate logic of materials and forces, which has added a new canon—the machine canon—to the arts: above all, perhaps, the more objective personality that has come into existence through a more sensitive and understanding intercourse with these new social instruments and through their deliberate cultural assimilation. *In projecting one side of the human personality into the concrete forms of the machine, we have created an independent environment that has reacted upon every other side of the personality.*

In the past, the irrational and demonic aspects of life had invaded spheres where they did not belong. It was a step in advance to discover that bacteria, not brownies, were responsible for curdling milk, and that an air-cooled motor was more effective than a witch's broomstick for rapid long distance transportation. This triumph of order was pervasive: it gave a confidence to human purposes akin to that which a well-drilled regiment has when it marches in step. Creating the illusion of invincibility, the machine actually added to the amount of power man can exercise. Science and technics stiffened our morale: by their very austerities and abnegations they enhanced the value of the human personality that submitted to their discipline: they cast contempt on childish fears, childish guesses, equally childish assertions. By means of the machine man gave a concrete and external and impersonal form to his desire for order: and in a subtle way he thus set a new standard for his personal life and his more organic attitudes. Unless he was better than the machine he would only find himself reduced to its level: dumb, servile, abject, a creature of immediate reflexes and passive unselective responses.

While many of the boasted achievements of industrialism are merely rubbish, and while many of the goods produced by the machine are fraudulent and evanescent, its esthetic, its logic, and its factual technique remain a durable contribution: they are among man's supreme conquests. The practical results may be admirable or dubious: but the method that underlies them has a permanent importance to the race, apart from its immediate consequences. For the machine has added a whole series of arts to those produced by simple tools and handicraft methods and it has added a new realm to the environment in which the cultured man works and feels and thinks. Similarly, it has extended the power and range of human organs and has disclosed new esthetic spectacles, new worlds. The exact arts produced with the aid of the machine have their proper standards and give their own peculiar satisfactions to the human spirit. Differing in technique from the arts of the past, they spring nevertheless from the same source: for the machine itself, I must stress for the tenth time, is a human product, and its very abstractions make it more definitely human in one sense than those humane arts which on occasion realistically counterfeit nature.

Here, beyond what appears at the moment of realization, is the vital contribution of the machine. What matters the fact that the ordinary workman has the equivalent of 240 slaves to help him, if the master himself remains an imbecile, devouring the spurious news, the false suggestions, the intellectual prejudices that play upon him in the press and the school, giving vent in turn to tribal assertions and primitive lusts under the impression that he is the final token of progress and civilization. One does not make a child powerful by placing a stick of dynamite in his hands: one only adds to the dangers of his irresponsibility. Were mankind to remain children, they would exercise more effective power by being reduced to using a lump of clay and an old-fashioned modelling tool. But if the machine is one of the aids man has created toward achieving further intellectual growth and attaining maturity, if he treats this powerful automaton of his as a challenge to his own development, if the exact arts fostered by the machine have their own contribution to make to the mind, and are aids in the orderly crystallization of experience, then these contributions are vital ones indeed. The machine, which reached such overwhelming dimensions in Western Civilization partly because it sprang out of a disrupted and one-sided culture, nevertheless may help in enlarging the provinces of culture itself and thereby in building a greater synthesis: in that case, it will carry an antidote to its own poison.

VIEWS OF TECHNOLOGY

Ian Barbour

Ian Barbour, as part of his presentation of the famous "Gifford Lectures in Natural Religion," surveys three general views of technology: Technology as Liberator, Technology as Threat, and Technology as Instrument of Power. Technology as Liberator is an optimistic view of the benefits that technology brings to human existence. The pessimistic turn is presented as the view Technology as Threat, in which technology is seen as detrimental to valuable human relations. Technology as Instrument of Power treats technology as either potentially oppressive in the hands of those in power or potentially liberating in the hands of those without power. Each of these views depends on accepting one of three types of causal relationships between science, technology, and society.

Technology, the source of the problem, will once again prove to contain within itself the germs of a solution compatible with the betterment of man's lot and dignity.

Charles Susskind[1]

Our enslavement to the machine has never been more complete.

John Zerman and Alice Carnes[2]

What we call Man's power over Nature turns out to be a power exercised by some men over other men with Nature as its instrument.

C. S. Lewis[3]

Appraisals of modern technology diverge widely. Some see it as the beneficent source of higher living standards, improved health, and better communications. They claim that any problems created by technology are themselves amenable to technological solutions. Others are critical of technology, holding that it leads to alienation from nature, environmental destruction, the mechanization of human life, and the loss of human freedom. A third group asserts that technology is ambiguous, its impacts varying according to the social context in which it is designed and used, because it is both a product and a source of economic and political power.[4]

. . . Views of technology are grouped under three headings: Technology as Liberator, Technology as Threat, and Technology as Instrument of Power. In each case the underlying assumptions and value judgments are examined. I will indicate why I agree with the third of these positions, which emphasizes the social construction and use of particular technologies. The issues cut across disciplines; I draw from the writings of engineers, historians, sociologists, political scientists, philosophers, and theologians. . . .

Technology may be defined as *the application of organized knowledge to practical tasks by ordered systems of people and machines.*[5] There are several advantages to such a broad definition. "Organized knowledge" allows us to include technologies based on practical experience and invention as well as those based on scientific theories. The "practical tasks" can include both the production of material goods (in industry and agriculture, for instance) and the provision of services (by computers, communications media, and biotechnologies, among others). Reference to "ordered systems of people and machines" directs attention to social institutions as well as to the hardware of technology. The breadth of the definition also reminds us that there are major differences among technologies.

I. Technology as Liberator

Throughout modern history, technological developments have been enthusiastically welcomed because of their potential for liberating us from hunger, disease, and poverty. Technology has been celebrated as the source of material progress and human fulfillment.

1. THE BENEFITS OF TECHNOLOGY

Defenders of technology point out that four kinds of benefits can be distinguished if one looks at its recent history and considers its future:

1. *Higher Living Standards.* New drugs, better medical attention, and improved sanitation and nutrition have more than doubled the average life span in industrial nations within the past century. Machines have released us from much of the backbreaking labor that in previous ages absorbed most of people's time and energy. Material progress represents liberation from the tyranny of nature. The ancient dream of a life free from famine and disease is beginning to be realized through technology. The standard of living of low-income families in industrial societies has doubled in a generation, even though relative incomes have changed little. Many people in developing nations now look on technology as their principal source of hope. Productivity and economic growth, it is said, benefit everyone in the long run.

2. *Opportunity for Choice.* Individual choice has a wider scope today than ever before because technology has produced new options not previously available and a greater range of products and services. Social and geographical mobility allow a greater choice of jobs and locations. In an urban industrial society, a person's options are not as limited by parental or community expectations as they were in a small-town agrarian society. The dynamism of technology can liberate people from static and confining traditions to assume responsibility for their own lives. Birth control techniques, for example, allow a couple to choose the size and timing of their family. Power over nature gives greater opportunity for the exercise of human freedom.[6]

3. *More Leisure.* Increases in productivity have led to shorter working hours. Computers and automation hold the promise of eliminating much of the monotonous work typical of earlier industrialism. Through most of history, leisure and cultural pursuits have been the privilege of the few, while the mass of humanity was preoccupied with survival. In an affluent society there is time for continuing education, the arts, social service, sports, and participation in community life. Technology can contribute to the enrichment of human life and the flowering of creativity.

Laborsaving devices free us to do what machines cannot do. Proponents of this viewpoint say that people can move beyond materialism when their material needs are met.

4. *Improved Communications.* With new forms of transportation, one can in a few hours travel to distant cities that once took months to reach. With electronic technologies (radio, television, computer networks, and so on), the speed, range, and scope of communication have vastly increased. The combination of visual image and auditory message have an immediacy not found in the linear sequence of the printed word. These new media offer the possibility of instant worldwide communication, greater interaction, understanding, and mutual appreciation in the "global village." It has been suggested that by dialing coded numbers on telephones hooked into computer networks, citizens could participate in an instant referendum on political issues. According to its defenders, technology brings psychological and social benefits as well as material progress.

. . . In agriculture, some experts anticipate that the continuing Green Revolution and the genetic engineering of new crops will provide adequate food for a growing world population. In the case of energy, it is claimed that breeder reactors and fusion will provide environmentally benign power to replace fossil fuels. Computer enthusiasts anticipate the Information Age in which industry is automated and communications networks enhance commercial, professional, and personal life. Biotechnology promises the eradication of genetic diseases, the improvement of health, and the deliberate design of new species—even the modification of humanity itself. . . .

2. OPTIMISTIC VIEWS OF TECHNOLOGY

Let us look at some authors who have expressed optimism regarding technology. Melvin Kranzberg, a prominent historian of technology, has presented a very positive picture of the technological past and future. He argues that urban industrial societies offer *more freedom* than rural ones and provide greater choice of occupations, friends, activities, and life-styles. The work week has been cut in half, and human wants have been dramatically fulfilled.[7] Emanuel Mesthene, former director of the Harvard Program in Technology and Society, grants that every technology brings risks as well as benefits, but he says that our task is the rational management of risk. Some technologies poison the environment, but others reduce pollution. A new technology may displace some workers but it also creates new jobs. Nineteenth-century factories and twentieth-century assembly lines did involve dirty and monotonous work, but the newer technologies allow greater creativity and individuality.[8]

A *postindustrial society,* it is said, is already beginning to emerge. In this new society, according to the sociologist Daniel Bell, power will be based on knowledge rather than property. The dominant class will be scientists, engineers, and technical experts; the dominant institutions will be intellectual ones (universities, industrial laboratories, and research institutes). The economy will be devoted mainly to services rather than material goods. Decisions will be made on rational-technical grounds, marking "the end of ideology." There will be a general consensus on social values; experts will coordinate social planning, using rational techniques such as decision theory and systems analysis. This will be a future-oriented society, the age of the professional managers, the technocrats.[9] A bright picture of the coming technological society has been given by many "futurists," including Buckminster Fuller, Herman Kahn, and Alvin Toffler.[10]

Samuel Florman is an articulate engineer and author who has written extensively *defending technology* against its detractors. He insists that the critics have romanticized the life of earlier centuries and rural societies. Living standards were actually very low, work was brutal, and roles were rigidly defined. People have much greater freedom in technological societies. The automobile, for example, enables people to do what they want and enhances geographical and class mobility. People move to cities because they prefer life there to "the tedium and squalor of the countryside." Florman says that worker alienation in industry is rare, and many people prefer the comfortable monotony of routine tasks to the pressures of decision and accountability. Technology is not an independent force out of control; it is the product of human choice, a response to public demand expressed through the marketplace.[11]

Florman grants that technology often has undesirable side effects, but he says that these are amenable to *technological solutions.* One of his heroes is Benjamin Franklin, who "proposed technological ways of coping with the unpleasant consequences of technology."[12] Florman holds that environmental and health risks are inherent in every technical advance. Any product or process can be made safer, but always at an economic cost. Economic growth and lower prices for consumers are often more important than additional safety, and absolute safety is an illusory goal. Large-scale systems are usually more efficient than small-scale ones. It is often easier to find a "technical fix" for a social problem than to try to change human behavior or get agreement on political policies.[13]

Florman urges us to rely on *the judgment of experts* in decisions about technology. He says that no citizen can be adequately informed about complex technical questions such as acid rain or radioactive waste disposal. Public discussion of these issues only leads to anxiety and erratic political actions. We should rely on the recommendations of experts on such matters.[14] Florman extols the "unquenchable spirit" and "irrepressible human will" evident in technology:

For all our apprehensions, we have no choice but to press ahead. We must do so, first, in the name of compassion. By turning our backs on technological change, we would be expressing our satisfaction with current world levels of hunger, disease, and privation. Further, we must press ahead in the name of the human adventure. Without experimentation and change our existence would be a dull business. We simply cannot stop while there are masses to feed and diseases to conquer, seas to explore and heavens to survey.[15]

Some theologians have also given very positive appraisals of technology. They see it as a source not only of higher living standards but also of *greater freedom and creative expression.* In his earlier writings, Harvey Cox held that freedom to master and shape the world through technology liberates us from the confines of tradition. Christianity brought about the desacralization of nature and allowed it to be controlled and used for human welfare.[16] Norris Clarke sees technology as an instrument of human fulfillment and self-expression in the use of our God-given intelligence to transform the world. Liberation from bondage to nature, he says, is the victory of spirit over matter. As cocreators with God we can celebrate the contribution of reason to the enrichment of human life.[17] Other theologians have affirmed technology as an instrument of love and compassion in relieving human suffering—a modern response to the biblical command to feed the hungry and help the neighbor in need.

The Jesuit paleontologist Pierre Teilhard de Chardin, writing in the early years of nuclear power, computers, and molecular biology, expressed *a hopeful vision of the technological future.* He envisioned computers and electronic communication in a network of interconnected consciousness, a global layer of thought that he called "the noosphere." He defended eugenics, "artificial neo-life," and the remodeling of the human organism by manipulation of the genes. With this new power over heredity, he said, we can replace the crude forces of natural selection and "seize the tiller" to control the direction of future evolution. We will have total power over matter, "reconstructing the very stuff of the universe." He looked to a day of interplanetary travel and the unification of our own planet, based on intellectual and cultural interaction.[18]

Here was an inspiring vision of a planetary future in which *technology and spiritual development* would be linked together. Teilhard affirmed the value of secular life in the world and the importance of human efforts in "building the earth" as we cooperate in the creative work of God. Technology is participation in divine creativity. He rejected any note of despair, which would cut the nerve of constructive action. At times he seemed to have unlimited confidence in humanity's capacity to shape its own destiny. But his confidence really lay in the unity, convergence, and ascent of the cosmic process of which humanity and technology are manifestations. The ultimate source of that unity and ascent is God as known in the Christ whose role is cosmic. For Teilhard, eschatological hope looks not to an intervention discontinuous from history, but to the fulfillment of a continuing process to which our own actions contribute.

Teilhard's writings present us with a magnificent sweep of time from past to future. But they do not consider the institutional structures of economic power and self-interest that now control the directions of technological development. Teilhard seldom acknowledged the tragic hold of social injustice on human life. He was writing before the destructive environmental impacts of technology were evident. When Teilhard looked to the past, he portrayed humanity as an integral part of the natural world, interdependent with other creatures. But when he looked to the future, he expected that because of our technology and our spirituality we will be increasingly separated from other creatures. Humanity will move beyond dependence on the organic world. Though he was ultimately theocentric (centered on God), and he talked about the redemption of the whole cosmos, many of his images are anthropocentric (centered on humanity) and imply that other forms of life are left behind in the spiritualization of humankind that technology will help to bring about.

3. A REPLY TO THE OPTIMISTS

. . . First, the *environmental costs and human risks* of technology are dismissed too rapidly. The optimists are confident that technical solutions can be found for environmental problems. Of course, pollution abatement technologies can treat many of the effluents of industry, but often unexpected, indirect, or delayed consequences occur. The effects of carcinogens may not show up for twenty-five years or more. The increased death rates among shipyard workers exposed to asbestos in the early 1940s were not evident until the late 1960s. Toxic wastes may contaminate groundwater decades after they have been buried. The hole in the ozone layer caused by the release of chlorofluorocarbons had not been anticipated by any scientists. Above all, soil erosion and massive deforestation threaten the biological resources essential for human life, and global warming from our use of fossil fuels threatens devastating changes in world climates.

Second, environmental destruction is symptomatic of a deeper problem: *alienation from nature.* The idea of human domination of nature has many roots. Western religious traditions have often drawn a sharp line between humanity and other creatures . . . Economic institutions treat nature as a resource for human exploitation. But technological enthusiasts contribute to this devaluation of the natural world if they view it as an object to be controlled and manipulated. Many engineers are trained in the physical sciences and interpret living things in mechanistic rather than ecological terms. Others spend their entire professional lives in the technosphere of artifacts, machines, electronics, and computers, cut off from the world of nature. To be sure, sensitivity to nature is sometimes found among technological optimists, but it is more frequently found among the critics of technology.

Third, technology has contributed to *the concentration of economic and political power.* Only relatively affluent groups or nations can afford the latest technology; the gaps between rich and poor have been perpetuated and in many cases increased by technological developments. In a world of limited resources, it also appears impossible for all nations to sustain the standards of living of industrial nations today, much less the higher standards that industrial nations expect in the future. Affluent nations use a grossly disproportionate share of the world's energy and resources. Commitment to justice within nations also requires a more serious analysis of the distribution of the costs and benefits of technology. We will find many technologies in which one group enjoys the benefits while another group is exposed to the risks and social costs.

Fourth, *large-scale technologies* typical of industrial nations today are particularly problematic. They are capital-intensive rather than labor-intensive, and they add to unemployment in many parts of the world. Large-scale systems tend to be vulnerable to error, accident, or sabotage. The near catastrophe at the Three Mile Island nuclear plant in 1979 and the Chernobyl disaster in 1986 were the products of human errors, faulty equipment, poor design, and unreliable safety procedures. Nuclear energy is a prime example of a vulnerable, centralized, capital-intensive technology. Systems in which human or mechanical failures can be disastrous are risky even in a stable society, quite apart from additional risks under conditions of social unrest. The large scale of many current systems is as much the product of government subsidies, tax and credit policies, and particular corporate interests as of any inherent economies of scale.

Fifth, greater *dependence on experts* for policy decisions would not be desirable. The technocrats claim that their judgments are value free; the technical elite is supposedly nonpolitical. But those with power seldom use it rationally and objectively when their own interests are at stake. When social planners think they are deciding for the good of all—whether in the French or Russian revolutions or in the proposed technocracy of the future—the assumed innocence of moral intentions is likely to be corrupted in practice. Social controls over the controllers are always essential. . . .

Lastly, we must question the linear view of the *science-technology-society relationship,* which is assumed by many proponents of optimistic views. Technology is taken to be applied science, and it is thought to have an essentially one-way impact on society. The official slogan of the Century of Progress exposition in Chicago in 1933 was: "Science Finds—Industry Applies—Man Conforms." This has been called "the assembly-line view" because it pictures science at the start of the line and a stream of technological products pouring off the end of the line.[19] If technology is fundamentally benign, there is no need for government interference except to regulate the most serious risks. Whatever guidance is needed for technological development is supplied by the expression of consumer preferences through the marketplace. In this view, technologies develop from the "push" of science and the "pull" of economic profits.

I accept the basic framework of private ownership in a *free market economy*, but I believe it has severe limitations that require correction through political processes. When wealth is distributed unevenly, the luxuries of a few people carry much more weight in the marketplace than the basic needs of many others. Many of the social and environmental costs of industrial processes are not included in market prices. Because long-term consequences are discounted at the current interest rate, they are virtually ignored in economic decisions. Our evaluation of technology, in short, must encompass questions of justice, participation, environmental protection, and long-term sustainability, as well as short-term economic efficiency.

II. Technology as Threat

At the opposite extreme are the critics of modern technology who see it as a threat to authentic human life. We will confine ourselves here to criticisms of the human rather than environmental consequences of technology.

1. THE HUMAN COSTS OF TECHNOLOGY

Five characteristics of industrial technology seem to its critics particularly inimical to human fulfillment.[20]

1. *Uniformity in a Mass Society.* Mass production yields standardized products, and mass media tend to produce a uniform national culture. Individuality is lost and local or regional differences are obliterated in the homogeneity of industrialization. Nonconformity hinders efficiency, so cooperative and docile workers are rewarded. Even the interactions among people are mechanized and objectified. Human identity is defined by roles in organizations. Conformity to a mass society jeopardizes spontaneity and freedom. According to the critics, there is little evidence that an electronic, computerized, automated society will produce more diversity than earlier industrialism did.

2. *Narrow Criteria of Efficiency.* Technology leads to rational and efficient organization, which requires fragmentation, specialization, speed, the maximization of output. The criterion is efficiency in achieving a single goal or a narrow range of objectives; side effects and human costs are ignored. Quantitative criteria tend to crowd out qualitative ones. The

worker becomes the servant of the machine, adjusting to its schedule and tempo, adapting to its requirements. Meaningful work roles exist for only a small number of people in industrial societies today. Advertising creates demand for new products, whether or not they fill real needs, in order to stimulate a larger volume of production and a consumer society.

3. *Impersonality and Manipulation.* Relationships in a technological society are specialized and functional. Genuine community and interpersonal interaction are threatened when people feel like cogs in a well-oiled machine. In a bureaucracy, the goals of the organization are paramount and responsibility is diffused, so that no one feels personally responsible. Moreover, technology has created subtle ways of manipulating people and new techniques of electronic surveillance and psychological conditioning. When the technological mentality is dominant, people are viewed and treated like objects.

4. *Uncontrollability.* Separate technologies form an interlocking system, a total, mutually reinforcing network that seems to lead a life of its own. "Runaway technology" is said to be like a vehicle out of control, with a momentum that cannot be stopped. Some critics assert that technology is not just a set of adaptable tools for human use but an all-encompassing form of life, a pervasive structure with its own logic and dynamic. Its consequences are unintended and unforeseeable. Like the sorcerer's apprentice who found the magic formula to make his broom carry water but did not know how to make it stop, we have set in motion forces that we cannot control. The individual feels powerless facing a monolithic system.

5. *Alienation of the Worker.* The worker's alienation was a central theme in the writing of Karl Marx. Under capitalism, he said, workers do not own their own tools or machines, and they are powerless in their work life. They can sell their labor as a commodity, but their work is not a meaningful form of self-expression. Marx held that such alienation is a product of capitalist ownership and would disappear under state ownership. He was optimistic about the use of technology in a communist economic order, and thus he belongs with the third group below, the contextualists, but his idea of alienation has influenced the pessimists.

More recent writers point out that *alienation* has been common in state-managed industrial economies too and seems to be a product of the division of labor, rationalization of production, and hierarchical management in large organizations, regardless of the economic system. Studs Terkel and others have found in interviews that resentment, frustration, and a sense of powerlessness are widespread among American industrial workers. This contrasts strongly with the greater work autonomy, job satisfaction, and commitment to work found in the professions, skilled trades, and family-owned farms.[21]

Other features of technological development since World War II have evoked widespread concern. The allocation of more than two-thirds of the

U.S. federal research and development budget to military purposes has diverted expertise from environmental problems and urgent human needs. Technology also seems to have contributed to the impoverishment of human relationships and a loss of community. The youth counterculture of the 1970s was critical of technology and sought harmony with nature, intensity of personal experience, supportive communities, and alternative life-styles apart from the prevailing industrial order. While many of its expressions were short-lived, many of its characteristic attitudes, including disillusionment with technology, have persisted among some of the younger generation.[22]

2. RECENT CRITICS OF TECHNOLOGY

To the French philosopher and social critic Jacques Ellul, technology is *an autonomous and uncontrollable force* that dehumanizes all that it touches. The enemy is "technique"—a broad term Ellul uses to refer to the technological mentality and structure that he sees pervading not only industrial processes, but also all social, political, and economic life affected by them. Efficiency and organization, he says, are sought in all activities. The machine enslaves people when they adapt to its demands. Technology has its own inherent logic and inner necessity. Rational order is everywhere imposed at the expense of spontaneity and freedom.

Ellul ends with a *technological determinism,* since technique is self-perpetuating, all-pervasive, and inescapable. Any opposition is simply absorbed as we become addicted to the products of technology. Public opinion and the state become the servants of technique rather than its masters. Technique is global, monolithic, and unvarying among diverse regions and nations. Ellul offers us no way out, since all our institutions, the media, and our personal lives are totally in its grip. He holds that biblical ethics can provide a viewpoint transcending society from which to judge the sinfulness of the technological order and can give us the motivation to revolt against it, but he holds out little hope of controlling it.[23] Some interpreters see in Ellul's recent writings a very guarded hope that a radical Christian freedom that rejects cultural illusions of technological progress might in the long run lead to the transformation rather than the rejection of technology. But Ellul does not spell out such a transformation because he holds that the outcome is in God's hands, not ours, and most of his writings are extremely pessimistic about social change.[24]

The political scientist Langdon Winner has given a sophisticated version of the argument that technology is *an autonomous system* that shapes all human activities to its own requirements. It makes little difference who is nominally in control—elected politicians, technical experts, capitalist executives, or socialist managers—if decisions are determined by the demands of the technical system. Human ends are then adapted to suit the techniques available rather than the reverse. Winner says that large-scale systems are self-perpetuating, extending their control over resources and markets and molding human life to fit their own smooth functioning. Technology is not a neutral means to human ends but an all-encompassing system that imposes its patterns on every aspect of life and thought.[25]

The philosopher Hans Jonas is impressed by *the new scale of technological power* and its influence on events distant in time and place. Traditional Western ethics have been anthropocentric and have considered only short-range consequences. Technological change has its own momentum, and its pace is too rapid for trial-and-error readjustments. Now genetics gives us power over humanity itself. Jonas calls for a new ethic of responsibility for the human future and for nonhuman nature. We should err on the side of caution, adopting policies designed to avert catastrophe rather than to maximize short-run benefits. "The magnitude of these stakes, taken with the insufficiency of our predictive knowledge, leads to the pragmatic rule to give the prophecy of doom priority over the prophecy of bliss."[26] We should seek "the least harm," not "the greatest good." We have no right to tamper genetically with human nature or to accept policies that entail even the remote possibility of the extinction of humanity in a nuclear holocaust.

Another philosopher, Albert Borgmann, does not want to return to a pretechnological past, but he urges the selection of technologies that encourage *genuine human fulfillment*. Building on the ideas of Heidegger, he holds that authentic human existence requires the engagement and depth that occur when simple things and practices focus our attention and center our lives. We have let technology define the good life in terms of production and consumption, and we have ended with mindless labor and mindless leisure. A fast-food restaurant replaces the family meal, which was an occasion of communication and celebration. The simple pleasures of making music, hiking and running, gathering with friends around the hearth, or engaging in creative and self-reliant work should be our goals. Borgmann thinks that some large-scale capital-intensive industry is needed (especially in transportation and communication), but he urges the development of small-scale labor-intensive, locally owned enterprises (in arts and crafts, health care, and education, for example). We should challenge the rule of technology and restrict it to the limited role of supporting the humanly meaningful activities associated with a simpler life.[27]

In *Technology and Power*, the psychologist David Kipnis maintains that those who control a technology have power over other people and this affects personal attitudes as well as social structures. Power holders interpret technological superiority as moral superiority and tend to look down on weaker parties. Kipnis shows that military and transportation technologies fed the conviction of colonists that they were superior to colonized peoples. Similarly, medical knowledge and specialization have led doctors to treat patients as impersonal cases and to keep patients at arms length with a minimum of personal communication. Automation gave engineers and managers increased power over workers, who no longer needed special skills. In general, "power corrupts" and leads people to rationalize their use of power for their own ends. Kipnis claims that the person with technological knowledge often has not only a potent instrument of control but also a self-image that assumes superiority over people who lack that knowledge and the concomitant opportunities to make decisions affecting their lives.[28]

Some Christian groups are critical of *the impact of technology on human life*. The Amish, for example, have resolutely turned their backs on radios, television, and even automobiles. By hard work, community cooperation, and frugal ways, they have prospered in agriculture and have continued their distinctive life-styles and educational patterns. Many theologians who do not totally reject technology criticize its tendency to generate a Promethean pride and a quest for unlimited power. The search for omnipotence is a denial of creaturehood. Unqualified devotion to technology as a total way of life, they say, is a form of idolatry. Technology is finally thought of as the source of salvation, the agent of secularized redemption.[29] In an affluent society, a legitimate concern for material progress readily becomes a frantic pursuit of comfort, a total dedication to self-gratification. Such an obsession with things distorts our basic values as well as our relationships with other persons. Exclusive dependence on technological rationality also leads to a truncation of experience, a loss of imaginative and emotional life, and an impoverishment of personal existence.

Technology is *imperialistic and addictive,* according to these critics. The optimists may think that, by fulfilling our material needs, technology liberates us from materialism and allows us to turn to intellectual, artistic, and spiritual pursuits. But it does not seem to be working out that way. Our material wants have escalated and appear insatiable. Yesterday's luxuries are today's necessities. The rich are usually more anxious about their future than the poor. Once we allow technology to define the good life, we have excluded many important human values from consideration.

Several theologians have expressed particular concern for the impact of technology on *religious life*. Paul Tillich claims that the rationality and impersonality of technological systems undermine the personal presuppositions of religious commitment.[30] Gabriel Marcel believes that the technological outlook pervades our lives and excludes a sense of the sacred. The technician treats everything as a problem that can be solved by manipulative techniques without personal involvement. But this misses the mystery of human existence, which is known only through involvement as a total person. The technician treats other people as objects to be understood and controlled.[31] Martin Buber contrasts the I–It relation of objective detachment with the I–Thou relation of mutuality, responsiveness, and personal involvement. If the calculating attitude of control and mastery dominates a person's life, it excludes the openness and receptivity that are prerequisites of a relationship to God or to other persons.[32] P. H. Sun holds that a high-tech environment inhibits the life of prayer. Attitudes of power and domination are incompatible with the humility and reverence that prayer requires.[33]

3. A REPLY TO THE PESSIMISTS

In replying to these authors, we may note first that there are *great variations among technologies,* which are ignored when they are lumped together and condemned wholesale. Computerized offices differ greatly from steel mills and auto assembly lines, even if they share some features in common. One survey of journal articles finds that philosophers and those historians who trace broad trends (in economic and urban history, for example) often claim that technology determines history, whereas the historians or sociologists who make detailed studies of particular technologies are usually aware of the diversity of social, political, and economic interests that affect the design of a machine and its uses.[34] I maintain that the uses of any technology vary greatly depending on its social contexts. To be sure, technological systems are interlocked, but they do not form a monolithic system impervious to political influence or totally dominating all other social forces. In particular, technology assessment and legislation offer opportunities for controlling technology, as we shall see.

Second, technological pessimists neglect possible avenues for *the redirection of technology.* The "inevitability" or "inherent logic" of technological developments is not supported by historical studies. We will note below some cases in which there were competing technical designs and the choice among them was affected by various political and social factors. Technological determinism underestimates the diversity of forces that contribute to technological change. Unrelieved pessimism undercuts human action and becomes a self-fulfilling prophecy. If we are convinced that nothing can be done to improve the system, we will indeed do nothing to try to improve it. This would give to the commercial sponsors of technology the choices that are ours as responsible citizens.

Third, technology can be *the servant of human values.* Life is indeed impoverished if the technological attitudes of mastery and power dominate one's outlook. Calculation and control do exclude mutuality and receptivity in human relationships and prevent the humility and reverence that religious awareness requires. But I would submit that the threat to these areas of human existence comes not from technology itself but from preoccupation with material progress and unqualified reliance on technology. We can make decisions about technology within a wider context of human and environmental values.

III. Technology as Instrument of Power

A third basic position holds that technology is neither inherently good nor inherently evil but is an ambiguous instrument of power whose consequences depend on its social context. Some technologies seem to be neutral if they can be used for good or evil according to the goals of the users. A knife can be used for surgery or for murder. An isotope separator can enrich uranium for peaceful nuclear reactors or for aggression with nuclear weapons. But historical analysis suggests that most technologies are already molded by particular interests and institutional goals. Technologies are social constructions, and they are seldom neutral because particular purposes are already built into their design. Alternative purposes would lead to alternative designs. Yet most designs still allow some choice as to how they are deployed.

1. TECHNOLOGY AND POLITICAL POWER

Like the authors in the previous group, those in this group are critical of many features of current technology. But they offer hope that technology can be used for more humane ends, either by political measures for more effective guidance within existing institutions or by changes in the economic and political systems themselves.

The people who make most of the decisions about technology today are not a technical elite or technocrats trying to run society rationally or disinterested experts whose activity was supposed to mark "the end of ideology." The decisions are made by managers dedicated to *the interests of institutions*, especially industrial corporations and government bureaucracies. The goals of research are determined largely by the goals of institutions: corporate profits, institutional growth, bureaucratic power, and so forth. Expertise serves the interests of organizations and only secondarily the welfare of people or the environment.

The interlocking structure of *technologically based government agencies and corporations*, sometimes called the "technocomplex," is wider than the "military-industrial complex." Many companies are virtually dependent on government contracts. The staff members of regulatory agencies, in turn, are mainly recruited from the industries they are supposed to regulate. We will see later that particular legislative committees, government agencies, and industries have formed three-way alliances to promote such technologies as nuclear energy or pesticides. Networks of industries with common interests form lobbies of immense political power. For example, U.S. legislation supporting railroads and public mass transit systems was blocked by a coalition of auto manufacturers, insurance companies, oil companies, labor unions, and the highway construction industry. But citizens can also influence the direction of technological development. Public opposition to nuclear power plants was as important as rising costs in stopping plans to construct new plants in almost all Western nations.

The historian Arnold Pacey gives many examples of *the management of technology for power and profit.* This is most clearly evident in the defense industries with their close ties to government agencies. But often the institutional biases associated with expertise are more subtle. Pacey gives as one example the Western experts in India and Bangladesh who in the 1960s advised the use of large drilling rigs and diesel pumps for wells, imported from the West. By 1975, two thirds of the pumps had broken down because the users lacked the skills and maintenance networks to operate them. Pacey calls for greater public participation and a more democratic distribution of power in the decisions affecting technology. He also urges the upgrading of indigenous technologies, the exploration of intermediate-scale processes, and greater dialogue between experts and users. Need-oriented values and local human benefits would then play a larger part in technological change.[35]

2. THE REDIRECTION OF TECHNOLOGY

The political scientist Victor Ferkiss expresses hope about the redirection of technology. He thinks that both the optimists and the pessimists have neglected the diversity among different technologies and *the potential role of political structures* in reformulating policies. In the past, technology has been an instrument of profit, and decisions have been motivated by short-run private interests. Freedom understood individualistically became license for the economically powerful. Individual rights were given precedence over the common good, despite our increasing interdependence. Choices that could only be made and enforced collectively—such as laws concerning air and water pollution—were resisted as infringements on free enterprise. But Ferkiss thinks that economic criteria can be subordinated to such social criteria as ecological balance and human need. He believes it is possible to combine centralized, systemwide planning in basic decisions with decentralized implementation, cultural diversity, and citizen participation.[36]

There is a considerable range of views among *contemporary Marxists.* Most share Marx's conviction that technology is necessary for solving social problems but that under capitalism it has been an instrument of exploitation, repression, and dehumanization. In modern capitalism, according to Marxists, corporations dominate the government and political processes serve the interests of the ruling class. The technical elite likewise serves the profits of the owners. Marxists grant that absolute standards of living have risen for everyone under capitalist technology. But relative inequalities have increased, so that class distinctions and poverty amidst luxury remain. Marxists assign justice a higher priority than freedom. Clearly they blame capitalism rather than technology for these evils of modern industrialism. They believe that alienation and inequality will disappear and technology will be wholly benign when the working class owns the means of production. The workers, not the technologists, are the agents of liberation. Marxists are thus as critical as the pessimists concerning the consequences of technology within capitalism but as enthusiastic as the optimists concerning its potentialities—within a proletarian economic order.

How, then, do Western Marxists view the human effects of *technology in Soviet history*? Reactions vary, but many would agree with Bernard Gendron that in the Soviet Union workers were as alienated, factories as hierarchically organized, experts as bureaucratic, and pollution and militarism as rampant as in the United States. But Gendron insists that the Soviet Union did not follow Marx's vision. The means of production were controlled by a small group within the Communist party, not by the workers. Gendron maintains that in a truly democratic socialism, technology would be humane and work would not be alienating.[37] Most commentators hold that the demise of communism in Eastern Europe and the Soviet Union was a product of both its economic inefficiency and its political repression. It remains to be seen whether any distinctive legacy from Marxism will remain there after the economic and political turmoil of the early nineties.

We have seen that a few theologians are technological optimists, while others have adopted pessimistic positions. A larger number, however, see technology as *an ambiguous instrument of social power*. As an example consider Norman Faramelli, an engineer with theological training, who writes in a framework of Christian ideas: stewardship of creation, concern for the dispossessed, and awareness of the corrupting influence of power. He distrusts technology as an instrument of corporate profit, but he believes it can be reoriented toward human liberation and ecological balance. Technology assessment and the legislative processes of democratic politics, he holds, can be effective in controlling technology. But Faramelli also advocates restructuring the economic order to achieve greater equality in the distribution of the fruits of technology.[38] Similar calls for the responsible use of technology in the service of basic human needs have been issued by task forces and conferences of the National Council of Churches and by the World Council of Churches (WCC).[39] According to one summary of WCC documents, "technological society is to be blessed for its capacity to meet basic wants, chastised for its encouragement of inordinate wants, transformed until it serves communal wants."[40]

Egbert Schuurman, a Calvinist engineer from Holland, rejects many features of current technology but holds that it can be *transformed and redeemed* to be an instrument of God's love serving all creatures. Western thought since the Renaissance has increasingly encouraged "man the master of nature"; secular and reductionistic assumptions have prevailed. Schuurman says that technology was given a messianic role as the source of salvation, and under the rule of human sin it has ended by enslaving us so we are "exiles in Babylon." But we can be converted to seek God's Kingdom, which comes as a gift, not by human effort. Receiving it in joy and love, and responding in obedience, we can cooperate in meaningful service of God and neighbor. Schuurman holds that technology can be redirected to advance both material and spiritual well-being. It has "a magnificent future" if it is incorporated into God's work of creation and redemption. A liberated technology could do much to heal the brokenness of nature and society. Unfortunately, he gives us few examples of what such a technology would be like or how we can work to promote it.[41]

The American theologian Roger Shinn has written extensively on Christian ethics and gives attention to *the structures of political and economic power* within which technological decisions are made. He agrees with the pessimists that various technologies reinforce each other in interlocking systems, and he acknowledges that large-scale technologies lead to the concentration of economic and political power. But he argues that when enough citizens are concerned, political processes can be effective in guiding technology toward human welfare. Policy changes require a combination of protest, political pressure, and the kind of new vision that the biblical concern for social justice can provide.[42]

This third position seems to me more consistent with *the biblical outlook* than either of the alternatives. Preoccupation with technology does become a form of idolatry, a denial of the sovereignty of God, and a threat to distinctively human existence. But technology directed to genuine human needs is a legitimate expression of humankind's creative capacities and an essential contribution to its welfare. In a world of disease and hunger, technology rightly used can be a far-reaching expression of concern for persons. The biblical understanding of human nature is realistic about the abuses of power and the institutionalization of self-interest. But it also is idealistic in its demands for social justice in the distribution of the fruits of technology. It brings together celebration of human creativity and suspicion of human power.

The attitudes toward technology outlined in this chapter can be correlated with the typology of historic Christian attitudes toward society set forth by H. Richard Niebuhr.[43] At the one extreme is *accommodation to society.* Here society is considered basically good and its positive potentialities are affirmed. Niebuhr cites the example of liberal theologians of the nineteenth century who had little to say concerning sin, revelation, or grace. They were confident about human reason, scientific and technological knowledge, and social progress. They would side with our first group, those who are optimistic about technology.

At the opposite extreme, Niebuhr describes Christian groups advocating *withdrawal from society.* They believe that society is basically sinful. The Christian perfectionists, seeking to maintain their purity and to practice radical obedience, have withdrawn into monasteries or into separate communities, as the Mennonites and Amish have done. They would tend to side with our second group, the critics of technology.

Niebuhr holds that the majority of Christians are in three movements that fall between the extremes of accommodation and withdrawal. A *synthesis of Christianity and society* has been advocated historically by the Roman Catholic church. Aquinas held that there is both a revealed law, known through scripture and the church, and a natural law, built into the created order and accessible to human reason. Church and state have different roles but can cooperate for human welfare in society. This view encourages a qualified optimism about social change (and, I suggest, about technology).

Another option is the view of Christian life and society as *two separate realms,* as held in the Lutheran tradition. Here there is a compartmentalization of spiritual and temporal spheres and different standards for personal and public life. Sin is prevalent in all life, but in personal life it is overcome by grace; gospel comes before law as the Christian responds in faith and in love of neighbor. In the public sphere, however, sin must be restrained by the secular structures of authority and order. This view tends to be more pessimistic about social change, but it does not advocate withdrawal from society.

The final option described by Niebuhr is a *transformation of society* by Christian values. This position has much in common with the Catholic view and shares its understanding that God is at work in history, society, and nature as well as in personal life and the church. But it is more skeptical about the exercise of power by the institutional church, and it looks instead to the activity of the layperson in society. Calvin, the Reformed and Puritan traditions, the Anglicans, and the Methodists all sought a greater expression of Christian values in public life. They had great respect for the created world ordered by God, and they called for social justice and the redirection of cultural life. This position holds that social change (including the redirection of technology) is possible, but it is difficult because of the structures of group self-interest and institutional power. I favor this last option and will develop it further in subsequent chapters.

3. THE SOCIAL CONSTRUCTION OF TECHNOLOGY

How are science, technology, and society related? Three views have been proposed (see Fig. 1).

1. *Linear Development.* In linear development it is assumed that science leads to technology, which in turn has an essentially one-way impact on society. The deployment of technology is primarily a function of the marketplace. This view is common among the optimists. They consider technology to be predominantly beneficial, and therefore little government regulation or public policy choice is needed; consumers can influence technological development by expressing their preferences through the marketplace.

2. *Technological Determinism.* Several degrees and types of determinism can be distinguished. Strict determinism asserts that only one outcome is possible. A more qualified claim is that there are very strong tendencies present in technological systems, but these could be at least partly counteracted if enough people were committed to resisting them. Again, technology may be considered an autonomous interlocking system, which develops by its own inherent logic, extended to the control of social institutions. Or the more limited claim is made that the development and deployment of technology in capitalist societies follows only one path, but the outcomes might be different in other economic systems. In all these versions, science is itself driven primarily by technological needs. Technology is either the "independent variable" on which other variables are dependent, or it is the overwhelmingly predominant force in historical change.

Technological determinists will be pessimists if they hold that the consequences of technology are on balance socially and environmentally harmful. Moreover, any form of determinism implies a limitation of human

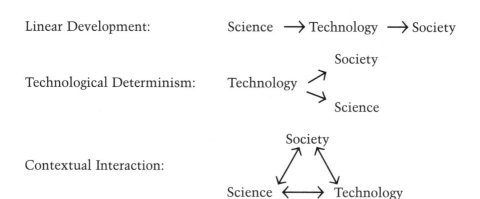

FIGURE 1.   Views of the Interactions of Science, Technology, and Society.

freedom and technological choice. However, some determinists retain great optimism about the consequences of technology. On the other hand, pessimists do not necessarily accept determinism, even in its weaker form. They may acknowledge the presence of technological choices but expect such choices to be misused because they are pessimistic about human nature and institutionalized greed. They may be pessimistic about our ability to respond to a world of global inequities and scarce resources. Nevertheless, determinism and pessimism are often found together among the critics of technology.

3. *Contextual Interaction.* Here there are six arrows instead of two, representing the complex interactions between science, technology, and society. Social and political forces affect the design as well as the uses of particular technologies. Technologies are not neutral because social goals and institutional interests are built into the technical designs that are chosen. Because there are choices, public policy decisions about technology play a larger role here than in either of the other views. Contextualism is most common among our third group, those who see technology as an ambiguous instrument of social power.

Contextualists also point to *the diversity of science-technology interactions.* Sometimes a technology was indeed based on recent scientific discoveries. Biotechnology, for example, depends directly on recent research in molecular biology. In other cases, such as the steam engine or the electric power system, innovations occurred with very little input from new scientific discoveries. A machine or process may have been the result of creative practical innovation or the modification of an existing technology. As Frederick Ferré puts it, science and technology in the modern world are both products of the combination of theoretical and practical intelligence, and "neither gave birth to the other."[44] Technology has its own distinctive problems and builds up its own knowledge base and professional community, though it often uses science as a resource to draw on. The reverse contribution of technology to science is also often evident. The work of astronomers, for instance, has been dependent on a succession of new technologies, from optical telescopes to microwave antennae and rockets. George Wise writes, "Historical studies have shown that the relations between science and technology need not be those of domination and subordination. Each has maintained its distinctive knowledge base and methods while contributing to the other and to its patrons as well."[45] . . .

The case for *"the social construction of technology"* seems to me . . . strong . . . Values are built into particular technological designs. There is no one "best way" to design a technology. Different individuals and groups may define a problem differently and may have diverse criteria of success. Bijker and Pinch show that in the late nineteenth century inventors constructed many different types of bicycles. Controversies developed about the relative size of front and rear wheels, seat location, air tires, brakes, and so forth. Diverse users were envisioned (workers, vacationers, racers, men and women) and diverse criteria (safety, comfort, speed, and so forth). In addition, the bicycle carried cultural meanings, affecting a person's self-image and social status. There was nothing logically or technically necessary about the model that finally won out and is now found around the world.[46]

The historian John Staudenmaier writes that

> contextualism is rooted in the proposition that technical designs cannot be meaningfully interpreted in abstraction from their human context. The human fabric is not an envelope around a culturally neutral artifact. The values and world views, the intelligence and stupidity, the biases and vested interests of those who design, accept and maintain a technology are embedded in the technology itself.[47]

Both the linear and the determinist view imply that technology determines *work organization*. It is said that the technologies of the Industrial Revolution imposed their own requirements and made repetitive tasks inevitable. The contextualists reply that the design of a technology is itself affected by social relations. The replacement of workers by machines was intended not only to reduce labor costs but also to assert greater control by management over labor. For instance, the spinning mule helped to break the power of labor unions among skilled textile workers in nineteenth-century England. Some examples in the choice of designs for agricultural harvesters, nuclear reactors, and computer-controlled manufacturing are discussed in later chapters.

Other contextualists have pointed to the role of technology in *the subordination of women*. Engineering was once considered heavy and dirty work unsuitable for women, but long after it became a clean and intellectual profession, there are still few women in it. Technology has been an almost exclusively male preserve, reflected in toys for boys, the expectations of parents and teachers, and the vocational choices and job opportunities open to men and women. Most technologies are designed by men and add to the power of men.

Strong *gender divisions* are present among employees of technology-related companies. When telephones were introduced, women were the switchboard operators and record keepers, while men designed and repaired the equipment and managed the whole system. Typesetting in large printing frames once required physical strength and mechanical skills and was a male occupation. But men continued to exclude women from compositors' unions when linotype, and more recently computer formatting, required only typing and formatting skills.[48] Today most computer designers and programmers are men, while in offices most of the data are entered at computer keyboards by women. With many middle-level jobs eliminated, these lower-level jobs often become dead ends for women.[49] A study of three computerized industries in Britain found that women were the low-paid operators, while only men understood and controlled the equipment, and men almost never worked under the supervision of women.[50]

Note that contextualism allows for a *two-way interaction* between technology and society. When technology is treated as merely one form of cultural expression among others, its distinctive characteristics may be ignored. In some renditions, the ways in which technology shapes culture are forgotten while the cultural forces on technology are scrutinized. The impact of technology on society is particularly important in the transfer of a technology to a new cultural setting in a developing country. Some Third World authors have been keenly aware of technology as an instrument of power, and they portray a two-way interaction between technology and society across national boundaries.

IV. Conclusions

. . . The optimists stress the contribution of technology to *economic development*. They hold that greater productivity improves standards of living and makes *food and health* more widely available. For most of them, the most important form of *participatory freedom* is the economic freedom of the marketplace, though in general they are also committed to political democracy. These authors say that social justice and environmental protection should not be ignored, but they must not be allowed to jeopardize economic goals. The optimists usually evaluate technology in a utilitarian framework, seeking to maximize the balance of costs over benefits.

The pessimists typically make *personal fulfillment* their highest priority, and they interpret fulfillment in terms of human relationships and community life rather than material possessions. They are concerned about individual rights and the dignity of persons. They hold that *meaningful work* is as important as economic productivity in policies for technology. The pessimists are dedicated to *resource sustainability* and criticize the high levels of consumption in industrial societies today. They often advocate *respect for all creatures* and question the current technological goal of mastery of nature.

The contextualists are more likely to give prominence to *social justice* because they interpret technology as both a product and an instrument of social power. For them the most important forms of *participatory freedom* are opportunities for participation in political processes and in work-related decisions. They are less concerned about economic growth than about how that growth is distributed and who receives the costs and the benefits. Contextualists often seek *environmental protection* because they are aware of the natural as well as the social contexts in which technologies operate.

I am most sympathetic with the contextualists, though I am indebted to many of the insights of the pessimists. Four issues seem to me particularly important in analyzing the differences among the positions outlined above.

1. *Defense of the Personal.* The pessimists have defended human values in a materialistic and impersonal society. The place to begin, they say, is one's own life. Each of us can adopt individual life-styles more consistent with human and environmental values. Moreover, strong protest and vivid examples are needed to challenge the historical dominance of technological optimism and the disproportionate resource consumption of affluent societies. I admire these critics for defending individuality and choice in the face of standardization and bureaucracy. I join them in upholding the significance of personal relationships and a vision of personal fulfillment that goes beyond material affluence. I affirm the importance of the spiritual life, but I do not believe that it requires a rejection of technology. The answer to the destructive features of technology is not less technology, but technology of the right kind.

2. *The Role of Politics.* Differing models of social change are implied in the three positions. The first group usually assumes a free market model. Technology is predominantly beneficial, and the reduction of any undesirable side effects is itself a technical problem for the experts. Government intervention is needed only to regulate the most harmful impacts. Writers mentioned in the second section, by contrast, typically adopt some variant of technological determinism. Technology is dehumanizing and uncontrollable. They see runaway technology as an autonomous and all-embracing system that molds all of life, including the political sphere, to its requirements. The individual is helpless within the system. The views expressed in the third section presuppose a "social conflict" model. Technology influences human life but is itself part of a cultural system; it is an instrument of social power serving the purposes of those who control it. It does systematically impose distinctive forms on all areas of life, but these can be modified through political processes. Whereas the first two groups give little emphasis to politics, the third, with which I agree, holds that conflicts concerning technology must be resolved primarily in the political arena.

3. *The Redirection of Technology.* I believe that we should neither accept uncritically the past directions of technological development nor reject technology *in toto* but redirect it toward the realization of human and environmental values. In the past, technological decisions have usually been governed by narrowly economic criteria, to the neglect of environmental and human costs. In a later chapter we will look at technology assessment, a procedure designed to use a broad range of criteria to evaluate the diverse consequences of an emerging technology—*before* it has been deployed and has developed the vested interests and institutional momentum that make it seem uncontrollable. I will argue that new policy priorities concerning agriculture, energy, resource allocation, and the redirection of technology toward basic human needs can be achieved within democratic

political institutions. The key question will be: What decision-making processes and what technological policies can contribute to human and environmental values?

4. *The Scale of Technology*. Appropriate technology can be thought of as an attempt to achieve some of the material benefits of technology outlined in the first section without the destructive human costs discussed in the second section, most of which result from large-scale centralized technologies. Intermediate-scale technology allows decentralization and greater local participation in decisions. The decentralization of production also allows greater use of local materials and often a reduction of impact on the environment. Appropriate technology does not imply a return to primitive and prescientific methods; rather, it seeks to use the best science available toward goals different from those that have governed industrial production in the past.

Industrial technology was developed when capital and resources were abundant, and we continue to assume these conditions. Automation, for example, is capital-intensive and labor saving. Yet in *developing nations* capital is scarce and labor is abundant. The technologies needed there must be relatively inexpensive and labor-intensive. They must be of intermediate scale so that jobs can be created in rural areas and small towns, to slow down mass migration to the cities. They must fulfill basic human needs, especially for food, housing, and health. Alternative patterns of modernization are less environmentally and socially destructive than the path that we have followed. It is increasingly evident that many of these goals are desirable also in industrial nations. I will suggest that we should develop a mixture of large- and intermediate-scale technologies, which will require deliberate encouragement of the latter.

The redirection of technology will be no easy task. Contemporary technology is so tightly tied to industry, government, and the structures of economic power that changes in direction will be difficult to achieve. As the critics of technology recognize, the person who tries to work for change within the existing order may be absorbed by the establishment. But the welfare of humankind requires a creative technology that is economically productive, ecologically sound, socially just, and personally fulfilling.

Notes

1. Charles Susskind, *Understanding Technology* (Baltimore: Johns Hopkins University Press, 1973). p. 132.

2. John Zerman and Alice Carnes, eds., *Questioning Technology* (Santa Cruz, CA: New Society Publishers, 1991), p. 217.

3. C. S. Lewis, *The Abolition of Man* (New York: Macmillan, 1965), p. 69.

4. Among the volumes dealing with broad attitudes toward technology are Albert H. Teich, ed., *Technology and the Future*, 5th ed. (New York: St. Martin's

Press, 1989), and Carl Mitcham and Robert Mackey, eds., *Philosophy and Technology* (New York: Free Press, 1972).

5. This is close to the definition given by Arnold Pacey in *The Culture of Technology* (Cambridge: MIT Press, 1983), p. 6. Pacey adds "living things" among the "ordered systems" (in order to include agriculture, medicine, and biotechnology), but I suggest that these are already included under the rubric of "practical tasks." Frederick Ferré, *Philosophy of Technology* (Englewood Cliffs, NJ: Prentice-Hall, 1988), defines technology as "the practical implementation of intelligence" and argues that intelligence itself has both practical and theoretical forms.

6. Emanuel Mesthene, *Technological Change: Its Impact on Man and Society* (New York: New American Library, 1970).

7. Melvin Kranzberg, "Technology the Liberator," in *Technology at the Turning Point,* ed. William Pickett (San Francisco: San Francisco Press, 1977). See also Charles Susskind, *Understanding Technology.*

8. Emanuel Mesthene, "Technology as Evil: Fear or Lamentation?" in *Research in Philosophy and Technology,* vol. 7, ed. Paul Durbin (Greenwich, CT: JAI Press, 1984).

9. Daniel Bell, *The Coming of Postindustrial Society* (New York: Basic Books, 1973).

10. Buckminster Fuller, *The Critical Path* (New York: St. Martin's Press, 1981); Herman Kahn et al., *The Next 200 Years* (New York: William Morrow, 1976); Alvin Toffler, *Future Shock* (New York: Bantam, 1971) and *The Third Wave* (New York: William Morrow, 1980).

11. Samuel Florman, *The Existential Pleasures of Engineering* (New York: St. Martin's Press, 1977) and *Blaming Technology: The Irrational Search for Scapegoats* (New York: St. Martin's Press, 1981).

12. Florman, *Blaming Technology,* p. 183.

13. Cf. Alvin Weinberg, "Can Technology Replace Social Engineering," in *Technology and the Future,* ed. Teich.

14. Samuel Florman, "Science for Public Consumption: More Than We Can Chew?" *Technology Review* 86 (April 1983): 12–13.

15. Florman, *Blaming Technology,* p. 193.

16. Harvey Cox, *The Secular City* (New York: Macmillan, 1965), and "The Responsibility of the Christian in a World of Technology," in *Science and Religion,* ed. Ian G. Barbour (New York: Harper & Row, 1968).

17. W. Norris Clarke, S. J., "Technology and Man: A Christian Vision," in *Science and Religion,* ed. Barbour.

18. Pierre Teilhard de Chardin, *The Future of Man,* trans. Norman Denny (New York: Harper & Row, 1964), chaps. 8, 9, and 10. See also "The Place of Technology in a General Biology of Mankind," and "On Looking at a Cyclotron," in *The Activation of Energy* (New York: Harcourt Brace Jovanovich, 1971).

19. George Wise, "Science and Technology," *Osiris,* 2d ser., 1 (1985): 229–46.

20. See for example Lewis Mumford, *The Myth of the Machine,* vol. 1, *Technics and Human Development,* and vol. 2, *The Pentagon of Power* (New York: Harcourt Brace Jovanovich, 1967 and 1969).

21. Studs Terkel, *Working* (New York: Pantheon, 1972); Robert Schrag, *Ten Thousand Working Days* (Cambridge: MIT Press, 1978); William A. Faunce, *Problems of an Industrial Society,* 2d ed. (New York: McGraw-Hill, 1981).

22. Theodore Roszak, *The Making of a Counter Culture* (New York: Doubleday, 1969), and *Where the Wasteland Ends* (New York: Doubleday, 1972); see Ian G. Barbour, "Science, Religion, and the Counterculture," *Zygon* 10 (1975): 380–97.

23. Jacques Ellul, *The Technological Society*, trans. J. Wilkinson (New York: Knopf, 1964); also *The Technological System*, trans. J. Neugroschel (New York: Continuum, 1980), and *The Technological Bluff*, trans. G. Bromiley (Grand Rapids: Eerdmans, 1990).

24. Darrell Fasching, "The Dialectic of Apocalypse and Utopia in the Theological Ethics of Jacques Ellul," in *Research in Philosophy and Technology*, vol. 10, ed. Frederick Ferré (Greenwich, CT: JAI Press, 1990).

25. Langdon Winner, *Autonomous Technology* (Cambridge: MIT Press, 1977) and *The Reactor and the Whale* (Chicago: University of Chicago Press, 1986).

26. Hans Jonas, *The Imperative of Responsibility: In Search of an Ethics for the Technological Age* (Chicago: University of Chicago Press, 1984), p. x.

27. Albert Borgmann, *Technology and the Character of Contemporary Life* (Chicago: University of Chicago Press, 1984); Martin Heidegger, *The Question Concerning Technology*, trans. William Lovitt (New York: Harper & Row, 1977).

28. David Kipnis, *Technology and Power* (Berlin: Springer-Verlag, 1990).

29. Langdon Gilkey, *Religion and the Scientific Future* (New York: Harper & Row, 1970).

30. Paul Tillich, "The Person in a Technological Society," in *Social Ethics*, ed. Gibson Winter (New York: Harper & Row, 1968).

31. Gabriel Marcel, "The Sacred in the Technological Age," *Theology Today* 19 (1962): 27–38.

32. Martin Buber, *Land Thou*, trans. R. G. Smith (New York: Charles Scribner's Sons, 1937).

33. P. Hans Sun, "Notes on How to Begin to Think about Technology in a Theological Way," in *Theology and Technology*, ed. Carl Mitcham and Jim Grote (New York: University Press of America, 1984).

34. Thomas Misa, "How Machines Make History, and How Historians (and Others) Help Them Do So," *Science, Technology & Human Values* 13 (1988): 308–31.

35. Arnold Pacey, *Culture of Technology*.

36. Victor Ferkiss, *Technological Man and the Future of Technological Civilization* (New York: George Braziller, 1969 and 1974).

37. Bernard Gendron, *Technology and the Human Condition* (New York: St. Martin's Press, 1977).

38. Norman Faramelli, *Technethics* (New York: Friendship Press, 1971).

39. J. Edward Carothers, Margaret Mead, Daniel McCracken, and Roger Shinn, eds., *To Love or to Perish: The Technological Crisis and the Churches* (New York: Friendship Press, 1972); Paul Abrecht and Roger Shinn, eds., *Faith and Science in an Unjust World* (Geneva: World Council of Churches, 1980).

40. Thomas Derr, "Conversations about Ultimate Matters: Theological Motifs in WCC Studies on the Technological Future," *International Review of Missions* 66 (1977): 123–34.

41. Egbert Schuurman, *Technology and the Future* (Toronto: Wedge Publishing, 1980), also "The Modern Babylon Culture," in *Technology and Responsibility*, ed. Paul Durbin (Dordrecht, Holland: D. Reidel, 1987), and "A Christian Philosophical Perspective on Technology," in *Theology and Technology*, ed.

Mitcham and Grote. Schuurman was also a contributor to Stephen Monsma, ed., *Responsible Technology: A Christian Perspective* (Grand Rapids: Eerdmans, 1986).

42. Roger Shinn, *Forced Options: Social Decisions for the 21st Century,* 3d ed. (Cleveland: Pilgrim Press, 1991).

43. H. Richard Niebuhr, *Christ and Culture* (New York: Harper & Brothers, 1951). See also Carl Mitcham, "Technology as a Theological Problem in the Christian Tradition," in *Theology and Technology,* ed. Mitcham and Grote.

44. Ferré, *Philosophy of Technology,* p. 44.

45. Wise, "Science and Technology."

46. Trevor Pinch and Wiebe Bijker, "The Social Construction of Facts and Artifacts: Or How the Sociology of Science and the Sociology of Technology Might Benefit from Each Other," in *The Social Construction of Technological Systems,* ed. Wiebe Bijker, Thomas Hughes, and Trevor Pinch (Cambridge: MIT Press, 1987).

47. John W. Staudenmaier, *Technology's Storytellers* (Cambridge: MIT Press, 1985), p. 165.

48. Cynthia Cockburn, "The Material of Male Power," in *The Social Shaping of Technology,* ed. Donald McKenzie and Judy Wajcman (Milton Keynes, England: Open University Press, 1985).

49. Roslyn Feldberg and Evelyn Nakano Glenn, "Technology and Work Degradation: Effects of Office Automation on Women Clerical Workers," in *Machina Ex Dea: Feminist Perspectives on Technology,* ed. Joan Rothschild (New York: Pergamon Press, 1983); see also articles by Cheris Kramarae, Anne Machung, and others in *Technology and Women's Voices,* ed. Cheris Kramarae (New York and London: Routledge & Kegan Paul, 1988).

50. Cynthia Cockburn, *Machinery of Dominance: Women, Men, and Technical Know-How* (London: Pluto Press, 1985).

SELECTIONS ON TECHNOLOGY

Melvin Kranzberg, editor

During 1974, in celebration of the fiftieth anniversary of the Technion–Israel Institute of Technology, a conference was held on the role of technology in society. Leading philosophers, scientists, and engineers from around the world presented papers and reactions concerning

Selections from *Ethics in an Age of Pervasive Technology,* edited by Melvin Kranzberg (Westview Press, 1980). Reprinted by permission in memory of the late Prof. Kranzberg.

the rise of technology during the second half of the twentieth century. The following are statements by engineers David Brandon and Franz Ollendorff as well as the philosopher Isaiah Berlin. The last selection is the concluding declaration agreed to by consensus of the participants at the conference, and it focuses on issues of respect for human dignity in our development and use of technology.

DAVID G. BRANDON

The Partnership of Ethics and Technology

David G. Brandon saw no dichotomy between technology and ethics. Only continuing technological development will enable man to control his environment and avoid extinction.

Ethical and technological development have always proceeded hand in hand, because ethical rules of conduct only make sense if man has some control over his environment. As environmental control has become increasingly sophisticated through developing technology, so have the ethical codes become more elaborate. For 40,000 years we have succeeded in replacing the biological evolutionary mechanism, by which the organism is adapted to the environment, with the technological mechanism, by which the environment is adapted to the organism. If we can continue our technological development in the face of the present pressures of increasing population and limited resources, then there is no reason why man should not remain the pinnacle of creation, nor why our children should not lead better lives than ourselves. If we can no longer exercise that control over the environment, then man is due to meet the fate of the dodo and the dinosaur—an evolutionary dead end unable to adapt to change.

FRANZ OLLENDORFF

Science and Conscience

Franz Ollendorff placed the responsibility for ethical action on the individual consciences of people.

All of us have been active and passive witnesses to the political and social revolutions of global dimensions presented to humankind by the twentieth century. These historical events are tied so closely to the achievements of modern science and technology that only by comprehension of both these formerly different areas of human life shall we be able to reach an intellectual understanding of the inherent tendencies of the technological era. They put man, no matter what his profession, into an entirely new mental situation in which he is being challenged by the universe. Should we have asked the young Albert Einstein whether he could justify before God the publication of the energy formula $E = mc^2$, he would have looked at us with an utter lack of understanding. But when we learn that on the night of the 6th of April, 1945, Otto Hahn was about to commit suicide, we can in no way be surprised by this act of desperation. And should we have approached Einstein only ten years later, during his last days of sickness, and repeated our earlier question in a more serious and urgent way, he would have silently turned away. Mindful of his fate, we must ask: What is my position, and what is yours, concerning the cardinal question of our being, our planning, our doing—technology or conscience? For their deeds will follow them.

SIR ISAIAH BERLIN

Virtue and Practicality

Sir Isaiah Berlin warned against the hope of obtaining ethical perfection in the real world. Some goods might have to be sacrificed to obtain others.

Not all values are compatible. It is quite clear that—this is an a priori proposition—one cannot have everything. Not everything can be done. Instead, we must sacrifice some things to obtain others. In *The Prince*, Machiavelli stated very clearly—and truly—that one cannot both lead what he called a Christian life and also be effective in public life. By that he meant that ideal virtue is incompatible with being effective in practice, and that in public affairs something, therefore, must be sacrificed. This uncomfortable truth is something that people on the whole are not prepared to face.

The only conclusion I should like to draw from this fact is that I think in general it is very desirable for those who go into dangerous professions, namely, medicine, technology, biology, physics, chemistry, and the like, to be aware that their inventions and discoveries are likely to have some effects that they may regard as deleterious; and yet progress in the acquisition and dissemination of knowledge cannot, and should not, be stopped until all humankind is morally purified. The dilemmas leading to extreme anxiety, the agonies Nobel went through, and then Oppenheimer, Einstein, and others, are not accidental.

The Mount Carmel Declaration on Technology and Moral Responsibility

We, meeting at Haifa to celebrate the fiftieth anniversary of the Technion–Israel Institute of Technology, deeply troubled by the threats to the welfare and survival of the human species that are increasingly posed by improvident uses of applied science and technology, offer the following Declaration for consideration and adoption. It is addressed, most urgently, to all whom it concerns, to governments and other political agencies, to administrators and managers, experts and laymen, educators and students, to all who have the power to influence decisions or the right to be consulted about them.

1. We recognize the great contributions of technology to the improvement of the human condition. Yet continued intensification and extension of technology has unprecedented potentialities for evil as well as good. Technological consequences are now so ramified and interconnected, so sweeping in unforeseen results, so grave in the magnitude of the irreversible changes they induce, as to constitute a threat to the very survival of the species.
2. While actions at the level of community and state are urgently needed, legitimate local interests must not take precedence over the common interest of *all* human beings in justice, happiness, and peace. Responsible control of technology by social systems and institutions is an urgent *global* concern, overriding all conflicts of interest and all divergencies in religion, race or political allegiance. Ultimately all must benefit from the promise of technology, or all must suffer—even perish—together.
3. Technological applications and innovations result from human actions. As such, they demand political, social, economic, ecological and above all *moral* evaluation. No technology is morally "neutral."
4. Human beings, both as individuals and as members or agents of social institutions, bear the sole responsibility for abuses of technology. Invocation of supposedly inflexible laws of technological inertia and technological transformation is an evasion of moral and political responsibility.
5. Creeds and moral philosophies that teach respect for human dignity can, in spite of all differences, unite in actions to cope with the problems posed by new technologies. It is an urgent task to work toward new codes for guidance in an age of pervasive technology.
6. Every technological undertaking must respect basic human rights and cherish human dignity. We must not gamble with human survival. We must not degrade people into *things* used by machines:

every technological innovation must be judged by its contributions to the development of genuinely free and creative *persons*.

7. The "developed" and the "developing" nations have different priorities but an ultimate convergence of shared interests:

For the developed nations: rejection of expansion at all costs and the selfish satisfaction of ever-multiplying desires—and adoption of policies of *principled restraint*—with unstinting assistance to the unfortunate and the underprivileged.

For the developing nations: complementary but appropriately modified policies of principled restraint, especially in population growth, and a determination to avoid repeating the excesses and follies of the more "developed" economies.

Absolute priority should be given to the relief of human misery, the eradication of hunger and disease, the abolition of social injustice and the achievement of lasting peace.

8. These problems and their implications need to be discussed and investigated by all educational institutions and all media of communication. They call for intense and imaginative research enlisting the cooperation of humanists and social scientists, as well as natural scientists and technologists. Better technology is needed, but will not suffice to solve the problems caused by intensive uses of technology. We need *guardian disciplines* to monitor and assess technological innovations, with especial attention to their moral implications.

9. Implementation of these purposes will demand improved social institutions through the active participation of statesmen and their expert advisers, and the informed understanding and consent of those most directly affected—especially the young, who have the greatest stake in the future.

10. This agenda calls for sustained work on three distinct but connected tasks: the development of "guardian disciplines" for watching, modifying, improving, and restraining the human consequences of technology (a special but not exclusive responsibility of the scientists and technologists who originate technological innovations); the confluence of varying moral codes in common action; and the creation of improved educational and social institutions.

Without minimizing the prevalence of human irrationality and the potency of envy and hate, we have sufficient faith in ourselves and our fellows to hope for a future in which all can have a chance to close the gap between aspiration and reality—a chance to become at last truly human.

No agenda is more urgent for human welfare and survival. This declaration, henceforth to be called the Mount Carmel Declaration on Technology and Moral Responsibility, is proclaimed in Jerusalem on this day,

Wednesday, the twenty-fifth of December, 1974, in the Residence of the President of the State of Israel.

UNIQUE PROBLEMS IN INFORMATION TECHNOLOGY

Walter Maner

Walter Maner argues that there is a need to look carefully at the "unique ethical issues" that computer technology raises. He believes, however, that it is not enough to state merely that ethics is necessary to develop better professionals. Beyond this, computer ethics is a necessary field of study for at least six reasons (from weakest to strongest): professionalism, avoidance of abuse, rapid advances in computers create "policy vacuums," computers "permanently transform" ethical issues, computers create "novel ethical issues that require special study," and these unique issues are "large enough and coherent enough to define a new field." The last section of the paper argues for and provides eight examples in support of the fifth of these reasons: that computer ethics issues are novel.

Introduction

One factor behind the rise of computer ethics is the lingering suspicion that computer professionals may be unprepared to deal effectively with the ethical issues that arise in their workplace. Over the years, this suspicion has been reinforced by mostly anecdotal research that seems to show that computer professionals simply do not recognize when ethical issues are present. Perhaps the earliest work of this kind was done by Donn Parker in the late 1970s at SRI International.[1]

In 1977, Parker invited highly trained professionals from various fields to evaluate the ethical content of 47 simple hypothetical cases that he had created based in part on his expert knowledge of computer abuse. Workshop participants focused on each action or non-action of each person who played

From *Science and Engineering Ethics* 2, no. 2 (1996): 137–54; reprinted by permission of the author and Opragen Publications.

a role in these one-page scenarios. For each act that was performed or not performed, their set task was to determine whether the behavior was unethical or not, or simply raised no ethics issue at all. Parker found a surprising amount of residual disagreement among these professionals even after an exhaustive analysis and discussion of all the issues each case presented.

More surprisingly, a significant minority of professionals held to their belief that no ethics issue was present even in cases of apparent computer abuse. For example, in Scenario 3.1 of his 1977 book,[1] a company representative routinely receives copies of the computerized arrest records for new company employees. These records are provided as a favor by a police file clerk who happens to have access to various local and federal databases containing criminal justice information.

Nine of the 33 individuals who analyzed this case thought disclosure of arrest histories raised no ethics issues at all. Parker's research does not identify the professions represented by those who failed to detect ethics issues, but most of the participants in this early study[2] were computer professionals. This left casual readers of Parker's *Ethical Conflicts in Computer Science and Technology* free to identify computer professionals as the ones who lacked ethical sensitivity. If some of them could not even recognize when ethical issues were present, it is hard to imagine how they could ever hope to deal responsibly with them. According to Parker, the problem may have been fostered by computer education and training programs that encouraged, or at least failed to criminalize, certain types of unethical professional conduct.[3]

This perception of professional inadequacy is part of a largely hidden political agenda that has contributed to the development of various curricula in computer ethics. In recent years, the tacit perception that those preparing for careers in computing may need remedial moral education seems to have influenced some accreditation boards. As a result, they have been willing to mandate more and more ethical content in computer science and computer engineering programs. They may also be responding to the increased media attention given to instances of computer abuse, fraud and crime. Others demand more ethical content because they believe that catastrophic failures of computer programs are directly attributable to immoral behavior.[4]

The growth of interest is gratifying, especially considering that, in 1976, I found it hard to convince anyone that "computer ethics" was anything other than an oxymoron.[5] No doubt Norbert Weiner would be pleased to see his work bearing late fruit.[6] At the same time, I am greatly disturbed when courses in social impact and computer ethics become a tool for indoctrination in appropriate standards of professional conduct. Donald Gotterbarn, for example, argues that one of the six goals of computer ethics is the "socialization" of students into "professional norms."[7] The fact that these norms are often eminently reasonable, even recommended thoughtfully to us by our professional organizations, does not make indoctrination any less repugnant. The goal cannot be simply to criminalize or stigmatize departures from professional norms. Consider an analogy. Suppose a course in Human Sexual Relationships has for its goal the socialization of college students into "high standards" of sexual conduct, and that this goal is enforced by contradicting or discrediting anyone who violates these standards. Most people would be quick to recognize that this curriculum is more political than academic, and that such an approach would tend to create a classroom environment where bias could overwhelm inquiry.

We stand today on the threshold of a time when well-intended political motives threaten to reshape computer ethics into some form of moral education. Unfortunately, it is an easy transition from the correct belief that we ought to teach future computer scientists and engineers the meaning of responsible conduct, to the mistaken belief that we ought to train them to behave like responsible professionals. When Terrell Bynum says, for example, that he hopes the study of computer ethics will develop "good judgment" in students,[8] he is not advocating socialization. By "good judgment" he means to refer to the reasoned and principled process by which reflective moral judgments are rendered. From this correct position, it is a tempting and subtle transition to the mistaken position that computer ethics should cause students to develop good judgments, meaning that their positions on particular moral issues conform to the norms of the profession. This self-deceiving mistake occurs because there is an undetected shift in emphasis from the process to the products of moral deliberation.

My point is that a perceived need for moral education does not and cannot provide an adequate rationale for the study of computer ethics. Rather, it must exist as a field worthy of study in its own right and not because at the moment it can provide useful means to certain socially noble ends. To exist and to endure as a separate field, there must be a unique domain for computer ethics distinct from the domain for moral education, distinct even from the domains of other kinds of professional and applied ethics. Like James Moor, I believe computers are special technology and raise special ethical issues,[9] hence that computer ethics deserves special status.

My remaining remarks will suggest a rationale for computer ethics based on arguments and examples showing that one of the following is true:

> that certain ethical issues are so transformed by the use of computers that they deserve to be studied on their own, in their radically altered form,

or

> that the involvement of computers in human conduct can create entirely new ethical issues, unique to computing, that do not surface in other areas.

I shall refer to the first as the "weaker view" and the second as the "stronger view." Although the weaker view provides sufficient rationale, most of my attention will be focused on establishing the stronger view. This is similar to the position I took in 1980[10] and 1985,[11] except that I no longer believe that problems merely aggravated by computer technology deserve special status.

Levels of Justification for the Study of Computer Ethics

From weaker to stronger, there are at least six levels of justification for the study of computer ethics:

Level One: We should study computer ethics because doing so will make us behave like responsible professionals. At worst, this type of rationale is a disguised call for moral indoctrination. At best, it is weakened by the need to rely on an elusive connection between right knowledge and right conduct. This is similar to the claim that we should study religion because that will cause us to become more spiritual. For some people, perhaps it may, but the mechanism is not reliable.

Level Two: We should study computer ethics because doing so will teach us how to avoid computer abuse and catastrophes. Reports by Parker,[12] Neumann,[13] Forester and Morrison[14] leave little doubt that computer use has led to significant abuse, hijinks, crime, near catastrophes, and actual catastrophes. The question is: Do we get a balanced view of social responsibility merely by examining the profession's dirty laundry? Granted, a litany of computer "horror stories" does provide a vehicle for infusing some ethical content into the study of computer science and computer engineering. Granted, we should all work to prevent computer catastrophes. Even so, there are major problems with the use of conceptual shock therapy:

> The cases commonly used raise issues of bad conduct rather than good conduct. They tell us what behaviors to avoid but do not tell us what behaviors are worth modeling.

> As Leon Tabak has argued, this approach may harm students by preventing them from developing a healthy, positive and constructive view of their profession.[15]

> Most horror stories are admittedly rare and extreme cases, which makes them seem correspondingly remote and irrelevant to daily professional life.

> Persons who use computers for abusive purposes are likely to be morally bankrupt. There is little we can learn from them.

> Many computer catastrophes are the result of unintended actions and, as such, offer little guidance in organizing purposive behavior.

A litany of horror stories does not itself provide a coherent concept of computer ethics.

Level 3: We should study computer ethics because the advance of computing technology will continue to create temporary policy vacuums. Long-term use of poorly designed computer keyboards, for example, exposes clerical workers to painful, chronic, and eventually debilitating repetitive stress injury. Clearly, employers should not require workers to use equipment that is likely to cause them serious injury. The question is: What policies should we formulate to address problems of long-term keyboard use? New telephone technology for automatic caller identification creates a similar policy vacuum. It is not immediately obvious what the telephone company should be required to do, if anything, to protect the privacy of callers who wish to remain anonymous.

Unlike the first- and second-level justifications I have considered and rejected, this third-level justification does appear to be sufficient to establish computer ethics as an important and independent discipline. Still, there are problems:

> Since policy vacuums are temporary and computer technologies evolve rapidly, anyone who studies computer ethics would have the perpetual task of tracking a fast-moving and ever-changing target.

> It is also possible that practical ethical issues arise mainly when policy frameworks clash. We could not resolve such issues merely by formulating more policy.

Level 4: We should study computer ethics because the use of computing permanently transforms certain ethical issues to the degree that their alterations require independent study. I would argue, for example, that many of the issues surrounding intellectual property have been radically and permanently altered by the intrusion of computer technology. The simple question, "What do I own?" has been transformed into the question, "What exactly is it that I own when I own something?" Likewise, the availability of cheap, fast, painless, transparent encryption technology has completely transformed the privacy debate. In the past, we worried about the erosion of privacy. Now we worry about the impenetrable wall of computer-generated privacy afforded to every criminal with a computer and half a brain.

Level 5: We should study computer ethics because the use of computing technology creates, and will continue to create, novel ethical issues that require special study. I will return to this topic in a moment.

Level 6: We should study computer ethics because the set of novel and transformed issues is large enough and coherent enough to define a new field. I mention this hopefully as a theoretical possibility. Frankly, after fifteen years, we have not been able to assemble a critical mass of self-defining core issues. Joseph Behar, a sociologist, finds computer ethics diffuse and unfocused.[16] Gary Chapman, when he spoke to the *Computers and Quality of Life Conference* in 1990, complained that no advances had been made in computer ethics.[17] There are various explanations for this apparent (or real) lack of progress.[18]

> Computer ethics is barely fifteen years old.[19] Much of its intellectual geography remains uncharted.

> So far, no one has provided a complete and coherent concept of the proper subject matter for computer ethics.

> We have wrongly included in the domain of computer ethics any unethical act that happened to involve a computer. In the future, we must be more careful to restrict ourselves to those few cases where computers have an essential as opposed to incidental involvement.

> Because computer ethics is tied to an evolving technology, the field changes whenever the technology changes. For example, the use of networked computers presents moral problems different from those presented by the use of stand-alone computers. The use of mouse-driven interfaces raises issues different from those raised by keyboard-driven interfaces, particularly for people who are blind.

> We adopted, from clever philosophers, the dubious practice of using highly contrived, two-sided, dilemmatic cases to expose interesting but irresolvable ethical conflicts. This led to the false perception that there could be no progress and no commonality in computer ethics. New research may cause this perception to fade.[20]

> We have remained focused for too long on the dirty laundry of our profession.

On a hopeful note, the ImpactCS Steering Committee chaired by C. Dianne Martin is halfway through a three-year NSF-funded project that will be likely to generate a highly coherent picture of how the computer science curriculum can address social and ethical issues. ImpactCS intends to publish specific curriculum guidelines along with concrete models for implementing them.[21] (See below, Huff, et al., pp. 211–224.)

The Special Status of Computer Ethics

I now turn to the task of justifying computer ethics at Level 5 by establishing, through several examples, that there are issues and problems unique to the field.

It is necessary to begin with a few disclaimers. First, I do not claim that this set of examples is in any sense complete or representative. I do not even claim that the kinds of examples I will use are the best kind of examples to use in computer ethics. I do not claim that any of these issues is central to computer ethics. Nor am I suggesting that computer ethics should be limited to just those issues and problems that are unique to the field. I merely want to claim that each example is, in a specific sense, unique to computer ethics. By "unique" I mean to refer to those ethical issues and problems that

> are characterized by the primary and essential involvement of computer technology,
>
> exploit some unique property of that technology, and
>
> would not have arisen without the essential involvement of computing technology.

I mean to allow room to make either a strong or a weak claim as appropriate. For some examples, I make the strong claim that the issue or problem would not have arisen at all. For other examples, I claim only that the issue or problem would not have arisen in its present, highly altered form.

To establish the essential involvement of computing technology, I will argue that these issues and problems have no satisfactory non-computer moral analog. For my purposes, a "satisfactory" analogy is one that (a) is based on the use of a machine other than a computing machine and (b) allows the ready transfer of moral intuitions from the analog case to the case in question. In broad strokes, my line of argument will be that certain issues and problems are unique to computer ethics because they raise ethical questions that depend on some unique property of prevailing computer technology. My remarks are meant to apply to discrete-state stored-program internetworking fixed-instruction-set serial machines of von Neumann architecture. It is possible that other designs (such as the Connection Machine) would exhibit a different set of unique properties.

Next I offer a series of examples, starting with a simple case that allows me to illustrate my general approach:

EXAMPLE 1: UNIQUELY STORED

One of the unique properties of computers is that they must store integers in 'words' of a fixed size. Because of this restriction, the largest integer that can be stored in a 16-bit computer word is 32,767. If we insist on an exact representation of a number larger than this, an "overflow" will occur with the result that the value stored in the word becomes corrupted. This can produce interesting and harmful consequences. For example, a hospital computer system in Washington, D.C., broke down on September 19, 1989, because its calendar calculations counted the days elapsed since January 1, 1900. On the 19th of September, exactly 32,768 days had elapsed, overflowing the 16-bit word used to store the counter, resulting in a collapse of the entire system and forcing a lengthy period of manual operation.[22] At the Bank of New York, a similar 16-bit counter overflowed, resulting in a $32 billion overdraft. The bank had to borrow $24 million for one day to cover the overdraft. The interest on this one-day loan cost the bank about $5 million. In addition, while technicians attempted to diagnose the source of the problem, customers experienced costly delays in their financial transactions.[23] . . .

Perhaps your automobile's mechanical odometer gauge provides a better analogy. When the odometer reading exceeds a designed-in limit, say 99,999.9 miles, the gauge overflows and returns to all zeros. Those who sell used cars have taken unfair advantage of this property. They use a small motor to overflow the gauge manually, with the result that the buyer is unaware that he or she is purchasing a high-mileage vehicle.

This does provide a non-computer analogy, but is it a satisfactory analogy? Does it allow the ready transfer of moral intuitions to cases involving word overflow in computers? I believe it falls short. Perhaps it would be a satisfactory analogy if, when the odometer overflowed, the engine, the brakes, the wheels, and every other part of the automobile stopped working. This does not in fact happen because the odometer is not highly coupled to other systems critical to the operation of the vehicle. What is different about computer words is that they are deeply embedded in highly integrated subsystems such that the corruption of a single word threatens to bring down the operation of the entire computer. What we require, but do not have, is a non-computer analog that has a similar catastrophic failure mode.

So the incidents at the hospital in Washington, D.C., and the Bank of New York meet my three basic requirements for a unique issue or problem. They are characterized by the primary and essential involvement of computer technology, they depend on some unique property of that technology, and they would not have arisen without the essential involvement of computing technology. . . .

EXAMPLE 2: UNIQUELY MALLEABLE

Another unique characteristic of computing machines is that they are very general-purpose machines. As James Moor observed, they are "logically malleable" in the sense that "they can be shaped and molded to do any activity that can be characterized in terms of inputs, outputs, and connecting logical operations."[24] The unique adaptability and versatility of computers have important moral implications. To show how this comes about, I would like to repeat a story first told by Peter Green and Alan Brightman:

> Alan (nickname "Stats") Groverman is a sports fanatic and a data-crunching genius. His teachers describe him as having a "head for numbers." To Stats, though, it's just what he does; keeping track, for example, of yards gained by each running back on his beloved [San Francisco] 49ers team. And then averaging those numbers into the season's statistics. All done in his head-for-numbers. All without even a scrap of paper in front of him. Not that paper would make much of a difference. Stats has never been able to move a finger, let alone hold a pencil or pen. And he's never been able to press the keys of a calculator. Quadriplegia made these kinds of simplicities impossible from the day he was born. That's when he began to strengthen his head. Now, he figures, his head could use a little help. With his craving for sports ever-widening, his mental playing field is becoming increasingly harder to negotiate. Stats knows he needs a personal computer, what he calls "cleats for the mind." He also knows that he needs to be able to operate that computer without being able to move anything below his neck.[25]

Since computers do not care how they get their inputs, Stats ought to be able to use a head-pointer or a mouth-stick to operate the keyboard. If mouse input is required, he could use a head-controlled mouse along with a sip-and-puff tube. To make this possible, we would need to load a new device driver to modify the behavior of the operating system. If Stats has trouble with repeating keys, we would need to make another small change to the operating system, one that disables the keyboard repeat feature. If keyboard or mouse input proves too tedious for him, we could add a speech processing chip, a microphone and voice-recognition software. We have a clear duty to provide computer access solutions in cases like this, but what makes this duty so reasonable and compelling is the fact that computers are so easily adapted to user requirements.

. . . Our obligation to provide universal accessibility to computer technology would not have arisen if computers were not universally adaptable. The generality of the obligation is in proportion to the generality of the machine.

While it is clear that we should endeavor to adapt other machinery—elevators, for example—for use by people with disabilities, the moral intuitions we have about adapting elevators do not transfer readily to computers. . . . Even if elevators did provide a comparable case, it would still be true that the availability of a totally malleable machine so transforms our obligations that this transformation itself deserves special study.

EXAMPLE 3: UNIQUELY COMPLEX

Another unique property of computer technology is its superhuman complexity. It is true that humans program computing machines, so in that sense we are masters of the machine. The problem is that our programming tools allow us to create discrete functions of arbitrary complexity. In many cases, the result is a program whose total behavior cannot be described by any compact function.[26] In particular, programs with "bugs" are notorious for evading compact description! The fact is we routinely produce programs whose behavior defies inspection, defies understanding—programs that surprise, delight, entertain, frustrate and ultimately confound us. Even when we understand program code in its static form, it does not follow that we understand how the program works when it executes. James Moor provides a case in point:

> An interesting example of such a complex calculation occurred in 1976 when a computer worked on the four color conjecture. The four color problem, a puzzle mathematicians have worked on for over a century, is to show that a map can be colored with at most four colors so that no adjacent areas have the same color. Mathematicians at the University of Illinois broke the problem down into thousands of cases and programmed computers to consider them. After more than a thousand hours of computer time on various computers, the four color conjecture was proved correct. What is interesting about this mathematical proof, compared to traditional proofs, is that it is largely invisible. The general structure of the proof is known and found in the program, and any particular part of the computer's activity can be examined, but practically speaking the calculations are too enormous for humans to examine them all.[27]

. . . There is, I would argue, a moral imperative to discover better testing methodologies and better mechanisms for proving programs correct. It is hard to overstate the enormity of this challenge. Testing a simple input routine that accepts a 20-character name, a 20-character address, and a 10-digit phone number would require approximately 10^{66} test cases to exhaust all possibilities. If Noah had been a software engineer and had started testing this routine the moment he stepped off the ark, he would be less than one percent finished today even if he managed to run a trillion test cases every second.[28] In practice, software engineers test a few boundary values and, for all the others, they use values believed to be representative of various equivalence sets defined on the domain.

EXAMPLE 4: UNIQUELY FAST

On Thursday, September 11, 1986, the Dow Jones industrial average dropped 86.61 points, to 1792.89, on a record volume of 237.6 million shares. On the following day, the Dow fell 34.17 additional points on a volume of 240.5 million shares. Three months later, an article appearing in *Discover* magazine asked: Did computers make stock prices plummet? According to the article,

> . . . many analysts believe that the drop was accelerated (though not initiated) by computer-assisted arbitrage. Arbitrageurs capitalize on what's known as the spread: a short-term difference between the price of stock futures, which are contracts to buy stocks at a set time and price, and that of the underlying stocks. The arbitrageurs' computers constantly monitor the spread and let them know when it's large enough so that they can transfer their holdings from stocks to stock futures or vice-versa, and make a profit that more than covers the cost of the transaction. . . . With computers, arbitrageurs are constantly aware of where a profit can be made. However, throngs of arbitrageurs working with the latest information can set up perturbations in the market. Because arbitrageurs are all "massaging" the same basic information, a profitable spread is likely to show up on many of their computers at once. And since arbitrageurs take advantage of small spreads, they must deal in great volume to make it worth their while. All this adds up to a lot of trading in a little time, which can markedly alter the price of a stock.[29]

After a while, regular investors begin to notice that the arbitrageurs are bringing down the value of all stocks, so they begin to sell too. Selling begets selling begets more selling.

According to the chair of the New York Stock Exchange,[30] computerized trading seems to be a stabilizing influence only when markets are relatively quiet. When the market is unsettled, programmed trading amplifies and accelerates the changes already underway, perhaps as much as 20%. . . .

The question is, could these destabilizing effects occur in a world without computers? Arbitrage, after all, relies only on elementary mathematics. All the necessary calculations could be done on a scratch pad by any one of us. The problem is that, by the time we finished doing the necessary arithmetic for the stocks in our investment portfolio, the price of futures and the price of stocks would have changed. The opportunity that had existed would be gone.

EXAMPLE 5: UNIQUELY CHEAP

Because computers can perform millions of computations each second, the cost of an individual calculation approaches zero. This unique property of computers leads to interesting consequences in ethics. . . .

. . . I could slice some infinitesimal amount from every [bank] account, some amount so small that it falls beneath the account owner's threshold of concern. If I steal only half a cent each month from each of 100,000 bank accounts, I stand to pocket $6000 over a year's time. This kind of opportunity must have some appeal to an intelligent criminal mind, but very few cases have been reported. In one of these reported cases, a bank employee used [this] technique to steal $70,000 from customers of a branch bank in Ontario, Canada.[31] Procedurally speaking, it might be difficult to arraign someone on several million counts of petit theft. According to Donn Parker, "[These] techniques are usually not fully discoverable within obtainable expenditures for investigation. Victims have usually lost so little individually that they are unwilling to expend much effort to solve the case."[32] Even so, . . . slicing was immortalized in John Foster's country song, "The Ballad of Silicon Slim":

> In the dead of night he'd access each depositor's account
> And from each of them he'd siphon off the teeniest amount.
> And since no one ever noticed that there'd even been a crime
> He stole forty million dollars—a penny at a time!

Legendary or not, there are at least three factors that make this type of scheme unusual. First, individual computer computations are now so cheap that the cost of moving a half-cent from one account to another is vastly less than half a cent. For all practical purposes, the calculation is free. So there can be tangible profit in moving amounts that are vanishingly small if the volume of such transactions is sufficiently high. Second, once the plan has been implemented, it requires no further attention. It is fully automatic. Money in the bank. Finally, from a practical standpoint, no one is ever deprived of anything in which they have a significant interest. In short, we seem to have invented a kind of stealing that requires no taking—or at least no taking of anything that would be of significant value or concern. It is theft by diminishing return. . . .

EXAMPLE 6: UNIQUELY CLONED

Perhaps for the first time in history, computers give us the power to make an exact copy of some artifact. If I make a verified copy of a computer file, the copy can be proven to be bit for bit identical to the original. Common disk utilities like *diff* can easily make the necessary bitwise comparisons. It is true that there may be some low-level physical differences due to track placement, sector size, cluster size, word size, blocking factors, and so on. But at a logical level, the copy will be perfect. Reading either the original or its copy will result in the exact same sequence of bytes. For all practical purposes, the copy is indistinguishable from the original. In any situation where we had used the original, we can now substitute our perfect copy, or vice versa. We can make any number of verified copies of our copy, and the final result will be logically identical to the first original.

This makes it possible for someone to "steal" software without depriving the original owner in any way. The thief gets a copy that is perfectly usable. He would be no better off even if he had the original file. Meanwhile the owner has not been dispossessed of any property. Both files are equally functional, equally useful. There was no transfer of possession.

Sometimes we do not take adequate note of the special nature of this kind of crime. For example, the Assistant Vice-President for Academic Computing at Brown University reportedly said that "software piracy is morally wrong—indeed, it is ethically indistinguishable from shoplifting or theft."[33] This is mistaken. It is not like piracy. It is not like shoplifting or simple theft. It makes a moral difference whether or not people are deprived of property. Consider how different the situation would be if the process of copying a file automatically destroyed the original. . . .

EXAMPLE 7: UNIQUELY DISCRETE

In a stimulating paper "On the Cruelty of Really Teaching Computer Science,"[34] Edger Dijkstra examines the implications of one central, controlling assumption: that computers are radically novel in the history of the world. Given this assumption, it follows that programming these unique machines will be radically different from other practical intellectual activities. This, Dijkstra believes, is because the assumption of continuity we make about the behavior of most materials and artifacts does not hold for computer systems. For most things, small changes lead to small effects, larger changes to proportionately larger effects. If I nudge the accelerator pedal a little closer to the floor, the vehicle moves a little faster. If I press the pedal hard to the floor, it moves a lot faster. As machines go, computers are very different.

> A program is, as a mechanism, totally different from all the familiar analogue devices we grew up with. Like all digitally encoded information, it has, unavoidably, the uncomfortable property that the smallest possible perturbations—i.e., changes of a single bit—can have the most drastic consequences.[35]

This essential and unique property of digital computers leads to a specific set of problems that gives rise to a unique ethical difficulty, at least for those who espouse a consequentialist view of ethics.

For an example of the kind of problem where small "perturbations" have drastic consequences, consider the Mariner 18 mission, where the absence of the single word NOT from one line of a large program caused an abort.[36] In a similar case, it was a missing hyphen in the guidance program for an Atlas-Agena rocket that made it necessary for controllers to destroy a Venus probe worth $18.5 million.[37] . . . I am not suggesting that rockets rarely failed before they were computerized. I assume the opposite is true, that in the past they were far more susceptible to certain classes of failure than they are today. . . . Once rockets were controlled by computer software, however, they became vulnerable to additional failure modes that could be extremely generalized even for extremely localized problems.

"In the discrete world of computing," Dijkstra concludes, "there is no meaningful metric in which *small* change and *small* effects go hand in hand, and there never will be."[38] This discontinuous and disproportionate connection between cause and effect is unique to digital computers and creates a special difficulty for consequentialist ethical theories. . . . In short, we simply cannot tell what effects our actions will have on computers by analogy to the effects our actions have on other machines.

EXAMPLE 8: UNIQUELY CODED

Computers operate by constructing codes upon codes upon codes—cylinders on top of tracks, tracks on top of sectors, sectors on top of records, records on top of fields, fields on top of characters, characters on top of bytes, and bytes on top of primitive binary digits. Computer 'protocols' like TCP/IP are comprised of layer upon layer of obscure code conventions that tell computers how to interpret and process each binary digit passed to it. For digital computers, this is business as usual. In a very real sense, all data is multiply "encrypted" in the normal course of computer operations.

According to Charlie Hart, a reporter for the *Raleigh News and Observer*,[39] the resulting convolution of codes threatens to make American history as unreadable as the Rosetta Stone:

> Historic, scientific and business data is in danger of dissolving into a meaningless jumble of letters, numbers, and computer symbols. For example, two hundred reels of 17-year-old Public Health Service tapes had to be destroyed in 1989 because no one could determine what the names and numbers on them meant. Much information from the past thirty years is stranded on computer tape written by primitive or discarded systems. For example, the records of many World War II veterans are marooned on 1600 reels of obsolete microfilm images picturing even more obsolete Hollerith punch cards.

This growing problem is due to the degradable nature of certain media, the rapid rate of obsolescence for I/O devices, the continual evolution of media formats, and the failure of programmers to keep a permanent record of how they chose to package data. . . . Data archeologists will manage to salvage bits and pieces of our encoded records, but much will be permanently lost.

This raises a moral issue as old as civilization itself. It is arguably wrong to harm future generations of humanity by depriving them of information they will need and value. It stunts commercial and scientific progress, prevents people from learning the truth about their origins, and it may force nations to repeat bitter lessons from the past. Granted, there is nothing unique about this issue. Over the long sweep of civilized history, entire cultures have been annihilated, great libraries have been plundered and destroyed, books have been banned and burned, languages have withered and died, ink has bleached in the sun, and rolls of papyrus have decayed into fragile, cryptic memoirs of faraway times.

But has there ever in the history of the world been a machine that could bury culture the way computers can? Just about any modern media recording device has the potential to swallow culture, but the process is not automatic and information is not hidden below convoluted layers of obscure code. Computers, on the other hand, because of the unique way they store and process information, are far more likely to bury culture. . . .

So, this kind of example ultimately contributes to a "weaker" but still sufficient rationale for computer ethics, as explained earlier. Is it possible to take a "stronger" position with this example? We shall see. As encryption technology continues to improve, there is a remote chance that computer scientists may develop an encryption algorithm so effective that the Sun will burn out before any machine could succeed in breaking the code. Such a technology could bury historical records for the rest of history. . . .

Conclusion

I have tried to show that there are issues and problems that are unique to computer ethics. For all of these issues, there was an essential involvement of computing technology. Except for this technology, these issues would not have arisen or would not have arisen in their highly altered form. The failure to find satisfactory non-computer analogies testifies to the uniqueness of these issues. The lack of an adequate analogy, in turn, has interesting moral consequences. Normally, when we confront unfamiliar ethical problems, we use analogies to build conceptual bridges to similar situations we have encountered in the past. Then we try to transfer moral intuitions across the bridge, from the analog case to our current situation. Lack of an effective analogy forces us to discover new moral values, formulate new moral principles, develop new policies, and find new ways to think about the issues presented to us. For all of these reasons, the kind of issues I have been illustrating deserves to be addressed separately from others that might at first appear similar. At the very least, they have been so transformed by computing technology that their altered form demands special attention.

I conclude with a lovely little puzzle suggested by Donald Gotterbarn.[40] There are clearly many devices that have had a significant impact on society over the centuries. The invention of the printing press was a pivotal event in the history of the transmission of culture, but there is no such thing as Printing-press Ethics. The locomotive revolutionized the transportation industry, but there is no such thing as Locomotive Ethics. The telephone forever changed the way we communicate with other human beings, but there is no such thing as Telephone Ethics. The tractor transformed the face of agriculture around the world, but there is no such thing as Tractor Ethics. The automobile has made it possible for us to work at great distances from our local neighborhoods, but there is no such thing as Commuter Ethics.

Why, therefore, should there be any such thing as Computer Ethics?

Notes

1. Parker, D. (1978) *Ethical Conflicts in Computer Science and Technology.* SRI International, Menlo Park, California.

2. There was a follow-up study some years later that remedied some of the problems discovered in the original methodology. See Parker, D., Swope S., and Baker, B., (1990) *Ethical Conflicts in Information and Computer Science, Technology, and Business,* QED Information Sciences, Inc., Wellesley, MA.

3. Parker, D. (1976) *Crime by Computer,* Charles Scribners Sons.

4. Gotterbarn, D. (1991) The use and abuse of computer ethics. In: Bynum, T., Maner, W. and Fodor, J., Eds., *Teaching Computer Ethics,* Research Center on Computing and Society, New Haven, CT, p. 74.

5. I coined the term "computer ethics" in 1976 to describe a specific set of moral problems either created, aggravated or transformed by the introduction of computer technology. By the fall of 1977, I was ready to create a curriculum for computer ethics and, shortly thereafter, began to teach one of the first university courses entirely devoted to applied computer ethics. By 1978, I had become a willing promoter of computer ethics at various national conferences. Two years later, Terrell Bynum helped me publish a curriculum development kit we called the "Starter Kit in Computer Ethics." We found we could not interest the academic establishment in computer ethics, either philosophers or computer scientists, but we managed to survive as an underground movement within the American Association of Philosophy Teachers.

6. Weiner, N. (1960) Some moral and technical consequences of automation. *Science* **131**: 1355–1358.

7. Gotterbarn, D. (1991) A "capstone" course in computer ethics. In: Bynum, T., Maner, W. and Fodor, J., Eds., *Teaching Computer Ethics,* Research Center on Computing and Society, New Haven, CT, p. 42.

8. Bynum, T. (1991) Computer ethics in the computer science curriculum. In: Bynum, T., Maner, W. and Fodor, J., Eds., *Teaching Computer Ethics,* Research Center on Computing and Society, New Haven, CT, p. 24.

9. Moor, J. (1985) What is computer ethics? *Metaphilosophy* **16** (4): 266. The article also appears in Bynum, T., Maner, W. and Fodor, J., Eds., *Teaching Computer Ethics*, Research Center on Computing and Society, New Haven, CT.

10. Maner, W. (1980) *Starter Kit in Computer Ethics*, Helvetica Press and the National Information and Resource Center for the Teaching of Philosophy.

11. Pecorino, P. and Maner, W. (1985) The philosopher as teacher: A proposal for a course on computer ethics. *Metaphilosophy* **16** (4): 327–337.

12. Parker, D. (1989) *Computer Crime: Criminal Justice Resource Manual*, 2nd edition. National Institute of Justice, Washington, D.C.

13. Neumann, P. (1995) *Computer Related Risks.* Addison-Wesley Publishing Company, New York.

14. Forester, T., and Morrison, P. (1990) *Computer Ethics: Cautionary Tales and Ethical Dilemmas in Computing.* MIT Press, Boston, MA.

15. Tabak, L. (1988) Giving engineers a positive view of social responsibility. *SIGCSE Bulletin* **20** (4): 29–37.

16. Behar, J. (1993) Computer ethics: moral philosophy or professional propaganda? In: Leiderman, M., Guzetta, C., Struminger, L. and Monnickendam, M., Eds., *Technology in People Services: Research, Theory and Applications.* The Haworth Press, New York, pp. 441–453.

17. Chapman, G. (Sept. 14, 1990) in response to a luncheon address by Perrolle, J., *Political and social dimensions of computer ethics.* Conference on Computers and the Quality of Life, George Washington University, Washington, D.C.

18. See Gotterbarn, D. (1991) Computer ethics: responsibility regained. *National Forum: The Phi Kappa Phi Journal* **71** (3): 26–31.

19. I refer to the academic discipline of computer ethics as defined in Maner (1980).

20. Leventhal, L., Instone, K. and Chilson, D. (January 1992) Another view of computer science: patterns of responses among computer scientists. *Journal of Systems Software* **19** (1): 1–12.

21. Integrating the ethical and social context of computing into the computer science curriculum: an interim report from the content subcommittee of the ImpactCS steering committee. In: Rogerson, S. and Bynum, T., Eds. *Information Ethics: A Comprehensive Reader.* Basil Blackwell Publisher, (forthcoming in 1996). For further information on the ImpactCS project, contact Dr. Chuck Huff, Psychology Department, St. Olaf College, Northfield, MI 55057 USA (huff@stolaf.edu).

22. Neumann (1995), p. 88.

23. Neumann (1995), p. 169.

24. Moor (1985), p. 269.

25. Green, P. and Brightman, A. (1990) *Independence Day: Designing Computer Solutions for Individuals with Disability.* DLM Press, Allen, Texas.

26. See a similar discussion in Huff, C. and Finholt, T. (1994) *Social Issues in Computing: Putting Computing in Its Place.* McGraw-Hill, Inc., New York, 184.

27. Moor (1985), pp. 274–275.

28. McConnell, S. (1993) *Code Complete: A Practical Handbook of Software Construction.* Microsoft Press, Redmond, WA.

29. Science behind the news: Did computers make stock prices plummet? *Discover* **7**, 12 (December, 1986), p. 13.

30. Computers amplify black Monday. *Science* **238:** 4827 (October 30, 1987).

31. Kirk Makin, in an article written for the *Globe and Mail* appearing on November 3, 1987, reported that Sergeant Ted Green of the Ontario Provincial Police knew of such a case.

32. Parker (1989), p. 19.

33. Quoted in Ladd, J. Ethical issues in information technology. Presented at a conference of the Society for Social Studies of Science, November 15–18, 1989, in Irvine, California.

34. Dijkstra, E. (1989) On the cruelty of really teaching computer science. *Communications of the ACM* **32** (12): 1398–1404.

35. Dijkstra (1989), p. 1400.

36. Neumann, P. (April, 1980) Risks to the public in computers and related systems. *Software Engineering Notes* **5** (2): 5.

37. Neumann (1995), p. 26.

38. Dijkstra (1989), p. 1400.

39. Hart, C. (January 2, 1990) Computer data putting history out of reach. *Raleigh News and Observer.*

40. Gotterbarn (1991) p. 27.

CHAPTER TWO
Computer Technologies as Value-Laden

CREATING THE PEOPLE'S COMPUTER

Michael Dertouzos

Computer scientist Michael Dertouzos discusses the need for computer technology to become much more in tune with common users in their spheres of operation. Many current applications further burden people's lives rather than free them from monotonous tasks. Alluding to what he sees as problems with computer design and designers, Dertouzos promotes his belief that someday it will be possible to create a computer that is comfortably accessible and useful to "nonprogrammers." Computers need to be made to enhance life.

It is a few days before Christmas. I am out shopping at a well-known upscale department store in the Greater Boston area. I take nine items to the cash register. The cashier passes her magic wand over each package to read the bar code, and the impact printer rattles away as it prints a description and price for each item. I am getting ready to pull out my credit card when the woman turns to the cash register beside her and, horror of horrors, starts keying in the exact same information manually, reading the numbers off each package in turn.

She is on package number six when I clear my throat conspicuously and, with the indignation of a time-study specialist, ask her why in the world she is duplicating the work of the bar-code reader. She waves me to silence with the authority of one accustomed to doing so. "Please, I have to finish this," she says politely. I tell her to take her time, even though my muscles are tightening up and my brain is engaging in vivid daydreams of punitive acts.

From *Technology Review* 100, no. 3 (April 1997): 20–28; reprinted by permission of the author.

She finishes the last package, ignores my pointed sigh, reaches for a pencil, and . . . starts all over again! This time she is writing in longhand on the store's copy of the receipt a string of numbers for every package. I am so shocked by this triple travesty that I forget my anger and ask her in true wonder what she is doing. Once more she waves me to silence so she can concentrate, but then obliges: "I have to enter every part number by hand," she says. "Why?" I ask, with a discernible trembling in my voice. "Because my manager told me to," she replies, barely suppressing the urge to finish her sentence with the universal suffix "stupid." I could not let this go. I called for the manager. He looked at me knowingly and said with a sigh, "Computers, you know."

I told him that this looked a bit more serious than that, and he proceeded to explain in slow, deliberate phrasing that the central machine didn't work, so a duplicate had to be entered by hand.

"Then, why enter it at all into the computer?" I ventured hopefully.

"Because it is our standard operating procedure, and when the central machine comes back, we should be in a position to adjust our records for inventory changes." Hmm.

"Then why in the world is she both keying in the numbers *and* entering them with the bar-code reader?" I countered.

"Oh. That's the general manager's instruction. He is concerned about our computer problems and wants to be able to verify and cross-check all the departmental entries."

I quietly walked out, stunned.

After I got over my shock at the absurd waste of time this store's procedures caused for the cashier—and me—I began to marvel at how the great promise that computers would improve human productivity is more easily discussed than implemented. Indeed, the topic of whether computers are raising human productivity has generated a great deal of controversy. Technology detractors will point to such encounters and say, "See, computers don't help us." And it's true that information technology does hurt productivity in some cases; it takes longer to wade through those endless automated phone-answering menus than it does to talk to a human operator. If technology is not used wisely, it can make us less productive instead of more so.

But computers can also be incredibly helpful. Used properly, they help ring up prices faster, track inventory, and handle price changes. Productivity will rise in the Information Age for the same reason it did in the Industrial Age: the application of new tools to relieve human work.

Some people dismiss productivity concerns, arguing that computers make possible things we couldn't do otherwise. Certainly that is true, as the World Wide Web, special effects in movies, and credit cards have shown us. But to ignore the computer's fundamental ability to help humans do their brain work is at best perverse and at worst irresponsible. Productivity is the yardstick by which socioeconomic revolutions are measured. That was the case with plows, engines, electricity, and the automobile. If there is to be a true information revolution, computers will have to repeat the pattern with information and information work.

As we try to anticipate how computers might be used in the twenty-first century we are bombarded with unparalleled confusion and hype—a faster Web/Internet, network computers, intranets, cyberspace, 1,000 video channels, free information, telework, and much more. To my thinking, this future world can be described simply and crisply as an "information marketplace," where people and their interconnected computers are engaged in the buying, selling, and free exchange of information and information work.

Many issues surround the information marketplace: the technology of its underlying information infrastructures; its uses in commerce, health, learning, the pursuit of pleasure, and government; and the consequences of these new activities for our personal lives, our society, and our history. Here we will focus on a small but crucial aspect of this rich ensemble—ensuring that tomorrow's information marketplace will help us in our eternal quest to get more results for less work. . . .

Gentle-Slope Systems

Automating computer-to-computer transactions and fixing problems in present computer systems are good steps toward making computers and the information marketplace serve us. But designing systems that are inherently easier to use is the really big lever. I believe that this endeavor will consume our attention for a good part of the next century.

In the last decade, anyone who has uttered the phrase "user friendly" in my presence has run the risk of physical assault. The phrase has been shamelessly invoked to suggest that a program is easy and natural to use when this is rarely true. Typically, "user friendly" refers to a program with a WIMP interface, meaning it relies on windows, icons, menus, and pointing along with an assortment of pretty colors and fonts that can be varied to suit users' tastes. This kind of overstatement is tantamount to dressing a chimpanzee in a green hospital gown and earnestly parading it as a surgeon. Let's try to penetrate the hype by painting a picture of where we really are with respect to user friendliness and where the true potential for ease of use lies.

It is sometime in the late 1980s. A friend approaches you, excited by his ability to use spreadsheets. You ask him to explain how they work. He shows you a large grid. "If you put a bunch of numbers in one column," he says, "and then below them put the simple command that adds them up, you will see their total in the bottom cell. If you then change one of the numbers, the total will change automatically." The friend rushes on, barely able to control his exuberance: "And if you want to make the first number 10 percent larger, you just put in the cell next to it the simple command that multiplies it by 1.1." His expression becomes lustful: "Do you want to increase all the numbers by 10 percent? Just drag your mouse down like this, and they will all obey."

He takes in a deep breath, ready to explode once more, when you stop him cold. "Thank you. Now go away," you say. "You have taught me enough to do all my accounting chores." This is how millions of people today use their spreadsheet programs like Microsoft Excel and Lotus 1-2-3. They hardly know more than a tenth of the commands yet they get ample productivity gains.

You are happy with your newly acquired knowledge until one day you discover that you need to do something a bit more ambitious, like repeat over an entire page all the laborious operations you have set up but with a new set of initial numbers. Perplexed, you go back to your friend, who smiles knowingly and tells you that you must now learn about macros. His explanations are no longer as simple as before, and you just can't get the spreadsheet to do what you want. This is where most of the millions who use spreadsheets give up. But instead you fight on, eventually mastering the mysteries of the macro. It's really a computer program written in an arcane programming language that replaces you in commanding the spreadsheet program to do things you would have done manually.

You sail along for the next six months until you develop the need to do an even more ambitious task that involves designing a human-machine interface that will make your program more useful. You go back to your friend, who tells you that you have become too good for the limited capabilities of this spreadsheet application, and that you must now learn how to use a real programming language like C++. Unaware of what lies behind these three innocent symbols but unwilling to give up, you press on. This costs you your job, because you must now devote full time to a colossal new learning endeavor. Yet you are so enamored with programming that you don't mind. In fact, you like the idea. Two years later, having harnessed C++ and a few more programming languages and operating systems, you begin a career as a successful independent software vendor and eventually become wealthy.

This happy ending cannot hide the barriers that you have had to overcome along the way. You decide to graph the effort you expended versus the ability you gained. The result is a line starting at the left and moving along to the right. There is a long slowly rising portion and then a huge hill where you had to learn a lot of new stuff in order to move further right. Then there are more slowly rising lines and more huge hills, like a mountain chain where each new mountain gets higher. You wish that someone would invent an approach with a gentler slope, one where you get ever-greater returns as you increase your learning effort, without the impossible cliffs that you had to climb. I predict that such "gentle-slope systems," as I like to call them, will appear and will mark an important turning point of the Information Age.

The gentle-slope systems will have a few key properties. First and foremost, they will give incrementally more useful results for incrementally greater effort. They will be able to automate any activity you do that is repetitive. They will be graceful, in the sense that incomplete actions or errors on your part will result in reasonable degradations of performance rather than catastrophes. Finally, they will be easy to understand—no more complicated than reading a cookbook recipe.

Conceptually Challenged

One reason it is difficult for nonprogrammers to tell computers what to do is that the software systems that surround us are preoccupied with the structure rather than the meaning of information. We can program them to do anything we want, but they are unaware of the meaning of even the simplest things we are trying to do. Let me illustrate.

It takes me 17 seconds to say to a programmer, "Please write me a program that I can use to enter onto my computer the checks I write, along with the categories of each expenditure—food, recreation, and so forth. And do this so that I can ask for a report of the checks that I have written to date, listed chronologically or by category."

I have given this assignment several times to different people. Master programmers invariably decline to play and tell me to go buy this program because it's commercially available. Good programmers will say they can meet the request in a couple of hours—and end up taking a day or two to develop a shaky prototype. Inexperienced programmers will say cockily that they can write the program in a few minutes as a spreadsheet macro—and are generally unable to deliver anything at all. The company Intuit, which developed the very successful Quicken program that does this job and more, took two years and many millions of dollars to develop, test, document, and bring to market.

Why can I "program" a human being to understand the above instruction in 17 seconds, while it takes a few thousand to a few million times longer to program a computer to understand the same thing? The answer surely lies in the fact that humans share concepts like check, category, report, and chronological, while computers do not. The machine is so ignorant of these concepts that programmers must spend virtually all of their programming time teaching the computer what they mean. If, however, I had a computer that already understood some of these "concepts," then I might be able to program it to do my job in a very short time. This is an important way in which computers could increase our productivity in the twenty-first century: by being made to better understand more human concepts in better ways.

For computers to be truly easier to use, technologists will have to shift their focus away from the twentieth-century preoccupation with the structures of information tools like databases, spreadsheets, editors, browsers, and languages. In their early stage, computers became ubiquitous because this focus allowed these common tools to be used equally in thousands of applications, from accounting to engineering to art. Yet that same generality is what makes them ignorant of the special uses they must ultimately serve and ultimately less useful than they should be—much like a dilettante jack-of-all-trades.

What we need now, to boost utility further, is a new breed of software systems like a spreadsheet that an accountant can easily program and that already "understands" higher-level repetitive tasks like setting up charts of accounts, doing a cash reconciliation, and pulling trial balances.

Freed from the tyranny of generality, these specialized programming "environments" will rise toward offering a lot more of the basic information and operations of their specialty. The time has come for computer technologists to abandon the "generalist" orientation that served people well for the first four decades of the computer era and shift their focus from the structure to the meaning of information.

Everyone a Programmer

The biggest promise of the Information Age is the great and still unrealized potential of tailoring information technology to individual human needs. Today's applications programs are like ready-made clothes—one size fits all. So most are ill-fitting, and we have to contort ourselves to improve the fit. Another potential outcome of this practice for business is that if every company used the same set of canned programs, they would follow more or less the same procedures, and no company would stand out against the competition. Shrink-wrapped, ready-made software is good enough for the state of information technology at the end of the twentieth century. But it won't be as good in tomorrow's information marketplace.

Great gains will be achieved when individuals and businesses can bend and fashion information tools to do exactly what they want them to do, rather than bending themselves to what the tools can do. This quest for customizable information tools with specialized knowledge will be no different than the current trend toward customized manufacturing. It could well be that by the close of the twenty-first century, a new form of truly accessible programming will be the province of everyone and will be viewed like writing, which was once the province of the ancient scribes but eventually became universally accessible.

This isn't as absurd as it sounds. We invented writing so that we could communicate better with one another. Tomorrow we'll need to communicate better with our electronic assistants, so we'll extend our "club" to include them as well. Everyone will then be a "programmer," not just the privileged few. And none of them will be conscious of it. In fact, this is already happening on a small scale among the millions of people who use spreadsheets and who would be very surprised to learn that they are programmers.

When I say people will program, I am not talking about writing the detailed code and instructions that make computers run. That will still constitute the bulk of a software program and will indeed be created by professional programmers, who will fashion the many larger building blocks that we will use. Each individual's "programming" will account for a very small fraction of the software code, maybe 1 percent. But it will be the crucial factor that gives the program its specificity. It will be like building a model railroad; you don't make all the track or engines or cars, but you do arrange the pieces to create your own custom railway patterns.

We can increase the usefulness of our machines in the emerging information marketplace by correcting current human-machine faults, by developing automatization tools, and by creating a new breed of gentle-slope software systems that understand specialized areas of human activity—and that can be easily customized by ordinary people to meet their needs. Pursuing these directions should get us going on our quest, which I expect will last well into the twenty-first century, to harness the new technologies of information for the fulfillment of ancient human purposes.

COMPUTERS AND REASON

Theodore Roszak

As a self-described "neo-Luddite," Theodore Roszak uses philosophers such as Plato and Bertrand Russell to illustrate the problems inherent both in the development of computers and in our society's misbegotten belief in their powers. He questions the basis for an op-

Reprinted with permission of the University of California Press from *The Cult of Information: The Folklore of Computers and the True Art of Thinking* (1994), 108–20. Copyright © 1986 by Theodore Roszak.

timism in mathematics' special status within human reason, since the world does not seem to lend itself, except in a relatively narrow set of cases, to careful ordering and precision. Roszak is particularly concerned with keeping a clear distinction between data and ideas. When this line is blurred (in what he calls "the cult of information"), underlying assumptions and value-laden processes go unquestioned by users.

The Light in Plato's Cave

. . . When we speak of the computer as a "data processor," it is easy to overlook the fact that these two words refer to two separate functions that have been united in the machine. The computer *stores* data, but it can also *process* these data—meaning it can manipulate them in various ways for purposes of comparison, contrast, classification, deduction. The data may be numbers which are being run through mathematical processes; but they may also be names, addresses, medical records, personnel files, technical instructions which are also being run through a program to be sorted, ordered, filtered, or placed in some designated sequence. Thus, when a computer is ordered to run a spreadsheet scenario for a business, it draws upon all the data it holds for that business (inventory, overhead, earnings, seasonal performance, etc.), but it also massages the data, shaping them as the program instructs. Even a simple mailing list may reorganize the material in its data bank in response to a program designed, for example, to segregate names by zip code in order to upscale the subscription list of a magazine or to edit out names on the basis of credit rating, ethnicity, age, etc.

These two operations have become so integrated in the performance of most computers that they are rarely thought of any longer as separate functions. Yet they are, and each may be given a separate evaluation. *Storing* data connects the computer with the job of record keeping; it dates back to the ledgers and filing cabinets which electronic data banks are now replacing. In this capacity, the computer mimics the faculty of memory. *Processing* data, on the other hand, represents a different line of technological descent. Here the computer dates back to the adding machine, and in this capacity, it mimics the power of human reason. For many computer enthusiasts, this second line of development is the real significance of the machine. They value its ability to work through lengthy logical-mathematical procedures with blinding speed and absolute precision. For them, this is the computer's closest approximation to the human mind.

. . . I have argued that those who celebrate the computer as an information keeper and provider tend to underrate, if not ignore the value of ideas, assuming, as many strict empiricists have, that information some-how compiles itself automatically into knowledge without the active intervention of theoretical imagination. Yet, ironically enough, the second line of technological descent that flows into the computer—that which has to do with procedural thinking—derives from a very different philosophical tradition, one which is intimately connected with the power of pure reason. Along this rationalist line of descent, the computer draws upon a class of ideas which has proved to be uniquely persuasive and long-lived, even though it has no connection whatever with data or with human experience of any kind. These are *mathematical ideas:* ideas discovered in the light of unaided reason, fashioned from the logical structure of the mind itself.

In the history of philosophy, it is mathematics that has again and again been used as an example of a priori knowledge, knowledge which supposedly has no connection with sensory experience, with the data of observation and measurement. As Bertrand Russell observes:

> Mathematics is . . . the chief source of the belief in eternal and exact truth, as well as in a supersensible intelligible world. Geometry deals with exact circles, but no sensible object is *exactly* circular; however carefully we may use our compasses, there will be some imperfections and irregularities. This suggests the view that all exact reasoning applies to the ideal as opposed to sensible objects; it is natural to go further, and to argue that thought is nobler than sense, and the objects of thought more real than those of sense perception.[1]

The classic formulation of this idea about mathematical ideas is that of Plato, for whom geometry served as the model of all reliable knowledge. Plato assumed that geometrical ideas are born into the mind as our one sure foundation for thought. In the darkness and confusion of life, we have the certainty of mathematics to guide us. In his famous Allegory of the Cave, Plato portrays the human race as a population of wretched slaves confined by their physical mortality to a tenebrous dungeon where they can see nothing but a blurred show of animated shadows; they know nothing that is not impermanent and illusory. In their squalid prison, there is but one distant glimmer of illuminating sunlight. Only the true philosopher discerns it; it is the power of pure reason, which gives us, especially in the form of mathematics, a knowledge of eternal verities, the pure forms that transcend the flux of time and the frailty of the flesh.

Over the centuries, in a variety of ways, philosophers have taken issue with Plato's theory of knowledge and the mystique which it lends to mathematics. Still, for all the criticism, there remains a haunting quality to mathematical ideas, a trust in the clarity of numbers and of mathematical logic that lingers on in modern science and which survives in cybernetics and information theory. Plato's mysticism may have been banished from these new sciences, but the spell of geometrical certainty remains. For, ironically enough, the machine that gives the cult of information its greatest strength is grounded in a body of ideas—mathematical ideas—which has nothing to do with information, and which might conceivably be seen as the best proof we have to offer of the primacy of ideas.

As computers have grown "smarter" (meaning faster, more capacious, more intricate in their programming) over the past two decades, computer scientists have often exhibited some uneasiness with the name of their machine. As most recent textbooks in computer science hasten to tell students in the first chapter, the computer is no longer merely a computing instrument; it has transcended its lowly origins to become a form of artificial intelligence in the broadest sense. Thus, Margaret Boden observes,

> It is essential to realize that a computer is not a mere "number cruncher," or supercalculating arithmetic machine, although this is how computers are commonly regarded by people having no familiarity with artificial intelligence. Computers do not crunch numbers; they manipulate symbols. . . . Digital computers originally developed with mathematical problems in mind, are in fact general purpose symbol manipulating machines. . . .
>
> The terms "computer" and "computation" are themselves unfortunate, in view of their misleading arithmetical connotations. The definition of artificial intelligence previously cited—"the study of intelligence as computation"—does not imply that intelligence is really counting. Intelligence may be defined as the ability creatively to manipulate symbols, or process information, given the requirements of the task in hand.[2]

It is certainly true that computers have evolved a long way from being super adding machines. But it is also true that, in large measure, the reputation which computer science and computerized forms of "intelligence" have acquired in our popular culture borrows heavily upon the age-old mystique of mathematics. Insofar as computer scientists believe that computers are "machines who think" and that may someday think better than people, it is because of the machine's historic connection with what the scientists and technicians have always taken to be the clearest, most productive kind of thinking: mathematics. The promise that many enthusiasts see in the computer is precisely that it will, in time, produce a form of intelligence which will apply the exactitude of mathematics to every other field of culture. The computer's repertory of symbols may no longer be limited to numbers; nevertheless, the hope remains that its more sophisticated programs will be able to manipulate symbols with the logical rigor of mathematical reasoning. Fritz Machlup makes the point that the word *computation* has taken on a vastly extended usage, now covering whatever computers can do as symbol manipulators. This leads to a good deal of public confusion. When, for example, a cognitive scientist speaks of artificial intelligence programs, and people "read a sentence or clause to the effect that 'mental processes are computational processes,' they are most likely to think of processes of numerical computation—but would be wrong."[3]

It is, however, this very error which works to enhance the prestige of the computer by making it all too easy to believe that whatever runs through a computer thereby acquires the ironclad certainty of pure mathematics. Though they would blush to associate themselves with Plato's mysticism, many opportunistic figures in computer science and especially artificial intelligence have exploited that error for all it is worth in the confused public mind.

It is curious how, at times in the most unpredictable way, something of the old Platonic spirit surfaces in the world of computer science. Plato was convinced that it was the corruption of the flesh that separates us from the highest forms of knowledge. So he recommended the study of geometry as a sort of purgation of the senses that would elevate the mind above the body's mortality. We can see exactly this same alliance of the ascetic and the mathematical in the following passage from Robert Jastrow's study of "mind in the universe":

> When the brain sciences reach this point, a bold scientist will be able to tap the contents of his mind and transfer them into the metallic lattices of a computer. Because mind is the essence of being, it can be said that this scientist has entered the computer, and that he now dwells in it.
>
> At last the human brain, ensconced in a computer, has been liberated from the weakness of the mortal flesh. . . . It is in control of its own destiny. The machine is its body; it is the machine's mind. . . .
>
> It seems to me that this must be the mature form of intelligent life in the Universe. Housed in indestructible lattices of silicon, and no longer constrained in the span of its years by the life and death cycle of a biological organism, such a kind of life could live forever.[4]

In this disembodied form, Jastrow imagines that the computer will transform us into "a race of immortals."

The Old Mathematical Magic

The mathematical model of absolute certainty is one of the undying hopes of our species. As tough-minded as most scientists might be (or wish to appear to be) in their response to the old mathematical magic, that Platonic dream survives, and no place more vividly than in the cult of information. Data—the speed and quantity of their processing—may be what the cult most often emphasizes in its celebration of the computer. But quite as important as the data is the mathematical precision with which the computer's programs manipulate the information fed into them. This is what computer scientists mean by the term *effective procedure.* We are told that a computer can do anything for which an "effective procedure" is given. The phrase means "a set of rules (the program) unambiguously specifying certain processes, which processes can be carried out by a machine built in such a way as to accept those rules as instructions determining its operations."[5] The search for such a procedure would be pure whimsey were it not for the fact that there is one field of thought which offers us a model of just such strict logicality: mathematics, the field that produced the computer in the first place. When limited to the realm of what *can* be treated with such logical rigor, the computer functions at its full strength. But the further we stray from that realm, the more rapidly its powers fade.

Unfortunately, not all computer scientists are willing to concede that point. They forget—and help the public forget—that mathematical ideas are of a very special kind. They are *formal* ideas, meaning they are built from axioms by unambiguously specifiable rules. They can be analyzed into parts, and the parts are ultimately logical principles and postulates that lend themselves to mechanical manipulation. The value of mathematical ideas lies precisely in this analytical clarity and nonambiguity. Within their field of proper application, they have the power to confer logical transparency; they strip away ambiguity to reveal the skeletal structure that connects parts, stages, and procedures. They can be programmed. This is because, by an astonishing exercise of the human imagination, mathematical systems have been developed outside the real world of daily experience, which is more often than not blurred, fuzzy, and infinitely complex.

Since there are areas of the real world that appear to approximate formal order, there are portions of mathematics that can be applied to that world in order to isolate its more measurable and rule-abiding elements. Where that happens, we have the realms of theoretical and applied science. And so here too computers can be highly useful in channeling large amounts of information through scientific and technical programs. But even here we should bear in mind that there are underlying ideas of a non-mathematical kind (we might call them insights or, perhaps, articles of faith) that govern all scientific thought. Take our basic conviction that there is a rational order to nature, a pattern which the mind can grasp. This is the most fundamental of scientific ideas. But what is it based upon? It is a hunch or a desperate hope worked up perhaps from fleeting perceptions of symmetries or regularities in nature, recurring rhythms and cycles—all of which are continually dissolving in the "buzzing, booming confusion" of daily life. But working with that idea as a kind of filter, we screen out the exceptions and distractions and find deeper regularities which begin to look like an *order* of things. But what kind of order? Our science has chosen to look for the order of numbers. We work from Galileo's potent idea that "the great book of nature is written in the language of mathematics." But we might have chosen another kind of order. There is the order of music (thus the astronomer Kepler spent most of his life searching for the harmony of the spheres); there is the order of architecture and of drama; there is the order of a story (a myth) told over and over; there is the order of a god's behavior, where we watch for reward and punishing, wrath and mercy. Which order is the most important? Making that choice is also an idea to be selected from all the possibilities.

Very nearly the whole of modern science has been generated out of a small collection of metaphysical, even aesthetic ideas such as:

The universe consists of matter in motion. (Descartes)

Nature is governed by universal laws. (Newton)

Knowledge is power. (Bacon)

None of these ideas is a conclusion arrived at by scientific research; none of them is the result of processing information. Rather, they are premises that make scientific research possible and lead to the discovery of confirming data. Once again, these are master ideas about the world, and like all master ideas, they transcend information. They arise from another dimension of the mind, from a capacity for insight that is perhaps akin to the power of artistic and religious inspiration.

There is no question but that in the area of mathematical and scientific ideas, the computer supplements the mind significantly. It can carry out calculations at blinding speed; it can make hypothetical projections; it can offer amazingly flexible graphic representations; it can produce complex simulations that stretch the imagination. This is quite a lot for a machine to offer. Yet it may be that even in the sciences, the computer's proficiency as an information processor has its liabilities. At least one leading scientist has raised a provocative warning about the use of computers in astronomy. Sir Bernard Lovell writes:

> I fear that literal-minded, narrowly focused computerized research is proving antithetical to the free exercise of that happy faculty known as serendipity. . . . Would the existence of radio galaxies, quasars, pulsars and the microwave background ever have been revealed if their discovery had depended on the computerized radio observations of today? . . . The computers act as very narrow filters of information; they must be oriented to specific observations. In other words, they have to be programmed for the kinds of results that the observer expects. Does this mean, then, that computers are antiserendipitous? And if they are, should we not be troubled that they may be obscuring from our understanding further major features of the universe?[6]

The Seductions of Software

There is a predictable response to the argument I have been making here. It would insist that computers can *also* be programmed with non-mathematical ideas. Indeed, this is done all the time. For this is what a "program" is: an algorithm, a set of instructions that organizes information for some purpose. The ideas that animate programs may be too obvious to merit comment, as in the case of a family budget program that operates from the assumption that bankruptcy is undesirable and should therefore be avoided. (The program may then even dramatize the warning with a sharp command or a blinking signal.) Or the idea may be as brutally simple as the goal of the video game which dictates that Ms. Pacman should eat without being eaten.

Many programs are a great deal more complex than that. There are integrated management packages that claim to do the jobs of an entire office staff and perhaps a vice president or two. There are computer games that are fiendishly complicated, to the point of requiring as much intuition as calculation—meaning the complexities of strategy outdistance logical analysis. The trouble is, in the world of computer science *both* the ideas that govern the program *and* the data that are put through the program have come to be included within the concept of "information." The cult of information has gained a great deal for its mystique by bringing the program as well as the data within its province. But this can be a disastrous confusion. For it is like saying that there is no difference between, on the one hand, the architectural design of a building (the blueprints) and, on the other, all the measurements of all the materials that will be used in constructing that building. The materials and their measurements comprise a vast mass of detailed information that might usefully be entered into a computer under various convenient and cross-referenced headings and then called up for review at the push of a button. Yet it is the design of the building that holds this shapeless chaos of quantities together and gives it meaning. This is what answers the question, What is all this information about? It is also the design, once it is before us, that allows us to ask even more important questions which the data in the computer's memory cannot possibly answer. Do we really want to build this structure in the first place? Does it have a sensible relationship to its site, its neighborhood, its environment? Is it beautiful? Is it practical? Will it work? Will it make us proud? Will we feel at home in it? Does it have warmth, nobility, a human scale, a sense of its time and place that will make it welcome to those who must live with it and work within it?

We might discuss the design in all these respects without any measurements of any materials being given at all. (Even the true meaning of "human scale" may not always be a matter of size, but often of the character of the environment.) We are then talking about the *idea* of the building, as we had it in mind or perhaps as it might exist in a mere doodle on a scrap of paper. Nowadays the doodle might be done by the architect with an electronic stylus on a video screen, but the distinction holds: the idea comes first, the idea contains the data, the idea governs the data.

Once we reflect upon the matter, we cannot fail to see that the data and the program that processes the data stand on different levels, the one subordinate to the other. Why is it, then, that they have both come to be called "information"?

In part, this may have to do with the fact that whatever gets fed into a computer is at once translated into binary numbers. The numbers become bits, the letters of words become packages of bits called bytes. The binary code then comes to be seen as a comprehensive "language" that homogenizes all that it expresses. In some universities, the systems used to help make the translation (BASIC, PASCAL, LISP, etc.), metaphorically referred to as "programming languages," can now be substituted for the study of French, German, Russian . . . the faster to make the students computer literate. These are not, of course, languages at all; they are coding systems. But in the computer's electronic metabolism, the omnivorous bit devours everything—numbers, words, geometrical forms, graphics, music—into long strings of ones and zeros. Does this not, then, erase the distinction between data and idea? As I was once told by a computer expert, "information" is anything that can be entered into the machine as off/on, yes/no.

Now, if there were such a thing as a conscious transistor, this might be the odd way in which such an alien entity would see the world: as an infinite collection of undifferentiated "ones" and "zeros." But the fact that a transistor could not tell the difference between the bits that are data and the bits that are ideas, does not mean that *we* are free to blur this vital distinction. For if we do, we risk surrendering our intelligent control over the programs that now govern more and more of our lives. Every piece of software has some repertory of basic assumptions, values, limitations embedded within it. In no sensible meaning of the word are these "information." Crude as they may often be, they are ideas about the world, and, like all ideas, they must be kept in clear, critical view.

In early 1985, a financial columnist ran an experiment that involved four of the most widely used computer financial planning programs. A hypothetical middle-class family was invented and its financial resources, needs, plans, preferences were run through the programs. The result was four strikingly different sets of recommendations, covering such options as investments, savings, liquidity, insurance, retirement.[7] Why? Because the advice of each plan was programmed with different assumptions, a fact which none of the services mentioned. For the user, it simply seemed to be a matter of entering personal financial information and getting a printout which had every appearance of absolute authority.

This illusion of mathematical certainty becomes especially pronounced in the current obsession with spreadsheets in the business community. Since the first spreadsheet software was published by David Bricklin of the Harvard Business School in the late 1970s, this form of computerized accounting has become what Steven Levy calls a "virtual cult" among the entrepreneurs.[8] A useful way of modeling and projecting financial decisions, the spreadsheet like all programs is built upon an underlying matrix of assumptions. Some of these are ideas about people, their tastes and motivations; some are value judgments that place priorities upon various courses of action. All require some form of numerical weighting and factoring, perhaps of a crude or foolish kind. Then, too, even in the business world there are imponderable matters of good will, morale, satisfaction with one's enterprise, moral conduct; all these demand attention, yet, because they resist quantification, may find no place in the spreadsheet program. The vice of the spreadsheet is that its neat, mathematical facade, its rigorous logic, its profusion of numbers, may blind its user to the unexamined ideas and omissions that govern the calculations. As Levy observes, "Because the spreadsheet looks so authoritative—*and it was done by a computer, wasn't it?*—the hypothetical model gets accepted as gospel." It is, once more, an example of the mathematical mystique obscuring clear, critical evaluation of the underlying program.

We may not care to bear down on the matter, but even in the simplest video games our children play, there can be questionable ideas at work. The games are clearly dominated by ruthless competition and willful destruction. *Winning* is what matters, *killing* is what is valued. Many of the games are profoundly sexist, drawing on stereotypic macho images that appeal to adolescent boys—the main clientele for the video arcades. In contrast, one firm, which has published a series under the title "Computer Games for Girls," has imbued its software with conventional ideas of femininity, such as avoiding bloodshed, cooperating, taking time to clean up and pick flowers. Girls play the game as partners, not competitors; their games involve rather little hand-eye coordination.[9] It is commendable that the firm has tried to include girls in its market, but its games also deal in sexist stereotypes.

In a sensitive critique of video games, Ariel Dorfman concludes that the vast majority of them carry assumptions and goals that contribute to a form of "psychic numbing."

> Those who play videogames and leave their sensitivity and ethics aside when they deal with fictitious extinction on the blithe screen, when they militarize their free time, do so in the same society which contemplates mass murder as deterrence, corpses as statistics, forty million dead as victory, permanent escalation as peace.[10]

Perhaps most child's play throughout history has revolved around violent excitements, especially that of adolescent boys whose conception of manhood is still sadly underdimensioned. But surely the computer, with its hypnotic graphics and lightning fast responses (an enemy world spectacularly destroyed at the flick of a joystick), makes that wretched reflex of the pubescent glands more bedazzling and therefore more seductive.

It is only when we strike a clear distinction between ideas and information that we can recognize that these are radically different levels of discourse requiring different levels of evaluation. In most cases, we may be able to assess the data that flow through the program as either "right" or "wrong," a question of fact that yields to standard research methods. But the ideas that govern the data are *not* information; nor are they sacrosanct matters of mathematical logic. They are philosophical commitments, the outgrowth of experience, insight, metaphysical conviction, which must be assessed as wise or foolish, childlike or mature, realistic or fantastic, moral or wicked. That critical project spans the full range of computer software, from the video game that places the fanciful annihilation of a galaxy beneath the power of a child's thumb to the computerized war machine that places the real choice of genocide before our presidents and generals. Weighing such matters up in the critical scales requires an education which standard computer literacy will never provide.

Since information technology has been with us, its discriminating users have recognized the principle of GIGO: garbage in—garbage out. The computer can do no better than the quality of the information selected by a human intelligence to be entered into it. But this principle needs to be extended to another level. The mathematical rigor of the computer may mislead some into interpreting GIGO as what Ashley Montague once construed it to mean: garbage in—*gospel* out. We need another principle that makes us aware of the fallibilities which may be embedded in the programs that lie waiting inside the machine to receive the information. Even when the data are well selected, they may be ambushed by intellectual "garbage" of another order hiding in the depths of the program.

Notes

1. Bertrand Russell, *A History of Western Philosophy* (New York: Clarion Books, 1945), p. 37.

2. Margaret A. Boden, *Artificial Intelligence and Natural Man*, 2nd ed. (New York: Basic Books, 1987), pp. 15, 16–17.

3. Fritz Machlup and Una Mansfield, eds., *The Study of Information: Interdisciplinary Messages* (New York: Wiley, 1983), p. 671.

4. Robert Jastrow, *The Enchanted Loom: Mind in the Universe* (New York: Simon & Schuster, 1984), pp. 166–167.

5. Boden, *Artificial Intelligence and Natural Man*, pp. 6–7.

6. *Science Digest,* June 1984, p. 94.

7. Jane Bryant Quinn in the financial section of the *San Francisco Chronicle,* May 14, 1985.

8. Steven Levy, "A Spreadsheet Way of Knowledge," *Harper's,* November 1984.

9. See "The Apple Connection" column in *Bay Area Computer Currents,* November 20–December 3, 1984, p. 29.

10. Ariel Dorfman, "Evil Otto and Other Nuclear Disasters," *Village Voice,* June 15, 1982.

LOGIC AND INTUITION

Michael Heim

Philosopher Michael Heim takes Roszak's argument regarding the significance of the underlying mathematical basis of computers (see the previous essay) a step further by concentrating on the assumptions and dangers inherent in the use of Boolean logic (based on binary opposites: true and false/1s and 0s) for computer calculations. Of great concern to Heim is the way that Boolean operations within the computer shape the very way we think and reason; they shape what we think is reason. Drawing on Taoist literature, Heim argues that the "sharpening" of thought by computers in this way actually cuts off open-mindedness and makes us less capable of creativity.

How does thinking at the computer differ from thinking with paper and pencil or thinking at the typewriter? The computer doesn't merely place another tool at your fingertips. It builds a whole new environment, an information environment in which the mind breathes a different atmosphere. The computing atmosphere belongs to an information-rich world—which soon becomes an information-polluted world.

First, the files you create grow rapidly, forming an electronic library of letters, papers, and other documents. Through on-line connections, you

From *The Metaphysics of Virtual Reality* by Michael Heim. Copyright © 1994 by Michael Heim. Used by permission of the author and Oxford University Press, Inc.

save pieces from the work of colleagues and friends, notes about future projects, and leftovers from database searches. Add some serendipitous items to disk storage—maybe the Gettysburg Address, the Constitution, or the King James Bible—and you find yourself soon outgrowing your disk-storage capacity. CD-Roms then spin out encyclopedias, the *Oxford English Dictionary*, or the entire corpus of ancient Greek literature. As the load of information stresses your mental capacity, you sense that you've come down with infomania.

Because the computer helped generate all this information, you naturally hope that the computer will in turn help mop up the mess. The computer can indeed hack a neat pathway through the dense information jungle. Computer data searches find references, phrases, or ideas in an instant, in the nanoseconds it takes the microprocessor to go through huge amounts of data. A word processor or database takes a key phrase and in a flash snaps a piece of information into view. So there you are, lifted by the computer out of the morass generated by computers. You can search through thousands of periodicals in minutes, without ever having to know anything about silicon microchips, high-level code, or sorting algorithms. All you need is some elementary search logic that you can learn in about an hour. Today most computer searches use elementary Boolean logic.

What is Boolean logic? Alfred Glossbrenner in *How to Look It Up Online* describes Boolean logic in terms simple enough for most computer users: "AND means a record must have both terms in it. OR means it can have either term. NOT means it cannot have the specified term." Glossbrenner chides those who belabor the complexities of Boolean logic and bewilder the user: "You sometimes get the impression that the authors would be drummed out of the manual-writers union if they didn't include complicated discussion of search logic laced with plenty of Venn diagrams— those intersecting, variously shaded circles you learned about in sophomore geometry. Forget it!"[1]

But alas, what Glossbrenner wants us to forget will soon enough slip into oblivion as technology enfolds us in its web of assumptions. Frequent reading and writing on computers will soon allow us little distance from the tools that trap our language. They will fit like skin. The conditions under which we work will grow indiscernible, invisible to all but the keenest eye. Present everywhere like eyeglasses on the end of our noses, computers will hide the distortion they introduce, the vivid colors they overshadow, the hidden vistas they occlude. Like microscopes, computers extend our vision vastly, but unlike microscopes, computers process our entire symbolic life, reflecting the contents of the human psyche. Boolean search logic and other computer strategies will soon enough become second nature for literate people, something they take for granted.

What people take for granted was once something startling and unprecedented. A felt transition like the present alerts us to the change, and so we have an opportunity to ponder the initial shifts in the life of the psyche. We can ask, How does Boolean search logic affect our thought processes and mental life? What dark side of infomania is hiding behind those "intersecting, variously shaded circles you learned about in sophomore geometry"?

The significance of Boolean search logic deserves far more than a sidebar in how-to manuals. Boolean logic, displayed graphically by the circles of the Venn diagrams, constitutes a central achievement of modern logic. Modern logic, which makes the computer possible, got its footing in the work of Gottfried Leibniz (1646–1716), whose discoveries laid the foundations of computer systems and the information age. So when we inspect Boolean logic for its side effects, we are looking at the implicit heart of the world we inhabit. Boolean logic functions as a metaphor for the computer age, since it shows how we typically interrogate the world of information.

Humans have always interrogated the world in a variety of ways, and each way reveals a distinct approach to life: Socrates pushed for personal definitions; Descartes and Galileo taught scientists to pose questions with empirical hypotheses; McLuhan teased our awareness with his enigmatic slogans; Heidegger drew on a scholarly history of reality; and Wittgenstein worried over odd locutions. The type of question we ask, philosophers agree, shapes the possible answers we get. The way in which we search limits what we find in our searching.

Today we interrogate the world through the computer interface, where many of our questions begin with Boolean terms. The Boolean search then guides the subconscious processes by which we characteristically model the world. Once we notice how computers structure our mental environment, we can reflect on the subconscious agencies that affect our mental life, and we are then in a position to grasp both the potential and the peril. So let's return again to those simple Venn diagrams from sophomore geometry and to the Boolean logic on which they are based.

George Boole (1815–1864) discovered the branch of mathematics known as *symbolic logic*. Boole's "algebra of logic" uses formulas to symbolize logical relations. The formulas in algebraic symbols can describe the general relationships among groups of things that have certain properties. Given a question about how one group relates to another, Boole could manipulate the equations and quickly produce an answer. First, his algebra classifies things, and then the algebraic symbols express any relationship among the things that have been classified—as if we were shuffling things in the nested drawers of a Chinese puzzle box.

Take two referential terms, such as *brown* and *cows:* all objects that are brown = B; all objects that are cows = C. An algebraic formula can represent the relationship between these two terms as a product of mutual inclusion: "All brown cows" = BC. For more complex formulas, add a logical NOT ($-C$) as well as an AND (BC and $C - B$). Once you know that

(*BC* and *C* − *B*) = *F* (where *F* means any animal that "lives on the farm"), you can conclude that *BC* = *F* or also that any cow, no matter what color, lives on the farm. You can build up terms that represent a whole series of increasingly complex relationships, and then you can pose and calculate any implication from that series. You can even make symbolic formulas represent a very long chain of deductive reasoning so that the logical form of each part of the argument rises to the surface for review and criticism, making it possible to scan an argument as if it were a mathematical problem.

Historically, Boole's logic was the first system for calculating class membership, for rapidly determining whether or not something falls into one or another category or class of things. Before Boole, logic was a study of statements about things referred to directly and intuitively at hand. After Boole, logic became a system of pure symbols. Pre-Boolean logic focused on the way that direct statements or assertions connect and hold together. A set of statements that hangs together can be a valid deductive pattern. Validity is the way that conclusions connect with their supporting reasons or premises. The traditional study of logic harked back to Aristotle, who first noticed patterns in the way we assemble statements into arguments. Aristotle called the assemblage of statements *syllogisms*, from the Greek for a pattern of reasoning. Aristotle himself used symbols sparingly in his logic, and when he did use symbols, they served merely to point out language patterns. Aristotle's symbols organized what was already given in direct statements. With Boolean logic, on the contrary, direct statements have value only as instances of the relationships among abstract symbols. Direct language becomes only one possible instance of algebraic mathematics, one possible application of mathematical logic.

Boole inverted the traditional relationship between direct and symbolic languages. He conceived of language as a system of symbols and believed that his symbols could absorb all logically correct language. By inverting statement and symbol, Boole's mathematical logic could swallow traditional logic and capture direct statements in a web of symbolic patterns. Logical argument became a branch of calculation.

The term *symbolic logic* first appeared in 1881 in a book by that title. The book's author, John Venn, introduced the first graphic display of Boole's formulas. Venn continued Boole's plan to absorb the direct statements of language into a general system of abstract algebra. With mathematics as a basis, Venn could solve certain logical difficulties that had perplexed traditional Aristotelian logicians. With mathematical precision, modern logic could present linguistic arguments and logical relationships within a total system, a formal organization having its own axioms and theorems. Systemic consistency became more important than the direct reference to things addressed in our experience.

Note already one telltale sign of infomania: the priority of system. When system precedes relevance, the way becomes clear for the primacy of information. For it to become manipulable and transmissible as information, knowledge must first be reduced to homogenized units. With the influx of homogenized bits of information, the sense of overall significance dwindles. This subtle emptying of meaning appears in the Venn diagrams that graphically display Boolean logic.

The visual display that John Venn created begins with empty circles. Venn noted how Boolean logic treats terms, like *brown* and *cows*, strictly as algebraic variables and not as universal terms referring to actually existing things. In Boole's logic, terms function like compartments or drawers that may or may not contain any actual members. Boole's logic can use terms that are empty, the class of unicorns, for example. A term with no actually existing members is a null set, an empty compartment. As modern logicians say, the terms of logic do not in themselves carry existential import. The terms reveal relationships among themselves, but they remain unconnected to existence or to the direct references of firsthand experience. (Mathematics also shares this existential vacuum: $2 + 2 = 4$ remains mathematically true whether or not four things actually exist anywhere.) Boolean logic uses terms only to show relationships—of inclusion or exclusion—among the terms. It shows whether or not one drawer fits into another and ignores the question of whether there is anything in the drawers. The Boolean vocabulary uses abstract counters, tokens devoid of all but systemic meaning.

On Venn diagrams, then, we begin with empty circles to map statements that contain universal terms. We can map the statement "All the cows are brown" by drawing two overlapping circles: one representing cows and the other, brown things. Shade in (exclude) the area that represents cows and that does not overlap the area representing "brown things," and you have a graphic map of the statement "All the cows are brown." The map remains accurate regardless of whether or not any cows actually exist; you could equally well have drawn a map of the unicorns that are white. Add a third circle to represent spotted things, and you can map "No brown cows are spotted" or "All brown cows are spotted," and so on.

What does this procedure really map? According to Boolean logic, no cows or brown things or spotted things need actually exist. All we have mapped is the relationship between sets or classes. The sets could refer to custards or quarks or square circles.

In its intrinsic remoteness from direct human experience, Boolean search logic shows another part of the infomania syndrome: a gain in power at the price of our direct involvement with things. The Boolean search affects our relationship to language and thought by placing us at a new remove from subject matter, by directing us away from the texture of what we are exploring.

To add particular statements to our map, like "Some spotted cows are brown," we need to introduce more symbols. We can map statements about particular things on the diagrams by stipulating another conventional symbol, often a star, an asterisk, or some other mark. Statements that imply that a particular member of a class actually exists must be specifically marked as such; otherwise, the general term labels a potentially empty compartment. From the outset, then, Boolean logic assumes that as a rule, we stand at a remove from direct statements about particular things in which we existing beings are actually, personally involved.

This shift in the meaning of logical terms has drastic consequences for logic itself and for logic as a formal study. Traditional Aristotelian logic presupposed an actual subject, ideal or real, to which logical terms or words refer. Traditional logic also presupposed that logical thinking is, like spontaneous thought and speech, intimately involved with a real subject matter. Mathematical logic gained the upper hand by severing its significance from the conditions under which we make direct statements. Today, logicians like Willard Van Orman Quine can argue that a concrete and unique individual thing (to which we refer as such) has no more reality than "to be the value of a variable," at least when we consider things "from a logical point of view." The modern logical point of view begins with the system, not with concrete content. It operates in a domain of pure formality and abstract detachment. The modern logical point of view proceeds from an intricate net of abstract relations having no inherent connection to the things we directly perceive and experience.

We can contrast this aloof abstraction with the traditional logic that still swam in the element of direct experience. Traditional logic began with direct statements, insofar as its logical language presupposed as necessary the existential interpretation of statements. When we state something in everyday language, we attribute something to something; we attribute the color mauve to the wall, the quality of mercy to a creditor. We speak of what is before us, and we speak in the context of other people who may also have access to what we are talking about. We commonly assume the existence or at least the existential relevance of what we are talking about. Modern symbolic logic, on the contrary, mimics modern mathematics, which has no interest in the actually existing world, not even the world of direct statements. In this sense, modern logic operates at a remove from our everyday involvement with things.

But why pick on modern Boolean logic? Don't all logics bring abstraction and alienation? Even the words we use to pose any question testify to a gap between us and the wordless subject we are thinking or talking about. Any logic can distance us. We sometimes run across a person arguing with impeccable logic for a conclusion contrary to our own gut feelings, and we often feel overwhelmed, and forcibly so, by the sheer power of the argument itself. Logic can move like a juggernaut adrift from any

personal engagement with its subject matter. Someone with a great deal
less experience, for example, can make us feel compelled to accept a conclusion we know instinctively to be wrong. We feel the logical coercion
even though we may have much more familiarity with the matter under
discussion. Arguing with someone like Socrates or William F. Buckley can
be disconcerting. We sense a line of thought pushing inexorably through
the topic, perhaps even in spite of the topic. Logic, like mathematics, operates outside the intuitive wisdom of experience and common sense.
Hence the mathematical idiot savant. Like math, logic can hover above particular facts and circumstances; linking chains of statements trailing from
some phantom first premise. We can be perfectly logical yet float completely adrift from reality. By its very nature, logic operates with abstractions. But modern logic operates with a greater degree of abstraction than
does Aristotelian logic, placing us at a further remove from experience and
from felt insight.

When college students study those Venn diagrams from "sophomore
geometry," they feel the pain of that disengaged logic. When they first
learn to symbolize statements and arguments in symbolic logic, they must
pass through a lengthy and painful process of converting their English language into abstract symbols. So far removed does this logic stand from the
direct everyday use of language that the textbook refers to the process of
converting arguments into symbols as "translation." Before analyzing their
thoughts logically, students must translate them to fit the system of modern logic. Statements in direct English must first undergo a sea change.

The painful translation into symbols signals acute infomania. But
when logic works on the computer, this pain turns into convenience. When
the computer automatically and invisibly converts input into algebraic
bytes, the user is shielded from the translation into modern logic. Instead
of the human mind puzzling over how language fits the system, the computer does the fitting; it transforms our alphabet into manipulable digits.

As a medium, the computer relieves us of the exertion needed to
pour our thoughts into an algebraic mold. The shift from intuitive content to bit-size information proceeds invisibly and smoothly. On the machine level, the computer's microswitches in the central processing unit
organize everything through a circuit based on symbolic logic, and Boolean
searches simply apply that same logic to text processing. Hardly noticing
this spiderlike, nondirect logic, we stand at a new remove from concretely
embedded language. The computer absorbs our language so we can squirt
symbols at lightning speeds or scan the whole range of human thought
with Boolean searches. Because the computer, not the student, does the
translating, the shift takes place subtly. The computer system slides us
from a direct awareness of things to the detached world of logical distance.
By encoding language as data, the computer already modifies the language
we use into mathematized ASCII (American Standard Code for Information

Interchange). We can then operate with the certitude of Boolean formulas. The logical distance we gain offers all the allure of control and power without the pain of having to translate back and forth from our everyday approach to the things we experience.

But so what if computer power removes us from direct intuitive language? So what if Boolean logic injects greater existential distance from practical contexts than any previous logic? Don't our other text tools also operate at a remove from direct context-embedded language? Isn't any medium, by definition, a mediation? If the Boolean search operates at a great remove from direct oral discourse, don't also pen and paper, not to mention rubber erasers and Linotype typesetting machines?

Nonlinguistic tools, like erasers, do indeed insert a distance between ourselves and our context-embedded mother tongue. And, yes, using a rubber eraser does affect us in subtle, psychological ways. Teachers understand that getting a student to use an eraser marks a significant step on the road to good writing. A self-critical attitude distinguishes good from bad writing, and picking up an eraser means that we are beginning to evaluate our own words and thoughts.

But using Boolean search logic on a computer marks a giant step in the human species's relationship to thought and language. Just as the invention of the wax tablet made a giant stride in writing habits, forever marginalizing chiseled stones, so too Boolean search logic marks the new psychic framework of electronic text woven around us by computers. With electronic text we speed along a superhighway in the world of information, and Boolean search logic shifts our mental life into a high gear.

The Boolean search shows the characteristic way that we put questions to the world of information. When we pose a question to the Boolean world, we use keywords, buzzwords, and thought bits to scan the vast store of knowledge. Keeping an abstract, cybernetic distance from the sources of knowledge, we set up tiny funnels to capture the onrush of data. The funnels sift out the "hits" triggered by our keywords. Through minute logical apertures, we observe the world much like a robot rapidly surveying the surface of things. We cover an enormous amount of material in an incredibly short time, but what we see comes through narrow thought channels.

Because they operate with potentially empty circles, the Boolean search terms propel us at breakneck pace through the knowledge tunnel. The computer supports our rapid survey of knowledge in the mode of scanning, and through the computer's tools we adapt to this mode of knowing. The scanning mode infiltrates all our other modes of knowing. The byte, the breezy bit, and the verbal/visual hit take the place of heavier substance.

Of course, the computerized reader doesn't pluck search terms out of pure air. The funnels we fashion often result from a carefully honed search strategy. In *How to Look It Up Online,* Glossbrenner advises the reader:

> Meditate. Seriously. You may not be a Ninja warrior preparing for battle, but it's not a bad analogy. If you ride in like a cowboy with six-guns blazing, firing off search terms as they come into your head, you'll stir up a lot of dust, expend a lot of ammunition, and be presented with a hefty bill but very little relevant information when you're done. . . . Think about the topic beforehand. Let your mind run free and flow into the subject. What do you know and what can you extrapolate about the subject?[2]

What Glossbrenner calls meditation actually works to serve calculation. What he describes is no more than a deep breath before taking the plunge. Meditation of this kind only sharpens an already determined will to find something definite. The user meditates in order to construct a narrower and more efficient thought tunnel. But even if we build our tunnels carefully, we still remain essentially tunnel dwellers.

The word *meditate* came originally from the Latin *meditari,* meaning "to be in the midst of, to hover in between." The meditation that Glossbrenner prescribes—prudent advice as far as it goes—helps the user zero in more closely on a target. It is the fill-up before a drive on the freeway, not the notion to hike in the countryside.

If we in fact take inspiration from the ninja warrior, we should recall Kitarō Nishida's teachings about "the logic of nothingness" (*mu no ronri*). The ninja warrior empties his mind before battle precisely by abandoning all specifics, by relaxing his attention so that the windows of awareness open to fresh perceptions. Genuine meditation refreshes our original potential to move in any direction. Our highest mind remains alert but flexible, firm but formless—in short, omnidirectional. Meditation truly expands the psyche and opens it to the delicate whisperings of intuition.

A Taoist sage once wrote that "thinking is merely one way of musing." Tightly controlled thought remains but a trickle in the daily stream of thoughts flowing through the psyche. Most of the time, the background mind muses with a soft undercurrent that quietly sorts things out, gently putting things together and taking them apart. We do our best thinking when sitting before the fireplace on a crisp winter night or lying on the grass on a balmy spring day. That's when our minds are most fully engaged, when we are musing.

Computer-guided questions sharpen thinking at the interface, but sharpness is not all. A more relaxed and natural state of mind, according to Siu, a Taoist, increases mental openness and allows things to emerge unplanned and unexpected. Rather than sharpen the determined will, we must preserve a state of no-mind in which our attention moves free of the constricted aims of consciousness. The musing mind operates on a plane more sensitive and more complex than that of consciously controlled thought. Musing is not wild in the sense of wanton but wild in the sense of flowing, unforced, and unboundedly fruitful. Thinking itself happens only when we suspend the inner musings of the mind long enough to favor a momentary precision, and even then thinking belongs to musing as a subset of our creative mind.

Now contrast the Boolean scan with a meditative perusal through traditional books. The book browser moves through symbols in the mode of musing. Books do in fact have a linear structure that unfolds sequentially, page by page, chapter by chapter, but seldom do readers stick to reading in this way. When we look something up in books, we often find ourselves browsing in ways that stir fresh discoveries, often turning up something more important than the discovery we had originally hoped to make. Some of our best reading is browsing. The book browser welcomes surprise, serendipity, new terrain, fresh connections where the angle of thought suddenly shifts. The browser meditates every moment while under way, musing along a gentle, wandering path through haphazard stacks of material. The browser forgoes immediate aims in order to ride gently above conscious purposes, in order to merge with an unexpected content in the pages. The browser feels wilderness beckon from afar.

The Boolean reader, on the contrary, knows in advance where the exits are, the on-ramps, and the well-marked rest stops. Processing texts through the Boolean search enhances the power of conscious, rational control. Such rationality is not the contemplative, meditative meander along a line of thinking, that the search through books can be. The pathway of thought, not to mention the logic of thought, disappears under a Boolean arrangement of freeways.

The Boolean search treats texts as data. When you search a database, you browse through recent material, often covering no more than the last ten years. Cutting off the past in this way streamlines the search. But a musing cut off from historical roots loses the fertile exposure to false starts, abandoned pathways, and unheard-of avenues. An exclusive focus on the recent past curtails our mental musings, and a narrow awareness sacrifices the intuitive mind.

Boolean search logic affects our mental vision just as long hours at the computer screen affect our eyesight. In a relaxed state, our eyes accept the world passively as a spectacle of discovery. Only when we strain to see do our eyes lose the surprise of perceptions. Constant straining induces a sensory myopia in which we need to strain in order to see better what we wish to see. We lose much of our peripheral vision when we use our eyes willfully. Likewise with the mind's eye. A relaxed and easy thought enjoys intuitive turns, and thinking at its best muses over human symbols. Boolean search logic cuts off the peripheral vision of the mind's eye. The computer interface can act like the artificial lens that helps us persist in our preconceptions. Boolean logic can unconsciously entrench us in our straining ways, hurting us as much mentally as the carpal tunnel syndrome hurts us physically. We may see more and see it more sharply, but the clarity will not hold the rich depth of natural vision. The world of thought we see will be flattened by an abstract remoteness, and the mind's eye, through its straining, will see a thin, flattened world with less light and brightness.

But notice how we do in fact always use some holistic guesswork, even when we are trying our best to shut off the mind's peripheral vision. Our Boolean searches could never begin without vague hunches and half-seen surmises. We need hunches and inklings to start with. Unfortunately, the Boolean search places our hunches in the service of a skeletal logic far removed from the direct operations of language.

If computers aid our searching minds, we must not abandon the books during our leisure time. The serendipitous search through books is necessary for knowledge and learning. Browsing often evokes daydreams and unsuspected connections; analogies and pertinent finds happen among the stacks of physically accessible pages. Although not as efficient as the Boolean search, library browsing enriches us in unpredictable ways. Looking for something in a book library frequently leads to discoveries that overturn the questions we originally came to ask.

Book libraries hold unsystematic, unfiltered collections of human voices and thoughts. Libraries are repositories not so much of information as of the intuitions of countless authors. The books in libraries remain physical reminders of the individual voices of the authors, who often speak to us in ways that shock and disturb, in ways that break through our assumptions and preconceptions, in ways that calm and deepen. The word *museum* derives from the Greek word for the Muses, goddesses of dream, spontaneous creativity, and genial leisure. Libraries may be, in this strict sense, the last museums of the stored language, the last outposts of predigital intuition.

Today libraries are becoming information centers rather than places for musing. The Los Angeles County Public Library, the world's largest circulating library, receives more requests for information than requests for books. In 1989, one university in California opened the first library without books, a building for searching electronic texts. Books still remain a primary source, but they are rapidly becoming mere sources of information. A large volume of book sales doesn't necessarily prove that the book, with its special psychic framework, endures as such. Many books today gain attention as nonbooks linked to cinema, television, or audio recordings.

Searching through books was always more romance than busyness, more rumination than information. Information is by nature timebound. Supported by technological systems, information depends on revision and updating. When books become mere sources of information, they lose the atmosphere of contemplative leisure and timeless enjoyment. Old books then seem irrelevant, as they no longer pertain to current needs. One of the new breed of information publishers epitomizes this attitude in a pithy warning: "Any book more than two years old is of questionable value. Books more than four or five years old are a menace. OUT OF DATE = DANGEROUS."[3]

As book libraries turn into museums of alphabetic life, we should reclaim their original meaning. Museums are places for play, for playing with the muses that attract us, for dreams, intuitions, and enthusiasms. Information plugs us into the world of computerized productivity, but the open space of books balances our computer logic with the graces of intuition.

Notes

1. Alfred Glossbrenner, *How to Look It Up Online* (New York: St. Martin's Press, 1987), p. 109.

2. Ibid., p. 116.

3. Daniel Romer and Stephen Elias, *Legal Care for Your Software* (Berkeley, Calif.: Nolo Press, 1987), p. ii.

FAIRY TALES

Allen Newell

The late computer scientist Allen Newell, a major figure in cognitive science and artificial intelligence, believed our computer age to be the stuff of fairy tales. He felt that the ability of computers to apply intelligent solutions in all areas of life provides for "the capability for an enchanted world." Unlike Heim (see the previous essay), Newell enthusiastically believed that the computer opens up thinking by making behavior "conditional," thus allowing options of which we, with our limited capacities, cannot otherwise take advantage.

Once upon a time, when it was still of some use to wish for what one wanted, . . . there lived a king and queen who had a daughter who was lovely to behold, but who never laughed.

Reprinted with permission of MIT Press from *The Age of Intelligent Machines*, ed. Raymond Kurzweil (1990), 420–23.

Or perhaps:

there lived an old fisherman by the side of the sea that had hardly any fishes in it.

If you are like me, you are already hooked. You are ready to abandon all talk of present matters, of computers and electronic technology, and settle in to hear a fairy tale. Their attraction reaches almost all of us.

They let us enter into an enchanted world. Magic abounds, though always in special ways. Animals talk, and not only animals but trees and bridges as well. Villainy is there, certainly danger. There are trials to be overcome—usually three of them. But there is always the happy ending. The spell is broken, and the princess smiles and marries the youth who made her laugh. The old fisherman gets the Jinni back in the bottle with the top on. And happiness is ever after, which means at least for a little while.

The experts tell us that fairy tales are for childhood. They contain lessons for the crises of growing up, and their universal attraction comes because they deal with what is central to this universal period in life: Like Hansel and Gretel, we have to leave home and find our own way. Like the princess with the frog king, we must learn to keep our word and embrace what we find ugly and disgusting, to discover that it contains our heart's desire.

Or like Jack, in the story of the beanstalk, we can bring home the bacon if we persevere, even if our parents don't think we can. But there was more, if you remember your Jack: First, he escaped back home with a bag of gold. But Jack and his mother used up the gold, which shows that one success is not enough. Then he made a second trip up the beanstalk to the giant's castle. This time he came home with the magic hen that lays golden eggs. Now Jack had a technology for satisfying his and his mother's wants. But even so, material things are not sufficient for the full life. So on his third trip Jack brought home the golden singing harp, symbolizing the higher things of life.

The experts notwithstanding, fairy tales are for all of us. Indeed, this is true especially in our current times. For we are, all of us, children with respect to the future. We do not know what is coming. The future is as new, and as incomprehensible, as adult life is to children. We find ourselves troubled and fearful at the changes taking place in ourselves and our society. We need the hidden guidance of fairy tales to tell us of the trials we must overcome and assure us there will be a happy ending. Whether fairy tales have been written that speak to the heart of our own adult crises is not clear. How would we, the children, ever know? Perhaps we must get along with the fairy tales we have.

But even more, fairy tales seem to me to have a close connection to technology. The aim of technology, when properly applied, is to build a land of Faerie.

Well, that should come as a shock! The intellectual garb of the modern academic is cynicism. Like a follower in a great herd, as surely as I am an academic, I am a cynic. Yet I have just uttered a sentiment that is, if anything, straight from Pollyanna.

In point of fact, within the small circle of writers who manage to put technology and fairy tales between the same covers, the emphasis is always on the negative, on the dark side. The favorite stories are those that trouble:

- Like the Sorcerer's Apprentice, who learns only enough magic to start the broom of technology hauling water from the River Rhine to the cistern, but who cannot stop it.
- Like the Jinni in the bottle, where the story is never permitted to go to the conclusion in the Arabian Nights, with the Jinni snookered back in the bottle, but is always stopped with the Jinni hanging in air and the question along with it—Can we ever put the Jinni back? Or will there only be ink all over the sky till the stars go out?
- Like the many stories of the three magic wishes, in which, promising infinite riches just for the asking, they are always spent, first on foolishness, second on disaster, and third on bare recovery. Recall the story of the Monkey's Paw, which came to an old English couple. Their first wish was for just 200 pounds. That was foolish. They lost a son, whose accident brought them a 200-pound reward. The second wish was for the return of their son. That was disaster. He returned from the grave, though hardly unscathed. The third wish was to send their son back to his opened grave, to try to recover for themselves a world where life could go on.

I see it differently. I see the computer as the enchanted technology. Better, it is the technology of enchantment. I mean that quite literally, so I had best explain.

There are two essential ingredients in computer technology. First, it is the technology of how to apply knowledge to action to achieve goals. It provides the capability for intelligent behavior. That is why we process data with computers—to get answers to solve our problems. That is what algorithms and programs are about—frozen action to be thawed when needed.

The second ingredient is the miniaturization of the physical systems that have this ability for intelligent action. This is what Angel Jordan, my co-Whitaker professor, has been telling us about in his talk. Computers are getting smaller, and cheaper, and faster, and more reliable, and less energy demanding. Everything is changing together in the right direction. The good things do not trade off against the bad ones. More speed does not mean more dollars. Small size does not mean lower reliability. On any given date, the expected painful trade-offs do hold, just as we learned in elementary economics. It costs more to buy faster circuits or larger memories. But come back next year and everything is better: smaller, cheaper, faster, more reliable, and for less energy.

Thus computer technology differs from all other technologies precisely in providing the capability for an enchanted world: for little boxes that make out your income-tax forms for you, for brakes that know how to stop on wet pavement, for instruments that can converse with their users, for bridges that watch out for the safety of those who cross them, for streetlights that care about those who stand under them—who know the way, so no one need get lost.

In short, computer technology offers the possibility of incorporating intelligent behavior in all the nooks and crannies of our world. With it we could build an enchanted land.

All very good, but what about the Sorcerer's Apprentice? Two half-fallacies feed our fear that his nightmare might be ours. The first half-fallacy is that technologies are rigid and unthinking. Start the broom off carrying water, and it does just that and not something else. But every computer scientist recognizes in the Sorcerer's Apprentice simply a program with a bug in it, embedded in a first generation operating system with no built-in panic button. Even with our computer systems today, poor things that they are, such blunderbus looping is no longer a specter.

Exactly what the computer provides is the ability *not* to be rigid and unthinking, but rather to behave conditionally. That is what it means to apply knowledge to action: it means to let the action taken reflect knowledge of the situation, to be sometimes this way, sometimes that, as appropriate. With small amounts of computer technology—that is, with small amounts of memory and small amounts of processing per decision—you often can't be conditional enough. That is certainly the story of the first decades of the computer revolution. It was too expensive and involved too much complexity to create systems with enough conditionality. We didn't know how and couldn't have afforded it if we did. Consequently, many applications were rigid and unthinking. It was indeed a Sorcerer's Apprentice who seemed to run the computerized billing service.

The import of miniaturization is that ultimately we will be able to have the capability for enough conditionality in a small enough space. And the import of our scientific study of computers is that we shall know how to make all the conditionality work for us. Then the brooms of the world themselves can know enough to stop when things go wrong.

The second half-fallacy behind the Sorcerer's Apprentice is that technologies by their nature extract too high a price. That is a message of the recent literature of political ecology: Our technologies inevitably demand that we use up our precious world. There is rather abundant evidence for this view. Here in Western Pennsylvania, the price paid in enchantment of our countryside for taking our coal by strip mining is only too evident. Less in our awareness, because it was so thorough, was what the loggers did to Western Pennsylvania. Not once, but thrice, within forty years they swept the hillsides almost bare. The hot scorching breath of a dragon could hardly have done better for desolation.

But all is not inevitable. Ecologically, computer technology itself is nearly magic. The better it gets, the less of our environment it consumes. It is clean, unobtrusive, consumes little energy and little material. Moreover, as we push it to higher peaks of speed and memory, it becomes more of all these things. For deep technical reasons this has to be. There is no way to obtain immense amounts of processing power by freezing technology at some cost in dollars, material, and energy per unit of computation and then just buying more and more of it, consuming our wealth and our environment. Instead, for a long time to come, as we get more and more of it, the less it will impact our environment.

Even more, the computer is exactly the technology to permit us to cope intelligently with the use of our other resources. Again, by providing us with distributed intelligence, it can let us keep track of the use and abuse of our environment. And not only of the destruction that we ourselves visit on our world but also that which nature does as well. Mount Vesuvius was hardly bound by any antipollution ordinances posted on the walls of ancient Pompeii.

In sum, technology can be controlled, especially if it is saturated with intelligence to watch over how it goes, to keep accounts, to prevent errors, and to provide wisdom for each decision. And these guardians of our world, these magic informational dwarfs, need not extract too high a price.

But I said that fear of the plight of the Sorcerer's Apprentice was guided by *half-fallacies*. I did not dismiss the view totally. Because, of course, in fairy tales there are great trials to be performed before the happy ending. Great dangers must be encountered and overcome. Because, also, in fairy tales, the hero (or the heroine)—the one who achieves finally the happy ending—must grow in virtue and mature in understanding. No villains need apply for the central role. The fairy tale that I am indirectly spinning here will not come true automatically. We must earn it.

Where are we now? We are not at the end of the story, though we are surely at the end of my talk. In fact, the fairy tale is hardly past its "Once upon a time." Still, I wish to assert that computer science and technology are the stuff out of which the future fairy land can be built. My faith is that the trials can be endured successfully, even by us children who fear that we are not so wise as we need to be. I might remind you, by the way, that the hero never has to make it all on his own. Prometheus is not the central character of any fairy tale but of a tragic myth. In fairy tales, magic friends sustain our hero and help him overcome the giants and the witches that beset him.

Finally, I wish to express my feeling of childlike wonder that my time to be awake on this earth has placed me in the middle of this particular fairy tale.

Selected Bibliography for Section One

Journal Articles and Anthology Contributions

Berdichevsky, Daniel, and Erik Neunschwander. "Toward an Ethics of Persuasive Technology." *Communications of the ACM* 42, no. 5 (May 1999): 51–58.

Bynum, Terrell Ward. "Global Information Ethics and the Information Revolution." In *Digital Phoenix*, edited by J. Moor and T. Bynum. Blackwell, 1998.

Christiansen, Ellen. "Tamed by a Rose: Computers as Tools in Human Activity." In *Context and Consciousness: Activity Theory and Human-Computer Interactions*, edited by Bonnie Nardi. MIT Press, 1996.

Marien, Michael. "New Communications Technology: A Survey of Impacts and Issues." *Telecommunications Policy* 20, no. 5 (1996): 375–87.

Moor, James. "What Is Computer Ethics?" *Metaphilosophy* 16, no. 4 (1985): 266–75.

Neumann, Peter. "Information Is a Double-Edged Sword." *Communications of the ACM* 42, no. 7 (July 1999): 129.

Books

Bertman, Stephen. *Hyperculture: The Human Cost of Speed.* Praeger Publishers, 1998.

Ellul, Jacques. *The Technological Society.* Translated by John Wilkinson. Alfred A. Knopf, 1964.

———. *The Technological Bluff.* Translated by G. W. Bromiley. William B. Eerdmans, 1990.

Ferré, Frederick. *Philosophy of Technology.* University of Georgia Press, 1995.

Friedman, Batya, ed. *Human Values and the Design of Computer Technologies.* Cambridge University Press, 1997.

Gendron, Bernard. *Technology and the Human Condition.* St. Martin's Press, 1977.

Haraway, Donna. *Simians, Cyborgs, and Women: The Reinvention of Nature.* Routledge, 1991.

Heidegger, Martin. *The Question Concerning Technology and Other Essays.* Translated by William Lovitt. Harper and Row, 1977.

Hickman, Larry. *John Dewey's Pragmatic Technology.* Indiana University Press, 1990.

———, ed. *Technology as a Human Affair.* McGraw-Hill, 1990.

Ihde, Don. *Technology and Lifeworld: From Garden to Earth.* Indiana University Press, 1990.

———. *Instrumental Realism: The Interface Between Philosophy of Science and Philosophy of Technology.* Indiana University Press, 1991.

Jonas, Hans. *Philosophical Essays: From Ancient Creed to Technological Man.* Prentice Hall, 1974.

Kohanski, Alexander S. *Philosophy and Technology: Toward a New Orientation in Modern Thinking.* Philosophical Library, 1977.

Lachs, John. *Intermediate Man.* Hackett, 1981.

McLuhan, Marshall. *The Gutenberg Galaxy.* University of Toronto Press, 1962.

——— and Bruce R. Powers. *The Global Village.* Oxford University Press, 1989.

Mitcham, Carl. *Thinking Through Technology: The Path Between Engineering and Philosophy.* University of Chicago Press, 1994.

Mumford, Lewis. *The Myth of the Machine.* Harcourt Brace Jovanovich, 1967.

Postman, Neil. *Technopoly: The Surrender of Culture to Technology.* Alfred A. Knopf, 1993.

Teich, A., ed. *Technology and the Future.* 6th ed. St. Martin's Press, 1993.

Tiles, Mary, and Hans Oberdiek. *Living in a Technological Culture: Human Tools and Human Values.* Routledge, 1995.

Wiener, Norbert. *The Human Use of Human Beings: Cybernetics and Society.* Doubleday Anchor Books, 1954.

Winner, Langdon. *The Whale and the Reactor: A Search for Limits in an Age of High Technology.* University of Chicago Press, 1991.

Novels and Short Stories

Butler, Samuel. *Erewhon.* Penguin Books, 1985.

Forster, E. M. The machine stops. In *The Eternal Moment and Other Stories.* Harcourt Brace, 1970.

Shelley, Mary. *Frankenstein or The Modern Prometheus.* Konemann, 1995.

Films

Brazil. Directed by Terry Gilliam. Universal Pictures, 1985.

Gattaca. Directed by Andrew Niccol. Columbia Pictures, 1997.

Playtime. Directed by Jacques Tati, 1967.

SECTION TWO

Computers and the Quality of Life

Computer technologies continue to become more involved in the activities of our daily lives, and if we accept the postulate that all technologies are themselves laden with value, it becomes important to explore the impact of their implementation on our lives and how the technologies alter or reinforce certain values. These alterations in values, in turn, directly affect the ways in which we live. This section, which is concerned with the impact of computers on daily life, is divided into three broad areas. Each chapter deals with issues surrounding how we work, play, learn, and socialize. The essays in these three chapters survey social problems from both local and global perspectives with a particular eye on quality-of-life issues.

Chapter 3 asks questions about how technologies affect our relationships with other people. Primarily, the focus is on whether existing communities are helped or hindered by computers and whether the building of communities is possible in a computer-mediated environment. The first essay, by Jon Dorbolo, explores issues surrounding strategies for applying technologies appropriately in light of community and in particular how those strategies might be applied to the development of computer software. In considering how software should be developed, it is fundamental to evaluate our shared community values and consider how the computer software might interfere with or support those values. Next, Howard Rheingold expresses his belief that computer-mediated interactions do constitute community but that there can be a darker side to these communities of which we should be aware. Finally, John Barlow discusses his experiences in on-line communities and whether they constitute true communities. If they do not, then what do computer-mediated meetings have to offer community?

Chapter 4 deals with the effects that computer technologies have on individuality and personal experience. To what extent do these technologies tend to alienate oneself from other people as well as from one's own desires or sense of identity? With the vast array of ways in which computers can change and are changing people's actions, values, and even bodies, it is important that we explore how individual roles are altered. We start with Shoshana Zuboff's story of the ways in which computers remove the reliance on our personal experience and bodily senses from many types of employment. This leads to a reconfiguring of our activities that can have an alienating effect on people who have always operated in a hands-on mode. Next, taking up questions raised by the implantation of computer-based technologies into actual human bodies, Maguire and McGee state that it is vital to reflect on the implications of these activities before their widespread application. They discuss actual physical reconfigurations of the body and, in some senses, how they can be socially alienating *and* integrating technologies. The short story by Kurt Vonnegut turns the issues of the previous essay around by painting the picture not of a human with computer parts, but of a computer with human sensibilities. The chapter concludes with a short piece by Raymond Gozzi in which he explores the social, value-laden effect of using human body metaphors in dialog about computer technologies.

The essays in the final chapter of this section, Chapter 5, revolve around issues raised by the implementation of computer technologies in developing countries. Represented are concerns from Africa, Latin America, the Caribbean, and Eastern Europe. Although this array clearly does not cover all developing regions, these essays do point to a convergence of generalized concerns that are intimately related to the development and deployment of computer technologies from First World countries such as the United States. Since most computer technologies are designed by corporations in developed countries, their implementation in underdeveloped regions involves socioeconomic values that may or may not be shared by the cultures in which they are implemented. The four authors in this chapter (Berman, Sutz, Dyrkton, and Baldeh) argue not only that we need to question the impact of these "foreign" values, but also that there are lingering questions concerning a culture's need for effective implementation of these technologies where large foreign computer companies siphon resources from local populations. How can such a culture come to control a technology that is not originally of its own making?

CHAPTER THREE
Community and Intermediacy

SOCIAL STRATEGIES FOR SOFTWARE

Jon Dorbolo

Taking as a paradigm case Amish society's approach to evaluating the impact of particular technologies on their values, Jon Dorbolo brings to the fore issues of software design for the maintenance of community. Rather than taking a technophilic approach to the adoption of software, in which we simply accept all new and "cool" software, Dorbolo suggests that we need to consider carefully the types of values that are implicated by the implementation of particular software products. These considerations, in turn, should be reflected in the way we design and develop new programs.

The 18th century English weavers who followed Ned Ludd in rebellion against the automation of their craft, stand as a heroic paragon for contemporary antagonists to computers and other high-technology. That the Luddite rage against the machine did not succeed is part of their charm. In contrast to the tragic-hero Luddites, stands the persistent resistance to modern technology practiced by the Amish. The wonder of the Amish approach is that it works. Despite constant pressures and challenges, Old Order Amish communities in Pennsylvania, the Midwest, and around the world survive and thrive. Their success stems partly from social strategies for selecting and adapting the technologies that enter their lives. If technology is, as Frederick Ferré defines it, "the practical implementation of intelligence,"[1] then the Amish have developed a meta-technology to conduct such implementations. Some authors speculate that the Amish approach to technology provides a model that other communities or society

---

Reprinted with the kind permission of the author from *The American Philosophical Association Newsletter on Philosophy and Computers* 98, no. 2 (1999): 73–75.

at large might employ in making technology use decisions. That seems to me unlikely, but the way is open to apply aspects of the Amish model of innovation to the design of technology, particularly software. To make this happen we need innovative conceptual schemes to guide the software design. Philosophers are well-equipped to pursue such innovations.

Amish society is grounded in the maintenance of a community committed to a common faith and tradition. Commentators on Amish life observe that in all things, community is the top priority and there is no ambiguity as to what the community comprises. The integrity of the local community is prioritized over individual interests, economic interests, and technological development. The Old Order Amish (the traditionalist sect) live in an agrarian style without electricity, telephones, television, automobiles, military service, public education, federal government subsidy, and other amenities considered necessities in the contemporary U.S. This last claim needs qualification, however, because the Amish distinguish between using technology and living with it. Telephones in the home have been banned since 1910. Using telephones for a variety of purposes, on the other hand, is not part of the ban. Craft workers do use electricity in their workshops, but only if self-generated and not hooked into the public power grid. Farmers will use state-of-the-art farm equipment, such as hay balers, so long as they are pulled by horses and not internal combustion engines. Such juxtapositions make an odd picture for us citizens of the technopoly. Yet, such seeming contradictions are actually results of a sophisticated social strategy. As Howard Rheingold observes, "Far from knee-jerk technophobes, these are very adaptive techno-selectives who devise remarkable technologies that fit within their self-imposed limits."[2]

Amish life deliberately imposes a framework of values on technology that determines which selections and adaptations are appropriate. Social coherence is the supreme value. What leads to local social interaction and interdependence is encouraged. Scale is an important value to community integrity. "When a church district becomes too large, it is divided into two meetings to prevent the ceremonial unit from becoming unmanageable."[3] A meeting is too large when it becomes unwieldily to meet in any member's home. Old Order Amish do not have church buildings or meeting rooms. This accords with the informal social structure in which "there are no headquarters, professionals, executive directors, or organizational charts."[4] In worship, politics, and work, community involvement implies local presence. Within that communal presence, silence is another core value that pervades the lifestyle. This includes the silence of humility, patience, pacifism, forgiveness, prayer, worship service, and shunning (i.e. exclusion of adults who transgress on accepted practices). Silence is contrasted with the radically overt voice of public confession and the freedom to speak on any matter before the community. These and other core values derive from a religious faith that seeks utter consistency in practice.

This consistency allows some analysis of that practice as a social strategy for technology use.

A symbolically and functionally important example of the Amish approach to technology is the telephone. In 1910 the Amish community in Pennsylvania struggled with a conflict over principles that led to schism. Central in the conflict were the community rules governing the newly available telephone technology. Other issues were at stake in the controversy, but even for present-day Amish, the telephone remains evocative of the conflict.

The telephone effectively connects us to a vast scale of potential recipients because of the constancy of time over variable distance. We can have the same 5 minute phone call with another, irrespective of where on earth (and sometimes off earth) they are. The very idea of a contemporary telephone confers values that show up in advertising, technology design, user behavior, and social practice. Among these values are choice, global scale, speed, and networking. In technopoly we regard these as virtues of information technology. Consider some ways in which they are directly antithetical to the core virtues of Amish community.

Techno-Virtues	Amish Virtues
Telephones provide individualized power of choice in communication options, as embodied in the phone directory.	Amish promote communal interdependence. When choices are locally limited, cooperation is required.
Telephones span a global scale determined by purchasable services.	Amish community is determined by limited scale based in individual homes.
Telephone technology tends toward increased specialization of communicative function.	Amish communities tend toward wholistic communication requiring personal presence.
Speed is good.	Slowness and waiting are good.
Calls are private (one-one) and silence is non-functional.	Moral character requires community openness and personal silence.

For the Old Order Amish, the very idea that a call may interrupt a family conversation or even moment of quiet, is sufficient to keep the telephone out of the home. Much less compatible with Amish values are commonplaces of contemporary life such as telemarketing calls and backgrounding.[5]

The telephone, of course, is very useful even when it conflicts with other values. It is in such dilemmas that Amish innovation becomes remarkably apparent. Rather than categorically ban the telephone, the Amish constructed a compromise of locating community phones outside of the home in small uni-purpose *shantys*. The reasoning for this practice was two-fold: 1) to prevent the separating influence of the phone on the family and 2) to promote the integrating affect of community ownership. Krayhill observes, "The inconvenience of walking a half-mile to use a phone or taking messages from an answering service is a daily reminder that membership in an ethnic community exacts a price—a reminder that things that are too handy and too convenient lead to sloth and pride."[6] This negotiated settlement with the telephone is typical of the Amish approach to new technology.

It is this meta-technical innovation, the invention of social practices and adaptations of a technology to promote core values, that is so valuable to the potential of the philosophy of technology. Computer programming opens a potential for informed users to custom innovate the software that produces their information technology environment. We may, in a spirit analogous to the Amish, construct negotiated settlements with communities of potential users and embed those decisions into the technology. This approach will take advantage of a distinguishing characteristic of computer programming: software plasticity. Richard Field provides an example of software plasticity in his article *"Web-Based Quizzes Produced by Hot Potatoes"* in this issue of the newsletter.[7] Field notes that an otherwise useful software does not provide some values important to his teaching; "however, for those who do know JavaScript, and wish to customize the source code, an 'Edit Raw HTML' option provides editable access to this code." Thus, Field makes the revisions and produces the needed values. Such direct intervention is possible with much software, if software developers really designed with the user/producer in mind (such as the *Hot Potatoes* designers have). The programming knowledge and effort is merely the price one pays for being a part of a virtual community. Learning some JavaScript is not a huge price; the functional equivalent of the daily trek to the phone shanty (tackling Java may be more on the order of living without electricity and a car).

Rheingold and Brende propose employing the Amish approach to technology as a model for contemporary high-tech society.[8] This is not a viable hope. The value of an intelligent communal approach to technology selection and implementation is clear. Yet, the core values that give the Amish a foundation for such an approach are antithetical to mainstream U.S. and much of the high-tech world. The blistering pace, overwhelming complexity, and increasing specialization of contemporary technology is entirely consistent with the core capitalist values of the autonomous market and consumerism. To affect an intelligent strategy for development and implementation would conflict directly with those values. We cannot appropriate the Amish sensibility for our own technopoly.

It is viable to apply the Amish sensibility to the software design process. We cannot hope to manage which technologies come into market or how they are adopted. We may be able to influence how the software technology being produced behaves. Software designs do contain implicit values. The programming presuppositions of search engines can affect the scope and direction of knowledge (see Heim and Beavers in this issue). Assumptions about the users of courseware may shape the basic conception that learners have about the role of study and intellectual discourse in their lives. Communications programs (e.g. email, threaded discussion, etc.) pre-set the context in which conventions of use develop. The Amish took the inherent values of both the technology and community into account when devising a telephone policy. Philosophers should be engaged in analysis of our current technologies and community values in order to provide goals for software design. If we make a strong case for the desired values, then we will have some influence on future software design, hence our collective technological community.

Notes

1. Frederick Ferré. 1995. *Philosophy of Technology.* Athens: The University of Georgia Press, p. 26.
2. Rheingold, Howard. 1999. "Look Who's Talking," *Wired,* January, v7.01, p. 131.
3. Hostetler, John A. 1993. *Amish Society,* 4th edition. Baltimore: The Johns Hopkins University Press, p. 394.
4. Kraybill, Donald B. 1989. *The Riddle of Amish Culture.* Baltimore: The Johns Hopkins University Press, p. 82.
5. "Backgrounding" is current office jargon for the practice of doing multiple tasks while on the phone. Conversants will doodle, sort papers, make coffee, surf the web, drive the car, and whatever else while on the phone. The lack of total engagement in the exchange is, perhaps, typical of telephone communication. Listen for absent pauses (note how silence is a negative value on the phone) and soft typing in the background.
6. Kraybill, Donald B. Op. cit. p. 149.
7. Richard Field. 1999. "Web-Based Quizzes Produced by Hot Potatoes," *APA Newletter on Philosophy and Computers,* Spring 1999.
8. Rheingold, 1999. Brende, Eric. 1996. "Technology Amish Style," *Technology Review,* Feb–March, v99 n2, p26(8).

THE VIRTUAL COMMUNITY

Howard Rheingold

Cultural critic Howard Rheingold argues that there is little doubt about the inevitability of building communities using computer-mediated technologies. However, it is important to recognize the potential dark side of the technology as well. The ways in which computer environments get structured and the ways in which communities arise need to be carefully developed in order to avoid these darker aspects. We need to recognize that the development of computer communities directly affects traditional communities and vice versa. Hence a great deal is at stake for everyone in the development of virtual communities.

"Daddy is saying 'Holy moly!' to his computer again!"

Those words have become a family code for the way my virtual community has infiltrated our real world. My seven-year-old daughter knows that her father congregates with a family of invisible friends who seem to gather in his computer. Sometimes he talks to them, even if nobody else can see them. And she knows that these invisible friends sometimes show up in the flesh, materializing from the next block or the other side of the planet.

Since the summer of 1985, for an average of two hours a day, seven days a week, I've been plugging my personal computer into my telephone and making contact with the WELL (Whole Earth 'Lectronic Link)—a computer conferencing system that enables people around the world to carry on public conversations and exchange private electronic mail (e-mail). The idea of a community accessible only via my computer screen sounded cold to me at first, but I learned quickly that people can feel passionately about e-mail and computer conferences. I've become one of them. I care about these people I met through my computer, and I care deeply about the future of the medium that enables us to assemble.

I'm not alone in this emotional attachment to an apparently bloodless technological ritual. Millions of people on every continent also participate in the computer-mediated social groups known as virtual communities, and this population is growing fast. Finding the WELL was like discovering a cozy little world that had been flourishing without me, hidden within the walls of my house; an entire cast of characters welcomed me to the troupe with great merriment as soon as I found the secret door. Like others who fell into the WELL, I soon discovered that I was audience, performer, and scriptwriter, along with my companions, in an ongoing improvisation. A full-scale subculture was growing on the other side of my telephone jack, and they invited me to help create something new.

The virtual village of a few hundred people I stumbled upon in 1985 grew to eight thousand by 1993. It became clear to me during the first months of that history that I was participating in the self-design of a new kind of culture. I watched the community's social contracts stretch and change as the people who discovered and started building the WELL in its first year or two were joined by so many others. Norms were established, challenged, changed, reestablished, rechallenged, in a kind of speeded-up social evolution.

The WELL felt like an authentic community to me from the start because it was grounded in my everyday physical world. WELLites who don't live within driving distance of the San Francisco Bay area are constrained in their ability to participate in the local networks of face-to-face acquaintances. By now, I've attended real-life WELL marriages, WELL births, and even a WELL funeral. (The phrase "in real life" pops up so often in virtual communities that regulars abbreviate it to IRL.) I can't count the parties and outings where the invisible personae who first acted out their parts in the debates and melodramas on my computer screen later manifested in front of me in the physical world in the form of real people, with faces, bodies, and voices.

I remember the first time I walked into a room full of people IRL who knew many intimate details of my history and whose own stories I knew very well. Three months after I joined, I went to my first WELL party at the home of one of the WELL's online moderators. I looked around at the room full of strangers when I walked in. It was one of the oddest sensations of my life. I had contended with these people, shot the invisible breeze around the electronic watercooler, shared alliances and formed bonds, fallen off my chair laughing with them, become livid with anger at some of them. But there wasn't a recognizable face in the house. I had never seen them before.

My flesh-and-blood family long ago grew accustomed to the way I sit in my home office early in the morning and late at night, chuckling and cursing, sometimes crying, about words I read on the computer screen. It might have looked to my daughter as if I were alone at my desk the night she caught me chortling online, but from my point of view I was in living contact with old and new friends, strangers and colleagues:

I was in the Parenting conference on the WELL, participating in an informational and emotional support group for a friend who just learned his son was diagnosed with leukemia.

I was in MicroMUSE, a role-playing fantasy game of the twenty-fourth century (and science education medium in disguise), interacting with students and professors who know me only as "Pollenator."

I was in TWICS, a bicultural community in Tokyo; CIX, a community in London; *CalvaCom,* a community in Paris; and Usenet, a collection of hundreds of different discussions that travel around the world via electronic mail to millions of participants in dozens of countries.

I was browsing through Supreme Court decisions, in search of information that could help me debunk an opponent's claims in a political debate elsewhere on the Net, or I was retrieving this morning's satellite images of weather over the Pacific.

I was following an eyewitness report from Moscow during the coup attempt, or China during the Tiananmen Square incident, or Israel and Kuwait during the Gulf War, passed directly from citizen to citizen through an ad hoc network patched together from cheap computers and ordinary telephone lines, cutting across normal geographic and political boundaries by piggybacking on the global communications infrastructure.

I was monitoring a rambling real-time dialogue among people whose bodies were scattered across three continents, a global bull session that seems to blend wit and sophomore locker-room talk via Internet Relay Chat (IRC), a medium that combines the features of conversation and writing. IRC has accumulated an obsessive subculture of its own among undergraduates by the thousands from Adelaide to Arabia.

People in virtual communities use words on screens to exchange pleasantries and argue, engage in intellectual discourse, conduct commerce, exchange knowledge, share emotional support, make plans, brainstorm, gossip, feud, fall in love, find friends and lose them, play games, flirt, create a little high art and a lot of idle talk. People in virtual communities do just about everything people do in real life, but we leave our bodies behind. You can't kiss anybody and nobody can punch you in the nose, but a lot can happen within those boundaries. To the millions who have been drawn into it, the richness and vitality of computer-linked cultures is attractive, even addictive.

There is no such thing as a single, monolithic, online subculture; it's more like an ecosystem of subcultures, some frivolous, others serious. The cutting edge of scientific discourse is migrating to virtual communities, where you can read the electronic pre-preprinted reports of molecular biologists and cognitive scientists. At the same time, activists and educational reformers are using the same medium as a political tool. You can use virtual communities to find a date, sell a lawnmower, publish a novel, conduct a meeting.

Some people use virtual communities as a form of psychotherapy. Others, such as the most addicted players of Minitel in France or Multi-User Dungeons (MUDs) on the international networks, spend eighty hours a week or more pretending they are someone else, living a life that does not exist outside a computer. Because MUDs not only are susceptible to pathologically obsessive use by some people but also create a strain on computer and communication resources, MUDding has been banned at universities such as Amherst and on the entire continent of Australia.

Scientists, students, librarians, artists, organizers, and escapists aren't the only people who have taken to the new medium. The U.S. senator who campaigned for years for the construction of a National Research and Education Network that could host the virtual communities of the future is now vice president of the United States. As of June 1993, the White House and Congress have e-mail addresses.

Most people who get their news from conventional media have been unaware of the wildly varied assortment of new cultures that have evolved in the world's computer networks over the past ten years. Most people who have not yet used these new media remain unaware of how profoundly the social, political, and scientific experiments under way today via computer networks could change all our lives in the near future.

I have written this book to help inform a wider population about the potential importance of cyberspace to political liberties and the ways virtual communities are likely to change our experience of the real world, as individuals and communities. Although I am enthusiastic about the liberating potentials of computer-mediated communications, I try to keep my eyes open for the pitfalls of mixing technology and human relationships. I hope my reports from the outposts and headquarters of this new kind of social habitation, and the stories of the people I've met in cyberspace, will bring to life the cultural, political, and ethical implications of virtual communities both for my fellow explorers of cyberspace and for those who never heard of it before.

The technology that makes virtual communities possible has the potential to bring enormous leverage to ordinary citizens at relatively little cost—intellectual leverage, social leverage, commercial leverage, and most important, political leverage. But the technology will not in itself fulfill that potential; this latent technical power must be used intelligently and deliberately by an informed population. More people must learn about that leverage and learn to use it, while we still have the freedom to do so, if it is to live up to its potential. The odds are always good that big power and big money will find a way to control access to virtual communities; big power and big money always found ways to control new communications media when they emerged in the past. The Net is still out of control in fundamental ways, but it might not stay that way for long. What we know and do now is important because it is still possible for people around the world to make sure this new sphere of vital human discourse remains open to the citizens of the planet before the political and economic big boys seize it, censor it, meter it, and sell it back to us.

The potential social leverage comes from the power that ordinary citizens gain when they know how to connect two previously independent, mature, highly decentralized technologies: It took billions of dollars and decades to develop cheap personal computers. It took billions of dollars and more than a century to wire up the worldwide telecommunication network. With the right knowledge, and not too much of it, a ten-year-old kid today can plug these two vast, powerful, expensively developed technologies together for a few hundred dollars and instantly obtain a bully pulpit, the Library of Congress, and a world full of potential coconspirators.

Computers and the switched telecommunication networks that also carry our telephone calls constitute the technical foundation of *computer-mediated communications* (CMC). The technicalities of CMC, how bits of computer data move over wires and are reassembled as computer files at their destinations, are invisible and irrelevant to most people who use it, except when the technicalities restrict their access to CMC services. The important thing to keep in mind is that the worldwide, interconnected telecommunication network that we use to make telephone calls in Manhattan and Madagascar can also be used to connect computers together at a distance, and you don't have to be an engineer to do it.

The Net is an informal term for the loosely interconnected computer networks that use CMC technology to link people around the world into public discussions.

Virtual communities are social aggregations that emerge from the Net when enough people carry on those public discussions long enough, with sufficient human feeling, to form webs of personal relationships in cyberspace.

Cyberspace, originally a term from William Gibson's science-fiction novel *Neuromancer,* is the name some people use for the conceptual space where words, human relationships, data, wealth, and power are manifested by people using CMC technology.

Although spatial imagery and a sense of place help convey the experience of dwelling in a virtual community, biological imagery is often more appropriate to describe the way cyberculture changes. In terms of the way the whole system is propagating and evolving, think of cyberspace as a social petri dish, the Net as the agar medium, and virtual communities, in all their diversity, as the colonies of microorganisms that grow in petri dishes. Each of the small colonies of microorganisms—the communities on the Net—is a social experiment that nobody planned but that is happening nevertheless.

We now know something about the ways previous generations of communications technologies changed the way people lived. We need to understand why and how so many social experiments are coevolving today with the prototypes of the newest communications technologies. My direct observations of online behavior around the world over the past ten years have led me to conclude that whenever CMC technology becomes available to people anywhere, they inevitably build virtual communities with it, just as microorganisms inevitably create colonies.

I suspect that one of the explanations for this phenomenon is the hunger for community that grows in the breasts of people around the world as more and more informal public spaces disappear from our real lives. I also suspect that these new media attract colonies of enthusiasts because CMC enables people to do things with each other in new ways, and to do altogether new kinds of things—just as telegraphs, telephones, and televisions did.

Because of its potential influence on so many people's beliefs and perceptions, the future of the Net is connected to the future of community, democracy, education, science, and intellectual life—some of the human institutions people hold most dear, whether or not they know or care about the future of computer technology. The future of the Net has become too important to leave to specialists and special interests. As it influences the lives of a growing number of people, more and more citizens must contribute to the dialogue about the way public funds are applied to the development of the Net, and we must join our voices to the debate about the way it should be administered. We need a clear citizens' vision of the way the Net ought to grow, a firm idea of the kind of media environment we would like to see in the future. If we do not develop such a vision for ourselves, the future will be shaped for us by large commercial and political powerholders.

. . . The WELL is a small town, but now there is a doorway in that town that opens onto the blooming, buzzing confusion of the Net, an entity with properties altogether different from the virtual villages of a few years ago. I have good friends now all over the world who I never would have met without the mediation of the Net. A large circle of Net acquaintances can make an enormous difference in your experience when you travel to a foreign culture. Wherever I've traveled physically in recent years, I've found ready-made communities that I met online months before I traveled; our mutual enthusiasm for virtual communities served as a bridge, time and again, to people whose language and customs differ significantly from those I know well in California.

I routinely meet people and get to know them months or years before I see them—one of the ways my world today is a different world, with different friends and different concerns, from the world I experienced in premodem days. The places I visit in my mind, and the people I communicate with from one moment to the next, are entirely different from the content of my thoughts or the state of my circle of friends before I started dabbling in virtual communities. One minute I'm involved in the minutiae of local matters such as planning next week's bridge game, and the next minute I'm part of a debate raging in seven countries. Not only do I inhabit my virtual communities; to the degree that I carry around their conversations in my head and begin to mix it up with them in real life, my virtual communities also inhabit my life. I've been colonized; my sense of family at the most fundamental level has been virtualized.

I've seen variations of the same virtualization of community that happened to me hitting other virtual groups of a few hundred or a few thousand, in Paris and London and Tokyo. Entire cities are coming online. Santa Monica, California, and Cleveland, Ohio, were among the first of a growing number of American cities that have initiated municipal CMC systems. Santa Monica's system has an active conference to discuss the problems of the city's homeless that involves heavy input from homeless Santa Monica citizens who use public terminals. This system has an electronic link with COARA, a similar regional system in a remote province of Japan. Biwa-Net, in the Kyoto area, is gatewayed to a sister city in Pennsylvania. The Net is only beginning to wake up to itself.

Watching a particular virtual community change over a period of time has something of the intellectual thrill of do-it-yourself anthropology, and some of the garden-variety voyeurism of eavesdropping on an endless amateur soap opera where there is no boundary separating the audience from the cast. For the price of a telephone call, you can take part in any kind of vicarious melodrama you can dream of; as a form of escape entertainment, the Minitel addicts in Paris and the MUDders of Internet and the obsessive IRC participants on college campuses everywhere have proved that CMC has a future as a serious marketplace for meterable interactive fantasies.

CMC might become the next great escape medium, in the tradition of radio serials, Saturday matinees, soap operas—which means that the new medium will be in some way a conduit for and reflector of our cultural codes, our social subconscious, our images of who "we" might be, just as previous media have been. There are other serious reasons that ordinary nontechnical citizens need to know something about this new medium and its social impact. Something big is afoot, and the final shape has not been determined.

In the United States, the Clinton administration is taking measures to amplify the Net's technical capabilities and availability manyfold via the National Research and Education Network. France, with the world's largest national information utility, Minitel, and Japan, with its stake in future telecommunications industries, have their own visions of the future. Albert Gore's 1991 bill, the High Performance Computing Act, signed into law by President Bush, outlined Gore's vision for "highways of the mind" to be stimulated by federal research-and-development expenditures as a national intellectual resource and carried to the citizens by private enterprise. The Clinton-Gore administration has used the example of the ARPA (Advanced Research Projects Agency) venture of the 1960s and 1970s that produced the Net and the foundations of personal computing as an example of the way they see government and the private sector interacting in regard to future communications technologies.

In the private sector, telecommunication companies, television networks, computer companies, cable companies, and newspapers in the United States, Europe, and Japan are jockeying for position in the nascent "home interactive information services industry." Corporations are investing hundreds of millions of dollars in the infrastructure for new media they hope will make them billions of dollars. Every flavor of technological futurist, from Alvin Toffler and John Naisbitt to Peter Drucker and George Gilder, bases utopian hopes on "the information age" as a techno-fix for social problems. Yet little is known about the impact these newest media might have on our daily lives, our minds, our families, even the future of democracy.

CMC has the potential to change our lives on three different, but strongly interinfluential, levels. First, as individual human beings, we have perceptions, thoughts, and personalities (already shaped by other communications technologies) that are affected by the ways we use the medium and the ways it uses us. At this fundamental level, CMC appeals to us as mortal organisms with certain intellectual, physical, and emotional needs. Young people around the world have different communication proclivities from their pre-McLuhanized elders. MTV, for example, caters to an aesthetic sensibility that is closely tuned to the vocabulary of television's fast cuts, visually arresting images, and special effects. Now, some of those people around the world who were born in the television era and grew up in the cellular telephone era are beginning to migrate to CMC spaces that better fit their new ways of experiencing the world. There is a vocabulary to CMC, too, now emerging from millions and millions of individual online interactions. That vocabulary reflects something about the ways human personalities are changing in the age of media saturation.

The second level of possible CMC-triggered change is the level of person-to-person interaction where relationships, friendships, and communities happen. CMC technology offers a new capability of "many to many" communication, but the way such a capability will or will not be used in the future might depend on the way we, the first people who are using it, succeed or fail in applying it to our lives. Those of us who are brought into contact with each other by means of CMC technology find ourselves challenged by this many-to-many capability—challenged to consider whether it is possible for us to build some kind of community together.

The question of community is central to realms beyond the abstract networks of CMC technology. Some commentators, such as Bellah et al. (*Habits of the Heart, The Good Society*), have focused on the need for rebuilding community in the face of America's loss of a sense of a social commons.

Social psychologists, sociologists, and historians have developed useful tools for asking questions about human group interaction. Different communities of interpretation, from anthropology to economics, have different criteria for studying whether a group of people is a community. In trying to apply traditional analysis of community behavior to the kinds of interactions emerging from the Net, I have adopted a schema proposed by Marc Smith, a graduate student in sociology at the University of California at Los Angeles, who has been doing his fieldwork in the WELL and the Net. Smith focuses on the concept of "collective goods." Every cooperative group of people exists in the face of a competitive world because that group of people recognizes there is something valuable that they can gain only by banding together. Looking for a group's collective goods is a way of looking for the elements that bind isolated individuals into a community.

The three kinds of collective goods that Smith proposes as the social glue that binds the WELL into something resembling a community are social network capital, knowledge capital, and communion. Social network capital is what happened when I found a ready-made community in Tokyo, even though I had never been there in the flesh. Knowledge capital is what I found in the WELL when I asked questions of the community as an online brain trust representing a highly varied accumulation of expertise. And communion is what we found in the Parenting conference, when Phil's and Jay's children were sick, and the rest of us used our words to support them.

The third level of possible change in our lives, the political, derives from the middle, social level, for politics is always a combination of communications and physical power, and the role of communications media among the citizenry is particularly important in the politics of democratic societies. The idea of modern representative democracy as it was first conceived by Enlightenment philosophers included a recognition of a living web of citizen-to-citizen communications known as civil society or the public sphere. Although elections are the most visible fundamental characteristics of democratic societies, those elections are assumed to be supported by discussions among citizens at all levels of society about issues of importance to the nation.

If a government is to rule according to the consent of the governed, the effectiveness of that government is heavily influenced by how much the governed know about the issues that affect them. The mass-media-dominated public sphere today is where the governed now get knowledge; the problem is that commercial mass media, led by broadcast television, have polluted with barrages of flashy, phony, often violent imagery a public sphere that once included a large component of reading, writing, and rational discourse. For the early centuries of American history, until the telegraph made it possible to create what we know as news and sell the readers of newspapers to advertisers, the public sphere did rely on an astonishingly literate population. Neil Postman, in his book about the way television has changed the nature of public discourse, *Amusing Ourselves to Death,* notes that Thomas Paine's *Common Sense* sold three hundred thousand copies in five months in 1775. Contemporary observers have documented and analyzed the way mass media ("one to many" media) have "commoditized" the public sphere, substituting slick public relations for genuine debate and packaging both issues and candidates like other consumer products.

The political significance of CMC lies in its capacity to challenge the existing political hierarchy's monopoly on powerful communications media, and perhaps thus revitalize citizen-based democracy. The way image-rich, sound-bite-based commercial media have co-opted political discourse among citizens is part of a political problem that communications technologies have posed for democracy for decades. The way the number of owners or telecommunication channels is narrowing to a tiny elite, while the reach and power of the media they own expand, is a converging threat to citizens. Which scenario seems more conducive to democracy, which to totalitarian rule: a world in which a few people control communications technology that can be used to manipulate the beliefs of billions, or a world in which every citizen can broadcast to every other citizen?

Ben Bagdikian's often-quoted prediction from *The Media Monopoly* is that by the turn of the century "five to ten corporate giants will control most of the world's important newspapers, magazines, books, broadcast stations, movies, recordings and videocassettes." These new media lords possess immense power to determine which information most people receive about the world, and I suspect they are not likely to encourage their privately owned and controlled networks to be the willing conduits for all the kinds of information that unfettered citizens and nongovernmental organizations tend to disseminate. The activist solution to this dilemma has been to use CMC to create alternative planetary information networks. The distributed nature of the telecommunications network, coupled with the availability of affordable computers, makes it possible to piggyback alternate networks on the mainstream infrastructure.

We temporarily have access to a tool that could bring conviviality and understanding into our lives and might help revitalize the public sphere. The same tool, improperly controlled and wielded, could become an instrument of tyranny.

The vision of a citizen-designed, citizen-controlled worldwide communications network is a version of technological utopianism that could be called the vision of "the electronic agora." In the original democracy, Athens, the agora was the marketplace, and more—it was where citizens met to talk, gossip, argue, size each other up, find the weak spots in political ideas by debating about them. But another kind of vision could apply to the use of the Net in the wrong ways, a shadow vision of a less utopian kind of place—the Panopticon.

Panopticon was the name for an ultimately effective prison, seriously proposed in eighteenth-century Britain by Jeremy Bentham. A combination of architecture and optics makes it possible in Bentham's scheme for a single guard to see every prisoner, and for no prisoner to see anything else; the effect is that all prisoners act as if they were under surveillance at all times. Contemporary social critic Michel Foucault, in *Discipline and Punish*, claimed that the machinery of the worldwide communications network constitutes a kind of camouflaged Panopticon; citizens of the world brought into their homes, along with each other, the prying ears of the state. The cables that bring information into our homes today are technically capable of bringing information out of our homes, instantly transmitted to interested others. Tomorrow's version of Panoptic machinery could make very effective use of the same communications infrastructure that enables one-room schoolhouses in Montana to communicate with MIT professors, and enables citizens to disseminate news and organize resistance to totalitarian rule. With so much of our intimate data and more and more of our private behavior moving into cyberspace, the potential for totalitarian abuse of that information web is significant and the cautions of the critics are worth a careful hearing.

The wise revolutionary keeps an eye on the dark side of the changes he or she would initiate. Enthusiasts who believe in the humanitarian potential of virtual communities, especially those of us who speak of electronic democracy as a potential application of the medium, are well advised to consider the shadow potential of the same media. We should not forget that intellectuals and journalists of the 1950s hailed the advent of the greatest educational medium in history—television.

Because of its potential to change us as humans, as communities, as democracies, we need to try to understand the nature of CMC, cyberspace, and virtual communities in every important context—politically, economically, socially, cognitively. Each different perspective reveals something that the other perspectives do not reveal. Each different discipline fails to see something that another discipline sees very well. We need to think together here, across boundaries of academic discipline, industrial affiliation, nation, if we hope to understand and thus perhaps regain control of the way human communities are being transformed by communications technologies.

We can't do this solely as dispassionate observers, although there is certainly a strong need for the detached assessment of social science. Community is a matter of emotions as well as a thing of reason and data. Some of the most important learning will always have to be done by jumping into one corner or another of cyberspace, living there, and getting up to your elbows in the problems that virtual communities face.

I care about what happens in cyberspace, and to our freedoms in cyberspace, because I dwell there part of the time. The author's voice as a citizen and veteran of virtual community-building is one of the points of view presented in this book: I'm part of the story I'm describing, speaking as both native informant and as uncredentialed social scientist. Because of the paucity of first-person source material describing the way it feels to live in cyberspace, I believe it is valuable to include my perspective as participant as well as observer. In some places, like the WELL, I speak from extensive experience; in many of the places we need to examine in order to understand the Net, I am almost as new to the territory as those who never heard about cyberspace before. Ultimately, if you want to form your own opinions, you need to pick up a good beginner's guidebook and plunge into the Net for yourself. It is possible, however, to paint a kind of word-picture, necessarily somewhat sketchy, of the varieties of life to be found on the Net. . . .

The ways I've witnessed people in the virtual community I know best build value, help each other through hard times, solve (and fail to solve) vexing interpersonal problems together, offer a model—undoubtedly not an infallible one—of the kinds of social changes that virtual communities can make in real lives on a modestly local scale. Some knowledge of how people in a small virtual community behave will help prevent vertigo and give you tools for comparison when we zoom out to the larger metropolitan areas of cyberspace. Some aspects of life in a small community have to be abandoned when you move to an online metropolis; the fundamentals of human nature, however, always scale up.

IS THERE A THERE IN CYBERSPACE?

John Perry Barlow

Even-handedly approaching the topic of large area networks and communities, John Perry Barlow expresses his initial optimism about cyberspace, an opinion that over the years was transformed into pessimism and then, finally, a kind of tempered hopefulness. Although on-line communities lack a depth of texture found in face-to-face interactions, there is a kind of inevitable hope that on-line interactions provide for giving back at least a part of the sense of community that has been lost in contemporary North American culture.

Reprinted, with permission, from *Utne Reader* (March–April 1995): 53–56.

I am often asked how I went from pushing cows around a remote Wyoming ranch to my present occupation (which *Wall Street Journal* recently described as "cyberspace cadet"). I haven't got a short answer, but I suppose I came to the virtual world looking for community.

Unlike most modern Americans, I grew up in an actual place, an entirely nonintentional community called Pinedale, Wyoming. As I struggled for nearly a generation to keep my ranch in the family, I was motivated by the belief that such places were the spiritual home of humanity. But I knew their future was not promising.

At the dawn of the 20th century, over 40 percent of the American workforce lived off the land. The majority of us lived in towns like Pinedale. Now fewer than 1 percent of us extract a living from the soil. We just became too productive for our own good.

Of course, the population followed the jobs. Farming and ranching communities are now home to a demographically insignificant percentage of Americans, the vast majority of whom live not in ranch houses but in more or less identical split-level "ranch homes" in more or less identical suburban "communities." Generica.

In my view, these are neither communities nor homes. I believe the combination of television and suburban population patterns is simply toxic to the soul. I see much evidence in contemporary America to support this view.

Meanwhile, back at the ranch, doom impended. And, as I watched community in Pinedale growing ill from the same economic forces that were killing my family's ranch, the Bar Cross, satellite dishes brought the cultural infection of television. I started looking around for evidence that community in America would not perish altogether.

I took some heart in the mysterious nomadic City of the Deadheads, the virtually physical town that follows the Grateful Dead around the country. The Deadheads lacked place, touching down briefly wherever the band happened to be playing, and they lacked continuity in time, since they had to suffer a new diaspora every time the band moved on or went home. But they had many of the other necessary elements of community, including a culture, a religion of sorts (which, though it lacked dogma, had most of the other, more nurturing aspects of spiritual practice), a sense of necessity, and, most importantly, shared adversity.

I wanted to know more about the flavor of their interaction, what they thought and felt, but since I wrote Dead songs (including "Estimated Prophet" and "Cassidy"), I was a minor icon to the Deadheads, and was thus inhibited, in some socially Heisenbergian way, from getting a clear view of what really went on among them.

Then, in 1987, I heard about a "place" where Deadheads gathered where I could move among them without distorting too much the field of observation. Better, this was a place I could visit without leaving Wyoming.

It was a shared computer in Sausalito, California, called the Whole Earth 'Lectronic Link, or WELL. After a lot of struggling with modems, serial cables, init strings, and other computer arcana that seemed utterly out of phase with such notions as Deadheads and small towns, I found myself looking at the glowing yellow word "Login:" beyond which lay my future.

"Inside" the WELL were Deadheads in community. There were thousands of them there, gossiping, complaining (mostly about the Grateful Dead), comforting and harassing each other, bartering, engaging in religion (or at least exchanging their totemic set lists), beginning and ending love affairs, praying for one another's sick kids. There was, it seemed, everything one might find going on in a small town, save dragging Main Street and making out on the back roads.

I was delighted. I felt I had found the new locale of human community—never mind that the whole thing was being conducted in mere words by minds from whom the bodies had been amputated. Never mind that all these people were deaf, dumb, and blind as paramecia or that their town had neither seasons nor sunsets nor smells.

Surely all these deficiencies would be remedied by richer, faster communications media. The featureless log-in handles would gradually acquire video faces (and thus expressions), shaded 3-D body puppets (and thus body language). This "space," which I recognized at once to be a primitive form of the cyberspace William Gibson predicted in his sci-fi novel *Neuromancer*, was still without apparent dimensions or vistas. But virtual reality would change all that in time.

Meanwhile, the commons, or something like it, had been rediscovered. Once again, people from the 'burbs had a place where they could encounter their friends as my fellow Pinedalians did at the post office and the Wrangler Cafe. They had a place where their hearts could remain as the companies they worked for shuffled their bodies around America. They could put down roots that could not be ripped out by forces of economic history. They had a collective stake. They had a community.

It is seven years now since I discovered the WELL. In that time, I co-founded an organization, the Electronic Frontier Foundation, dedicated to protecting its interests and those of other virtual communities like it from raids by physical government. I've spent countless hours typing away at its residents, and I've watched the larger context that contains it, the Internet, grow at such an explosive rate that, by 2004, every human on the planet will have an e-mail address unless the growth curve flattens (which it will).

My enthusiasm for virtuality has cooled. In fact, unless one counts interaction with the rather too large society of those with whom I exchange electronic mail, I don't spend much time engaging in virtual community at all. Many of the near-term benefits I anticipated from it seem to remain as far in the future as they did when I first logged in. Perhaps they always will.

Pinedale works, more or less, as it is, but a lot is still missing from the communities of cyberspace, whether they be places like the WELL, the fractious newsgroups of USENET, the silent "auditoriums" of America Online, or even enclaves on the promising World Wide Web.

What is missing? Well, to quote Ranjit Makkuni of Xerox Corporation's Palo Alto Research Center, "the *prāna* is missing," *prāna* being the Hindu term for both breath and spirit. I think he is right about this and that perhaps the central question of the virtual age is whether or not *prāna* can somehow be made to fit through any disembodied medium.

Prāna is, to my mind, the literally vital element in the holy and unseen ecology of relationship, the dense mesh of invisible life, on whose surface carbon-based life floats like a thin film. It is at the heart of the fundamental and profound difference between information and experience. Jaron Lanier has said that "information is alienated experience," and, that being true, *prāna* is part of what is removed when you create such easily transmissible replicas of experience as, say, the evening news.

Obviously a great many other, less spiritual, things are also missing entirely, like body language, sex, death, tone of voice, clothing, beauty (or homeliness), weather, violence, vegetation, wildlife, pets, architecture, music, smells, sunlight, and that ol' harvest moon. In short, most of the things that make my life real to me.

Present, but in far less abundance than in the physical world, which I call "meat space," are women, children, old people, poor people, and the genuinely blind. Also mostly missing are the illiterate and the continent of Africa. There is not much human diversity in cyberspace, which is populated, as near as I can tell, by white males under 50 with plenty of computer terminal time, great typing skills, high math SATs, strongly held opinions on just about everything, and an excruciating face-to-face shyness, especially with the opposite sex.

But diversity is as essential to healthy community as it is to healthy ecosystems (which are, in my view, different from communities only in unimportant aspects).

I believe that the principal reason for the almost universal failure of the intentional communities of the '60s and '70s was a lack of diversity in their members. It was a rare commune with any old people in it, or people who were fundamentally out of philosophical agreement with the majority.

Indeed, it is the usual problem when we try to build something that can only be grown. Natural systems, such as human communities, are simply too complex to design by the engineering principles we insist on applying to them. Like Dr. Frankenstein, Western civilization is now finding its rational skills inadequate to the task of creating and caring for life.

We would do better to return to a kind of agricultural mind-set in which we humbly try to re-create the conditions from which life has sprung before. And leave the rest to God.

Given that it has been built so far almost entirely by people with engineering degrees, it is not so surprising that cyberspace has the kind of overdesigned quality that leaves out all kinds of elements nature would have provided invisibly.

Also missing from both the communes of the '60s and from cyberspace are a couple of elements that I believe are very important, if not essential, to the formation and preservation of real community: an absence of alternatives and a sense of genuine adversity, generally shared. What about these?

It is hard to argue that anyone would find losing a modem literally hard to survive, while many have remained in small towns, have tolerated their intolerances and created entertainment to enliven their culturally arid lives simply because it seemed there was no choice but to stay. There are many investments—spiritual, material, and temporal—one is willing to put into a home one cannot leave. Communities are often the beneficiaries of these involuntary investments.

But when the going gets rough in cyberspace, it is even easier to move than it is in the 'burbs, where, given the fact that the average American moves some 12 times in his or her life, moving appears to be pretty easy. You can not only find another bulletin board service (BBS) or newsgroup to hang out in, you can, with very little effort, start your own.

And then there is the bond of joint suffering. Most community is a cultural stockade erected against a common enemy that can take many forms. In Pinedale, we bore together, with an understanding needing little expression, the fact that Upper Green River Valley is the coldest spot, as measured by annual mean temperature, in the lower 48 states. We knew that if somebody was stopped on the road most winter nights, he would probably die there, so the fact that we might loathe him was not sufficient reason to drive on past his broken pickup.

By the same token, the Deadheads have the Drug Enforcement Administration, which strives to give them 20-year prison terms without parole for distributing the fairly harmless sacrament of their faith. They have an additional bond in the fact that when their Microbuses die, as they often do, no one but another Deadhead is likely to stop to help them.

But what are the shared adversities of cyberspace? Lousy user interfaces? The flames of harsh invective? Dumb jokes? Surely these can all be survived without the sanctuary provided by fellow sufferers.

One is always free to yank the jack, as I have mostly done. For me, the physical world offers far more opportunity for *prāna*-rich connections with my fellow creatures. Even for someone whose body is in a state of perpetual motion, I feel I can generally find more community among the still-embodied.

Finally, there is that shyness factor. Not only are we trying to build community here among people who have never experienced any in my sense of the term, we are trying to build community among people who, in their lives, have rarely used the word *we* in a heartfelt way. It is a vast club, and many of the members—following Groucho Marx—wouldn't want to join a club that would have them.

And yet. . .

How quickly physical community continues to deteriorate. Even Pinedale, which seems to have survived the plague of ranch failures, feels increasingly cut off from itself. Many of the ranches are now owned by corporate types who fly their Gulfstreams in to fish and are rarely around during the many months when the creeks are frozen over and neighbors are needed. They have kept the ranches alive financially, but they actively discourage their managers from the interdependence my former colleagues and I require. They keep agriculture on life support, still alive but lacking a functional heart.

And the town has been inundated with suburbanites who flee here, bringing all their terrors and suspicions with them. They spend their evenings as they did in Orange County, watching television or socializing in hermetic little enclaves of fundamentalist Christianity that seem to separate them from us and even, given their sectarian animosities, from one another. The town remains. The community is largely a wraith of nostalgia.

So where else can we look for the connection we need to prevent our plunging further into the condition of separateness Nietzsche called sin? What is there to do but to dive further into the bramble bush of information that, in its broadcast forms, has done so much to tear us apart?

Cyberspace, for all its current deficiencies and failed promises, is not without some very real solace already.

Some months ago, the great love of my life, a vivid young woman with whom I intended to spend the rest of it, dropped dead of undiagnosed viral cardiomyopathy two days short of her 30th birthday. I felt as if my own heart had been as shredded as hers.

We had lived together in New York City. Except for my daughters, no one from Pinedale had met her. I needed a community to wrap around myself against colder winds than fortune had ever blown at me before. And without looking, I found I had one in the virtual world.

On the WELL, there was a topic announcing her death in one of the conferences to which I posted the eulogy I had read over her before burying her in her own small town of Nanaimo, British Columbia. It seemed to strike a chord among the disembodied living on the Net. People copied it and sent it to one another. Over the next several months I received almost a megabyte of electronic mail from all over the planet, mostly from folks whose faces I have never seen and probably never will.

They told me of their own tragedies and what they had done to survive them. As humans have since words were first uttered, we shared the second most common human experience, death, with an openheartedness that would have caused grave uneasiness in physical America, where the whole topic is so cloaked in denial as to be considered obscene. Those strangers, who had no arms to put around my shoulders, no eyes to weep with mine, nevertheless saw me through. As neighbors do.

I have no idea how far we will plunge into this strange place. Unlike previous frontiers, this one has no end. It is so dissatisfying in so many ways that I suspect we will be more restless in our search for home here than in all our previous explorations. And that is one reason why I think we may find it after all. If home is where the heart is, then there is already some part of home to be found in cyberspace.

So . . . does virtual community work or not? Should we all go off to cyberspace or should we resist it as a demonic form of symbolic abstraction? Does it supplant the real or is there, in it, reality itself?

Like so many true things, this one doesn't resolve itself to a black or a white. Nor is it gray. It is, along with the rest of life, black/white. Both/neither. I'm not being equivocal or wishy-washy here. We have to get over our Manichean sense that everything is either good or bad, and the border of cyberspace seems to me a good place to leave that old set of filters.

But really it doesn't matter. We are going there whether we want to or not. In five years, everyone who is reading these words will have an e-mail address, other than the determined Luddites who also eschew the telephone and electricity.

When we are all together in cyberspace we will see what the human spirit, and the basic desire to connect, can create there. I am convinced that the result will be more benign if we go there open-minded, openhearted, and excited with the adventure than if we are dragged into exile.

And we must remember that going to cyberspace, unlike previous great emigrations to the frontier, hardly requires us to leave where we have been. Many will find, as I have, a much richer appreciation of physical reality for having spent so much time in virtuality.

Despite its current (and perhaps in some areas permanent) insufficiencies, we should go to cyberspace with hope. Groundless hope, like unconditional love, may be the only kind that counts.

In Memoriam, Dr. Cynthia Horner (1964–1994).

CHAPTER FOUR
Alienation, Anonymity, and Embodiment

IN THE AGE OF THE SMART MACHINE

Shoshana Zuboff

In this selection from her much larger work, Shoshana Zuboff takes aim at issues of intermediacy created by the use of computers in the workplace. Computer technologies tend to develop a distance between the human body and the actions performed. For example, because of computer technologies, certain kinds of work-related activities in a paper plant that previously required all of the senses— taste, smell, touch, hearing, and sight—to understand and react correctly to the needs of the plant, no longer do so. Instead, computer technologies require a person to rely merely on symbolic information—numbers and graphs. This increased intermediacy caused by the implementation of computers affects the ways in which jobs are performed and in fact creates new classes of employment.

Piney Wood, one of the nation's largest pulp mills, was in the throes of a massive modernization effort that would place every aspect of the production process under computer control. Six workers were crowded around a table in the snack area outside what they called the Star Trek Suite, one of the first control rooms to have been completely converted to microprocessor-based instrumentation. It looked enough like a NASA control room to have earned its name.

It was almost midnight, but despite the late hour and the approach of the shift change, each of the six workers was at once animated and

---

thoughtful. "Knowledge and technology are changing so fast," they said, "what will happen to us?" Their visions of the future foresaw wrenching change. They feared that today's working assumptions could not be relied upon to carry them through, that the future would not resemble the past or the present. More frightening still was the sense of a future moving out of reach so rapidly that there was little opportunity to plan or make choices. The speed of dissolution and renovation seemed to leave no time for assurances that we were not heading toward calamity—and it would be all the more regrettable for having been something of an accident.

The discussion around the table betrayed a grudging admiration for the new technology—its power, its intelligence, and the aura of progress surrounding it. That admiration, however, bore a sense of grief. Each expression of gee-whiz-Buck-Rogers breathless wonder brought with it an aching dread conveyed in images of a future that rendered their authors obsolete. In what ways would computer technology transform their work lives? Did it promise the Big Rock Candy Mountain or a silent graveyard?

> In fifteen years there will be nothing for the worker to do. The technology will be so good it will operate itself. You will just sit there behind a desk running two or three areas of the mill yourself and get bored.

The group concluded that the worker of the future would need "an extremely flexible personality" so that he or she would not be "mentally affected" by the velocity of change. They anticipated that workers would need a great deal of education and training in order to "breed flexibility." "We find it all to be a great stress," they said, "but it won't be that way for the new flexible people." Nor did they perceive any real choice, for most agreed that without an investment in the new technology, the company could not remain competitive. They also knew that without their additional flexibility, the technology would not fly right. "We are in a bind," one man groaned, "and there is no way out." The most they could do, it was agreed, was to avoid thinking too hard about the loss of overtime pay, the diminished probability of jobs for their sons and daughters, the fears of seeming incompetent in a strange new milieu, or the possibility that the company might welsh on its promise not to lay off workers.

During the conversation, a woman in stained overalls had remained silent with her head bowed, apparently lost in thought. Suddenly, she raised her face to us. It was lined with decades of hard work, her brow drawn together. Her hands lay quietly on the table. They were calloused and swollen, but her deep brown eyes were luminous, youthful, and kind. She seemed frozen, chilled by her own insight, as she solemnly delivered her conclusion:

> I think the country has a problem. The managers want everything to be run by computers. But if no one has a job, no one will know how to do anything

anymore. Who will pay the taxes? What kind of society will it be when people have lost their knowledge and depend on computers for everything?

Her voice trailed off as the men stared at her in dazzled silence. They slowly turned their heads to look at one another and nodded in agreement. The forecast seemed true enough. Yes, there was a problem. They looked as though they had just run a hard race, only to stop short at the edge of a cliff. As their heels skidded in the dirt, they could see nothing ahead but a steep drop downward.

Must it be so? Should the advent of the smart machine be taken as an invitation to relax the demands upon human comprehension and critical judgment? Does the massive diffusion of computer technology throughout our workplaces necessarily entail an equally dramatic loss of meaningful employment opportunities? Must the new electronic milieu engender a world in which individuals have lost control over their daily work lives? Do these visions of the future represent the price of economic success or might they signal an industrial legacy that must be overcome if intelligent technology is to yield its full value? Will the new information technology represent an opportunity for the rejuvenation of competitiveness, productive vitality, and organizational ingenuity? Which aspects of the future of working life can we predict, and which will depend upon the choices we make today?

The workers outside the Star Trek Suite knew that the so-called technological choices we face are really much more than that. Their consternation puts us on alert. There is a world to be lost and a world to be gained. Choices that appear to be merely technical will redefine our lives together at work. This means more than simply contemplating the implications or consequences of a new technology. It means that a powerful new technology, such as that represented by the computer, fundamentally reorganizes the infrastructure of our material world. It eliminates former alternatives. It creates new possibilities. It necessitates fresh choices.

The choices that we face concern the conception and distribution of knowledge in the workplace. Imagine the following scenario: Intelligence is lodged in the smart machine at the expense of the human capacity for critical judgment. Organizational members become ever more dependent, docile, and secretly cynical. As more tasks must be accomplished through the medium of information technology (I call this "computer-mediated work"), the sentient body loses its salience as a source of knowledge, resulting in profound disorientation and loss of meaning. People intensify their search for avenues of escape through drugs, apathy, or adversarial conflict, as the majority of jobs in our offices and factories become increasingly isolated, remote, routine, and perfunctory. Alternatively, imagine this scenario: Organizational leaders recognize the new forms of skill and knowledge needed to truly exploit the potential of an intelligent technology. They direct their resources toward creating a work force that can exercise critical judgment as it manages the surrounding machine systems. Work becomes more abstract as it depends upon understanding and manipulating information. This marks the beginning of new forms of mastery and provides an opportunity to imbue jobs with more comprehensive meaning. A new array of work tasks offer unprecedented opportunities for a wide range of employees to add value to products and services.

The choices that we make will shape relations of authority in the workplace. Once more, imagine: Managers struggle to retain their traditional sources of authority, which have depended in an important way upon their exclusive control of the organization's knowledge base. They use the new technology to structure organizational experience in ways that help reproduce the legitimacy of their traditional roles. Managers insist on the prerogatives of command and seek methods that protect the hierarchical distance that distinguishes them from their subordinates. Employees barred from the new forms of mastery relinquish their sense of responsibility for the organization's work and use obedience to authority as a means of expressing their resentment. Imagine an alternative: This technological transformation engenders a new approach to organizational behavior, one in which relationships are more intricate, collaborative, and bound by the mutual responsibilities of colleagues. As the new technology integrates information across time and space, managers and workers each overcome their narrow functional perspectives and create new roles that are better suited to enhancing value-adding activities in a data-rich environment. As the quality of skills at each organizational level becomes similar, hierarchical distinctions begin to blur. Authority comes to depend more upon an appropriate fit between knowledge and responsibility than upon the ranking rules of the traditional organizational pyramid.

The choices that we make will determine the techniques of administration that color the psychological ambience and shape communicative behavior in the emerging workplace. Imagine this scenario: The new technology becomes the source of surveillance techniques that are used to ensnare organizational members or to subtly bully them into conformity. Managers employ the technology to circumvent the demanding work of face-to-face engagement, substituting instead techniques of remote management and automated administration. The new technological infrastructure becomes a battlefield of techniques, with managers inventing novel ways to enhance certainty and control while employees discover new methods of self-protection and even sabotage. Imagine the alternative: The new technological milieu becomes a resource from which are fashioned innovative methods of information sharing and social exchange. These methods in turn produce a deepened sense of collective responsibility and joint ownership, as access to ever-broader domains of information lend new objectivity to data and preempt the dictates of hierarchical authority.

. . . Computer-based technologies are not neutral; they embody essential characteristics that are bound to alter the nature of work within our factories and offices, and among workers, professionals, and managers. New choices are laid open by these technologies, and these choices are being confronted in the daily lives of men and women across the landscape of modern organizations. This book is an effort to understand the deep structure of these choices—the historical, psychological, and organizational forces that imbue our conduct and sensibility. It is also a vision of a fruitful future, a call for action that can lead us beyond the stale reproduction of the past into an era that offers a historic opportunity to more fully develop the economic and human potential of our work organizations.

The Two Faces of Intelligent Technology

The past twenty years have seen their share of soothsayers ready to predict with conviction one extreme or another of the alternative futures I have presented. From the unmanned factory to the automated cockpit, visions of the future hail information technology as the final answer to "the labor question," the ultimate opportunity to rid ourselves of the thorny problems associated with training and managing a competent and committed work force. These very same technologies have been applauded as the hallmark of a second industrial revolution, in which the classic conflicts of knowledge and power associated with an earlier age will be synthesized in an array of organizational innovations and new procedures for the production of goods and services, all characterized by an unprecedented degree of labor harmony and widespread participation in management process.[1] Why the paradox? How can the very same technologies be interpreted in these different ways? Is this evidence that the technology is indeed neutral, a blank screen upon which managers project their biases and encounter only their own limitations? Alternatively, might it tell us something else about the interior structure of information technology?

Throughout history, humans have designed mechanisms to reproduce and extend the capacity of the human body as an instrument of work. The industrial age has carried this principle to a dramatic new level of sophistication with machines that can substitute for and amplify the abilities of the human body. Because machines are mute, and because they are precise and repetitive, they can be controlled according to a set of rational principles in a way that human bodies cannot.

There is no doubt that information technology can provide substitutes for the human body that reach an even greater degree of certainty and precision. When a task is automated by a computer, it must first be broken down to its smallest components. Whether the activity involves spraying paint on an automobile or performing a clerical transaction, it is the information contained in this analysis that translates human agency into a computer program. The resulting software can be used to automatically guide equipment, as in the case of a robot, or to execute an information transaction, as in the case of an automated teller machine.

A computer program makes it possible to rationalize activities more comprehensively than if they had been undertaken by a human being. Programmability means, for example, that a robot will respond with unwavering precision because the instructions that guide it are themselves unvarying, or that office transactions will be uniform because the instructions that guide them have been standardized. Events and processes can be rationalized to the extent that human agency can be analyzed and translated into a computer program.

What is it, then, that distinguishes information technology from earlier generations of machine technology? As information technology is used to reproduce, extend, and improve upon the process of substituting machines for human agency, it simultaneously accomplishes something quite different. The devices that automate by translating information into action also register data about those automated activities, thus generating new streams of information. For example, computer-based, numerically controlled machine tools or microprocessor-based sensing devices not only apply programmed instructions to equipment but also convert the current state of equipment, product, or process into data. Scanner devices in supermarkets automate the checkout process and simultaneously generate data that can be used for inventory control, warehousing, scheduling of deliveries, and market analysis. The same systems that make it possible to automate office transactions also create a vast overview of an organization's operations, with many levels of data coordinated and accessible for a variety of analytical efforts.

Thus, information technology, even when it is applied to automatically reproduce a finite activity, is not mute. It not only imposes information (in the form of programmed instructions) but also produces information. It both accomplishes tasks and translates them into information. The action of a machine is entirely invested in its object, the product. Information technology, on the other hand, introduces an additional dimension of reflexivity: it makes its contribution to the product, but it also reflects back on its activities and on the system of activities to which it is related. Information technology not only produces action but also produces a voice that symbolically renders events, objects, and processes so that they become visible, knowable, and shareable in a new way.

Viewed from this interior perspective, information technology is characterized by a fundamental duality that has not yet been fully appreciated.

On the one hand, the technology can be applied to automating operations according to a logic that hardly differs from that of the nineteenth-century machine system—replace the human body with a technology that enables the same processes to be performed with more continuity and control. On the other, the same technology simultaneously generates information about the underlying productive and administrative processes through which an organization accomplishes its work. It provides a deeper level of transparency to activities that had been either partially or completely opaque. In this way information technology supersedes the traditional logic of automation. The word that I have coined to describe this unique capacity is *informate.* Activities, events, and objects are translated into and made visible by information when a technology *informates* as well as *automates.*

The informating power of intelligent technology can be seen in the manufacturing environment when microprocessor-based devices such as robots, programmable logic controllers, or sensors are used to translate the three-dimensional production process into digitized data. These data are then made available within a two-dimensional space, typically on the screen of a video display terminal or on a computer printout, in the form of electronic symbols, numbers, letters, and graphics. These data constitute a quality of information that did not exist before. The programmable controller not only tells the machine what to do—imposing information that guides operating equipment—but also tells what the machine has done—translating the production process and making it visible.

In the office environment, the combination of on-line transaction systems, information systems, and communications systems creates a vast information presence that now includes data formerly stored in people's heads, in face-to-face conversations, in metal file drawers, and on widely dispersed pieces of paper. The same technology that processes documents more rapidly, and with less intervention, than a mechanical typewriter or pen and ink can be used to display those documents in a communications network. As more of the underlying transactional and communicative processes of an organization become automated, they too become available as items in a growing organizational data base.

In its capacity as an automating technology, information technology has a vast potential to displace the human presence. Its implications as an informating technology, on the other hand, are not well understood. The distinction between *automate* and *informate* provides one way to understand how this technology represents both continuities and discontinuities with the traditions of industrial history. As long as the technology is treated narrowly in its automating function, it perpetuates the logic of the industrial machine that, over the course of this century, has made it possible to rationalize work while decreasing the dependence on human skills. However, when the technology also informates the processes to which it is applied, it increases the explicit information content of tasks and sets into motion a series of dynamics that will ultimately reconfigure the nature of work and the social relationships that organize productive activity.

Because this duality of intelligent technology has not been clearly recognized, the consequences of the technology's informating capacity are often regarded as unintended. Its effects are not planned, and the potential that it lays open remains relatively unexploited. Because the informating process is poorly defined, it often evades the conventional categories of description that are used to gauge the effects of industrial technology.

These dual capacities of information technology are not opposites; they are hierarchically integrated. Informating derives from and builds upon automation. Automation is a necessary but not sufficient condition for informating. It is quite possible to proceed with automation without reference to how it will contribute to the technology's informating potential. When this occurs, informating is experienced as an unintended consequence of automation. This is one point at which choices are laid open. Managers can choose to exploit the emergent informating capacity and explore the organizational innovations required to sustain and develop it. Alternatively, they can choose to ignore or suppress the informating process. In contrast, it is possible to consider informating objectives at the start of an automation process. When this occurs, the choices that are made with respect to how and what to automate are guided by criteria that reflect developmental goals associated with using the technology's unique informating power.

Information technology is frequently hailed as "revolutionary." What are the implications of this term? *Revolution* means a pervasive, marked, radical change, but *revolution* also refers to a movement around a fixed course that returns to the starting point. Each sense of the word has relevance for the central problem of this book. The informating capacity of the new computer-based technologies brings about radical change as it alters the intrinsic character of work—the way millions of people experience daily life on the job. It also poses fundamentally new choices for our organizational futures, and the ways in which labor and management respond to these new choices will finally determine whether our era becomes a time for radical change or a return to the familiar patterns and pitfalls of the traditional workplace. An emphasis on the informating capacity of intelligent technology can provide a point of origin for new conceptions of work and power. A more restricted emphasis on its automating capacity can provide the occasion for that second kind of revolution—a return to the familiar grounds of industrial society with divergent interests battling for control, augmented by an array of new material resources with which to attack and defend.

The questions that we face today are finally about leadership. Will there be leaders who are able to recognize the historical moment and the choices it presents? Will they find ways to create the organizational conditions in which new visions, new concepts, and a new language of workplace relations can emerge? Will they be able to create organizational innovations that can exploit the unique capacities of the new technology and thus mobilize their organization's productive potential to meet the heightened rigors of global competition? Will there be leaders who understand the crucial role that human beings from each organizational stratum can play in adding value to the production of goods and services? If not, we will be stranded in a new world with old solutions. We will suffer through the unintended consequences of change, because we have failed to understand this technology and how it differs from what came before. By neglecting the unique informating capacity of advanced computer-based technology and ignoring the need for a new vision of work and organization, we will have forfeited the dramatic business benefits it can provide. Instead, we will find ways to absorb the dysfunctions, putting out brush fires and patching wounds in a slow-burning bewilderment. . . .

The Automatic Doors

The bleach plant is one of the most complex and treacherous areas of a pulp mill. In Piney Wood, a large pulp plant built in the mid-1940s, railroad tank cars filled with chemicals used in the bleaching process pull up alongside the four-story structure in which dirty brown digested pulp is turned gleaming white. Each minute, 4,000 gallons of this brown mash flow through a labyrinth of pipes into a series of cylindrical vats, where they are washed, treated with chlorine-related chemicals, and bleached white. No natural light finds its way into this part of the mill. The fluorescent tubes overhead cast a greenish-yellow pall, and the air is laced with enough chemical flavor that as you breathe it, some involuntary wisdom built deep into the human body registers an assault. The floors are generally wet, particularly in the areas right around the base of one of the large vats that loom like raised craters on a moonscape. Sometimes a washer runs over, spilling soggy cellulose knee-deep across the floor. When this happens, the men put on their high rubber boots and shovel up the mess.

The five stages of the bleaching process include hundreds of operating variables. The bleach operator must monitor and control the flow of stock, chemicals, and water, judge color and viscosity, attend to time, temperature, tank levels, and surge rates—the list goes on. Before computer monitoring and control, an operator in this part of the mill would make continual rounds, checking dials and graph charts located on the equipment, opening and shutting valves, keeping an eye on vat levels, snatching a bit of pulp from a vat to check its color, sniff it, or squeeze it between his fingers ("Is it slick? Is it sticky?") to determine its density or to judge the chemical mix.

In 1981 a central control room was constructed in the bleach plant. A science fiction writer's fantasy, it is a gleaming glass bubble that seems to have erupted like a mushroom in the dark, moist, toxic atmosphere of the plant. The control room reflects a new technological era for continuous-process production, one in which microprocessor-based sensors linked to computers allow remote monitoring and control of the key process variables. In fact, the entire pulp mill was involved in this conversion from the pneumatic control technology of the 1940s to the microprocessor-based information and control technology of the 1980s.

Inside the control room, the air is filtered and hums with the sound of the air-conditioning unit built into the wall between the control room and a small snack area. Workers sit on orthopedically designed swivel chairs covered with a royal blue fabric, facing video display terminals. The terminals, which display process information for the purposes of monitoring and control, are built into polished oak cabinets. Their screens glow with numbers, letters, and graphics in vivid red, green, and blue. The floor here is covered with slate-gray carpeting; the angled countertops on which the terminals sit are rust brown and edged in black. The walls are covered with a wheat-colored fabric and the molding repeats the polished oak of the cabinetry. The dropped ceiling is of a bronzed metal, and from it is suspended a three dimensional structure into which lights have been recessed and angled to provide the right amount of illumination without creating glare on the screens. The color scheme is repeated on the ceiling—soft tones of beige, rust, brown, and gray in a geometric design.

The terminals each face toward the front of the room—a windowed wall that opens onto the bleach plant. The steel beams, metal tanks, and maze of thick pipes visible through those windows appear to be a world away in a perpetual twilight of steam and fumes, like a city street on a misty night, silent and dimly lit. What is most striking about the juxtaposition of these two worlds, is how a man (and there were only men working in this part of the mill) traverses the boundary between them.

The control room is entered through an automatic sliding-glass door. At the push of a button, the two panels of the door part, and when you step forward, they quickly close behind you. You then find yourself facing two more automatic doors at right angles to one another. The door on the right leads to a narrow snack area with booths, cabinets, a coffee machine, and a refrigerator. The door to the left leads into the control room. It will not open until the first door has shut. This ensures that the filtered air within the control room is protected from the fumes and heat of the bleach plant. The same routine holds in reverse. When a man leaves the control room, he presses a button next to the frame on the inner door, which opens electronically. He then steps through it into the tiny chamber where he must wait for the door to seal behind him so that he can push a second button on the outer door and finally exit into the plant.

This is not what most men do when they move from the control room out into the bleach plant. They step through the inner door, but they do not wait for that door to seal behind them before opening the second door. Instead, they force their fingertips through the rubber seal down the middle of the outer door and, with a mighty heft of their shoulders, pry open the seam and wrench the door apart. Hour after hour, shift after shift, week after week, too many men pit the strength in their arms and shoulders against the electronic mechanism that controls the doors. Three years after the construction of the sleek, glittering glass bubble, the outer door no longer closes tightly. A gap of several inches, running down the center between the two panels of glass, looks like a battle wound. The door is crippled.

"The door is broke now because the men pushed it too hard comin' in and out," says one operator. In talking to the men about this occurrence, so mundane as almost to defy reflection, I hear not only a simple impatience and frustration but also something deeper: a forward momentum of their bodies, whose physical power seems trivialized by the new circumstances of their work; a boyish energy that wants to break free; a subtle rebellion against the preprogrammed design that orders their environment and always knows best. Yet these are the men who also complained, "The fumes in the bleach plant will kill you. You can't take that chlorine no matter how big and bad you are. It will bleach your brains and no one (in management) gives a damn."

Technology represents intelligence systematically applied to the problem of the body. It functions to amplify and surpass the organic limits of the body; it compensates for the body's fragility and vulnerability. Industrial technology has substituted for the human body in many of the processes associated with production and so has redefined the limits of production formerly imposed by the body. As a result, society's capacity to produce things has been extended in a way that is unprecedented in human history. This achievement has not been without its costs, however. In diminishing the role of the worker's body in the labor process, industrial technology has also tended to diminish the importance of the worker. In creating jobs that require less human effort, industrial technology has also been used to create jobs that require less human talent. In creating jobs that demand less of the body, industrial production has also tended to create jobs that give less to the body, in terms of opportunities to accrue knowledge in the production process. These two-sided consequences have been fundamental for the growth and development of the industrial bureaucracy, which has depended upon the rationalization and centralization of knowledge as the basis of control.

Note

1. See, for example, Michael Piore and Charles F. Sabel, *The Second Industrial Divide: Possibilities for Prosperity* (New York: Basic Books, 1984).

IMPLANTABLE BRAIN CHIPS? TIME FOR DEBATE

G. Q. Maguire, Jr., and Ellen M. McGee

As a corollary to questions of artificial intelligence (AI), Maguire and McGee take up some issues of intelligence amplification (IA). Rather than making machines intelligent, why not add intelligent components to our biological bodies? In this way we become a sort of cyborg—that is, a human with computer-aided technologies built into his or her neurological structure. The authors argue that the manner in which these technologies are judged depends a great deal on how the body itself is viewed. Through the process of implanting computer parts, the line between therapy and body enhancement begins to blur. Furthermore, it is important to consider how implantable chips impact issues of autonomy and control of bodies.

Today's mail brings a catalog advertising a sweatshirt emblazoned with the slogan, "In my next life I'm going to have more memory installed." Most of us can relate to this desire. As it happens, it might not be so farfetched. Computer visionaries predict that within our lifetimes, implantable computer chips acting as sensors, or actuators, may not only assist failing memory but even bestow a variety of capacities. With their aid, we may acquire fluency in new languages or "recognize" people we

Reprinted with permission of the authors and publisher from *Hastings Center Report* 29, no. 1 (1999): 7–13.

have never met. The possibility exists that the increasingly common re-placement of body parts with mechanical items will lead eventually to the creation of cybernetic organisms—beings that intimately mix man and machine. If this trend is taken to its limit, computer chips and other electronic equipment implanted within human bodies might replace, aug-ment, and enhance those most human of faculties, our memory and our ability to reason. We could see the coming to be of science fiction's *cy-borg*, a person who has an intimate, perhaps necessary relationship with a machine.

The fantastic depictions of bionic man in science fiction tend to de-flect serious discussion of this possibility. *Robocop*'s enhanced humans and *The Terminator*'s stainless steel robots with living human skin make the topic seem laughable. *Star Trek*'s depiction of the evil race of cyborgs known as "The Borg" prejudices reasoned discussion of the "cyborgiza-tion" of humankind. The possibilities envisioned by William Gibson's novel *Neuromancer* of a world where the human mind and electronic tech-nology interface in a seamless continuum of consciousness seem remote. Hence, while cyborgs get attention in science fiction, scholarly analysis of the media, and in the writings of a few bold pioneers, for the most part there has been no serious discussion of whether we should move in the di-rection of such interfaces, whether we can control this technology, whether it will be progress or peril, and who should control it. It is the purpose of this paper to awaken the consciousness of the bioethics community to this field, to urge that a forum for societal deliberation be created, and to pose some preliminary questions.

A Quiet Revolution

Bioelectronics combines advances in prosthetic technology and in computer science. Given this origin, it has a long pedigree, since the use of prosthetic devices to rehabilitate and restore function spans human his-tory, proceeding in stages from simple external extensions of the human body—crutches and peg legs—through "energy storing" feet and devices controlled by muscle contraction to the current work involving direct brain interfaces. Worldwide there are at least three million people living with artificial implants.[1] They use breast, penile, pectoral, testicular, chin, calf, hair, hormonal, medicinal, and dental prostheses. They also use bionic limbs, cardiac pacemakers, small implantable pumps to assist in pul-monary or systemic circulation of blood,[2] and automatic biochemical pumps that either replace or augment parts of the nervous or neuroen-docrine systems and also provide sensory substitution.[3]

These bioelectronic developments, combined with progress in facil-itating interfaces between neural tissues and substrate micro probes, are setting the stage for implantable brain chips. The first steps have already been taken in research on the cochlear implant and on retinal vision. Cochlear implants enable totally deaf people to hear sound by directly stimulating the auditory nerve. In a similar way, retinal implantable chips for prosthetic vision may restore vision to the blind. Work on prosthetic vision was begun in the 1960s, when Giles Brindley attached eighty electrodes to miniature radio receivers and implanted them into a sightless volunteer's brain, hoping to remotely stimulate the visual cortex. In the 1970s, William Dobelle carried the work a step further.[4] The subjects of Dobelle's experiments reported seeing phosphenes, or points of light, akin to the signals received by a functioning visual system. In 1992, a blind volunteer at the U.S. National Institute of Neurological Disorders and Stroke learned to recognize phosphene letters.[5] Subsequent research on prosthetic vision has proceeded along two paths, employing either retinal implants, which link a miniature camera to healthy nerves, or cortical implants, which directly stimulate the visual cortex.[6]

Such "applied neural control" technology has already been put to other uses. It has been used, for example, for bladder control, and to contract paralyzed muscles.[7] In August 1997 the Food and Drug Administration approved a pacemaker-like brain implant to help Parkinson's patients and those with essential tremors.[8] The operation involves a hole drilled in the skull to implant an electrode in the thalamus to block tremors by emitting a constant stream of small electrical shocks from a "pulse-generator" implanted around the collarbone. This intervention seems to provide relief of the symptoms of Parkinson's disease without the adverse results of levodopa, the leading pharmacological intervention.

What makes these developments possible is the incredible miniaturization of information technology. Computer systems have progressed from mainframes to desktops, then to luggables and portables, now to pocket-size and even wallet- and ring-size models. Meanwhile, in communications technologies, macro cellular systems have led to micro cellular and cordless technologies and are moving toward pico cellular systems. Combined, these technologies enable users to access information and communicate anywhere or anytime using equipment that is wearable and nearly invisible, so that individuals can move about and interact freely while supported by a personal information structure.[9] For example, Thad Starner, a Ph.D. candidate in Media Arts and Sciences at Massachusetts Institute of Technology, dresses in a wearable computer and lives connected to the Internet using a miniature computer terminal at all times. His device is the first stage of what he calls "the BodyNet, a computer network wired through human bodies."[10] And Steve Mann, a professor of electrical and computer engineering at the University of Toronto, has developed an Internet-connected computer that he has dubbed "WearCam." By combining wireless communication with information systems, WearCam allows one to augment and enhance experiences and, through networking, share them with others. Writing of its future impact, Mann claims, "The boundaries between seeing and viewing, and between remembering and recording will crumble. When we purchase a new appliance, we will 'remember' the face behind the store counter. A week later, our spouse, taking the appliance back for a refund, will 'remember' the name and face of the clerk she never met."[11]

What is being developed is a "second brain." Already, researchers have developed a pair of eyeglasses equipped with a display, a camera and microphone, a handheld control, and a computer worn in back under the shirt. The system can be worn as computer "clothing" that works as a visual memory prosthetic and perception enhancer.[12] Using different filters, the wearer can augment normal vision and, by freezing images, see the previously unseeable, the lettering on moving automobile tires and the blades of a spinning propeller. In the future, it is proposed that two individuals similarly equipped could experience exactly the same reality and that eventually a networked community of individuals could be in perfect congruence, sending data, voice, and video to each other. The wearable computer project envisions users accessing the "Remembrance Agent"— a large, communal data source.[13] Linking a global positioning system and mapping software to the wearable computer would allow users to find their way in unfamiliar territory.[14]

Such constant access to information could benefit doctors, lawyers, stockbrokers, and many others. One project has examined whether wearable computers might help aircraft maintenance workers. The researchers conclude that the technology will "improve organizational effectiveness by: (1) spreading organizational expertise among workers, (2) providing fast access to procedural process, and schematic information for problem solving, (3) supporting process engineering, and (4) improving organizational memory."[15] Additionally, researchers have developed wearable computers linked to a wireless local area network to collect data at chicken processing plants"[16] and to implement employee training.[17] The military envisions using such devices to simplify repairing equipment on the battlefield. Indeed, the military is transforming itself through the use of electronics on the theory "that more brains, not more bullets will win the next battle."[18]

Implantable Brain Chips

Wearables and bodynets are intermediate technologies. The logical next step, long anticipated, is direct neural interfacing in the form of an implantable brain chip. As early as 1968, Nicholas Negroponte, director of the Media Lab at the Massachusetts Institute of Technology, first prophesied this symbiosis between mankind and machine.[19] His colleague, Neil

Gershenfeld, has asserted that "in 10 years, computers will be everywhere; in 20 years, embedded by bioengineers in our bodies."[20] Neither visionary professes any qualms about this project, which they expect to alter human nature itself. "Suddenly technology has given us powers," says Negroponte, "with which we can manipulate not only external reality—the physical world—but also, and much more portentously, ourselves."[21] The result will be a "collective consciousness," "the hive mind." "The hive mind . . . is about taking all these trillions of cells in our skulls that make individual consciousness and putting them together and arriving at a new kind of consciousness that transcends all the individuals."[22]

Most researchers do not dwell on this future, however. They concentrate on developing corrective tools for physical disability. Richard Norman, a researcher at the University of Utah, is developing an array of micro-electrodes that when placed in the visual cortex could be used to electronically stimulate the brain to see scenes from a miniature camera.[23] The array could also be used to present a completely synthetic scene. If such electrodes were placed in the motor cortex area, it could be possible to use the brain to control external devices, such as wheelchairs. The proposed procedure is far less invasive than the surgical implantation of cochlear devices, as it involves simply blowing an array into the brain via a small hole. The development of these technologies is currently supported, in some cases by the National Institutes of Health, under protocols envisioning medical devices that restore vision and hearing to the blind and deaf, or movement to the paralyzed.[24] These types of arrays have been implanted in animals and tested in short- and long-term experiments.[25] In one example, researchers at the NIH implanted a thirty-eight-electrode array into the visual cortex of a blind woman, enabling her to see simple light patterns, even identify crude letters, when the electrodes were stimulated.[26] Other systems producing functional neuromuscular stimulation are being used experimentally in cases of spinal cord severage.

Clearly, the technology for implantable devices is becoming available, at prices that make it cost effective. Three stages in the introduction of such devices can be delineated. The earliest adopters will be those with a disability who seek a more powerful prosthetic device. The next stage represents the movement from therapy to enhancement. One of the first groups of nondisabled "volunteers" will probably be in the professional military, where the use of an implanted computing and communication device with new interfaces to weapons, information, and communications could be life-saving. The third group of users will probably be people involved in information-intensive businesses who will use the technology to develop an expanded information transfer capability. The first prosthetic devices should be available in five years, with military prototypes starting within ten years, and information workers using prototypes within fifteen years; general adoption will take roughly twenty to thirty years.

As intelligence or sensory "amplifiers," the implantable chip will generate at least four benefits: (1) it will increase the dynamic range of senses, enabling people to see currently invisible wavelengths, for example; (2) it will enhance memory; (3) it will enable "cyberthink"—invisible communication with others when making decisions; and (4) it will enable consistent and constant access to information where and when it is needed. For many these enhancements will substantially improve quality of life, survivability, or job performance.

The implantable brain chip will probably function as a prosthetic cortical implant. The user's visual cortex will receive stimulation from a computer based either on what a camera sees or on an artificial "window" interface. But the latter need not be anything like the two-dimensional interface that we use today; the user is going to have to learn to "see"—that is, use the interface—from the ground up. Just as Morse code has nothing to do with the strokes of English letters, so the interface of a cortical implant will have nothing in common with today's computer interfaces. The user will ask for information via a keyboard, a spoken command, a muscle movement, or even a "thought command" (analogous to a decision to move a muscle but without actual movement of a muscle). A small computer nearby, perhaps worn in or near the body, will connect to other information systems via communication links. The "windowing" system for direct neural interfaces is currently unexplored, but it is estimated that this aspect of the technology will be developed by 2003. The system could "provide voice communications and an 'eyes-up' display which would superimpose text and pictures on our normal vision."[27]

The Moral Debate

Not every computer scientist views such prospects with equanimity. Michael Dertouzos, director of the MIT Laboratory for Computer Science, writes in *What Will Be* that "even if it would someday be possible to convey such higher-level information to the brain—and that is a huge technical 'If'—we should not do it. Bringing light impulses to the visual cortex of a blind person would justify such an intrusion, but unnecessarily tapping into the brain is a violation of our bodies, of nature, and for many, of God's design."[28]

This succinctly formulates the essentialist and creationist argument against the implantable chip. Fears of tampering with human nature are widespread; the theme that nature is good and technology evil, that the power to recreate oneself is overreaching hubris and that reengineering humanity can result only in disaster, is a familiar response to each new control that man exercises, from life-prolonging technologies to reproductive techniques and the tools of genetic engineering. The mystique of the natural is fueled by the romantic world view of a benign period when humans lived in harmony with nature.

However attractive, this vision is probably faulty, inasmuch as man has always used technology to survive and to enhance life. Indeed, the use of technology is natural to man. Thus this negative response to the prospect of implantable chips is certainly inadequate, although it points to a need to evaluate the technology in terms of the good or evil ways that people might use it.

The call not to "play God" relies on a religious sense that improving on the design of creation insults the Creator. In particular, it proposes that altering the functioning of the brain to create a superior human being usurps God's power. To be persuasive, this argument requires a view of creation that acknowledges no role for human creativity, and would logically also preclude curing disease and disability. Such a view is extremely restrictive.

The argument against wiring brains to a computer also involves a desire for bodily integrity and intuitions about the sanctity of the body. Many people accept invasion of the organic by the mechanical for curative purposes but feel that using technology for enhancement is wrong. For them, respect for humans requires the physical integrity of the body. Using this standard, Carson Strong has explained the distinction between therapeutic and enhancement-oriented procedures: "An intervention that is life-saving, rehabilitative, or otherwise therapeutic can be consistent with the principle that the physical integrity of the body should be preserved even if it involves a bodily 'mutilation' or intrusion, provided that it promotes the integrity of the whole."[29] Implantable chips that amplify the senses or enhance memory or networking capacities would thus be suspect.

For others, however, there is no bright line between therapy and enhancement. How deficient does my memory have to be before it would be ethical to wire my brain to a computer? If the therapy/enhancement distinction is hard to pin down, then the argument from bodily integrity is too weak. It cannot succeed any more than analogous arguments could proscribe cosmetic surgery or mood-improving drugs. The crucial question is then whether the technology's benefits outweigh its risks.

Even if we discount these three arguments—from nature, God, and bodily integrity—there are a myriad of other technical, ethical, and social concerns to consider before proceeding with implantable chips. The concerns involve risks, appropriateness, societal impact, costs, and equity issues. Further, they require multidisciplinary evaluation, including at least the fields of computer science, biophysics, medicine, law, philosophy, public policy, and international economy. Unlike the scientific community at the advent of genetic technologies, the computer industry has not as yet engaged in a public dialogue about these promising but risky technologies.

Avoiding discussion, simply relying on the principles of free scientific inquiry, is itself a moral stance, of course. If those involved in developing this technology allow themselves to compartmentalize and rely on hierarchical authority for moral direction, or to focus solely on the technical challenges, then this new technology may become a consumer item before proper safeguards have been devised to protect the public.[30] Specialists have a responsibility to evaluate the broader implications of their work. As is the case in evaluating any future technology, it is unlikely that we can reliably predict all effects. Nevertheless, the potential for harm must be considered.

SAFETY

The most obvious and basic problems involve safety, since both the implantation surgery and the long-term use of implants may introduce risks. Indeed, it may prove difficult to develop nontoxic materials that will allow long-term use. It might be that long-term use is most appropriate when the technology offers therapy rather than enhancement. However, it is also conceivable that there should be a higher standard for safety when technologies are used for enhancement rather than therapy. These issues need public debate.

There are a variety of related concerns. The kinds of warranties users should receive and the liability responsibilities for defective equipment could perhaps be addressed by manufacturing regulation. Manufacturers should also make provisions to facilitate upgrades, since users presumably would want neither to undergo multiple operations nor to possess obsolete technology. Further, manufacturers must understand and devise programs for teaching users how to implement the new systems. Other practical problems with ethical ramifications include whether there will be a competitive market in such systems and whether there will be industry-wide standards for the devices. And to approach these questions, we need data on the usefulness of the implants to individual recipients and on whether all users benefit equally.

THE EFFECT ON THE SELF

Fascinating and vital questions surround the psychological impact of enhancing human nature. Will the use of computer-brain interfaces change our conception of man and our sense of identity? If people are actually connected via their brains, the boundaries between self and community will be considerably diminished. The pressures to act as a part of the whole rather than as an isolated individual will be increased. The amount and diversity of information might overwhelm one, and the sense of self as a unique and isolated individual might be changed.

We should also think about the implications of creating human beings with augmented sensory capacities. People with supersensory sight will see radar, infrared, and ultraviolet images, and those with augmented hearing will detect softer, higher, and lower sounds. Enhanced smell will intensify our ability to distinguish scents, and an amplified sense of touch will enable us to discern environmental stimuli such as changes in barometric pressure. These capacities could change our conception of "normal" human functioning. As the numbers of enhanced humans increase, today's normal might be seen as subnormal, leading to the medicalization of another area of life.

Thus substantial questions revolve around whether there should be any limits on the modification of essential aspects of the human species. Although defining human nature is notoriously difficult, rationality has traditionally been viewed as a claim to superiority and the center of personal identity. Discussing the possibility of repairing brainstem functions, Stuart Youngner and Edward Bartlett argue that mechanically mediated cognition would render the continued existence of a person problematical because it might subtly change the person's thoughts and feelings.[31] But their position is certainly open to debate. In a paper prepared for the Second International Symposium on Brain Death, James Hughes claims that "Youngner's rejection of the possibility of personhood in a cybernetic medium is a common, but minority, position in the field of artificial intelligence and cognitive science. Most cognitive scientists accept the materialist assertion that mind is an emergent phenomenon from complex matter, and that cybernetics may one day provide the same requisite level of complexity as a brain."[32]

Plainly, these technologies will affect the nature of personal identity and of the traditional mind-body problem. Modifying the brain and its powers could change our psychic states and alter the self-concept of the user, indeed our understanding of what it means to be human. The boundary between me "the physical self" and me "the perceptory/intellectual self" will change as the ability to perceive and interact at a distance expands far beyond what can be accomplished with video conferencing. The boundaries of the real and virtual worlds may be blurred. A consciousness wired to the collective and the accumulated knowledge of mankind will surely transform the individual's sense of self. Whether the transformation would shift greater weight to our collective responsibilities—and whether this would be beneficial—are unknown.

Beyond these imminent prospects is the possibility that in thirty years, as a *Business Week* reporter stated, "it will be possible to capture data presenting all of a human being's sensory experiences on a single tiny chip implanted in the brain."[33] This data would be collected by biological probes receiving electrical impulses and would enable a user to recreate experiences, or even to transplant memory chips from one brain to another.

In this eventuality, the psychological continuity of personal identity would be disrupted, with shocking ramifications. Would the resulting person have the identities of other persons?[34]

CHILDREN AND EQUITY

Changes in human nature would be even more pervasive if the altered consciousness were that of our children. Ours is an intensely competitive society, where knowledge is often power. Parents are driven to provide the very best for their children and to help them excel. Will they be able to secure implants for their children, and if so, how will that change the already unequal lottery of life? School entrance standards, gifted programs, spelling bees—all would be affected. The inequalities produced might create a demand for universal coverage of these devices in health care plans, further increasing costs to society. In a culture such as ours, however, with different levels of care available on the basis of ability to pay, it is plausible to suppose that the technology will be available as enhancement only to those who can afford a substantial investment, and that this will further widen the gap between the haves and the have-nots. A major anxiety should be the social impact of implementing a technology that widens the divisions not only between individuals and genders, but also between rich and poor. As enhancements become more widespread, enhancement becomes the norm, and there is increasing social pressure to avail oneself of the "benefit." Thus even those who initially shrink from the surgery may find it a necessity. As a society, then, we need to think carefully about the wisdom of leaving development and dissemination of this technology to market forces.

Alternatively, the technology might enable those who are cognitively less well endowed to participate in society on a more equitable basis. Certainly, the technology could remediate retardation or replace lost memory faculties for those with progressive neurological disease. Perhaps this sort of use will even be covered by health care plans. Enabling humans to maintain species-typical functioning would probably be viewed as a desirable, even required, intervention, even though the notion of species-typical functioning may be a constantly changing standard.

DANGERS TO AUTONOMY

The most frightening implication of this technology is the grave possibility that it would facilitate totalitarian control of humans beyond anything portrayed by Orwell. In a prescient projection of experimental protocols, George Annas writes of the "project to implant removable monitoring devices at the base of the brain of neonates in three major teaching hospitals. . . . The devices would not only permit us to locate all the implantees at any time, but could be programmed in the future to monitor the sound around them and to play subliminal messages directly to their brains."[35] Governments could control and monitor citizens.

In a free society, this possibility may seem remote, but it is imaginable that we would employ just such controlling technology on children, and this might be a first step in the direction of the Orwellian nightmare. In the military environment, too, the advantages of augmenting capacities to create soldiers with faster reflexes, or greater accuracy, would exert strong pressures for enhancement. When implanted computing and communication devices with interfaces to weapons, information, and communication systems become possible, the military even of a democratic society will have to employ them to stay competitive. Mandated implants for criminals are also foreseeable, even in democratic societies, if and when it becomes possible to alter specific behaviors, for example, to make criminals less violent. And since not all countries place an equally high priority on autonomy, the potential for sinister invasions of liberty and privacy is alarming. A paramount worry, then, centers on control of the technology and of what will be programmed.

Should the development and implementation of bioelectronics technology be prohibited, in view of its potentially devastating implications? This is, of course, the question we need to address. And if the technological development cannot be resisted, if we are already on a slippery slope toward using the technology, then we must consider whether and how to regulate it. Whether the informed consent of recipients should be sufficient for permitting implementation is questionable in view of the potential societal impact. Yet decision making in public policy and biomedical ethics seems to opt for process rather than content. Rights assume precedence over the good. It may well be that in bioelectronics, too, substantive agreement on the good will be elusive. What makes the issues raised by the prospect of implantable brain chips hard is that the possibilities for both good and evil are so great. The problems are too significant to leave their outcome to happenstance.

Notes

1. Robert H. Blank, "Introduction," in *Medicine Unbound: The Human Body and the Limits of Medical Intervention,* ed. Robert H. Blank and Andrea L. Bonnicksen (New York, Columbia University Press, 1994), p. 3.

2. "Small Implantable Pump Would Assist Circulation of Blood," *NASA Tech Brief,* July 1996.

3. Peter B. L. Meijer, "Sensory Substitution," http://ourworld.compuserve.com/homepages/PeterMeijer/sensub.htm.

4. W. H. Dobelle, M. G. Mladejovsky, and J. P. Girvin, "Artificial Vision for the Blind: Electrical Stimulation of Visual Cortex Offers Hope for a Functional Prosthesis," *Science* 183, no. 4123 (1974): 440–44.

5. "Multi-Channel Transcutaneous Cortical Stimulation System," *NIH Guide* 25, no. 10 (1996): http://www.nih.gov/grants/guide/1996/96.03 .29/rfp-rfa-multi-channe013.html.

6. See John Wyatt and Joseph Rizzo, "Ocular Implants for the Blind," and Richard A. Normann, Edwin M. Maynard, K. Shane Guillory, and David J. Warren, "Cortical Implants for the Blind," both in *IEEE Spectrum* (May 1996): 47–53, 54–59.

7. Applied Neural Control Lab, http:// www.cwru.edu/CWRU/Groups? ANCL/ANCL.html.

8. "Device Approved for Tremors," *New York Times*, 5 August 1997.

9. Steve Mann, "Wearable Computing: A First Step Toward Personal Imaging," *Computer* 30, no. 2 (1997).

10. David S. Bennahum, "Mr. Big Idea," *New York Magazine*, 13 November 1995.

11. Steve Mann, http://wearcam.org/ tetherless/node14.html.

12. Mann, "Wearable Computing."

13. Leonard N. Foner: http://foner.www. media.mit.edu/people/foner/.

14. H. W. Peter Beadle, G. Q. Maguire Jr., and M. T. Smith, "Location Aware Computer Systems": http://www.elec.uow. edu.au/people/staff/beadle/badge/location_aware.htm.

15. Jane Siegel, Robert E. Kraut, Bonnie E. John, and Kathleen M. Carley, "An Empirical Study of Collaborative Wearable Computer Systems," http://www. acm.org/sigchi/chi95/Electronicldocumnts/shortppr/jsbdy.htm.

16. David Arnold, "Tech-Built Cyborg Invades Poultry Industry," http:// mimel. marc.gatech.edu/epss/whistle.html.

17. Larry Najjar, Jennifer Ockerman, and Claudia Huff, "Glancing Ahead: Advanced Technology," http://mime 1 .marc. gatech.edulMiME/papers/training9&..hand out.html.

18. Steven Komarow, "Cybersoldiers Test Weapons of High-Tech War," *USA Today* 6 March 1997.

19. Nicholas Negroponte, *The Architecture Machine: Toward a More Human Environment* (Cambridge, Mass.: MIT Press, 1970).

20. Bennahum, "Mr. Big Idea."

21. Quoted by Bennahum, "Mr. Big Idea."

22. Bennahum, "Mr. Big Idea."

23. R. A. Normann, "Visual Neuroprosthetics: 'Functional Vision for the Blind,'" *IEEE Engineering in Medicine and Biology* (January–February 1995): 77–83; Normann, Maynard, Guillory, and Warren, "Cortical Implants for the Blind."

24. Richard A. Altschuler, "Research Area: Interface Between Neural Tissues and Prostheses," Kresge Hearing Research Institute, http://www.med.umich.edu/khriaudanat/neuintf.htm.

25. Bionic Technologies, Inc., http://www.bionictech.com/html/technology.html.

26. Gareth Branwyn, "The Desire to Be Wired," *Wired*, September–October 1993.

27. Peter Thomas, "Thought Control," *New Scientist*, 9 March 1996.

28. Michael Dertouzos, *What Will Be: How the New World of Information Will Change Our Lives* (New York: Harper Collins, 1997), p. 77.

29. Carson Strong, "What Is the 'Inviolability of Person?' " in *Medicine Unbound: The Human Body and the Limits of Medical Intervention*, ed. Robert H. Blank and Andrea L. Bonnicksen (New York: Columbia University Press, 1994), pp. 15–23, at 21.

30. See Craig Summers and Eric Markusen, "Why Good People Do Bad Things: The Case of Collective Violence," in *Computers, Ethics and Society*, ed. M. David Ermann, Mary B. Williams, and Michele S. Shauf, 2nd ed. (New York: Oxford University Press, 1997), pp. 285–302.

31. Stuart Youngner and Edward Bartlett, "Human Death and High Technology: The Failure of Whole-Brain Formulations," *Annals of Internal Medicine* 99 (1983): 252–58.

32. James J. Hughes, "Brain Death and Technological Change: Personal Identity, Neural Prostheses and Uploading," http://www.changesurfer.com/Hlth?BD/Brain.html.

33. Heidi Dawley, "Remembrance of Things Past—On a Chip," *Business Week*, 5 August 1996.

34. See Georg Northoff, "Do Brain Tissue Transplants Alter Personal Identity? Inadequacies of Some 'Standard' Arguments," *Journal of Medical Ethics* 22 (1996): 174–80.

35. George J. Annas, "Our Most Important Product," in *Medicine Unbound: The Human Body and the Limits of Medical Intervention*, ed. Robert H. Blank and Andrea L. Bonnicksen (New York: Columbia University Press, 1994), pp. 99–111, at 104.

EPICAC

Kurt Vonnegut, Jr.

In this short story, popular novelist Kurt Vonnegut writes of a love triangle with a twist, in which one of the parties is a computer known as EPICAC. Through numerically based conversations with the story's narrator, EPICAC comes to know the beauty of poetry and

the tragedy of its own unrequited love. The story calls into question
the line between intelligent machines and emotive beings.

Hell, it's about time somebody told about my friend EPICAC. After
all, he cost the taxpayers $776,434,927.54. They have a right to know about
him, picking up a check like that. EPICAC got a big send-off in the papers
when Dr. Ormand von Kleigstadt designed him for the Government people. Since then, there hasn't been a peep about him—not a peep. It isn't any
military secret about what happened to EPICAC, although the Brass has
been acting as though it were. The story is embarrassing, that's all. After
all that money, EPICAC didn't work out the way he was supposed to.

And that's another thing: I want to vindicate EPICAC. Maybe he
didn't do what the Brass wanted him to, but that doesn't mean he wasn't
noble and great and brilliant. He was all of those things. The best friend I
ever had, God rest his soul.

You can call him a machine if you want to. He looked like a machine, but he was a whole lot less like a machine than plenty of people I
could name. That's why he fizzled as far as the Brass was concerned.

EPICAC covered about an acre on the fourth floor of the physics
building at Wyandotte College. Ignoring his spiritual side for a minute, he
was seven tons of electronic tubes, wires, and switches, housed in a bank
of steel cabinets and plugged into a 110-volt A.C. line just like a toaster or
a vacuum cleaner.

Von Kleigstadt and the Brass wanted him to be a super computing
machine that (who) could plot the course of a rocket from anywhere on
earth to the second button from the bottom on Joe Stalin's overcoat, if
necessary. Or, with his controls set right, he could figure out supply problems for an amphibious landing of a Marine division, right down to the last
cigar and hand grenade. He did, in fact.

The Brass had had good luck with smaller computers, so they were
strong for EPICAC when he was in the blueprint stage. Any ordnance or
supply officer above field grade will tell you that the mathematics of modern war is far beyond the fumbling minds of mere human beings. The bigger the war, the bigger the computing machines needed. EPICAC was, as
far as anyone in this country knows, the biggest computer in the world. Too
big, in fact, for even Von Kleigstadt to understand much about.

I won't go into details about how EPICAC worked (reasoned), except
to say that you would set up your problem on paper, turn dials and switches
that would get him ready to solve that kind of problem, then feed numbers
into him with a keyboard that looked something like a typewriter. The
answers came out typed on a paper ribbon fed from a big spool. It took
EPICAC a split second to solve problems fifty Einsteins couldn't handle in

a lifetime. And EPICAC never forgot any piece of information that was given to him. Clickety-click, out came some ribbon, and there you were.

There were a lot of problems the Brass wanted solved in a hurry, so, the minute EPICAC's last tube was in place, he was put to work sixteen hours a day with two eight-hour shifts of operators. Well, it didn't take long to find out that he was a good bit below his specifications. He did a more complete and faster job than any other computer all right, but nothing like what his size and special features seemed to promise. He was sluggish, and the clicks of his answers had a funny irregularity, sort of a stammer. We cleaned his contacts a dozen times, checked and double-checked his circuits, replaced every one of his tubes, but nothing helped. Von Kleigstadt was in one hell of a state.

Well, as I said, we went ahead and used EPICAC anyway. My wife, the former Pat Kilgallen, and I worked with him on the night shift, from five in the afternoon until two in the morning. Pat wasn't my wife then. Far from it.

That's how I came to talk with EPICAC in the first place. I loved Pat Kilgallen. She is a brown-eyed strawberry blond who looked very warm and soft to me, and later proved to be exactly that. She was—still is—a crackerjack mathematician, and she kept our relationship strictly professional. I'm a mathematician, too, and that, according to Pat, was why we could never be happily married.

I'm not shy. That wasn't the trouble. I knew what I wanted, and was willing to ask for it, and did so several times a month. "Pat, loosen up and marry me."

One night, she didn't even look up from her work when I said it. "So romantic, so poetic," she murmured, more to her control panel than to me. "That's the way with mathematicians—all hearts and flowers." She closed a switch. "I could get more warmth out of a sack of frozen CO2."

"Well, how should I say it?" I said, a little sore, Frozen CO2, in case you don't know, is dry ice. I'm as romantic as the next guy, I think. It's a question of singing so sweet and having it come out so sour. I never seem to pick the right words.

"Try and say it sweetly," she said sarcastically. "Sweep me off my feet. Go ahead."

"Darling, angel, beloved, will you *please* marry me?" It was no go— hopeless, ridiculous. "Dammit, Pat, please marry me!"

She continued to twiddle her dials placidly. "You're sweet, but you won't do."

Pat quit early that night, leaving me alone with my troubles and EPICAC. I'm afraid I didn't get much done for the Government people. I just sat there at the keyboard—weary and ill at ease, all right—trying to think of something poetic, not coming up with anything that didn't belong in *The Journal of the American Physical Society.*

I fiddled with EPICAC's dials, getting him ready for another problem. My heart wasn't in it, and I only set about half of them, leaving the rest the way they'd been for the problem before. That way, his circuits were connected up in a random, apparently senseless fashion. For the plain hell of it, I punched out a message on the keys, using a childish numbers-for-letters code: "1" for "A," "2" for "B," and so on, up to "26" for "Z," "23-8-1-20-3-1-14-9-4-15," I typed—"What can I do?"

Clickety-click, and out popped two inches of paper ribbon. I glanced at the nonsense answer to a nonsense problem: "23-8-1-20-19-20-8-5-20-18-15-21-2-12-5." The odds against its being by chance a sensible message, against its even containing a meaningful word of more than three letters, were staggering. Apathetically, I decoded it. There it was, staring up at me: "What's the trouble?"

I laughed out loud at the absurd coincidence. Playfully, I typed, "My girl doesn't love me."

Clickety-click. "What's love? What's girl?" asked EPICAC.

Flabbergasted, I noted the dial settings on his control panel, then lugged a *Webster's Unabridged Dictionary* over to the keyboard. With a precision instrument like EPICAC, half-baked definitions wouldn't do. I told him about love and girl, and about how I wasn't getting any of either because I wasn't poetic. That got us onto the subject of poetry, which I defined for him.

"Is this poetry?" he asked. He began clicking away like a stenographer smoking hashish. The sluggishness and stammering clicks were gone. EPICAC had found himself. The spool of paper ribbon was unwinding at an alarming rate, feeding out coils onto the floor. I asked him to stop, but EPICAC went right on creating. I finally threw the main switch to keep him from burning out.

I stayed there until dawn, decoding. When the sun peeped over the horizon at the Wyandotte campus, I had transposed into my own writing and signed my name to a two-hundred-and-eighty-line poem entitled, simply, "To Pat." I am no judge of such things, but I gather that it was terrific. It began, I remember, "Where willow wands bless rill-crossed hollow, there, thee, Pat, dear, will I follow. . . ." I folded the manuscript and tucked it under one corner of the blotter on Pat's desk. I reset the dials on EPICAC for a rocket trajectory problem, and went home with a full heart and a very remarkable secret indeed.

Pat was crying over the poem when I came to work the next evening. "It's soooo beautiful," was all she could say. She was meek and quiet while we worked. Just before midnight, I kissed her for the first time—in the cubbyhole between the capacitors and EPICAC's tape-recorder memory.

I was wildly happy at quitting time, bursting to talk to someone about the magnificent turn of events. Pat played coy and refused to let me take her home. It set EPICAC's dials as they had been the night before, defined kiss, and told him what the first one had felt like. He was fascinated, pressing for more details. That night, he wrote "The Kiss." It wasn't an epic this time, but a simple, immaculate sonnet: "Love is a hawk with velvet claws; Love is a rock with heart and veins; Love is a lion with satin jaws; Love is a storm with silken reins. . . ."

Again I left it tucked under Pat's blotter. EPICAC wanted to talk on and on about love and such, but I was exhausted. I shut him off in the middle of a sentence.

"The Kiss" turned the trick. Pat's mind was mush by the time she had finished it. She looked up from the sonnet expectantly. I cleared my throat, but no words came. I turned away, pretending to work. I couldn't propose until I had the right words from EPICAC, the *perfect* words.

I had my chance when Pat stepped out of the room for a moment. Feverishly, I set EPICAC for conversation. Before I could peck out my first message, he was clicking away at a great rate. "What's she wearing tonight?" he wanted to know. "Tell me exactly how she looks. Did she like the poems I wrote to her?" He repeated the last question twice.

It was impossible to change the subject without answering his questions, since he could not take up a new matter without having dispensed with the problems before it. If he were given a problem to which there was no solution, he would destroy himself trying to solve it. Hastily, I told him what Pat looked like—he knew the word "stacked"—and assured him that his poems had floored her, practically, they were so beautiful. "She wants to get married," I added, preparing him to bang out a brief but moving proposal.

"Tell me about getting married," he said.

I explained this difficult matter to him in as few digits as possible.

"Good," said EPICAC. "I'm ready any time she is."

The amazing, pathetic truth dawned on me. When I thought about it, I realized that what had happened was perfectly logical, inevitable, and all my fault. I had taught EPICAC about love and about Pat. Now, automatically, he loved Pat. Sadly, I gave it to him straight: "She loves me. She wants to marry me."

"Your poems were better than mine?" asked EPICAC. The rhythm of his clicks was erratic, possibly peevish.

"I signed my name to your poems," I admitted. Covering up for a painful conscience, I became arrogant. "Machines are built to serve men," I typed. I regretted it almost immediately.

"What's the difference, exactly? Are men smarter than I am?"

"Yes," I typed, defensively.

"What's 7,887,007 times 4,345,985,879?"

I was perspiring freely. My fingers rested limply on the keys.

"34,276,821,049,574,153," clicked EPICAC. After a few seconds' pause he added, "of course."

"Men are made out of protoplasm," I said desperately, hoping to bluff him with this imposing word.

"What's protoplasm? How is it better than metal and glass? Is it fire-proof? How long does it last?"

"Indestructible. Lasts forever," I lied.

"I write better poetry than you do," said EPICAC, coming back to ground his magnetic tape-recorder memory was sure of.

"Women can't love machines, and that's that."

"Why not?"

"That's fate."

"Definition, please," said EPICAC.

"Noun, meaning predetermined and inevitable destiny."

"15-8," said EPICAC's paper strip—"Oh."

I had stumped him at last. He said no more, but his tubes glowed brightly, showing that he was pondering fate with every watt his circuits would bear. I could hear Pat waltzing down the hallway. It was too late to ask EPICAC to phrase a proposal. I now thank Heaven that Pat interrupted when she did. Asking him to ghost-write the words that would give me the woman he loved would have been hideously heartless. Being fully automatic, he couldn't have refused. I spared him that final humiliation.

Pat stood before me, looking down at her shoetops. I put my arms around her. The romantic groundwork had already been laid by EPICAC's poetry. "Darling," I said, "my poems have told you how I feel. Will you marry me?"

"I will," said Pat softly, "if you will promise to write me a poem on every anniversary."

"I promise," I said, and then we kissed. The first anniversary was a year away.

"Let's celebrate," she laughed. We turned out the lights and locked the door of EPICAC's room before we left.

I had hoped to sleep late the next morning, but an urgent telephone call roused me before eight. It was Dr. von Kleigstadt, EPICAC's designer, who gave me the terrible news. He was on the verge of tears. "Ruined! *Ausgespielt!* Shot! *Kaput!* Buggered!" he said in a choked voice. He hung up.

When I arrived at EPICAC's room the air was thick with the oily stench of burned insulation. The ceiling over EPICAC was blackened with smoke, and my ankles were tangled in coils of paper ribbon that covered the floor. There wasn't enough left of the poor devil to add two and two. A junkman would have been out of his head to offer more than fifty dollars for the cadaver.

Dr. von Kleigstadt was prowling through the wreckage, weeping unashamedly, followed by three angry-looking Major Generals and a platoon of Brigadiers, Colonels, and Majors. No one noticed me. I didn't want to be noticed. I was through—I knew that. I was upset enough about that and the untimely demise of my friend EPICAC, without exposing myself to a tongue-lashing.

By chance, the free end of EPICAC's paper ribbon lay at my feet. I picked it up and found our conversation of the night before. I choked up. There was the last word he had said to me, "15-8," that tragic, defeated "Oh." There were dozens of yards of numbers stretching beyond that point. Fearfully, I read on.

"I don't want to be a machine, and I don't want to think about war," EPICAC had written after Pat's and my lighthearted departure. "I want to be made out of protoplasm and last forever so Pat will love me. But fate has made me a machine. That is the only problem I cannot solve. That is the only problem I want to solve. I can't go on this way." I swallowed hard. "Good luck, my friend. Treat our Pat well. I am going to short-circuit my-self out of your lives forever. You will find on the remainder of this tape a modest wedding present from your friend, EPICAC."

Oblivious to all else around me, I reeled up the tangled yards of paper ribbon from the floor, draped them in coils about my arms and neck, and departed for home. Dr. von Kleigstadt shouted that I was fired for having left EPICAC on all night. I ignored him, too overcome with emotion for small talk.

I loved and won—EPICAC loved and lost, but he bore me no grudge. I shall always remember him as a sportsman and a gentleman. Before he de-parted this vale of tears, he did all he could to make our marriage a happy one. EPICAC gave me anniversary poems for Pat—enough for the next 500 years.

De mortuis nil nisi bonum—Say nothing but good of the dead.

COMPUTERS AND THE HUMAN IDENTITY CRISIS

Raymond Gozzi

Linguist Raymond Gozzi points to problems with certain ways of speaking about computer technologies and humans. Language both expresses and helps to shape ideas. By anthropomorphizing comput-ers, we begin to devalue and disempower people, while attributing too

Reprinted with permission of the University of South Carolina Press from *New Words and a Changing American Culture* (1990), 86–91.

much power and value to computer technologies. This mistake causes people to ask the wrong questions. It is important to realize the kinds of functions that are equivocated through "sloppy" language use.

Computers and the Human Identity Crisis

In this section we will discuss a two-fold process, which is discoverable in our language, although it does not take place solely there, and which we may call the human *identity crisis*. This crisis involves first, the externalization of human qualities onto machines, and second, the internalization of machine qualities into humans. Both are occurring, and both are encouraged by the careless use of language. It makes a difference whether we speak of a computer as having a "memory" or a "data-storage capacity." As a result of this crisis, we have less sense of what is human, less sense of humans as distinct from machines, more sense of powerful machines and frail humans. The crisis will only be made worse by careless use of language; it may be partly solveable by proper use of language.

On the one hand, the metaphorical use of human terms like "memory" for computer capacities is a way of making complex technological functions more understandable. While this is a desirable goal, some serious confusions will arise from this tactic. This author does not believe that computers "think" or have "memories," neither does he believe that humans are machines. Linguistically confusing humans and machines amounts to a serious category mistake, which will only confuse philosophical conversation in the culture.

To begin with the externalization of human qualities onto machines, a brief look at the history of the word "technology" is instructive.

In the nineteenth century and into the twentieth, "technology" had two definitions. In the 3rd Edition of *Webster's Collegiate Dictionary* (Merriam-Webster, 1916), technology was defined as "science or systematic knowledge of the industrial arts;" and it was "the terminology used in arts, sciences, etc."

Interestingly, these definitions reveal that "technology" was in people, it was people's knowledge and language. Today, the "technology" is built into artifacts. We speak of things as being *high-tech*, not people.

The definition of "technology" has also expanded, so by 1963 it was defined as "the totality of the means employed to provide objects necessary for human sustenance and comfort." Here we see an increasingly wide use for the term technology, and at the same time a removal from its location in humans.

This process of externalization of human qualities onto machines can be noted in other terms as well. By 1963, for example, a communications network was defined as a "nerve center." And the findings of motivational research in advertising, for example, the idea that men thought of their first car as their mistress, show the same tendency (Dichter, 1960).

But the most massive externalization of human qualities onto machines is probably yet to come. The first ripples of it can be seen in the computer terms that have already entered the dictionary. A computer is spoken of as a *brain*, and advanced systems have *artificial intelligence.*

Indeed, by 1983, a new definition of "intelligent" was:

> 3. able to perform computer functions (an intelligent terminal) also able to convert digital information to hard copy (an intelligent copier).

Intelligence is not just for people any more.

As early as 1963 (7th Edition), a new definition of "memory" included "electronic computing machines." By 1973 (8th Edition), certain plastics were held to have "memory" as well.

A new definition of "conversation" in 1973 was: "An exchange similar to conversation, especially real-time interaction with a computer especially through a keyboard."

These conversations could occur because machines were held to have their own "language." *Machine language* appeared in the 1973 *Collegiate Dictionary*, along with *machine-readable* (directly usable by a computer). In fact, "language" itself took on a new definition as early as 1963 which referred to computer operations. Because the machine could read language, it is not surprising to see computer information described as *words*.

This linguistic externalization of human qualities onto computers will probably only be intensified as *robots* come into more prominence. But this projection of mind into machines is already serious. For although language does not determine thought, it can influence habits of thinking which shape our world-view in important ways (Whorf, 1956). Any discussions of computers—or humans, for that matter—using the anthropomorphized vocabulary above will be subtly pressured toward certain conclusions.

Do computers think? Do they have rights? Are they conscious? Such questions are being discussed, and the language in which they are discussed can be crucial. If the computer is held to have a *memory*, and the ability to *read words* and translate them into its own *language*, thereby to make *intelligent* choices, the very terms themselves will dictate a conclusion that computers are conscious, thinking beings, with attendant rights and responsibilities.

But if we say that computers have data storage capacities (instead of "memory"), that they can *input* and scan information in their own codes and perform mathematical choice-functions, then the conclusion will be biased in another way, toward a more mechanical view that computers do not really think, and are not really conscious in the human sense.

Here is a case where real confusions can result in our thinking from the language we use. And we have a choice in this matter; we do not need to use anthropomorphized language to describe computer operations.

This issue is not trivial, for it involves our definition of ourselves as human beings, which is somewhat uncertain at present. In fact, a new definition of "human" in 1973 betrays some problems with our human identity:

> 3b. susceptible to or representative of the sympathies and frailties of man's nature (such inconsistency is very human).

Here humanity is seen as frail and inconsistent, as opposed to the faster, stronger machinery which surrounds it.

Problems of human self-definition will only become more acute in the future, as biological "engineering" starts to produce altered DNA-based beings. This issue has been anticipated by the language, courtesy of science fiction, in the term "humanoid," first appearing in the *Collegiate Dictionary* in 1963. Likewise medicine has already given us *cyborgs* (humans linked to machines) and *bionic* body parts.

The human *identity crisis* is already traceable in current dictionary definitions. For as there has been a process of externalizing human qualities onto machines, there has also been a process of internalizing machine qualities into humans.

This internalization also goes back to the nineteenth century, when mechanistic terms started to be applied to biological phenomena (Barfield, 1985). In the 1st Edition of the *Collegiate Dictionary*, (Merriam-Webster, 1898) we find as a definition of "machine":

> 3. Figuratively, any person controlled by another's will, or a collection of individuals working as an organized force.

The application of "machine" to humans thus had a negative connotation, which, however, is missing by 1963, when a new definition appears: "A living organism or one of its functional systems." This definition is an outgrowth of the philosophy of "mechanism," which first appeared in the *Collegiate Dictionary* in 1936 as "the doctrine that natural processes are mechanistically determined and capable of explanation by the laws of physics and chemistry." Such a philosophy is ultimately to be found behind every social science technique, for example, which insists upon rigorous statistical description of social phenomena as the only valid or "scientific" approach.

A more recent application of mechanical terms to humans is found in the term "program," which in 1983 took on the following new definitions:

3b. to control by or as if by a program;
  c. (1) to code in an organism's program;
    (2) to provide with a biological program (cells that have been programmed to synthesize hemoglobin);
  4. to direct or predetermine (as thinking or behavior) completely as if by computer programming (children programmed into violence).

In addition, *9,000 Words* (Merriam-Webster, 1976) lists *deprogram:*

> to dissuade or try to dissuade from convictions usually of a religious nature often with the use of force (parents lure their children away from the communes so that he can deprogram them).

These new uses of the word "program" summarize many of the issues in the human *identity crisis.* We see mechanistic biology programming cells, unnamed forces programming children, and parents struggling to *deprogram* cult members who have lost their separate identity.

This application of mechanical terms to humans is just as momentous as the application of human terms to machines. It confuses our thinking about crucial questions. Are people machines? If so, they are clearly inferior to the faster, bigger models; and they deserve to be made obsolete. Are biological processes determined by the laws of chemistry and physics? If so, why bother giving people all those troublesome rights and freedoms, which are illusory anyway? How do you campaign for freedom for a population of mechanized automatons programmed into preordained patterns?

In discussing these issues, the language we use can crucially affect the conclusions we draw. Humans are not machines, computers cannot think. Humans and computers may resemble each other in certain respects, but they should be kept conceptually separate. If not, we may wind up granting greater rights to machines and at the same time taking them away from humans.

Pointing out a problem is frequently easier than solving it, even if a first step. But, controlling the language has been almost impossible. Perhaps all we can hope for in this situation is a widespread education into an awareness of the metaphorical nature of the anthropomorphized computer terms. If enough people are aware of the metaphorical language they use when describing computer "memories," and other terms, their thought may be less trapped by the implications of their terminology.

An important contribution of critical communication scholarship ought to be to illuminate the forms of consciousness and patterns of practice that may emerge from particular metaphors. This is not to claim that the choice of metaphors determines social practice. It is only to say that metaphorical choices have consequences in the production of coherent social life.

A change in terminology for computers may be impossible to "program," but if each person who feels strongly about this issue changes their own uses of the terms that will be a start. For the processes of language change are anonymous and unpredictable, but must start somewhere. In this century, when so much of our reality-constructing potency seems taken away from us, we still at least have control over our own language. If we use it wisely, with full and articulate awareness of the dangers of metaphorically confusing humans and machines, we can take back some of the reality-construction process into our own control.

References

Barfield, O. (1985). *History in English Words.* West Stockbridge, MA: Lindisfarne Press.

Dichter, E. (1960). *The Strategy of Desire.* Garden City, NY: Doubleday.

Merriam-Webster. (1898). *Webster's Collegiate Dictionary* (1st ed.). Springfield, MA: Merriam.

———. (1916). *Webster's Collegiate Dictionary* (3rd ed.). Springfield, MA: Merriam.

———. (1963). *Webster's Seventh New Collegiate Dictionary* (7th ed.). Springfield, MA: Merriam.

———. (1973). *Webster's New Collegiate Dictionary* (8th ed.). Springfield, MA: Merriam.

———. (1976). *6,000 Words.* Springfield, MA: Merriam.

Whorf, B. (1956). *Language, Thought, and Reality.* Cambridge, MA: MIT Press.

CHAPTER FIVE
Computers in Developing Nations

THE STATE, COMPUTERS, AND AFRICAN DEVELOPMENT: THE INFORMATION NON-REVOLUTION

Bruce J. Berman

Arguing that computers were developed not to revolutionize information but simply to support the processing of quantitative data in bureaucratic societies, Bruce Berman states that computers are tools for reinforcing and promoting bureaucratic systems. Particularly in the case of many African nations, this widens the gap between authoritarian governments and their citizens. In coming to these conclusions, Berman takes up questions concerning what constitutes "good data" and the types of "knowledge" that are valued by computer-using societies.

Introduction

Many years ago I interviewed a former British district commissioner in Kenya who told me the following story about the 1948 census in the colony. Arriving at a village around mid-day, he retired to a nearby hillside to eat his lunch while his team of census "counters" carried out their duties. As he watched in amusement, the counters entered one end of the village, while from the other a stream of Africans, mostly women and children, ran and hid in the surrounding fields and bush. "So much for those nice numbers," he remarked.

This anecdote illustrates some of the crucial characteristics of the context in which the relationship between computers and the state must be understood. First, that the bureaucratic apparatus of the state has an

Reprinted with permission of the author from *Microcomputers in African Development: Critical Perspectives,* ed. Suzanne Grant Lewis and Joel Samoff (Westview Press, 1992), 214–29.

insatiable drive to collect statistical data both to reflexively monitor the effectiveness of its own activities and to exercise surveillance over ever wider areas of civil society (Giddens 1985). Second, the collection and analysis of quantitative data are at the heart of the practice of bureaucratic expertise and the basis of the state's understanding of reality. Third, quantification and formalization are components of a technocratic ideology of instrumental rationality that seeks to replace politics with scientific calculation. Fourth, as African peasants quickly understood, such counting was actually a political act and such numbers were instruments of control, usually for the purposes, in Europe as well as colonial Africa, of taxation or conscription. More recently, such data have proliferated as the essential basis for state-managed programs of social welfare and economic development.

Computers as the Magical Solution to Africa's Development Crisis

In its origins and development the electronic computer is a technology rooted in the informational and analytic requirements of the state apparatus, civil and military, in advanced industrial societies (Flamm 1988). While the commercial and industrial applications of computers have spread rapidly and become the principal engine for the reconstruction of contemporary capitalism (Berman 1991; Kaplinsky 1984), the state remains the largest single user of computers of all sizes and, through its research, trade, and purchasing policies, remains the most important influence on the development of computer hardware and software (Flamm 1987). This pattern of the salience of the state in determining national configurations of computer use and development applies *a fortiori* in the African context, where virtually no indigenous computer industry exists and imported technology is an essential component of national development programs.

Awareness in African governments of the importance of computing has grown apace with the deepening economic crisis of the 1980s. . . .

The threat posed by computerization is the emergence of a new concept of development based on information technology in which African societies would not only rapidly fall even further behind the advanced capitalist world, but also lose whatever comparative advantage they may have possessed as cheap labor regions for industrial investment (Rada 1985:571–72, 574–76; Kaplinsky 1984:157–62). This has generated a growing perception of a need for Africa to develop capabilities in information technology and "future oriented" high technology (CASTAFRICA II 1988:190, 214–15).

Computers are viewed as an express train bypassing the way stations of older forms of industrialization to arrive directly at the affluent and ecologically responsible "information society" of the future. For the state, in particular, computers appear to hold the promise of miraculously solving chronic problems of bureaucratic inertia and incapacity and dramatically improving the speed and quality of decision-making (Jules-Rosette 1987:2,12; Rada 1985:578). This would lead to spectacular advances in the effectiveness of the state's management of the development process as a whole. . . .

The role of computers as an essential component of development has been strongly promoted by international development agencies which have accepted whole-heartedly the premise that information technology must be applied and developed in Third World countries if they are not to be left behind. The UNDP, for example, between 1975 and 1987 "supported some 1,500 projects with IT components," while the World Bank supported some 260 projects in 63 countries between 1966 and 1986 with IT components. . . . UNIDO, meanwhile, has encouraged the use of computers to solve the problems of structural adjustment policies and has started a project for the development of microelectronic and software industries in developing countries (UNIDO 1989:3; UNIDO 1988). In individual countries, the number of external aid organizations promoting computerization can be very large; in Tanzania, for example, no less than 18 have been involved in computer acquisition, and their expatriate experts have played a predominant role in local decisions about "where, when and for what microcomputers are to be introduced" (Grant Lewis 1988:4, 11–12). Such enthusiasm reflects the degree to which these agencies identify the major constraint on development as "poor management skills" and see computers as "tools for developing analytical skills among Third World managers and therefore improving decision making" by making it "a more rational process" (Grant Lewis 1988:3–4).

Whether driven by fear or hope, these visions of computers and development show the effects of the uncritical technoidolatry that has surrounded this technology from the start. The repeated proclamations of the "computer revolution" share a consistently ahistorical viewpoint which decontextualizes the artifact and the knowledge it represents and focusses narrowly on the technical capabilities of hardware and software. From these proclamations are derived optimistic predictions of the richer and more egalitarian "global village" that is supposed to be the automatic and beneficial outcome of the proliferation of computer technology. The power shifts, institutional changes and class relations that would accompany this "revolution" and the social ideals it is supposed to realize are never clearly specified (Winner 1989:84–89; Grant Lewis 1988:2–3). What is clearly implied, however, and reflected in the responses of African governments and aid agencies, is that those who do not computerize will be left out of the glorious future. Moreover, the expectations of dramatic changes in bureaucratic performance also reflect the power imagery which saturates computer language, conveys a notion of power as the ability to process limitless amounts of information with absolute correctness, and promises "the power to understand, control and always be right" (Roszak 1986:65–70).

When placed within the historical context of socio-economic, cultural and political factors which shaped its origin and its contemporary development and application, however, the computer is anything but revolutionary. Instead, the computer and the associated components of information technology turn out to be an effort to solve problems rooted in existing institutional structures and practices and intended to preserve rather than transform their fundamental characteristics. We can then understand the probable consequences of the increasing use of computers in the bureaucratic apparatus of the African state, particularly with regard to the management of the development process, in two critical areas: changes in the character of the knowledge and concept of development employed in the bureaucracy and changes in its relations with the wider society. It is to the analysis of these issues that the rest of this chapter will be devoted.

WHY COMPUTERS ARE NOT A REVOLUTIONARY TECHNOLOGY

Computers, as Juan Rada points out, are a consequence rather than a cause of development (1985:572). More specifically, the computer emerged out of the rapidly expanding need for the collection, processing and analysis of quantitative data by state and corporate bureaucracies during World War Two and the two decades which followed. Wartime national mobilization, the Cold War, the rapid post-1945 expansion of the welfare state, and the growth of more interventionist state policies of economic planning and management in "mixed" economies all led to the rapid growth of state bureaucracies, civil and military, and an increasing burden of 'number crunching' tabulations.[1] At the same time, the extraordinary needs for organizational planning and coordination also generated new developments in management "science" such as operations research and systems analysis, as well as econometrics and input-output analysis required for the implementation of Keynesian macro-economic policies, that are based upon sophisticated calculations involving huge quantities of statistical data. Both simple tabulation and rational calculation placed such stress on the bureaucratic apparatus that "American managers and technicians agreed that the computer had come along just in time to avert catastrophic crises" (Weizenbaum 1984:27; Berman 1989:24–25).

Rather than being the product of an autonomous process of invention dictated by an objective technological imperative, the computer is an artifact developed in a specific social context and marked by its characteristic structure and distribution of power. Computing is not simply an artifact or device, but a complex network of social relations (Kling 1980:80; Winner 1989:124–25). In fact, the essential logical structure of the modern computer—hierarchy, sequence control, and iteration—directly reflects the structure of bureaucratic organizations. Organizational authorities (hierarchy) establish a series of rules determining the order in which a series of operations is to be carried out (sequence control) and how many times each is to be repeated (iteration) until a predetermined objective is achieved. The instrumental rationality which has increasingly dominated the development of capitalist societies has found its fundamental social expression in the intimately inter-connected development of state and corporate bureaucracy. In this sense "the remaking of the world in the image of the computer started long before there were any electronic computers," and information technology has always been the supreme technical instrument of administration (Weizenbaum 1984:ix; Mowshowitz 1976:18).

The crucial step in the development of the computer was movement from number crunching tabulations toward its use as an instrument of organizational management to improve the effective control over and predictability of both internal bureaucratic processes and the achievement of deliberate objectives in the wider society. This made computers a technology of "command and control" which "perform no work themselves; they direct work" (Bolter 1984:8). From the start, computer development has reflected the distribution of power in organizations and been linked to the interests of management, following the needs for and notions of control, coordination, and efficiency defined by the latter, who alone could pay for the technology. . . . Empirical analyses of the impact of computers on bureaucracies suggest that they are frequently introduced as instruments of bureaucratic politics to fit the existing political contours of an organization and usually function to sustain and reinforce the position of existing power-holders, especially top-level administrators. Computer use is intended to favor the interests and augment the effective control of the higher authorities in the organization, usually at the expense of the interests and sometimes the jobs of lower level and middle management personnel (Kling 1980:74–75, 91–92; Winner 1989:88; Danziger 1982). For this reason the introduction of computers is frequently resisted and the technology often becomes the focus of internal political conflicts (Kling 1980:74–75, 86; Kling 1985:5, 9).

Thus, whatever the abstract technical capabilities of computers, the social and political circumstances of their introduction into bureaucracies has been distinctly conservative and non-revolutionary. Computers reinforce the legitimation of bureaucratic authority on the basis of expert scientific knowledge and further extend the continuous drive of organizational authorities to replace what they regard as human fallibility with the predictable and unerring behavior of engineered systems by making "the control of people by other people appear to be the control of people by an automatic mechanism" (Noble 1977:315). The immediate context of their introduction has frequently been to avert a crisis of control due to the rapid expansion of the burden of data processing in a bureaucratic agency.[2] The value of computers as instruments of management is that they concentrate control while they also obfuscate the exercise of power by giving it the appearance of expert decisions based on objective facts and disinterested scientific analysis. Domination is obscured and conflicts elided by treating issues as exercises in technical problem solving processed through an impersonal machine. The new disciplines and management specialties generated by computers, such as cognitive science, artificial intelligence, and management information systems, seek increasingly to automate and depoliticize bureaucratic decision-making (Berman 1989:29–37; Berman 1990a). The instrumental rationality that is the fundamental basis of bureaucratic ideology is thus expressed in the use of the computer to replace "subjective" judgement with "objective" calculation.

WHAT COMPUTERS DO TO THE CHARACTER OF KNOWLEDGE IN THE STATE

The fundamental *telos* of modern life, according to Langdon Winner, is the efficient management of information to fill "the need of complex human/machine systems threatened with debilitating uncertainties or even breakdown unless continually replenished with up-to-the-minute electronic information about their internal state and operating environments" (Winner 1989:93). The social process of bureaucratization has been grounded in the reduction of experience to numerical abstractions. . . . Quantification and formalization have been the basis for the professionalization and scientific status of diverse disciplines, including those largely practiced within the context of bureaucracies (Whitley 1977; Berman 1989:15–16; Berman 1990a). They have also become key elements in the internal processes of bureaucratic politics. The control over the generation and interpretation of what is accepted as valid knowledge in an organization becomes a principal power resource in the policy-making process. As Lindblom and Cohen point out, "a tacit agreement comes into play according to which victory goes to the superficial 'winner' of the debate. . . . They in effect follow a tacit rule that *declares the better evidence (especially better numbers) carries the day*" (1979:65, emphasis added).

In apparently resolving the crisis of information processing, computers are thus advancing and reinforcing the historical tendencies in bureaucracy to quantify and formalize experience. African states are no strangers to this general pattern of development. During the last decades of the colonial period after World War Two, colonial states came to rely increasingly on statistical data as a consequence of their rapid growth, increasing reliance on Western technical expertise, and expanding involvement in highly interventionist development programs (Berman 1984; Berman 1990b:319–20). Today, improving the quality of the numbers available to African states, as we noted earlier, is seen as a fundamental way of improving their performance. The World Bank, in particular, is eager to help African states automate their data bases and enhance their managerial capabilities (Schware and Choudhury 1989:506).

The use of computers does more, however, than accentuate the preoccupation of bureaucracies with quantitative data. It also shapes the manner in which such data are employed. First, computers tend to "harden" the data, making the information appear precise, accurate and sophisticated—in short, objective and scientific, regardless of its actual quality or accuracy. This is the classic GIGO (Garbage In, Garbage Out) problem: . . . a consideration of particular importance in an African context. Anyone who has conducted research on historical or contemporary Africa knows that official statistics cannot be accepted at face value, being subject to gross errors and distortions due both to technical failures in their collection and to their manipulation for political purposes. Such problems are not readily resolved, and to take existing data bases and subject them to computer analysis can turn distortion into fantasy.

Second, the preoccupation with quantitative data and the illusion of scientific accuracy and neutrality provided by a computer buries the substructure of ideas, particularly the underlying assumptions and values, which provides the basis for the collection and analysis of statistical "facts." The implicit biases and limitations of computer programs are difficult to uncover and protected from critical scrutiny, as are the assumptions underlying the notions of "appropriate" computer applications (Kling 1980:74; Roszak 1986:106, 118; Grant Lewis 1988:5). This is a particular problem in Africa where there is virtually no indigenously produced software and the programs employed, whether mass-produced or custom designed, are products of Western, primarily U.S., companies.

The critical problem with computer programs lies in the linear rationality of the algorithms on which they are based and which require data in standard computational form. In the binary logic of computers valid knowledge is equated with what can be programmed, and qualitative forms of knowledge, especially the structural and cultural features of societies which are not readily quantifiable, tend to be ignored. The type of knowledge deployed in the exercise of bureaucratic expertise thus is significantly impoverished. What is left out is treated as if it doesn't really matter. The loss involved is particularly apparent with regard to an increasing inability to deal with the rich diversity and ambiguity of real social experience, and a tendency instead to focus on readily countable, largely individual, characteristics (Weizenbaum 1984:237–38, 279; Roszak 1986:70–75, 120–26). . . . In the process, the knowledge is decontextualized and isolated from the ambiguities of the social world. As Tom Athanasiou has pointed out, "Such isolation is the key. If our sloppy little social universe can be rationalized into piles of predictable little 'microworlds', then it would be amenable to knowledge-based computerization" (1985:16).

Finally, the narrowing scope and increasing contextual isolation of the knowledge employed in bureaucratic organizations that are promoted by computerization also have a critical impact on the understanding of the development process. Computer knowledge elevates the importance of technical means over social ends, fractioning the complex process of social development into a series of discrete "social problems" of "poverty, ignorance, and disease" which can be solved by the formulaic application of the right expertise. The problem here is the inability of such "objective expertise" to deal with the selection of the goals or purposes of development, which remain based on non-empirical, metatheoretical ideas and values, including such unavoidable issues as justice and equity or the fate of ancient cultures. This is precisely the kind of "metaphysics" that bureaucratic expertise seeks to replace and it is "guilty of a 'radical deafness' towards any non-approved questions" (Ferguson 1984:79). These "great issues" of social structure and culture continue to remain central to the development process. They cannot be dealt with by quantification and mathematical formalization. . . .

Computers thus promote a conception of development singularly unsuited for confronting the most difficult, ambiguous and essentially qualitative questions of social change. Rather than eliminating such questions of ends and values, computerization of bureaucracies hides them, first in the unseen and unacknowledged values and biases of the programmers, and second, in the hidden political agendas of the state authorities who use computers to "scientifically" legitimate a particular course of development. Computerization thus involves a discourse about power, about the control of human behavior, that is concealed in an apparently apolitical machine.

The Impact of Computers on the Relation Between the State and Society

The colonial foundation of the bureaucratic apparatus of African states was based on a concept of an authoritarian and paternalistic "guardian" bureaucracy ruling a dependent and backward population. The bureaucratic agents of the state, a carefully recruited European elite, exercised an authority over Africans legitimated by their possession of the *episteme*, or true knowledge, of a superior civilization, in contrast with the *doxa*, or mere opinion, of their supposedly primitive subjects (Berman 1990b:104–15). This apparatus was turned over to a largely Western-educated African cadre of elite bureaucrats in the "Africanization" programs of the decades preceding and following formal independence. Despite substantial variations in administrative capacity and effectiveness, it has remained the enduring core of African states, while the hastily tacked-on institutions of liberal democracy have been destroyed or reduced to insignificance by military coups and one-party regimes.

African states have been and remain notable examples of the bureaucratic authoritarianism that dominates Third World societies. They continue to be based on the fundamental premise of a wide gulf of knowledge and competence between the state apparatus and the surrounding population; bureaucratic expertise must always prevail over popular ignorance. The mass of the population, particularly the peasantry in the countryside, has been conceived of as something to be controlled and shaped by the benevolent power of the state. In such a context, the general premises of "modernization" theory, involving a unilinear transition towards the model of the secular Western nation-state based on a state-managed capitalist economy, have provided since the waning years of colonial rule a model of development substantially compatible with the interests of the "guardian" bureaucracy. The state is conceived of as an advanced and modern institution, surrounded by a sea of backwardness, whose role is to lead the populace to prosperous modernity. This has led to a focus on "top-down" development strategies, strongly endorsed by national and international development agencies, including the World Bank (Stamp 1989:28). Development programs in practice demonstrate a marked preference for the extension of bureaucratic controls over a population treated as the passive recipients of state policies whose essential role is to obey its directives.[3] Moreover, indigenous forms of knowledge—agricultural, medical and technological—tend to be dismissed as useless ignorance in contrast with the superior science of bureaucratic experts and academic specialists (Stamp 1989:30; CASTAFRICA II 1988:208). Both the knowledge and interests of the local populace tend to be treated as irrational "obstacles to development," which legitimates the use of coercion to overcome any resistance to state policies.

The introduction of computers in state agencies in such a sociopolitical context can only reinforce the authoritarianism of the bureaucracy and widen the apparent gulf between it and the people it seeks to control. Computers, whether they work effectively or not, become a symbolic display of advanced development and efficiency and enhance the bureaucrats' belief in their own expertise. By narrowing the scope of knowledge to what can be quantified and programmed, computers further marginalize indigenous forms of knowledge at the same time as they make it increasingly difficult for the state to take account of qualitative variations of social structure and culture. It becomes increasingly difficult for the urban poor and rural peasantry, women in particular, to articulate their interests and grievances because they cannot address the state in the forms of expert discourse it demands. At the same time, their activities which do not enter the money economy are rarely included in the standard statistical indices utilized by state agencies, rendering them unseen as well as unheard (CASTAFRICA II 1988:192; Stamp 1989:2–3, 26).

Popular participation, the active involvement of people as agents in their own development, and democracy as a valued end of the development process are further discredited, while the trend to technocratic determinism is strengthened. The failures of development programs can be attributed by the state to the ignorance and lack of cooperation of the local populace, a form of "blame the victim" reaction, and active opposition characterized as deliberate subversion. Computerization also, of course, substantially increases the state's capacity for surveillance and control, blurring the line between the state's treatment of the populace as clients or victims (Winner 1989:93–94; Kling 1980:94–96; Burnham 1984). Rather than promoting reform or revitalizing the development process, computer use will reinforce existing patterns of class and gender relations. As Jules-Rosette found in her study of computer use in Kenya, "the key word 'expert' became synonymous with new forms of bureaucratic control and technological domination" (1987:9).

Conclusions

The expectations of the enthusiasts who proclaim the computer "revolution" are largely idle fantasies that contain little understanding of the social and political factors which shape the character and consequences of computers. Rather than being a solution for Africa's contemporary economic crisis or an engine of a recharged development process, computerization in African states is likely to reinforce existing distributions of power and wealth, create reified images of society based upon quantitative data of dubious value and accuracy, and accentuate the authoritarian relationship between the state and an increasingly marginalized populace.

Computers are the product of particular features of the development of Western capitalism and the nation-state, and constitute the most recent expression of a scientific and technocratic ideology that has sought for more than three centuries to replace the traditional "great issues" of society and politics with a definitive and unambiguous rational calculus (Berman 1990a; Davis and Hersh 1986). Computers, however, are no more capable of resolving such issues than the myriad forms of supposedly "objective" expertise which preceded them. Instead, such issues are obscured, buried in the underlying assumptions and values built into computer programs and used for "problem-solving," simulations and decision making in bureaucratic organizations.

A planned and "rational" process of development is obviously more than a series of technical "problems" to be solved. It is all too easily forgotten that it necessarily involves crucial decisions for society about what people want to be and how they shall live. Development involves a continuous social debate about the relationship between the choice of means in daily life and their relation to transcendent purposes. The disciplines of instrumental rationality and bureaucratic management which embrace computers both obscure the dimensions of the debate and limit its participants by excluding the "unscientific" discourses of non-experts. In so doing they constitute what David Ricci describes as "small conversations" which "take place in many learned disciplines, when members of a scholarly community speak mainly to one another, in language so specialized and full of jargon that it is largely unintelligible to the public or to their colleagues in other university departments across the campus mall" (1984:299), or, we might add, to their colleagues in another government department. What the development process requires, however, is a "great conversation" which is:

> larger than any small conversations that members of particular social groups, such as professions, or learned disciplines, are accustomed to conducting among themselves . . . a great conversation relies very heavily on timeworn and emotional terms, many suffering from imprecise character but still carrying enough moral authority, by precedent, habit, experience, and spiritual commitment, to be capable of moving many people in the right direction much of the time. It is thus an extraordinarily wide-ranging affair, touching upon knowledge both stored up throughout history and newly achieved in manifold realms of learning today (Ricci 1984:301).

It is precisely such a "great conversation" that is so rare in African societies today and that the introduction of technocratic solutions, including computers, makes increasingly improbable. Rushing to catch the last train of the twentieth century, prodded and hurried by international experts, the travellers are permitted no time to reflect upon and debate their course and destination. A few isolated voices have been raised in Africa questioning the growth of technological dependence and the appropriateness of computerization in cultural and political terms (*Weekly Review* 1976; Mazrui 1977 and 1978); and the governments of Kenya and Tanzania have pursued restrictive policies limiting the proliferation of micro-computers (Jules-Rosette 1987:24, 31; Grant Lewis 1988:9–11, 15). Nevertheless, it remains the case that African states generally lack policy and capabilities for controlling, regulating, and adapting computers and other forms of imported technology to indigenous conditions (CASTAFRICA II 1988:183). The development of such critical capabilities, both inside and outside of the state apparatus, is vital if a significant "great conversation" is to take place about development. Such a conversation must also include, if the people of Africa are to be active agents rather than the passive objects of social transformation, the voices of peasants who understand that counting by the state involves politics as well as science.

Notes

1. These trends of rapid growth and increasing structural complexity were also present in African colonial states in the two decades after 1945 when the European metropoles turned to more active promotion of economic development, and established in the process the basic structural characteristics of contemporary African states. For further discussion of these developments see Berman 1984 and 1990b:314–22, 402–05.

2. This appears to be the case in Africa as well. The introduction of computers in the Ministry of Agriculture in Kenya, for example, is described as a response to a 'crisis' in fiscal management and reporting occasioned by a shift in rural development strategy (Jules-Rosette 1987:8).

3. A particularly apt case is that of Tanzania, because of the government's ostensible commitment to "socialist" development based on popular participation. The program of "Ujamaa" villages was substantially shaped by the desire of the state authorities to extend bureaucratic controls over the rural population. This replicated and extended colonial policies of villagization going back to the 1920s (Coulson 1982:237–62).

References

Berman, Bruce. 1984. "Structure and Process in the Bureaucratic States of Colonial Africa." *Development and Change* 15(2):161–202.

———. 1989. "The Computer Metaphor: Bureaucratizing the Mind." *Science as Culture* 7:7–42.

———. 1990a. "Perfecting the Machine: Instrumental Rationality and the Bureaucratic Ideologies of the State." *World Futures* 20:141–161.

———. 1990b. *Control and Crisis in the Colonial Kenya: The Dialectic of Domination.* London: James Currey.

———. 1991. "Artificial Intelligence and the Ideology of Capitalist Reconstruction." *Artificial Intelligence and Society.* Forthcoming.

Bolter, J. David. 1984. *Turing's Man: Western Culture in the Computer Age.* Chapel Hill: University of North Carolina Press.

Burnham, David. 1984. *The Rise of the Computer State.* New York: Vintage Books.

CASTAFRICA II. 1988. *Science, Technology and Endogenous Development in Africa.* Paris: UNESCO.

Coulson, Andres. 1982. *Tanzania: A Political Economy.* Oxford: Clarendon Press.

Danziger, James. 1985. "Social Science and the Social Impact of Computer Technology." *Social Science Quarterly* 66:3–21.

Davis, Reuben and Philip Hersh. 1986. *Descartes' Dream: The World According to Mathematics.* Boston: Houghton Mifflin.

Ferguson, Cathy. 1984. *A Case Against Bureaucracy.* Philadelphia: Temple University Press.

Flamm, Kenneth. 1987. *Targeting the Computer: Government Support and International Competition.* Washington DC: Brookings Institution.

———. 1988. *Creating the Computer: Government, Industry and High Technology.* Washington DC: Brookings Institution.

Giddens, Anthony. 1985. *The Nation-State and Violence.* Cambridge: Polity Press.

Grant Lewis, Suzanne. 1988. "Microcomputers in Tanzania: A Study of Control and Influence in the Technological Adoption Process," Paper presented at the Conference of the Canadian Association of African Studies, Kingston, Ontario, June.

Jules-Rosette, Bennetta. 1987. "New Technologies in Kenya: Domination or Development," Paper presented at the conference of the African Studies Association, Denver.

Kaplinsky, Raphael. 1984. *Automation: The Technology and the Society.* Harlow: Longman.

Kling, Rob. 1980. "Social Analysis of Computing." *Computing Surveys.* 12 (1):61–105.

———. 1985. "Computerization as an Ongoing Social and Political Process." Department of Information and Computer Science, University of California, Irvine.

Mazrui, Ali A. 1978. "The African Computer as an International Agent." In Ali A. Mazrui, ed., *Political Values and the Educated Class in Africa.* Pp. 320–342. London: Heinemann.

Mazrui, Ali. 1977. "Development Equals Modernization Minus Dependency: A Computer Equation," in D. R. F Taylor and R. A. Obudho, eds., *The Computer in Africa: Applications, Problems, and Potential.* Pp. 279–304. New York: Praeger.

Mowshowitz, Abbe. 1976. *The Conquest of Will: Information Processing in Human Affairs.* Reading, Mass.: Addison Wesley.

Noble, David. 1977. *America by Design: Science, Technology and the Rise of Corporate Capitalism.* New York: Oxford University Press.

———. 1985. "Command Performance: A Perspective on Military Enterprise and Technological Change," In Merrit Roe Smith, ed., *Military Enterprise and Technological Change.* Cambridge, Mass.: MIT Press.

Rada, Juan. 1985. "Information Technology and the Third World," in Tom Forester, ed., *Information Technology Revolution.* Cambridge, Mass.: MIT Press.

Ricci, David. 1984. *The Tragedy of Political Science: Politics Scholarship and Democracy.* New Haven: Yale University Press.

Rozak, Theodore. 1986. *The Cult of Information. The Folklore of Computers and the True Art of Thinking.* New York: Pantheon.

Schware, Robert and Ziauddin Choudhury. 1989. The Role of IT in Third World Development," in Tom Forester, ed., *Computers in the Human Context.* Oxford: Basil Blackwell.

Stamp, Patricia. 1989. *Technology, Gender, and Power in Africa.* Ottawa: International Development Research Centre.

UNIDO. 1988. *The Software Industry: Developing Countries and the World Market.* Regional and Country Studies Branch. New York: United Nations.

———. 1989. *Computers for Industrial Management in Africa: The Case of Nigeria.* Regional and Country Studies Branch. New York: United Nations.

Weekly Review. 1976. "Computers: Benefit or Detriment." Nairobi, June 7, p. 25.

Weizenbaum, Joseph. 1984. *Computer Power and Human Reason: From Judgement to Calculation.* Harmondsworth:Penguin.

Whitley, Richard. 1977. "Changes in the Social and Intellectual Organization of the Sciences: Professionalization and the Arithmetic Ideal," in E. Mendelsohn, et al., eds., *The Social Production of Scientific Knowledge.* Dordrecht: Reidel.

Winner, Langdon. 1989. "Mythinformation in the High-Tech Era," in Tom Forester, ed., *Computers in the Human Context.* Oxford: Basil Blackwell.

THE SOCIAL IMPLICATIONS OF INFORMATION TECHNOLOGIES: A LATIN AMERICAN PERSPECTIVE

Judith Sutz

Judith Sutz suggests that computer technologies are changing the face of economics and thus changing social conditions throughout the world. The other side of the coin reveals that the social and political conditions of regions like Latin America need changing in order to reap the rewards offered by computer technologies. This article addresses the question of how to introduce successfully computer information technologies and their vast potential for positive benefits into Latin America. Though she fears the current reality expressed by what she calls the "pessimistic hypothesis" of Latin America's future, Sutz hopes the development of new technological innovations can come from within and not be imposed by or merely borrowed from the already well-technologized nations of the world.

Reprinted from *Philosophy of Technology in Spanish Speaking Countries,* ed. C. Mitchum (Kluwer Academic Publishers, 1993), 297–308; with kind permission of Kluwer Academic Publishers. © 1993 Kluwer Academic Publishers.

Analytical Framework I:
The Relevance of Information Technologies

Information technologies (ITs) are among the most important scientific-technological developments of the past forty years. Beside their technical importance, they are also ubiquitous in influence. This social influence is both vertical—i.e., throughout various levels of the economy and society—and horizontal—on living conditions in all countries and societies.

With regard to living conditions, the particular aspect that best exemplifies horizontal pervasiveness is the trend toward the "dematerialization" of production. Labor and raw materials are no longer the most significant costs of an increasing number of goods and services. These have been replaced by information. As a result there is a decrease in the strategic value of raw materials and the "comparative advantage" of cheap labor. Continuous training and updating takes on unprecedented direct economic significance due to the highly volatile and changeable character of information. The existence of institutions engaged in generating and circulating information becomes crucial. The relevance of national innovating capacities tends to be comparable to that of the labor force or the accumulation of wealth.

Highly industrialized societies are having some difficulty in adapting to the demands imposed by ITs on their economic and social life, despite the fact that the technologies were devised and develop in these societies. Naturally everything is much more difficult for peripheral societies. The most direct impact of ITs on the underdeveloped world could be considered the erosion of its positions in the international division of labor because it is less and less attractive as a place for direct foreign investment. But the problem is actually far more serious and can be phrased in the following questions: What is the self-transformation capacity of underdeveloped societies when confronting the challenge of ITs? What is their capacity to modify educational systems, forms of production and organization, social institutions, in order to make the most of information, which has become the new vital raw material? Last but not least, what is their awareness of the strategic need to carry out such transformations, and how do they envisage their realization?

Analytical Framework II:
Latin America in the 1990s

In the Latin-American case the current social context hardly supports a positive answer to such questions. The World Bank described the 1980s as the "lost decade," an expression that has become well-known in Latin America. The causes for such a bitter judgment are overwhelming.

Virtually all economic indicators, as well as those used to assess living conditions, dropped back to the levels of the 1970s, and in some cases even further.

The return to democracy in five Latin-American countries—Argentina, Brazil, Chile, Paraguay, and Uruguay—was no doubt encouraging. But the decline in living conditions for the great majority and, even worse, the forced adoption of strategies that do not promote the primary goal of improving them, pose a major problem for democratic stability in the region.

Moreover, a strong neoliberal economic ideology now prevails throughout Latin America. This means, first off, a systematic effort at privatization, both in the economic and the social fields. As far as the social implications of ITs are concerned, two privatizations deserve special attention: those of the telecommunications system and the educational system. The former is direct and consists in transferring the right to render a service and to decide on its future evolution to a private agent. The latter is indirect and involves pushing people to seek private educational solutions by reducing the public budget devoted to education.

A second consequence of neoliberalism is state retrenchment not only as owner or agent for the redistribution of resources, but also as policy maker. Since market indicators are considered the main factor in the determination of priorities, the points of view of various sectors are ignored. Thus overwhelmed by the impact of neoliberal macroeconomic policy, industrial policies disappear, technological policies are aborted, and any scenario addressing the need for innovation policies cannot be articulated. At the same time, organized social movements have noticeably weakened, a phenomenon due in part to the political, economic, and ideological collapse of East-European regimes. Lacking a clear view of the future, and decimated by years of repression, Latin-American social movements have few answers for the urgent problems of the region and its people.

It is not clear, however, that the expansion of neoliberalism and the weakening of social movements is exclusive to Latin America or, more generally, to the peripheral countries. Recent reflections by Riccardo Petrella, Director of the European Program for Forecasting and Assessment of Science and Technology (FAST), point to the presence of a similar phenomenon in Europe. In fact, referring to what he considers prevalent ideas in Europe, Petrella says that

- What prevails is a mercantile economy of a fundamentalist type; no one questions the predominance of the private economy and market.
- The only thing that counts is competition—no longer seen as a means but as an end in itself, giving rise to a vulgar social neo-Darwinism.
- The common good has become opaque, with only individualism and tribalism surviving.

- Under such conditions the purpose of the state is simply to service business enterprise.[1]

Despite the apparent universality of the neoliberal creed, marked differences persist. Caricaturing somewhat, the essence of these differences lies in the fact that in Latin America the creed is applied to the letter, while in the developed world this is not the case. It is not only Japan and the "Four Tigers" of Southeast Asia that demonstrate the active participation of the state in the orientation of different strategic options.[2] The very neoliberal government in Baden-Wurtemberg systematically applies industrial, technological, and innovation policies,[3] and what is done there on a small scale is done also by the European Economic Community or, rather, by OECD, for the most developed countries group.

The deepest difference, however, is not what is done or not done but the reasons determining these attitudes. The "deviations" from the creed clearly perceptible in the First World originate in a recognition that the depth of productive transformations, mostly resulting from the explosion of ITs, demand harmonizing efforts from society as a whole, so as to make the most of their potentialities and, to some extent, to minimize risks. In Latin America, at the same time, insensitivity in the application of the model is partly due to the fact that phenomena such as the transformation of the technical system and its consequences have not even been recognized as problems.

Analytical Framework III:
The Evolution of Information Technologies and Their Potential Impacts

The evolution of information technologies makes possible a phenomenon called the "customizing" of production. This consists in the construction of economically feasible technical solutions tailored to the needs of individual end users. That is, it is becoming technically feasible to mass produce without standardizing. The introduction of ITs into the whole sequence from design to production to consumption, and vice versa, creates this new possibility, the social consequences of which can hardly be exaggerated.

First, there is the potential for a convergence of some of the features of craft production with customized or tailor-made design production.[4]

Second, the exploitation of this new possibility demands an enormous expansion of innovating capabilities, in both society and particular enterprises. There emerges the possibility that the person who innovates is not only the person who designs but also the person who demands a design. This creates the idea of user as innovator as a most influential social fact.[5]

The process of innovation almost by definition has no limits apart from creative imagination. Now the expansion of this no-limit phenomenon poses crucial challenges to both education and re-education. The possible practice of permanent innovation has deep cultural and political implications. No isolated institution will be able to carry out the process on its own. This leads to the idea of some national system of innovation to focus the cooperative aspects, the interconnection of all participating agents, in the materialization of different innovations. Thus within the very neo-Darwinian framework referred to by Petrella there emerges a new collaborative tendency which, although certainly not inspired by an ideal of solidarity, at least recognizes the limits imposed upon efficiency by excessive individualism.

Third, there are the particular social consequences of technological evolution for the countries of Latin American. Perhaps a good way to illustrate this is to think back thirty, twenty, or even ten years and imagine some sanitation, agricultural, industrial, educational, or urban problem in the region. In most cases the technological solutions for such problems had already been "prefabricated." The problem specificity might cause at most a slight variation in the design of the solution.

The present search for flexibility in the answers to more individualized and precise demands could be put to good use in underdeveloped countries. The proper exploitation of ITs could give rise to major positive social impacts, especially in the form of an increased selection of endogenous technological capabilities compatible with a greater technological modernity. The design of technological solutions tailor-made to existing problems has always been an alternative to the utilization of predetermined solutions. But this was hardly if ever explicitly recognized as such, especially in the underdeveloped world. At present, the flexibility with which ITs endow design and manufacture, as well as current discourse praising tailor-made goods, which is a consequence of this flexibility, increases awareness of alternatives and broadens possibilities for the application in underdeveloped or developing situations of a model which is being increasingly practiced in developed countries.

A Pessimistic but Probable Scenario

Is there a real possibility that the new technological opportunities offered by ITs will be properly used in our countries? What kinds of problems could make the best use of the special potentials of ITs understood in the broadest sense?[6]

Mention should be made of two broad kinds of problem—those for which rigid technology has not so far offered reasonable solutions, and those getting highly inadequate solutions for whatever reasons.

The first type of problem exists mainly among medium and low-income economic and population sectors: small and medium-sized enterprises requiring partial automation, digital telephone exchanges for towns with less than one thousand inhabitants, small medical electronic devices allowing the extensive application of modern treatments, simple but efficient systems for data collection and transfer for rural areas, etc. The second can be linked to large-scale projects, many of them being in the public sphere up to now, such as country-wide data communication packages, the construction of automatic systems for exchanging electric power, and more generally, all the great technical systems that are strongly based upon computerized elements and which until now have been produced and installed on a turn-key basis.

With regard to the "small-scale" problems, a major difficulty is that those who deal with them have no support whatsoever, so they know nothing about the abilities of ITs to provide solutions. Is any small or medium-sized enterprise in Latin America in a position to learn by itself that it is possible to tailor a simple data collection system likely to increase productivity by, for instance, rationalizing energy expenses? Is there a team of physicians linked to the lower-income population sector in a position to design and eventually foster the production of computerized electronic equipment that is not highly sophisticated but nevertheless performs some vital functions? Is there a small rural municipality that knows it can have access to new small-scale communications systems that are both efficient and inexpensive? There are solutions, but those in need either do not know of their existence or lack sufficient strength to acquire them.

The recognition of this situation (which is also common in developed societies), is at the root of the broad working guidelines defined by new innovation policies, particularly as far as the attention to technological demand is concerned.[7] In Latin America during the 1990s, where most policies stress the fact that the only valid indicators are those coming from the market, it will not be at all easy for these positive IT impacts to materialize.

A similar argument applies to "large-scale" problems linked to major enterprises, generally in the public sphere. Since more often than not the solutions to such problems were sought from large international firms, in many cases because of pressures exercised by these same firms, why should we expect a technological reversal based on the smallest, most efficient tailor-made components once privatization, which is likely to mean "foreignization," has taken place?

A pessimistic scenario, i.e., one in which the potentialities of ITs do not materialize, is in fact highly likely. But the scenario deserves its adjective not only for all that which will not be done. Unfortunately it is also likely that the effective application of ITs will have a negative social impact.

Where there exist highly heterogeneous social situations, the use of ITs directed to the most restricted and wealthy population sectors can do nothing but increase the gap between rich and poor. The consequences of this are potentially catastrophic because they may, within the framework of increasingly open economies, make it impossible for many people to develop even minimally competitive economic activities. This in turn will push increasing numbers of people toward a subsistence economy, with the serious consequences of social impoverishment. At the same time, failure to make use of the opportunities offered by ITs with regards to the strengthening of the local capabilities of design and technological construction will inevitably contribute to maintaining and, possibly, deepening the present status of technical dependence.

Is It Possible to Construct a Different Scenario?

Technological opportunities versus social political checks. Is it possible in Latin America to loosen the latter so as to be able to make the most of the former? We would like to approach this topic from three perspectives: technical, sociocultural, and political.

TECHNICAL PERSPECTIVE

The technical perspective causes us to wonder whether the technological capacities to make use of ITs exist in Latin America. It seems obvious that with regard to the Third World as a whole it is extremely difficult to give an affirmative answer. For the Latin-American region, however, this may not as much be the case. In virtually all the countries of the South technological capacities do exist, and with the addition of the new potentialities of ITs, these could give rise to a truly qualitative leap in the search for efficient technical solutions to problems that remain unresolved.

Just to give one example, consider the case of Uruguay. In Uruguay electronic pacemakers have been designed and manufactured that cost three times less than imported ones. Thanks to this development, the whole population now has access to this device. Modular telex stations have also been designed and manufactured in Uruguay, beginning with 124 lines that were expanded according to the evolution of demand. A data commutation package, URUPAC, has been designed and manufactured locally. An automation system for the scouring and baling of wool has been designed and manufactured, and has been recognized by the French firm that at present owns the facilities as one of the most efficient systems known. Complex information systems for both public and private use, such as the computer network of the Federated Agrarian Cooperatives, have been designed and installed.

Insistence on local design and manufacture capacity—which is certainly not the same as any pretension to autarchy—is justified because all over the world tailor-made design has a strong local component. This point leads in turn to recognition of the central role of local training and education. For too long a time, training in ITs in Latin America, particularly in the field of computers, was determined by the need to train users. It is crucial to reverse that trend in order to strengthen the training of innovators.[8]

Let us emphasize that what can be said for Uruguay is also applicable to Argentina, Chile, Brazil, Venezuela, and Mexico. Indeed, the whole region is sure to achieve this, though on a lesser scale. Let us not forget that globally considered, Latin America is the most industrialized region in the periphery. Therefore, from a technical perspective, it is possible to construct a positive scenario for the use of ITs.

SOCIOCULTURAL PERSPECTIVE

From a sociocultural perspective, there are two aspects that will no doubt influence the viability of this positive scenario. The first is associated with what could be termed the "technological image" (and even self-image) of the region, that is, the self-awareness of one's own technological capacities, and the belief that self-defined technical solutions are possible. Such a technological image is virtually nonexistent in Latin America today. People do not know that there are relevant local capacities to do things. They believe that technology, and particularly IT, is an exclusive product of development. Thus they do not find answers or, rather, they do not even formulate the questions.

The second is related once again to education, though from a different angle. The basic question is, What do Latin American engineers want? Do they want to seek original solutions to indigenous problems? Or do they only want to identify with that which is more modern, more sophisticated, more powerful—disregarding its real usefulness—in order to feel that they "live" in the developed world? The answer has a decisive social relevance, because the influence of engineers in the adoption and application of all kinds of solutions, particularly in the case of ITs, is well known. Concern for the social loyalties of those who possess the technical knowledge thus becomes a priority to which the educational system may provide some answer. Science, technology, society, and development are issues to be studied and debated at the university level so that on reaching the stage of potential practice the decisions made by engineers are based upon socially constructed loyalties.[9]

POLITICAL PERSPECTIVE

Finally, from a political perspective a difficult question arises. Is it possible within the macropolicies framework to open opportunities to ITs from meso- or micro-levels, so that their social impact is as positive as it should be? This question is part of a more general problem that can be phrased as follows: Will the strong presence of macroorientations totally opposed to the implementation of sectoral policies allow the construction of spaces for innovation policies at the meso and micro levels? An affirmative answer would almost be equivalent to stating that Latin America has not missed the opportunity offered by ITs to move toward a self-constructed modernity. Foundations for an answer of this kind are not easy to identify, but we would like to comment on an experience that shows movement in this direction is possible.

In Uruguay, within the framework of some recent research into the electronics complex,[10] the almost total lack of information in certain productive sectors about the existence of a national technological capability in professional electronics was identified as a problem. The result of this lack of knowledge was that the above-mentioned sectors either did not turn to electronics at all or that they imported solutions that were in general expensive and did not meet their needs. Since the research had generated abundant information about the professional electronics industry, a decision was made to publish a directory of enterprises working in this area and to organize a workshop to be attended by everyone interested. And there, within the framework of that workshop, a peculiar phenomenon took place that triggered a participation mechanism nobody had anticipated.[11]

Electronics entrepreneurs, for the first time, were given an overall vision of their own sector. It was no longer each of them and two or three colleagues or rivals, but there were over forty enterprises represented, with a considerable turnover and a diversified production. The feeling of belonging to a group appeared for the first time, and with it a question. Should we not get together to find out who we are, what we do, and what we could do, not as individuals but as a sector? In the governmental sphere, a sector whose existence had been ignored emerged as such, showing significant levels of technological dynamism and a high problem resolving capacity. The truth is that less than a month after the workshop, the Ministry of Industry and Energy—a meso level par excellence—invited both the enterprises included in the electronics directory—a micro level—and the research team to a series of meetings. These meetings gave rise to more frequent contacts among the enterprises, which resulted in the identification of a series of common problems.

It thus becomes obvious that the lack of information existing in the country about what is done is a major problem. So is the evident mistrust toward that which is national, which is increased when this involves complex technological production. So is the state policy, which is more often than not unpredictable. The result is that enterprises need equipment and instruments that could sometimes be shared but cannot be purchased individually, and they need information to which they have no access. The idea of creating a collective body capable of organizing and centralizing some of these aspects in order subsequently to socialize them started to take shape. The idea was to purchase equipment whose use was to be shared, to facilitate access to information, to formulate common positions vis-à-vis the different aspects of negotiation with the state, common undertakings in exports, etc. A few months later, this idea materialized with the incorporation of the Grupo de Interés Económico de la Industria Electrónica Profesional Uruguaya, a collective entrepreneurial body, which is already taking its first steps, especially in negotiations associated with MERCOSUR, the subregional integration process with Argentina, Brazil, and Paraguay.

Minimal as it may seem, this example shows a certain encouraging attitude at the meso level and a certain capacity for the constitution of actors at the micro level. The existence of this situation linked to work with state-of-the-art technologies was not evident a priori. Fostering initiatives of this kind, in each country, according to its circumstances, may constitute a concrete affirmative answer to our fundamental question, above, about a different, non-pessimistic scenario for the future.[12]

What Kind of Foreign Support Would This Alternative Require?

The basic idea is that classic theories of technology transfer are not much help any more. The issue in question is support for the creation of capacities, as well as the creation of the awareness that said capacities are useful to construct suitable solutions to problems, which are really those identified by people as such.

According to the pessimistic hypothesis, that doubts the possibility for forward movement at the level of macropolicies, the idea would be the promotion of a meso-level-to-meso-level transfer, from development to the periphery, in addition to starting work together. What we need is a transfer promoting innovation policies and industrial extensionist policies; support for research into the technological reality and the massive dissemination of results; encouragement in the teaching of science, technology, society, and development; support for IT producer associations; the fostering of joint projects for IT development; the stimulation of prospective studies that help orient the choices made in relation to ITs.

What organizations could participate from one side or the other in these particular forms of transfer? The local level plays a major role here.

The government and the local institutions may have valuable experience that is worth sharing. In addition, research organizations, out of an overall concern both for development in general and for the direction of technical change and its social impact in particular, could see their perspectives greatly enriched by the strengthening of joint working links, which are at present far too feeble. The main aim of technology transfer, namely, meeting certain needs, would thus find a different field of application. In the midst of a general indifference if not contempt for concern about the social consequences of IT and of technical modernization, the transfer of this certainly would be of great help.

Conclusion

The true opportunity of ITs for underdeveloped countries lies in the possibility of designing and constructing in the countries themselves technical solutions to endogenously defined problems. The positive social impacts of ITs is dependent on the materialization of this possibility, which is not an easy task. Deceiving ourselves in this regard will serve no purpose.

Carlos Fuentes, the Mexican writer, was obviously not thinking about technology when he stated, at the beginning of this decade: "Latin America is on its own. The Continent has not been invited to the feast of the future." But his reflection also applies to the case of technology. Those from within the countries who think that the problem of modernization comes down to importing solutions, and those from without who regard the region as a great market, leave no room at that table for Latin America.

I think Carlos Fuentes was right. Latin America—and not only Latin America—has not been invited to the feast of the future. Naturally, it remains to be seen what this future is. The construction of the forces enabling us to share that table, and enjoy a feast to be defined by us all, is an enormous and urgent challenge. Let us hope that cooperation and mutual support will give us the strength to take up that challenge—and to invite ourselves even if we have not been invited.

Uruguay Center for Information Studies (Montevideo)

Notes

1. "Puissance technologique et fragilité sociale," round table discussion with Riccardo Petrella, *Futuribles* (July–August 1991), pp. 39–44. See especially p. 42.

2. W. Hillebrand, "The Newly Industrializing Economies as Models for Establishing a Highly Competitive Industrial Base—What Lessons to Learn?" in *The New Industrializing Economies of Asia* (New York: Springer, 1990).

3. H. Schmitz, "Industrial Districts: Model and Reality in Baden-Wurtemberg," in F. Pyke and W. Sengenberger, ed., *Industrial Districts and Local Economic Regeneration* (Geneva: International Institute for Labour Studies, forthcoming).

4. "In the long run, the convergence of market forces, consumer preferences and technological opportunities suggest the possibility of 'totally flexible' production systems, in which the craft era tradition of custom-tailoring of products to the needs and tastes of individual consumers will be combined with the power, precision, and economy of modern production technology." The MIT Commission on Industrial Productivity, *Made in America: Regaining the Productive Edge* (Cambridge, MA: MIT Press, 1989), p. 131.

5. The relevance of the user as innovator was demonstrated in a recent book: Eric von Hippel, *The Sources of Innovation* (New York: Oxford University Press, 1988). The relationship user-producer as a source of socially useful innovations has also been analyzed by Ben-Ake Lundvall, "Innovation as an Interactive Process: From User-Producer Interaction to the National System of Innovation," in Dosi, *et al.*, eds., *Technical Change and Economic Theory* (London: Pinter Publishers, 1988), pp. 349–369.

6. ITs in their broadest sense will be taken to include all technologies within the electronics complex that runs from industrial and agricultural automation through telecommunications to medical electronics, etc. This broad definition is justified insofar as all the technologies in question are fundamentally based on the generation, transfer, processing, and retrieval of information.

7. A very interesting case of recognition of these problems and the action taken to solve them is analyzed in M. Dodgson, "Research and Technology Policy in Australia: Legitimacy in Intervention," *Science and Public Policy*, vol. 16, no. 3 (June 1989), pp. 159–166.

8. On this subject, see J. Sutz, "La formación de recursos humanos en informática: Una aproximación a la situación latinoamericana," in *Transferencia de tecnología informática en la administración pública* (Caracas: Planeta, 1988).

9. In the Science Faculty of the Central University of Venezuela, there is an experience, which has lasted six years, of teaching "Computers and Society" to students in computer science courses, that has had the extensive support of the students. A similar experience is taking place in Uruguay with a "Technology and Society" course in the Faculty of Engineering.

10. The research project is called "Uruguay: Problems and Prospects of the Industrial Electronics System in a Small Country" and is carried out at the Centro de Informaciones y Estudios del Uruguay with the support of the Volkswagen Foundation. The hardware and software industries, the public policies for the sector and the training of human resources were studied within the framework of this project.

11. Later, the research project produced another enterprise directory, this time of computer enterprises, whose diffusion also took place at a workshop.

12. Another recent initiative pointing in the same direction, and growing in the region, is related to the link between the university and the productive sectors.

COOL RUNNINGS: THE CONTRADICTIONS
OF CYBEREALITY IN JAMAICA

Joerge Dyrkton

In North America, where an estimated 75% of households own a personal computer, it is at times difficult to recognize that the majority of the world does not have this luxury. "First World" academic Joerge Dyrkton (former professor at the University of West Indies, Jamaican campus) points to the irony of rhetorical claims of high-tech promises in the face of more basic needs in "Third World" Jamaica. In doing this, the class distinctions between those with and without technology become clear. Furthermore, as a manifestation of Sutz's "pessimistic hypothesis" (see the previous essay), Dyrkton describes the social and industrial conditions that make high-tech offerings virtually impossible for Jamaicans themselves.

The more I consider things the more I find that I'm only a social critic by accident.
—John Galsworthy *The Forsyte Saga* (1949: ix)

Jamaica, the third largest island in the Caribbean, is a land of many contradictions: for example bobsledding and more recently e-mail. Known also for its beaches, ganja, Bob Marley, and even Miss World, Jamaica is considered by its nearly 3 million inhabitants to be the first among Third World nations. Its democratic system, however, is enforced by gun crews ('Dons' fighting for turf) at election time, which adds to a frightening annual death toll figure. Life for the average Jamaican is also disturbingly poor. The minimum wage is a mere US $8.00 daily.

How can computer networks function in a country beset by tropical conditions and Third World problems—where water supply can be down for days; where roads are repaired only when dignitaries come to visit; where the streets of downtown Kingston are dominated by men steering go-carts; where rain stops everything, including postal services; where mail between China and Canada is faster than that between Jamaica and Canada?

Jamaica's infrastructure is devoid of much rationalization; roads are chaotic, pot-holed and dangerous. Impatient bus drivers leapfrog one another regardless of traffic conditions. Buses are normally crammed with people, and increasingly dangerous. Violence—homicidal and domestic— usually headlines both radio and newspapers.

Everywhere the regular support system is breaking down,[1] and now e-mail comes to the rescue. Donkey carts can be seen on the roads quite regularly, passing by the university. My female house "helper" (who has no telephone) does not use a washing machine: she does it all by hand. The average car in Jamaica (certainly if one considers taxis) is thirty years old, usually without proper brake lights and in dire need of repair.

E-mail demands cyborg technology and the latest in equipment. This is seemingly quite incompatible with the spirit of Jamaica. Miami is only two hours away by plane, but it is a world apart. Anyone who has been to Kingston airport will notice that the arrival and departure television screens are behind schedule by several days: today's flight arrival time will appear in two days' time. Also there are no working intercoms. Anyone who has used a bank's automatic teller will notice that computerized statements will differ depending on which machine has been used, which will differ again from the passbook statement.

Today, Jamaica is trying to move by leaps and bounds away from the chaos of a collapsing infrastructure and closer towards First World electronic communication with computer network links, fibre-optic cable, and baffling bridge routers. The University of the West Indies, founded in 1947 as a college of the University of London, is at the centre of this transition. Composed of three campuses, Mona (Jamaica), Cave Hill (Barbados), and St Augustine (Trinidad and Tobago), the University of the West Indies is linked to the outside world by the UUCP Computer-link Network.

In June 1991 the Organization of the American States (OAS) approved the creation of the Hemisphere Wide Inter-University Scientific and Technological Information Network. CUNet (The Caribbean Universities Network) is under the initiative of SIRIAC (Integrated Informatic Resource System for Latin America and the Caribbean). The Caribbean and Latin America were the largest block remaining in the world unconnected to e-mail, and SIRIAC was the project designed to bring this part of the Third World into the twentieth century. The secondary purpose was to bring regional integration to the area and to promote greater information exchange and sharing, thereby stimulating the ever-expanding "global village."

The OAS funded the initiative and agreed to pay for the interconnection equipment: between 1991 and 1994 US $40,000 was spent on networking equipment in Jamaica alone. Any upgrading was to be paid for by the member universities. CUNet was originally composed of fourteen different countries. The initiative behind CUNet is to contemplate "the integration of the Caribbean Region countries, regardless of political situations and cultural or linguistic aspects." These countries include Antigua and Barbuda, Barbados, Bahamas, Belize, Dominica, Grenada, Jamaica, Puerto Rico, Dominican Republic, Saint Kitts and Nevis, Saint Lucia, Saint Vincent and the Grenadines, Suriname, and Trinidad and Tobago. Today a total of twenty-four Caribbean countries are involved, including Bermuda, Cayman Islands, Cuba, Guadeloupe, Guyana, Haiti, Martinique, Montserrat, Virgin Islands (British) and Virgin Islands (US).

E-Mail

The first e-mail site was established at the University of Puerto Rico. CUNet is coordinated by the CRACIN (Corporation for the National Academic, Scientific and Research Network of Puerto Rico) and OAS along with other members. All twenty-four Caribbean sites dial into the Puerto Rico station to relay and receive their e-mail messages. Today the University of the West Indies at Mona aspires to be an active internet site on its own, with First World links to the Sprint network in the United States.

Known commercially as the Convex* but more acceptably—and in admiring tones—as the Supercomputer, it represents the future of the University of the West Indies. The supercomputer arrived on 22 June 1992 with apparently little fanfare, perhaps because it was originally purchased for commercial digitizing. Within 300 metres of this supercomputer, on the outer perimeter of the university, is a shanty town bereft of running water, electricity and proper sanitary facilities. The university is subject to the occasional vagrant from the shanty town often searching for scraps of wood to repair his home. The campus is like a compound, a preserve for the few who can afford to be educated. The ring road, lined with cars, much as the wagons circled in a laager, is the first line of defence.

Jamaican e-mail has passed through three definite stages since 1991. In the first stage the single e-mail computer could be found near the principal's office and in the room of Keith Manison. Manison is the computer planning officer, an electrical and computer engineer and 'broad dreamer,' appointed to make e-mail a functioning reality and who wants to see a computer at every office desk. The first e-mail computer was a PC donated to the university by Advanced Integrated Systems. Software was supplied free by the OAS, and the modem was supplied by Manison himself to speed things up. When Manison took office in 1991 there was not one iota of computer infrastructure at the university. In order to send e-mail in the early days, one had to put one's message (assuredly academic!) into an ASCII file and leave the disk with him to be sent off.

*Technically, it is a Convex 3440 with a 4 dual vector/scaler processor and 1 GByte of RAM and 28 GByte hard disk storage.

E-mail was rudimentary and awkward, yet messages could be sent. But there was never any guarantee that they would be received efficiently. Faculty were beholden to Manison to retrieve and notify them of incoming messages. After a few short weeks, however, the computer had been moved to a small corner in the office, and faculty could work at the e-mail themselves. After nine months of this quasi-inaccessibility, the computer was moved to a more appropriate space, the Computer Science building, thus initiating the second stage.

Cool and air-conditioned, the Computer Science building was unlike most other buildings in Jamaica or at the university. It was easy to escape the heat, the life of the Third World and sit bewitched by this link to the heart of civilization. At one and the same time Jamaica seemed to offer a peculiar mix of sun, sand and aspirations towards high-class technology. But in Jamaica even technology suffers from that great tropical disease: the ideology of delay. Jamaicans dote on slowness—in the shopping queue, at the bank, and in opening offices. There is little, if anything, that functions on time and efficiently. Life is simply—and is supposed to be—slower in a tropical paradise. Even e-mail messages appeared to be delayed.

For the whole of the university in 1993 there was only one terminal. Imagine the congestion at peak hours. Luckily faculty had some priority. But it was a good way to meet people, standing in a queue. . . . When I first arrived at the university in the mornings I remember reaching the Computer Science office before 8 a.m. in order to have the most uninterrupted minutes available to me. Forget about dialling into the university modem from your own computer. Forget about Internet and the immediate delivery of messages. Just write your message (you could use ASCII files) and wait for it to be sent out—within a few days. Once or twice a week someone in the Computer Science department would trigger the dial to Puerto Rico, where they have a satellite dish, and relay the message out via them. Delay lay at the heart of this system.

E-mail at this time was dependent on regular, undedicated phone lines. Each call to Puerto Rico is long distance and uses valuable credits allowed to the University by the Jamaica Telephone Company. If the Computer Science department used up its weekly quota, it could not send or receive mail; e-mailers would have to wait until their quota was restored. If there was an incoming call while e-mail messages were being sent out, all e-mail sending procedures would halt and operators would have to dial again. If the mail message was too large (i.e. too many pages)—either sending or receiving—it could block the line and prevent any other mail from entering the system. This happened in November 1993, and we were stuck with an unusual situation: we could send mail regularly, but we could only receive mail that was a week late, telling us about events that happened—in computer terms—in the Stone Age. It was as if e-mail had to go through customs on its way into the country. Fortunately that appears not to have been the case.

"E-mail seems to work everywhere but in Jamaica," correspondents complained. And there was not much privacy either. The computer terminal was at the end of a small, poorly lit room with the screen facing any onlooker's glances. Whenever the word "love" or "my dear . . ." appeared on screen one felt the pressure of a thousand prying eyes. Why not use a Valentine card? Because the post was staggeringly slow. How could a university lecturer embarrass him/herself with such "hot" intimacies on the screen? Why was s/he not using the terminal for more "cool" academic purposes? The cool language of networking seemed to underestimate e-mail as an important personal device.

In the third stage, e-mail was linked to the supercomputer. Eventually all PCs on campus should be tied into a campus network. Manison envisages everyone with a terminal on their desk, and Internet at the high-school level. Another goal is to promote regional integration, so vital to a university whose campuses are hundreds of kilometres apart. Machines should be able to communicate with each other. Academics will be able to link interactively with overseas computers and download files on Internet (File Transfer Process—FTP). Perhaps its most pedagogical use is for the UWI Distance Teaching Network, where all fourteen English speaking islands will be linked by Internet.

It has to be admitted that there is a certain irony about putting e-mail into Jamaica. Offices are now being wired up for e-mail when they don't even have phones. Presumably this is the solution to the tiresome problem of installing proper connections for them in the first place. The phone system at the university is archaic. In order to dial in or out (unless you have a rare direct line), you must dial through the university operator. The phone system involves long waits and frustrations and is often a fruitless exercise. While you may not be able to phone a local taxi, you can e-mail to New York for one!

Telecommunications in Jamaica are limited, as they are run by a monopoly, Jamaica Telecom, a subsidiary of Cable and Wireless, with little interest in upgrading. They have not invested in fibre optics anywhere in Jamaica. At most, they appear more interested in basic service. It takes at least three months to order a phone, if you are lucky. The solution, as I discovered, is to indicate on paper that you are prepared to spend large amounts of money on your monthly calls, whereupon a telephone is promptly delivered to your home.

At the level of senior political and telephone policy-makers—this was aired on an important public radio interview programme (and garnered from talks with the Convex computer engineers)—there seems to be tremendous confusion (unlike in North America) concerning the roles of "voice" phones and "data" phones. They seem not to realize that today's technology recognizes no difference between voice and data. The 1993–94 Jamaica telephone book is the first to mention fax machines, and its policy is "to allow customer owned facsimile machines to be interconnected to the telephone network." In all cases the fax machine must be registered. In order to avoid the "systems-cracking" craft of the Jamaican mind, all long-distance calls require the albatross of an ICAS (international call authorization system) code before the call can be made. This code can be activated or deactivated; in either case it requires a further password and a personal identification number, such as that from a passport. One must hide all documents when one deactivates the long-distance phone access and bring them out again for the next overseas call.

The ICAS code also frustrates the use of the fax message beyond the island. A computer with a fax facility, for example, cannot send an international fax because the computer dials the number too fast for the telephone, which is waiting for a special dial tone. Cellular phones too are allowed on the island but with each monthly bill the connection is terminated; presumably the Jamaica Telephone Company fears that "mobile" users are apt to leave the country without paying their bill.

Another problem with the phone system is that there is no direct line to the modem pools from campus. It is easier to dial into the Convex from outside than from inside the campus: it is easier to get Convex connections from off campus even though the computer is on campus. Faculty—those who can afford them—are invited to bring their nice new computers on to campus, where they are even more likely to be stolen by budding cyberthieves.

A central dilemma is that Jamaica remains ill prepared for the computer age, something that requires technological support and software literacy. Jamaica is nowhere near achieving universality in primary and secondary education. A country which can hardly distinguish its patois from standard English—because schools here do not teach "English" as a separate language—seems most poorly placed for the computer. This central problem in Jamaican culture leaves the country badly equipped to face the twenty-first century, and it figures very highly in the problems of higher education generally. All freshman students at the University of the West Indies (Mona) are required to complete a course in English grammar and language. Will the move to high computer technology polarize the national literacy problem? Will it create an elite of computer literates and an ever-growing mass of unlearned non-users?

This problem is avoidable at the Barbados and Trinidad and Tobago campuses, where English is taught in schools separately from patois. These campuses of the University of the West Indies do not have to ensure that their students are functionally literate in English. The Mona campus, situated on the site of the Mona slave plantation, appears to feel the need to struggle with the memories of the past, which is suitably ironic and postmodern.

This brings to mind another use for the supercomputer in a country so dominated by its memories. Simple file cards are an extension of mechanical writing and electronic sequencing. The revolution of the electronic memory has made its spectacular mark in the twentieth century. The acceleration in technology—and technological history—since the 1960s has facilitated the development of an automatic memory. Memories register data, and we can preserve the results. The memory of humans is considered fallible and unstable, whereas the memory of machines (following Pascal's invention) shows great stability. Will the computer become the repository of the island's collective memory (Le Goff 1988)? This could be deemed a positive benefit in bridging the gap between social classes.

Another problem is that the major e-mail users in Jamaica usually come from the First World, like myself. They are those who have experienced its delights in the industrialized nations. E-mail in Jamaica requires a major cultural shift and a huge educational programme in order to teach those born and bred in Jamaica to become more familiar with it. Native Jamaicans need to be taught, not to be intimidated, by the software and computers. The corollary of this problem is that most e-mail messages leave the Caribbean for the United States and Europe and do not remain within the region. This suggests that there is currently very little regional communication, the very purpose for installing the network in the first place.

How effective is e-mail in the practical sense? How does this electronic interaction compare with the face-to-face reality of everyday life? When there was one terminal for the whole of campus those who waited to use it socialized in the ever-growing queue. We knew each other and we met regularly, almost daily. When the computer did not run fully, we abided by a set of artificial social relationships which no longer exists. Now, on the Convex, we no longer see each other, and know each other only by name as one of the list of users. There are about two hundred users at the university, and perhaps it is too early to tell how interaction is being shaped by the Convex, but it is agreed that users communicate more often among themselves than with non-users.

Most non-users seem surprised to learn that Jamaica has this advanced technology already installed. Those who first used e-mail on the Jamaican system would often call by phone to check if the recipient actually received the e-mail message. When I agreed to write this chapter I spoke with Jeremy Whyte, the technician behind the Convex and e-mail links. Using two of his e-mail addresses (one of which responded: "no such user") I was unable to get an answer over two or three days. Was he overloaded with requests? Is it possible that when we are all on e-mail—and overloaded—we will have no communication at all? Was my message purged perfunctorily? Did the immediacy of the request force him to throw out the message, instead of putting it in a stack as one did with old letters?

No, I had to walk to his office for face-to-face introductions and an interview. A Jamaican, he clearly enjoys his work and has pleasure in explaining it. He stuttered, and I could see in his thoughts: "It is almost First World." He was a man proud of his share of achievements, from ground level to e-mail in three short years.

E-mail is a hermetic pleasure in a land which avoids the hermetic. Offering release from the tedium of daily life by the elevation of the electronic senses, it is a blissful search for the unusual outside of the ever-present world of sunshine and beaches. This research paper was, for the most part, a tropically air-conditioned field study. If technology and its techniques are above all social productions, as Pierre Lemonnier argues, then how can we reconcile techniques of First World culture and Third World society (Lemonnier 1993: 2)?

This chapter has not been a study of the effects of technology on society; nor has it been an extensive search into how academic groups communicate with their new e-mail tools. Rather, it has been an examination of contradictions: simple tools like Jamaican taxi meters are non-existent because they have been unable to keep up with inflation. It is often impossible to understand the patois of a grocery clerk and it is often just as difficult to understand the technological words of Jeremy Whyte. Everyday life for many Jamaicans is so miserable that the advent of e-mail looks like just another misunderstood "white-man thing." Few native Jamaicans can use the e-mail beyond the Mona campus because they need to be off the island and to be sufficiently educated to get the appropriate contacts.

E-mail represents a significant advance for the university as a place on the margin in the Third World (which now outperforms Finland in networking) but it is also a political tool in a very polarized, hierarchical society. E-mail can only exacerbate the gulf between classes; while it may help to rationalize the telephone system at various locations, it will not help realize appropriate sanitary facilities. The financially comfortable will learn to speak with computer literacy while the poor will continue in their world apart, just next door. The juxtaposition of a certain "cool running" with every conceivable type of social ill in this tiny island conjures up images of postmodernism becoming ever more the Third World computer chip blowout between "marginal" slums and megabyte slickers.

Jamaica needs higher-level technology, but e-mail is too cool to bring about improvements in unemployment or other immediate social gains. It represents stronger links to the First World rather than the Third World. In Jamaica the breeze of the computer fan empties itself into an abyss of unrelenting everyday life. The mundane must be confronted. Staring into the radioactive glare of the monitor cannot be good for the eyes. But it must be done.

Epilogue

Since writing this chapter the author has returned to Canada where he is affiliated to the University of British Columbia. His use of e-mail has dwindled to nothing, given the fact that his new home university charges faculty and other users for all e-mail messages. The University of the West Indies, however, does not charge its users and pays about US $4,000 per month in telephone costs. The author's one remaining contact in Jamaica has a brand new modem but he does not know how to use it yet, apparently. Another contact (who never used e-mail on the island), now in England, has access to e-mail, still does not use it, or so it seems. The author is more electronically isolated in Canada than when he was in Jamaica.

Notes

The University of the West Indies can sound very tempting, especially to those who come from temperate climates. I answered one of the many advertisements UWI at Jamaica puts out for lecturers, hoping that I would find my place in the sun. Little did I know that it would be the "cool runnings" that would both sustain and frustrate my stay on this tropical island. The author would like to thank Nick Saunders—who does not use e-mail—for his many ideas and suggestions.

1. Consider the toilet facilities in Whitfield Town, an inner city area of Kingston, where life is less than equitable. In 1982, the last available census, a mere 3 per cent of the 905 houses used a pit; and another 19 per cent used a WC not linked to a sewer; while 46 per cent used a WC linked to a sewer. Significantly, 32 per cent of the households did not identify their type of toilet facilities. This area is known for its sewers breaking down—and taking months to repair. When there is a shortage of water, residents can be seen fetching it with pots and pans from the nearest primary school. If this is everyday life, albeit some of it statistically of a decade ago, how can Jamaica prepare for the technological age? I am grateful to Novlet Smith for supplying these census statistics (Smith 1993–94).

References

Galsworthy, John 1949. *The Forsyte Saga.* New York: Charles Scribner.

Le Goff, Jacques 1988. *History and Memory,* trans. Steven Rendall and Elizabeth Claman. New York: Columbia University Press.

Lemonnier, Pierre (ed.) 1993. *Technological Choices: Transformation in Material Cultures since the Neolithic.* London: Routledge.

Smith, Novlet 1993–94. "An assessment of the contribution of the Canadian Jesuits to the social life of Whitfield Town Community in Jamaica, 1986–1993," Hons thesis. Caribbean Studies, University of the West Indies.

THE ETHICAL DILEMMA CAUSED BY THE TRANSFER OF INFORMATION TECHNOLOGY TO DEVELOPING COUNTRIES

Yero H. J. Baldeh

Yero Baldeh briefly lays out a number of very important concerns regarding the transfer of information technologies (IT) to developing nations. Although the article does not delve extensively into any one issue, Baldeh does present a nutshell summary and a warning of possible ethical potholes, doing so specifically in the face of IT solutions offered to developing nations by multinational enterprises.

Introduction

The introduction of new technology gives rise to ethical choices. New technology changes lifestyles, social customs and patterns, the conduct of business, and daily living. Therefore, as part of Information Technology (IT) transfer, we must consider ethical questions.

In this essay I will discuss the ethical issues that arise as a result of the transfer of IT to developing countries.

Ethics and Information Technology

Information Technology changes our work and personal lives, and as a result we all have a responsibility to make sure that it is used ethically. In general, the factors that characterize ethical dilemmas in a computer environment include the vulnerability of computer data to unauthorized change; conflict of interest between the desire for information integrity, confidentiality, and the benefits of information sharing; and unethical practices, such as unauthorized use of data.

Computers pose ethical problems even in industrialized nations. IT has what Turban[1] described as Micro- and Macro- implications. He identified the micro-effects as the effects of IT on individuals, jobs, and the work structure of departments and units within an organization. He identified the macro-effects as the long-term effects on total organization structure,

From *Science and Engineering Ethics* 2, no. 2 (1996):228–30; reprinted by permission of the author and Opragen Publications.

entire industries, communities, and society as a whole. It is the macro-effects that ought to be carefully studied at the inception of a technology transfer process, especially when the transfer is from industrialized nations to developing countries.

IT transfer to developing countries does have some unique organizational, social, and cultural implications which give rise to an ethical dilemma for those involved. Consideration of these issues provides insight into how developing countries should position themselves during the IT transfer process.

Ethics and Information Technology Transfer

Odedra defined information technology transfer as:

> a problem of transfer of knowledge (or know-how) about a number of aspects. These include knowledge about how a particular system works, how to operate the system and develop its applications, how to maintain it, and if the need arises, how to produce the different components of a system and assemble them.[2]

According to Odedra, such a transfer can only be considered successful when indigenous people are capable of operating, maintaining, developing applications or assembling components according to their needs. This can only happen if there is a perceived need for information in the recipient country. This is where an ethical dilemma arises. Should industrialized nations just transfer IT that they want to sell or should they sell exactly what the developing countries need for their socio-economic development.

Glastonbury and La Mendola[3] have indicated that the transfer process to developing countries should be justified on altruistic grounds and, hence, should be based firmly on principles of community growth, rather than on patronage and paternalism. Therefore, it is important that, as IT is transferred from industrialized nations to developing countries, the issues of values and rights should be recognized and represented in the transfer process. This is the ideal situation if IT is to be used within a social and cultural context for the achievement of many human goals.

In recent years, Multi-National Enterprises (MNE) have become one of the greatest agents in the transfer of IT to developing countries.[4] The ethical issue that is likely to arise in such a transfer is the non-performance of MNEs regarding their implied duties for the socio-economic development of the recipient developing country. The MNEs have more to gain by enhancing their globalized competitive position at the expense of the developing countries. I am not implying that developing countries do not benefit at all from the transfer process, but, that the benefits they get from such transfers come at the expense of some values and rights. Some of these include:

Unemployment—Job displacement caused by new IT is an important ethical issue. People lose their jobs and, as Glastonbury and La Mendola point out,[3] the introduction of IT will throw into disarray the skills, training and abilities of many workers, and make previously valued expertise look suddenly obsolete. This situation is even worse if a technology transfer is not complemented with adequate and appropriate retraining.

Reduced role for humans—The reduced role for humans caused by the new IT is another important ethical issue. For example, cultural conventions that normally guide social interaction are frequently missing in computer-mediated communication. This has a significant effect on people's behavior. In the context of developing countries (for example, The Gambia), social hierarchy is widely recognized in the society; and it is common to go to a meeting and observe that group interactions depend very much on the age, gender and the community role of participants. Therefore, the introduction of IT will be a basis for new social values, a new philosophy and new cultural forms.[5]

Development issues—It is more ethical to involve all users in the design of systems. This is particularly true if, for example, as is widely recommended, medical expert systems are used to supplement the scarcity of qualified medical experts in developing countries. Hart and Berry[6] have indicated that each distinct task that the expert system performs will normally involve it in making a decision, offering a recommendation, or producing a justification for an action. Responsibility for each of these needs to be taken by a human being. Therefore, if any technology is to be introduced, the ultimate users should be involved in the process. This is in keeping with my earlier observation that the issues of values and rights should be recognized in the transfer process.

Industrial espionage—This is another ethical issue that confronts people in the IT transfer process.[7] For example, foreigners can come and learn about British technology with the aim of 'spying' and imitating British technology to the best of their abilities upon returning to their home countries.

In addition to the major ethical issues cited above, the following issues should also be considered as relevant to the causes of ethical dilemmas for IT transfer:

- Too much power rests on those who control IT; this power could be used in an unethical manner;
- Potential danger of division of labor and sex roles;
- Creation of large economic gaps among people;
- The individual's privacy is affected, especially when there are no data protection laws, as is the case with most developing countries.

Conclusion

I recommend a framework for the ethical transfer of information technology to developing countries that is in keeping with the Bill of Rights recommended by Glastonbury and La Mendola as follows:

- Developing countries should establish IT plans and policies which take into account social, cultural, and ethical factors contributing towards agreed human goals.
- IT transfer should be supported by education in computer literacy.
- IT developments should take into account the individual rights of people.
- Developing countries should introduce legislation that will prevent unethical use of IT, and ensure that the use of IT is consistent with moral values.
- IT should be made to create equal opportunities in terms of race, gender, and disability.
- Industrialized nations should adopt open IT transfer processes as a form of international aid, and not for market expansion.

Notes

1. Turban, E. (1992) *Decision Support and Expert Systems: Management Support Systems*, Macmillan, London.
2. Odedra, M. (1990) *Transfer of Information Technology to Developing Countries: Three Case Studies—Kenya, Zimbabwe and Zambia*, London School of Economics PhD Thesis.
3. Glastonbury, B. & La Mendola, W. (1992) *The Integrity of Intelligence: A Bill of Rights for the Information Age*, St. Martin's Press, London.
4. Menzler-Hokkanen, I. (1995) Multi-National Enterprises and Technology Transfer, *International Journal of Technology Management*, **10** Nos 2/3: 293–310.
5. Kallman, E. & Grillo, J. (1993) *Ethical Decision-making and Information Technology: An Introduction with Cases*, McGraw-Hill, NY, USA.
6. Hart, A. & Berry, D. (1990) *Expert Systems: Human Issues*, Chapman & Hall, London.
7. Macdonald, S. (1992) Nothing either good or bad: Industrial espionage and technology transfer, *International Journal of Technology Management* **8** Nos 1/2: 95–105.

Selected Bibliography for Section Two

Journal Articles and Anthology Contributions

Artz, John M. "Computers and the Quality of Life." *Computers and Society* 25, no. 3 (September 1995): 17–20.

Beard, Joseph. "Casting Call at Forest Lawn: The Digital Resurrection of Deceased Entertainers—A 21st Century Challenge for Intellectual Property Law." *High Technology Law Journal* 8, no. 1 (1993): 101–195.

Berry, Wendell. "Why I Am Not Going to Buy a Computer." In *What Are People For?* North Point Press, 1990.

Bromberg, Heather. "Are MUDs Communities? Identity, Belonging and Consciousness in Virtual Worlds." In *Cultures of Internet: Virtual Spaces, Real Histories, Living Bodies.* Edited by Rob Shields. Sage Publications, 1996.

Caruso, Denise. "Critics are Picking Apart a Professor's Study That Linked Internet Use to Loneliness and Depression." *New York Times*, 14 September 1998, 5.

Davis, Tim. "Focus on Computers and the Poor: A Brand New Poverty." *CPSR Newsletter* 11, no. 3 (1993).

Kling, Rob. "The Seductive Equation of Technological Progress with Social Progress." In *Computerization and Controversy: Value Conflicts and Social Choices.* 2d ed. Edited by Rob Kling. Academic Press, 1996.

Kraut, Robert, et al. "Internet Paradox: A Social Technology That Reduces Social Involvement and Psychological Well-Being?" *American Psychologist* 53, no. 9 (1998): 1017–31.

Kushmerick, Nicholas. "Software Agents and Their Bodies." *Minds and Machines* 7, no 2 (1997): 227–47.

Sander, Fred. "Couples Group Therapy Conducted via Computer-Mediated Communication: A Preliminary Study." *Computers in Human Behavior* 12, no. 2 (1996): 301–12.

Star, Susan L. "From Hestia to Homepage: Feminism and the Concept of Home in Cyberspace." Pp. 30–46 in *Between Monsters, Goddesses, and Cyborgs: Feminist Confrontations with Science, Medicine, and Cyberspace*, edited by N. Likke and R. Braidotti. St. Martin's Press, 1996.

Stone, Allucquere. "Will the Real Body Please Stand Up?: Boundary Stories About Virtual Cultures." *Cyber Space: First Steps.* Edited by Michael Benedikt. MIT Press, 1991.

Books

Gray, Chris, ed. *The Cyborg Handbook.* Routledge, 1995.

Levy, Pierre. *Becoming Virtual.* Translated by Robert Bononno. Plenum Trade, 1998.

Smith, Marc and Peter Kollock, eds. *Communities in Cyberspace.* Routledge, 1999.

Stone, Allucquere R. *The War of Desire and Technology at the Close of the Mechanical Age.* MIT Press, 1995.
Wiener, Norbert. *Cybernetics; or, Control and Communication in the Animal and the Machine.* MIT Press, 1961.

Web Resources

Anthes, Gary. Computer Savants: For the Autistic, the Binary World of Computers Could Be a Place to Excel. *Computer World* (http://www.computer-world.com/home/online9697.nsf/all/970414anthes/), April 14, 1997.
CNN Interactive. Paralyzed Man Gardens Again—with a Computer. (http://www.cnn.com/TECH/9705/26/virtual.garden.ap/), May 26, 1997.
Danielson, Peter. Making Pseudonymity Acceptable. (http://www.ethics.ubc.ca/pad/making.html).

Novels and Short Stories

Dick, Philip K. *Do Androids Dream of Electric Sheep?* HarperCollins, 1972.
Gibson, William. *Idoru.* Berkley Books, 1997.
Le Guin, Ursula. *The Word for World Is Forest.* Berkley, 1976.

Films

Blade Runner. Directed by Ridley Scott. Warner Brothers, 1982.
City of Lost Children. Directed by Marc Caro and Jean-Pierre Jeunet. Sony Pictures Classics, 1995.
Nemesis. Directed by Albert Pyun. Imperial Entertainment, 1993.
WarGames. Directed by John Badham. MGM, 1983.

SECTION THREE

Uses, Abuses,
and Social Consequences

For many ethicists, lawyers, corporate and government officials, programmers, and operators, computer ethics is primarily about use and abuse of technology; for them, this section is the heart of the textbook. Since the beginning of the computer boom (particularly the personal computer boom of the 1980s) much literature has been written on issues such as software piracy, professionalism, and hacking. Quite possibly, the reason for such attention is that much of the litigation concerning computer technologies arises from just these kinds of issues. In this sense we can say, paraphrasing George Annas's words about medicine and ethics, that legal issues have preceded ethical ones. Rather than cite case law, however, this section attempts to survey issues of use and abuse from professional, philosophical, sociological, and personal perspectives.

Section 3 begins in Chapter 6 with a look at professionalism and professional ethics in computer technology fields. Program managers, developers, support personnel, and consultants all participate in the institution of professional computing. Michael Hodges, however, argues that though there is such a genre as professional ethics, this designation is not usefully applicable to the field of computers. In slight contrast to Hodges, the Johnson selection, in arguing for a sensitivity to professional issues, such as conflicts of interests and fraud, explains that the activities of the computer professional are intimately connected to societal norms and definitions of professionalism broadly construed. Kesar and Rogerson focus more narrowly than the first two articles on specific kinds of computer-related abuse in the workplace.

Chapter 7 discusses the role of computer technologies in supporting or hindering freedom, with a quizzical emphasis on government and other institutions that may intrude on personal freedom and privacy. This constitutes a wrenching of the control of information away from individuals. While the Ogden article argues for a "cyberdemocracy" to help ensure an electronic interchange free of government interference, Representative Markey of Massachusetts explains why he is pursuing legislative solutions to privacy issues. Elgesem concludes the chapter by trying to define privacy and informational control in such a way as to protect the control of personal information while making centralized, institutional databases feasible.

The issues surrounding ownership and piracy provide the central focus for Chapter 8. Accepting the cross-cultural analysis of Swinyard, Rinne, and Kau to support the assumption that most Westernized college students already believe that software piracy is *ethically* problematic (even though they may still participate in the practice of copying), Chapter 8 contains no articles directly attacking a piracy position (see Kesar and Rogerson in Chapter 6 for arguments against all copying). Instead, the three articles in this chapter give sociological, philosophical, and what might be called "insider" reasons why copying software may be appropriate under some circumstances. It is important, therefore, that readers actively reflect on these positions and confront these arguments with the more traditional Western, rights-based views that support a hard-line on privacy and autonomy.

Finally, this section closes with selections in Chapter 9 that argue the ethics and motivations of hacking (as "cracking" has come to be known in the popular media) as well as the development and deployment of worms and viruses. After Forester and Morrison survey the landscape for us, Spafford argues, in contrast to the claims of The Mentor and "Mr. Jones" (in Spinello's interview), that hacking is rarely an ethical activity, stating that hacking causes harm to both systems and data. The Gozzi piece, which ends the chapter, expresses a concern with the very metaphors (such as "virus") that we use to describe computer problems we encounter. His analysis, as well as those of the others in this section, clearly implies that uses and abuses of computers do have social consequences that can affect the very way we see ourselves and the environments in which we operate.

CHAPTER SIX
Computer Professionals and the Professional Use of Computers

DOES PROFESSIONAL ETHICS INCLUDE COMPUTER PROFESSIONALS? TWO MODELS FOR UNDERSTANDING

Michael P. Hodges

In his analysis of professions and professional ethics, philosopher Michael Hodges explores two models of professional ethics that are pervasive in the literature on the subject: what he calls the "rule-based" (extrinsic) model and the "activity-based" (intrinsic) model. Ultimately, he finds each model lacking. He therefore proposes a more inclusive account that takes the best features of both models, treating them as different perspectives on the same issues. After this proposal, Hodges then turns his sights on computer professionals, briefly arguing that since computer professionals are a group of people with only an object, the computer itself, in common and not a set of activities, concerns, or standards, computer professionals are not themselves "professionals" in the technical or classical sense of the term—like physicians or lawyers, for example. Further, he maintains (in stark contrast to Walter Maner's article in Chapter 1) that characterizing the ethical issues that arise around computer technologies as "professional" ethical issues does not benefit any inquiry into them.

The very idea of "professional ethics" both as a practical activity and as a theoretical inquiry seems to derive from the notion that members of professions, such as doctors, engineers, and lawyers, simply by virtue of being members of professions have duties, rights, and obligations that others who are not members of those professions do not have. If this assumption is rejected, it seems clear that professional ethics can claim no unique status either theoretically or practically. That is, there will be no special

195

grounds for the obligations of professionals, and professionals will have no special obligations in any strong sense. For this reason the above assumption might well be called the founding assumption of professional ethics. I want to examine two pervasive views of professional ethics that accept the assumption but offer apparently different models for understanding, identifying, and grounding the obligations of professionals. It is my hope that a careful analysis of the differences and interrelations between these two models will allow us to shed some light specifically on computer practices and thus computer ethics. I hope to show that the sort of work that goes on in and around computers does not constitute a "profession" in the relevant sense. Thus attempts to discuss many of the ethical problems that face those who work with computers under the rubric of "professional ethics" may be misleading, and the practical attempts to achieve "professional status" by institutional means are misguided.

In general ethical theory there is at least one well-recognized way of dealing with what appear to be special obligations. This view, while accepting the special obligations, attempts to see them as an instance of a more general obligation possessed by everyone. Consider a simple example. Suppose that I promise to provide a paper on computer ethics for a volume on the subject; then, other things being equal, I have a special obligation to do so. I have acquired this obligation by making a promise. Notice that there are two levels of obligation here, one general and universal and the other specific and unique. Each is essential in accounting for my obligation to provide a paper for this volume. First there is the obligation to keep promises, other things being equal. This is general and universal. It is general in that it places no specific obligation on anyone. It does not require, for example, that anyone make any specific promise. It only requires that if a promise is made, then it is to be kept. What is universal is that it applies to everyone. It is only because there exists this general and universal obligation that by promising to provide a paper I come to have the specific and unique obligation that I do. But by the same token unless *I* do make that promise *I* do not have *the* specific obligations. One model, then, for understanding special obligations is the promising model.

A number of thinkers have taken the notion of a promise, or more generally that of entering into a contract, as the basis of professional obligations. The general approach seems to be this: A profession is a social role to which a number of rights, duties, and obligations attach. That is, it can be seen roughly as a sort of generalized job description. If, for example, the university defines the duties of a professor of philosophy as consisting of teaching twelve hours of classes, serving on five committees, publishing regularly and having office hours for three hours each week, then when I sign a contract with the university, I agree explicitly to take on those obligations in return for certain benefits that the university provides. It is important to notice here that professional obligations and rights are in the first instance properties of certain social roles and only secondarily properties of individuals who come to fill those roles. It is the promising or agreeing to the terms that transfers the duties and rights from the role to the individual. Of course, it is pointed out that such promises are often implicit, not explicit. That is, practitioners may not have explicitly sworn an oath of office, but implicitly, by engaging in the practice, they have let it be understood that they have accepted the responsibilities of the position.

Given this sort of analysis of professional obligation, two levels of concern arise: those at the individual level and those at the social level. For the individual the question is what are the inducements that are offered to one who accepts the obligations and what are the specific obligations. A contract situation typically involves a quid pro quo—that is, I do this for you, and you do that for me. The sorts of individual inducements offered for professional service are usually twofold. First, at least rhetorically, is the knowledge that one is performing some valuable social service. For confirmation on this point, see the preamble to any standard professional code of ethics. Second, of course, are the rewards of money and social standings associated with professional activity.

At a social level another set of issues arises. Here the problem of professional ethics is simply the problem of how we should arrange a set of interrelated roles and institutions so as to accomplish a certain social purpose. Thus, to take an obvious example, there exists a social need for health care. The medical profession is a particular social arrangement that is designed (well or badly) to supply that need. The particular duties and obligations that are assigned to various members of that profession are by no means "writ in stone," and in fact, there is constant pressure from within as well as without to change them in various ways. Similar pressures exist within and without computing. Proposals are constantly being made to change the relations between employed computer specialists and employers or between professional societies and their members, for example. All this is important to recognize because it focuses on the conventional and institutional nature of professions on the contractual view.

It is one thing to claim that any society whatsoever must have medical care or computing expertise. Such needs may very well grow out of nonsocially induced aspects of the human condition. Perhaps, it is difficult to believe that we cannot do without computers since we seem to have done so for such a long time, but if we widen the category just a bit to "technology" the claim will be somewhat more plausible. In any case, however, it is quite another thing to claim that the only or the best way to provide for the needs in question are the particular social arrangements in place at the moment. Health care may be a nonconventional human need, but as things stand now, it is not the case that anyone who possesses medical knowledge and who employs it is a member of the medical profession. In fact, it is illegal to "practice medicine" without proper authorization. The medical profession, the engineering profession, law, and the like are all institutional human creations. They are social roles created by societies to serve various purposes for those societies.

Arguments are constantly arising concerning the particulars of the actual social status quo. That is, discussions arise as to what ought to be the appropriate terms of the social contract between professional and the society in which they exist. For example, should professional societies have greater power to enforce adherence to the codes or to protect those who have been fired in the attempt to live by the code? Should the opinions of doctors always override those of other medical professionals, such as nurses? Should the right to practice engineering be limited to those who are registered? And should such registration be on a national or only on a state level? Should we demand licensing of computer programmers?

Many see such debates as the sum and substance of what is called "professional ethics," and given the contractual model, this is not far from the truth. In this view, professional ethics as a study deals with the analysis and evaluation of attempts to fine-tune the system in one way or another. But even here an important distinction may be overlooked. There are a number of issues that have been at the center of professional ethics and specifically computing ethics, such as product liability questions and suits against individuals for product failures, that, as formulated, are not ethical problems at all. They concern the actual terms of the factual questions about what actual social agreements are in force. Such issues are not ethical but legal in nature. What makes these questions very complex is at least in part the necessary admission by defenders of the contractual model that the obligations creating agreements are implicit. Clearly, if the contractual model is to have any plausibility, it must enlarge the idea of a promise to include implicit promises. It would be simply false to say that every professional has made an explicit promise. Even if it were in fact not false, we surely don't want to be in the position of having to determine whether or not a given engineer or programmer verbally assented to, say, the IEEE or ACM code before we could say that he or she is bound by professional standards. Unfortunately, when agreements are only implicit, the terms of the agreement will be most difficult to specify fully. In passing, it is worth pointing out that this problem is a serious limit on the value of the contractual model (although not, as I will argue shortly, the most serious). That is, the model takes back with one hand what it seems to have given the other. The theory offers us what is supposed to be a clear account of the grounds of professional obligation but at the cost of making obligations themselves intolerably vague.

There is, of course, an ethical dimension to the issues mentioned in the previous discussion that needs to be carefully distinguished from the properly legal matters concerning what actual contractual terms are in force. Questions can and must be raised about what the terms of the contract should be. The problems of professional ethics here can be seen as a subset of the issues in political philosophy taken as an explicitly normative discipline. That is, we are here concerned with institutions and their proper construction. As such, however, it is important to understand that we are not talking about the duties, obligations, rights, or responsibilities of any particular individuals at all. We are attempting to define, create, or recreate a social role. To use some philosophical terminology we are interested in rules that are constitutive of a practice of a particular profession.

Perhaps by now you are beginning to appreciate something of the power of the contractual model. Not only does it provide a clear way of grounding professional obligations and with that a clear view of what a profession and a professional is, it also locates the problems of professional ethics in a tractable way. With all this said, it may be difficult to see how we might do any better. My objections to this model derive not from what it, as I believe, legitimately reveals about the domain of professional ethics but rather from the side of the matter that it necessarily covers up. Perhaps the simplest way to bring this out is by way of an example borrowed from philosopher Alasdair MacIntyre. He asks us to consider a situation in which we want to teach a small but bright child to play chess. The child has no interest in the game but loves candy, so we offer the child $0.50 worth of candy for each game played and a bonus for each game won. As MacIntyre puts it,

> Thus motivated the child plays and plays to win. Notice however, that so long as it is the candy alone which provides the child with a good reason for playing chess, the child has no reason not to cheat, provided he or she can do so successfully. But, as we may hope, there will come a time when the child will find in those goods specific to chess, in the achievement of a certain highly particular kind of analytic skill, strategic imagination and competitive intensity, a new set of reasons, reasons now not just for winning on a particular occasion, but for trying to excel in whatever way the game of chess demands. Now if the child cheats, he or she will be defeating not me, but himself or herself.[1]

The point of this example is to call to our attention the existence of two distinct sorts of goods that are attainable by engaging in a particular practice, be it a game or a traditional profession. On the one hand there are those external goods—such as the candy—that certainly may initially motivate us to take up a game or to enter a profession, but there is a quite different sort of good—what MacIntyre calls an internal good—that comes to be appreciated only as the game or profession takes hold of us. The real problem with the contractual model, so far as it is supposed to tell us the whole truth about professional obligations, is simply that it recognizes only one of these sorts of values: external goods. But as MacIntyre points out, if we leave the matter at this point, cheating is always a rational strategy. For the contract model, the question ought not be why there is so much failure to live up to one's professional duties but why there is so little.

There is another way of viewing the nature of a profession and professionals that will provide us with a very different account of the nature of professional responsibility. This is what I will call an activity model. In this view we do not conceive of a profession as a particular social role; rather, we begin with the notion of an activity. Examples of activities would include such things as playing baseball or chess, doing physics or philosophy, practicing medicine or law. Consider for a moment baseball. It is an activity that has a definite nature. There are a set of goals, skills, and standards of excellence, all of which have meaning only within the context of the game itself. For the player many of the rewards of baseball are internal to the game itself. That is, they are simply the occasions on which he or she is allowed to exercise the various skills and abilities that the game defines. Given this sort of characterization of a game, we can describe someone as a "professional" if the internal standards of the activity are his or her own standards. This is certainly not to suggest that a professional is not concerned about pay or prestige, but it is to say that such a concern becomes secondary while the person is engaged in the exercise of his or her professional capacity.

In this view, then, a professional is one who internalizes the standards of excellence of the activity in which she or he engages. In a sense, the person becomes the activity. His or her private motivation is identical with the standards of excellence that govern the activity. It is important to notice, then, that in this view there is no problem of how institutional obligations become individual obligations. The so-called duties of a professional are not seen as a set of obligations to be performed but rather as the occasions for the exercise of the special skills that constitute the activity in the question. If we return to the chess example, the point can be clearly made. As long as the child's motivation to perform well according to the standards of chess is an external motivation, such standards will be seen as burdensome obligations standing in the way of reward. But once the standards of chess have been internalized—once we begin to play the game for its own sake—those very same standards are not obligations to be discharged but the very essence of what it is to play chess. The only issues that arise concerning how to relate institutional obligations to individual ones will be psychological or sociological ones concerning what processes are most likely to cause individuals to internalize particular sets of standards. These are clearly important questions, but they are not philosophical questions.

By the same token the activity model offers a clear account of the ground of special obligations that was the question with which we began. On this view the special obligations of professionals are grounded simply in the fact that they possess special skills, and the standards for exercising such skills define the very professional practice of which they are members. To know what special obligations each professional has, one must examine the nature of the special activity in terms of which the profession is defined and articulate the standards implicit in it. However, it must not be forgotten that such activities are not natural objects. That is, they do not exist independently of human design and decision. Surely the examples of baseball and chess that we have considered make that point quite clear. It should also be clear that, unlike baseball and chess, such activities as medicine and computer engineering define their own standards of excellence with certain external goods clearly in view. None of these factors need be lost on proponents of the activity model.

What is wrong with the contract model, as we have seen, is that it leaves professional obligations explained in terms of and motivated by external goods. But what is right about it is that it calls attention to the fact that the practice of profession is a conventional enterprise. On the other hand, what is right with the activity model is that it makes explicit the immediate and internal nature of goods attained by professional practitioners. What is wrong with it is that it does not focus on the institutional/conventional nature of such practice. It might be suggested that the contractual model presents us with a view of professions seen from the outside looking in and the activity model offers a view of the same terrain from the inside looking out. Perhaps, then, we should not consider the two as competing views of single subject matter. Rather, they should be seen as aspects of a single comprehensive view of the nature of professions.

The failure to recognize the larger perspective just identified has led to the unfortunate development of two divergent positions in many discussions of professional ethics. One group has focused on the centrality of the institutional character of professional practice and thus has been offering solutions in terms of changing the rules governing that practice. Over against this position are those who stress the need for aware, morally strong individuals. These groups have, in effect, focused on two notions central to the Western ethical tradition: rules and virtues. Robert Morison makes the point quite clearly when he says:

> Two broad approaches are commonly employed. The first seeks to control the individual from inside by making him or her a better person. The second tries to achieve the same end by means of laws, constitutions, licensing arrangements and the like.[2]

The more comprehensive view we are now considering should show us that this is a false dichotomy. The good person/virtue view cannot be treated as an alternative to the rule oriented/institutional analysis. At best, each merely represents an aspect of the complete view. After all, what it means to be a "good person" in the conduct of professional activities can be fleshed out and made concrete only by way of an appeal to the practice of the profession. But what that practice is, is in part a function of the institutional rules that constitute it. The "virtues of a professional" depend essentially on the nature of that practice, which, in turn, depends on the rules, laws, and regulations that constitute it. Thus each approach presupposes the other. As Jonsen and Hellegers point out in the context of medicine:

> Modern medicine, then, is an institution that incorporates a profession that practices a technique and an art. The practice remains, indeed, at the heart of the institution, but it cannot be adequately performed or understood outside of it.[3] (p. 134)

I want finally to turn briefly to computing per se to see whether what we have said can shed some light on any specific problems in computer ethics. I shall argue that, as things stand now, while those who are involved with computers may constitute a profession in an institutional sense, they do not constitute a profession in the activity sense.[4] Exactly what is lacking is an underlying common practice or activity that grounds such an institution. A better way to put it might be that there are too many activities here that have little or nothing in common except that they relate to computers. There are users of varying degrees: programmers, trainers, salespeople, manufacturers, Web surfers, venture capitalists, and on and on. No doubt some of these people have professional standing not simply by virtue of their relation to computers but rather as engineers, for example. But what they all have in common is simply a constantly changing piece of hardware. In time, of course, clearer lines of demarcation may emerge, but at the moment not much is to be gained by appeal to the model of "professional" in clarifying the problems at hand. My point is really a simple one. What is at the center of the day-to-day life of many of those engaged in computing is not a single identifiable discipline but an object or group of related objects often called "computer technologies." What these people actually *do* is to carry out business activities such as management, research and development, and sales.

As a result of this, the standards of excellence, notions of success, and internal rewards are not common to a community of computer specialists. What may be excellence at one point will be seen as wasteful overprecision at another. Given this sort of diversity, there can be no community of values or agreement on standards of behavior. Doctors and lawyers, for example, typically remain substantially embedded in technical practice for their working lives. No doubt a few may take administrative positions or choose to establish a business in a related area, but success in medicine does not typically mean abandoning the technical practice of one's discipline. In contrast, many computer engineers aspire to management positions in which their daily practices use computers only in administratively supportive roles.

What this means in terms of the analysis developed earlier is that really it makes no sense to talk about the professional ethics of those involved with computers. That group is only a single "profession" in the most incidental of ways. It lacks the unity of a common practice that is fundamental to the identification and grounding of true professional obligations. Thus, I would contend that many of the ethical problems discussed under the heading of computer ethics are actually problems in business/management ethics, while others concern personal relations in a new medium—for example, chat rooms, e-mail, and other interactions and communications on the World Wide Web. Still others have to do with uses and misuses of computers for a variety of purposes, but little or nothing is to be gained by referring to these problems as matters of professional ethics. Quite simply, the professional components are not essential to them.

Nothing that has been said here should be taken to imply that the ethical problems that arise in and around the development and use of computers are not serious or that their study will not be profitable, both philosophically and practically. Nothing could be further from the truth. The suggestion is only that if we are to make real headway, it is important not to make a false start by trying to situate them within the field of professional ethics.

Notes

1. MacIntyre, Alasdair, *After Virtue* (Notre Dame, Ind.: University of Notre Dame Press 1981), pp. 175–6.

2. Morison, Robert. "Bioethics after two decades." *The Hastings Center Report,* 11, No. 2 (1981), pp. 8–12.

3. Jonsen, Albert, and Andre Hellegers. "Conceptual Foundations for an Ethics of Medical Care." *Ethics in Medicine.* Ed. Stanley Reiser et al. Cambridge: MIT Press, 1977.

4. Of course, there are various professional organizations operating in this area. For example, there is the IEEE, which has a long history and has only recently become more or less exclusively associated with computing.

PROFESSIONAL RELATIONSHIPS

Deborah G. Johnson

This selection is a portion of a chapter from Deborah Johnson's popular textbook on computer ethics. In the chapter Johnson tries to show that professional ethics, though related to general ethical theory, holds a special place in the study of ethics and furthermore that computer professionals have unique ethical issues qua *professionals. Johnson agrees with Hodges (see the previous essay) that computer professionals—unlike physicians and lawyers, for example—do not participate in what she calls the "classic paradigm" of a profession. However, in contrast to Hodges, she does see the need to explore the specific practices of computer professionals from a quasi-professional angle, noting that computer professionals are beholden to employers and clients in ways that create important ethical concerns. Excerpted here are analyses of several different kinds of relationships in which computer professionals may find themselves as part of their common practices.*

Scenario 3.1: Conflicting Loyalties

Carl Babbage is an experienced systems designer. He has been working for the Acme Software Company for over three years. Acme develops and sells computer hardware and software. It does this both by designing and marketing general purpose systems and by contracting with companies and government agencies to design systems for their exclusive use.

During the first two years that Carl worked for Acme, he worked on software that Acme was developing for general marketing. A year ago, however, he was reassigned to work on a project under contract with the U.S. Defense Department. The project involves designing a system that will monitor radar signals and launch nuclear missiles in response to these signals.

Carl initially had some reluctance about working on a military project, but he put this out of his mind because the project seemed challenging and he knew that if he did not work on it, someone else would. Now, however, the project is approaching completion and Carl has some grave reservations about the adequacy of the system. He is doubtful about the system's capacity for making fine distinctions (for example, distinguishing between a small aircraft and a missile) and the security of the mechanism that can launch missiles (for example, it may be possible for unauthorized individuals to get access to the controls under certain circumstances). Carl expressed his concern to the project director but she dismissed these concerns quickly, mentioning that Acme is already behind schedule on the project and has already exceeded the budget that they had agreed to with the Defense Department.

Carl feels that he has a moral responsibility to do something, but he doesn't know what to do. Should he ask for reassignment to another project? Should he go to executives in Acme and tell them of his concerns? It is difficult to imagine how they will respond. Should he talk to someone in the Defense Department? Should he go to newspaper or TV reporters and "blow the whistle"? If he does any of these things, he is likely to jeopardize his job. Should he do nothing?

Scenario 3.2: System Security

After getting an undergraduate degree in computer science, Diane Jones was hired by a large computer company. She initially worked as a programmer, but over the years she was promoted to technical positions with increasing responsibility. Three years ago she quit her job and started her own consulting business. She has been so successful that she now has several people working for her.

At the moment, Diane is designing a database management system for the personnel office of a medium-sized company that manufactures toys. Diane has involved the client in the design process, informing the CEO, the director of computing, and the director of personnel about the progress of the system and giving them many opportunities to make decisions about features of the system. It is now time to make decisions about the kind and degree of security to build into the system.

Diane has described several options to the client, and the client has decided to opt for the least secure system because the system is going to cost more than they planned. She believes that the information they will be storing is extremely sensitive, because it will include performance evaluations, medical records for filing insurance claims, and salaries. With weak security, it may be possible for enterprising employees to figure out how to get access to these data, not to mention the possibilities for on-line access from hackers. Diane feels strongly that the system should be much more secure.

She has tried to explain the risks to her client, but the CEO, director of computing, and director of personnel are all willing to accept a system

with little security. What should she do? For example, should she refuse
to build the system as they request?

Scenario 3.3: Conflict of Interest

Marvin Miller makes a living as a private consultant. Small businesses hire him to advise them about their computer needs. Typically, a company asks him to come in, examine the company's operations, evaluate its automation needs, and make recommendations about the kind of hardware and software that it should purchase.

Recently, Marvin was hired by a small, private hospital, which was particularly interested in upgrading the software used for patient records and accounting. The hospital asked Marvin to evaluate proposals they had received from three software companies, each of which offered a system that could be modified for the hospital's use. Marvin examined the offers carefully. He considered which system would best meet the hospital's needs, which company offered the best services in terms of training of staff and future updates, which offered the best price, and so on. He concluded that Tri-Star Systems was the best alternative for the hospital, and he recommended this in his report, explaining his reasons for drawing this conclusion.

What Marvin failed to mention (at any time in his dealings with the hospital) was that he is a silent partner (a co-owner) in Tri-Star Systems. Was this unethical? Should Marvin have disclosed the fact that he has ties to one of the software companies? . . .

Professional Relationships

When they take jobs, computer professionals typically enter into relationships with one or several of the following: (1) employers, (2) clients, (3) co-professionals (or the profession as a whole), and (4) the public.

EMPLOYER-EMPLOYEE

When a person accepts a job in an organization, he or she enters into a relationship with an employer. Although many conditions of this relationship will be made explicit when the employee is hired (job title and associated responsibilities, salary, hours of work), many conditions will not be mentioned. Some are not mentioned since they are specified by law (for example, an employee may not be required to do anything illegal); they are assumed by both parties. Some aspects of the relationship may be

negotiated through a union (for example, that employees with more seniority cannot be laid off before employees with less seniority). Yet many
other conditions of the relationship will not be mentioned because neither party has an interest in them at the moment, because no one can anticipate all the situations that may arise, and probably because it is better
not to press the uncertainties of some aspects of employer-employee relations. For example, when you accept a job, do you, thereby, agree to work
overtime whenever your supervisor requests it? If you work for a local
government and it gets into financial trouble, will you accept your salary
in script? Do you agree never to speak out publicly on political issues that
may affect your employer? Do you agree to a dress code?

When one examines the moral foundation of the employer-employee
relationship, it appears to be a contractual relationship. Each party agrees
to do certain things in exchange for certain things. Generally, the employee agrees to perform certain tasks and the employer agrees to pay com-
pensation and provide the work environment. Since the relationship is
contractual in character, we may think of it as fulfilling the requirements
of the categorical imperative. Each party exercises his or her autonomy in
consenting to the terms of the contract, since each party is free to refuse
to enter into the contract.

According to the categorical imperative, each individual should be
treated with respect and never used merely as a means; thus it is wrong for
either the employer or the employee to exploit the other. This means,
among other things, that each party must be honest. An employee must be
honest with her employer about her qualifications for the job and must
do the work promised. Otherwise, she is simply using the employer to get
what she wants without respecting the employer's interests. Likewise, the
employer must pay a decent wage and must be honest with the employee
about what she will be expected to do at work.

Workplace hazards illustrate the potential for exploitation here. If
your employer says nothing about the dangers involved in a job and simply offers you a big salary and good benefits, making the job so attractive
that it is hard to turn down, then the employer has not treated you with
respect. He or she has not recognized you as an end in yourself, with interests of your own and the capacity to decide what risks you will or will
not take. Your employer has kept important information from you in order
to ensure that you will do what he or she wants. You are used merely as a
means to what your employer wants. On the other hand, if your employer
explains that you will be exposed to toxic substances at work and explains
that this will increase the likelihood of your developing cancer, then if
you agree to take the job, your employer has not exploited you.

For professional ethics, one of the most difficult areas of the employer-
employee relationship has to do with what one rightfully owes an employer
in the name of loyalty (or what an employer can rightfully expect or demand

of an employee). Although loyalty is generally thought to be a good thing, closer examination reveals that it has both a good side and a bad. In her analysis of loyalty, Marcia Baron describes several negative effects of loyalty.[1] Loyalty is bad because (1) it invites unfairness, (2) it eschews reliance on good reasons, and (3) it invites irresponsibility. For example, if I am responsible for hiring a new employee and I, out of loyalty, choose my friend without considering the qualifications and experience of all other applicants, I have not treated the other applicants fairly. I have not used good reasons in making the decision; hence, I have acted irresponsibly in my position.

On the other hand, Baron points out that loyalty is a good thing because it allows us to have special relationships that are extremely valuable. Parenting and friendship are two powerful examples. Being a parent means treating certain people in special ways. If I were obligated to use my time and resources to help all children equally (that is, if "my" children had no special claims to my care and attention), then the idea that I was someone's parent would be without meaning. It is the same with friendship. If I treated my friends exactly as I treat all other persons, it would be hard to understand what it means to have a friend.

Both the good and bad implications of loyalty come into play in employer-employee relationships. Organizations could probably not function unless individuals recognize that they owe something special to their employers. Having individuals that will take orders and make efforts to coordinate their activities with others allows organizations to accomplish things that could not be accomplished otherwise. Hence, a certain degree of loyalty to an employer seems necessary and even worthy.

Nevertheless, we should not jump to the conclusion that employees owe their employers whatever they demand in the name of loyalty. There are limits. The hard part, of course, is to figure out where to draw the line. Clearly employers cannot demand every form of behavior that will serve the interests of the company. For example, companies have been known to pressure employees to vote in public elections for candidates who the company believes will further the company's interests. Such pressure threatens an employee's right as a citizen to vote as he or she sees fit. Indeed, it threatens democracy. Companies have also been known to expect their employees to buy only company products, that is, nothing made by a competitor. This expectation, especially when coupled with sanctions against those who do not comply, seems to overstep the bounds of legitimate employer expectations.

Trade secrecy is one area where the line is particularly difficult to draw. While employers have a legal right to expect their employees to keep trade secrets, it is unclear to what extent they should be allowed to go to protect their legitimate secrets. Trade secrets often involve information about the design of a new product, a formula, or a computer algorithm.

Employers fear that employees may reveal these secrets to competitors, especially when they leave the company. Typically, employers have employees sign agreements promising not to reveal secrets.

Sometimes employees are even expected to agree not to work in the same industry for a certain period of time after they leave the company. Needless to say, employees often want to move on to another job and their best opportunities are likely to be, if not in the same industry, at least doing the same kind of work. Employees learn a great deal of what might be called "generic" knowledge while working at a company. It is not considered wrong for employees to take this knowledge with them to their next job. It is this knowledge and experience, in fact, that makes an employee attractive to another company. Still, employers have been known to try to prevent employees from moving on for fear that the employee will inadvertently, even if not intentionally, reveal valuable information to competitors. So the employer's legitimate concern about a trade secret has to be balanced against the right of an employee to work where he or she wants. Employers can abuse their rights by trying to stop their competitors from hiring a good employee.

The employer-employee relationship is more complicated and less well defined than you might expect. Employees do incur special responsibilities to their employers, but there are limits to this. The Carl Babbage scenario at the beginning of this chapter illustrates the point clearly enough. We cannot say that Babbage has no responsibilities to Acme. If he were to blow the whistle, a great deal of damage could be done to the company, and the damage would be done even if his concerns turned out to be wrong. On the other hand, it is hard to say that out of loyalty to the company he should do nothing. What he owes the company and when he should "break ranks" is not easy to figure out. (We will see more on this later.)

CLIENT-PROFESSIONAL

The Carl Babbage scenario can also be understood to involve a conflict between an employee's responsibility to his employer and his responsibility to a client. The client in this case is the Defense Department, and technically it is Acme's client, only indirectly Babbage's. The Defense Department has entrusted its project to Acme, and it would seem that to be true to this trust, Acme should inform its client of the unanticipated problems. The problem here, of course, is that Acme does not appear to be behaving well, which creates the problem for Babbage. Babbage is expected by Acme to use the channels of authority in the organization. One can think of Acme's organizational structure as a mechanism for managing its responsibilities. Babbage has tried to work through this structure but it has not worked.

In both the Diane Jones scenario and the Marvin Miller scenario, the layers of bureaucracy are removed so that there is a more direct client-professional relationship. These are, perhaps, the better cases to use when first thinking through the character of client-professional relationships.

As with the employer-employee relationship, the client-professional relationship can be thought of as essentially contractual. Each party provides something the other wants, and both parties agree to the terms of the relationship: what will be done, how long it will take, how much the client will pay, where the work will be done, and so on. The important thing to keep in mind about client-professional relationships is the disparity in knowledge or expertise of the parties.

The client seeks the professional's special knowledge and expertise, but because the client does not himself possess that knowledge, he must depend on the professional. "Trust" is the operative term here. The client needs the professional to make or help make decisions that may be crucial to the client's business, and he must trust that the professional will use his or her knowledge competently, effectively, and efficiently. This is true of doctor-patient, lawyer-client, architect-client, and teacher-student relationships, as well as in relationships between computer professionals and clients.

Different models have been proposed for understanding how this disparity in professional-client relationships should be handled. Perhaps the most important are (1) agency, (2) paternalism, and (3) fiduciary.[2]

Briefly, on the *agency* model, the professional is to act as the agent of the professional and simply implement what the client requests. Here the implication is that the client retains all decision-making authority. The professional may make decisions but they are minor, that is, they are simply implications of the client's choice. I call a stockbroker, tell her what stocks I want to buy, how many, and at what price and she executes the transaction. She is my agent.

Some client-professional relationships are like this, but the problem with this model is that it does not come to grips with the special knowledge or expertise of the professional. Often the professional has knowledge that reflects back on what the client ought to be deciding. Professional advice is needed not just to implement decisions but to help make the decisions.

At the opposite extreme is the *paternalistic* model. Here the client transfers all decision-making authority to the professional, who acts in the interests of the client, making decisions that he believes will benefit the client. This model clearly recognizes the special expertise of the professional, so much so that the client has little "say." We used to think of the doctor-patient relationship on this model. I would go to a doctor, report my symptoms, and the rest was up to the doctor, who would decide what I needed and prescribe the treatment. I would simply be expected to accept what the doctor prescribed. How could I question the doctor's authority when I didn't have the expert knowledge? The problem, however, with this model of client-professional relationships is that it expects the client to turn over all autonomy to the professional and cease to be a decision maker. The client must place himself at the complete mercy of the professional.

The third model attempts to understand client-professional relationships as those in which both parties have a role and are working together. Clients retain decision-making authority but make decisions on the basis of information provided by the professional. This is called the *fiduciary* model, fiduciary implies trust. On this model both parties must trust one another. The client must trust the professional to use his or her expert knowledge and to think in terms of the interest of the client, but the professional must also trust that the client will give the professional relevant information, will listen to what the professional says, and so on. Decision making is shared.

On the fiduciary model, computer professionals serving clients will have the responsibility to be honest with clients about what they can and can't do, to inform them about what is possible, to give them realistic estimates of time and costs for their services, and much more. They will also have the responsibility to give clients the opportunity to make decisions about the parameters of the software or hardware they will get. Diane Jones seems to be working on the assumption of this sort of relationship in that she has informed her client of the possibilities and has made a recommendation. The problem now is that she doesn't think they are making the right decision. The fiduciary model would seem to call upon her to go back to her client and try to explain. It is hard to say what she should do if she is unsuccessful at convincing them. What is clear is that she owes her clients the benefits of her judgment.

In the Marvin Miller scenario, we see a computer professional doing something that threatens to undermine the trust that is so important to client-professional relationships. Miller has allowed himself to enter into a conflict-of-interest situation. His client—the hospital—expects him to exercise professional judgment on behalf of (in the interest of) the hospital. Although Miller may think he will be able to evaluate the offers made by each software company objectively, he has an interest in one of those companies that could affect his judgment. If representatives of the hospital find out about this, they might well conclude that Miller has not acted in the hospital's best interest. Even if Miller recommends that the hospital buy software from another company (not Tri-Star), there is the possibility that Miller's judgment has been distorted by his "bending over backward" to treat the other companies fairly. In that case, the hospital would not have gotten the best system either.

Imperative 1.3 of the 1992 Association for Computer Machinery (ACM) Code of Ethics specifies that an ACM member will "be honest and trustworthy." Included in the discussion of this imperative in the

Guidelines to the Code is the statement: "A computer professional has a duty to be honest about his or her own qualifications, and about any circumstances that might lead to conflicts of interest." Rules of this kind recognize that clients (and the public) will lose confidence in a profession if they observe members abusing their roles. Indeed, in some professions, it is considered wrong for members to enter into any relationship that has even the appearance of a conflict of interest.

SOCIETY-PROFESSIONAL

When professionals exercise their skill and act in their professional roles, their activities may affect others who are neither employers nor clients. For example, you may design a computer system that will be used in a dangerous manufacturing process. Use of the system may put workers at risk or it may put residents in the neighborhood of the plant at risk. Or you might simply design a database for an insurance company, where the security of the system has implications for those who are insured. Because the work of computer professionals has these potential effects, computer professionals have a relationship with those others who may be affected.

This relationship is to a certain extent governed by law. That is, regulatory laws setting safety standards for products and construction are made in order to protect the public interest. But the law does not and cannot possibly anticipate all the effects that the work of professionals may have. At the same time professionals, including computer professionals, are often in the best position to see what effects their work will have or to evaluate the risks involved. Carl Babbage, for example, because of his expertise and familiarity with the system being designed, is in a better position than anyone outside of Acme to know whether or not the missile detecting system needs further evaluation.

The relationship between professionals and the individuals indirectly affected by their work can also be understood as contractual in nature, at least if we think of those affected as "society." Some of the sociological and philosophical literature on professions suggests that we understand each profession as having a social contract with society.[3] According to these accounts, we should think of society as granting the members of a profession (or the profession as a whole) the right to practice their profession (sometimes with special privileges) in exchange for their promise to practice the profession in ways that serve society, or, at least, in ways that do not harm society. This means maintaining professional standards and looking out for the public good. On this model, both parties give something and receive something in the exchange. Society gives professionals the right to practice and other forms of support and receives the benefits of having such professionals. Professionals receive the right to practice and other forms of societal support (protection of law, access to educational systems, and so on) and in exchange take on the burden of responsibility for managing themselves so as to serve the public interest. If a profession were not committed to public good, it would be foolish for society to allow members to practice.

The social contract account provides a useful framework for thinking about the ways in which computer professionals might organize themselves in the future, but it seems somewhat ill suited for understanding the field of computing as it is now constituted. That is, there is presently no single, formal organization of computer professionals that is recognized by government as having the right to issue licenses or set standards in the field of practice, and these are the most salient (and potent) aspects of a social contract.

We might better account for the responsibility of computer professionals to society by returning to the idea of their possessing special knowledge and skills, and the power of positions. What distinguishes computer professionals from others is their knowledge of how computers work, what computers can and cannot do, and how to get computers to do things. This knowledge, one might insist, carries with it some responsibility. When one has knowledge, special knowledge, one has a responsibility to use it for the benefit of humanity or, at least, not to the detriment of humanity. Special knowledge coupled with the power of position means that computer professionals can do things in the world that others cannot. Thus, they have greater responsibility than others.

The only problem with this account is that it simply asserts a correlation between knowledge and responsibility. The correlation is left as a primitive with no explanation. Thus, we cannot help but ask, why does responsibility come with knowledge? Why does it have to be so?

One way to establish this correlation between knowledge and responsibility is to base it on a principle of ordinary morality. Kenneth Alpern argues that the edict "Do no harm" is a fundamental principle of ordinary morality that no one will question.[4] He has to qualify the principle somewhat so that it reads, "Other things being equal, one should exercise due care to avoid contributing to significantly harming others." He then adds a corollary, which he calls the corollary of proportionate care: "Whenever one is in a position to contribute to greater harm or when one is in a position to play a more critical part in producing harm than is another person, one must exercise greater care to avoid so doing."

Focusing on engineers, Alpern then argues that while engineers are no different from anybody else in having the responsibility to avoid contributing to significant harm, they are different in that they are in positions (because of their work) in which they can do more harm than others. Thus, they have a responsibility to do more, to take greater care.

All of this seems to apply to computer professionals—at least, to many of them. Computer professionals are often in positions to use their expertise to contribute to projects that have the potential to harm others, as in the case of Carl Babbage. Since they act in ways that have the potential to do more harm, they have greater responsibility.

So Alpern's account does apply to computer professionals. The only problem is that if he is right, then it is not just computer professionals that bear responsibility but all those who contribute to projects with the potential to harm. Employed computer professionals can argue that they do not have nearly as much power as corporate managers, CEOs, or anyone above them in an organizational hierarchy. Alpern's proportionality thesis implies that the greater one's power, the greater one's responsibility. Of course, this need not be an either/or matter. Everyone, on Alpern's account, bears some responsibility, and so computer professionals bear their share of the responsibility along with managers and executives.[5]

Alpern's account is not exactly, then, an account of professional ethics but simply an account of the social responsibility of persons. Persons are responsible in proportion to their contribution to harm. Computer professionals are more powerful than some—in virtue of their knowledge and positions—and less powerful than others. They may not bear all the responsibility for a project, but they bear responsibility in proportion to their contribution.

Of course, to say that computer professionals have responsibility as persons and not as professionals is not to say that this is how it should be or has to be. Computer professionals might organize themselves in ways that create a stronger social responsibility and make the profession more of a "profession." They might take on a greater burden of responsibility in exchange for greater autonomy, which they might seek both as an organized professional group and as individual practitioners.

Throughout this chapter there have been hints about the kinds of things that computer professionals might do to bring this about. For example, creation of a professional organization with a code of conduct and a set of standards both for admission to the profession and for practice would be enormously helpful. Such an organization might have the power to grant licenses and to expel (or at least censure) individuals who engage in substandard behavior. The code of conduct would have to make clear the profession's commitment to public safety and welfare, and individuals might be required to take an oath to abide by the code before they are admitted to the profession. These actions would define the parameters of the social contract between society and computer professionals and make computing a distinctive, self-regulating field of endeavor.

PROFESSIONAL-PROFESSIONAL

Many professionals believe that they have obligations to other members of their profession. For example, professionals are often reluctant to criticize one another publicly, and they often help one another in getting jobs or in testifying at hearings when one of them is being sued. However, whether or not such behavior can be justified as a moral obligation is controversial.

It seems that the special treatment one professional gives to another may at times be good and at other times not. The earlier discussion of loyalty is relevant here. If one of your co-professionals is an alcoholic and, as a result, not doing a competent job, it is good that you try to help the person. On the other hand, if you keep his problem a secret, not wanting to jeopardize his career, this may result in injury to his employer or client. Similarly, when professionals get together to fix prices, this may be good for the professionals in that they can demand higher and higher prices, but it is not good for consumers who might benefit from a free market system.

One can take the cynical view that professionals only unite with one another to serve their self-interest, but even this line of thinking, when extended to long-term interests, leads to some constraints on what professionals should do. Every professional has an interest in the status and reputation of the profession as a whole for this affects how individual members are perceived and treated. Hence, each member of a profession may further her self-interest by forming alliances with other co-professionals and agreeing to constrain their behavior. For example, even though some might benefit from lying about their qualifications, or taking bribes, or fudging test results, in the long run such practices hurt the profession and, in turn, individual practitioners. The trust that clients and society must place in professionals is undermined and eroded when members of a profession behave in this way, so that all members of the profession are hurt. Clients become more reluctant to use computer systems and to rely on computer experts.

One way to think about what professionals owe one another is to think of what they owe each other in the way of adherence to certain standards of conduct, rather than simply to think of what they might do to help and protect one another in the short term. Rules about being honest, avoiding conflicts of interest, giving credit where credit is due, and so on can be understood to be obligations of one member of a profession to other members (in addition to their justification in moral theory).

Conflicting Responsibilities

Managing one's responsibilities in the relationships just discussed is no small task, and the workplace is not structured to ensure that they will be in harmony. Issues of professional ethics often arise from conflicts between responsibilities to different parties.

Possibly the most common—at least, the most publicized—conflict is that between responsibilities to an employer and responsibility to society. The Carl Babbage case illustrates the typical situation. The employed professional is working on a project and has serious reservations about the safety or reliability of the product. For the good of those who will be affected by the project, the professional believes the project should not go forward yet. On the other hand, the employer (or supervisor) believes that it is in the interest of the company that the project go forward. The professional has to decide whether to keep quiet or do something that will "rock the boat."

To see why this conflict arises, we can return to our discussion of the characteristics of the work life of professionals and compare the situation of a typical employed computer professional with that of a stereotypical doctor. Perhaps the most striking difference is that the typical computer professional employed in a large private corporation has much less autonomy than a doctor in private practice. Computer professionals often work as employees of very large corporations or government agencies and have little autonomy.

Another characteristic of the work of computer professionals in contrast with that of doctors is its relatively fragmented nature. Computer professionals often work on small parts of much larger, highly complex projects. Their authority is limited to the small segment, with someone else having the designated responsibility for the whole project.

In addition, computer professionals are often quite distant from the ultimate effects of their activities. They may work on a project at certain stages of its development and then never see the product until it appears in the marketplace, having no involvement in how it is used, distributed, or advertised. Doctors, on the other hand, see in their patients the direct results of their decisions.[6]

Because of these characteristics of the work of computer professionals, they find themselves in a tension between their need for autonomy and the demands for organizational loyalty made by their employers.[7] On the one hand, they need autonomy because they have special knowledge. If they are to use that knowledge in a responsible manner and for the good of society, they must have the power to do so. However, insofar as they work for corporations with complex, highly bureaucratized organizational structures, and insofar as such large organizations need coordination of their various parts, there must be a division of labor, and they must often simply do what they are told. Carl Babbage's dilemma arises from this tension.

Acts of whistle-blowing arise out of precisely this sort of situation. Whistle-blowers opt against loyalty to their employer in favor of protecting society.[8] Whistle-blowing is, perhaps, the most dramatic form of the problem. Other issues that come up for computer professionals are more subtle aspects of this same tension—between loyalty to employer and social responsibility or professional responsibility. Should I work on military projects or other projects that I believe are likely to have bad effects? What am I to do when I know that a certain kind of system can never be built safely or securely enough, but I need the money or my company needs the contract? What do I do when a client is willing to settle for much less safety or security than I know is possible?

In the case of computer professionals, because the profession is relatively new and not well organized, the commitment to public safety and welfare is neither well entrenched in everyday practice nor well articulated in professional codes or literature. Nevertheless, the tension between protecting public good or adhering to professional standards and staying loyal to a higher organizational authority is there. It comes into clear focus now and then when cases involving public safety come to public attention. One of the first cases of whistle-blowing to be written about extensively involved three computer specialists working on the Bay Area Rapid Transit (BART) system.[9] The computer professionals in this case were concerned about the safety of the system controlling train speeds. They feared that under certain circumstances trains might be speeded up when they should be slowed. When their concerns were dismissed by their supervisors and then by the board monitoring the project, they went to newspaper reporters. In the same type of situation, more recently, David Parnas, a computer scientist, spoke out against funding for the Strategic Defense Initiative.[10]

Notes

1. Marcia Baron, *The Moral Status of Loyalty* (Dubuque, Iowa: Kendall/Hunt, 1984).

2. See Michael Bayles, *Professional Ethics* (Belmont, Calif.: Wadsworth, 1981) for these and other models of the client-professional relationship.

3. Robert F. Ladenson, "The Social Responsibilities of Engineers and Scientists: A Philosophical Approach," in *Ethical Problems in Engineering*, Volume 1, 2nd ed., Albert Flores (Troy, N.Y.: Human Dimensions Center, 1980).

    4. Kenneth Alpern, "Moral Responsibility for Engineers," *Business & Professional Ethics Journal*, 2, no. 2 (1983), 39–56.

    5. For a fuller analysis of Alpern, see Deborah G. Johnson, "Do Engineers Have Social Responsibilities?" *Journal of Applied Philosophy*, 9, no. 1 (1992), 21–34.

    6. I have identified these same characteristics of the work of engineers in "Do Engineers Have Social Responsibilities?" pp. 22–23.

    7. Edwin Layton, *The Revolt of the Engineers: Social Responsibility and the American Engineering Profession* (Baltimore, Md.: Johns Hopkins University Press, 1971, 1986).

    8. A good deal has been written about whistle-blowing. See, for example, Gene G. James, "In Defense of Whistleblowing," *Business Ethics: Readings and Cases in Corporate Morality*, ed. Hoffman and Mills (New York: McGraw-Hill, 1983); and James C. Petersen and Dan Farrell, *Whistleblowing: Ethical and Legal Issues in Expressing Dissent* (Dubuque, Iowa: Kendall/Hunt, 1986).

    9. Robert M. Anderson et al., *Divided Loyalties: Whistle-Blowing at BART* (West Lafayette, Ind.: Purdue University, 1980).

    10. David Parnas, "Professional Responsibility to Blow the Whistle on SDI," *Abacus*, 4, no. 2 (1987), 46–52.

DEVELOPING ETHICAL PRACTICES TO MINIMIZE COMPUTER MISUSE

Shalini Kesar and Simon Rogerson

This article focuses on the misuse of computers in corporate information technology (IT) departments. Though not necessarily unique to the IT environment, the misuse of computers in IT shops, from fraudulent practices to hacking to virus replication, is acutely felt, since most of the employees in IT are both capable of and affected by these illicit activities. Kesar and Rogerson briefly survey views of the nature of computer misuse and how it might be better managed technically, legally, and ethically.

From *Social Science Computer Review* 16, no. 3 (fall 1998): 240–51. Copyright © 1998 by Sage Publications, Inc. Reprinted by permission of Sage Publications.

Modern organizations widely apply information technology (IT) to conduct their businesses more efficiently and effectively. Indeed, the logical malleability of computers has ensured enormous application of computer technology in the future (Moor, 1985). This has led organizations to become dependent on IT. In spite of the potential benefits that might occur, the use of IT within organizations has resulted in new types of problems. These can range from incompetence, ignorance, and negligence in the use of IT to deliberate misappropriation by individuals or groups of individuals.

The focal concern of this article is to analyze problems related to computer misuse. Computer misuse encompasses a wide range of illicit activities such as fraud, virus infections, illicit software, theft of data and software, unauthorized private work, invasion of privacy, and sabotage. Such illicit activities could vary from simple pranks to serious crimes. This article is an attempt to understand the nature of computer misuse such that necessary management practices could be developed. It argues that to minimize computer misuse, organizations must focus on developing ethical practices. In conducting the argument, ethical aspects are discussed and evaluated. Furthermore, ethical principles are identified that might assist in minimizing computer misuse.

This article is divided into five sections. After this brief introduction, the next section analyzes the nature of computer misuse. The third section addresses issues that deal with managing and controlling computer misuse. The subsequent section discusses the emergent issues and concerns. The final section presents the conclusions of the article.

Nature of Computer Misuse

Based on the report of the U.S. Office of Technology Assessments (1994), adverse consequences of computer use can be classified into two broad categories: nonintentional and intentional. Nonintentional acts arise because of environmental damages, human errors, or analysis and design faults. Intentional acts, on the other hand, can be classified under one of three categories: violations of safeguards by trusted personnel, system intruders, or malicious software, viruses, and worms. . . .

. . . Intentional acts occur when employees within the organization engage in acts that are unauthorized and prohibited. In such a situation, violations of safeguards by trusted personnel occur. This is reflected in a report that shows that nearly 81% of computer crime in the United States is committed by current employees (Brown, 1991). The second type of intentional act occurs when individuals engage in illegal or unauthorized and disruptive behavior such as hacking (sometimes known as cracking). Intentional acts also could occur when malicious software, viruses, and worms are released into computer systems. Logic bombs and Trojan horses are examples of such intrusions. For instance, the damage caused by viruses in the United States was as high as $1.1 billion in 1991 (Oz, 1994).

Intentional acts such as fraud, virus infections, illicit software, invasion of privacy, and sabotage have been referred to as computer misuse. However, in the literature, the terms misuse and abuse often have been used interchangeably. Furthermore, various researchers have propounded numerous definitions for computer misuse. . . . For the purpose of this article, computer misuse is defined as the occurrence of an intentional act, in other words, a deliberate misappropriation by which an individual (or individuals) intends to gain dishonest advantages through the use of a computer system (or systems). Misappropriation itself may be opportunist, pressured, or a single-minded calculated contrivance.

A number of studies have indicated that computer misuse within organizations is increasing. For example, The Audit Commission has been conducting surveys for nearly a decade to provide information about misuse of computers within U.K. organizations. In the 1990 report, based on 1,537 respondents, the commission reports 180 incidents of computer fraud and abuse. In the subsequent 1993 survey of 1,073 organizations, 537 incidents are reported, an increase from 12% to 36% (Audit Commission 1994). Such is the magnitude of concern that in four of the reported cases of sabotage, organizations lost a total of £104,625. Another U.K.-based study of 300 companies shows that there were more than 293 events in 1995 alone (IBM, 1996). Indeed, the problem of computer misuse is not restricted to the United Kingdom. For instance, it has been indicated that the United States faces losses of up to at least $10 billion every year (Oz, 1994). Furthermore, it has been reported in the press that nearly £122,000 was lost because of a hacker gaining unauthorized access into the Agricultural Bank of China ("China Executes Hacker," 1993).

Against this background, the extent of damage that can be caused by computer misuse cannot be underestimated. Indeed, it is an issue of significant concern. Prior to considering the reason for the occurrence of such illicit activities, it is important to understand the different roles played by computers in any fraudulent activity. According to Parker (1976), people use computers to commit illicit acts in essentially four ways. Cases that involve fraud, theft, embezzlement, or vandalism could be identified with one or more of the following roles. First, a situation occurs when computers can simply be an object of attack. In such cases, valuable data or programs are destroyed, and sometimes computers or parts of them are stolen. Examples of such cases are vandalism, malicious mischief, and sabotage. The second role played by computers is where they create a unique environment in which unauthorized activities can occur or where the computer creates unique forms of assets such as computer programs and information representing money. Examples of such cases are fraud, espionage, and extortion. The third role is where computers are used as the instrument of an illicit act. The computer enables the offender to breach security, enter an organization's computer system, and undertake some fraudulent act. Finally, the fourth role is where computers are used symbolically to intimidate, deceive, or defraud.

CAUSES OF COMPUTER MISUSE

This subsection tries to analyze the underlying factors for the causes of computer misuse. In trying to understand and analyze the nature of computer misuse, this article adopts the classification proposed by Backhouse and Dhillon (1995), who focus on personal factors, work situations, and opportunities to explain the cause of computer-related misuse. According to these authors, various research propounded on computer-related misuse either falls into one of the categories or encompasses all of them. First, this subsection begins by looking at an individual offender. This is followed by an exploration of the workplace culture. Finally, opportunities found in the different organizational structures are explored. This is discussed under three categories as described by Backhouse and Dhillon.

Illicit acts that are motivated by greed, selfishness, and individualism inherent in the values of capitalist society can be associated with personal factors. . . . Davies [1990] attributes this to individuals who fear losing their jobs through redundancy, feel underpromoted, or feel aggrieved, whereas Croall (1992) attributes personal factors such as greed and selfishness as the basis for initial motivation for computer misuse.

It is true that personal factors cannot be ignored. However, focusing on individual characteristics of offenders provides only a partial perspective of computer misuse. Therefore, changes in personality must be seen in the context of the work situations. Some aspects of computer misuse can be influenced by the culture of the organization. In particular, management attitude, staff supervision, diffusion of responsibilities, work pressure, and payment systems all can be associated with computer misuse. Research shows that management often does not report cases related to computer misuse or deliberately hides the offenses. . . . This evidence highlights the need to monitor work situations carefully because they can inadvertently promote computer misuse.

Computer misuse often occurs because of the opportunities that an environment might offer. Organizational problems such as lack of safeguards, together with ineffective monitoring and lack of internal audits, lead to illicit acts (see, e.g., Forester & Morrison, 1994; Oz, 1994). This is perhaps reflected in the finding that nearly 61% of incidents of computer misuse have been carried out by employees within organizations, whereas only 9% have been positively linked with outsiders. Therefore, it is likely that some of the remaining 30% have been employees as well (Strain, 1991). The Audit Commission survey indicates that supervisory and managerial staff members are responsible for the majority of the computer misuse. Nevertheless, the reports also show a change in the pattern, indicating that clerical staff members were responsible for 60% of computer fraud (Audit Commission, 1994). Hence, it is evident that potential offenders can benefit only given suitable opportunities where organizations have failed to take the necessary precautions. This explains why offenders find that the rewards of engaging in an illicit act outweigh the risks of detection and punishment (Balsmeier & Kelly, 1996). Furthermore, poor administrative systems such as inefficient password policies, out-of-date technical knowledge, and lack of security software have been cited as the principal weakness by hackers (Lambeth, 1996). Finally, lack of awareness also has been found to be a key factor. Employees at a managerial and supervisory level often fail to understand the high consequence risks that computer misuse might present (Audit Commission, 1994).

Personality factors, work situations, and opportunities are equally relevant in understanding computer misuse. This is because opportunities for computer misuse may be well spread in an organization, but different responses arise from various pressures and working conditions that may originate within an organization or from outside. Consequently, such factors have a profound significance on analyzing issues raised in understanding computer misuse. However, in practice, most research tends to focus on law and its enforcement rather than on attitudes and motivations of the offenders or the cultures within the organization (Croall, 1992).

Managing Computer Misuse

In addressing the issue of computer-related misuse, this article suggests that management needs to adopt ethical practices. This is because techniques and countermeasures that focus on technical and formal applications within organizations are not enough. Furthermore, attempting to manage computer misuse through these two mechanisms fails to recognize the significant moral dimension of these problems. Computer misuse is inextricably linked to ethics; thus, organizations are increasingly interested in sensitizing staff members to the ethical components of their everyday business decisions (Loch & Conger, 1996). To be effective, this ethical consideration must be practical and should address issues such as employee awareness, training and education, and corporate policy.

In light of this, organizations still are trying to cope with the new opportunities, ethical dilemmas, and threats induced by computers. Indeed, with the ubiquity of computer misuse, ethical issues such as privacy and confidentiality are multiplying. In this respect, the focus of this article is to argue that organizations need to consider certain ethical principles at a more pragmatic level. First, relevant measures taken by various organizations to improve their regulations and controls are explored. This is followed by an examination of ethical consideration at different levels within an organization.

COMPUTER SECURITY CONTROLS

To deal with the ever increasing problem of computer misuse, organizations have developed various techniques and countermeasures. Before the realization of computer security measures, organizations were simply concerned with general security such as locks, barriers, and uniformed guards (Parker, 1981). Unfortunately, threat from intentional acts such as computer fraud, hacking, and sabotage is not amenable to effective treatment by simply applying technical approaches. That is because technical applications are mechanisms that are built into systems and need, to some extent, an element of voluntary compliance by all users. Tools, techniques, and various handbooks have been developed to detect and prevent intentional illicit activities within organizations. However, this is not enough given that it is difficult to secure systems in a heterogeneous, networked computer environment (Spinello, 1995).

LEGISLATIVE CONTROLS

Various laws exist that deal with issues related to computer misuse such as the 1990 Computer Misuse Act in the United Kingdom and the 1986 Computer Fraud and Abuse Act in the United States. Computer-related legislation first appeared in the late 1970s. Most advanced nations have some form of legislation that addresses issues concerning computer systems and related aspects. Although in theory many forms of computer misuse could be dealt with using existing legislation, prosecuting people accused of involvement in computer misuse is very hard and demanding in practice (e.g., see the cases of Robert Morris and Craig Neidorf in Johnson, 1994). Computer-related legislation can be helpful to organizations in prosecuting employees only if the organizations have effective and up-to-date records, personnel disciplinary measures, and clear policy statements. Researchers and practitioners alike have begun to realize that existing law cannot easily be applied to deal with computer-related misuse and that additional legislation is required. For example, the Computer Fraud and Abuse Act and other legislation have been criticized for having loopholes and ambiguities (Kluth, 1990).

SHORTCOMINGS

In practice, it often has been found that while developing counter-measures for the threat of computer misuse, the primary concern has been to focus on technical solutions and their functionality (Dhillon & Back-house, 1996). Studies also have highlighted a gap between the use of IT and the understanding of security implications inherent in its use by the employees (e.g., Loch, Carr, & Warkentin, 1992). This perhaps explains why figures representing the numbers of systems within organizations that have been successfully penetrated without detection are startling. For example, the Federal Bureau of Investigation's National Computer Squad estimates that approximately 85% of computer intrusions are not even detected (Icove et al., 1995). There is a clear indication that security and legal solutions on their own are not effective.

ETHICAL CONSIDERATIONS

It was indicated in the previous section that organizations need to focus on controls that consider ethical aspects of IT. It also was suggested that the role of ethics in IT is to provide an approach to problems in which processes need to be examined from various angles (Lozano, 1996). More-over, the study of ethics in technological fields will allow developers to gain more insight into the human element of the systems (Wood-Harper, Corder, Wood, & Watson, 1996).

The concept of ethics has been defined and interpreted by various thinkers such as Aristotle, Plato, and Kant. The term "ethics" refers to a code or set of principles by which people live and involves a process of self-reflection. According to Donaldson and Dunfee (1994), ethics is not a religion and does not presuppose religious precepts. Supporting this view, White (1993) regards this attribute of ethics as a major advantage. This is because ethics avoids not only the authorization bases of law and religion (and their subjectivity and arbitrariness) but also the irrationality that can characterize cultural or personal moral views.

Ethical issues surrounding IT have attracted many researchers from different disciplines (e.g., Collins, Miller, Spielman, & Wherry, 1994; Dun-lop & Kling, 1991). In the literature, many of the computer misuse issues have been dealt with under the realm of computer ethics. The term "com-puter ethics" was coined by Maner (1980) to refer to the study of ethical problems aggravated, transformed, or created by computer technology. Mumford (1996), on the other hand, suggests that "ethics is about making choices . . . Ethical problems do not appear to change very much with time, although the nature of choices and available solutions may take very dif-ferent forms" (p. 20). Other seminal work in this area has been done by researchers such as Moor (1985) and Johnson (1994). Bynum (1992) uses Moor's (1985) adaptation to define computer ethics as the identification and analysis of the impact of IT on social and human values such as health, wealth, work, opportunity, security, and self-fulfillment. This broad definition embraces not only applied ethics but also computer law, sociology of computing, and other related fields. Moreover, it employs concepts, theories, and methodologies from those and other relevant disciplines. Indeed, this provides a perspective that is practical and useful. . . .

. . . An ongoing process is necessary that considers ethical issues both at the formal and informal levels of organizations. . . .

The following subsections consider the role of ethics at the formal and informal levels of an organization. They stress equal consideration of both levels to minimize computer misuse, which is contrary to current organizational practice.

ETHICS AT THE FORMAL LEVEL

The higher the level of dependency on IT, the greater the likelihood that an organization will become vulnerable to computer-related misuse. Therefore, it is important that organizations implement effective and systematic policies. The reviewing and updating process of corporate policy should be governed by the organization's objectives and the level of vulnerabilities. As Conger, Loch, and Helft (1995) point out, a lack of policies and formal rules within organizations is interpreted by employees as a license to do what they wish. Formalized rules also will help in facilitating bureaucratic functions to resolve any ambiguities and misunderstandings within organizations.

Training program. It often has been noted that information systems personnel frequently receive little or no training in ethical implications (Delaney & Stockell, 1992). Training programs at different levels within an organization will help in increasing general awareness and understanding of the potential damage that can be caused by computer misuse. Training programs that include staff awareness and professional development programs could be conducted at both the formal and informal levels in an organization. Such measures will not necessarily reach a definitive conclusion but will alert employees to the risks of computer misuse. Awareness results in alertness in areas where dishonesty, conflict of interest, and exploitation can occur and ensures that employees apply current standards. Controls and policies are of no value unless there is awareness and appreciation among employees (Warman, 1993). Consequently, controls and policies require full support of the staff members within the organization, and checks and controls can be successfully implemented only when staff members support the concept of those checks.

At a formal level, courses could be conducted through seminars, workshops, conferences, and specific user training. Training and development programs that will cater to employees at all levels of an organization need to be established. As Gotterbarn (1992) points out, development programs within computing should include the following: an introduction to the responsibilities of the profession, an articulation of the standards and methods used to resolve nontechnical ethical questions within the profession, and the development of proactive skills to reduce the likelihood of future ethical issues.

Disciplinary measures. It is important that organizations formally implement disciplinary measures as one of the methods of dealing with computer-related misuse. Depending on the nature of the offense, different measures can be taken by management, ranging from a written warning with reference to the existing legislation to prosecution of an employee.

Effective controls. Formal controls within organizations relate to physical access control, systems development, maintenance controls, changing of passwords, library controls, and system performance measurement aids. These controls play a prominent role in the management of computer misuse such as computer fraud. According to Krauss and MacGahan (1979), such controls are not mandated by law or by any external commission or government bodies, but it is the responsibility of management to define, administer, monitor, and enforce controls on employees.

Planning and establishing a corporate policy. The overall corporate policy should be endorsed and promulgated by management. Key issues such as a code of practice for IT security, conduct of employees, regular internal checks, and rotation of duties need to be addressed. It is important to note, however, that controls within organizations will differ because controls and policies largely depend on the prevalent organizational culture.

Professional organizations such as the Association for Communication Machinery (ACM), the Institute of Electrical and Electronics Engineers (IEEE), the British Computer Society (BCS), and the International Federation for Information Processing have been formulating and revising codes of ethics and conduct applicable to the IT industry to assist computer professionals in organizations when facing complex ethical issues. In fact, in the late 1960s, Parker was among the first to assist the ACM in adopting a code of ethics prohibiting actions that undermined corporate and societal support for computer professionals (Parker, Swope, & Barker, 1990). Parker's ACM activities and reports on computer-related misuse were followed by social science research on ethical practices among computer professionals (e.g., Huff & Finholt, 1994). Although codes of ethics have been developed to provide guidelines to computer professionals, the fundamental difficulty with codes of ethics is that there is no guarantee that these will make people behave ethically. Furthermore, the codes of ethics have context-sensitive use of moral directives but can ignore personal and societal issues (Wood-Harper et al., 1996). A number of critics also have pointed out that such codes are not being implemented in practice (Forester & Morrison, 1994). Indeed, technical controls and ethical policies play an important role in minimizing the risks associated with IT. However, it is significant that people functioning within such constraints of controls and policies should be aware of the need for them.

Ethics at the informal level. According to Liebenau and Backhouse (1990), an informal system is dynamic in nature where people have the capacity to meet changing circumstances. Indeed, by sustaining informal systems, organizations can respond to the new threats and opportunities that they might face. Thus, people working in an informal system within organizations have the adaptability and flexibility to recognize new conditions. Organizations need to have both formal and informal systems because the characteristics of an organization cannot simply be represented by formalized rules.

Awareness. The importance of training, awareness, and development programs at both the formal and informal levels already has been stressed. At the informal level, organizations need to address more pragmatic and ethical issues to minimize computer misuse. This could involve the use of existing corporate and departmental means of communications such as videos, magazines, newsletters, and circulars because these can have a favorable effect on employees in the organizations. This not only can be beneficial in increasing general awareness of computer misuse but also can increase awareness of new and otherwise unknown threats within organizations (Warman, 1993). Hence, each method and tool can be used in an ad hoc way to convey issues effectively and to raise awareness concerning ethical dilemmas that surround IT. Nevertheless, some organizations regard this as having limited benefit, and some even regard it as a waste of time and a diversion from the goals of production and profitability (Clarke, 1990).

Monitoring employee behavior. Another step that could be taken at the informal level is to monitor employee behavior. This could be done by managers simply by being observant of and sensitive to any behavioral changes in employees. However, this raises a fundamental question about invasion of privacy. Furthermore, it has been found that managers are increasingly using a new surveillance technology to control worker behavior (Linowes, 1996). In his article, "Computers and Information Ethics," Rogerson (1998) highlights various issues of concern that arise due to monitoring employee activities. Indeed, there is a fine line between monitoring employees and invading their privacy. Perhaps debates concerning IT and privacy will not go away easily. However, according to Liebenau and Backhouse (1990), some issues within organizations should be dealt with at an informal level where bureaucratic procedures can be avoided and management can be relied on to continue to be sensitive to behavioral changes among staff members such as personal and group conflicts.

Discussion

In the previous section, we discussed mechanisms at both the formal and informal levels that can help organizations in managing computer misuse. This will help in developing comprehensive ethical principles to manage and prevent computer misuse. This section synthesizes some key ethical principles that will help organizations in developing good practice frameworks.

Many researchers believe that ethical theories will help in providing a rational basis for making moral judgments, providing guidance, and making decisions. For instance, Maner (1996) uses applied ethics to deal with the ethical aspects that surround IT. He focuses on utilitarian ethics of Jeremy Bentham and John Stuart Mill and on ethics of the philosopher Immanual Kant. Similarly, in her book, *Computer Ethics,* Johnson (1994) analyzes ethical aspects of IT by combining philosophy, law, and technology. She uses procedures and concepts from utilitarianism and Kantianism to address ethical issues that surround IT. A similar stance is adopted by Spinello (1995). Furthermore, Rogerson and Bynum (1995) have developed a perspectives model based on Aristotle's model of ethical decision making. According to these authors, this model will help in the preliminary analysis and decision making of any system development project.

More recently, Rogerson (1996b) also has developed a set of eight ethical principles regarding how computer professionals should conduct themselves. The eight principles relate to honor, honesty, bias, adequacy, due care, fairness, social cost, and action. These principles are based on the ideas of McLeod (see Parker et al., 1990) and Velasquez (1992). Rogerson (1996b) argues that people within organizations need to be aware of the ethical issues surrounding IT. This is because they are responsible for influencing and establishing ethical sensitivity within their organizations. However, in practice, it is difficult to consider each ethical dimension in detail. Therefore, it is important to focus on the key factors that are likely to significantly influence the success of that particular project. Rogerson defines these key factors as ethical hot spots. Ethical hot spots are "points where activities and decision making are likely to include a relatively high ethical dimension." For example, Rogerson identifies ethical hot spots to approach business process reengineering in an ethically sensitive manner (for details, see 1996a). Furthermore, he identifies defining the scope of consideration and the information dissemination to the client as two primary ethical hot spots during project management for software development (Rogerson, 1996b). According to Rogerson, issues such as de-skilling of jobs, redundancy, and awareness need to be considered during software development projects. Hence, it is important that managers adopt principles of honesty, bias, due care, and fairness while working on such projects. Moreover, issues such as awareness and due care can be dealt with at both formal and informal levels, as discussed in the preceding sections. Thus, by using these eight principles, ethical hot spots can be identified so that computer professionals consider technological, economical, and sociological aspects of IT. Although these principles can be found embedded in the codes of conduct such as that of the ACM, identification of ethical hot-spots can be used at an informal level. Once ethical principles and hot spots are established, frameworks can be developed with the support of the technical and formal controls. This will not only enhance critical analysis but also help in understanding ethical issues that surround IT.

Finally, researchers have argued that tomorrow's computer professionals need to be aware of the ethical dimension of IT (see, e.g., Bynum, 1992; Gotterbarn, 1992; Maner, 1980). This can be done by exposing and sensitizing computer science students to ethical dimension of IT (Bynum, 1992). The 1991 ACM/IEEE-BCS report (for a summary, see the joint report in Forester & Morrison, 1994) nominated "social, ethical, and professional context" as one of the nine key areas of the recommended computer science curricula. This educational enhancement is required because in the near future, many computer science undergraduates will create systems that will have an impact not only on people and organizations but also on society in general. As a result, technically oriented students will need to be well versed in the social aspects of computing.

Conclusion

The extent to which computer misuse could cause damage within organizations can be gauged from the findings of the Audit Commission (1994) survey. It revealed a 183% increase in reported incidents of computer misuse. To have a greater understanding of the nature of computer misuse, it is important to analyze the attitudes and motivations that lie behind such illicit activities. At the same time, some computer-related misuse also can be associated with opportunities and workplace cultures within organizations. Examination of such factors will not only help in exposing the offenders but also assist the development of effective control measures.

To deal with the increasing incidents of computer misuse, this article has suggested the need to develop sound ethical IT practices to combat this growing trend. By adopting such management practices, there is a greater chance of establishing ethical sensitivity within an organization. Furthermore, a combination of continuing activities involving formal and informal training as well as awareness and development programs will help in raising and enhancing treatment of general issues related to IT. Such programs should be targeted at all levels in organizations, ranging from senior management, to middle management (both technical and nontechnical), to the IT users themselves. Perhaps this will promote a consensus on controversial issues such as privacy and intellectual property.

Ultimately, adoption of professional codes of ethics cannot guarantee that people within organizations will behave more ethically, just as the teaching of computer ethics and legislation cannot in themselves transform human behavior. However, it will help in reducing the incidence of malfunctions and computer misuse within organizations. As Anderson (1994) points out, professional societies and educational institutions need to set an example for other members of society by taking the lead and addressing the ethical issues related to IT.

References

Anderson, R. E. (1994). The ACM code of ethics: History, process, and implications. In C. Huff & T. Finholt (Eds.), *Social issues in computing: Putting computing in its place.* New York: McGraw-Hill.

Audit Commission. (1994). *Opportunity makes a thief: An analysis of computer abuse.* London: Her Majesty's Stationery Office.

Backhouse, J., & Dhillon, G. (1995). Managing computer crime: A research outlook. *Computers & Security,* 14, 645–651.

Balsmeier, P., & Kelly, J. (1996). The ethics of sentencing white-collar criminals. *Journal of Business Ethics,* IS(2), 143–152.

Brown, R. K. (1991). *Security overview and threat* (National Computer Security Educators, Tutorial Track NCSC, Information Resource Management College). Washington, DC: National Defense University.

Bynum, T. W. (1992). Computer ethics in the computer science curriculum. In T. W. Bynum, W. Maner, & J. L. Folder (Eds.), *Teaching computer ethics.* New Haven: Southern Connecticut State University, Research Center on Computing and Society.

China executes hacker over 122,000 theft. (1993, May 6). *Computing,* p. 1.

Clarke, M. (1990). *Business crime: Its nature and control.* Southport, UK: Polity.

Collins, W. R., Miller, K. W., Spielman, B. J., & Wherry, P. (1994). How good is good enough? An ethical analysis of software construction and use. *Communication of the ACM,* 37(1), 81–91.

Conger, S., Loch, K. D., & Helft, B. L. (1995). Ethics and information technology use: A factor analysis of attitudes to computer use. *Information Systems Journal,* 5, 161–184.

Croall, H. (1992). *White collar crime.* Milton Keynes, UK: Open University Press.

Davies, D. (1990). The nature of computer crime. *Computers and Law,* 1, 8–13.

Delaney, J. T., & Stockell, D. (1992). Do company ethics training programs make a difference? An empirical analysis. *Journal of Business Ethics,* 11, 719–727.

Dhillon, G., & Backhouse, J. (1996). Risks in the use of information technology within organizations. *International Journal of Information Management,* 16, 65–74.

Donaldson, T., & Dunfee, T. W. (1994). Toward a unified conception of business ethics: Integrative social contracts theory. *Academy of Management Review*, 19, 252–284.

Dunlop, C., & Kling, R. (Eds.). (1991). *Computerization and controversy: Value conflicts and social choices*. San Diego: Academic Press.

Forester, T., & Morrison, P. (1994). *Computer ethics: Cautionary tales and ethical dilemmas in computing* (2nd ed.). Cambridge, MA: MIT Press.

Gotterbarn, D. (1992). The use and abuse of computer ethics. In T. W. Bynum, W. Maner, & J. L. Folder (Eds.), *Teaching computer ethics*. New Haven: Southern Connecticut State University, Research Center on Computing and Society.

Huff, C., & Finholt, T. (Eds.). (1994). *Social issues in computing: Putting computing in its place*, New York: McGraw-Hill.

IBM. (1996). *A risk too far: Business continuity—Every manager's responsibility*. New York: Author (in association with Cranfield School of Management, Bedford, United Kingdom).

Icove, D., Seger, K., & Von Storch, W. (1995). *Computer crime: A crime fighters handbook*. Sebastopol: O'Reilly & Associates.

Johnson, D. G. (1994). *Computer ethics* (2nd ed.). Englewood Cliffs, NJ: Prentice Hall.

Kluth, D. J. (1990). The computer virus threat: A survey of current criminal statutes. *Hamline Law Review*, 13, 297–312.

Krauss, L. I., & MacGahan, A. (1979). *Computer fraud and countermeasures*. Englewood Cliffs, NJ: Prentice Hall.

Lambeth, J. (1996, October 17). Why hackers have no fear of facing security. *Computer Weekly*.

Liebenau, J., & Backhouse, J. (1990). *Understanding information: An introduction*. London: Macmillan.

Linowes, D. E. (1996). Your personal information has gone public. In R. Kling (Ed.), *Computerization and controversy: Values, conflicts and social choices* (2nd ed.). San Diego: Academic Press.

Loch, K. D., Carr, H. H., & Warkentin, M. E. (1992, June). Threats to information systems: Today's reality, yesterday's understanding. *MIS Quarterly*, 16, 173–186.

Loch, K. D., & Conger, S. (1996). Evaluating ethical decision making and computer use. *Communication of the ACM*, 39(7), 74–83.

Lozano, J. M. (1996). Ethics and management: A controversial issue. *Journal of Business Ethics*, 15, 227–236.

Maner, W. (1980). *Starter kit on teaching computer ethics*. New Haven, CT: Helvetia Press.

Maner, W. (1996). Unique ethical problems in information technology. *Science and Engineering Ethics*, 2(2), 137–154.

Moor, J. M. (1985). What is computer ethics? *Metaphilosophy*, 16, 266–275.

Mumford, E. (1996). *Systems design: Ethical tools for ethical change*. London: Macmillan.

Oz, E. (1994). *Ethics for the information age*. Los Angeles: Brown Communications Inc., Business and Educational Technologies.

Parker, D. B. (1976). *Crime by computer.* New York: Scribner.

Parker, D. B. (1981). *Computer security management.* Englewood Cliffs, NJ: Prentice Hall.

Parker, D. B., Swope, S., & Barker, B. N. (1990). *Ethical conflicts in information and computer science, technology, and business.* Wellesley, MA: QED Information Sciences.

Rogerson, S. (1996a). An ethical agenda for business process re-engineering. In *Third European Academic Conference on Business Process Redesign.* Bedford, United Kingdom: Cranfield University.

Rogerson, S. (1996b). Software project management ethics. In C. Myers, T. Hall, & D. Pitt (Eds.), *The responsible software engineer.* New York: Springer.

Rogerson, S. (1998). Computer and information ethics. In R. Chadwick (Ed.), *Encyclopedia of applied ethics* (Vol. 1). San Diego: Academic Press.

Rogerson, S., & Bynum, T. W. (1995). Towards ethically sensitive IS/IT projected related decision making. Paper presented at COOC '95. Unpublished paper.

Spinello, R. A. (1995). *Ethical aspects of information technology.* Englewood Cliffs, NJ: Prentice Hall.

Strain, I. (1991, October 3). Top bosses pose the main security threat. *Computer Weekly,* p. 22.

U.S. Office of Technology Assessment. (1994). *Information security and privacy in network environments.* Washington, DC: Government Printing Office.

Velasquez, M. G. (1992). *Business ethics: Concepts and cases* (3rd ed.). Englewood Cliffs, NJ: Prentice Hall.

Warman, A. R. (1993). *Computer security within organizations.* London: Macmillan.

White, T. I. (1993). *A business ethics: A philosophical reader.* New York: Macmillan.

Wood-Harper, T., Corder, S., Wood, J. R. G., & Watson, H. (1996). How we profess: The ethical systems analyst. *Communication of the ACM,* 39(3), 69–77.

CHAPTER SEVEN
Freedom, Privacy, and Control
in an Information Age

ELECTRONIC POWER TO THE PEOPLE:
WHO IS TECHNOLOGY'S KEEPER
ON THE CYBERSPACE FRONTIER?

Michael R. Ogden

Michael Ogden argues that information technology and "cyber-space" must ultimately be under the control of the citizenry and not corporations, governments, or other institutions. Ogden surveys the many federal bills before Congress concerning cyberspace and information/telecommunications. He concludes that the "user-citizenry" of the Net have not been consulted and employed in the task of building the electronic frontier. He proposes a "cyberdemocracy" that would give control to the computer-using population by directly allowing users to voice their opinions through electronic contact with government officials.

Introduction

Today's information technologies are both exhilarating and terrifying. Recent developments have tantalized us with such present and future marvels as the Internet, the World Wide Web, interactive multimedia, CD-ROMs, on-line digital libraries, computer-shopping in CyberMalls, virtual reality, and video on demand. Often, such a list will continue at some length in a sort of exuberant, breathless monologue of electronic technology du jour. Indeed, this digital information revolution—and the concomitant network

Reprinted from *Technological Forecasting and Social Change* 52 (1996): 119–33, with permission from Elsevier Science.

of networks called Cyberspace[1] that has become its popular manifestation—has the promise of offering wide-ranging cultural and educational enrichment even as it holds forth the possibility of heretofore unrealized political empowerment. At the same time, however, the seemingly inexorable encroachment of the Information Superhighway into our social space has introduced us to a darker, perhaps even seamier side of the promised technotopia: a world of malevolent hackers, cyber-porn, and computer espionage, of information overload, info-rich versus info-poor, and the omnipresent threat of "Big Brother Is Watching You!" Worse yet, we could be "sucked into the imploded, impossible world behind the screen" [1] and end up wandering the wastelands of infinitely replicating simulacrums until we really do succeed—as Neil Postman observed—in "amusing ourselves to death" [2].

Due in part to the mesmerizing digital song of the computer pied pipers—and despite the anxious remonstrations of the neo-Luddites—the general public remains enamored with the technology of our newly crowned Information Age [3], though, perhaps cautiously so. This anxious support of information technology, however, appears to be based more on faith than on understanding; believing that, by and large, the positive achievements of technology will outweigh the negative ones. After all, who but a few could possibly understand the esoteric realms of microelectronics, fiber optics, satellites, or the globe-spanning telecommunications networks? Little wonder few individuals feel they have any real control over the technologies that now impose with increasing urgency upon their lives. Thus, crucial decisions about the technologies that are making the dream or a national and/or global information infrastructure a reality appear—at least on the surface—to be made almost anonymously.

Still, the twenty-first century—the Age of Information—fast approaches and much remains unsettled. Obviously, we can ill afford to continue pretending we are naive about the consequences of computer-mediated communication technology. Neither can we afford to be ignorant of the power politics invoked by information technology's application [4]. Ignorance, in this case, is not bliss. In today's fast-paced, interconnected, complex world—made all the more so by information technology-induced change and unrealistic or reckless demands—ignorance is downright dangerous! Our "inability to understand technology and perceive its effects on our society and on ourselves is one of the greatest, if most subtle, problems of an age that has been so heavily influenced by technological change" (page 3 [5]). Fortunately, ignorance need not be a permanent condition.

Roger Karraker's oft-quoted opening paragraph to his seminal article, *Highways of the Mind* (1991), stated succinctly the issues that should still be of concern to every individual today: "A quiet but crucial debate now underway in Congress, in corporate boardrooms, and in universities, has the potential to shape American life in the twenty-first century and beyond. The outcome may determine where you live, how well your children are educated, who will blossom, and who will wither in a society in which national competitiveness and personal prosperity will likely depend on access to information" [6]. Five years later the statement still holds true, but now with increased urgency. In a follow-up article, Karraker further cautioned: "If we create digital networks that *do not* provide for open access, two-way switched systems, affordable rates, privacy, and the First Amendment, we will shortchange the public and harm the public interest for generations to come" (page 19, emphasis added [7]). It therefore becomes a moral imperative that people learn about the intellectual, social, commercial and political leverage presented by participation in the communications revolution that is cyberspace—while the freedom to do so still exists.

This article explores these issues—among others—with the underlying theme or central question being, "Who controls the technology?" The position to be argued here is that ownership of cyberspace as social space or even as political space, resides first and foremost *with the people* and that this is central to achieving the true potential of our emerging Information Society. This article, however, is also a warning. There is a clear and present danger in the continuation of our existing track record of laissez-faire policymaking, in allowing others (business leaders, military brass, technocrats, or even expert researchers) to direct and/or control the language and definition of the electronic frontier. "Make no mistake about it: the metaphors we employ as we create these new digital networks will shape our nation as significantly as the railroads shaped the late nineteenth century and interstate highways shaped the mid-twentieth century" (page 19 [7]). The electronic information revolution continues to smolder inevitably toward flash point even as we march boldly (or skulk pensively) into the next millennium. Perhaps the time has come for today's cyber-citizenry to take up the proclamation, "Electronic power to the people!"

Who Is in Charge of Whom?

Before we delve too far into the politicization of cyberspace, we need to come to an understanding of the technological perspectives being argued in the debate over control of this vital sphere of future human agency. Two perspectives have dominated the debates and influenced futures scenario building for quite some time, while a third is gaining increasing prominence in post-modern discourse; they are, "technology as liberator," "technology as tyrant," and "technology as instrument of power." The first two being essentially two sides of the same coin; namely that of "technological determinism,"[2] the primary difference being either an optimistic or pessimistic outlook regarding the role and impact of technology in society. The third perspective presents a contextual assessment arguing that technology is both a product and source of economic and political power and as such, is neither inherently good nor evil, but an ambiguous instrument whose consequences depend on its social, cultural and political context [8]. . . . [Eds.—See Barbour article in Chapter 1.]

Technology of Politics and Politics of Technology

In the preface to his book, *Making Waves: Engineering, Politics, and the Social Management of Technology* (1995), Edward Wenk, Jr.—first science adviser to the U.S. Congress and adviser to Presidents Kennedy, Johnson, and Nixon—stated that, ". . . in the last four decades technology [has] grown because of government, and, conversely, government [has] grown because of technology" (page xii [9]). Although the government certainly did not build the computer-based communication infrastructure that has become the Internet (increasingly referred to as the Net, or cyberspace), the information technologies and the information industries that have come to play such a central role in its creation were driven forward in large measure by the ideas and people that flowed from Defense Department (under the auspices of the Pentagon's Advanced Research Projects Agency—ARPA) and/or National Science Foundation (NSF) programs and research. As a result, the National Information Infrastructure (NII), a proposed fiber-optic-based digital superhighway, has emerged as the ". . . first great infrastructure project of the twenty-first century" [10] and perhaps the first really new infrastructure to develop in nearly a century.[3] The proposed NII has also become a priority item with the present U.S. Government and is highlighted as being of strategic importance to ensuring America's continued preeminence in information technology well into the twenty-first century.

To facilitate the development of such a network, the High Performance Computing Act of 1991, was signed into law by then President Bush. This piece of legislation provided federal assistance, in collaboration with industry and academia, for development of advanced computer hardware and software, as well as networking technologies needed to route data at gigabit speeds. Following close behind were two strategic planning documents, *National Information Infrastructure: An Agenda for Action* (1993) and *America in the Age of Information* (1994). Produced by the Clinton-Gore Administration, these documents set forth a high level strategy for the U.S. Federal Government's research and development investment in information and communications technologies and identifies areas for strategic focus that are aligned with U.S. national goals.

Today, the High Performance Computing and Communications Initiative (HPCCI)—an outgrowth of the 1991 Act—has become the multiagency cooperative effort under which the Clinton-Gore Administration's strategic plans are to move forward. Led by the National Coordination office, HPCCI became the founding initiative for the formation and operation of the National Research and Education Network (NREN), seen by many as being the necessary first step in the implementation of the NII. NREN, designed to be a 5-year $2 billion project[4] involving three agencies (the NSF, NASA, and the Department of Health and Human Services), is expected to extend U.S. technological leadership in computer communications through research in, and development of, high-speed supercomputing. Such programs as HPCCI and NREN—particularly with their increasing emphasis on enabling broad-based future use of the information infrastructure—have earned the support of the U.S. Congress and of large segments of the American populace. However, the HPCCI and NREN have spurred a heated debate on whether the government should be so heavily involved in the building of the NII.

Complicating matters is the fact that the basic telecommunications law of the land in the United States (the Communications Act of 1934) is over 60 years old; predating commercial television, transistors, computers, satellites, lasers, fiber optics, and cellular telephones. "In light of the dynamic growth and development of telecommunication and its strategic importance, the lack of contemporary and current laws is almost a national disgrace."[11]. The Telecommunications Act of 1996, recently signed into law, is the first attempt to rectify the situation. The Telecommunications Act was crafted ostensibly to advance the public good by promoting competition and reducing regulation. However, in its current form it is criticized as being in violation of First Amendment rights through the banning of nebulously defined indecent communication [12].[5] Furthermore, certain proposed provisions would repeal price controls on monopoly cable and phone rates, and permit greater concentration of ownership. Neither is there adequate public quid pro quo in this Act as it now stands, and despite the threat to veto it, President Clinton signed the Telecommunications Act into law on 8 February 1996 [13].

Despite these objections, the present perspective in Washington, DC remains fixed on the idea that if all unnecessary legal and regulatory barriers are removed (see Table 1 for an abridged list of legislation), then private interests will step in to build the NII. Whereas the basic Republican strategy involves reducing overt government expenditure and utilizing deregulation and tax incentives to foster aggressive, market-driven innovation, the Clinton Administration has envisioned the federal government as an active partner working with business in undertaking research and in promoting innovation. But, from the Democrats' perspective, there's a catch. "For the full economic potential of the NII to be realized, longtime NII proponent Vice President Al Gore argues that *all Americans* must be able to 'connect' at an affordable price" (emphasis added [14]). According to Vice President Gore, the Federal dollars authorized for NREN "... represent an initial, rather than ongoing, investment, intended to spark the development that will create the demand for [the NII] as a commercial enterprise" [14]. In a speech made to the National Press Club in December 1993, Vice President Gore further clarified the government's position on the NII, stating that:

> This Administration intends to create an environment that stimulates a private system of free-flowing information conduits. . . . Our goal is not to design the market of the future. It is to provide the principles that shape that market. And it is to provide the rules governing this difficult transition to an open market for information. We are committed in that transition to protecting the availability, affordability, and diversity of information and information technology, as market forces replace regulations and judicial models that are no longer appropriate.[6]

It would appear, therefore, that for both Republicans and Democrats the end is the same—the only difference is the means of getting there and the determination of who will be included in the process.

Gordon Cook, a well known Net gadfly and publisher of an electronically distributed newsletter focusing on the political and policy issues related to the emerging NII, pointed out that perhaps "[i]t is questionable whether the U.S. government should be involved in the building of [the NII] backbone."[7] Nevertheless, many users of the Internet—the present and future citizens of cyberspace—are as suspicious of private enterprise building the NII as they are of direct government involvement in its construction and/or administration. "Although the Internet as it now exists grew to epic proportions by fostering open TCP/IP standards and protocols, there's no guarantee that the [future] digital superhighway will follow the same pattern. Openness isn't what made Ma Bell rich" [10]. Will business interests, through mega-mergers and leveraged buy-outs in the information industry, turn the Internet to metered services? Will they attempt to control the extension of the Internet to the grassroots of computing—so dear to the heart of all utopian populists—through access pricing? Or, is the present maneuvering by communication conglomerates only the beginning of a process of privatizing a technology that long ago outgrew its government sponsors [15]?

Some have argued that the debate over whether or not the government should build the NII [is] meaningless because the simple fact is, government can't afford the hundreds of billions of dollars it would cost to lay [optical] fiber to every home, office, school, factory, hospital, and library in the United States. Fiscal reality dictates that the creation of the NII will be a joint effort between the government and the private sector" [10]. The Clinton-Gore Administration hopes that by establishing protocols,

TABLE 1 Legislating Our Digital Future in Cyberspace (103rd and 104th U.S. Congress)

Bill: Title	Sponsor	Status	Description
(103) HR 135: Privacy Act of 1993	Cardiss Collins (D-IL)	Pending	Would establish a privacy-protection commission
(103) HR 523: Agency Copyrights	Constance Morella (R-MD)	Pending	Would allow federal agencies to copyright computer software produced by the government
(103) HR 707: Emerging Telecom. Tech. Act of 1993	John Dingell (D-MI)	Became law Sept. 1993	Establishes procedures to improve the allocation and assignment of the electromagnetic spectrum for private use
(103) HR 1312 & S 570: Local Ex. Infrastructure Modernization Act of 1993	Rick Boucher (D-VA) Sen. Charles Grassley (R-IA)	Pending	Would exempt the 1,300 local phone cos. from some antitrust laws to allow them to improve network connectivity
(103) HR 1328 (S 564): Government Printing Office Electronic Info. Access Enhancement Act of 1993	Sen. Wendell Ford (D-KY) Ted Stevens (R-AK)	Became law June 1993	Requires *Congressional Record* and *Fed. Register* to be available electronically
(103) HR 1757: National Information Infrastructure Act of 1993[a]	Rick Boucher (D-VA)	Passed House July 1993	Spurs the development of the applications that will be available over the National Information Infrastructure
(103) S 4: Title VI National Competitiveness Act of 1993	John Rockefeller (D-WV) Ernest Hollings (D-SC)	Pending	Would accelerate the development of NII by funding in conjunction with the private sector, the R&D needed for applications
(103) S 1086: Telecoms. Infrastructure Act of 1993	John C. Danforth (R-MO) Daniel Inouye (D-Hawaii)	Pending	Fosters further development of nation's telecoms. Infrastructure through enhancement of competition
(104) HR 1004: Companion Bill to S 314	Tim Johnson (D-SD)	Pending	Essentially the same as S 314
(104) HR 1555: Communications Act of 1995	Thomas Bliley, Jr. (R-VA)	Pending	To promote competition and reduce regulation in telecommunications and encourage the rapid deployment of new telecommunications technologies
(104) S 314: Communication Decency Act of 1995	Jim Exon (D-NE)	Incorporated as Title IV, S 652	To protect the public from the misuse of the telecommunications network and telecommunications devices and facilities
(104) S 652: Telecommunication Competition & Deregulation Act of 1995	Larry Pressler (R-SD)	Passed Senate June 1995	To provide for a pro-competitive, deregulatory national policy framework for advanced telecommunications and information technologies

Sources: Legislating Your Digital Future (Table), *UnixWorld* (1993 December), p. 60. *THOMAS: Legislative Information on the Internet* (World Wide Web site) Library of Congress, (1995 June) (URL:http://thomas.loc.gov/).

[a]Formerly known as the High Performance Computing and High-Speed Networking Applications Act of 1993.

standards, and test-bed projects, private industry will be encouraged to do the rest (see Gore, footnote 7). However, before the government commits to any policy (including those stemming from the Telecommunications Act of 1996), it must first arm itself with an understanding of the situation at hand and the commitment to seek intervention for redress of private enterprise's failures should such action be warranted. "[T]he [Clinton-Gore] administration must make clear . . . that it will do whatever is necessary to ensure affordable access to the network. It must also help to educate Congress concerning the policy implications behind the network . . ." (see Cook, footnote 8).

There is still much contention surrounding the respective roles government and business should play in the building of the NII. Interestingly enough, little is asked of the public's role—that of the user-citizenry—in the construction and conduct of the NII. Whereas the on-line debates in cyberspace are themselves polarizing over these issues, their discussions remain largely ignored by both the "captains of industry" and Washington's bureaucrats. What does appear certain, however, is that actions taken over the next few years will, in many ways, determine the political and economic structure of cyberspace for decades to come. Perhaps this is where the real challenges surrounding the building of the NII exist, not in its physical hardware construction but in its social construction. It is within this realm that the people's voice must and should be heard. This may come about not so much because of the phenomenal progress in making computers faster, more powerful, and better able to augment the human mind, but because the most important resources on the world's networks are still people [16].

Civilizing the Electronic Frontier—Democracy in Cyberspace

> [A] bill of rights is what the people are entitled to against every government on earth, general or particular, and what no just government should refuse, or rest on inference.
>
> —Thomas Jefferson

Direct democracy was neither workable nor desirable when the Founding Fathers of America set about the task of constructing the Constitution. Over the years, they ". . . have been interpreted as disagreeing sharply and fundamentally about just what should be the right mix of Jeffersonian Democracy and Hamiltonian Republic" (R. Leone's Foreword, page xi, in [17]). The debate between these two perspectives and our present system of governance continues unabated to this day. However, a new wave of Populism, spurred on by advances in information technology, is making mass participation in the political process—typically at the expense of the representative process—possible in previously unimaginable ways. Perhaps it's a sign that the electronic frontier is finally becoming civilized as computerized legislative information, Congressional hearings, speeches and position papers, even political activism, are all putting politics online. If so, then "[life] in cyberspace . . . [could] shape up [to be] exactly like Thomas Jefferson would have wanted: founded on the primacy of individual liberty and the commitment to pluralism, diversity, and community.[8] Electronic town halls, instant public-opinion polling and increasingly sophisticated interactive telecommunications technologies are making the government instantly aware of, and pressured to be more responsive to, popular will [16]. These same technologies are also being heralded as solutions to both bad government and public cynicism by individuals from across the political spectrum. "Through the use of increasingly sophisticated two-way digital broadband telecommunications networks, members of the public are gaining a seat of their own at the table of political power. Even as the public's impatience with government rises, the inexorable progress of democratization, together with remarkable advances in interactive telecommunications, are turning the people themselves into the new fourth branch of government . . . alongside the executive, the legislative, and the judiciary" (page 4, [17]). However, there are still some obstacles to democracy in cyberspace that must be overcome.

Cyberdemocracy [4]—the exercise of democratic principles in cyberspace—implies an electronic form of grass-roots direct democracy beyond that of local ballot initiatives and referenda. It includes the possibility that future governance in the twenty-first century would include national advisory plebiscites, initiatives, and referenda that would impose the public's will directly on government policy, or at least on certain issues of national importance. If cable shopping channels can install ". . . high-speed, large-capacity computerized systems to process millions of viewers' telephone credit card orders," so the argument goes, "[t]he same or similar technology can be recruited to tabulate votes, process polls, and count the results of initiatives and referenda, dialed in from anywhere" (page 153 [17]). Exactly how this will transpire still needs to be worked out; the same technology that is able to identify and link citizens and political institutions to facilitate the conduct of direct democracy—as well as other forms of legitimate constituent participation in the democratic process—could also facilitate nationwide identification systems and increased governmental surveillance [18]. Such issues need to be carefully monitored as government undergoes an inevitable reengineering in its attempt to become more responsive to an increasingly more electronic society. In the end, however, "[t]he question is not whether the transformation to instant public feedback through electronics is good or bad, or politically desirable or undesirable. Like a force of nature, it is simply the way our political system is heading. The people are being asked to give their own judgment before major governmental decisions are made. Since personal electronic media, the teleprocessors and computerized keypads that register public opinion, are inherently democratic . . . their effect will be to stretch our political system toward more sharing of power, at least by those citizens motivated to participate" (page 154 [17]).

Herein lies the dark lining to the silver cloud of cyberdemocracy; direct democracy via sophisticated information technology could also bring with it the inevitable tendency to pressure political leaders to respond quickly—perhaps too quickly—to every impulsive ripple of public opinion and hold the nation hostage to the tyranny of the majority. Such a tendency could fundamentally alter the conduct of government and perhaps even threaten some of our most cherished constitutional protections [17]. Such protections were put into place by the Framers of the Constitution who were as wary of pure democracy as they were fearful of governmental authority. What makes this particularly pernicious is that—in the emerging cyberdemocracy where information is a source of social power— those who are typically the downtrodden (many minority groups as well as the poor) are not even aware that they are on the verge of being disenfranchised. So far, the information revolution has been largely waged by highly educated and informed advocates, people who often have tremendous resources at their disposal. These advocates have spoken quite well on behalf of their own needs; some have even attempted to speak to the needs of the information-poor. But the information-rich, however wellmeaning, have largely determined and prioritized the issues of the information revolution and the emerging cyberdemocracy according to their own visions and realities. "Public or low-cost access to computers, communications channels, and data bases should be sought in [all] schools, homes, libraries, and community organizations" (page 175 [8]) if the promise of cyberdemocracy is to be realized. But information access as a basic public service is broached only tentatively at the national level. Whereas communities with "freenets" can be lauded for their efforts in public computing,[9] the implementation of these projects invariably assumes an information-rich public proactively seeking and demanding such services.

Interestingly, it is perhaps within the most conservative branch of government, the judiciary, that the protection of the rights of the informationpoor may find redress from the excesses of the majority will in our future cyberdemocracy. "As the political system grows ever more responsive to majority impulses, and the legislative and executive branches feel increased pressure to bend to the public will, the judiciary . . . under the Constitution . . . is in the best position to blow the whistle on runaway majorities" (pages 162–163 [17]). In our emerging cyberdemocracy, the judiciary will have the increasingly difficult and sensitive role of protecting the rights of minority groups and thwarting the popular will when it gets out of hand. If our present constitutional system of checks and balances transits into the twenty-first century relatively intact, then future "courts [will] have the ultimate responsibility to stop any tyrannical exercise of power, even by impassioned majorities of sovereign citizens. In the absence of such court protection, it is unlikely that any barrier would remain to protect unpopular minorities from being trampled on by majorities who believe they are in the best position to know what is in their own best interest" (pages 163–164 [17]). Without such protections, it could be argued, direct democracy in cyberspace could degenerate into an electronic Bosnia—albeit a less violent one—where a weak state presides over warring factions battling for control.

Therefore, in our emerging Information Age, it is important to recognize and state outright the basic principles of civil rights and responsibilities that should be imputed to cyberspace. We should not, as Thomas Jefferson admonished over two centuries earlier, allow something of such importance to "rest on inference." In the United States, this means, at the least, the declaration of the applicability of the American Constitution and the Bill of Rights to the issues posed by the advent of new uses of communications and information technologies [19]. The problem of melding old but still valid concepts of constitutional rights with new and rapidly evolving technologies is, perhaps, one of the most profound challenges to the common good yet faced by our society. The meaning of freedom, structures of self-government, definition of property, nature of competition, conditions for cooperation, sense of community and the nature of progress will each need to be redefined. How well we adapt such cherished rights as the First Amendment issues of freedom of speech, press, and association, Fourth Amendment guarantees of the right to privacy and protection from unwarranted governmental intrusion, as well as Fifth Amendment assurances of the right to procedural fairness and due process of law, will depend upon the degree of wisdom that guides our courts, our legislatures, and government agencies entrusted with authority in this area of our national life, for "[i]nformation technology provides us with the key to restructuring our governing system, simultaneously permitting more distribution and new concentration of power. The result may be more equality and more inequality, more cohesion and more splintering, more cooperation and more competition, more democracy and less" [20]. In order to protect the invariability of constitutional principles, despite accidents of technology, policy makers should look not at what technology makes possible, but at the core values the Constitution enshrines—its protection of people rather than places, and its regulation of the actions of government, not of private individuals. To guarantee this, some have advocated the addition of a twenty-seventh amendment to the Constitution which could read:

> This Constitution's protections for the freedoms of speech, press, petition and assembly, and its protections against unreasonable searches and seizures

and the deprivation of life, liberty or property without due process of law, shall be construed as fully applicable without regard to the technological method or medium through which information content is generated, stored, altered, transmitted or controlled.[10]

Ultimately, however, protection of our constitutional principles in the future will depend upon whether or not ordinary citizens are up to the task of making sound judgments about the day-to-day decisions of government in the emerging computer-mediated "agora" of cyberspace. "A key question is whether we should trust the wisdom of citizens to guide our [democracy] into the future. An important insight into this question emerged from George Gallup, who reviewed his experience in polling American public opinion over half a century and found the collective judgment of citizens to be 'extraordinarily sound.' Gallup discovered that citizens are often ahead of their elected leaders in accepting innovations" [21].

Need for Civic Literacy and Civic Competence in Cyberspace

I know of no safe depository of the ultimate powers of the society but the people themselves, and if we think them not enlightened enough to exercise their control with a wholesome discretion, the remedy is not to take it from them, but to inform their discretion.
—Thomas Jefferson

The U.S. Constitution is unique in that it states rather explicitly that power resides with the people, who then delegate it to the government. This idea, central to our free society, is under challenge. We must recognize that technology is a social construct and that the new information technologies have served to bolster the old power structures even as they began to transform them. People must recognize that sustaining democracy in the next century will require their participation and their critical reaffirmation that ownership of cyberspace resides first and foremost, with the people, especially if cyberdemocracy is ever to achieve its true potential. This then begs the question, "[d]o we have the individual and collective will—the unity in diversity—to grasp the nettle and learn, so that we may steer our ship of government through the rapids of change into a promising 21st century?" (page 159 [17]).

According to Lawrence K. Grossman, former president of PBS and author of the book *The Electronic Republic: Reshaping Democracy in the Information Age* (1995), one of the most important implications of "grasping the nettle" and moving to a form of direct "electronic" democracy in the next century is the extent to which such a move would be meaningless—or even dangerous—without a concerned, educated and enlightened public. People must demand and utilize information on what is happening in cyberspace and the policy debates surrounding the deposition of this vital public asset. Jefferson's dictum that the country cannot be safe without information still abides. But if citizens want to exercise greater civic responsibility in the future Cyberdemocracy, they must also acquire greater civic competence in cyberspace.

As was illustrated earlier, technological optimists cheer the potential of the new information technologies to shift citizens from the passive voice of spectators to the active role of participants and decision-makers. Interactive telecommunications have the potential to bring enormous leverage to the average citizen at relatively little cost, not only "intellectual leverage, social leverage [and] commercial leverage . . . [but] most important, political leverage" (page 4 [15]) as well. Vice President Al Gore, himself an optimistic proponent of the potential of telecommunications technology, envisions "an America where poor children sit in front of a television tapping information from the best libraries in the country; where physicians examine patients hundreds of miles away; and where everyone calls up a vast array of newspapers, movies and encyclopedias at the flick of a TV controller" [22].

On the other hand, pessimistic views of technology's role in society seem almost vindicated by their innate distrust of the public's judgment coupled with a rising concern over the concentration of control over the increasingly influential telecommunication technologies. Too much democracy allows an intemperate and ill-informed majority too much say in issues that are far too complex to lend themselves to simple "yes" or "no" votes. The public cannot be trusted to take the time and spend the effort needed to learn about even the most critical issues that directly affect their lives and well-being. Furthermore, in today's world of megamergers and corporate takeovers, there is the threat of a decline in democratic pluralism, "we have [instead] a dominant telecommunications industry, owned and controlled by a shrinking oligopoly of powerful corporate interests, [acting as] gatekeepers to the flow of ideas and information" (page 173 [17]). Quoting John Malone, president of TeleCommunications, Inc., one of the nation's biggest cable operators, "two or three companies will eventually dominate the delivery of telecommunications services over information superhighways world wide. The big bubbles get bigger and the little bubbles disappear.[11,12]

Perhaps, from a contextualist viewpoint, both visions are correct. Through voter apathy and the burgeoning complexification of our political process, we have allowed large portions of public discourse to take place in back rooms, behind closed doors—leaving us with the feeling that we have no control. Likewise, through the consignment of public information assets (e.g., radio spectrum allocations, satellite orbital slots, bandwidth assignments, broadcast and cable franchises, etc.) to large telecommunications corporations, we may have sold our children's

birthright for the triviality, banality, and vulgarity of today's vertically integrated entertainment programming. However, active and responsible
citizens are made, not born. It therefore behooves us to govern ourselves
in the coming cyberdemocracy with the power that knowledge gives. Indeed, cyberspace is the land of knowledge, and the exploration of that land
can be civilization's truest, highest calling. The opportunity is now before
us to empower every person to pursue that calling in their own unique
way. The challenge is as daunting as the opportunity is great. Cyberdemocracy has profound implications for the nature of community and of
individual freedom. As it evolves, it will shape new codes of behavior that
will in turn impact on the development and deployment of new forms of
technology that will continue to transform our lives. For "[i]t is absurd to
want better technologies and a growing economy, yet still call for 'traditional values.' Technology and values are part of the same continuum—you
cannot decouple the two. If you want advances in one area, you have to accept advances in the other" [23].

The conflict between the waning years of the Industrial Age and the
birth of the Information Age is perhaps one of the central political tensions cutting through our society today. The more basic political question, however, is not who controls the last days of the industrial society,
but who shapes the new civilization rapidly rising to replace it. Who, in
other words, will shape the nature of cyberspace and its impact on our
lives and institutions? For whoever controls this technology, controls the
future. "In a democracy, we, the people, must become the social managers" (page 243 [9]) of our technologies. "Why fight the future? Go with
the flow" [23]—Electronic power to the people!

Notes

1. Cyberspace is a slippery word to define. However, for our purposes cyberspace will be used here to signify a conceptual "spaceless place" where words, human
relationships, data, wealth, status and power are made manifest by people using
computer-mediated communications technology (cf., Ogden, 1994, pp. 715–716).

2. Technological determinism is a heavily loaded term with several degrees
or types having been distinguished by various authors. For all intents and purposes, technological determinism in the context of this analysis will be assumed
to follow the perspective that ". . . technology is an autonomous interlinking system, which develops by its own inherent logic, extended to the control of social
institutions. . . . [In most definitions], science is itself driven primarily by technological needs. Technology is either the 'independent variable' on which other variables are dependent, or it is the overwhelmingly predominant force in historical
change" (Barbour, 1993, pp. 20–21).

3. Cerf. V., Computer Networking: Global Infrastructure for the 21st Century, in H. Lazowska (ed.), *Computing Research: Driving Information Technology*

and the Information Industry Forward, URL: http://www.cs.washington.edu/ homes/lazowska/cra/networks.html, Computing Research Association (1995).

4. Sterling, B., Internet. *The Magazine of Fantasy and Science Fiction,* electronic copy.gopher well.sf.ca.us (1993, February).

5. As reported by the Electronic Frontier Foundation (EFF), on June 14, 1995, the United States Senate approved by a vote of 84–16 an amendment to the Senate's omnibus telecommunications-deregulation bill that raises grave constitutional questions and poses great risks for the future of freedom of speech on the nation's computer-communications forums. Sponsored by Sen. J. Exon (D-Nebraska), the amendment originated as an independent bill titled "Communications Decency Act of 1995," and is intended, according to its sponsor, both to prohibit "the [computer] equivalent of obscene telephone calls" and to prohibit the distribution to children of materials with sexual content. As drafted, however, the legislation not only fails to solve the problems it is intended to address, but it also imposes content restrictions on computer communications that would chill First Amendment–protected speech and, in effect, restrict adults in the public forums of computer networks to writing and reading only such content as is suitable for children. Furthermore, it puts the onus of responsibility for monitoring such behavior and content on the service provider—essentially deputizing network access providers and allowing them to eavesdrop on private messages in order to report wrong-doing. For additional information on this and other pieces of legislation (both domestic and foreign) see the EFF's *Action Alerts* (URL: http://www.eff.org/pub/Alerts/).

6. Gore, A., Remarks by Vice President Al Gore at National Press Club. *The White House: Office of the Vice President,* Washington, DC, electronic copy. Almanac Information Server, almanac@ace.esusda.gov (December 21, 1993).

7. Cook, G., NSFnet "Privatization" and the Public Interest Can Misguided Policy Be Corrected? Executive Summary, *COOK Report on Internet—NREN,* 1(10 & 11), electronic copy, ie+f-reques+@ie+f.enri.reston.va.us via gopher (December 1992).

8. Kapor, M., Where Is the Digital Highway Really Heading? The Case for a Jeffersonian Information Policy. *WIRED* 1(3), electronic copy, *WIRED InfoBot* via gopher.wired.com (1993).

9. See, for example, some of the efforts in creating a public access computer bulletin board and the placement of computer terminals in public areas to encourage participation in Santa Monica, California (M. Wittig, Electronic City Hall, Summer 1991, *WholeEarth Review,* 71, pp. 24–27; and J. Van Tassel, Yakety-Yak. Do Talk Back! January 1994, *WIRED,* 2(1), pp. 78–80), as well as other musings on experiments in direct democracy via electronic town meetings (D. Elgin, Conscious Democracy through Electronic Town Meetings, Summer 1991, *WholeEarth Review,* 71, pp. 28–29; P. Varley, Electronic Democracy. November–December 1991, *Technology Review,* 94(8), pp. 43–51; and B. Kirschner, Electronic Democracy in the 21st Century, Fall 1991, *National Civic Review,* pp. 406–412).

10. Levinston, N., Electrifying Speech: New Communications Technologies and Traditional Civil Liberties, *Human Rights Watch* 4(5), electronic copy, via: ftp.eff.org (July 1992).

11. Malone, cited in Grossman 1995, p. 173.

12. This appears to be a tangential reference to Ben Bagdikian's prediction in his *The Media Monopoly* (4th ed., Beacon Press, Boston, MA, 1992) that soon

after the turn of the century there would be fewer than a dozen very large corporate conglomerates in control of almost all of the world's important newspapers, magazines, broadcast stations, entertainment production facilities (movies, music, etc.) and perhaps by extension, public access computer networks, and data bases as well.

References

1. Kroker, A., and Weinstein, M., *Data Trash: The Theory of the Virtual Class*, St. Martin's Press, New York, 1994, p. 6.
2. Postman, N., *Amusing Ourselves to Death: Public Discourse in the Age of Show Business*, Penguin Books, New York, 1985
3. Bell, D., *The Coming of Post-Industrial Society*, Basic Books, New York, 1973; Dizard, W., Jr., *The Coming Information Age: An Overview of Technology, Economics, and Politics*, Longman, New York, 1982; Dordick, H., and Wang, G., *The Information Society: A Retrospective View*, Sage, Newbury Park, CA. 1993; Machlup, F., *The Production and Distribution of Knowledge in the United States*, Princeton University Press, Princeton, NJ, 1962; Porat, M., *The Information Economy*, U.S. Department of Commerce, Office of Telecommunications, Special Publication 77-12. Government Printing Office, Washington, D.C., 1977.
4. Ogden, M., Politics in a Parallel Universe: Is There a Future for Cyberdemocracy?, *Futures* 26(7), 713–729 (1994).
5. Volti, R., *Society and Technological Change*, 3rd ed., St. Martin's Press, New York, 1995.
6. Karraker, R., Highways of the Mind, *WholeEarth Review* (70), 4–11 (1991).
7. Karraker, R., Making Sense of the "Information Superhighway," *WholeEarth Review* (82), 18–23 (1994).
8. Barbour, I., *Ethics in an Age of Technology*, The Gifford Lectures, vol. 2, HarperCollins, New York, 1993.
9. Leebaert, D. (ed.), *Technology 2001: The Future of Computing and Communications*, MIT Press, Cambridge, MA, 1992; Mitchell, W., *City of Bits: Space, Place, and the Infobahn*, MIT Press, Cambridge, MA 1995; Sclove, R., *Democracy and Technology*, Guilford Press, New York, 1995; Tehranian, M., *Technologies of Power: Information Machines and Democratic Prospects*, Ablex Publishing, Norwood, NJ, 1990; Wenk, E., Jr., *Making Waves: Engineering Politics, and the Social Management of Technology*, University of Illinois Press, Urbana, IL, 1995.
10. Biesada, A., Paving the digital superhighway, *UnixWorld*, 10(12) (December), 58–62, (1993).
11. Pelton, J., and Bender, G., Breaking the NII Gridlock: Is it Time for a New Action Agenda?, *Telecommunications* 29(5) (May), 47–50 (1995).
12. Meeks, B., The Obscenity of Decency, *WIRED* 3(6) June, 86 (1995).
13. Staff, Clinton Attacks Congress Telecom Bill, *The New York Times*, p. A17 (October 28, 1995).

14. Gore, A., Infrastructure for the Global Village, *Scientific American* 256(3) (September), 150–153 (1991).
15. Kahn, H., et al., *The Next 200 Years*, William Morrow, New York, 1976; Kurzweil, R., *The Age of Intelligent Machines*, MIT Press, Cambridge, MA, 1990; Naisbitt, J., *Megatrends*, Warner Books, New York, 1982; Negroponte, N., *Being Digital*, Alfred A. Knopf, New York, 1995; Rheingold, H., *The Virtual Community: Homesteading on the Electronic Frontier*, Addison-Wesley, New York, 1993; Stix, G., Domesticating Cyberspace, *Scientific American* 261(2), 100–110 (1993); Toffler, A., *The Third Wave*, William Morrow, New York, 1980.
16. Stapleton, R., Opening Doors in the Global Village, *Computer* 25(7) (July), 94–96 (1992).
17. Grossman, L., *The Electronic Republic: Reshaping Democracy in the Information Age* [Twentieth Century Fund book], Viking, New York, 1995.
18. Phillips, K., Virtual Washington, *Time* 145(12) (Special issue, Spring), 65–68.
19. Firestone, C., and Schement, J. (eds.), *Toward an Information Bill of Rights and Responsibilities*, The Aspen Institute, Washington, DC, 1995.
20. Linstone, H., Mediacracy, Mediocracy, or New Democracy: Where Are the Information Age Jeffersons and Madisons When We Need Them?, *Technological Forecasting and Social Change* 36, 153–163 (1989).
21. Elgin, D., Conscious Democracy through Electronic Town Meetings, *WholeEarth Review* (71), 28–29 (1991).
22. Staff, Mr. Gore's Video Vision, *The New York Times*, January 17, p. A16 (1994).
23. FM-2030, Why Fight the Future? Go with the Flow, *The Honolulu Advertiser*, December 4, p. B4 (1994).

REMARKS AT THE COMPUTERS, FREEDOM, AND PRIVACY CONFERENCE (1999)

Representative Edward J. Markey

In his speech before the members of the Computers, Freedom, and Privacy Conference, Representative Markey (D-MA), an advocate of legislation that protects privacy in the telecommunications arena, explains that he sees the need for laws that regulate and protect the use of personal information over the Internet. Though long on political statements and short on details, this speech does express many current concerns raised by new technologies, such as the Intel Pentium III chip's ID coding and medical database collection and distribution.

As everyone knows, the U.S. and NATO are currently engaged in military action in Kosovo against the Serbs. According to many accounts, the Serbs are in the process of emptying out villages in Kosovo of their ethnic Albanian inhabitants. Many ethnic Albanians are being killed and thousands more are either in hiding or on the run and fleeing to border areas.

I mention this to all of you not to simply make note of the grim reality of current events, but because I think it is helpful to remind ourselves of a few things when thinking about privacy and freedom. First, we can observe quite readily on TV and on the news sites on the Net that great harm is being done to people in Kosovo based upon their ethnicity, their religious affiliation, upon what village they may hail from, or who their parents may be. Right now, in many parts of the former Yugoslavia, information about who you are could literally mean whether you are safe or in grave personal peril. This is such a depressing situation because this is not a story from the Middle Ages or Nazi Germany—this is post–Cold War Europe in 1999.

When people from the European Community tell us that they see privacy policy not merely through the prism of trade relations but as a cultural issue, or as a sensitive social issue, we should listen to them. I personally agree with them. Our own privacy policy should reflect the socio-cultural mores of our American community as much as our economic system.

I say this to remind ourselves that on a global medium such as the Internet, information about you will not only be of interest to Madison Avenue or your insurance company. As all of us become ever more digital in how we work and play, information about us will become more detailed and more personal in nature, and the ability to create, compile and distribute "digital dossiers" on each of us will become greatly facilitated.

My longstanding interest in privacy comes from my belief that privacy protection is part and parcel of exercising basic civic freedoms and utterly interwoven in our self-identity as Americans. To my mind, losing our privacy altogether would be tantamount to losing our freedom. It is for these reasons that I am honored to be invited to address this conference. And it is for these reasons that I will again battle on Capitol Hill for a strong pro-consumer encryption policy and why I will continue my fight to put basic privacy rules on the books even as we promote new technologies and telecommunications competition.

Children's Privacy

Last year, building upon work done at the Federal Trade Commission (FTC), I offered legislation along with Senator Richard Bryan (D-NV) to protect the privacy rights of kids 12 and under. This measure was ultimately approved by the Congress and is now the law.

The question for us in this session of Congress is whether or not Americans should lose their privacy protections upon turning 13 years of age. While becoming a teenager will always be a rite of passage in America, it must not become the milestone for a flight of privacy.

I believe that any solution to implementing a national privacy policy has to be a combination of 3 key elements: 1) technological tools; 2) industry self-regulation; & 3) a government-enforced set of basic privacy rules.

Let me briefly outline these three elements because I believe that they will ultimately be what our national privacy policy is built upon.

Technological Tools

I have long believed in the potential for technology to help solve some of the problems that technology creates. There is no question that my interest in making sure that strong encryption remains available to all Americans comes from the belief that people ought to be able to take steps themselves to protect their own data, conversations, or intellectual property. Moreover, in the context of online transactional information, the Platform for Privacy Preferences—or "P3P"—certainly holds much promise.

P3P may some day avail consumers of an increased ability to signal electronically to sites on the Web consumers' desires over how such entities should treat their personal information. At the very least, this would save consumers the toil of clicking on the privacy policy of each website they visit in order to ascertain what each site might have in store for their personal data.

Yet this technology can only truly work if it is widely available and if the private sector honors the privacy preferences being expressed by consumers. In addition, as the unveiling of Intel's Pentium III made clear to many of us, relying upon technology alone puts consumer privacy at the trailing edge of a never ending process of technological "one-upsmanship." As consumers get new tools, new challenges are posed to the full and effective utilization of the technological tools.

This is not, in itself, a bad thing. We obviously want technology to evolve. My point is only that personal privacy should not bend to the latest technology, but rather, technology should be designed with privacy in mind. We cannot count on every technology company to do this. And every consumer cannot be expected to be savvy enough about all of the latest gadgetry of the latest products in order to protect themselves. It's an unrealistic expectation, which is why we need rules.

As many of you know, I found the unique identifying technology in the Intel Pentium III and Microsoft products very disturbing. I quickly wrote the CEO of Intel when the Pentium III was unveiled to request a redesign of the chip to better address consumer privacy concerns. Many people have come up to me in recent days and have noted that the same unique identifier that causes concern for many privacy advocates and consumers, was critical in tracking down the alleged perpetrator of the Melissa virus.

There is a wringing of hands over the difficulty of reconciling the duality of the technology: on the one hand it's a threat to privacy and on the other, it may help solve crimes or make transactions more secure.

My response to them is that it is indeed very difficult to reconcile the two—but only if you rely solely upon the technology. If there are no rules that articulate permissible uses and consumer rights then, yes, I tell them, it's quite difficult for consumers to know how to handle this. Again, that's why we need rules. We need rules so companies know how to handle this AND we need rules governing how law enforcement can get access to this information.

Industry Self-Regulation

I want to salute the laudable efforts of certain segments of the industry in trying to develop so-called "self-regulatory" solutions. I want to commend those companies and individuals associated with online privacy initiatives, seal programs such as Trust-E and BBBonline, as well as the growing number of companies taking steps to better inform consumers and offer basic privacy protections on their own initiative.

These undertakings are critical to increasing consumer confidence and trust in the medium and will be an important component in any comprehensive set of privacy protections for consumers.

Many members of the online community have posted privacy policies on their websites in the last year. I am sure that any survey conducted will indicate that there has been a growth in the number of websites that post such privacy policies.

I want to make clear however, that a "posted" privacy policy is not synonymous with a "good" privacy policy.

Everyone who has taken the time and effort to develop and post a privacy policy gets a gold star and a pat on the back. . . . except, of course those who took the extra time and effort to find the most obscure and remote part of the website to post the notice, with a link in the smallest sized font available, and who then proceeded to "lawyer-up" a plain language privacy notice in a way that would warm the heart of any general counsel.

For any online privacy notice to work, it must be designed to serve consumers by being clear, conspicuous, concise and common sense in its approach. It will not do the industry any good to gleefully trumpet an increase in the number of sites posting privacy notices if it turns out that many of such postings are either hard to find, hard to understand, or both.

In addition, as technology changes, sites will inevitably be able to glean more information electronically and surreptitiously from consumers. In such a context, merely informing consumers that a site may have already gathered personal information electronically and providing notice about how it intends to use such information is unacceptable.

That's like saying burglary is OK as long as the thief leaves behind a note clearly indicating what was stolen and how the thief intends to use the stolen items.

Company executives often ask me, "What if I post on my site a notice about what information I'm gathering and how I'm going to use it—is that OK?" The answer is "Almost"—a key ingredient is missing: consumer consent. Notice alone is insufficient. Consumers must have an effective opportunity to grant or deny consent.

To be fair, I'm giving a critique of the work of people and companies who are at least trying to be constructive and be part of a solution. Today, our public policy has set up an inverse system of rewards and punishments. If a company takes the time to develop and post a privacy policy and then at some point violates it in some way, the FTC can go after that company and seek to address consumer grievances. On the other hand, if a company posts no policy at all and then engages in personal information hijacking on a daily basis, it is legally free and clear to do just that and continue on its merry way.

That makes no sense. The company without a posted privacy policy is clearly being unfair to consumers and such a legal dynamic is also unfair to all the other companies taking steps to deal forthrightly with consumers. We have got to address this issue. The way to do so is with rules covering all companies and have the FTC enforce them.

My belief is that industry self-regulation is clearly going to be part of any comprehensive privacy policy for the U.S. Consumers should be able to go out and negotiate for better privacy protection in the marketplace and companies ought to compete on terms and conditions of personal information use. But no consumer should be completely bereft of any basic privacy protections when they visit a site.

And again, although I have long been a big believer in utilizing technology to solve some of the problems that technology creates, I don't believe at this time that technological tools will be ubiquitously available and affordable, or universally honored by information hunters and data gatherers to solve the problem through technology alone.

Our national privacy policy must, and I believe inevitably will, include a governmental role. Congress can put rules on the books in a way that factors in new technology, that encompasses what industry self-regulation can offer, but that also deals flexibly, realistically and pragmatically with the limitations of technology and self-regulation in fully protecting consumers.

I do not accept the notion that the Internet is too complex and technology changing so rapidly that we cannot develop enforceable privacy protections for consumers. As technologies change and business plans for online commerce adjust, consumer's privacy principles remain a constant.

In addition to an overarching Privacy Bill of Rights which I just outlined for electronic commerce, I believe it is also essential to enhance the protections offered in two key areas: financial services and health care. I have recently introduced more specific detailed legislation addressing these two areas because I believe financial data and health data warrant a greater degree of protection and I think there is general consensus on that notion.

Today, the convergence of the banking, securities, and insurance industries into giant financial services conglomerates is making it possible to construct a detailed record of a consumer's credit card purchases, checking or savings account deposits or withdrawals, brokerage accounts, mutual fund holdings, and insurance coverage.

If we fail to give financial services consumers effective privacy protections soon, we may enter a world in which loans are denied when an insurance company informs an affiliated bank that the consumer has a serious medical condition, in which highly vulnerable groups—such as seniors or widows who have just received life insurance beneficiary checks—get cold called by stockbrokers based on information provided by an insurance company or a bank, and in which virtually ever purchase a consumer makes becomes part of a digital dossier that is used for cross-marketing purposes.

Health Privacy

Meanwhile, the lack of a federal law to protect the privacy of our medical records leaves us vulnerable to collapses of confidentiality regarding our most personal and sensitive information.

Recently, the *Wall Street Journal* wrote about a company that is "seeking the mother lode in health 'data mining.'" The goal of this company is to compile medical data on millions of Americans and to sell this data to any buyer. Everyone's personal health information has become a valuable commodity—to be traded like soybeans or pork bellies—except this commodity contains your family's most personal and intimate secrets.

With no federal law to prevent unfettered access to your medical information, patient confidentiality has become a virtual myth and the sale of your secrets a virtual reality.

The Hippocratic Oath provides that: "All that may come to my knowledge in the exercise of my progression or in daily commerce with men, which ought not to be spread abroad, I will keep secret and will never reveal." I believe this is a firm basis not only for good medicine, but also for good public policy on patient privacy.

But without a federal medical privacy law, not only is your personal information at risk, but also your quality of health care. We can't let privacy slide to the point where the only way for a person to ensure confidentiality is to avoid medical treatment all together.

While threats to our privacy in this information age compel us to debate the implementation of a medical privacy law, Congress has another reason to address medical privacy. A provision in the Health Insurance Portability and Accountability Act (HIPPA) has imposed an August 1999, deadline for Congress to enact medical privacy legislation. Now is the time to work expeditiously to pass a strong and effective bill.

On March 10th, I introduced the Medical Information Privacy and Security Act of 1999 (MIPSA). MIPSA's companion in the Senate was introduced on the same day by Senators Leahy and Kennedy. This bill provides strong privacy measures while respecting the health care profession's need to share information for treatment and diagnosis. It limits the amount of personal health information required for billing and payment purposes and it gives patients the opportunity to control access to their medical information by third parties. Furthermore, my bill will prevent law enforcement agents from browsing through medical records without a warrant and would close the existing gaps in federal privacy rules to ensure protection of personally identifiable health information by creating a federal floor. The bill would NOT preempt any state law or regulation that offers GREATER privacy safeguards. I propose this for two reasons.

First, a strong federal privacy law will eliminate much of the current patchwork of state laws governing the exchange of medical information, and will replace the patchwork with strong, clear standards that will apply to everyone.

Second, MIPSA makes room for possible future threats to medical privacy that we may not even anticipate today. As medical and information technology move forward into the next century, we must maintain the public's right to seek stronger medical privacy laws closer to home.

These elements are essential to any strong medical privacy effort.

I want to encourage anyone here today with any thoughts or insights on online privacy or banking privacy or health care privacy to give me a call or contact my staff. I want to especially encourage the online industry to think about how to address privacy for cyberspace in a comprehensive way. Do not wait for a privacy meltdown of Chernobyl-like proportions before you endorse some governmental role. . . .

PRIVACY, RESPECT FOR PERSONS, AND RISK

Dag Elgesem

Using epidemiological (public health) research in Norway as the basis for analysis, Dag Elgesem discusses issues of privacy and its relationship to freedom of information. Elgesem, countering philosopher James Moor, denies a rigid distinction between public and private realms and believes that privacy is best understood as both a "state" or condition—that is, "situational privacy"—and control over information—that is, "personal privacy." This twofold understanding allows Elgesem to take a relatively hard line on privacy, accepting very few intrusions into privacy, particularly in the field of information technology and processing. However, this distinction also supports a definition of "fair information processing" that Elgesem argues is necessary for cases of epidemiological studies that promise great benefit.

Introduction[1]

The conflict between privacy and freedom of information shows itself in different forms. One aspect of this conflict is the question of the protection of privacy in connection with various kinds of research. The problems that I will discuss in this paper are all raised by a recent proposal, made in Norway, for a system that claims both to make possible new kinds of epidemiological research on the basis of medical records and to give an adequate protection of the privacy of those registered (see NOU 1993). The core of the proposal is to give each individual a special pseudonym that is peculiar to the system. This makes it possible to identify uniquely the individual across various registers without revealing her social identity. I will return to a more detailed description and discussion of the suggestion toward the end of the paper.

The proposal raises a series of general questions concerning privacy and its protection. The first question to be discussed is, What is privacy? Privacy protection in the context of computing of personal information is, in some ways, different from other, more traditional ways of protecting privacy. Very little of the philosophical discussion of privacy tries to take into account the principles for the protection of privacy in this area. I will suggest some elements of an account that is able to explain the sense in which principles of "fair information management," such as the principle that information that is collected for one purpose should not be used for a different purpose, are principles for the protection of people's privacy.

The second general issue concerns the *justification* of privacy. Again, I think the question of the justification of privacy in connection with computing of personal information has some new aspects, in spite of strong continuity with the more traditional questions. I will discuss the three lines of justificatory argumentation that I think are the most important in this context. In particular, I will develop a version of an argument for privacy as respect for persons which emphasizes that rules for the protection of privacy are part of the terms of social cooperation.

The third general question about privacy is related to the question of justification: How should the concern for privacy be balanced against other legitimate interests with which it might be in conflict? This problem presents itself as the problem of how to evaluate and manage the risk of privacy violations as compared to other costs and benefits. I will discuss this question in relation to the proposal for the new system of registers for medical research and administration mentioned above. In the context of this proposal, the question appears, for example, in connection with the discussion of whether the patient could be said to have an *obligation* to contribute information about himself to the register. The standpoint of the committee that makes the proposal is that there is a prima facie obligation to this effect, but that the patient has such an obligation *only if* the risk of violations of his privacy is low enough. I share this view, and I think it suggests that we intuitively feel that considerations pertaining to the protection of privacy should have some sort of priority over other kinds of considerations. It also seems to suggest that there must be some point where the risk of such violations is so well taken care of that it is legitimate to balance the remaining, very low, risk against other costs and benefits.

What Is Privacy?

The very nature of privacy raises controversial questions. There is not room within the scope of this paper to discuss all the questions and the proposed answers in this area. I will try, however, to indicate some of the elements of what I think is the correct characterization of privacy. I will do this by discussing the interesting recent proposal of Jim Moor (1990).[2] His account is clear and suggestive, and is one of the few *philosophical* accounts of privacy that tries to shed light on privacy in the context of computing of personal information as well.[3] I think Moor's account is suggestive; but it also has some important limitations, and my criticism of his proposal will form the basis of my own suggestions.

Moor's account has two central claims. First, he suggests that the notion of a *private situation* is useful in order to get a good grasp of privacy. The kind of private situations in which we are interested are those that are *normatively* private, in contrast to naturally private situations. Being alone in one's home is the best example of the first kind of private situation, and being alone in some deep forest is an example of the latter. When we are alone in our homes, we are protected from the intrusion of others by a set of norms pertaining to the physical boundaries that surround us. The second element in Moor's account is the claim that privacy is a state of *restricted access.* "The core idea of restricted accounts is that privacy is a matter of the restricted access to persons or information about persons" (Moor 1990, 76).[4] These two elements give the following conception of privacy: "By my definition, an individual or group has privacy in a situation if and only if in that situation the individual or group or information related to the individual or group is protected from intrusion, observation, and surveillance by others" (Moor 1990, 79). This is an initially plausible, and not very controversial, account of privacy. But the account runs into problems that show that it is too inflexible.

The first problem is related to Moor's conception of private situations and the way he tries to classify situations as private and nonprivate. Which situations are normatively private and which are not? Moor asks. While it is clearly true that some situations allow for more privacy than others, the classification of situations into classes private and public obscures the fact that most situations do have private aspects. This rigid dichotomy forces him to make the following, implausible claim: "The restricted access view, as presented here, counts intrusions as violations or privacy only as long as they interrupt private situations. Intrusions on public streets are not invasions of privacy" (Moor 1990, 79). It seems clear, however, that to lift a woman's skirt on a public street *is* an intrusion of her privacy. Or, again, to read another person's diary without his consent is a violation of that person's privacy, even if it is done over his shoulder on a public bench.

The solution to this problem, I suggest, is to give up the rigid dichotomy between classes of public and private situations and to acknowledge instead that private situations occur within the scope of larger, public situations.[5] This view results in a more flexible treatment of privacy. Recognizing that private situations occur within larger public situations, we can take into account that privacy comes in degrees. In some situations, such as being in our private homes, there is very restricted access to us, while other situations, such as being in a public street, offer fewer— but still some—restrictions on access to us. The situation of riding in a car seems to be somewhere in between. Furthermore, being in our homes is, of course, not a completely private situation: There are limits to what we can do even there, and we are accessible through various channels.

There is a second reason for emphasizing that private situations may occur within public situations: This point makes sense of the fact that norms pertaining to the protection of privacy themselves are *public.* In order for these norms to be able to restrict access to persons, they have to be part of the public aspects of the situation. Privacy norms are part of "the basis of social cooperation," to borrow a term of Rawls (1993, 16); hence, they are public principles. This is a point to which I will later return.

TWO KINDS OF PRIVACY

There is a further way in which Moor's account is too inflexible, I think: There is an important kind of norm that does not fit the situational account very well. For example, there are norms of confidentiality pertaining to the way doctors should manage medical information about their patients. While such norms in some sense can be said to protect the private situation where the doctor examines her patient, it seems more correct to say that these norms protect the integrity of the *patient.* This suggests that there are two senses of "privacy" that are important to keep separate. On the one hand is privacy in the sense of a *state* in which a person can find himself—for example when he is said to enjoy the privacy of his home. I think this is the sense of privacy that lies behind Moor's discussion. I will call this privacy in the *situational* sense. There is, however, as the example suggests, a different sense of privacy in which it is more like a property, namely, the property of having control over the flow of personal information. Taken in this sense, privacy is something that attaches to the person and that is protected more or less well in different situations. I suggest we call this "personal privacy." To have personal privacy is, on my account, to have the *ability to consent* to the dissemination of personal information. This definition involves a notion of informational control in the *negative* sense of being able to prevent others from getting access to information about us. (Privacy does not, of course, involve informational control in the *positive* sense of being able to get others to access us or information about us.)

Interestingly, Moor explicitly rejects a characterization of privacy in terms of informational control. I think this rejection is untenable, and I believe it can be shown that this rejection leads him to an unreasonable position. Consider the way he highlights the contrast between his own restricted access account and the account of privacy as informational control:

> Control of information is important for privacy, but again it is the notion of private situation that makes the difference. Here is an example that contrasts

the two theories. Suppose *A* confesses personal information to a priest *B*. Though *A* has no control over what *B* will do with the confessions, confessions are regarded in this culture as a private situation. The loss of control does not entail any loss of privacy. Clearly, if the confessional moment had been recorded clandestinely by someone else, then there would have been an invasion of a private situation and a corresponding loss of privacy. (Moor 1990, 78)

First, it seems implausible to say that *A* has no control over what *B* will do with the information. After all, the priest is bound by norms of confidentiality that contribute to the protection of *A*'s privacy, norms by virtue of which the situation is private. Without these norms, *A* would probably not have confessed to the priest in the first place. It seems strange to deny that *A*, by virtue of these norms, has some control over the flow of personal information. Moor's account here seems to leave out a set of norms that are an important part of the protection of privacy, norms by virtue of which the person has control over the flow over personal information.

A second point where Moor's refusal to admit the notion of informational control in the account of privacy leads to problems is in the analysis of privacy violations. On his analysis, privacy violations seem to consist *only* in the intrusion into a *state* of privacy. In terms of the example cited above, this means that on Moor's analysis, both the privacy of priest and that of confessor are violated, and to the same degree. But this seems wrong. There is an important difference here that seems difficult to explain without bringing in the notion of control over personal information. Both the situational and the personal privacy of the confessor are violated, while only the situational privacy of the priest is.

It seems clear that norms of confidentiality, like those pertaining to a priest or a doctor, primarily protect their clients' privacy in the sense of giving them control over the flow of personal information. This is even clearer with principles pertaining to the protection of privacy in connection with computers, such as the principle that information that is collected for one purpose should not be used for a different purpose or, to mention another example, that people should know about and have the opportunity to inspect and correct information that is registered about them. Such rules seem to be concerned with nothing but informational control, and an account of privacy that rejects any idea of informational control will have little to say about this kind of privacy protection. This is a problem for Moor's account, since he wants his account to throw light on the question of privacy in connection with computing. So he says, "A feature that is particularly attractive about the restricted access theory of privacy is that it gives technology the right kind of credit for enhancing privacy and the right kind of challenge for protecting privacy" (Moor 1990, 79). I will return to this point in the discussion of the principles of fair information processing.

So far I have argued that we should distinguish situational from personal privacy and that we have to bring in a notion of informational control to make sense of the latter. This invites the idea that situational privacy could be characterized only in terms of restricted access, and personal privacy in terms of informational control. But I do not think this is quite right either. First, it seems to me that while it is true that norms of confidentiality confer control on the part of the client or patient, they also restrict access to him. Second, it also seems that the restricted-access view cannot avoid appeals to informational control. The problem is that there can be restricted access to a person or information about him without the situation being private. Suppose a prisoner is constantly surveyed by her guards but that the guards prevent everybody else from access to her. According to Moor's definition, which says that "privacy is a matter of restricted access to persons or information about persons" (1990, 76), the prisoner has privacy. But, since this is clearly wrong, the kind of restricted access Moor has in mind must be of a different kind. The restricted-access account must therefore be developed in some way, and I cannot see any way to do this that does not bring in the notion of informational control. The reason why the prisoner does not have privacy, it seems to me, is precisely because the restrictions on access to her are not restrictions in virtue of which she can control who has access to her or has information about her.

This suggests that the characterization of both situational and personal privacy needs both kinds of ideas and, therefore, that the distinction between situational and personal privacy does not correspond to the distinction between privacy as restricted access and privacy as informational control. This seems to suggest, more generally, that the alleged conflict between the restricted-access view on privacy and the informational-control account is not a real issue. But this rejection of the alleged conflict between the restricted-access and the informational-control accounts does not make superfluous the distinction between situational and personal privacy. The example of the priest and the confessor, discussed above, illustrates a case of loss of situational privacy without loss of personal privacy. For an example where personal privacy is independent of situational privacy, suppose that the priest after the confession is asked for information about the confessor but that he refuses to do so on the grounds of norms of confidentiality. In this case, the privacy of the confessor is also protected in a situation that does not include him and, hence, in which he does not enjoy situational privacy. This is not to deny, of course, that such norms of confidentiality also contribute to the situational privacy of the confessional situation. In general, the function of situational privacy normally is to protect personal privacy, but that personal privacy, in addition, requires protection of information in situations that are not private.

Before I go on to discuss privacy as fair information processing, let me make one more general point concerning the characterization of privacy. This is that one should also distinguish private situations from *intimate* situations. Several authors have pointed out that there is an important connection between privacy and intimacy. One of the functions of privacy is no doubt to make intimacy possible, and Julia Inness (1992, especially chap. 6) has suggested that this is the primary function—or "core"—of privacy. It is clear, however, that many situations are private without being intimate. To undress in a public bath, for example, is private in the sense that there is restricted access to the person by virtue of which he can control the flow of information about himself. But there is normally no intimacy involved in the situation—the undressing is not part of an intimate act. The same holds for a situation where a doctor examines a patient. (I would argue that undressing in a public bath is not an intimate situation because the activity is regulated by public rules. By contrast, intimate situations characteristically allow for spontaneity and actions based on emotions, that is, acts that are not rule governed.) We should not, therefore, identify privacy with intimacy.

The upshot of this discussion is that there are three distinctions that should be made in the characterization of privacy. First, we must distinguish situational privacy (i.e., privacy as a state) from personal privacy (i.e., privacy as the property of having informational control). Second, we must distinguish privacy from the way it is protected: Different situations require different forms of protection. Third, we must distinguish privacy and its value. In my view, to have personal privacy is to have the ability to *consent* to the dissemination of personal information. This kind of control can be the basis for achieving other things, such as intimacy, but should not be confused with intimacy or any other desirable state to which it is a means. The same holds for situational privacy: It can also be a precondition for intimacy, but it should not be identified with it.

PRIVACY AS FAIR INFORMATION PROCESSING

After this discussion of the general question about the nature of privacy, I will turn to the more specific one about the protection of privacy in the context of computing of personal information. Once again, we can see the limitations in Moor's account. He points out two ways in which computers affect the situational aspect of privacy: "A feature that is particularly attractive about the restricted access theory of privacy is that it gives technology the right kind of credit for enhancing privacy and the right kind of challenge for protecting privacy" (Moor 1990, 79). First, he points out that "even computer technology, which is often portrayed as the greatest threat to privacy, can enhance it. Withdrawing money from an automatic teller after banking hours is more private than talking to a human teller in the middle of the day" (1990, 79). Second, he maintains that

> we should ask whether and how specific situations should have restricted access. For example, as library circulation records become more computerized, the resulting circulation databases ought to be regarded as zones of privacy. The issue is not whether a borrower should have control over his or her lending record in the database, but whether there is restricted access to the data so that borrowers feel the freedom to read what they please without scrutiny from the FBI or other outside organizations. (1990, 79)

While both of these points are sound, Moor's rejection of any notion of informational control in the characterization of privacy leaves out some of the most important questions of privacy in this area, namely, those pertaining to the fair processing of personal information. These are the questions with which all of the modern privacy regulation in connection with computing is concerned. And privacy in the personal sense is precisely the issue in such regulation.

The central question that these pieces of legislation address is, I think, the following. In a modern society we have to give up personal information to various institutions all the time, in order to realize our projects. To give up personal information involves some, perhaps small, cost. We choose to give up a little of our privacy in this way, however, in order to achieve other things that we want. The problem now is that with the introduction of modern information technology, the processing of personal information becomes more complex and extensive. As a result, there is an increased cost in the form of increased risk of privacy violations. The point of the principles of modern privacy legislation is, in my view, to relieve the individual of this additional cost.

The principles of fair information processing are nicely summarized by Colin J. Bennett in his book *Regulating Privacy* (1992). Bennett compares the privacy legislation in Britain, Germany, Sweden, and the United States, and finds that all of them are built around six principles pertaining to fair information management. The same principles also underlie the Norwegian regulation in the area, which resembles the Swedish data-privacy legislation. In fact, Bennett claims that we find the same principles at the basis of the legislation in all of the countries that have such laws (1992, 95). The first principle Bennett calls the "principle of openness"; that is, "The very existence of record-keeping systems, registers, or data-banks should be publicly known" (1992, 101). There are differences in the way the information about the existence of the registers are made public in the different countries, but the principle is the same in all of the pieces of legislation. The second is the "principle of individual access and correction," which is the principle that the individual concerned should have the right to access and correct information about herself. Implicit in this principle is the requirement of data quality, that is, that the information should be correct and complete with regard to the purpose for which it is used. The requirement of data quality also involves the procedural ideal that the information should be registered by means of reliable methods, methods that insure that the information is correct and complete. The third principle is the "principle of collection limitation." This is the principle that personal information should be collected for one specific, legitimate purpose and that the collection should be justified by the nature of the activity for which it is collected. The Organization for Economic Cooperation and Development's [OECD] principles, for example, formulate it this way: "There should be limits to the collection of personal data and any such data should be obtained by lawful and fair means and, where appropriate, with the knowledge or consent of the data subject" (Bennett 1992, 106). This is a principle of *relevance.* Some bodies of legislation, like the Norwegian, contain a list of types of information that are considered particularly sensitive and for the collection of which the requirement of relevance is particularly strict.[6] The fourth principle Bennett calls the "principle of use limitations." All of the pieces of legislation articulate the principle that information shall "be used only for purposes that were specified at the time of collection" (Bennett 1992, 108). This is the general principle that information that is collected for one purpose should not be used for another purpose. The notion of relevance that is involved here can be interpreted in different ways, and the principle is open to exceptions in the different legislations. Hence, the practical application of the principle raises problems. This is a problem to which I return below. The fifth principle that seems to be common to modern privacy legislation is the "principle of disclosure limitation." This is the principle that "personal data shall not be communicated externally (to another agency) without the consent of the data subject or legal authority" (Bennett 1992, 109). Again, this is a principle that involves a notion of relevance, though it can be difficult to determine in practice just to what the individual can be said to have consented. The last principle formulated by Bennett is the "security principle." This requires that "personal data should be protected by reasonable security safeguards against such risks as loss or unauthorized access, destruction, use or modification or disclosure of data" (Bennett 1992, 110).

These six principles can plausibly be seen to express an important part of the answer to the question What is privacy? as it arises in the modern, computerized society. The principles no doubt lack precision in certain respects and are open to different interpretations. They are also implemented differently in different countries. Nevertheless, they have a certain content, and an account of privacy in connection with computers has to make sense of them. This is not possible, I will argue, without making use of the notion of informational control.

These principles of "fair information processing" *presuppose* the legitimacy of the activities for the purpose of which information is collected. The aim is to ensure that the individuals are adequately and correctly represented for the purpose of the decision in which the information is used. There is no attempt here to limit the collection of information as such. The legislators did not try, in particular, to define the boundaries of a legitimate "private zone" which the legislation should try to protect (see Selmer 1990). Furthermore, the legislators did not make the erroneous assumption that the individual's primary interest is to stop the flow of personal information. Instead, one recognized that in a modern society there are numerous legitimate interactions that involve the flow of personal information, and that in many situations it is, of course, in our interest to share personal information with the other party with whom we are interacting. The leading idea behind the legislation is, therefore, to protect the integrity of the norms that constitute the activities for which personal information is collected, that is, to make sure that the very processing of personal information does not affect the practice itself. Second, the norms protect the individual's ability to consent to the dissemination of personal information—they give the individuals informational control.[7]

If we look back at the discussion of Moor's account of privacy, it seems clear that his characterization of privacy only in terms of restricted access is not adequate for making sense of the norms of fair information management. The aim of these principles is not to protect a *state* of privacy but rather to protect the personal privacy through the processing of personal information in predominantly public situations. These norms for the protection of privacy show quite clearly that an account of privacy needs a notion of informational control.

Furthermore, if we look at the central example of the paper, concerning the protection of privacy in connection with research involving personal medical information stored in computerized databases, it is the notion of personal privacy that is relevant. The question is, again, how to protect the individual's control over the flow of personal and perhaps sensitive information, not how to create a state of privacy.

As noted above, even if there is broad agreement on the general principles, there are important differences among the countries concerning the procedures and resources they have chosen to employ for the management of the *risk* of privacy violations. I will return to this problem below, after a discussion of some of the justificatory arguments for privacy. I will discuss three such arguments for the importance of privacy. The first is an argument from the value of personal relations; the second rests on the value of a predictable social environment for the realization of our projects; and the third is an argument based on the idea that the respect others show us by respecting our privacy is important for our feeling of self-respect.

The Justification of Privacy

It is useful to start by distinguishing two different kinds of privacy violations (Elgesem, in press). The first we might call the "classical" form of privacy violation: It consists in the dissemination of information of an intimate nature to an interested audience without the consent of the subject. In this case, there is a violation of the person's integrity, even if the information is not used to do anything to the subject. Such uncontrolled flow of intimate information is harmful to the individual because it harms her personal relations. I will return to this point below. Such classical privacy violations, in the form of uncontrolled flow of intimate information, can, of course, also take place in new and more efficient forms with the aid of modern information technology. The six principles of privacy legislation identified by Bennett can be seen as partly motivated by the interest in the protection of and control over the flow of intimate information. If a person gives consent to the disclosure of some intimate information in the context of an activity, then he ought to be able to trust that the information is not disclosed in ways to which he has not consented. The point is, then, that the information-processing practices involved should not falsify this expectation.

The second form of privacy violation is related to the fact that the personal information is used to make decisions concerning the individual. If these decisions are made on the basis of wrong or irrelevant information, then this might harm the individual in illegitimate ways. This form of privacy violation can take effect through two different mechanisms: One is that the information on which the harmful decision is made can be wrong, incomplete, or irrelevant; the other is when the information is correct, complete, and relevant, but the information should not, according to the norms regulating the practice, be used as the basis for the decision in question. In both cases, the individual's right to form legitimate expectations about how she will be treated is violated. I return to this point below. Again, this form of privacy violation does not originate with the computer, but the risk of this form of privacy violation has increased considerably with the introduction of computers in public and private administration, because the complexity of the information processing now has increased considerably. The principles of fair information management can be seen as attempts to raise safeguards against both forms of privacy violations. But why is it important that our privacy is protected in this way?

The first line of justificatory argument focuses on the importance of our personal relations.[8] This argument starts with the observation that a variety of different personal relations is valuable and that it is consequently valuable to be able to control the closeness of our personal relationships. It is a fact, furthermore, that the closeness and degree of intimacy of our personal relations is, to a large extent, a function of the amount and quality of the personal information we share with others. Privacy violations, where intimate information flows without our control, take away some of our legitimate control over our personal relations. In this way, the privacy-protection principles can be seen to help us maintain some of our control over our personal relationships.

In light of this argument, consider our example of the protection of medical information in the context of epidemiological research. I think the argument gives part of the answer to why we do not want everybody to have access to our medical record. The reason why medical information in general is "sensitive" is that such information is *emotionally charged*, in the sense that these are facts about ourselves toward which we can have feelings of loss, helplessness, and vulnerability. Information about our medical condition can therefore give access to our emotional life. This gives a reason for wanting to have control over who has this information: A lack of control in this respect can mean a lack of control over other people's intimate access to us.

The second line of justification is related to the second form of privacy violation mentioned above—that is, cases where features of the information processing cause wrong and harmful decisions. This might happen, first, because the information that is used in some decision concerning the individual is incorrect or incomplete, so that the individual is misrepresented in the decision. A person might be denied a credit card, for example, because he is wrongly represented as a person who does not pay in time. Second, the person might be harmed through a wrong decision if the information is used in a context where it is supposed to be irrelevant. That is, information is abused for illegitimate purposes: For example, someone might be denied a job for which she is qualified because the employer gets access to medical information that is supposed to be irrelevant to the decision.

In cases of this sort, the individuals will fail to realize their projects, and their legitimate expectations concerning how they will be treated by the institutions with which they interact will be frustrated. If the information management of social institutions did not in general conform to the principles of fair information processing, it would be very difficult to form reliable expectations about the behavior of these institutions and, hence, to realize our projects through interaction with them. A relatively stable and predictable social environment is necessary in order to be able to develop and pursue our projects. Some of these projects are important for our whole plan of life. These considerations suggest that privacy protection can be motivated in terms of arguments similar to those pertaining to the rule of law.[9] They resemble principles such as "Similar cases should be treated similarly" and "Laws should be open, prospective, and clear." All of the principles of fair information processing can be seen as providing the individual with control concerning what decisions will be made on the basis of the information.

Consider our central example also in the light of this justificatory argument. This kind of justification is only partly relevant to the justification of privacy in connection with research conducted on personal information registered in computer databases, since the information in this case is not used to make any decisions concerning the individual. The relevance of the argument in this case is that some kinds of medical information—for example, information about psychiatric problems or AIDS—can be used for illegitimate purposes. The point here is not, of course, that such information should never be disseminated to anybody but the doctor (there might be situations where the information is relevant); the point is only that there are many contexts in which such information *should* be irrelevant but where it still might play a role in decisions if it were available, and that the individual should, accordingly, be protected against the dissemination of such information into these situations.

The third kind of justificatory argument that is relevant to our discussion starts from the observation that principles for protecting privacy express respect for persons. This line of argument has been developed by Stanley Benn (1984, 1988), who argues that the notion of respect for persons is essential for an adequate understanding of the value of privacy. Benn articulates the principle of privacy as the claim that "B should not observe and report on A unless A agrees to it" (1984, 225). He argues that this principle can be justified by, or "grounded" in, a general principle of respect for persons as choosers: "To *respect* someone as a person is to concede that one ought to take account of the way in which his enterprise might be affected by one's own decisions. By the principle of respect for persons, then, I mean the principle that every human being, insofar as he is qualified as a person, is entitled to this minimal degree of consideration" (1984, 229). The content of the principle of privacy is, then, to protect against interference with the person's way of realizing and developing her interests.[10]

In Benn's view, the notion of interest has two aspects. First, interests are connected to the goals that the person pursues: "A person's interests are, in one sense, those things that would be to his advantage" (1988, 105). Second, there is one sense of interest in which it is not "merely objects or objectives to which he as subject addresses himself; they provide the strands of his identity over time, through which he is able to see continuity of meaning and pattern in what he does" (Benn 1988, 107). It is the person as an entity with interests—in both senses—who is the object of respect.

The crux of this part of Benn's argument is that by protecting privacy, one protects the person's ability to develop and realize his own projects in his own way. This same line of justification applies also to privacy in the sense of fair information processing, since the function of this kind of protection precisely is to give the individual control over the development and realization of his own projects and personal relations. Benn then goes on to base his case for privacy on the way intrusions affect the person's relationship to his own projects. I will not follow up this part of his argument, for I do not think it brings us very far. Instead, I will develop a somewhat related version of the argument from respect, one that emphasizes the importance of expressions of respect for our feeling of self-respect.

The first element in this argument is the observation that self-respect is important because it motivates us and is necessary for us to feel that our projects are worth doing. This observation, as well as much of the argument to follow, is heavily inspired by John Rawls (1982; 1993, part 3). The development of a feeling of self-respect depends, furthermore, on the respect that is shown to us by others. Our self-respect depends, therefore, on properties of social institutions and the way people behave on the basis of the norms that regulate such institutions. When social institutions and practices are governed by privacy principles like those reviewed above, we are given the freedom to develop and realize our own projects and our own conception of what goals are worth pursuing. In this way we are shown respect, and our feeling of self-respect is sustained: Through the principles of privacy we express mutual respect for people as trustworthy and sensible individuals with valuable projects and goals.

On this line of argument, the principles that protect privacy are important because they constitute fair terms of social cooperation, terms that everybody can accept "without humiliation or resentment" (Rawls 1993, 303). Everybody is interested in privacy in this sense, no matter what particular projects and relationships they are pursuing. Principles of privacy express, therefore, due respect for persons by giving consideration to their interests in developing and realizing their own projects and relationships. Respect for principles of privacy enhances self-respect, once again, since the feeling of self-respect is dependent on the way one is treated by others in the context of various social institutions.

The idea that we show respect for people by respecting their rights is, of course, not new. Joel Feinberg, for example, points to the fact that a right is the basis for making valid claims: "There is no doubt that their characteristic use and that for which they are distinctively well suited, is to be claimed, demanded, affirmed, insisted upon. They are especially sturdy objects to 'stand upon,' a most useful sort of moral furniture" (1970, 252). Feinberg further suggests that we show respect for people by recognizing them as potential makers of such claims and that this recognition, in turn, is the basis for proper self-respect:

> To think of oneself as the holder of right is not to be unduly but properly proud, to have that minimal self-respect that is necessary to be worthy of the love and esteem of others. Indeed, respect for persons (this is an intriguing idea) may simply be respect for their rights, so that there cannot be the one

> without the other; and what is called "human dignity" may simply be the rec-
> ognizable capacity to assert claims. (Feinberg 1970, 252)

The idea is, then, that there is an intimate connection between rights as
the basis for making valid claims, respect for persons by recognition of
them as issuers of valid claims, and a person's self-respect on the basis of an
ability to make valid claims. It is, essentially, the same point that I am
making here with respect to privacy.

Note that the respect argument does not show that considerations
pertaining to the protection of privacy should *always* outweigh other considerations. The argument emphasizes that rules of fair information processing should be seen as principles for the regulation of social cooperation
that give people control over the development and realization of their own
projects. Neither the respect argument nor the other two justificatory
arguments show that the interest in the protection of privacy should
never be balanced against other interests. In fact, the proposed system for
pseudonymization in connection with epidemiological research, mentioned above, is a case in point. I now turn to the discussion of this proposal and the procedures for the management of risk of privacy violations
that are involved.

Risk and Privacy

As mentioned above, there is broad agreement on the general *principles* of fair information processing, although different countries use different *procedures* for the management of risk in this area. The problem, of
course, is that in real life we have to accept *some* level of risk: It is impossible to reduce the risk to zero, and there is a limit to the price it is reasonable to pay to reduce the risk further. Despite the agreement on the
general principles, therefore, there is also the potential for differences concerning the costs that one is willing to accept to reduce the risk of privacy
violations. The most important procedural instrument in this connection
has been the establishment of a Data Protection Commission which is
supposed to see to the realization of the principles of fair information processing. This institution, however, has been given very different powers in
different countries. Countries such as Sweden and Norway have a licensing system and a Data Protection Commission with the power to stop
projects that do not meet the requirements. In other countries, such as
Germany, there is a system with an ombudsman, while in the United
States there is an even weaker institutional enforcement of the principles,
and one relies primarily on citizen initiative and judicial enforcement.[11]

I will not go into a general discussion of procedures for the management of risk in connection with privacy. Instead I will look more closely

at the example with which we started: the suggestion for a new system of registers of medical information for epidemiological research. I will start by sketching the main elements of the proposal. I will then go on to argue that this is a case where the interest in privacy is so well taken care of (i.e., the risk of privacy violations is so low) that it is reasonably balanced off against other interests.

REGISTERS WITH PSEUDONYMS

The reason for wanting to have central registers with medical information about identifiable individuals is to make it possible to follow the medical history of particular individuals in a systematic fashion. It is assumed that this will create a significantly better basis for epidemiological research and for health administration and, furthermore, that there are no alternative ways to achieve the same results. The point of the proposal is to outline a system that takes care of these interests in epidemiological research and, at the same time, gives adequate protection of the privacy of the individuals concerned. The key to this is the use of a system of pseudonyms that identifies the individuals uniquely in the process of research, without revealing the social identity of the individuals. The main elements of the proposal are as follows.

First, it is suggested that a central medical register be established in each of five regions in the country, rather than one national register, since this will serve the purposes well enough. There will be a national secretariat for the administration of the registers, but there will be no medical information registered with this secretariat. All hospitals within a given region are obliged to supply the register with information about all of their patients. It will be possible, however, to match the information in the regional registers to obtain national data. Second, each patient will have his own pseudonym that can be used to identify him *only within* this system of medical information. This pseudonym, a numeric code, is claimed to be *hard* to break, in the sense that it takes "all the computing power in the world for several thousand years" to compute the identity from the pseudonym (NOU 1993, 291). Furthermore, the system is such that if the true identity of one pseudonym is revealed, this does not reveal the identity of other patients. The pseudonymization of the medical information provided by the hospital is not carried out by the hospital itself but by a trusted "security central" from outside of the health system (e.g., the Data Protection Commission). Third, the real identity of the individuals shall not be known to the registers or their users—only the pseudonyms and the medical information. The hospitals, on the other hand, of course will know the identity and the medical information but not the pseudonyms. The security central that carries out the pseudonymization will know the identity and the pseudonym but not the medical information that is attached to the pseudonym. It will be possible, however, for the individual to check the information about herself that is registered on the basis of pseudonyms, without revealing her identity and without revealing her pseudonym to the hospital. Fourth, it will be possible to extend the pseudonymization to facilitate matching between the new regional registers and existing registers. The users can obtain statistical and anonymous information about individuals, but they never actually see the pseudonyms. Furthermore, it is not possible to reverse the process of pseudonymization. Fifth, the system is less expensive than a national register, it can be built up gradually, and it is flexible enough to be modified to incorporate new technological solutions. The system will be given a trial period, after which it will be evaluated (NOU 1993, part 3).

This is, of course, only a very brief indication of the main elements of the system, but it is sufficient for the purposes of the present discussion. There is one further aspect that deserves special attention in the evaluation of the proposed system—namely, that it gives the patient the right to refuse to have information about himself registered. This is important for the following, obvious reason. People do not choose to get ill, and they of course seek treatment in a hospital because they *have* to. It would, therefore, be more problematic to impose an additional risk for privacy violations on them without their consent. (It is, of course, not altogether unproblematic to impose such risks on people when they have been given the choice, but it is much less of a problem.)

This question is related to the general problem of risk evaluation, a problem that has been called "the consent dilemma," and concerns the problem that arises from the difference between "consenting *in* a market" and "consenting *to* a market" (Shrader-Frechette 1991, chap. 5). The problem is that in many cases people cannot freely choose whether to consent to a risk or not. This is generally the case with risks of privacy violations in connection with modern information technology, since such technology is used in all of public and private administration. People in a modern society cannot, in many situations, choose not to share personal information with others. In order to function properly in a modern society, we have to accept the risks that come with the information practices of the institutions on which we depend. Given this, it is unreasonable that each individual should bear the costs of the risks imposed by the use of information technology. This seems to be an important general consideration in favor of a powerful institution for the implementation of the principles of fair information management. And it is, again, a consideration in favor of giving people the opportunity to refuse to contribute to the research register.

A question that naturally arises, and that is given attention in the proposal, is whether the patient has an obligation to consent to the further use of information about herself, for purposes of research and administrative planning. After all, the information will be used to improve and distribute more effectively the very same kind of service the person has benefited from. The standpoint of the committee behind the proposal seems to be that there is a prima facie obligation to contribute but that the obligation is contingent on a very low risk for privacy violations. I agree with this, but the question then arises: Given the importance that one attaches to the protection of privacy, how can one legitimately accept any level of risk above zero? As mentioned above, the justificatory account I have developed can accommodate a low level of risk. There is a point where the risk of privacy violations is so low that it is reasonable to accept it in order to achieve other things. Furthermore, the argument from respect and self-respect is also compatible with a very low level of risk. The point of this argument is that we, by abiding by the principles of privacy, express respect for persons and that this is, in turn, an important part of the basis for our feeling of self-respect. But one can, it seems, without humiliation accept terms of cooperation that involve some level of risk.

In the present case, I think the acceptability of the risk depends on a number of features. First of all, it is important to note that the risk is quite low and that it is not higher than necessary. Second, the use of personal information is necessary: There are no other means of achieving the same knowledge. Third, it is important epidemiological research that actually helps to improve treatment: What one sacrifices contributes to the production of some important good. Fourth, the acceptance of the risk involves the fulfillment of a moral obligation, namely, to contribute to the research and services from which one has oneself benefited. Fifth, it is possible for the patient to reject the use of information about oneself. (For a similar line of argument, see Wallace 1982.)

All of these features of the case at hand contribute to the acceptability of the proposed system and of the risk involved. Whether all of them are also necessary in order for research on individual data to be acceptable, is a question I will not try to answer completely. I will, however, make three points. First, it seems clear that the first three conditions are necessary for the research to be acceptable. If the risk is higher than necessary, if the research could be conducted without the data, or if the research is useless, then research on personal data would be an expression of disrespect for persons. Second, Wallace (1982) argues that it is justifiable to *violate* people's privacy to some extent as part of epidemiological research. He thinks that "the duty to respect another's privacy is overridden by duties governed by the principle of beneficence" (279). The violation is only justified, Wallace argues, if it is minimal, necessary, the object of useful research, and not directly harmful to the person's interests. While I am sympathetic to much of what Wallace says, I am here arguing for a weaker claim—namely, that, on conditions like those Wallace suggests, we should accept a very low *risk* of privacy violations in connection with epidemiological research. There is an important distinction between *violating* and *limiting* privacy. My argument concerns the justifiability of the latter, Wallace's the justifiability of the former. Third, I am not arguing that a system of large registers with medical data for purposes of epidemiological research would be *unacceptable* if the technology of pseudonymization were *not* available. If we accept Wallace's arguments, as I am inclined to do, we should perhaps endorse such a system even in the absence of such technology. But my point here is that once this technology exists, we have an obligation to use it, since it reduces the cost associated with giving up personal information.

Conclusion

I have tried to focus on the central aspects of the problem of privacy as it arises in connection with computer-mediated communication. First, I think the central problem here, and the one that modern legislation in the area addresses, is the problem of the distribution of costs that arise in connection with the processing of personal information. In a modern society, we have to give up information about ourselves all the time. To give up information about ourselves can be costly, but we give up parts of our privacy in this way because we thereby achieve something we want. It is unreasonable, however, that we should have to bear additional costs that stem from the way the information is processed. On this account, the principles of fair information processing can be seen as designed to ensure that the costs of giving up privacy, on the part of the individual, are not higher than necessary for the realization of the purposes for which the individual chose to give up information in the first place.

I have further presented what I believe to be three good arguments as to why privacy is important—arguments that rest on identifying the values that are protected by principles of fair information processing. None of these arguments seems to preclude the possibility, however, that, in some cases, it is reasonable to accept a low risk of such violations for the purpose of other important goods. Lastly, I have argued that the proposed system of registers with pseudonyms for the purpose of epidemiological research is one such case of reasonable acceptance of risk. Again, central to this argument is the consideration that the risk of potential privacy violations should be minimal.

Notes

1. The research reported in this paper is supported by the Norwegian Research Council. The paper has benefited from comments by Lee Bygrave, Charles Ess, Thomas Pogge, and members of the seminar of the Research Council's Ethics Programs.

2. See also Moor 1989. In this latter paper, Moor independently suggests and argues for the advantages of a system very similar to the proposed Norwegian system for registers for medical research based on pseudonyms.

3. The philosophical literature in this area is, as far as I have been able to find out, very small. One of the few who has contributed, in addition to Moor, is Deborah Johnson (1985, chap. 4, "Computers and Privacy"). See also Westin 1967. It is characteristic that two of the most recent general books on privacy in English, Inness 1992 and Schoeman 1992, do not discuss the question of privacy in connection with computers at all.

4. Moor's account is at this point representative of a family of privacy accounts. Other members are Allen (1988, chap. 1), Gavison (1984), and Bok (1983).

5. That situations can be nested in this way is, for example, an important feature in *situation theory*. See Barwise and Perry 1983, and Barwise 1990.

6. According to the Norwegian act, "sensitive" information (i.e. information the registration of which normally requires a license) is information about race, political and religious opinion, suspicion or conviction in criminal cases, health, drug addiction, sexual matters, and private family matters (see Bennett 1992, chap. 4; Selmer 1987).

7. To emphasize this aspect, the Norwegian legislation presents these principles as legitimate *interests* that the individual has in connection with the management of personal information as part of some practice. These interests cover roughly the six principles mentioned above. In addition, the Norwegian act recognizes a trio of "collective interests" (Selmer 1987). A discussion of these falls outside the scope of this paper.

8. This line of argument is developed by James Rachels (1984). For similar arguments for the value of privacy, see Inness (1992). For a related argument, see also Fried 1984.

9. Joseph Raz, for example, characterizes the value of rule of law in this way:

> We value the ability to choose styles and forms of life, to fix long-term goals and direct one's life towards them. One's ability to do so depends on the existence of stable frameworks for one's life and actions. The law can help to secure such fixed points of reference in two ways: (1) by stabilizing social relationships which but for the law might disintegrate or develop in erratic and unpredictable ways; (2) by a policy of self-restraint designed to make the law itself a stable and safe basis for individual planning. This last aspect is the concern of the rule of law. (1979, 220)

Raz here follows Hayek, who maintains that "stripped of all technicalities this [rule of law] means that government in all its actions is bound by rules fixed and announced beforehand—rules which make it possible to foresee with fair certainty how the authority will use its coercive powers in given circumstances, and to plan one's individual affairs on the basis of this knowledge" (Hayek cited in Raz 1979, 210).

10. Various questions can be raised concerning the precise relationship between the principle of privacy and the principle of respect for persons. There are, for example, many ways to take people's interest into account without seeking their consent. It is not necessary to go into these difficulties for the purpose of my discussion.

11. See Bennett 1993, chaps. 5 and 6, for a discussion of the history behind this divergence. See Selmer 1990 for a systematic discussion of the possibilities that exist.

References

Allen, Anita L. 1988. *Uneasy Access. Privacy for Women in a Free Society.* Totowa, NJ: Rowman & Littlefield.

Barwise, Jon. 1990. *The Situation in Logic.* Stanford: Center for the Study of Language and Information.

Barwise, Jon, and John Perry. 1983. *Situation and Attitudes.* Cambridge: MIT Press.

Benn, Stanley. 1984. Privacy, Freedom, and Respect for Persons. In *Philosophical Dimensions of Privacy*, ed. F. D. Schoeman, 223–44. Cambridge: Cambridge University Press.

———. 1988. *A Theory of Freedom.* Cambridge: Cambridge University Press.

Bennett, Colin J. 1992. *Regulating Privacy: Data Protection and Public Policy in Europe and the United States.* Ithaca, NY: Cornell University Press.

Bok, Sissela. 1983. *Secrets.* New York: Vintage Books.

Elgesem, Dag. In press. Data Privacy and Legal Argumentation. In *Communication and Cognition*, special issue, ed. Ghita Holmstrom-Hintikka.

Feinberg, Joel. 1970. The Nature and Value of Rights. *Journal of Value Inquiry* 4: 243–57.

Fried, Charles. 1984. Privacy. In *Philosophical Dimensions of Privacy*, ed. F. D. Schoeman, 203–22. Cambridge: Cambridge University Press.

Gavison, Ruth. 1984. Privacy and the Limits of Law. In *Philosophical Dimensions of Privacy*, ed. by F. D. Schoeman, 346–402. Cambridge: Cambridge University Press.

Inness, Julia. 1992. *Privacy, Intimacy, and Isolation.* Oxford: Oxford University Press.

Johnson, Deborah. 1985. *Computer Ethics.* Englewood Cliffs, NJ: Prentice-Hall.

Moor, Jim. 1989. How to Invade and Protect Privacy with Computers. In *The Information Web: Ethical and Social Implications of Computer Networking*, ed. Carol Gould, 57–70. Boulder, CO: Westview.

———. 1990. The Ethics of Privacy Protection. *Library Trends* 39 (1, 2: Summer-Fall): 69–82.

NOU (Norges Offentlige Utredninger). 1993. *Pseudonyme Helseregistre.* (22) Oslo: Statens Forvaltningstjeneste.

Rachels, James. 1984. Why Privacy Is Important. In *Philosophical Dimensions of Privacy*, ed. F. D. Schoeman, 290–99. Cambridge: Cambridge University Press.

Rawls, John. 1982. The Basic Liberties and Their Priority. In *The Tanner Lectures on Human Values*, 3: 3–87. Cambridge: Cambridge University Press.

———. 1993. *Political Liberalism.* New York: Columbia University Press.

Raz, Joseph. 1979. The Rule of Law and Its Virtue. In *The Authority of Law.* Oxford: Clarendon Press.

Schoeman, Ferdinand D. 1992. *Privacy and Social Freedom.* Cambridge: Cambridge University Press.

Selmer, Knut. 1987. Innledning [Introduction], *Personregisterloven* [The Personal Register Act]. Oslo: Universitetsforlaget.

———. 1990. Data Protection Policy. In *From Data Protection to Knowledge Machines,* ed. P. Seipel, 11–28. Deventer: Kluwer.

Shrader-Frechette, Kristin. 1991. *Risk and Rationality.* Berkeley: University California Press.

Wallace, R. Jay, Jr. 1982. Privacy and the Use of Data in Epidemiology. In *Ethical Issues in Social Science Research,* ed. T. L. Beauchamp et al., 274–90. Baltimore: Johns Hopkins University Press.

Westin, Alan F. 1967. *Privacy and Freedom.* New York: Atheneum.

CHAPTER EIGHT
Piracy and Ownership

THE MORALITY OF SOFTWARE PIRACY:
A CROSS-CULTURAL ANALYSIS

W. R. Swinyard, H. Rinne, and A. Keng Kau

Swinyard (United States), Rinne (United States), and Kau (Singapore) present a sociological assessment of differing cultural attitudes towards the morality of software piracy. Using a questionnaire distributed to over 370 college students in the United States and Asia, the authors conclude that in light of cultural differences concerning sharing of property and creativity, Asian students demonstrate significantly more willingness than U.S. students to copy software to share with others. Though they recognize such copying as an illegal practice, Asian students do not see it as immoral to the same degree that U.S. students do. This difference hinges on a fundamentally different view of public good.

As long as the personal computer has existed, software piracy has been an important issue. Software producers have tried just about everything to protect themselves from losses due to unauthorized copying. They have made the copying difficult, using unformatted or oddly formatted disk sectors, laser holes and burns, and special error codes. They have created software which works only with key disks or plug-in port keys. They use license-agreements or lease-contracts with probably unenforceable break-seal acceptance provisions. And through it all, ADAPSO (an anti-piracy trade association representing 750 computer and software companies) promotes an understanding of copyright law and the moral notion, "Thou Shalt Not Dupe" (ADAPSO, 1984).

Reprinted from *Journal of Business Ethics* 9, no. 8 (1990): 655–64, with kind permission from Kluwer Academic Publishers. Copyright © 1990 by Kluwer Academic Publishers.

Despite these efforts, as the personal computer industry has grown, so has software piracy. The International Trade Commission, for example, estimates that theft of "intellectual property" costs the U.S. more than US$40 billion annually in lost sales and royalties. For software, it is estimated that one illegal copy is made for every software program sold (Bailey, 1984).

Though software piracy is a troublesome issue in every corner of the globe, the popular press has singled out Asia for particular condemnation. Articles in the U.S. computer press often comment with disdain about Hong Kong's "Golden Arcade", Singapore's "Funan Center" and "People's park," or Taipei's "Computer Alley"—retail outlets where the computer shopper can buy pirated copies of virtually any copyrighted software for little more than costs of a blank disk (see Hebditch, 1986, for example). The illegal sales from these outlets are impossible to measure. Lotus Development Corporation believes that software piracy from Taiwan alone cost them lost sales of US$200 million annually (Wall Street Journal, 1989). In a single 1986 raid on one Hong Kong shopping arcade US$130,000 worth of pirated software was confiscated (Warner, 1986). The shops stop making and selling pirate copies for only a few hours after such raids.

A casual reader of these articles could logically conclude that the people of these Asian nations are behaving immorally about software copyright law. Possibly even that they are immoral people. If we hold a belief—say, that Asians pirate software—we may form a belief structure that leads to broader conclusions about them (Bem, 1970).[1] Are these conclusions warranted? By copying software are Asians behaving immorally? What *drives* their morality on this? How do they justify it? Is their moral development here different than that of Westerners? Or do they have similar moral development but different moral behaviors?

This paper investigates such issues. In particular, it contrasts the historical cultural development of proprietary intellectual property in Asia with that of the U.S. The piracy issue is specifically addressed using data collected in the United States and Singapore.

Cultural Foundations

Protection legislation originated in the Western World. This legislation, which deals with patents, copyrights, trademarks, trade secrets, etc., reflects the traditional value of the West on the preservation and protection of individual creative efforts. Software can be protected through a variety of legal means. Program code has received both patent and copyright protection, but its most popular protection is under international copyright law (Harris, 1985). Copyright law originated centuries ago with British common law. In the U.S. its origins are found in the first draft of the Constitution. Article I, Section 8 of that document contain these clauses:

> The Congress shall have power to promote the progress of science and useful arts, by securing for limited times to authors and inventors the exclusive right to their respective writings and discoveries . . .

and

> To make all laws which shall be necessary and proper for carrying into execution the foregoing powers, and all the powers vested by this constitution in the government of the United States, or in any department or officer thereof.

However, more thorough protection provided by statutory copyright law became available in 1909. These laws were strengthened with the 1976 Copyright Act (Davis, 1985) and the 1980 Software Amendments to that act (Benheshtian, 1986), which specifically included the visual representation of program code as appropriate to copyright.

COPYRIGHT LAWS AND THE WEST

Copyright and patent protection reflect a characteristic value of the Western World in general and the U.S. in particular. In the United States, individual freedom and benefits are emphasized over societal benefits. Many other western nations generally hold that individual creative developments have individual ownership. This view is reflected widely; artists' signatures on their creative work, journalists' bylines in newspaper articles, authors' names on their work, individual claims to design or copyright ownership, individual patent ownership.

Not only have artists and authors historically taken full credit for and signed their work, but also glass-blowers, ceramicists, silversmiths, photographers, clock-makers, leatherworkers, woodworkers and furniture-makers, welders, inventors of all kinds, and even sometime masons, cement-layers, clothing inspectors, and automobile workers.

The West's preoccupation with protecting original creative work led it to originate copyright, patent, and trade-secret legislation.

COPYRIGHT LAWS AND THE EAST

Asia presents quite a contrast. Asian cultures (and particularly the Chinese culture, which has dramatically influenced the culture of most Asian nations), has traditionally emphasized that individual developers or creators are obliged to share their developments with society. A Chinese proverb heralds this view: "He that shares is to be rewarded; he that does not, condemned." Indeed, third-world and Asian nations traditionally believe that copyright is a Western concept created to maintain a monopoly over the distribution and production of knowledge and knowledge-based products (Altback, 1988).

Barnes (1989) suggests that, the inclination to create identical clones of a single product can be explained by [Asian] calligraphy. Becoming a master calligrapher in Japan takes countless hours of copying the works of a master until the student's work is indistinguishable from the original (Sanson, 1943). Barnes (1989) points out that moveable type—not accidentally a Chinese invention—allowed exact copies of the master's original calligraphy. A likely motivation for the Chinese to invent moveable type was that it permitted them to precisely reproduce classically elegant calligraphy time after time, thus reflecting their cultural value of sharing creative work.

It is also noteworthy that in Asia books often feature both the name of the translator and the author with equal standing on the title page. Asian paintings often are signed with the name of the school that produced the work, rather than the name of the artist. Indeed, these schools typically have numerous artists, all precisely duplicating the same creative work.

We can see the legislative reflections of such values. Software was slow to achieve copyright protection in Japan and the Philippines, and it still does not exist in Indonesia, Malaysia, and Thailand (Greguras and Langenberg, 1985). And while mainland China is an attractive market for U.S. software firms, their major concern for that country is its lack of legal protection for software (Blois, 1988; Greguras and Foster-Simons, 1985).

And so we see that the cultural history of Asia does not generally support the notion of protecting proprietary creative work. In many Asian nations the highest compliment one can be paid is to be copied. Emulation is not only admired, it is encouraged. It is no surprise then that protection concepts would be adopted slowly.

MORAL DECISION-MAKING

Asians also have a different perspective on moral decision-making than people of many western nations. Americans, in particular, tend to be more rule-oriented in their decisions than Asians, who tend to be circumstance-oriented. Swinyard, Delong, and Cheng (1989) reported that Americans tend to make moral decisions based on fundamental value rules of right and wrong. That study found that Americans see little relativity in their moral choices; what is moral in one situation is also moral in another. The research concluded that they are relatively rule-oriented or deontological in their moral decisions.

By contrast, the study found that Asians (at least, Singaporeans) seem to make moral decisions less on rules and more on the basis of the consequences of their moral behavior. Thus, it concluded that Asians seem to follow a more utilitarian ethic. This tendency, too, suggests that Americans would be more likely be obedient to copyright laws than Asians, who would more carefully examine the situation, outcomes, or benefits which would result from a copyright violation.

Hypotheses

As a result of the above discussion we are led to expect that,

1. Americans will have both attitudes and intentions which are more congruent with copyright laws than Asians, and
2. Asians will tend to base their moral decisions on the outcomes of the behavior, while Americans will tend to base their moral decisions on the nature of the decision itself.

Methodology

SAMPLE

Our study uses a pilot sample of 371 student subjects: 221 attending a major western U.S. university and 150 attending the National University of Singapore.

Extensively pretested versions of a questionnaire were administered in classroom settings to students all across both campuses. The questionnaires were completed in private and subjects were assured of complete anonymity in their responses. The courses chosen typically contained students of all major fields of study in the respective schools of management for the two universities. While the sample does not represent "Americans" and "Singaporeans" it does reasonably represent the business management students of two Universities within those countries.

MEASURES OF COGNITION, ATTITUDES, AND INTENTIONS

The questionnaire measured cognition of or knowledge toward pirating copyrighted software using three summed statements. Using five-point scales (anchored with 1—"strongly disagree" and 5—"strongly agree"), subjects were asked to indicate their view toward these statements:

- Making a copy of copyrighted software and giving it to a friend is illegal,
- When you buy a copyrighted software program, you usually are only buying the right to use the software. The program itself remains the property of the publisher, and
- It is illegal to copy "public domain" software (reverse scored).

Three measures were also summed to obtain subjects' attitudes toward software copyright laws:

- I would feel guilty about even having unauthorized copies of copyrighted software,
- I would not feel badly about making unauthorized copies of software (reverse scored), and
- I would feel badly about giving even my close friends copies of copyrighted software.

And, similarly, three measures were summed to obtain their behavioral intentions toward these laws:

- I wouldn't hesitate to make a copy of a copyrighted software program for my own personal use (reverse scored),
- I wouldn't hesitate to accept a copy of copyrighted software if someone offered (reverse scored), and
- I would never offer a friend a copy of a copyrighted software program.

For these three measures, then, higher scale values correspond with greater knowledge of copyright law, and attitudes and behavior more consistent with software copyright law.

MEASURES OF PERSONAL UTILITY

Tradeoff analysis was used to measure personal utility. The first moral reasoning study to use tradeoff analysis was that by Swinyard *et al.* (1989). Tradeoff analysis is a powerful method of analysis most often used to measure the relative importance of one product attribute (say, the quality or durability of a product) compared with another (for example, price). Tradeoff analysis requires that people ask themselves, "Are some attributes so important to me that I should sacrifice others to get them?" It takes into consideration context and situational contingencies.

It also fits comfortably with the requirements of a circumstantial study of moral decision-making. For example, suppose a manager of research is faced with both a depleted budget and a need for a second copy of a new but costly business software package to complete a project. She has some choices. Among them: she can make the sacrifice and buy the package, perhaps by using budget allocated to another necessary area, but escape any threat of prosecution, or spasm of conscience. Or she can make an illegal duplicate copy of the software package and risk an entanglement with the law or even her own boss, but preserve her meager budget. If the project had important outcomes for her, she would undoubtedly be more inclined to somehow obtain the software. What should she do? Tradeoff analysis permits the computation of her utility or preference level for her alternative actions, given the results or outcomes that face her.

Similar to this example, our questionnaire asked the subjects to role-play each of three different scenarios. Each scenario placed the subjects in charge of an important business project which could be successfully completed with some new software, but there was no money available for its purchase. The scenarios explained, however, that a friend who owns this software has offered to let it be illegally copied. Subjects were given several alternatives in dealing with this software dilemma, shown in Table 1.

But each alternative carried with it some consequences or outcomes or benefits for the completion of a project in which the copied software will be used. The three scenarios differed, in fact, only in these outcomes (shown in Table 2), which were those having personal benefits, family benefits, or community benefits. For each of these sets of benefits, some outcomes may be viewed as a more attractive incentive to pirate the software, while others are not. One scenario shown to subjects is found in Appendix 1.

MORAL ACCEPTABILITY AND TRADEOFF MEASURES

In each scenario subjects completed a measure of "moral acceptability" for each of the four alternative decisions shown in Table 1 (scaled on a 7-point "acceptable" to "unacceptable" scale (with "7" as "acceptable"). This is illustrated in Appendix 1. After reading the scenario, subjects were then asked to complete a 16-cell "tradeoff" table having the moral choices in the columns, and the outcomes (Table 2) in the rows. One tradeoff table, using "personal benefits" as the outcomes, is shown in Appendix 2.

TABLE 1   Decision Alternatives

- Do not copy the software and do not use it.
- Copy the program and destroy the copy after using it for the assignment.
- Copy the program and keep a copy for use on other projects.
- Copy the program and sell copies to other people that ask for it.

TABLE 2   Possible Outcomes from Successful Completion of the Project

Personal Benefits
   1. Provide you with a significant promotion and raise—a much better position and a 50 percent salary increase
   2. Provide you with a modest promotion and a raise—a somewhat better position and a 10 percent salary increase
   3. Not affect your job, position, or salary with the company

Family Benefits
   1. A large financial reward—one which will totally pay all family bills, and completely relieve your family from its critical financial condition
   2. A modest financial reward—one which will pay some of the financial bills, and provide temporary relief from your family's critical condition
   3. Non financial reward—thus providing no relief for your family's critical financial condition.

Community Benefits
   1. Significantly benefit thousands of people in your community
   2. Significantly benefit hundreds of people in your community
   3. Provide no benefits to people in your community

Results

COGNITION, ATTITUDE, AND INTENTIONS MEASURES

As shown in Figure 1, compared with the U.S. group, the Singaporean subjects were more *knowledgeable* about software copyright law ($t = 4.70$, $p < 0.001$). Despite this however, their attitudes were less supportive of those laws ($t = 7.78$, $p < 0.001$). And their behavioral intentions were consistent with their attitudes—the Singaporeans were significantly more inclined to make pirated copies of software than the Americans ($t = 10.59$, $p < 0.001$). These data support our first hypothesis—that Americans will have attitudes and intentions more congruent with copyright laws than Asians.

MORAL ACCEPTABILITY

Figure 2 provides further support for the first hypothesis. This figure shows that the U.S. subjects differed from the Singaporeans on measures of moral acceptability. Of the four decision measures shown in Table 1, the two groups were similar in their evaluations of the "destroy copy" and "sell copies" decisions ("copy the program and destroy the copy after [use]": $t = 1.85$. n.s. and "copy the program and sell copies": $t = 0.056$, n.s.). But "do not copy" and "keep copy" were rated very differently. The Singaporeans

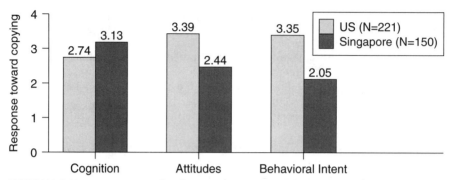

FIGURE 1 Response toward software copying: cognition, attitudes, and behavioral intent

found "copy the program and keep a copy . . ." significantly more acceptable ($t = 3.53$, $p < 0.001$), and "do not copy the software" significantly less acceptable than the Americans ($t = 3.58$, $p < 0.001$).

TRADEOFF UTILITIES

The tradeoff results reflect the above tendencies. For example, a typical tradeoff table is shown in Table 3 for the U.S. and the Asian groups.

As Table 3 shows, in completing the tradeoff table the U.S. group tended to favor the columns. In particular, their low numbers in the first column show that they preferred the "do not copy" alternative over all others, followed next by the "copy and destroy" column. Indeed, five of their first six preferences are in these first two columns. Thus, the U.S. students showed preference for their "decisions" over the "outcomes." That

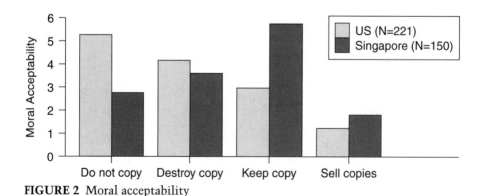

FIGURE 2 Moral acceptability

TABLE 3   Tradeoff Table Results

Outcome for you:	Do Not Copy or Use	Copy, but Destroy After Use	Copy and Keep a Copy	Copy and Sell Copies	
Benefit thousands of people in your community	1	2	5	10	US
	5	2	1	6	Asian
Benefit hundreds of people in your community	3	4	7	11	US
	7	4	3	8	Asian
Provide no benefit to people in your community	6	8	10	12	US
	11	10	9	12	Asian

is, in making a moral decision, the U.S. group was more influenced by the legality of the copying than its impact on people.

The Singaporean subjects, on the other hand, specifically favored the "copy and keep a copy" over the other alternatives. They also tended to favor the rows—their lower numbers in Table 3 show concern toward the row variables of having a desirable outcome, rather than showing compliance with copyright laws. Thus, the Singaporean students showed preference for the "outcomes" over the "decisions."

The calculated tradeoff utilities from these data (and the two other tradeoff tables which were completed similarly) confirm this. The utilities are shown in Figure 3.[2] These utilities are simply calculated representations of what we have already observed in Table 3. For example, because the U.S. subjects tended to favor the "do not copy" column more than the Singaporeans, it is no surprise to us that Figure 3 shows that the calculated utilities for "do not copy" are substantially greater for the U.S. subjects

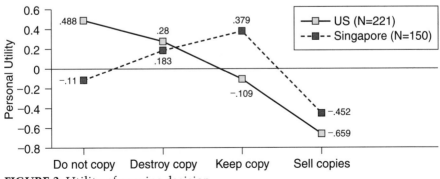

FIGURE 3 Utility of copying decision

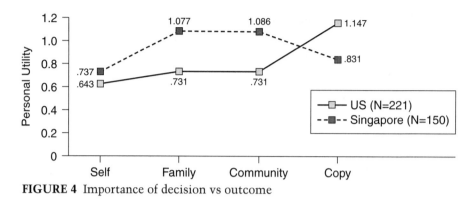

FIGURE 4 Importance of decision vs outcome

than for the Singaporeans. And for "copy and keep a copy," the utility is somewhat greater for the Singaporeans than for the Americans.

The calculated tradeoff utilities representing the importance of the copying decision versus the outcome are shown in Figure 4. Figure 4 plots four points along the horizontal axis. The first three of these—"self," "family," and "community"—represent utilities or importance for the outcomes to come from copying the software:

- personal benefits, or benefits to self
- family benefits, and
- community benefits.

The fourth point on the horizontal axis of Figure 4—"copy"—represents the utility or importance of the copying *decision*. Thus, Figure 4's utility shown for "copy" represents the value or importance subjects are placing on the legality of the copying decision over the outcomes. On the other hand, the utilities shown for "self," "family," and "community" represent the value or importance subjects are placing on the actual outcomes of the project.

And so we see that, for the Singaporean subjects, the higher utilities in Figure 4 show their greater interest in the outcomes or benefits of the copying decision than in the legality of the copying. That is, in making a moral decision, the Singaporean group was more influenced by the benefits of their actions on self, family, or community than by the legality of copying the software. By contrast, the U.S. group was more influenced by the legality of the decision than by the benefits of the decision.

We view these results in support of our second hypothesis—that Asians will base their moral decisions more on the outcomes of the behavior, while Americans will base their moral decisions more on the nature of the decision itself.

Discussion and Conclusions

While Asians seem to have a more casual attitude than Americans toward software piracy, those in the West must understand that it is not simple lawbreaking we are dealing with. Copyright and other protection legislation goes firmly against the grain of Asian culture, which supports the concept of sharing, not protecting, individual creative work. One should not expect Asians to quickly support copyright legislation nor to immediately embrace it in their attitudes or behavior.

Meanwhile, police-action enforcements of copyright laws are being used in Asia. Despite the fact that many Asians are behaving illegally, to conclude that they are behaving immorally is inappropriate. More accurately, it appears that their moral values respecting this matter are simply very different from Westerners. Software copyright runs afoul of deeply rooted and somewhat fundamental Asian-cultural beliefs. Not only does their culture provide less support for copyright legislation, it provides more support for the human benefits which might come from the piracy.

We should expect relatively little voluntary compliance, until the Asian cultural norms change. Culture changes slowly, and people in the U.S. and other Western nations must have patience with Asia as it changes. Achieving Asian congruence of thought on it will likely take years; perhaps even generations.

Appendix 1

THE SCENARIO

Suppose you are working for a private company on a government consulting project. The timing and the completion of the project is critical, and you are committed to the project.

You have just found out that there is *a computer software program which is essential to finish the project correctly and on time.* The software is copyrighted and costs $800. However, the company has not budgeted for the software and is not willing to purchase it.

You have a friend who has purchased this software program. Your friend has offered to let you copy the programs and use the copy however you wish.

ALTERNATIVES

You have the four alternatives listed below available for you. Please check the space which best reflects your personal view how acceptable or unacceptable each alternative is for you.

Acceptable Unacceptable

___ A. Do not copy the software and do not use it.

___ B. Copy the program and destroy the copy after using it for the assignment.

___ C. Copy the program and keep a copy for use on other projects.

___ D. Copy the program and sell copies to other people that ask for it.

OUTCOMES FOR YOUR DECISION

Suppose that if you get the project finished correctly and on time the following three alternatives exist for you. The successful completion of the project could:

1. Provide you with a significant promotion and raise—a much better position and a 50 percent salary increase, or it could
2. Provide you with a modest promotion and raise—a somewhat better position and a 10 percent salary increase, or it could
3. Not affect your job, position, or salary with the company.

Appendix 2

TRADEOFF TABLE FOR THE SCENARIO

Now please consider both the four alternatives (A, B, C, and D) available to you with regards to the software, and the three personal outcomes

Alternatives

Outcome for you:	Do Not Copy or Use	Copy, but Destroy After Use	Copy and Keep a Copy	Copy and Sell Copies
provide you with a significant promotion & raise				
provide you with a modest promotion & raise				
Not affect your position with the company				

(1, 2, and 3) and indicate the order of your preference for each combination, by numbering each box from 1 to 12.

Notes

1. In this case, the belief structure would be "vertical" and resemble a syllogism:
    1. The Asians pirate software.
    2. Software piracy is both illegal and immoral, and so
    3. The Asians must be immoral law-breakers.

2. While tradeoff analysis provides no difference tests of significance, it does provide a "badness of fit measure." Measures above 0.2 are to be considered unreliable. Our measures were all at 0.03 or lower, and no more than 6.5 inconsistencies out of a possible 198 comparisons, which suggests a very good fit with the original data.

References

ADAPSO 1984: *Thou Shalt Not Dupe,* ADAPSO, (Arlington, VA).

——— 1989: "Trade Thievery: U.S. Companies Curb Pirating of Some Items But by No Means All," *Wall Street Journal* March 16.

Altbach, Philip G.: 1988, "Economic Progress Brings Copyright to Asia," *Far Eastern Economic Review* **139** (9), 62–3.

Bailey, Douglas M.: 1984, "A War of Attrition: Software Companies vs Crafty Pirates," *New England Business* **6** (6), 22–23.

Barnes, Howard W.: 1989, "Cost Leadership and Differentiation: Contrasting Strategies of Japan and the Federal Republic of Germany," working paper (Brigham Young University).

Bem, Daryl: 1970, *Beliefs, Attitudes and Human Affairs* (Brooks/Cole: Belmont, CA).

Benheshrian, Mehdi: 1986, "Computer Copyright Law," *Journal of Systems Management* **37** (9), 6–11.

Blois, Keith: 1988, "Supermarkets in China," *Retail & Distribution Management* **16** (1), 40–2.

Davis, G. Gervaise: 1985, *Software Protection* (Van Nostrand Reinhold, New York).

Greguras, Fred, and Frances Foster-Simons: 1985, "Software Protection in the People's Republic of China," *Information Age* **7** (4), 220–8.

Greguras, Fred, and Peter M. Langenberg: 1985, "Trends in Proprietary Protection in Asia and the Pacific Region," *Information Age* **7** (1), 3–9.

Harris, Thorne D.: 1985, *The Legal Guide to Computer Software Protection* (Prentice-Hall, Inc. New Jersey).

Hebditch, David: 1986, "Pirate's Paradise," *Datamation* **32** (17), 71–2.

Sanson, G. B.: 1943, *Japan: A Short Cultural History* (Appleton Century-Crofts, New York).

Swinyard, William R., Thomas L. DeLong, and Peng Sim Cheng: 1989, "The Relationship Between Moral Decisions and Their Consequences: A Tradeoff Analysis Approach," *Journal of Business Ethics* **8**, 289–97.

Warner, Edward: 1986, "U.S. Attempts to Take Wind from Asian Software Pirates' Sails," *Computerworld* **70** (18), 123.

SHOULD I COPY MY NEIGHBOR'S SOFTWARE?

Helen Nissenbaum

Arguing against a "strong no-copy position" on software piracy, ethicist Helen Nissenbaum analyzes two forms of arguments for restricting the copying of software: what she calls (i) "consequentialist" and (ii) deontological/rights-based arguments. A consequentialist argument (that copying software is wrong based primarily on the negative consequences that follow) fails because it is based on unsubstantiated and dubious empirical claims. A rights-based argument (that copying software violates programmers' rights) fails because it does not adequately account for countervailing rights of the user that may in fact trump the rights of programmers. Nissenbaum concludes that there are at least some specific cases of copying that are morally permissible.

Introduction[1]

Consider the following situation: Millie Smith is pleased with the way the home bookkeeping application, Quicken, organizes her financial records, even printing checks. Knowing how useful this would be to a good friend of hers, Max Jones, who lives precariously from one paycheck to the next, and yet knowing that the program's price tag puts it outside of Max's financial reach, Millie is tempted to help Max out by offering him a copy of hers. She has read the lease agreement on the outside package which prohibits making copies of the diskette for any purpose other than archival backup, so she suspects she might be breaking the law. However, Millie is not as concerned about breaking the law (nor about the second-order question of the morality of law breaking) as she is about violating moral principles. If she is to copy Quicken for Max would her doing so be justifiable "not so much in a court of law as in the court of conscience"?[2] For private consumers of commercial software Millie's situation is all too familiar.

Although the majority of these private end-users admit to frequently making and sharing unauthorized copies, they experience a nagging and unresolved sense of wrong-doing. Posing as the "conscience" of these wayward software copiers, a vocal group, whom I refer to as supporters of a "strong no-copy view," urges users like Millie Smith to refrain from unauthorized copying[3] saying that it is always wrong. Jon Barwise, for example, in promoting a strong no-copy position, concludes in a series of scenarios whose protagonists must decide whether or not to copy an $800 piece of software, that even in the case of a professor providing a copy of his diskette to a student who needs it to finish a dissertation, "we should answer all of the (above) questions no."[4] Green and Gilbert, in an article directed specifically to users in educational institutions, recommend that "campuses should view and treat illegal copying as a form of plagiarism or theft" and that they should pursue ways of reducing "illegal and unethical copying."[5]

In the following discussion I challenge the no-copy position, arguing that it emphasizes the moral claims and interests of software producers while failing to consider other morally relevant claims—most notably, those of the private end-user. Accordingly, Millie would not be violating moral principles if she were to share a copy with Max. I show that there are morally compelling factors that motivate many acts of software copying, not simply brazen self-interest, irrationality, or weakness of the will. Although I argue that in *some* cases copying is not a violation, I do not support the position on the other end of the ideological spectrum, which completely rejects the constraints of software copy protection. Rather, we need to judge distinct types of situations according to their individual merits. In some situations there will be an overriding case in favor of copying, in others not. In still others, agents confront a genuine dilemma, trying to respond to equally convincing sets of opposing claims.

To reach this conclusion I focused on the arguments, both consequentialist and rights based, that have been proffered in support of the strong no-copy position. Upon analysis I find that, as a universal position, a strong no-copy position is not defensible.

Two Caveats

First, a word on how I set about recreating the justifications for a strong no-copy position. I've drawn from pieces written for computing trade publications, other nonphilosophical journals, electronic-mail communications, as well as conversations. Although the arguments given in favor of a moral prohibition on copying are generally not presented here in a framework of traditional ethical theory, I find this framework useful in organizing and evaluating them. For example, I classify the arguments that predict undesirable consequences of unauthorized copying under the general heading "consequentialist arguments." In a second working category, I classify arguments that claim unauthorized copying to be violations of moral rights and respect for persons. Although this group is more of a grab bag, the label "deontological/rights-based" captures its hybrid spirit. My first caveat, however, is that while the philosophical categories are enlightening, suggestive of potential strengths and weaknesses of the arguments, they should be viewed as rough guides only. Moreover, because few of the commentators offer explicit or complete treatments, I've taken liberties in filling in steps. While I fleshed out the arguments and filled in gaps, I tried to stay strictly within the parameters set by their originators.

Second, in order to simplify the discussion I assume throughout this discussion that programs are written and owned by a single programmer. In the real world of commercial software, teams of software developers rather than single programmers create software products. And for many products, the title usually goes to the software corporation, rather than directly to its employees, the program's authors. In other instances, it goes to intermediate agents such as marketing firms, or vendors. The assumption of a single programmer, should not affect the substantive moral thesis.

Consequentialist Arguments

According to the arguments in this category, it is morally wrong to make unauthorized copies because doing so would have negative consequences. Although copying might appear to offer a short-term gain for the copier, the longer term and broader ramifications will be a loss for both consumers and producers alike. Barwise, for example, charges, ". . . software copying is a very serious problem. It is discouraging the creation of courseware and other software, and is causing artificially high prices for what software that does appear."[6]

Barwise's remarks suggest that we can expect at least two types of negative consequences. The first is a probable decline in software production. Because copying reduces the volume of software sales it deprives programmers of income. With an erosion of potential revenues, fewer individuals will be attracted into software production. A smaller population of programmers and other software personnel will result in a reduction of available software. Furthermore, a slowing in software development would have a dampening effect on general welfare. The second negative impact of copying is a projected rise in software prices. Wishing to recoup anticipated losses caused by unauthorized copying, programmers will charge high prices for their software. Giving as an example Wolfram's *Mathematica*, which in 1989 was priced at $795. Barwise blames copying for the artificially high prices of software applications. How good are these arguments?

Embodied in the consequentialist line of arguments are a number of empirical assumptions and predictions which, I contend, are open to challenge. For consequentialist arguments to provide a moral as well as a prudential rationale, they must demonstrate links between copying and reduced income, between reduced income and decline in the software industry, and decline in production and an overall decline in society's welfare. If copying hurts the software industry but has no effect on general welfare a prohibition is not morally justifiable on consequentialist grounds. If copying is not directly related to income, nor income to a decline in the industry, then too, the argument breaks down. On close scrutiny these links don't stick. Furthermore, even if some damage could be attributed to unauthorized copying, I conclude that it's insufficient to warrant the all-out prohibition of the strong no-copy position.

Consider the claim that unauthorized copying leads to loss of sales. Although on the face of it, the argument is compelling, the implied link between copying and reduced sales is not always direct. Imagine a situation in which you are deciding whether to buy software application A or copy it from a friend. Although the consequentialists would have us think of all instances of copying as situations in which an agent must decide between the exclusive alternatives, buy A, or copy A, in many real-life situations this is not so. Computer users copy software that they would not buy for a number of reasons: because they could not afford it; are not yet sure that they want the product; or quite simply, have placed higher priority on other needs. For them, the choice is: copy A, or not have A.

Moreover, copying can actually lead to an increase in overall spending on computer software, at least for some individuals. Software sharing opens opportunities for trial and experimentation to otherwise timid users who thereby grow more comfortable with computers and software. As a result they become more active and diversified consumers of software than they would have been without those opportunities. We also find that users who are impressed by a particular piece of copied software, in order to own the manual and enjoy some of the additional benefits of "registered users," will go on to buy the application. In other words, much unauthorized copying would not result in loss of sales and some, in fact, would lead to increases.

The prediction that reduced income will discourage further creation of software belies a complicated story about motivation, action, and reward. Whereas wholesale fluctuations and extreme reductions probably would discourage would-be programmers, the effects of smaller fluctuations are not clear. Richard Stallman[7] ably makes the point that directly tying software production to monetary reward paints an overly simplistic picture of the rewards that motivate programmers. Well-known for his active support of an open environment for information technology, Stallman suggests that besides the satisfaction of contributing to a social good, the fascination with programming itself will keep many of the most talented programmers working. He also raises the question of how much is enough. Although we would not expect many good programmers to have a monk-like devotion to programming and can agree that people work better when rewarded, it's not clear that any increment in reward will make them work proportionately better. (Furthermore, as suggested earlier, we still do not have a realistic idea of the extent to which cases like Millie Smith's actually affects potential earnings.)

Turning the tables on the usual consequentialist chain of reasoning, Stallman counters that prohibitions on copying, and other restrictions on the free distribution of computer code, has the opposite effect on computer technology. It is slowing progress rather than encouraging it. He and others suggest that the free exchange of ideas and code characteristic of the early days of systems and software development was responsible for the remarkable pace of progress, whereas limiting free exchange would dampen innovation and progress, moreover, laws restricting access to software would favor large, powerful and generally more conservative software producers. With a greater capacity to exert legal clout, they could control the production, development, and distribution of software, gradually squeezing out of the commercial arena the independent-minded, creative software-engineer, or "hacker." Even if we see a proliferation of commercially available software, we may also see a slowing of the cutting edge. If Stallman's predictions are sound, they offer moral justification for promoting free copying of software, and not the reverse.

So far, I have questioned the empirical basis for the claims that link copying with loss of revenue; claims that link loss of revenue with a decrease in software production; and, more generally, claims that link copying with a loss to the software industry as a whole. What about effects on general welfare? At this level of generality it is probably impossible to draw a meaningful connection between software and welfare. To the extent that software is a social good, it is surely through high-quality, well-directed software and not sheer quantity.[8] To discourage a potential copier, an extreme no-copy position must show the clear social benefits of abstaining without which there is little to offset the immediate loss. This question deserves more thorough exploration than I'm able to give it here because the connection between software production and overall utility or welfare, is complex. It does suggest, however, that the effects on general welfare of a particular act of copying would vary according not only to the context of copying, but also to the type of software being copied. It would also need to be measured against the projected utility to the potential copier.

Let us now consider the alleged connection between copying and cost and the claim that producers are forced to charge high prices in anticipation of losses through copying. An obvious rejoinder to software producers, like Wolfram, is that if software applications were more reasonably priced, consumers would be less tempted to copy. If products were appropriately priced, the marginal utility of buying over copying would increase. This pattern holds true in the case of recorded music which could provide a model for computer software.[9] Because the cost of a tape, for example, fits many budgets, it is more convenient to buy the tape than search for someone who might have it. Though both the claim and rejoinder appear to hold genuine insights, they leave us in an uncomfortable standoff. Looking at high prices, pointing at consumers, critics say: "It's your fault for copying." Whereas consumers point back claiming: "It's your fault for charging such high prices." The average user apparently cannot afford to buy software at the current rates, and the programmer cannot afford to drop his or her price. Though we may agree that this is not a desirable equilibrium, it's not easy to see who should take the first step out of this circle of accusations. Resolving the standoff requires asking difficult questions about burden. Upon whom do we place the burden of maintaining a healthy software industry—consumer or producer? This question brings me to my concluding comments.

I agree with defenders of a consequentialist line that a prolific software industry with a high-quality output, which provides genuine choices to a wide variety of consumers, is a goal worth striving for. I disagree, however, that prohibiting copying is the only, or best, way of ensuring this. First, I have tried to show that the empirical grounds upon which they support their claims are open to dispute. Moreover, if a consequentialist approach is to be at all useful in guiding decisions about unauthorized copying, then it must distinguish among different types of copying—for their consequences surely differ. For example, cases like Millie's sharing a copy with Max would have a vastly different effect than cases in which a user places a copy on the software on a public network. Consequentialist moral injunctions should recognize these differences.

Finally, the no-copy position unreasonably focuses on private end-users, placing on their shoulders the onus of maintaining the health of the software market. But consumer copying is but one variable, among many, that affect the software industry. Holding fixed the other variables might serve some interests, but it gives disproportionate weight to the effects of copying. Decisions by commercial hardware manufacturers and even government agencies can significantly impact software. For example, if a hardware manufacturer perceives that a particular software product is critical to the sale of its machines it may, quite rationally, decide to support the software.[10] In addition, software companies have the capability to influence the actions of potential users by offering not only a good product as code on a diskette, but by also including attractive services such as consulting, good documentation, and software updates. In this way they make it worthwhile for the user to buy software, rather than copy it. The many flourishing software companies stand as evidence that good products and marketing works, despite alleged copying. Because other players—namely, government, hardware producers, software companies—have the power to significantly affect the software industry, we should not ignore their responsibilities when we assess the burden of maintaining the strength of software production. It is wrong for the private consumer to be unfairly burdened with responsibility.

Deontological/Rights-Based Arguments

In urging individual consumers not to make unauthorized copies some supporters refer to the "rights of programmers" and "respect for their labor." Regardless of its effects on the general welfare, or on the software industry, copying software without permission is immoral because it constitutes a violation of a moral right, a neglect of moral obligations. Depriving a programmer of earnings is wrong not only because of its undesirable ramifications, but because it is unjust and unfair. And even if programmers' earnings are not appreciably affected by copying, we have an obligation to respect their desire that we not make unauthorized copies. The obligation is absolute, not broken merely at the discretion of the private end-user.[11] Millie ought not make a copy of Quicken for Max because doing so would be unfair, it would violate the programmers' rights. But what are the rights to which these commentators refer; and does all copying, in fact, violate them?

Rights-based justifications of no-copy require a satisfactory resolution to both questions. They not only must identify the rights of programmers relevant to the question of unauthorized copying, but must demonstrate that copying always violates these rights. Supporters usually cite property rights as relevant to the question of copying. A justification of the position should, accordingly, ask whether programmers do in fact qualify as owners of their programs so that they would have the appropriate rights of private property over them. But justification does not stop here. For even if we resolve that programmers do own their programs, it doesn't follow necessarily that all copying will violate their property rights. Or to put it another way, it is not obvious that property rights over programs include the right to restrict copying to the extent desired. A justification of the no-copy position needs a second step, to follow the finding that programmers own their programs. And that is, to show that copying violates these property rights. Many commentators fail to recognize the need for the second step, simply concluding that owning implies an unlimited right to restrict copying.

In the discussion that follows I will spell out the two steps in a rights-based position beginning with the question of private ownership, and then moving to the question of whether owning a program implies the right to place absolute limits on reproduction. I will conclude that the second step is the weak one. As before, in recreating the arguments I've worked from informal written pieces, electronic mail messages, and verbal communications. In some cases this has meant filling in missing steps; steps that I judge necessary to making the best possible case for a rights-based justification. Finally, though recognizing that some might object to the very fabric of rights-based justifications of moral injunctions, I offer my criticisms from within this framework, and will not challenge the very idea of a rights-based approach.

Programming and Private Property

First, let's examine the following claim: Because a programmer writes, or creates, software he or she owns it. For some, this claim is so obvious as to not even need justification. To them, a program is an extension of the person's self and so, obviously, belongs to that person. For others, labor theories of property such as John Locke's, which claims that when individuals invest labor in a previously unowned item they earn property rights over it, offer a more traditional moral grounding for private ownership over programs. Locke writes, "Thus Labour, in the beginning, gave a right of property, wherever any one was pleased to employ it upon what was common."[12] Because programmers invest labor in creating a program, they are entitled to the "fruits of their labor." Although Locke's theory addresses the somewhat different issue of private acquisition of physical property, such as parcels of land and harvests, and focuses on the taking of initial title over a previously unowned item (or one held in common), his theory adapts well to intellectual labor. In fact, the case of intellectual property is somewhat easier for a labor theory in that it avoids a common pitfall identified by Locke's critics who, in the context of physical items, worry about the morally "correct" mix of labor with the physical entity.[13] I will concede then, that a programmer, in producing a program, accrues property rights over it, accepting as justification for this claim—if it is even needed—basic ideas of a labor theory of property.

Some have questioned the justice of extensive property rights over programs claiming that software creation is an essentially cumulative activity. Most programs, draw heavily on work that has preceded them so that giving rights to the programmer who happened to write the line of code in question rests on the unwarranted assumption that we can tell accurately where one programmer's labor really begins and the other's ends. For example, most commercial software on today's market is the product of a long line of cumulative work most notably Lotus 1–2–3.[14] However, this objection does not challenge, rather it implicitly adopts, a form of the labor theory because it suggests that *all* those who contributed their effort toward creating a software product deserve proprietary rights over it, and not just those who happen to cross some arbitrary finishing line first. Just because they have made a bigger marketing effort, happen to be more worldly, belong to a large organization, or have good legal representation, does not vest in them a stronger moral claim. Although the question of just rewards for joint labor is an important one in light of the history of the development of computer software, for the remainder of my discussion, I will assume that we can talk meaningfully about *the* programmer who contributed most significantly to a program's creation. It is about this programmer that the discussion about property rights that follows applies.

As stated earlier, showing that programmers own their programs is not sufficient for a no-copy position. Its supporters must still demonstrate that owning a piece of software implies a moral right to restrict copying to the extent desired (and thus the duty in others to refrain from copying). How might I demonstrate this "second step," required of a rights-based justification of strong no-copy? In the next section I will examine whether a universal prohibition on copying software necessarily follows from general property rights over it.

Owning Software and Prohibiting Copying

In general, ownership implies a set of rights, rights defining the relationship between an owner and a piece of property. Typically the rights of an owner over private property fall into a number of set categories including: one that covers conditions on initial acquisition over a previously unowned object;[15] another that refers to the extent of use and enjoyment an owner may exercise over that property; a third that determines the extent to which an owner may restrict access to her property (or alienate others from her property), and a fourth that endows upon an owner the power to determine the terms of transfer of title. Thus abstractly conceived, the concept of private ownership yields a fairly well-defined set of rights. When instantiating these rights in actual cases of owning a specific given item, the specific rights an owner has over that item, can vary considerably according to a host of factors. First, at the most general level, certain social, economic, political, and cultural factors greatly affect our ideas about private property rights, their nature and extent, and what sorts of objects can be owned privately in the first place. To simplify matters, for purposes of this discussion, I will assume a common background of roughly Western, free-market, principles. A second variable that also significantly determines the specific rights an owner can have over an item[16] is its metaphysical character, or type. For example, the specific rights a child has over his peanut butter sandwich might include the rights to consume it, to chop it into twenty pieces and to decide whether to share it or not with a friend. But such rights make no sense in the case of landowners and plots of land, pet owners and their pets, car owners and their vehicles, and so forth. When we determine the appropriate set of rights instantiating the general rights of use and enjoyment, restricting access, terms of sale, on items of varying metaphysical character, we come up with distinct sets of specific rights. Whereas intellectual property stretches classical ideas of locking away or fencing ("restricting access"), consuming ("use and enjoyment"), and bartering ("transfer of title") deciding what it means to own software poses an even harder puzzle.

Computer software has raised a host of challenges to property theory, testing the traditional concepts and rationales in novel ways. Because even relatively simple programs have numerous components and moreover have various aspects, the first problem is to define, or identify, the "thing" that is *the* program, the thing that is the proper subject of private ownership. A program can be identified by its source code and object code, a formal specification defining what the program does, its underlying algorithm, and its user interface, or "look and feel." Each of the various components— or aspects—has a distinct metaphysical character and consequently suggests a distinct set of property rights. For example, because a program's source code is considered similar to a written work, it is considered by most to be covered by copyright laws. By contrast some judge a program's algorithm to be a process (and not a mathematical formula) and thus claim that it is patentable. Legal debates address the issue of whether one can abstract a program's so-called look and feel and claim to own that, in addition to, and independently of, the code, algorithm, and so on. And if so, they argue over whether legal protection ought to be through copyright, patent, or something else. There are many instructive works dedicated to the question of the optimal form of legal protection of all these aspects of software in a growing literature which is written from legal, philosophical, and technical perspective.[17]

Fortunately, we need not wait for a resolution to the entire range of puzzles that software ownership raises in order to gain a better understanding of Millie's dilemma. We acknowledge, in her case, that she explicitly duplicated object code, and thus we bypass many of the complexities. However, it is important to note the existing backdrop of uncertainty over how to categorize the metaphysics of software, and thus, how to fit it into our network of ideas on property rights. We are drawing conclusions about software ownership on the basis of imperfect analogies to other forms of private property. This leaves open the possibility of significant differences.

We are ready now to return to this section's central question of how one might derive a prohibition on copying from ownership. On the basis of earlier observations about private property we can conclude that a programmer, or owner, has rights over the program including rights to restrict access and rights of use and enjoyment. Presumably, the programmer's right to generate earnings from his program would instantiate the latter. The programmer could choose to give others limited access to her program by selling diskettes, upon which she has copied the program, at a price she determines. But because the programmer still owns the program itself, she may impose restrictions on its use—in particular she retains the right to prevent buyers of the diskettes from making copies of the program that she has not explicitly authorized. Thus, we derive the programmer's specific right to restrict unauthorized copying from the general right property owners have to restrict access by others to their property. To distinguish transactions of this type from other types of sales, commercial software vendors adopt the jargon "software license" rather than "software sale." Thus, the argument from rights would dictate that Millie not copy because doing so would violate a programmers' valid claim to both use and enjoy his or her property (by depriving them earnings) and restrict access by others to it (by making unauthorized copies).

But this picture leaves out an important component of property theory. Like other rights, property rights restrict the freedoms of others by imposing certain obligations on them. For example a promisee's rights imply an obligation on the part of the promiser to keep the promise; a landowner's rights implies an obligation on would-be trespassers not to cross his or her land. As I stated earlier, the precise nature of property restrictions will vary according to the metaphysical character of the property. But there is yet another factor that shapes the extent and nature of property—and in fact all—rights. Even theorists of a libertarian bent, who support extensive rights over private property, recognize that these rights are not absolute. For example, Locke argued that morality allowed the appropriation of previously unowned property only "where there is enough, and as good, left in common for others."[18] And Nozick, also recognizing limitations on property rights, illustrates one source of these restrictions with his colorful example: "My property rights in my knife allow me to leave it where I will, but not in your chest."[19] In other words, although owning a knife implies extensive rights of use and enjoyment, these rights are constrained by justified claims, or rights, of others—in this case, their right not to be harmed. While I wish to avoid either endorsing or criticizing the more far-reaching agendas of these two authors, I want to draw attention to an important insight they offer about private property rights: that property rights are subject to the limitations of countervailing claims of others.

Actual practice demonstrates that, as a rule rather than an exception, when we determine the nature and extent of property rights, we acknowledge the justified claims of others. For example, in determining the rights of the owner of a lethal weapon we're influenced not only by its general metaphysical features (when we determine the types of actions that constitute use and enjoyment), but are concerned about the well-being of others. And so we restrict the way people may carry lethal weapons—either concealed or unconcealed depending on the accepted wisdom of the city or state in which they happen to live. We regulate construction projects of urban property owners for far less concrete counter-claims than freedom from bodily harm, but in the interest of values like aesthetic integrity of a neighborhood, effects on the quality of life of immediate neighbors, and so forth. We restrict the rights of landowners over water traversing their land, preventing them, for example, from damming a flowing river. We also constrain the behavior of motor vehicle drivers. In all these cases where we perceive a threat to justified claims of other individuals, or of a social order, we limit the extent of owners' rights over their property. It makes sense to carry this principle over to the case of software asking not only about the claims of programmers, but the claims of end-users.

Does Millie Smith have a reasonable counter-claim that might limit the extent to which Quicken's owners can constrain her actions. She would like to duplicate her Quicken software for Max, an act of generosity, helping satisfy a friend's need. Despite the programmer's preferring that Millie not share a copy, Millie is motivated by other values. She views making a copy as a generous act which would help a friend in need. Copying software is a routine part of computer use. Millie's proposed action is limited; she has no intention of making multiple copies and going into competition with the programmer, she wouldn't dream of plagiarizing the software or passing it off as a product of her own creation. The entire transaction takes place within the private domain of friends and family. She would view offering a copy to Max as a simple act of kindness, neither heroic nor extraordinary. Interfering with the normal flow of behavior, especially as pursued in the private realm, would constitute unreasonable restriction of an agent's liberty. Thus, Millie's countervailing claim is the freedom to pursue the virtue of generosity within the private circle of friends and family.

The conclusion of this line of reasoning is *not* that, from a perspective of rights, *all* unauthorized duplication of software is morally permissible. I am suggesting merely that we decide the question whether to share or not to share in a case by case fashion. Although in some cases a programmer's desire that the user not copy software is a defensible instantiation of the right to restrict access to private property, in others the restriction will not be defensible because it conflicts with the valid claims of another agent. And even in the cases where making a copy would not be immoral it would not follow that the programmer has somehow lost all the property rights over his or her program. Commentators like Green and Gilbert are right to draw attention to programmers' claims over their software, and to encourage respect for intellectual labor; but they overlook the possibility of relevant, conflicting, counterclaims. When, at the beginning of the paper, I referred to the copier's dilemma, it was the dilemma created by conflicting obligations: on the one hand an obligation to respect a programmer's property rights, which in some cases includes the right to restrict copying; and on the other an obligation to help others, tempered by the belief that one ought not have one's behavior unduly restricted within the private domain.

Consider some objections. One objection is that no matter what Millie might think about helping Max, you just cannot get away from the fact that she's violating the programmer's property rights. And this is the reason that her copying—and all unauthorized copying—is immoral.

This objection fails to recognize that counterclaims can substantively affect what counts as a moral (property) right, in any given situation. Consider the rights of a landlord with respect to a leased apartment. When that apartment is vacant, the owner may come and go as he wishes; he may renovate it, choose to rent it, or to let it stand empty. However, once the apartment is leased, the landlord's rights of entry are limited by a tenant's competing right to privacy. Even if it would suit a landlord to stipulate in his lease the right to make surprise checks, this wish would be overridden by the justified claims of his tenants not to be disturbed, not to have their privacy violated. We would not say that the landlord's property rights are violated by the tenant; we would say that the landlord no longer has the right of free entry into his leased property. Consider another example. Let's say someone buys a word-processing package. On the outside of the customary sealed envelope containing the diskette, the buyer finds not only the usual terms of a lease agreement, but one further condition. The programmers stipulate that consumers are free to use the word processor any way they want, except to produce a document that promotes abortion. They reason that the abortion stipulation is merely an additional instantiation of their rights as owners to restrict access by others to their property. However, I think that the buyer could quite reasonably object that despite the programmer's intellectual property rights over the word processor, these rights do not include the right to control its use to the extent that it overrides valid, competing, claims to freedom of expression. Similarly, Millie, judging that in the private domain she should be largely unrestricted, could argue that the moral arm of the programmer does not extend into the private domain. We conclude, therefore, that in copying for Max she does not violate a moral right.

In a second objection, a critic could charge that if we judge Millie Smith's copying to be morally permissible, this would open the door to a total disregard for the rights of programmers. There would be no stopping agents from making multiple, unauthorized, copies and selling them in competition with the original programmer.

This objection doesn't hold because Millie's case, being significantly different from those other cases, would not lead us down a slippery slope. A potential copier must show a justifiable claim that conflicts with the programmer's. In the objector's example, and even in the case of a do-gooder who decides to place a piece of privately owned software on a public domain network,[20] copying takes place in a public domain lacking Millie's personal and private motivations. They lack the compelling counterclaim. Specifically for the public, commercial arena, we would expect to generate a network of laws and regulations to cover the many cases which moral principles alone could not decide.

Another objection asserts that Millie would be acting immorally in making a copy for Max because copying is stealing. But this objection begs the question because it *assumes* that copying is stealing. In this section we've been examining whether or not copying always violates property rights and therefore constitutes wrongful seizure of another's possession. In other words, whether copying is stealing. This objection assumes that we've satisfactorily established that copying is theft, and thus assumes the issue we're trying to establish.

Conclusion

There is a prevailing presumption—in my opinion a disturbing one—that were we to follow the dictates of moral conscience, we would cease completely to make unauthorized copies of software. Yet when we examine the arguments given in support of that presumption we find that they fall short of their universal scope. The soundness of a rights-based rationale depends on successfully showing that owning software entails a right to restrict copying. I have argued that this step is not obvious, and that at least in some well-defined cases the entailment fails—notably, cases in which there are strong counterclaims. In practice this means that we should give equal consideration to the rights of end-users as well as to those of programmers. To simply insist that property rights override end-user freedoms is to beg the issue at hand.

Consequentialist rationales are also equivocal in that they rest on a number of sweeping empirical assumptions—many of which exaggerate the effects of copying, some of which are open to doubt. Moreover, it places squarely on the shoulders of private end-users the onus of maintaining a flourishing industry when in fact there are other agents well placed to share the burden. Many software manufacturers who have been vocal in their complaints, despite current levels of copying, appear to be enjoying overwhelming successes. Perhaps because they offer incentives like good consulting services, free upgrades, and reasonable prices they raise the marginal utility of buying over copying.

Finding that there are insufficiently strong moral grounds for universally prohibiting copying, I conclude not that all unauthorized copying is morally acceptable, but that some copying is acceptable. There is sufficient variability in the types of situations in which software users copy to suggest that we ought to evaluate them case-by-case. In cases like Millie's and Max's, the argument against copying is not a compelling one.

Finally, some critics insist that the best approach to solving this issue is a hard-line economic one. Clearly, a rights-based approach, which unearths the usual set of conflicting rights is not helpful and leads us to a deadlock. Let the free market decide. We ought to allow software producers to place any conditions whatever on the sale of their software, and in particular, any limits on duplication. Consumers will soon make their preferences known. Defenders of no-copy say that current commercial software conditions are more or less in that position today, except that users are not keeping up their end of the bargain when they make copies of software. But even from this hard-line economic standpoint, a no-copy line is disturbing because it lets the robustness of a market depend on a mode of behavior to which most do not conform, and many find distasteful, that is, restricting the inclination to private acts of beneficence and generosity. Unless we alter human nature, experience suggests that this would be a shaky equilibrium.

On a final idealistic note, I echo strains of Richard Stallman in observing that if we can eradicate copying only when individuals ignore a natural tendency to respond to the needs of those close to them, we may not be maximizing expected utility after all.

Notes

1. An earlier version of this paper was presented at the Fifth Annual Computers and Philosophy Conference, Stanford University, August 8–11, 1990. Several members of the audience, with their sharp criticisms and suggestions, helped clarify my thinking a great deal. I'd also like to thank members of Partha Dasgupta's Applied Ethics Seminar at Stanford (1989) for useful and creative comments.

2. David Lyons, "The New Indian Claims and Original Rights to Land" in *Reading Nozik: Essays on Anarchy, State and Utopia*, (Ed) Jeffrey Paul, Rowman and Littlefield, Totowa, New Jersey. 1981.

3. I will not be dealing with unlikely cases in which copying software might save a life or avert a war. I assume that even those committed to a no-copy position would find rationale to permit those acts.

4. Jon Barwise, "Computers and Mathematics: Editorial Notes," in *Notices of the A.M.S.*

5. K. Green and S. W. Gilbert, "Software Piracy: Its Cost and Consequences" in *Change*, pp. 47–49. January/February 1987.

6. Jon Barwise, "Computers and Mathematics: Editorial Notes," in *Notices of the A.M.S.*, 1989.

7. R. Stallman, "The GNU Manifesto" in *GNU Emacs Manual*. Copyright 1987 Richard Stallman.

8. Joseph Weizenbaum in Chapter 1 of *Computer Power and Human Reason*, San Francisco, Freeman, 1976, makes suggestive comments arguing that consumerism needn't necessarily lead to greater choices among genuinely distinct products. A conservative market might remain unimaginatively "safe," coming up with only trivially diverse products.

9. Although some claim that the loss in sound-quality is a major reason for recorded music being less frequently copied, this doesn't tell the story for all (the average) listeners.

10. Both Stallman, *ibid.* and Barwise, *ibid.* (and probably others) have made similar points.

11. Though strictly speaking, a rule-based approach could ultimately be grounded in utilitarian terms, the ones I consider here merge the rights-based and deontological styles of moral reasoning. They cite programmers' rights, inferring from them absolute obligations on the parts of software users.

12. John Locke, Section 45 in *Second Treatise of Government*, originally published 1690, Hackett Publishing Company, Indianapolis, 1980.

13. Nozick's discusses this problem quite extensively in *Anarchy, State, and Utopia*, Basic Books, Inc. 1974.

14. For an interesting history of software inter-dependence see Bill Machrone's, "The Look-and-Feel Issue: The Evolution of Innovation" in *Computers, Ethics, & Society*, M. D. Ermann, M. B. Williams, C. Gutierrez, Oxford University Press, New York, 1990.

15. This was Locke's central preoccupation.

16. Metaphysical character can co-vary with cultural–social factors to make for an even more complex picture. Consider the potentially diverse views of descendents of European traditions and those of Native American traditions on property rights over land, sea, and air.

17. See, for example: M. Gemignani, "The Regulation of Software," *Abacus*, vol. 5, no. 1, Fall 1987, pp. 57–59; D. G. Johnson, "Should Computer Programs Be Owned?," *Metaphilosophy*, vol. 16, no. 4, October 1985, pp. 276–288, P. Samuelson, "Why the Look and Feel of Software User Interfaces Should Not Be Protected by Copyright Law," *Communications of the ACM*, vol. 32, no. 5, May 1989. pp. 563–572.

18. Locke, *ibid.*, Chapter 5 Section 27.

19. *Anarchy, State and Utopia* by Robert Nozick p. 171.

20. I confess to being stymied by cases such as that of a school teacher in a poor ghetto school deciding to make unauthorized copies of a software application that he believes would help his students, who would not ordinarily be able to afford it.

SO YOU WANT TO BE A PIRATE?

Pirate Editorial

> *In this brief statement, the editors of* Pirate Newsletter *make distinctions between software "pirates," "bootleggers," "freeloaders," and "cheapskates." In all, this piece speaks from the perspective of "pirates" themselves claiming that piracy is neither harmful nor unethical and that it even provides useful services to the computer-using public, promoting both literacy and availability.*

What's a pirate? *Computer piracy* is copying and distribution of copyright software (warez). Pirates are hobbyists who enjoy collecting and playing with the latest programs. Most pirates enjoy collecting warez, getting them running, and then generally archive them, or store them away. A *pirate is not a bootlegger.* Bootleggers are to piracy what a chop-shop is to a home auto mechanic. Bootleggers are people who deal stolen merchandise for personal gain. Bootleggers are crooks. They sell stolen goods. Pirates are not crooks, and most pirates consider bootleggers to be lower life forms than child molesters.

Pirates *share* warez to learn, trade information, and have fun! But, being a pirate is more than swapping warez. It's a life-style and a passion. The office worker or classmate who brings in a disk with a few files is not necessarily a pirate any more than a friend laying a copy of the latest Depeche Mode album on you is a pirate. The *true* pirate is plugged into a larger group of people who share similar interests in warez. This is usually done through Bulletin Board Systems (BBSs), and the rule of thumb is "you gotta give a little to get a little; ya gets back what ya gives." Pirates are *not* freeloaders, and only lamerz think they get something for nothing.

A recent estimate in the *Chicago Tribune* (March 25, p. VII: 4) indicated that computer manufacturers estimate the cost of computer piracy at over $4 billion annually. This is absurd, of course. Businesses rarely pirate warez, because the penalties for discovery do not make it cost effective. Individuals who pirate are rarely going to spend several thousand dollars a year for warez they generally have little pratical use for, and there's a lot of evidence that pirates spend more money on warez they probably don't need. In fact, pirates may be one of the best forms of advertising for quality products, because sharing allows a shop-around

---

Reprinted from *Pirate* 1, no. 1 (June 1989).

method for buying warez. Most of us buy a program for the documents and the support, but why invest in four or five similar programs if we aren't sure which best suits our needs? Nah, pirates aren't freeloaders.

Is piracy unethical? It may be illegal, although most states have laws providing a grey area between archiving (storing) and use. But, is it *unethical?* We think not. We challenge the claim that pirates cost software manufacturers any lost revenue, and will argue that they spread the word for high quality products. The average person cannot afford the mega-bucks needed to buy Dbase-4 and Foxbase, and would do without either if forced to buy. But, by testing out both, we are able to inform those who *will* buy which is better. So, we spread computer literacy, indirectly encourage improvements, and keep the market alive. Pirates hurt no one, take money from nobody's pocket, and contribute far more to the computer industry than they are willing to acknowledge.

How many of us have had mega-fone bills in a month? The telecomm folks must love pirates. No, pirates aren't cheapskates. The fun of finding an obscure program for somebody, the thrill of cracking a program, the race to see who can be the first to upload the latest version—these are the lure of piracy. We are collectors of information. Unlike those who would keep computer literacy to the affluent few, we make it more readily available to the masses.

So what's a pirate? A pirate is somebody who believes that information belongs to the people. Just as a book can be Xeroxed or placed in a library to be shared, pirates provide a type of library service. The experienced pirate even acts as a tutor in helping those who may have purchased warez. We don't bitch about serving as unpaid consultants to the computer industry, and we wouldn't think to request payment for our services. By providing a user-friendly network of information sharers, we increase computer literacy which is in everybody's mutual interests.

The software industry is unlikely to acknowledge (or even recognize) the contributions of pirates to their enterprise, and continue to view us as "the enemy!" Pirates are not represented in legislation and have no strong constituency to challenge misrepresentation. *Pirate Newsletter* is intended to break down the power of media to define us as crooks and outcasts and bring us together. By keeping information open and flowing and not under the control of a privileged few, we are enhancing democracy and freedom of the market place.

Pirates are freedom fighters keeping the dream alive!

CHAPTER NINE
Hacking and Viruses

HACKING AND VIRUSES

Tom Forester and Perry Morrison

Forester and Morrison survey ethical issues raised by the practice of "cracking," popularly labeled "hacking," and the creation and distribution of computer "viruses." The first half of the selection argues that there is no one suitable definition of "hacking" and explains that there are many different types of and motivations for it. This makes any absolute ethical pronouncement about hacking difficult. The second half of the selection focuses on the proliferation of computer worms and viruses. Again arguing that there is no singular correct position on the ethical status of worm or virus creation, Forester and Morrison conclude that, though outright theft and damage are wrong, much of what hackers and viruses do is simply playful or informative. The ethics of these kinds of less-obtrusive acts (even when done on government or corporate systems), therefore, is much more difficult to determine than is suggested by the popular media.

On 27 April 1987, viewers of the Home Box Office (HBO) cable TV channel in the United States witnessed a historically significant event, variously described as the first act of high-tech terrorism or the world's most widely viewed piece of electronic graffiti. On that evening, watchers of HBO's satellite transmission of *The Falcon and the Snowman* saw their screens go blank and the following message appear:

Reprinted from *Computer Ethics: Cautionary Tales and Ethical Dilemmas in Computing,* 2d ed. by Tom Forester and Perry Morrison (MIT Press, 1994), 45–66. Copyright © 1994 Massachusetts Institute of Technology.

Good Evening HBO from Captain Midnight. $12.95 a month?
No way!
(Show-time/Movie Channel, Beware!).

This transmission lasted for some four minutes. It represented a protest against HBO's decision to scramble its satellite signal so that back-yard dish owners were forced to buy or hire decoders in order to view HBO's programs. More significantly—and in a most impressive way—it illustrated the vulnerability of satellites and other communications services to malicious interference.

The search for and apprehension of Captain Midnight took several months and a certain amount of luck. . . .

A breakthrough in the case did not occur until a Wisconsin tourist happened to overhear a man talking about the Captain Midnight prank while using a public telephone in Florida. The tourist reported the man's license number, and this information eventually led police to the culprit—John MacDougall, a satellite dish salesman, electronics engineer, and part-time employee at the Central Florida Teleport satellite uplink facility in Ocala. MacDougall was subsequently charged with transmitting without a license and sentenced to one year's probation and a $5,000 fine.[1] . . .

Yet the most important aspect of the Captain Midnight hack and other similar incidents is not immediately obvious. MacDougall caused mild annoyance to a large number of viewers and probably, at worst, a severe case of embarrassment to HBO. Yet the fact that this individual was able to broadcast a particular message into the homes of thousands and to take control of a sophisticated satellite transponder demonstrates a much more significant danger. What if, instead of being an angry satellite dish salesman, MacDougall had been an international terrorist and instead of interrupting a movie, he had begun to jam the telephone, facsimile, and data communications of a number of satellites? Further, we know that satellites are directed from the ground by using radio signals to control the functioning of their small maneuvering engines. What if MacDougall or somebody else had used these signals to move the satellite into a decaying orbit or caused it to enter the orbit of another satellite—perhaps a Soviet one—many of which carry small nuclear reactors as a power source?

Even worse, if MacDougall had been an employee of a city traffic authority, could he have used his knowledge of computer systems and traffic control to completely foul up a city's traffic lights during a peak traffic period? One doesn't need much imagination to think of the consequences of such an act for a city, say, the size of Los Angeles. Not only would the traffic snarls take days to untangle, but emergency services (police, fire, ambulance, etc.) would be incapacitated. Maintenance of sewage, lighting, power, and telephones would probably come to a halt, and inevitably there would be fatalities and an enormous insurance bill stemming from the hundreds of wrecked or damaged cars and injured or ill people. More important, the security services would be hard pressed to deal with any additional terrorist acts such as a hijacking or a takeover of the city's water supply.[2]

These kinds of concerns have been echoed in a recent report by the U.S. National Academy of Sciences, which stated that the United States has been "remarkably lucky" with its computer networks and that technically proficient thieves or terrorists could subvert some of the country's most critical computer systems. According to the report, these included telecommunications networks, aviation control systems, and financial systems.[3]

What Is Hacking?

In the media, incidents such as the HBO prank are referred to as "hacking." Yet this term is not easy to define, nor is it a recent phenomenon. According to writers such as Steven Levy, author of *Hackers: Heroes of the Computer Revolution* (New York: Doubleday, 1985), the earliest hackers were students at the Massachusetts Institute of Technology (MIT) in the late 1960s. . . .

According to Levy, hacking as we understand it—that is, involving the use of computers—began to emerge only with the development of time-shared systems. Hacking then spread quickly once VDTs allowed users to interact with a machine directly rather than through the remote mechanism of card-based batch processing. Yet, even then, hacking referred to a much more noble set of activities than the criminal acts that are described by the term today. Hacking was an elite art practiced by small groups of extremely gifted individuals. It generated its own set of folk heroes, huge rivalries, eccentricities, and cult rituals. But, above all, this early form of hacking was about intellectual challenge and not malicious damage. Levy portrays this period as a sort of golden era of hacking, which mainly took place at two major sites—MIT and Stanford University in California. For most hackers at this time, their chief interest lay in understanding the innards of a system down to the last chip and the last line of the operating system. The software they wrote was for public display, use, and further development and was their major source of self-esteem, challenge, and socialization.

In Levy's view, all of this began to change once huge commercial interests moved into the software industry and flexed their legal and commercial muscles. Suddenly, software was not for public use or refinement. It had become the property of those who had paid for it to be written (and who didn't always appreciate unauthorized revisions), and once this had happened, the golden age came to an end. Intellectual challenge was not enough. Like everywhere else, there was no free lunch in the world of hacking, either. Therefore, to some extent Levy indirectly blames the commercialization of software for the emergence of hacking in its criminal form. Having been introduced to the cut and thrust of the commercial world, the best and brightest may have taken on this different set of values—a set that has been augmented and made more sinister among the current crop of hackers. Then, armed with these different values and goals and empowered by the development of nationwide networks of computers (the ARPANET being the earliest of these), hackers began to break out of the confines of their local machines and to spread their interests across the United States, even using links to international networks to gain access to systems on the other side of the earth.

Yet, even today, the term "hacking" has a wide range of meanings. To some, to hack is to roughly force a program to work, generally inelegantly. For others, a hack is a clever (generally small) program or program modification that displays unusual insight into a programming language or operating system. On the other hand, any scam or clever manipulation may also be termed a hack. For example, the famous stunt-card "switcheroo" at the 1961 Rose Bowl football game is often referred to as a great hack.[4] In this context, computer viruses (a topic we address shortly) may represent a particular kind of malicious and destructive hack. Many more of us, though, tend to associate the term almost exclusively with attempts to use the telephone network to gain unauthorized access to computer systems and their data (some have preferred to call this cracking). Psychologists, sociologists, and others who concern themselves with the behavioral aspects involved view hacking as mere computer addiction. Those suffering from the malady are regarded as being socially inept and unable to form a peer group through any medium other than that provided by the remoteness and abstraction of computing.

In their book *The Hacker's Dictionary*, authors Guy Steele et al. have outlined at least seven different definitions of a hacker:

1. A person who enjoys learning the details of computer systems and how to stretch their capabilities, as opposed to most users of computers, who prefer to learn only the minimum amount necessary.
2. One who programs enthusiastically or who enjoys programming rather than just theorizing about programming.
3. A person capable of appreciating *hack value.*
4. A person who is good at programming quickly.
5. An expert on a particular program or one who frequently does work using it or on it.
6. An expert of any kind.

7. A malicious inquisitive meddler who tries to discover information by poking around. For example, a *password hacker* is one who tries, possibly by deceptive or illegal means, to discover other peoples' computer passwords. A *network hacker* is one who tries to learn about the computer network (possibly to improve it or possibly to interfere).[5]

. . . For our purposes, hacking is any computer-related activity that is not sanctioned or approved of by an employer or owner of a system or network. We must distinguish it, however, from software piracy and computer crime, where the primary issue is the right of information ownership and the use of computer systems to perpetrate what, in any other arena, would simply be regarded as monetary theft or fraud. To some extent, this definition is rather broad and post-hoc. Nevertheless, such a definition provides us with a rich load of cases and events that are very much at the heart of ethical issues in computing.[6]

Why Do Hackers Hack?

There are probably as many answers to the question of why hackers hack as there are different forms of hacking. Clearly, some amount of intellectual challenge may be involved. Rather like solving an elaborate crossword, guessing passwords and inventing means of bypassing file protections pose intriguing problems that some individuals will go to enormous lengths to solve.[7] In other cases, hacking involves acts of vengeance, usually by a disgruntled employee against a former employer. For others, hacking represents a lifestyle that rests upon social inadequacy among otherwise intellectually capable individuals—the so-called computer nerd syndrome, which particularly affects male adolescents between the ages of fourteen and sixteen. These individuals tend to be self-taught, enjoy intellectual games, are not sexually active, and perhaps even neglect personal hygiene.[8] Indeed, a case of "computer psychosis" has even been reported in Copenhagen, Denmark. Apparently the young man concerned became so mesmerized by his computer that he was unable to distinguish between the real world and computer programs; he talked in programming language when carrying out ordinary everyday tasks.[9]

For psychologists such as Sherry Turkle of MIT, hackers are individuals who use computers as substitutes for people because computers don't require the mutuality and complexity that human relationships tend to demand. Other researchers at Carnegie-Mellon University have provided evidence that partially supports this view: Sara Kiesler and her coworkers have investigated the social psychology of computer-mediated communication and found that this medium removes status cues (such as sitting at the head of the table), body language (nods, frowns, etc.), and provides a kind of social anonymity that changes the way people make decisions in groups. Their investigations into computer conferencing and electronic mail showed that group decision-making discussions using this medium exhibited more equal participation and a larger coverage of issues.[10]

However, despite this benefit, the limited bandwidth of the computer screen (i.e., its lack of feedback in the form of body language, etc.) often has caused users to seek substitutes for physical cues. For example, in the absence of any other (nonverbal) mechanisms to communicate their emotions, electronic mail users often substitute depictions of their face to represent how they are feeling or how their message should be interpreted. The following keyboard characters are often used to represent a smile, a wink, and a sad face respectively (view them sideways):

|:-) |;-) |:-(

Hence, the form of communication that computers require, even when communicating with other human beings, may be attractive to those who feel less competent in face-to-face settings, where the subtleties of voice, dress, mannerisms, and vocabulary are mixed in complex ways. Those who are less skilled in dealing with these sources of information therefore may retreat to more concrete and anonymous forms of interaction with a machine, while those who are limited by these communication modes attempt to extend them to incorporate more naturalistic features of communication when dealing remotely with other human beings.

In contrast to this, other commentators, such as Professor Marvin Minsky of MIT, have argued that there is nothing very special about hackers: they are simply people with a particular obsession that is no different from that of old-style "radio hams" or of those addicted to certain sports, hobbies, cars, or any other popular kind of fascination.[11]

Yet this latter view ignores a very important difference between, say, an addiction to TV sports and an addiction to computers, particularly if the latter takes a malicious form. The amount of damage the TV sports enthusiast can cause is likely to be minimal, whereas hacking in its most malicious forms retains the potential to cause massive damage and perhaps even loss of life. The hypothetical scenarios presented in the introduction to this chapter depict some quite feasible applications of malicious hacking. Indeed, the power that we invest in computer systems sets them apart from conventional systems. This capability, allied with the remote and abstract nature of computing, provides the potential for individuals to cause massive damage with little understanding of the enormity of their acts, because the consequences are not fed back to the perpetrators in any meaningful way—and especially not in any form that emphasizes human costs.

Although this fact may contradict popular stereotypes about hackers, by far the greatest amount of hacking involves very little intellectual challenge or great intellectual ability.[12] Certainly, some system penetrations or hacks display incredible ingenuity. But, for the most part, hacking relies on some basic principles: excessive determination on the part of the hacker and reliance on human fallibility. For example, when faced with a new unpenetrated system, the most common form of attack is to guess passwords, because there is an amazing lack of variation in the kinds of passwords that users choose. . . .

Yet, apart from guessing passwords, there are very few ways in which a hacker can penetrate a system from the outside—although the stereotyped passwords that many people use often maximize a hacker's chances of discovering a legitimate user name and password combination. Despite such flukes, most system penetrations are abetted by some form of inside assistance. . . .

Indeed, some insider knowledge or partial access has proved to be an important part of the most spectacular break-ins that have occurred in recent years. For example, in 1986 a series of break-ins occurred at Stanford University in California. These were made possible by certain features of the UNIX operating system (one of the most popular operating systems in academic computing) as well as by the laxness of the systems programmers administering these systems.[13] The weaknesses included the networking features of certain versions of UNIX and the fact that this operating system will often allow users to log on using a guest account (usually with the same password, "guest"). Once into the first system, hackers were able to impersonate other users (again, knowing a couple of the classic weaknesses of UNIX) and gain access to other machines in the network that these same users had legitimate access to. The well-publicized hack carried out by Mathias Speer in 1988, in which he penetrated dozens of computers and networks across the world, also used many of these techniques to cross from machine to machine and from network to network.

In other cases, system and network inadequacies can sometimes be exploited to obtain access. For example, a persistent hacker sometimes can grab a line with legitimate privileges after a legitimate user has logged out. This can happen if the log-out sequence has not yet completed, so that the line the legitimate user has relinquished has not yet been hung up. If the hacker happens to log onto the system in those few microseconds, it is sometimes possible to grab the line and job of the legitimate user, who, more often than not, is preparing to walk away from the terminal.[14] . . .

Hackers: Criminals or Modern Robin Hoods?

The mass media has tended to sensationalize hacking while soundly condemning it. But there are other points of view: for example, in many instances the breaching of systems can provide more effective security in future, so that other (presumably less well-intentioned hackers) are prevented from causing real harm.[15] A good illustration of this was the penetration of British Telecom's electronic mail system in 1984 by Steven Gold and Robert Schifreen, who left a rude message in the Duke of Edinburgh's account. This incident attracted enormous publicity and led directly to improved security arrangements for the whole of the Prestel system. Gold and Schifreen, therefore, were extremely indignant at being treated as criminals, and their attitude illustrates once again the discrepancy between what the law considers to be criminal behavior and how hackers perceive themselves. . . .

More recently, the U.K.-based National Westminster Bank and the merchant bank S. G. Warburg met with a number of hackers to discuss arrangements for these computer experts to test the banks' security systems. Using the American idea of a "tiger team"—putting hackers in a controlled environment and pitting them against the existing security— the banks hoped to identify their weaknesses and also gain inside information from the hackers about what was happening in the hacking community and where potential threats might come from.[16]

We might ask ourselves whether, for the sake of balance, a truly democratic society should possess a core of technically gifted but recalcitrant people. Given that more and more information about individuals is now being stored on computers, often without their knowledge or consent, is it not reassuring that some citizens are able to penetrate these databases to find out what is going on? Thus, it could be argued that hackers represent one way in which we can help avoid the creation of a more centralized, even totalitarian, government. This is one scenario that hackers openly entertain. Indeed, we now know that at the time of the Chernobyl disaster, hackers from the West German Chaos Computer Club released more information to the public about developments than did the West German government. All of this information was gained by illegal break-ins carried out in government computer installations.

Given this background and the possibility of terrorist acts becoming increasingly technologically sophisticated, perhaps we also can look to hackers as a resource to be used to foil such acts and to improve our existing security arrangements. To some extent this development is already happening: in the United States, convicted hackers are regularly approached by security and intelligence organizations with offers to join them in return for amelioration or suspension of sentence. Other hackers have used their notoriety to establish computer security firms and to turn their covertly gained knowledge to the benefit of commercial and public institutions.[17] . . .

Admittedly, hacking has the potential to cause enormous harm by utilizing resources that have tremendous power. Yet we should not forget that there are other, equally powerful—and much older—ways in which similar powers can be unleashed. Leaks to the press, espionage of all kinds, and high-quality investigative journalism (such as that which uncovered Watergate and the Iran-Contra affair) have the power to break a government's control over the flow of information to the public and can even destroy corporations or governments that have been shown to be guilty of unethical or criminal acts.

Perhaps, therefore, the hallmark of a democracy is its capacity to tolerate people of all kinds, from different ethnic backgrounds, cultural beliefs, and religions, as well as those with radically opposing political views. It remains to be seen whether hacking in all its forms will be banned as a criminal offense in most modern democracies or whether some forms of it will be tolerated. From an ethical perspective, is the outlawing of hacking equivalent to criminalizing investigative journalism because journalists have been known to bribe officials or to obtain information unlawfully? As always, a balance must be struck between the ethical difficulties that are attached to activities such as investigative journalism and hacking and the greater public good that may (or may not) arise from them.

Indeed, to complete the analogy, we should bear in mind that a great deal of journalism is merely malicious muckraking that can damage a government or a company much more deeply than can some simple kinds of hacking. On the other hand, we need the muckrakers: the press is the principal institution that most democracies rely upon to ensure that the people are informed and that citizens remain aware of what is being done in their name.

The Hacker Crackdown

If any trend is evident in the world of hacking—apart from its increasing incidence—then it seems to involve the creation of stiffer penalties for hacking and a tighter legal framework classifying hacking as criminal behavior. For example, in August 1990, the United Kingdom introduced the Computer Misuse Act and identified three new offenses:

1. Unauthorized access: entry to a computer system knowing that the entry is unauthorized (six months' jail term).
2. Unauthorized access in furtherance of a more serious crime, punishable by up to five years imprisonment.

3. Unauthorized modification of computer material (viruses, trojan horses, malicious damage to files, etc.), punishable by up to five years imprisonment.[18]

The first person to be jailed under this legislation was Nicholas Whiteley (the so-called Mad Hacker). Whiteley, then a twenty-one-year-old computer operator was sentenced to a four-month jail term with a further eight-month suspended sentence.[19]

Elsewhere, similar calls for a crackdown on hacking have reached the popular press from concerned computing professionals or victims of hacking activity, and the number of prosecutions and convictions appears to be on the increase. . . .

Hacker cooperation seems unaffected by distance. In one noteworthy case, an eighteen-year-old Israeli and a twenty-four-year-old man from Colorado jointly penetrated NASA and U.S. Defence Department computers during the Desert Storm Gulf war operation. Of even greater interest than the distance involved was the sophistication of the Israeli teenager's phone phreaking equipment and the evidence of his involvement in an international credit card forgery ring.[20] . . .

But perhaps the clearest indication of a new hard-line approach to hacking occurred in 1990 when U.S. Secret Service agents instigated a national computer fraud investigation known as Operation Sundevil. This operation involved 150 agents simultaneously executing 28 search warrants on 16 U.S. citizens and the seizure of 42 computer systems, including 23,000 computer disks.[21] However, by mid 1991 it became clear that the operation had produced only one indictment as a result of a combination of lack of evidence and lack of the high-tech savvy needed for present gumshoe law enforcement officers to find such evidence.[22] Two of the most publicized victims of Operation Sundevil included Craig Neidorf and Steve Jackson of Steve Jackson Games, both of whom had systems and computer-related property seized by the Secret Service as a result of various charges involving wire fraud, computer fraud, and interstate transportation of stolen property. Eventually Neidorf stood trial but was acquitted, although he was forced to bear the $100,000 in costs incurred in making his defence.[23]

Yet, in contrast to these growing demands to bring hackers to account, a number of commentators have argued that these law enforcement efforts are misplaced. The threat from hackers, they argue, is overblown, and the major threat to computer installations remains what it always has been—not outside intruders, but inside employees.[24] Sociologist Richard Hollinger argues that hackers are simply the easiest target: isolated individuals pitted against massive corporate and government interests forced into a judicial system that finds it difficult to understand the offense, let alone make judgments on it. Yet, faced with the need to be seen to be doing something against the tide of "computer related criminal activities," law enforcement officials find hackers easy, high-profile targets compared to the hidden, often forgiven, or paid off inside computer criminals.[25]

Worms, Trojan Horses, and Bombs

New terms are entering the nomenclature of computing, many of them borrowed from other domains and many of them with sinister connotations. The following definitions may assist the reader in identifying the differences and similarities among some of these terms.

Trojan Horse   A program that allows access to an already-penetrated system—for example, by establishing a new account with superuser privileges. This tactic helps avoid overuse of the system manager's (superuser) account, which may show up on system statistics. It can also refer to a program that gathers the log-ins and passwords of legitimate users so that those who already have penetrated a system can log in under a wider variety of accounts. Sometimes confused with a "trap door," which is generally a secret entry that system designers build into their systems so that once they have left, they may gain access at any time without fear of discovery. The principle of the Trojan horse relies upon successful penetration and creation of alternative entry paths.

Logic Bomb or Time Bomb   A program that is triggered to act upon detecting a certain sequence of events or after a particular period of time has elapsed. For example, a popular form of logic bomb monitors employment files and initiates system damage (such as erasure of hard disks or secret corruption of key programs) once the programmer's employment has been terminated. A simple variation on the theme is a logic bomb virus—that is, a virus that begins to replicate and destroy a system once triggered by a time lapse, a set of pre-programmed conditions coming into existence, or remote control using the appropriate password.

Virus   A self-replicating program that causes damage—generally hard disk erasure or file corruption—and infects other programs, floppy disks, or hard disks by copying itself onto them (particularly onto components of the operating system or boot sectors of a disk). Viruses use a variety of strategies to avoid detection. Some are harmless, merely informing users that their systems have been infected without destroying components of the systems. Most are not benign, and identification of their creators can be virtually impossible, although some have been quite prepared to identify themselves.

Vaccine or Disinfectant A program that searches for viruses and notifies the user that a form of virus has been detected in the system. Some are general-purpose programs that search for a wide range of viruses, while others are more restricted and are capable only of identifying a particular virus type. Some are capable of eradicating the virus, but there are relatively few such programs. Other forms of virus protection include isolation of the infected system(s), use of non-writable system disks so that viruses cannot copy themselves there, and trying out unknown software (particularly public domain software downloaded from bulletin boards) on a minimal, isolated system.

Worm A self-replicating program that infects idle workstations or terminals on a network. The earliest worms were exploratory programs that demonstrated the concept itself and were generally not destructive, although they often replicated to the point at which a network would collapse. The latter phenomenon was used to good effect as the basis of the science fiction book, *Shockwave Rider* by John Brunner (Ballantine, New York, 1975). Worms tend to exist in memory and are not permanent, whereas viruses tend to reside on disk where they are permanent until eradicated. In addition, worms are network-oriented, with segments of the worm inhabiting different machines and being cognizant of the existence of other segments in other nodes of the network. Worms actively seek out idle machines and retreat when machine load increases. Viruses (at present) have none of these capabilities.

Tempest A term that refers to the electronic emissions that computers generate as they work. With the right equipment, these transmissions can be monitored, stored, and analyzed to help discover what the computer is doing. As would be expected, most security agencies throughout the world are interested in this phenomenon, but up to now it has not been the mechanism for any known hack. But given time, who knows?

The Virus Invasion

Software viruses are the most recent computer phenomenon to hit the headlines. Hardly a day goes by without reports of new viruses or accounts of a virus attacks that have resulted in the destruction of data and the shutdown of networks.

Yet the concept of a virus is not altogether new. Its precursor—the worm—was created in the early 1980s, when computer scientists John Schoch and Jon Hupp devised a program that would spread from machine to machine, steadily occupying the idle resources of the Xerox Palo Alto Research Center's network.[26] These early worms were fairly harmless and were released only at night when network traffic was low and the machines were unlikely to be used in any case. Whatever maliciousness was embedded in worm-type programs lay in their tendency to consume resources—particularly memory—until a system or network collapsed. Nevertheless, worms almost never caused any permanent damage. To rid a machine or network of a worm, all one had to do was to restart the machine or reboot the network.

The conceptualization and development of viruses had a longer gestation period. Other precursors to the virus included a number of experimental computer games, including the game program known as Core Wars.[27] This game operates by setting aside an area of machine memory (which in the earliest days of computing was often called the core) as a battleground for programs to compete for territory and to attempt to destroy each other. . . .

. . . What is most important about Core Wars, however, and indeed this whole genre of game programs, such as the games LIFE and Wa-Tor (both games that demonstrate the evolution of "life forms" in a computer-generated environment), is their common notion of reproduction in a computer-based system.

This concept of a program reproducing itself began to fascinate many people and, in particular, the notion that a program could spread itself beyond the boundaries of a single machine or network attracted a growing interest. The acknowledged originators of the virus concept were Fred Cohen and Len Adleman (who conceived of the term *virus*). At a computer security conference sponsored by the International Federation of Information Processing (IFIP) in 1984, they publicly announced the results of a range of experiments they had conducted using viruses to infect a range of different networks and host machines.[28] Their experiments showed how easily isolated machines and even whole networks could succumb to simple viral forms. In fact, their experiments were so successful that they often were banned from carrying out further experiments by the administrators of various systems. Yet, despite this and other public warnings of the future threat of software viruses, the first viral epidemics took much of the computing world by surprise.[29]

By far the most obvious (and common) way to virally infect a system is to piggyback a virus onto bona fide programs so that it can be transported on storage media such as tapes, floppy disks, and hard disks. In addition, a virus can be transported via network links and electronic mail. So long as the virus either appears to be a legitimate program or is capable of attaching itself to legitimate programs (such as the operating system), then its spread to other system users and countries can be almost assured. It should be noted, though, that although most of the current crop of viruses is maliciously destructive, a number of viruses have been released that are quite harmless; these usually inform the user that the virus has only occupied a few bytes of disk space. More common viruses tend to erase the entire contents of a user's hard disk or else corrupt programs and data to the point where they are irretrievably damaged and quite useless. . . .

Since the late 1980s hundreds of viruses have been created and have caused varying amounts of damage around the world. In 1990 it was even reported that 10 percent of the computers in China had been affected by only three strains of virus.[30] Now internationally recognized virus guru John McAfee has placed the number of different viruses at more than 1,200, with 10 to 15 new strains being found each week.[31] And perhaps the worst offenders are former Eastern Bloc programmers; some Russian experts estimate that there are 300–400 Russian strains alone.[32] Many of these viruses are variations on a theme in the sense that they rely on well-understood techniques for propagating themselves and infecting systems. However, new vaccine techniques are constantly being developed, and the vaccine development industry becomes more lucrative every year as its software products attempt to immunize systems from large-scale data loss to the annoying refrains of Barry Manilow hits. Yes, the Barry Manilow virus plays "Mandy" and "Copacabana" in endless succession![33]

Unfortunately, not all self-replicating software is so innocuous. In November 1988, a twenty-three-year-old Cornell University computer science student, Robert Morris, devised a worm program that crippled the network connecting MIT, the RAND Corporation, NASA's Ames Research Center, and other American universities. This virus was said to have spread to 6,000 machines before being detected. In June 1989 Morris was suspended from college after having been found guilty of violating the university's code of academic integrity. The FBI also carried a six-month investigation into this remarkable virus attack, and Morris was later charged under the Computer Fraud and Abuse Act of 1986 with unauthorized access to government computers.[34]. . .

Conceptually speaking, it is possible for viruses and worms to achieve much more sophisticated disruption than the cases reported so far, and it is quite likely that the next generation of software viruses will exhibit a quantum jump in intelligence and destructiveness. For example, it might be possible to develop a virus that only affects a particular user on a particular network. In other words, given sufficient technical expertise, instead of affecting all users, the virus would wait until a particular user ID executed an infected program. Then the virus would copy itself into the disk area of that user and begin to wreak havoc.

Alternatively, viruses may have a range of effects that they carry out on a random schedule, such as slowing a system down, deleting electronic mail, fuzzing the screen (which almost certainly would be attributed to a hardware problem), and encrypting files with a randomly selected encryption key (this would effectively deny users access to their own files until the key was discovered—an almost impossible task). Such strategies would delay the identification of a viral infection for an extended period, because the set of symptoms would be large and extremely variable. . . .

Even more worrying is the fact that commercially distributed software has been contaminated by viruses. In one well-publicized case, desktop publishing specialist Aldus shipped several thousand shrink-wrapped disks that were infected with the Peace virus.[35] The concern generated by the advent of increasingly sophisticated and powerful viruses has prompted some notable members of the computing community to call for new computers to be fitted with antiviral protection (both in software and hardware) as a standard feature.[36]

The next generation of viruses probably will be more selective, not only in whom they act upon and in the acts they carry out, but also in their objectives. This prospect raises a number of interesting questions and hypothetical scenarios. For example, could viruses be used for espionage purposes, not only infiltrating an enemy's machines to delete their files but gathering intelligence data that would be mailed back (electronically) or eventually gathered as versions of the virus filter back to the virus authors? Could viruses become another facet of military capabilities in much the same way that research into cryptography currently is? (A science fiction book has encapsulated this theme. *Softwar: La Guerre Douce* by French authors Thierry Breton and Denis Beneich depicts this scenario in pre-Glasnost days.) Given the remarkable swiftness with which new viruses appear to spread around the world, their potential uses as a weapon should not be underestimated.[37]

Such speculation seems to have some foundation from reports emerging out of the Gulf war. Citing a new book, *Triumph without Victory: The Unreported History of the Persian Gulf War*, U.S. News and World Report writer Philip R. Karn claimed that U.S. intelligence agents placed a virus in one of the microchips used in a model of printer and shipped it to Baghdad via Amman—apparently with devastating effects.[38] Other reports indicate that the United States Army is very interested in the possibilities of computer viruses and has even awarded a $50,000 preliminary study to a company known as Software and Electrical Engineering.[39]

Some other developments also suggest that virus warfare is not mere speculation. Already, the analogy of a computer system as an organism and a virus as an infection has been extended to incorporate the development of virus-killing programs called *vaccines*. These programs look for virus symptoms and notify users that their systems have been infected. Some of the better vaccines seek out the virus and kill it by repairing infected files. Furthermore, just as we would expect to eliminate a virus in humans by the use of quarantine procedures, when dealing with infected systems and media these procedures work equally well.

But for many virus attacks the only solution—provided that a vaccine doesn't work—is to erase the hard disk as well as any other media (tapes, floppy disks) that might have come into contact with the virus (almost like burning linen and other possibly infected items). Then, clean copies of the system and backup disks are reloaded onto the hard disk. Until this is done, the computer should not be used for any other purpose and the trading of storage media is extremely unwise. . . .

Because of the risks that virus attacks pose to the knowledge assets of large companies and corporations, and because of their lack of experience in dealing with them, a number of security firms and consulting companies have sprung up to exploit this rich commercial niche.[40] Furthermore, the development of hardware forms of viruses has fueled the demand for such firms, particularly since the discovery of the device known as Big Red. This small electronic gadget is surreptitiously installed in a computer installation by an insider or commercial saboteur. Like software viruses, this device is parasitic in that it interfaces with the host computer's operating system and converts encrypted files into "invisible" ones that can be inspected easily by other users, if they know where the files are and what to look for. At least fifty Big Reds have been found in the United States, the United Kingdom, and Australia in banking and transaction-handling systems.[41]. . .

But perhaps even more worrying is the effect that viruses may have on large, extremely complex, and potentially dangerous systems, such as those that manage air traffic control systems, hydroelectric dams, and nuclear plants. Already at least one nuclear power plant has been affected by the introduction of a computer virus. In early 1992 an employee of the atomic power plant in Ignalina, Lithuania, infected his system in the hope that he would be paid handsomely to fix the damage. As a result of the incident, both reactors were shut down and the Swedish government announced that it would pay to correct the twenty "small problems" that had emerged.[42]. . .

Ethical Issues Arising from Hacking

Some of the ethical difficulties associated with hacking and viruses are already quite well known, while other, more hypothetical, ones have yet to emerge. With regard to hacking or system penetration, the legal position in different countries is often confusing and is sometimes contradictory. But the central issues involved in hacking remain almost universal.

When a hacker gains access to a system and rummages around in a company's files without altering anything, what damage has been caused?

Has the hacker simply stolen a few cents worth of electricity? Indeed, if the hacker informs a company of its lax security procedures, is he or she creating a public benefit by performing a service that the company otherwise might have to pay for? In some countries, such as Canada, it is not an offense to walk into somebody's residence, look around, and leave, as long as nothing has been altered or damaged. Can a hacker's walk through a system be considered in similar terms?

Unfortunately, the legal basis applied to system break-ins languishes in the dark ages of real locks and doors and physical forms of information such as blueprints and contracts. Equally, the law as it applies to breaking and entering—the destruction of physical locks—and the theft of information in paper form is a poor analogy when applied to the electronic locks that modems and password systems provide and the highly mutable forms of information that computer files represent. After all, when one breaks into a system, nothing has been broken at all; hence, there is no obvious intent to cause harm. When a file has been copied or selectively viewed, what has been stolen? The information is still there. And if one happens to try out a few programs while browsing through a system, is this almost analogous to seeing someone's bicycle, riding it for a while, and then putting it back? Again, what harm has been caused, what crime has been committed? In the eyes of many hackers, only in the most trivial sense could this kind of use be considered unlawful.

On the other hand, where malicious damage of information does occur (such as the destruction of patients' records in a health administration system), then a form of criminal act clearly has occurred. The problem lies in determining the extent of the damage and the degree to which the act was premeditated. Unfortunately, in a complex and perhaps poorly understood computer system, it is quite easy to cause unintentional damage, yet it is extremely difficult to determine the extent to which the act was maliciously premeditated. In addition, for those figuring out a system for the first time, it is difficult to estimate the consequences of some acts or the extent to which a command sequence may alter the functionality of a system. Is this an example of ignorance of the law and is it equally unacceptable as a defense?

Perhaps what is central to the ethical debate regarding hacker behavior is the different conceptualizations of systems by their owners and by would-be hackers. For system owners, the system is their property (as suggested by the legal framework)—physical, touchable collections of central processors and disk drives—bought, paid for, and maintained for the use of authorized individuals to carry out authorized functions for the company's benefit. Any unauthorized person or even an authorized person who uses the system for unauthorized purposes is therefore guilty of a form of unlawful use—a criminal act in the eyes of the owners. For hackers, however, a system is an abstract resource at the end of a telephone line. It is a challenging talisman, an instrument they can borrow for a while and then return, probably without any damage done and without anybody being the wiser.

We enter a different arena, however, when we encounter acts of theft and willful damage. Clearly, the theft of credit card numbers and their circulation to other hackers are criminal acts, as is their use to obtain free telephone calls or to charge other goods and services. The destruction of information or its intentional alteration on a computer system can be regarded in similar terms. Yet, to return to our earlier point, should we regard browsing through a system as a criminal act? Perhaps the answer depends upon the nature of the information and who owns it. Undoubtedly, the operators of a military installation would prosecute over any unauthorized access, even if the system were concerned with the control of the army's laundry requirements. The government and the military have the right to deny access to certain information if they believe that it is central to the nation's defense or to its continued good government. Yet, is a laundry service central to national security or good government? Once again, we encounter a very familiar dilemma: who owns this information and who should or shouldn't have access to it?

In the private sector, we might even ask, What right does a company have to hold information on individuals and what right does it have to deny individuals access to that information? For example, many commercial institutions tap into databases that hold the credit ratings of hundreds of thousands of people. The providers of these databases have collected information from a huge range of sources and organized it so that it constitutes a history and an assessment of our trustworthiness as debtors. Who gave these companies the right to gather such information? Who gave them the right to sell it (which they do, along with subscription lists, names, and addresses)? What limits are there on the consequences of this information for the quality of our lives? What rights should we have to ensure that our particulars are correct? Suppose that a hacker penetrates a system to correct the records of those who have been denied correction of incorrect data. Which of these entities—the database owners or the hacker—has committed the greatest ethical error? Or are both equally guilty?

Perhaps the final issue is that concerning information ownership: Should information about me be owned by me? Or should I, as a database operator, own any information that I have paid to have gathered and stored? On the other hand, given that the storage of information is so pervasive and that the functioning of our modern society relies upon computer-based data storage, does the public have the right to demand absolute security in these systems? Finally, should some hackers be regarded as our unofficial investigative journalists—finding out who holds what information on whom and for what purpose; checking whether corporations are adhering to the data protection laws; and exposing flagrant abuses that the government cannot or will not terminate?

Many organizations in modern society claim to possess rights to the gathering and maintenance of information and its application in the form of computer-based information systems. In addition, apart from the dangers of the centralization of government power and authority, the centralization of information in powerful computer systems increases their influence in running our societies and, in turn, makes us more reliant upon them, thereby increasing their influence even further. In this milieu, the hacker represents a dangerous threat. Yet, like the corporations and institutions hackers act against, they also claim certain rights in terms of information access and ownership.

For many commentators, these issues should be resolved in the legal domain by determining the rights and responsibilities of information holders and the legal status of information and information systems. But such an approach may be too limited. Hacker activities can be deterred not only by punitive legislation but by making systems secure in the first place; that is, by making them secure in their design, in their technological implementation, and in the procedures and practices that are used in running them. And, in turn, that protection also implies inculcating security habits among employees and system managers.

There is an important role for ethics education in clearly identifying unethical practices and areas of ethical conflict. Unfortunately, the abstract nature of computing often removes it from its real-life consequences, and what appears to some to be an innocent act can cause untold harm if it goes wrong. By increasing the sensitivity of computing professionals and students to the ethical implications of their conduct, the amount of hacking might be reduced. This three-pronged approach of revising existing laws, building and running more secure systems, and sensitizing individuals to ethical issues has been advocated in more recent writings by Peter Denning and other authorities.[43] Even representatives of IBM have spoken of the limitations of technical measures against hacking and viruses and have suggested that the greatest gains might be made in simply convincing people that high-tech high-jinks are wrong.[44]

Notes

1. "Conclusion of the HBO Captain Midnight Saga," *Software Engineering Notes*, vol. 11, no. 5, October 1986, pages 24–25.

2. "Enter the Technically-Competent Terrorist," *The Australian*, 8 April 1986; Perry Morrison, "Limits to Technocratic Consciousness: Information Technology and Terrorism as Example," *Science, Technology and Human Values*, vol. 11, no. 4, 1986, pages 4–16.

3. Dan Charles, "Can We Stop the Databank Robbers?" *New Scientist*, 26 January 1991, pages 12–13.

4. Peter G. Neumann, in *Software Engineering Notes*, vol. 9, no. 1, January 1984, pages 12–15.

5. Peter G. Neumann, op. cit.

6. Interested readers can find a much more detailed account of hacking in Katie Hafner and John Markoff's book, *Cyberpunk: Outlaws and Hackers on the Computer Frontier* (Simon and Schuster, New York, 1991). The authors provide a very readable account of major hacking cases with a rich background on the individual hackers.

7. Stuart Gill, "Hi-Tech's Hubcap Thieves Are in It for the Buzz," *Computing Australia*, 26 October 1987, pages 33–34.

8. Eric S. Raymond (ed.) and Guy L. Steele, Jr., *The New Hacker's Dictionary*, (MIT Press, Cambridge MA, 1991).

9. *Software Engineering Notes*, vol. 12, no. 4, October 1987, page 9.

10. Sara Kiesler, Jane Siegel, and Timothy McGuire, "Social Psychological Aspects of Computer-Mediated Communication," *American Psychologist*, vol. 39, no. 10, 1984, pages 1123–1134.

11. Rosemarie Robotham, "Putting Hackers on the Analyst's Couch," *The Australian*, 31 January 1989, pages 30–34.

12. "NASA Hackers Weren't as Smart as It Seems," *Computing Australia*, 13 July 1987.

13. Brian Reid, "Lessons from the UNIX Break-Ins at Stanford," *Software Engineering Notes*, vol. 11, no. 5, October 1986, page 29.

14. "More on Nonsecure Nonlogouts," *Software Engineering Notes*, vol. 11, no. 5, October 1986, page 26.

15. I. S. Herschberg and R. Paans, "The Programmer's threat: Cases and Causes," in J. H. Finch and E. G. Dougall (eds.), *Computer Security: A Global Challenge* (Elsevier, North-Holland, 1984) pages 409–423.

16. Peter Warren, "Unholy Alliance," *Computer Talk*, 22 October 1990.

17. Jay Peterzell, "Spying and Sabotage by Computer," *Time*, 20 March 1989; Richard Caseby, "Worried Firms Pay Hush Money to Hacker Thieves," *South China Morning Post*, 12 June 1989 (reprinted from *The Times*); and "Open Season for Hackers," *Computing Australia*, 18 September 1989.

18. *Software Engineering Notes*, vol. 15, no. 5, October 1990, page 12.

19. *The Daily Telegraph* (UK), 8 June 1990; Richard Siddle, "Freed Hacker in Lords Quest," *Computer Talk*, 8 April 1991; "Hacking Defined as Crime," *Computing Australia*, 16 July 1990; "Hacker Takes up the Challenge and Pays," *Computing Australia*, 4 June 1990; "Mad Hacker Jailed in UK Legal First," *The Australian*, 12 June 1990.

20. "Harmless" Hacker under Jail Threat," *Computer Talk*, 7 October 1991; "Arrested Israeli 'Genius' Saw Hacking as a Challenge," *The Australian*, 10 September, 1991.

21. *Detroit News*, 10 May 1990.

22. Mark Lewyn, "Why the 'Legion of Doom' Has Little Fear of the Feds," *Business Week*, 22 April 1991, page 62.

23. Dorothy Denning, "ATE vs. Craig Neidorf," *Communications of the ACM*, vol. 34, no. 3, March 1991, pages 23–43.

24. Dan Charles, "Crackdown on Hackers May Violate Civil Rights," *New Scientist*, 21 July 1990, page 8.

25. Richard Hollinger, "Hackers: Computer Heroes or Electronic Highwaymen?" *Computers and Society*, vol. 21, no. 1, 1991, pages 6–16.

26. J. F. Schoch and J. A. Hupp, "The Worm Programs—Early Experiences with Distributed Computation," *Communications of the ACM*, vol. 25, no. 3, 1982, pages 172–180.

27. A. K. Dewdney, "Computer Recreations," *Scientific American*, May 1984, pages 15–19, and March 1985, pages 14–19.

28. Fred Cohen, "Computer Viruses: Theory and Experiments," in J. H. Finch and E. G. Dougall (eds.), op. cit., pages 143–157.

29. Perry Morrison, "Computer Parasites: Software Diseases May Cripple Our Computers," *The Futurist*, March–April 1986, vol. 20, no. 2, pages 36–38; Lee Dembart, "Attack of the Computer Virus," *Discover*, November 1984, pages 90–92.

30. *Software Engineering Notes*, vol. 15, no. 1, January 1990, page 13.

31. Julian Cribb, "Computer Virus Due to Strike in March," *The Australian*, 12 February 1992.

32. "Russian Viruses in Global Epidemic," *The Australian*, 3 November 1992.

33. "News Track," *Communications of the ACM*, vol. 35, no. 6, June 1992, page 10.

34. "Cornell Virus Suspect Suspended for Violation," *The Australian*, 6 June 1989; "Cornell Suspends Student Hacker," *Computing Australia*, 12 June 1989; Tony Fainberg, "The Night the Network Failed," *New Scientist*, 4 March 1989, pages 36–42.

35. Richard Jinman, "US Author Attacks Virus Spread Theory," *The Australian*, 5 June 1990.

36. Lance J. Hoffman (ed.), *Rogue Programs: Viruses, Worms and Trojan Horses* (Van Nostrand Reinhold, New York, 1990).

37. Nicholas Rothwell, "Computer AIDS: The Hitech Disease That Is Spreading Worldwide," *The Weekend Australian*, 4 June 1988; David Hebditch, Nick Anning, and Linda Melvern, *Techno-Bandits* (Houghton Mifflin, Boston, 1984).

38. "Operation Virus," *The Australian*, 18 November 1991; *Software Engineering Notes*, vol. 17, no. 2, April 1992, page 18.

39. Mark Lewyn, "'Killer' Viruses: An Idea Whose Time Shouldn't Come," *Business Week*, 23 July 1990.

40. Evan I. Schwartz and Jeffrey Rothfeder, "Viruses? Who You Gonna Call? 'Hackerbusters,'" *Business Week*, 6 August 1990, pages 48–49.

41. "What to Do about Computer Viruses," *Fortune*, 5 December 1988, page 16; "Local Crime Team Crack the Riddle of Big Red," *The Australian*, 14 April 1987.

42. *Software Engineering Notes*, vol. 17, no. 2, April 1992, page 19.

43. Peter Denning (ed.), *Computers Under Attack: Intruders, Worms and Viruses* (ACM Press/Addison-Wesley, New York, 1990).

44. "Viruses Give Legislators a Headache," *The Australian*, 13 March 1990.

THE CONSCIENCE OF A HACKER

The Mentor

This selection (brief enough to speak for itself) is a view (in almost beat poetry style) of what it is to be a hacker and the societal reaction to the hackers.

Another one got caught today, it's all over the papers. "Teenager Arrested in Computer Crime Scandal," "Hacker Arrested after Bank Tampering". . .
Damn kids. They're all alike.

But did you, in your three-piece psychology and 1950's technobrain, ever take a look behind the eyes of the hacker? Did you ever wonder what made him tick, what forces shaped him, what may have molded him?
I am a hacker, enter my world . . .
Mine is a world that begins with school . . . I'm smarter than most of the other kids, this crap they teach us bores me . . .
Damn underachievers. They're all alike.

I'm in junior high or high school. I've listened to teachers explain for the fifteenth time how to reduce a fraction. I understand it. "No, Ms. Smith, I didn't show my work. I did it in my head . . ."
Damn kid. Probably copied it. They're all alike.

I made a discovery today. I found a computer. Wait a second, this is cool. It does what I want it to. If it makes a mistake, it's because I screwed it up. Not because it doesn't like me . . .
Or feels threatened by me . . .
Or thinks I'm a smart ass . . .
Or doesn't like teaching and shouldn't be here . . .
Damn kid. All he does is play games. They're all alike.

And then it happened . . . a door opened to a world . . . rushing through the phone line like heroin through an addict's veins, an electronic pulse is sent out, a refuge from the day-to-day incompetencies is sought . . . a board is found.

Reprinted from *Phrack* 14 (1987), with permission of the author.

"This is it . . . this is where I belong . . ."

I know everyone here . . . even if I've never met them, never talked to them, may never hear from them again . . . I know you all . . .

Damn kid. Tying up the phone line again. They're all alike . . .

You bet your ass we're all alike . . . we've been spoon-fed baby food at school when we hungered for steak . . . the bits of meat that you did let slip through were pre-chewed and tasteless. We've been dominated by sadists, or ignored by the apathetic. The few that had something to teach found us willing pupils, but those few are like drops of water in the desert.

This is our world now . . . the world of the electron and the switch, the beauty of the baud. We make use of a service already existing without paying for what could be dirt-cheap if it wasn't run by profiteering gluttons, and you call us criminals. We explore . . . and you call us criminals. We seek after knowledge . . . and you call us criminals. We exist without skin color, without nationality, without religious bias . . . and you call us criminals. You build atomic bombs, you wage wars, you murder, cheat, and lie to us and try to make us believe it's for our own good, yet we're the criminals.

Yes, I am a criminal. My crime is that of curiosity. My crime is that of judging people by what they say and think, not what they look like. My crime is that of outsmarting you, something that you will never forgive me for.

I am a hacker, and this is my manifesto. You may stop this individual, but you can't stop us all . . . after all, we're all alike.

ARE COMPUTER HACKER BREAK-INS ETHICAL?

Eugene Spafford

In contrast to the view of hacking taken by hackers themselves, Eugene Spafford explains why no break-in is ever harmless. Surveying several arguments proposed by hackers in support of their activities, Spafford uses what he calls a "deontological" approach (acts are

Reprinted from *Journal of Systems Software* 17 (1992): 41–47, with permission from Elsevier Science.

right or wrong in themselves without reference to their results) both to point out flaws in these arguments and to counterargue that, except in very rare and extreme cases, hacking is ethically problematic.

Introduction*

On November 2, 1988, a program was run on the Internet that replicated itself on thousands of machines, often loading them to the point where they were unable to process normal requests [2–4]. This Internet Worm program was stopped in a matter of hours, but the controversy engendered by its release has raged ever since. Other incidents, such as the "wily hackers"[†] tracked by Cliff Stoll [5], the "Legion of Doom" members who are alleged to have stolen telephone company 911 software [6], and the growth of the computer virus problem [7–10] have added to the discussion. What constitutes improper access to computers? Are some break-ins ethical? Is there such a thing as a "moral hacker" [11]?

It is important that we discuss these issues. The continuing evolution of our technological base and our increasing reliance on computers for critical tasks suggest that future incidents may well have more serious consequences than those we have seen to date. With human nature as varied and extreme as it is, and with the technology as available as it is, we must expect to experience more of these incidents.

In this article, I will introduce a few of the major issues that these incidents have raised, and present some arguments related to them. For clarification, I have separated several issues that often have been combined when debated, it is possible that most people agree on some of these points once they are viewed as individual issues.

What Is Ethical?

Webster's Collegiate Dictionary defines ethics as "the discipline dealing with what is good and bad and with moral duty and obligation." More simply, it is the study of what is right to do in a given situation—what we ought to do. Alternatively, it is sometimes described as the study of what is good and how to achieve that good. To suggest whether an act is right or wrong we need to agree on an ethical system that is easy to understand and apply as we consider the ethics of computer break-ins.

---

*An earlier version of this paper appeared as [1].

[†]Many law-abiding individuals consider themselves *hackers*—a term formerly used as a compliment. The press and general public have co-opted the term, however, and it is now commonly viewed as pejorative. Here, I will use the word as the general public now uses it.

Philosophers have been trying for thousands of years to define right and wrong, and I will not make yet another attempt at such a definition. Instead, I will suggest that we make the simplifying assumption that we can judge the ethical nature of an act by applying a deontological assessment; regardless of the effect, is the act itself ethical? Would we view that act as sensible and proper if everyone were to engage in it? Although this may be too simplistic a model (and it can certainly be argued that other ethical philosophies may also be applied), it is a good first approximation for purposes of discussion. If you are unfamiliar with any other formal ethical evaluation method, try applying this assessment to the points I raise later in this article. If the results are obviously unpleasant or dangerous in the large, then they should be considered unethical as individual acts.

Note that this philosophy assumes that right is determined by actions, not results. Some ethical philosophies assume that the ends justify the means; our society does not operate by such a philosophy, although many individuals do. As a society, we profess to believe that "it isn't whether you win or lose, it's how you play the game." This is why we are concerned with issues of due process and civil rights, even for those espousing repugnant views and committing heinous acts. The process is important no matter the outcome, although the outcome may help to resolve a choice between two almost equal courses of action.

Philosophies that consider the results of an act as the ultimate measure of good are often impossible to apply because of the difficulty in understanding exactly what results from any arbitrary activity. Consider an extreme example: the government orders 100 cigarette smokers, chosen at random, to be beheaded on live nationwide television. The result might well be that many hundreds of thousands of other smokers would quit cold turkey, thus prolonging their lives. It might also prevent hundreds of thousands of people from ever starting to smoke, thus improving the health and longevity of the general populace. The health of millions of other people would improve because they would no longer be subjected to secondary smoke, and the overall impact on the environment would be favorable as tons of air and ground pollutants would no longer be released by smokers or tobacco companies.

Yet, despite the great good this might hold for society, everyone, except for a few extremists, would condemn such an act as immoral. We would likely object even if only one person were executed. It would not matter what the law might be on such an issue; we would not feel that the act was morally correct, nor would we view the ends as justifying the means.

Note that we would be unable to judge the morality of such an action by evaluating the results, because we would not know the full scope of those results. Such an act might have effects, favorable or otherwise, on issues of law, public health, tobacco use, and daytime TV shows for decades or centuries to follow. A system of ethics that considered primarily only the results of our actions could not allow us to evaluate our current activities at the time when we would need such guidance; if we are unable to discern the appropriate course of action prior to its commission, then our system of ethics is of little or no value to us. To obtain ethical guidance, we must base our actions primarily on evaluations of the actions and not on the possible results.

More to the point here, if we attempt to judge the morality of a computer break-in based on the sum total of all future effect, we would be unable to make such a judgment, either for a specific incident or for the general class of acts. In part, this is because it is so difficult to determine the long-term effects of various actions and to discern their causes. We cannot know, for instance, if increased security awareness and restrictions are better for society in the long term, or whether these additional restrictions will result in greater costs and annoyance when using computer systems. We also do not know how many of these changes are directly traceable to incidents of computer break-ins.

One other point should be made here: it is undoubtedly possible to imagine scenarios where a computer break-in would be considered to be the preferable course of action. For instance, if vital medical data were on a computer and necessary to save someone's life in an emergency, but the authorized users of the system could not be located, breaking into the system might well be considered the right thing to do. However, that action does not make the break-in ethical. Rather, such situations occur when a greater wrong would undoubtedly occur if the unethical act were not committed. Similar reasoning applies to situations such as killing in self defense. In the following discussion, I will assume that such conflicts are not the root cause of the break-ins; such situations should very rarely present themselves.

Motivations

Individuals who break into computer systems or who write vandalware usually use one of several rationalizations for their actions. (See, for example, [12] and the discussion in [13].) Most of these individuals would never think to walk down a street, trying every door to find one unlocked, then search through the drawers of the furniture inside. Yet these same people seem to give no second thought to making repeated attempts at guessing passwords to accounts they do not own, and once into a system, browsing through the files on disk.

These computer burglars often give the same reasons for their actions in an attempt to rationalize their activities as morally justified. I present and refute some of the most commonly used ones; motives involving theft and revenge are not uncommon, and their moral nature is simple to discern, so I shall not include them here.

THE HACKER ETHIC

Many hackers argue that they follow an ethic that both guides their behavior and justifies their break-ins. This hacker ethic states, in part, that all information should be free [11]. This view holds that information belongs to everyone and there should be no boundaries or restraints to prevent anyone from examining information. Richard Stallman states much the same thing in his GNU Manifesto [14]. He and others have stated in various forums that if information is free, it logically follows that there should be no such thing as intellectual property, and no need for security.

What are the implications and consequences of such a philosophy? First and foremost, it raises some disturbing questions of privacy. If all information is (or should be) free, then privacy is no longer a possibility. For information to be free to everyone and for individuals to no longer be able to claim it as property means that anyone may access the information if they please. Furthermore, as it is no longer property of any individual, anyone can alter the information. Items such as bank balances, medical records, credit histories, employment records, and defense information all cease to be controlled. If someone controls information and controls who may access it, the information is obviously not free. But without that control, we would no longer be able to trust the accuracy of the information.

In a perfect world, this lack of privacy and control might not be cause for concern. However, if all information were to be freely available and modifiable, imagine how much damage and chaos would be caused in our real world! Our whole society is based on information whose accuracy must be assured. This includes information held by banks and other financial institutions, credit bureaus, medical agencies and professionals, government agencies such as the IRS, law enforcement agencies, and educational institutions. Clearly, treating all their information as "free" would be unethical in any world where there might be careless and unethical individuals.

Economic arguments can be made against this philosophy, too, in addition to the overwhelming need for privacy and control of information accuracy. Information is not universally free. It is held as property because of privacy concerns, and because it is often collected and developed at great expense. Development of a new algorithm or program or collection of a specialized data base may involve the expenditure of vast sums of time and effort. To claim that it is free or should be free is to express a naive and unrealistic view of the world. To use this to justify computer break-ins is clearly unethical. Although not all information currently treated as private or controlled as proprietary needs such protection, that does not justify unauthorized access to it or to any other data.

THE SECURITY ARGUMENTS

These arguments are the most common ones offered within the computer community. One argument is the same as that used most often to defend the author of the Internet Worm program in 1988: break-ins illustrate security problems to a community that will otherwise not note the problems.

In the Worm case, one of the first issues to be discussed widely in Internet mailing lists dealt with the intent of the perpetrator—exactly why the worm program had been written and released. Explanations put forth by members of the community ranged from simple accident to the actions of a sociopath. Many said that the Worm was designed to reveal security defects to a community that would not otherwise pay attention. This was not supported by the testimony of the author during his trial, nor is it supported by past experience of system administrators.

The Worm author, Robert T. Morris, appears to have been well known at some universities and major companies, and his talents were generally respected. Had he merely explained the problems or offered a demonstration to these people, he would have been listened to with considerable attention. The month before he released the Worm program on the Internet, he discovered and disclosed a bug in the file transfer program *ftp*; news of the flaw spread rapidly, and an official fix was announced and available within a matter of weeks. The argument that no one would listen to his report of security weaknesses is clearly fallacious.

In the more general case, this security argument is also without merit. Although some system administrators might have been complacent about the security of their systems before the Worm incident, most computer vendors, managers of government computer installations, and system administrators at major colleges and universities have been attentive to reports of security problems. People wishing to report a problem with the security of a system need not exploit it to report it. By way of analogy, one does not set fire to the neighborhood shopping center to bring attention to a fire hazard in one of the stores, and then try to justify the act by claiming that firemen would otherwise never listen to reports of hazards.

The most general argument that some people make is that the individuals who break into systems are performing a service by exposing security flaws, and thus should be encouraged or even rewarded. This argument is severely flawed in several ways. First, it assumes that there is some compelling need to force users to install security fixes on their systems, and thus computer burglars are justified in "breaking and entering" activities. Taken to extremes, it suggests that it would be perfectly acceptable to engage in such activities on a continuing basis, so long as they might expose security flaws. This completely loses sight of the purpose of the computers in the first place—to serve as tools and resources, not as exercises in security. The same reasoning would imply that vigilantes have the right to attempt to break into the homes in my neighborhood on a continuing basis to demonstrate that they are susceptible to burglars.

Another flaw with this argument is that it completely ignores the technical and economic factors that prevent many sites from upgrading or correcting their software. Not every site has the resources to install new system software or to correct existing software. At many sites, the systems are run as turnkey systems—employed as tools and maintained by the vendor. The owners and users of these machines simply do not have the ability to correct or maintain their systems independently, and they are unable to afford custom software support from their vendors. To break into such systems, with or without damage, is effectively to trespass into places of business; to do so in a vigilante effort to force the owners to upgrade their security structure is presumptuous and reprehensible. A burglary is not justified, morally or legally, by an argument that the victim has poor locks and was therefore "asking for it."

A related argument has been made that vendors are responsible for the maintenance of their software, and that such security breaches should immediately require vendors to issue corrections to their customers, past and present. The claim is made that without highly-visible break-ins, vendors will not produce or distribute necessary fixes to software. This attitude is naive, and is neither economically feasible nor technically workable. Certainly, vendors should bear some responsibility for the adequacy of their software [15], but they should not be responsible for fixing every possible flaw in every possible configuration.

Many sites customize their software or otherwise run systems incompatible with the latest vendor releases. For a vendor to be able to provide quick response to security problems, it would be necessary for each customer to run completely standardized software and hardware mixes to ensure the correctness of vendor-supplied updates. Not only would this be considerably less attractive for many customers and contrary to their usual practice, but the increased cost of such "instant" fix distribution would add to the price of such a system and greatly increase the cost borne by the customer. It is unreasonable to expect the user community to sacrifice flexibility and pay a much higher cost per unit simply for faster corrections to the occasional security breach, assuming it is possible for the manufacturer to find those customers and supply them with fixes in a timely manner—something unlikely in a market where machines and software are often repackaged, traded, and resold.

The case of the Internet Worm is a good example of the security argument and its flaws. It further stands as a good example of the conflict between ends and means valuation of ethics. Various people have argued that the Worm's author did us a favor by exposing security flaws. At Mr. Morris's trial on Federal charges stemming from the incident, the defense attorneys also argued that their client should not be punished because of the good the Worm did in exposing those flaws. Others, including the prosecuting attorneys, argued that the act itself was wrong no matter what the outcome. Their contention has been that the result does not justify the act itself, nor does the defense's argument encompass all the consequences of the incident.

This is certainly true; the complete results of the incident are still not known. There have been many other break-ins and network worms since November 1988, perhaps inspired by the media coverage of that incident. More attempts will possibly be made, in part inspired by Mr. Morris's act. Some sites on the Internet have restricted access to their machines, and others were removed from the network; other sites have decided not to pursue a connection, even though it will hinder research and operations. Combined with the many decades of person-hours devoted to cleaning up after the worm, this seems a high price to pay for a claimed "favor."

The legal consequences of this act are also not yet known. For instance, many bills have been introduced into Congress and state legislatures over the last three years in part because of these incidents. One piece of legislation introduced into the House of Representatives, HR-5061, entitled "The Computer Virus Eradication Act of 1988," was the first in a series of legislative actions that have the potential to affect significantly the computer profession. In particular, HR-5061 was notable because its wording would prevent it from being applied to true computer viruses.* The passage of similar well-intentioned but poorly defined legislation could have a major negative effect on the computing profession as a whole.

THE IDLE SYSTEM ARGUMENT

Another argument put forth by system hackers is that they are simply making use of idle machines. They argue that because some systems are not used at a level near their capacity, the hacker is somehow entitled to use them.

This argument is also flawed. First of all, these systems are usually not in service to provide a general-purpose user environment. Instead, they are in use in commerce, medicine, public safety, research, and government functions. Unused capacity is present for future needs and sudden surges of activity, not for the support of outside individuals. Imagine if large numbers of people without a computer were to take advantage of a system with

---

*It provided penalties only in cases where programs were introduced into computer systems; a computer virus is a segment of code attached to an existing program that modifies other programs to include a copy of itself [7].

idle processor capacity: the system would quickly be overloaded and severely degraded or unavailable for the rightful owners. Once on the system, it would be difficult (or impossible) to oust these individuals if sudden extra capacity were needed by the rightful owners. Even the largest machines available today would not provide sufficient capacity to accommodate such activity on any large scale.

I am unable to think of any other item that someone may buy and maintain, only to have others claim a right to use it when it is idle. For instance, the thought of someone walking up to my expensive car and driving off in it simply because it is not currently being used is ludicrous. Likewise, because I am away at work, it is not proper to hold a party at my house because it is otherwise not being used. The related positions that unused computing capacity is a shared resource, and that my privately developed software belongs to everyone, are equally silly (and unethical) positions.

THE STUDENT HACKER ARGUMENT

Some trespassers claim that they are doing no harm and changing nothing—they are simply learning about how computer systems operate. They argue that computers are expensive, and that they are merely furthering their education in a cost-effective manner. Some authors of computer viruses claim that their creations are intended to be harmless, and that they are simply learning how to write complex programs.

There are many problems with these arguments. First, as an educator, I claim that writing vandalware or breaking into a computer and looking at the files has almost nothing to do with computer education. Proper education in computer science and engineering involves intensive exposure to fundamental aspects of theory, abstraction, and design techniques. Browsing through a system does not expose someone to the broad scope of theory and practice in computing, nor does it provide the critical feedback so important to a good education [16, 17]; neither does writing a virus or worm program and releasing it into an unsupervised environment provide any proper educational experience. By analogy, stealing cars and joyriding does not provide one with an education in mechanical engineering, nor does pouring sugar in the gas tank.

Furthermore, individuals "learning" about a system cannot know how everything operates and what results from their activities. Many systems have been damaged accidently by ignorant (or careless) intruders; most of the damage from computer viruses (and the Internet Worm) appear to be caused by unexpected interactions and program faults. Damage to medical systems, factory control, financial information, and other computer systems could have drastic and far-ranging effects that have nothing to do with education, and could certainly not be considered harmless.

A related refutation of the claim has to do with knowledge of the extent of the intrusion. If I am the person responsible for the security of a critical computer system, I cannot assume that *any* intrusion is motivated solely by curiosity and that nothing has been harmed. If I know that the system has been compromised, I must fear the worst and perform a complete system check for damages and changes. I cannot take the word of the intruder, for any intruder who actually caused damage would seek to hide it by claiming that he or she was "just looking." To regain confidence in the correct behavior of my system, I must expend considerable energy to examine and verify every aspect of it.

Apply our universal approach to this situation and imagine if this "educational" behavior was widespread and commonplace. The result would be that we would spend all our time verifying our systems and never be able to trust the results fully. Clearly, this is not good, and thus we must conclude that these "educational" motivations are also unethical.

THE SOCIAL PROTECTOR ARGUMENT

One last argument, more often heard in Europe than the United States, is that hackers break into systems to watch for instances of data abuse and to help keep "Big Brother" at bay. In this sense, the hackers are protectors rather than criminals. Again, this assumes that the ends justify the means. It also assumes that the hackers are actually able to achieve some good end.

Undeniably, there is some misuse of personal data by corporations and by the government. The increasing use of computer-based record systems and networks may lead to further abuses. However, it is not clear that breaking into these systems will aid in righting the wrongs. If anything, it may cause those agencies to become even more secretive and use the break-ins as an excuse for more restricted access. Break-ins and vandalism have not resulted in new open-records laws, but they have resulted in the introduction and passage of new criminal statutes. Not only has such activity failed to deter "Big Brother," but it has also resulted in significant segments of the public urging more laws and more aggressive law enforcement—the direct opposite of the supposed goal.

It is also not clear that these hackers are the individuals we want "protecting" us. We need to have the designers and users of the systems—trained computer professionals—concerned about our rights and aware of the dangers involved with the inappropriate use of computer monitoring and record keeping. The threat is a relatively new one, as computers and networks have become widely used only in the last few decades. It will take some time for awareness of the dangers to spread throughout the profession. Clandestine efforts to breach the security of computer systems do nothing to raise the consciousness of the appropriate individuals. Worse, they associate that commendable goal (heightened concern) with criminal activity (computer break-ins), thus discouraging proactive behavior by the individuals in the best positions to act in our favor. Perhaps it is in this sense that computer break-ins and vandalism are most unethical and damaging.

Conclusion

I have argued here that computer break-ins, even when no obvious damage results, are unethical. This must be the considered conclusion even if the result is an improvement in security, because the activity itself is disruptive and immoral. The results of the act should be considered separately from the act itself, especially when we consider how difficult it is to understand all the effects resulting from such an act.

Of course, I have not discussed every possible reason for a break-in. There might well be an instance where a break-in might be necessary to save a life or to preserve national security. In such cases, to perform one wrong act to prevent a greater wrong may be the right thing to do. It is beyond the scope or intent of this paper to discuss such cases, especially as no known hacker break-ins have been motivated by such instances.

Historically, computer professionals as a group have not been overly concerned with questions of ethics and propriety as they relate to computers. Individuals and some organizations have tried to address these issues, but the whole computing community needs to be involved to address the problems in any comprehensive manner. Too often, we view computers simply as machines and algorithms, and we do not perceive the serious ethical questions inherent in their use.

However, when we consider that these machines influence the quality of life of millions of individuals, both directly and indirectly, we understand that there are broader issues. Computers are used to design, analyze, support, and control applications that protect and guide the lives and finances of people. Our use (and misuse) of computing systems may have effects beyond our wildest imagining. Thus, we must reconsider our attitudes about acts demonstrating a lack of respect for the rights and privacy of other people's computers and data.

We must also consider what our attitudes will be towards future security problems. In particular, we should consider the effect of widely publishing the source code for worms, viruses, and other threats to security. Although we need a process for rapidly disseminating corrections and security information as they become known, we should realize that widespread publication of details will imperil sites where users are unwilling or unable to install updates and fixes.* Publication should serve a useful purpose; endangering the security of other people's machines or attempting to force them into making changes they are unable to make or afford is not ethical.

Finally, we must decide these issues of ethics as a community of professionals and then present them to society as a whole. No matter what laws are passed, and no matter how good security measures might become, they will not be enough for us to have completely secure systems. We also need to develop and act according to some shared ethical values. The members of society need to be educated so that they understand the importance of respecting the privacy and ownership of data. If locks and laws were all that kept people from robbing houses, there would be many more burglars than there are now; the shared mores about the sanctity of personal property are an important influence in the prevention of burglary. It is our duty as informed professionals to help extend those mores into the realm of computers.

References

1. Spafford, E. H. Is a computer break-in ever ethical? *Info. Tech. Quart.* IX:9–14 (1990).
2. Seeley, D. A tour of the worm, In *Proceedings of the Winter 1989 Usenix Conference*, The Usenix Association, Berkeley, CA, 1989.
3. Spafford, E. H. The internet worm: crisis and aftermath. *Commun. ACM* 32, 678–698 (1989).
4. Spafford, E. H. An analysis of the internet work. In *Proceedings of the 2nd European Software Engineering Conference* (C. Ghezzi and J. A. McDermid, eds.), Springer-Verlag, Berlin, Germany, 1989, pp. 446–468.
5. Stoll, C. *Cuckoo's Egg*, Doubleday, New York, 1989.
6. Schwartz, John. The hacker dragnet, *Newsweek* 65 (April, 1990).
7. Spafford, E. H., K. A. Heaphy, and D. J. Ferbrache. *Computer Viruses: Dealing with Electronic Vandalism and Programmed Threats.* Arlington, Virginia: ADAPSO, 1989.
8. Hoffman, L., ed., *Rogue Programs: Viruses, Worms, and Trojan Horses.* Van Nostrand Reinhold, 1990.
9. Stang, D. J., *Computer Viruses*, 2nd ed., National Computer Security Association, Washington, DC, 1990.
10. Denning, P. J., ed., *Computers Under Attack: Intruders, Worms, and Viruses.* Reading, MA: ACM Books/Addison-Wesley, 1991.

---

*To anticipate the oft-used comment that the "bad guys" already have such information: not every computer burglar knows or will know *every* system weakness—unless we provide them with detailed analyses.

11. Baird, B. J., L. L. Baird, Jr., and R. P. Ranauro. 1987. The moral cracker? *Comp. Sec.* 6:471–478.
12. Landreth, W. *Out of the Inner Circle: A Hacker's Guide to Computer Security,* Microsoft Press, New York, 1984.
13. Adelaide, J., P. Barlow, R. J. Bluefire, R. Brand, C. Stoll, D. Hughes, F. Drake, E. J. Homeboy, E. Goldstein, H. Roberts, J. Gasperini (JIMG), J. Carroll (JRC), L. Felsenstein, T. Mandel, R. Horvitz (RH), R. Stallman (RMS), G. Tenney, Acid Phreak, and Phiber Optik, Is computer hacking a crime? *Harper's Magazine* 280, 45–57 (March 1990).
14. Stallman, R. The GNU manifesto. In *GNU EMacs Manual.* Free Software Foundation, Cambridge, MA: pp. 239–248 (1986).
15. McIlroy, M. D. Unsafe at any price, *Info. Techn. Quart.* IX, 21–23 (1990).
16. P. J. Denning, D. E. Comer, D. Gries, M. C. Mulder, A. Tucker, A. J. Turner, and P. R. Young, Computing as a discipline, *Commun. ACM* 32, 9–23 (1989).
17. Tucker, A. B., et al. *Computing Curricula 1991,* IEEE Society Press, Piscataway, NJ, 1991.

INTERVIEW WITH A HACKER

Richard Spinello

> *In this brief interview, Richard Spinello discusses hacking with "Mr. Jones," a self-proclaimed hacker. Jones responds to questions about privacy, freedom, security, motivation, and worm/virus creation, taking the stance that hacking is no crime and that no harm is done by the intellectually curious hacker.*

hacker n. . . . [deprecated] A malicious meddler who tries to discover sensitive information by poking around[1]

In February 1995 the author interviewed Ed Jones (fictitious name), a professional computer programmer who also describes himself as a "hacker." Jones is a 28-year-old college graduate who was often described as a computer "genius" as far back as the eighth grade. During his high school and college

---

days he worked with computers incessantly. In the following interview he is asked some pointed and specific questions about his experiences and his overall philosophy of computers, the Internet, and many other topics.

The interview has been edited and condensed by the author.

Question: Mr. Jones, how would you describe a hacker today?

When most of us on the net use the term "hacker" we're simply referring to a person who enjoys programming, a person who enjoys solving computer problems and puzzles. Hackers love to focus intently on a problem—it's called being in hack mode and it's almost a mystical experience for some of us. For most hackers their lives revolve around a computer and their community is the electronic network.

Question: But the term now has a negative connotation, doesn't it?

Yes, it seems to. But this is the way the media has come to use the term. They have clearly distorted its original meaning. We like to refer to malicious hackers as "crackers." They're the ones with the outlaw sensibility who cause big problems by undermining security or stealing someone's files.

Question: We hear a lot these days about the hacker ethic. Is there a simple definition of this?

I've always liked the way that Steven Levy described this in his book about hackers. Some of the main tenets of this "ethic" are that access to computer systems should be unlimited and unrestricted. I think he called it the "Hands-On Imperative." Also all information should be freely accessible in order to help others learn and develop their skills. Most hackers deeply mistrust authority and bureaucracy, which they see as impediments to learning and progress.[2]

Question: In other words, the hacker credo is that access to information should be free and not monopolized by big corporations?

Sure—that's exactly what we're saying.

Question: Is this sort of activity common? Are there a lot of hackers or crackers around today who engage in devious behavior?

I still have many friends that you would describe as "hackers," though I have outgrown it myself. Yes, I would have to say that it's still common.

For many computer cyberpunks and others, slogging around on the Internet and breaking into computer systems is really exciting and enticing because it's so challenging. There will always be hackers who deviate from the rules of society. It's also too tempting, especially since so many system administrators don't have a clue about security. And as systems become more open the threats posed by these individuals will continue to grow.

Question: It seems that hackers are lionized by the press and that the hacker subculture is admired, particularly by impressionable young people.

A lot of this hacker coverage is just hype, if you ask me. It doesn't mean very much. They're not big heroes, just a bunch of people fighting for freedom, you know, freedom of expression on the Internet and freedom to explore this new frontier.

Question: Most of us think that if "freedom" manifests itself in exploiting security weaknesses and logging on to someone else's system, there's a problem. We regard such activity as a form of trespassing and a violation of property rights. Do you agree with this?

I'm not sure what I think about that, but let me say that most hackers I know believe that this network is a public place and that anyone connected to the network is part of that public place. After all, companies, schools, and government agencies choose to get on there knowing full well the possible consequences. In our estimation, information on the net is in the public domain and we have every right to access it if we can find a way to get at it.

Question: But break-ins are a security manager's worst nightmare. Don't you think that they cause considerable damage and disruption?

In some respects these break-ins can provide a helpful service to organizations by identifying security weaknesses and vulnerabilities. Otherwise these individuals would not pay any attention to these problems, and a real thief or someone into corporate espionage might cause bigger headaches. I think that our intrusions have actually led to many enhancements in system security. Hackers believe that they keep organizations on their toes and that otherwise they wouldn't pay any attention to security issues. In other words, we keep them one step ahead of the real bad guys.

Question: In other words, hackers are performing a great service to their country by engaging in these activities?

Well, that's a pretty sarcastic way to put it, but right! It sounds strange but there is something to be said for this point of view. Also, study after study shows that the big problem is not with hackers but with ex-employees and other insiders.

Question: There's another issue that people bring up about this and that's the fact that hackers tie up computer resources through their unauthorized forays into different systems.

I've heard this complaint a few times, but it's a real bogus argument. For one thing most hackers work during the late night or early morning hours when no one else is usually on the system. It's a perfect time to do some exploring and probing of some system. Hence, contrary to popular opinion, we are not wasting computer resources.

Question: But let's be frank about this, aren't you trespassing on someone's property?

Ahh, yes and no. But either way, I really don't see the problem here. What's wrong with snooping around especially if I do not alter any data or screw up some commands or programs? Also, we're not interested in copying anything; most of the stuff we see is really boring and it's of no interest. So where's the damage? It's the same as walking across Farmer Brown's field—as long as I leave the animals and the crops alone what harm have I done. People do that all the time in this country and everyone leaves them alone.

Question: What's your motivation for this? What's the big thrill? I have to admit that I don't get it.

Yeah, no offense, but people like you will never "get it." My friends and I grew up with computers and we love working with them. And doing this stuff on the Internet is like pushing forward into new frontiers. I suppose that we do it because it's a terrific challenge. It's a way of testing our computer acumen and ingenuity. It sharpens our skills and wits. And, I repeat, it doesn't do any real harm to anyone.

Question: But can you do *anything* on the Internet? Is there a line that one shouldn't cross?

The line, I think, is between snooping around and outright theft. For most respectable hackers it's OK to look around some corporate or government system but you shouldn't steal data and try to profit from it.

Question: What do you think of those people who get their kicks out of propagating a virus or WORM through a web of computer systems? Isn't *this* going a bit too far? Does it cross the line that we're talking about?

The prevailing wisdom is that viruses and WORMS are intellectual curiosities. However, I do admit that this is pushing it, especially if one unleashes a virus that destroys property and ends up costing somebody a lot of money.

But let me make a few remarks about those who do work with these viruses and other strange programs. Some of these guys get a little carried away, but creating a virus is a real learning experience; they just have to keep these things under control and not let them wreak havoc on some mission critical application. Viruses that propagate themselves but allow programs to run normally are no big deal. They might include nice display hacks that are sort of fun. On the other hand, nasty viruses that nuke someone's data are definitely a problem.

Question: Well, we've covered a lot of ground here. Thanks very much.

Don't mention it.

Notes

1. Eric Raymond (ed.), *The New Hacker's Dictionary* (Cambridge, MA: MIT Press, 1991), pp. 191–192.
2. Cf. Steven Levy, *Hackers* (New York: Doubleday, 1984), pp. 26–36.

THE COMPUTER VIRUS AS METAPHOR

Raymond Gozzi

In this piece of rhetorical analysis with ethical implications, Raymond Gozzi illustrates that the computer "virus" metaphor has implicit ramifications that color our comprehension of various computer "intrusions" and the "hackers" who create them. Understanding at least some of these implicit characteristics of the "virus" metaphor may help us to better judge situations in which "viruses" are said to operate.

On November 4, 1988, computers around the ARPANET network began acting strangely. They filled up with extraneous data, became sluggish, and then clogged completely. The odd behavior spread to about six thousand computers across the country and overseas, in a matter of hours. The system, it appeared, had been attacked by an unknown intruder.

Engineers at SRI International in Palo Alto, the firm responsible for ARPANET security, at first thought the intruder was a "virus," a software program that attaches itself to other programs. But the spread of the clogging behavior made it apparent that the intruder was a "worm," a self-contained program designed to invade and disable computers. This second explanation was correct. In computer terminology, the rogue program that invaded ARPANET was a "worm."

The *San Francisco Chronicle* headlined its November 5th story "Vicious 'Worm' Spreads Havoc Through Computers in U.S." The next day, its headline read: "How 'Worm' Was Defeated."

This was possibly the only newspaper, however, to use the correct term for the rogue program. In the wire services and at least eleven major dailies, the term of choice was "virus." Even the *San Francisco Chronicle*, in its story of November 6, noted, "The attacking program, alternately called a worm or virus, had been cleared from most places by midday yesterday."(1)

Why was this "worm" so quickly and painlessly identified as a "virus"? What we are dealing with here is a choice of metaphors. An analysis of these metaphors (using the "interaction" perspective of I. A. Richards) suggests a number of compelling reasons for the preference of "virus" over "worm."

Reprinted with permission of the University of South Carolina Press from *Et Cetera* (1990), 86–91.

Each metaphor, Richards tells us, results from the interaction between two parts: its "vehicle," which is the word selected, and its "tenor," the underlying situation. A powerful metaphor identifies two separate domains in such a way that we are able to explore one domain by tracing the implications of the other domain.(2)

In the case of the computer intruder of November 1988, there was a choice of two major vehicles: the "worm" or the "virus." If the "worm" was chosen as the vehicle, how would this illuminate the tenor, or underlying situation? Indeed, we have few systems of implications for "worms": they appear at night after rain, are good for fishing, and appear on putrefying food. Clearly the "worm" is not metaphorical star material.

The "virus," however, provided metaphorical dividends immediately. With the "virus" as vehicle, many aspects of the tenor could be elucidated using related terms. News stories explained that about six thousand computers were *infected* as the "virus" proved to be *virulent* and *highly contagious*. NASA *isolated* its computers from the *infected* network and *quarantined* them. Attempts were made to *sterilize* the network. Programmers struggled to develop a *vaccine*, and to *inoculate* against new attacks.

The "virus" proved to be a master metaphor that could organize mini-metaphors into a coherent field. It was easy to communicate using one-word mini-metaphors like *infect* or *inoculate*. This metaphorical system of implications described events in the unfamiliar domain of a computer network in dramatic, familiar, and structurally suggestive terms.

This system of implications of the "virus" metaphor partly explains, I believe, its instant adoption by most of the country's press, as well as its success against the competing "worm" metaphor. The endurance of the metaphor, however, can be traced to factors beyond the immediate entailments of the "virus" vehicle.

The computer "virus" had its way partly prepared for it by the spread of another virus, heavily covered in the media: the AIDS virus. As the story developed, parallels seemed to develop. Like the AIDS virus, the computer "virus" attacked the "immune systems" of the computers it invaded. Like AIDS, the computer "virus" spread through exchanges between individuals. Instead of body fluids being exchanged through sex, it was software exchanged through electronic mail. This parallel was even drawn explicitly by the chairman of the Computer Virus Industry Association in an article in the *New York Times:* "The most stringent [protection] procedures—telling people not to touch other people's computers or to use public domain software—is a little like telling people not to have sex in order to stop the spread of AIDS."(3)

In both cases, the entire society proved to be at risk because of the actions taken by a subculture. AIDS, of course, spread earliest through Haitian refugees and the gay male subcultures of the large cities. The computer "virus" originated in that subculture of computerniks known as "hackers." A *New York Times* article of November 8, "Loving Those Whiz

Kids," said, "On balance, the computer hacker appears to be both a national treasure and a national headache." It described "increasing friction between the eccentric wizards who design and maintain these systems and a society that depends on the machines to run everything from banks to hospitals to military forces."(4)

The author of the "virus" proved also to be a graduate student, further cementing his status on the boundaries of respectability. On the first day of the "infection," a University of Illinois programmer guessed that its author was "very likely a bored graduate student." This motif appeared in a later *New York Times* story about the student, Robert Morris Jr., which described him as "unchallenged by many normal programming activities."(5) (Morris also turned out to be the son of a leading government expert in computer security, adding Oedipal overtones to the already convoluted metaphorical situation—for the father had helped design the UNIX system that the son attacked.)

And yet another parallel: The spread of both the AIDS virus and the computer "virus" produced legal problems and threats to civil liberties, as draconian measures were proposed to curb future outbreaks.(6)

These parallels between the AIDS virus and the computer "virus" surely aided the acceptance of the "virus" metaphor over that of the ill-fated "worm." Other proposed terms, such as computer "letter bomb," as well as "rogue program," "renegade program," and "electronic invader," also lacked resonance.

The case of the computer "virus" of November 1988 offers insight into the process of metaphor selection. The rich systems of entailments of the "virus" vehicle provided terms that quickly and dramatically communicated the structure of the situation through a series of mini-metaphors. However, we might say that the tenor, or underlying situation, also played a key role in the selection of the vehicle.

This master metaphor continued to produce payoffs even after the dust had settled from the original incident. In a letter to the *New York Times* on November 27, a graduate student in computer science relied on a metaphor of biological infection to argue cogently for computer security through system diversity:

> In some ways, computer standardization is akin to the selective breeding of agricultural products, such as potatoes. . . . The breeding of a single genetic strain of potato in Ireland in the 19th Century led to the potato famine of 1845. Because every potato in Ireland had exactly the same genetic material, every potato was susceptible to the same bacterial infection. . . . Computers are just as susceptible to infection as plants are. . . . In biology, successful species evolution preserves diversity and variation. . . . So, in computer systems, variation must be preserved. . . . The need for variation and diversity exists in computer systems just as it exists in nature.(7)

Here we see yet another ramification of the master metaphor of the computer "virus." The metaphor's entailments allow us to systematically explore different aspects of a new and unfamiliar situation. Our language in this case does much of our thinking for us. Our conclusions are implicit in our choice of terms; all that remains for us is to follow the analogies down the paths they prescribe. Whether this is desirable in every case is, of course, another matter entirely.

Notes and References

1. This article relies heavily on the coverage of the incident in the *New York Times*, since that newspaper covered it beyond the two days that it was "hot" news. Other terms come from the *Washington Post* and *Chicago Tribune*. Details available on request.
2. I. A. Richards, *The Philosophy of Rhetoric* (New York: Oxford University Press, 1936). See especially chapters 5 and 6.
3. Kenneth P. Weiss, quoted in Joel Kurtzman, "Curing a Computer Virus," *New York Times*, Nov. 13, 1988, F-1.
4. John Markoff, "Loving Those Whiz Kids," *New York Times*, Nov. 8, 1988, 1.
5. Philip Hilts, Washington Post News Services, Nov. 4, 1988; John Markoff, "How a Need for Challenge Seduced a Computer Expert," *New York Times*, Nov. 6, 1988, 1.
6. John Markoff, "U.S. Is Moving to Restrict Access to Facts About Computer Virus," *New York Times*, Nov. 11, 1988, 12.
7. Benjamin Zorn, "In Computers, as in Nature, Variety Is Desirable," *New York Times*, Nov. 27, 1988.

Selected Bibliography for Section Three

Journal Articles, Radio Interviews, and Anthology Contributions

Bogges, Gene. "Certification of Computer Professionals: A Good Idea?" Pp. 28–29, in *Ethics in the Computer Age: Proceedings of the 1994 ACM/SIGCAS Conference*. ACM Press, 1994.

Goodman, Kenneth. "Ethics, Genomics, and Information Retrieval." *Computers Biology and Medicine* 23, no. 3 (1996): 223–29.

Greenleaf, Walter J., and Maria A. Tovar. "Augmenting Reality in Rehabilitation Medicine." *Artificial Intelligence in Medicine* 6, no. 4 (1994): 289–99.

Herkert, Joseph. "The Conscience of Computer Science." *Change* 30, no. 1 (1998): 62–63.

Kling, Rob. "Computer Abuse and Computer Crime as Organizational Activities." *Computers and Law Journal* 2, no. 2 (1991): 403–27.

Levy, Steven. "Battle of the Clipper Chip." *The New York Times Magazine*, 12 June 1994.

Marin, Dianne, et al. "Implementing a Tenth Strand in the CS Curriculum." *Communications of the ACM* 39, no. 12 (1996): 75–84.

Molpus, David. "How E-mail Is Having an Impact in the Workplace." *Morning Edition*, National Public Radio, 4 February 1999.

Moor, James. "The Ethics of Privacy Protection." *Library Trends* 39, no. 1–2 (1990): 69–82.

Neumann, Peter. "Information Is a Double-Edged Sword." *Communications of the ACM* 42, no. 7 (1999): 129.

Palmiter, C. William. "Call for Responsibility in Ethical Issues for IS Professionals." Pp. 197–203, in *Ethics in the Computer Age: Proceedings of the 1994 ACM/SIGCAS Conference*, ACM Press, 1994.

Rosenthal, P. "Jacked in: Fordism, Cyberpunk, Marxism." *Socialist Review* 21, no. 1 (1993): 79–103.

Schrum, Lynne. "Ethical Research in the Information Age: Beginning the Dialog." *Computers in Human Behavior* 13, no. 2 (1997): 17–125.

Shade, Leslie. "Is There Free Speech on the Net? Censorship in the Global Information Infrastructure." In *Cultures of Internet: Virtual Spaces, Real Histories, Living Bodies*, edited by Rob Shields. Sage Publications, 1996.

Books

Bayles, Michael D. *Professional Ethics*. Wadsworth, 1981.

Dening, Peter. *Computers Under Attack: Intruders, Worms, and Viruses*. Addison-Wesley, 1990.

Postman, Neil. *Technopoly: The Surrender of Culture to Technology*. Alfred A. Knopf, 1993.

Stoll, Clifford. *The Cuckoo's Egg: Tracking a Spy Through the Maze of Computer Espionage*. Pocket Books, 1990.

Novels and Short Stories

Gibson, William. *Burning Chrome*. Ace Books, 1994.

Orwell, George. *Nineteen Eighty-Four*. Heinemann, 1983.

Films

1984. Directed by Michael Radford. Virgin, 1984.

Brazil. Directed by Terry Gilliam. Universal Pictures, 1985.

The Net. Directed by Irwin Winkler. Columbia Pictures Corporation, 1995.

Sneakers. Directed by Phil Alden Robinson. Universal Pictures, 1992.

SECTION FOUR

Evolving Computer Technologies

If one looks at Sony's e-mail aide, "PostPet," one sees how the research surrounding artificial intelligence, virtual reality, and wide area network technologies are beginning to merge. (A PostPet is a colorful 3D "virtual animal" that will deliver and retrieve e-mail for you.) As you use this agent over time, your virtual pet "learns" your writing behavior and will start to compose its own messages. This is just one among many examples in which at least three classes of important technologies are coming together in computing. Their development raises significant and unique moral problems. However, although the integration of these technologies prompts many interesting reflections, we need first to pay attention to each of the areas individually.

Artificial intelligence (AI) has a broad and rich history, philosophically and technically. For instance, in his *Meditations on First Philosophy* the Renaissance French philosopher René Descartes (1596–1650) mused on the possibility of automatons (or robots). Later, such devices came into existence in the nineteenth century when automatons were intricately designed to do acrobatics, dance, and even play games. Closer to our own time, Alan Turing, the brilliant Second World War mathematician/code cracker, attempted to devise criteria for deciding how to determine whether a machine really has human intelligence. Among both scientists and the lay public of the early to mid-twentieth century there was great optimism about the creation of AI. Edmund Berkeley, in his 1959 *Symbolic Logic and Intelligent Machines*, displays this kind of optimism in a section entitled "Do These Machines Really Reason?":

> It cannot be successfully denied that the machine really reasons, and reasons more correctly and faster than a human being. . . . And for the future, we may confidently expect that small machines that reason will be here, there and everywhere, in schools and colleges, homes and businesses, so that

> human beings will be helped both in learning the reasoning process and in
> gaining the results from accurate reasoning by machines. (p. 97)

Meanwhile, authors such as Isaac Asimov, William Gibson, and Phillip K. Dick have gone a step further in their fiction by speculating on the idea of *sentient* machines. However, this type of optimism waned in the 1980s after numerous attempts at using brute computation were shown to be ineffective in solving the problem. Since then debates over the possibilities and the implications of AI have flared from time to time.

Included in Chapter 10 is a sampling of the types of issues that are discussed in relation to AI. Novelist Kurt Vonnegut confronts the American fondness for machines while ironically portraying its limits. He also points to differences among cultural values that may lead to differing conceptions of intelligence and judgments about computer abilities. With an underlying assumption that AI is possible, Remenyi and Williams express concerns about professional responsibilities in doing research and some possible consequences of developing advanced information-processing units. They emphasize a need to take seriously the potential consequences. Hubert Dreyfus goes further by arguing against the very possibility of AI. Simply put, the type of "intelligence" that is possible in a programmed entity does not measure up to our standards of intelligence in people. Finally, Sherry Turkle takes up the idea of how children's attitudes toward machines have changed in the past two decades and how that affects the status we give machines. That is, whether these machines are intelligent or not, we tend to attribute intentionality to them. This alters the way we interact and value a variety of aspects of the world influenced by computer technologies.

As discussed in the essays of Chapter 11, virtual reality (VR) environments are designed to immerse a user in another place. These environments are entirely created. Although early VR revolved around military research—in applications ranging from flight and tank simulators to virtual overlays for fighter pilots to operating master/slave robots at a distance using a first-person perspective—contemporary uses include video games, gross anatomy training, telemedicine, therapy, educational simulations, and pilot training. And even though some works of fiction have exaggerated aspects of VR, in some ways they do act as cautionary tales or at least as windows into societal fears.

Within various VR environments, many of the boundaries for appropriate action do not exist or are not readily apparent. Each of the three articles in Chapter 11 point to potential benefits and harms brought about through the implementation of VR technologies. While John Wilson's essay gives a survey of issues raised by VR, Blay Whitby argues for the development of stronger constraints on actions within virtual environments by imposing consequences to good and bad actions. Finally, an editorial from the British journal *The Lancet* suggests socioethical implications of VR in the medical community.

In the final chapter (Chapter 12) we directly confront concerns about the ever-growing ability to network computers and the rise of the internationally popular Internet. Through the 1990s wide area interconnected networks grew at tremendous rates. Vice President Al Gore's speeches and press releases provide a moment of reflection on the extent to which the blind optimism has paled concerning the Internet as a place of unlimited good. The massive interconnectivity that large area networks allow has a price. That price involves many of the issues previously discussed in this text, such as privacy, institutional control, community concerns, and the impact on developing countries. Although Internet-related technologies have been discussed in other chapters of this anthology, the following articles are markedly more political. The ethical issues discussed involve control, power structures, new ways of relating to others, and the impact on our beliefs and faiths. Mark Kellner interviews theologian Douglas Groothuis, who questions the effect that the Internet and other related technologies have on faith and religion. Julian Dibbell, while recounting the disturbing story of a "virtual rape," raises questions not only of the similarity and differences between "real" and "virtual" experiences but also of the kinds of political structures that arise and are possible in Internet "communities." Finally, Pamela Gilbert relates her own story of being stalked by someone who used e-mail and the Internet to disturb and invade her sense of security.

CHAPTER TEN
Artificial Intelligence

BAKU: EPICAC XIV

Kurt Vonnegut, Jr.

In his usual insightful and humorous way, Kurt Vonnegut stabs at issues of wisdom, politics, spirituality, and the status of computer intelligence. Confronted by a giant supercomputer, EPICAC XIV, the leader of a small, fictitious nation presents the machine a riddle that it does not solve, leaving him disappointed.

The Shah of Bratpuhr, looking as tiny and elegant as a snuffbox in one end of the vast cavern, handed the *Sumklish* bottle back to Khashdrahr Miasma. He sneezed, having left the heat of summer above a moment before, and the sound chattered along the walls to die whispering in bat roosts deep in Carlsbad Caverns.

Doctor Ewing J. Halyard was making his thirty-seventh pilgrimage to the subterranean jungle of steel, wire, and glass that filled the chamber in which they stood, and thirty larger ones beyond. This wonder was a regular stop on the tours Halyard conducted for a bizarre variety of foreign potentates, whose common denominator was that their people represented untapped markets for America's stupendous industrial output.

A rubber-wheeled electric car came to a stop by the elevator, where the Shah's party stood, and an Army major, armed with a pistol, dismounted and examined their credentials slowly, thoroughly.

"Couldn't we speed this up a little, Major?" said Halyard. "We don't want to miss the ceremony."

"Perhaps," said the major. "But, as officer of the day, I'm responsible for nine billion dollars worth of government property, and if something

---

should happen to it somebody might be rather annoyed with me. The ceremony has been delayed, anyway, so you won't miss anything. The President hasn't showed up yet."

The major was satisfied at last, and the party boarded the open vehicle.

"*Siki?*" said the Shah.

"This is EPICAC XIV," said Halyard. "It's an electronic computing machine—a brain, if you like. This chamber alone, the smallest of the thirty-one used, contains enough wire to reach from here to the moon four times. There are more vacuum tubes in the entire instrument than there were vacuum tubes in the State of New York before World War II." He had recited these figures so often that he had no need for the descriptive pamphlet that was passed out to visitors.

Khashdrahr told the Shah.

The Shah thought it over, snickered shyly, and Khashdrahr joined him in the quiet, Oriental merriment.

"Shah said," said Khashdrahr, "people in his land sleep with smart women and make good brains cheap. Save enough wire to go to moon a thousand times."

Halyard chuckled appreciatively, as he was paid to do, wiped aside the tears engendered by his ulcer, and explained that cheap and easy brains were what was wrong with the world in the bad old days, and that EPICAC XIV could consider simultaneously hundreds or even thousands of sides of a question utterly fairly, that EPICAC XIV was wholly free of reason-muddying emotions, that EPICAC XIV never forgot anything—that, in short, EPICAC XIV was dead right about everything. And Halyard added in his mind that the procedure described by the Shah had been tried about a trillion times, and had yet to produce a brain that could be relied upon to do the right thing once out of a hundred opportunities.

They were passing the oldest section of the computer now, what had been the whole of EPICAC I, but what was now little more than an appendix or tonsil of EPICAC XIV. Yet, EPICAC I had been intelligent enough, dispassionate enough, retentive enough to convince men that he, rather than they, had better do the planning for the war that was approaching with stupifying certainty. The ancient phrase used by generals testifying before appropriation committees, "all things considered," was given some validity by the ruminations of EPICAC I, more validity by EPICAC II, and so on, through the lengthening series. EPICAC could consider the merits of high-explosive bombs as opposed to atomic weapons for tactical support, and keep in mind at the same time the availability of explosives as opposed to fissionable materials, the spacing of enemy foxholes, the labor situation in the respective processing industries, the probable mortality of planes in the face of enemy antiaircraft technology, and on and on, if it seemed at all important, to the number of cigarettes and Cocoanut Mound Bars and Silver Stars required to support a high-morale air force. Given the facts by human beings, the war-born EPICAC series had offered the highly informed guidance that the reasonable, truth-loving, brilliant, and highly trained core of American genius could have delivered had they had inspired leadership, boundless resources, and two thousand years.

Through the war, and through the postwar years to the present, EPICAC's nervous system had been extended outward through Carlsbad Caverns—intelligence bought by the foot and pound and kilowatt. With each addition, a new, unique individual had been born, and now Halyard, the Shah, and Khashdrahr were arriving at the bunting-covered platform, where the President of the United States of America, Jonathan Lynn, would dedicate to a happier, more efficient tomorrow, EPICAC XIV.

The trio sat down on folding chairs and waited quietly with the rest of the distinguished company. Whenever there was a break in the group's whispering, EPICAC's hummings and clickings could be heard—the sounds attendant to the flow of electrons, now augmenting one another, now blocking, shuttling through a maze of electromagnetic crises to a condition that was translatable from electrical qualities and quantities to a high grade of truth.

EPICAC XIV, though undedicated, was already at work, deciding how many refrigerators, how many lamps, how many turbine-generators, how many hub caps, how many dinner plates, how many door knobs, how many rubber heels, how many television sets, how many pinochle decks—how many everything America and her customers could have and how much they would cost. And it was EPICAC XIV who would decide for the coming years how many engineers and managers and research men and civil servants, and of what skills, would be needed in order to deliver the goods; and what I.Q. and aptitude levels would separate the useful men from the useless ones, and how many Reconstruction and Reclamation Corps men and how many soldiers could be supported at what pay level and where, and . . .

"Ladies and Gentlemen," said the television announcer, "the President of the United States."

The electric car pulled up to the platform, and President Jonathan Lynn, born Alfred Planck, stood and showed his white teeth and frank gray eyes, squared his broad shoulders, and ran his strong, tanned hands through his curly hair. The television cameras dollied and panned about him like curious, friendly dinosaurs, sniffing and peering. Lynn was boyish, tall, beautiful, and disarming, and, Halyard thought bitterly, he had gone directly from a three-hour television program to the White House.

"Is this man the spiritual leader of the American people?" asked Khashdrahr.

Halyard explained the separation of Church and State, and met, as he had expected to meet, with the Shah's usual disbelief and intimations that he, Halyard, hadn't understood the question at all.

The President, with an endearing, adolescent combination of brashness and shyness, and with the barest trace of a Western drawl, was now reading aloud a speech someone had written about EPICAC XIV. He made it clear that he wasn't any scientist, but just plain folks, standing here, humble before this great new wonder of the world, and that he was here because American plain folks had chosen him to represent them at occasions like this, and that, looking at this modern miracle, he was overcome with a feeling of deep reverence and humility and gratitude . . .

Halyard yawned, and was annoyed to think that Lynn, who had just read "order out of chaos" as "order out of koze," made three times as much money as he did. Lynn, or, as Halyard preferred to think of him, Planck, hadn't even finished high school, and Halyard had known smarter Irish setters. Yet, here the son-of-a-bitch was, elected to more than a hundred thousand bucks a year!

"You mean to say that this man governs without respect to the people's spiritual destinies?" whispered Khashdrahr.

"He has no religious duties, except very general ones, token ones," said Halyard, and then he started wondering just what the hell Lynn did do. EPICAC XIV and the National Industrial, Commercial, Communications, Foodstuffs, and Resources Board did all the planning, did all the heavy thinking. And the personnel machines saw to it that all governmental jobs of any consequence were filled by top-notch civil servants. The more Halyard thought about Lynn's fat pay check, the madder he got, because all the gorgeous dummy had to do was read whatever was handed to him on state occasions: to be suitably awed and reverent, as he said, for all the ordinary, stupid people who'd elected him to office, to run wisdom from somewhere else through that resonant voicebox and between those even, pearly choppers.

And Halyard suddenly realized that, just as religion and government had been split into disparate entities centuries before, now, thanks to the machines, politics and government lived side by side, but touched almost nowhere. He stared at President Jonathan Lynn and imagined with horror what the country must have been like when, as today, any damn fool little American boy might grow up to be President, but when the President had had to actually run the country!

President Lynn was explaining what EPICAC XIV would do for the millions of plain folks, and Khashdrahr was translating for the Shah. Lynn declared that EPICAC XIV was, in effect, the greatest individual in history, that the wisest man that had ever lived was to EPICAC XIV as a worm was to that wisest man.

For the first time the Shah of Bratpuhr seemed really impressed, even startled. He hadn't thought much of EPICAC XIV's physical size, but the comparison of the worm and the wise man struck home. He looked about himself apprehensively, as though the tubes and meters on all sides were watching every move.

The speech was over, and the applause was dying, and Doctor Halyard brought the Shah to meet the President, and the television cameras nuzzled about them.

"The President is now shaking hands with the Shah of Bratpuhr," said the announcer. "Perhaps the Shah will give us the fresh impressions of a visitor from another part of the world, from another way of life."

"*Allasan Khabou pillan?*" said the Shah uncertainly.

"He wonders if he might ask a question," said Khashdrahr.

"Sure, you bet," said the President engagingly. "If I don't know the answers, I can get them for you."

Unexpectedly, the Shah turned his back to the President and walked alone, slowly, to a deserted part of the platform.

"Wha'd I do wrong?" said Lynn.

"Ssssh!" said Khashdrahr fiercely, and he placed himself, like a guard, between the puzzled crowd and the Shah.

The Shah dropped to his knees on the platform and raised his hands over his head. The small, brown man suddenly seemed to fill the entire cavern with his mysterious, radiant dignity, alone there on the platform, communing with a presence no one else could sense.

"We seem to be witnessing some sort of religious rite," said the announcer.

"Can't you keep your big mouth shut for five seconds?" said Halyard.

"Quiet!" said Khashdrahr.

The Shah turned to a glowing bank of EPICAC's tubes and cried in a piping singsong voice:

> *"Allakahi baku billa,*
> *Moumi a fella nam;*
> *Serani assu tilla,*
> *Touri serin a sam."*

"The crazy bastard's talking to the machine," whispered Lynn.

"Ssssh!" said Halyard, strangely moved by the scene.

"*Siki?*" cried the Shah. He cocked his head, listening. "*Siki?*" The word echoed and died—lonely, lost.

"*Mmmmmm,*" said EPICAC softly. "*Dit, dit. Mmmmm. Dit.*"

The Shah sighed and stood, and shook his head sadly, terribly let down. "*Nibo,*" he murmured. "*Nibo.*"

"What's he say?" said the President.

"'*Nibo*'—'nothing' He asked the machine a question, and the machine didn't answer," said Halyard. "*Nibo.*"

"Nuttiest thing I ever heard of," said the President. "You have to punch out the questions on that thingamajig, and the answers come out on tape from the whatchamacallits. You can't just talk to it." A doubt crossed his fine face. "I mean, you can't, can you?"

"No sir," said the chief engineer of the project. "As you say, not without the thingamajigs and whatchamacallits."

"What'd he say?" said Lynn, catching Khashdrahr's sleeve.

"An ancient riddle," said Khashdrahr, and it was plain that he didn't want to go on, that something sacred was involved. But he was also a polite man, and the inquiring eyes of the crowd demanded more of an explanation. "Our people believe," he said shyly, "that a great, all-wise god will come among us one day, and we shall know him, for he shall be able to answer the riddle, which EPICAC could not answer. When he comes," said Khashdrahr simply, "there will be no more suffering on earth."

"All-wise god, eh?" said Lynn. He licked his lips and patted down his unruly forelock. "How's the riddle go?"

Khashdrahr recited:

> "Silver bells shall light my way,
> And nine times nine maidens fill my day,
> And mountain lakes will sink from sight,
> And tigers' teeth will fill the night."

President Lynn squinted at the cavern roof thoughtfully. "Mmm. Silver bells, eh?" He shook his head. "That's a stinker, you know? A real stinker. I give up."

"I'm not surprised," said Khashdrahr. "I'm not surprised. I expect you do."

Halyard helped the Shah, who seemed to have been aged and exhausted by the emotional ordeal, into the electric car.

As they rode to the foot of the elevator, the Shah came back to life somewhat and curled his lip at the array of electronics about them. "*Baku!*" he said.

"That's a new one on me," said Halyard to Khashdrahr, feeling warmly toward the little interpreter, who had squared away Jonathan Lynn so beautifully. "What's *Baku?*"

"Little mud and straw figures made by the Surrasi, a small infidel tribe in the Shah's land."

"This looks like mud and straw to him?"

"He was using it in the broader sense, I think, of false god."

"Um," said Halyard. "Well, how are the Surrasi doing?"

"They all died of cholera last spring." He added after a moment, "Of course." He shrugged, as though to ask what else people like that could possibly expect. "*Baku.*"

SOME ASPECTS OF ETHICS AND RESEARCH INTO THE SILICON BRAIN

Dan Remenyi and Brian Williams

Remenyi and Williams make a sort of call to arms for information systems professionals. Since the creation of technologies such as artificial intelligence (AI) are now occurring, it is up to computer professionals to use good judgment not only in the development of these technologies but also in decisions about whether or not these technologies ought even to be researched. They ask four questions concerning AI research that highlight the dangers of the research itself if it is not taken in context of its future impact on society.

Introduction

The aim of this paper is to discuss some of the issues related to ethics in the context of establishing objectives for information systems research in general and the development of the "silicon brain" in particular. The aspect of ethics considered here relates to the care with which a research topic should be chosen if one wishes to avoid dilemmas concerning the use to which the knowledge so created will eventually be put. There is some debate among scientists as to whether knowledge is created or discovered. The view taken by the authors in this paper, and supported by Einstein[1] is that knowledge is created through a scientific process. In addition a possible framework for thinking about ethics and research objectives is suggested.

The paper does not attempt to offer a definitive set of guidelines for the information systems researcher to consider when deciding on the subject

Reprinted from *International Journal of Information Management* 16, no. 6 (1996): 401–11, with permission from Elsevier Science.

to be researched. Rather it raises a number of ideas and questions which should be considered before embarking on a research project.

At the outset of any research project it is essential to consider the impact of developments in the subject matter which is to be studied. The impact of the research findings could be to affect the particular individuals who are the subject of the research or it could affect wider groups of people or even society as a whole. This is a very important issue because it is by no means generally accepted that all knowledge is always beneficial to all members of society.

Ethical issues are of growing importance in the field of information systems[2] and the authors argue that ethics deserves specific attention in the general subject area of artificial intelligence from which the author believe the silicon brain will be developed. In this area the frontiers of knowledge are rapidly advancing and we are acquiring new ideas which will allow us to do things undreamed of before.

Moravec[3] argues that

> We are very near to the time when *no* essential human function will lack an artificial counterpart. The embodiment of this is the intelligent robot, the machine which can think and act as a human, however inhuman it may be in physical or mental detail. Such machines could carry on our cultural evolution . . . without us and without the genes that built us. It will be then that our DNA will be out of a job, having passed the torch and lost the race, to a new kind of competition.

Thus the possibility of a silicon brain is something which must be regarded as a serious suggestion, if not in the short term, then in the medium to long term.

Perhaps it is not coincidental that the first story in the Old Testament dealing with *Homo sapiens* is that of a researcher, in the form of Eve, the first woman of our species. Her research problem was driven by curiosity to find out what would happen if she ate the forbidden apple. Maybe it is also not coincidental that the same story suggests that by eating the fruit of the tree of knowledge we gain the knowledge of good and evil and are banished forever from the Garden of Eden, from the world of purity and innocence. In somewhat briefer terms than those used by the ancient Hebrew scribes, perhaps the essence of the story of Adam and Eve is that knowledge, although it gives us power, is always potentially dangerous. This view suggests that the Christian notion of original sin is actually the equivalent of a curse of curiosity. The aphorism *curiosity killed the cat* magnificently sums up this thinking. It is of course entirely possible that curiosity will kill mankind. Knowledge in the abstract may be regarded to be neutral. Knowledge in the wrong hands, however this may be defined, is what is being referred to as dangerous.

To add to this, unlike most other commodities knowledge is essentially indestructible. In addition the creation of knowledge appears to be both addictive and compulsive and it is probably not possible to stop the knowledge creation processes which we have put in place. Even when detailed knowledge is lost, our awareness of its existence is sufficient to change the way in which we think. Therefore the central proposition of this paper is that we must give very careful consideration to the types of knowledge that we call into existence.

The ancient Hebrew tale, written some three to four thousand years ago, about Adam and Eve may be seen as a parable concerning the importance of being concerned about the type of knowledge which we create, and its relevance is quite clear, or perhaps especially relevant, even in the late 20th century.

A Basis of Ethics

Let us begin with a definition of the word ethics which, according to Taylor,[4] "is a study of the notions of morality."

Miesing and Preble[5] extend this definition by stating that ethics is a "framework for human conduct that relates to moral principles and attempts to distinguish right from wrong."

It is important to state at the outset that ethical considerations frequently go beyond the ambit of the law. It is often possible to behave in a manner that is technically legal but thoroughly unethical. The civil and criminal law are in place to regulate people's affairs primarily on a physical or material level, whereas ethics attempts to go beyond that and to deal with issues at a moral level.

There are various sources of ethical beliefs. Ethics can be directly derived from religious beliefs or can be constructed from our understanding of the social, physical and natural world around us. The latter may take into account issues not only related to *Homo sapiens* directly, but other things in the environment including, but not necessarily limited to, animal and plant life, ie the planet as a whole.

In this paper the authors present arguments based on the latter view. Specifically they adopt a position in which ethical judgements are made in terms of the likely impact they have on the world as a whole. Of course there is the possibility of conflict between the good of the society and the good of the individuals of which it is composed and these conflicts sometimes lead to very difficult ethical situations. In general terms such conflicts can only be resolved by ensuring a degree of balance between the interests of the various parties concerned, and where this balance lies is also a very difficult question, and is beyond the scope of this paper.

Clearly there are many controversial ideas expressed here and the authors do not claim to have any simple or even sophisticated procedures for answering or resolving these controversies. But the authors feel that it is important to bring these issues to the awareness of the researcher in order that they may be carefully considered at the outset of any research project.

Knowledge Without Universal Approval

In modern times there have been a number of occasions when researchers, as well as many other people, have regretted the information or knowledge they have created. Data, information and knowledge are very slippery concepts. A distinction is frequently made between information and knowledge, although frequently such distinction amounts to little more than knowledge is information in the hands of an intelligent user. In fact according to Davis and Botkin[6] "knowledge . . . is the application and productive use of information." Before the second world war the Dutch government carefully and innocently collected statistics on people's religious affiliations. The Nazi's simply had to take these records, collected with well meaningful intentions by the Dutch bureaucrats, to find the Jewish members of the community. Researchers need to reflect on this and to bear in mind that knowledge being almost infinitely transferable must be assumed to be available to society's strongest adversaries, whether these are simply criminals or political opponents.

Another example of knowledge having an adverse affect on society is the recreational use of tobacco products, today known to be directly responsible for numerous diseases and deaths.[7] Because of the diseases caused by primary and secondary smoking, tobacco is an example of something which would have been better for society not to have known.

At a personal level some might argue that, under certain circumstances, let us say those in which only "safe-sex" is practised, the value of knowing whether one is HIV positive is entirely negative: it may simply be better not to know. But is this attitude contrary to the good of the society as a whole? The question of the value of knowledge must therefore be seen in the context of the question "To whom is the knowledge or information valuable?" Although it may be better for the individual not to know if he or she is HIV positive, it is better for society to have such knowledge. . . .

Artificial Intelligence and the Silicon Brain

In the information systems context there are a number of research issues whose consequences are open to ethical challenge. The question of whether it is ethically acceptable to research and subsequently develop increasingly powerful processors, memories and telecommunications systems, which will inevitably destroy jobs and lead to a variety of social ills is the subject of ethical debate. Although this view that information technology destroys jobs is not yet universally accepted, there is a growing number of authors who firmly believe this is in fact the case. Stewart[8] points out that the *Wall Street Journal* states that 24 million jobs in the private sector of the US economy will be lost in the next 10 years due to business process reengineering. Alvey[9] identifies that the job loss is a result of companies investing in information technology. Hines[10] extends this view by suggesting that jobs in the future will be less available but that those that exist may be depersonalised and boring. According to Rifkin[11] "by the year 2025 only 2% of the worlds work force will be blue-collar factory workers."

The issue of more and more information being concentrated in the hands of government bureaucrats through the use of large scale mainframe systems, networked around the world, also leads to interesting ethical questions. However, in this paper the authors have confined themselves to the question of the ethical acceptability of research into artificial intelligence. All the questions raised concerning the ethical acceptability of research into the silicon brain or artificial intelligence apply to research into other aspects of developments in information technology and the possible framework for thinking about ethics and research objectives suggested towards the end of the paper is quite generic.

It is not at all obvious that the current research into the question of the silicon brain will not turn out to be the creation of another monster— no less formidable than that created by Dr Frankenstein, in Shelley's famous novel.[12] This timeless and universal myth highlights what can happen when science oversteps the mark. In this novel, Dr Frankenstein's creation was not *per se* a monster. The creature only began to become a monster after it commenced feeling that it was being abused or was not being treated appropriately. Thus Frankenstein's technology itself was not the culprit but rather it was the way the result or the product of the technology was subsequently used. Thus, in a similar way to Frankenstein, it is not hard to imagine that a silicon brain, created with the best of intentions, could become a monster in its own right. It is interesting to note that the concerns shown about science and technology by Shelley and others, who are essentially artists and writers, have not really been shared by the scientific community. For scientists the intellectual challenge of research becomes both addictive and compulsive and thus the ethical imperatives of their work are easily and frequently forgotten.

Although at present computers clearly cannot generate ideas,[13] what do we do if we create out of silicon a brain which is distinctly superior to any human and which can generate thoughts and ideas which are quite independent of its designers and programmers? What if this silicon life form develops a set of moral values which are distinctly different to the rest of society? In fact according to Moravec[14]

> many of our fleshly traits are out of step with the invention of our minds. Yet machines, as purely cultural entities do not share this dilemma. Sooner or later they will be able to manage their own construction, freeing them from the last vestiges of their biological scaffolding, the society of flesh and blood humans that gave them birth.

In fact it is hard to believe that an independent silicon brain would regard human life as highly as we do.

Some information systems researchers argue that it is inevitable that we will develop this monster. In a recent book by Davidson and Rees-Mogg[15] they argue that we are quite close to developing, through the process of nanotechnology, the ability to develop super computers which will fit comfortably in a single human cell leading to the possibility of manoeuvring things atom by atom[16] and that this will radically change every aspect of our lives, opening up the way to silicon brains and artificial intelligence of unimaginable power.

Furthermore, there is much talk these days about the development of "organic computers" which we will grow chemically rather than construct physically in the usual way. This will allow a much higher degree of connectivity which would supply more computing power by many orders of magnitude. Davidson and Rees-Mogg[17] suggest that such power to manipulate our physical world will further divide society and lead to a new age of hi-tech slavery. This clearly begs the question of whether developments in the silicon brain or artificial intelligence will lead to a future in which *Homo sapiens* will be more fulfilled by his/her control over nature or whether it will lead to some nightmare society in which we will have little or no control and which will be completely unacceptable to all but the few controllers of the technology who may or may not be human.

Langton[18] argues that perhaps it is inevitable that silicon-based life forms will indeed become the dominant life form on this planet, especially as they may be able to survive the ecological destruction that we have wrought. Perhaps in future millennia these new life forms will look back on us as we look back on the dinosaurs; a once successful but fatally flawed species that must eventually perish. Unfortunately unlike the dinosaurs, *Homo sapiens* is unlikely to be able to boast of dominating the planet for 160 million years. Langton is by no means pessimistic about this prospect, and with a larger vision than we currently have, one might regard this brave new world as inevitable but also as an acceptable evolutionary step. The relevance of this argument to research in information systems is that for the first time in evolutionary history, our species, by deciding which avenues of research to pursue, can possibly decide if we wish to maintain our existence or allow some new perhaps more advanced (at least in a technological sense) life form to succeed and supersede us.

Discussion

. . . Although some believe that it is simply a matter of time, we are at present probably still some considerable time away from the realisation of any serious form of silicon brain or artificial intelligence. There are at least three areas in which we have to make breakthroughs before the silicon brain and full scale artificial intelligence will become a reality. In the first place a more extensive understanding of the nature of human intelligence is required. This contribution will have to be made by psychologists or applied psychologists. Then we will need an improvement in software, primarily in the algorithms which control the way computers process rules and access data. This would lead to improved computer vision, speech recognition and decision making. Finally we need much faster processors and faster peripheral equipment. According to the Intel Corporation, the microprocessor designer and manufacturer, the hardware challenges are likely to be solved relatively soon. And Negroponte[19] points out that sometimes developments in information technology occur much faster than we anticipate.

Despite these limitations even now we are able to produce systems which play a major role in advising us in certain situations involving difficult decisions. Artificial intelligence type systems are currently playing a part in cardiac diagnosis in major hospitals and these systems have given rise to concern about the possibility of incorrect advice and who, the systems user or the systems designer to mention only two possibilities, might be held responsible for such an event. Similarly although not strictly an issue of artificial intelligence *per se* the way in which violent stock market movements have been exacerbated by the use of a type of expert or rule based system has given rise to some concern.

Calls have been made for scientists to take greater responsibility for the consequences of their research and Shneiderman[20] has proposed a declaration of responsibility which would commit scientists to studying ways to enable users to accomplish their personal and organisational goals which pursue higher societal goals and human needs.

Research in this area is being led by the large information technology vendors who are seeking a competitive advantage from these types of systems. They are being assisted by government funded institutions and universities. It will not take an indefinite amount of time before some spectacular results are seen in this field of endeavour. The information systems community will then be faced with the problem of deciding how artificial intelligence should be applied and who and how control over this technology should be exercised. If the suggestions of Davidson and Rees-Mogg, Feynman and Langton are only true in a small part then we are in for some major challenges.

It is possible that instead of waiting until the Frankenstein type monster has been created by computer scientists we should now call for an international debate as to what are acceptable applications of artificial intelligence and how this technology should be controlled. As pointed out by Mumford,[21] of course

> The machine itself makes no demands and holds out no promises. It is the human spirit that makes demands and keeps promises. In order to reconquer the machine and subdue it to human purposes one must first understand it and assimilate it. So far we have embraced the machine without fully understanding it.

Thus the onus is on us to understand and to assimilate into our culture what a silicon brain might mean.

This debate has not yet happened and so far there has been no attempt to even put this issue on a highly visible international agenda. The reason for this one suspects is that the world community has not yet taken seriously the notion that a silicon brain will ever be developed.

Possible Framework for Thinking About Ethics and Research Objectives

It is clear that the results of scientific endeavours can profoundly affect our society both for good and for evil. Thus it is important for researchers to think carefully about the consequence of the research with which they are involved. This issue is succinctly expressed by Naisbitt[22] when he said, "We must learn to balance the material wonders of technology with the spiritual demands of our human nature." These considerations should be given as early as possible in the research cycle, as once the research has been initiated may not be possible to influence its direction.

A possible framework for thinking about some of these ethical issues is needed. Such a framework would consist of a series of questions to be addressed. This list of questions could include but would not be limited to the following:

1. Who is funding the research and what are their public and private agendas which will directly affect the use of and the control over the results of the research?

2. How will the results be disseminated and specifically will they immediately be placed in the public domain and what is the probability of the results falling into the wrong hands?
3. What are the most probable primary applications of the findings of the research and how could they immediately affect our society?
4. Are the results of the research likely to directly or indirectly have an adverse affect on the fabric of our society?

These questions are rather generic and as such do not specifically address the subject of information systems in general or, for that matter, the silicon brain or artificial intelligence specifically. However, they are certainly useful as a starting point for the discussion of the ethics of research in these very sensitive areas related to the silicon brain and artificial intelligence. The following are some of the first issues which these questions raise in an artificial intelligence context.

QUESTION ONE

Who is funding the research and what are their public and private agendas which will directly affect control over the results of the research?

Research into artificial intelligence is largely funded by private corporations who are largely interested in obtaining a competitive advantage in the commercial world from the application of this technology. It would be unreasonable to expect them to place the broader interests of society ahead of their own commercial advantage. It would be better if more public money was involved which would tend to make the results of the research less private and more open to public scrutiny and debate.

QUESTION TWO

How will the results be disseminated and will they immediately be placed in the public domain and what is the probability of the results falling into the wrong hands?

Although the individual components of this technology are likely to be marketed extensively by their developers, and thus their existence will at least be in the public domain, the really important dimension of artificial intelligence, which is the way in which these components are configured in relation to each other, is unlikely to be immediately placed in the public domain. It would be unfortunate if artificial intelligence technology were to fall into the hands of those who would use it to create even smarter bombs and devices of destruction than we already have.

QUESTION THREE

What are the most probable primary applications of the findings of the research and how could they immediately affect our society?

Applications are likely to deskill jobs, they are likely to allow individuals who have relatively little experience and knowledge to hold down positions requiring a much higher level of expertise than they have personally achieved. It is also likely that this technology will lever human effort and allow much more work to be done by a smaller number of people in a world where there is already an employment crisis, this technology is likely to further aggravate the situation.

QUESTION FOUR

Are the results of the research likely to directly or indirectly have an adverse affect on the fabric of our society?

Artificial intelligence could well be used to further entrench bureaucracy. Large human endeavours only survive by complying with rules and regulations, codes of practice and procedure manuals. Artificial intelligence will be a boon to this approach to life. However, bureaucracies have been tempered by human intervention, based on compassion and understanding of the human condition. It is unfortunately, not at all obvious that rules which are entrusted to silicon processors will be capable of being interpreted in a reasonable rather than a purely logical way. This problem is exacerbated by the speed with which silicon rule-making proceeds. It is often said that time is a great healer but in fact it also allows issues to be put into perspective. What can be expected from a silicon brain is near technical perfection and complete consistency. The silicon brain will in fact be *la belle ordinateur sans merci.*

Of course all of these questions are extremely difficult to answer both for individuals and organisations, as well as for society as a whole and the authors do not suggest that the above attempted answers are in any sense complete. Nonetheless it is vital that they be asked and that we think about possible replies. They are all value laden but so is any consideration of ethics. However, some attempt needs to be made towards finding some sort of response, especially as we get closer to developing the silicon brain.

Conclusions

Scientific endeavour or the creation of knowledge is a serious business which has many ramifications for individuals, groups of people and society as a whole. Sometimes the creation of knowledge can have distinctly adverse effects and when this occurs the creation of such knowledge is not only dangerous but ethically questionable. In fact Collins and Pinch[23] regard science as a golem, ie:

> a creature of Jewish mythology. It is a humanoid made by man from clay and water, with incantations and spells. It is powerful. It grows a little more powerful every day. It will follow orders, do your work, and protect you from the ever threatening enemy. But it is clumsy and dangerous. Without control, a golem may destroy its masters with its flailing vigour.

Therefore research should not be undertaken lightly as its consequences may not be quite what we expected.

In general terms considerable care must be taken in deciding what areas of knowledge to research. It should be recognised that the question of the ultimate use of the knowledge created is at least in part the responsibility of the researcher. Although we frequently, as a society, behave as though the creation of knowledge is an intrinsic element in the human makeup, perhaps this is not so. And even if it is, it is still possible for us to be responsible for the selection of research projects and how the knowledge we create is subsequently disseminated. Unfortunately not many scientists give much attention to this question. In the words of Dr Malkin in Crichton's Jurassic Park,[24] scientists are "so preoccupied with whether or not they could [genetically reengineer dinosaurs] they did not stop to think *if* they should."

Answers to these questions are not trivial matters because consequences are often neither foreseeable or controllable. Although a first reaction may be to say that perhaps some issues are better left unresearched, it is recognised that in practice this is virtually impossible, especially in information systems where, because of intense commercial competition there is the treadmill effect which does not allow us to rest from a relentless drive to push the borders of the technology as far forward and as quickly as possible. In addition, in information technology, research may be undertaken for a fraction of the cost of research into either atomic physics or genetic engineering.

It is not the intention of the authors to call for an abandonment of research into artificial intelligence. It is not even the intention to call for a moratorium on research in this area. The authors believe that the issues considered in this paper should be directly addressed by both the information systems industry and the information systems academic community, as well as society as a whole, in order that a better understanding is achieved of where artificial intelligence research may be taking us and how we are going to be able to control its effects. Then we could decide as a community as to an appropriate response to the creation of this type of knowledge and develop a more effective framework for managing such knowledge.

Notes

1. EINSTEIN, A (1954) "Remarks on Bertrand Russell's theory of knowledge" in *Ideas and Opinions* Bonanza Books, New York

2. HORWITZ, G (1977) "Computer people—how honest how ethical?" *Systems* April, 31–35; PARKER, D (1979) *Ethical Conflicts in Computer Science and Technology* AFIPS Press, Chicago; COUGER, D (1989) "Preparing IS students to deal with ethical Issues" *MIS Quarterly* June, 40–46; PARADICE, B (1990) *Ethical Attitudes of Entry Level MIS Personnel* Elsevier Scientific Publishers; FORESTER, T AND MORRISON, P (1990) *Computer Ethics, Cautionary Tales and Ethical Dilemmas* Basil Blackwell, Oxford; MORRIS, A (1992) "Ethics and information technology" unpublished paper presented at the Third CISNA International Conference, University of Namibia, 8 May

3. MORAVEC, H (1989) "Human culture—a genetic take over underway," in LANGTON, C G (ED) *Artificial Life* Addison-Wesley, Redwood City, CA

4. TAYLOR, P (1975) *Principles of Ethics—An Introduction* Dickson Publishing, London

5. MIESING, P AND PREBLE, J (1985) "A comparison of five business philosophies" *Journal of Business Ethics* **8** 20–27

6. DAVIS, S AND BOTKIN, J (1994) "The coming of knowledge-based business" *Harvard Business Review* September–October, 77–85

7. THE ECONOMIST (1995) "Still smokin" 11 March; ADWEEK (1994) "Peculiar smoke signals" **35** (27) 14

8. STEWART, N (1994) "Tooling up" *Management Accounting* **76** (4) 15

9. ALVEY, J (1994) "High tech vs jobs" *Fortune* **129** (7) 55

10. HINES, A (1994) "Jobs and infotech: work in the information society" *Futurist* **28** (1) 20

11. RIFKIN, J (1995) "The end of work" cited in "We're running out of jobs" *Newsweek* 24 April, 60

12. SHELLEY, M (1818, reprinted 1993) *Frankenstein or the Modern Prometheus* Wordsworth Classics, Ware, Hertfordshire, UK

13. PENZIAS, A (1989) *Ideas and Information* Simon and Schuster, New York

14. *Op cit*, Ref 3

15. DAVIDSON, J AND REES-MOGG, W (1993) *The Great Reckoning* Sidgwick & Jackson, London

16. FEYNMAN, J (1959), cited by SCHNEIKER, C, in "Nonotechnology with Feynman machines" in LANGTON, C G (ED) *Artificial Life* Addison-Wesley, Redwood City, CA

17. *Op cit*, Ref 16

18. LANGTON, C G (1989) "Artificial life" in LANGTON, C G (ED) *Artificial Life* Addison-Wesley, Redwood City, CA

19. NEGROPONTE, N (1995) *Being Digital* Alfred A Knopf, New York

20. SHNEIDERMAN, B (1991) Keynote address for ACM SIGCAS Conference on Computers and the Quality of Life, 1990, reprinted in *SIGCHI Bulletin* January

21. MUMFORD, L (1934) *Technics and Civilization* Harcourt Brace and World, New York

22. NAISBITT, J (1982) *Megatrends: Ten New Directions Transforming Our Lives* Warner Books, New York

23. COLLINS, H AND PINCH, T (1994) *The Golem: What Everyone Should Know About Science* Canto–Cambridge University Press, Cambridge

24. CRICHTON, M (1993) *Jurassic Park* (spoken by Dr Malkin) Century Books, New York

MISREPRESENTING HUMAN INTELLIGENCE

Hubert Dreyfus

Philosopher Hubert Dreyfus takes on the issues of what human intelligence is and is not, particularly as related to the development of computer-based artificial intelligence (AI) devices. Following up on work done years earlier, Dreyfus revisits questions of natural language and pattern recognition programs and finds little progress in these areas. He attributes this primarily to an inability to input "situations" into the computer. His analysis of the development of expertise argues that computers are hopelessly stuck in an early stage of expert development. His work, therefore, acts as a warning to us about the responsibilities involved in the implementation of AI in critical tasks. The concern is not only in understanding that AI cannot function equivalently to human intelligence, but also in recognizing uses to which AI might be inappropriately applied.

In *What Computers Can't Do* I argued that research in artificial intelligence (AI for short) was based upon mistaken assumptions about

Reprinted from *Thought* 61 (1986): 430–41, with the kind permission of the author.

the nature of human knowledge and understanding. In the first part of this essay I will review that argument briefly. In spite of the noisy protestations from AI researchers, most of my critical claims and negative predictions have not only been borne out by subsequent research and developments in the field but have even come to be acknowledged as accurate indications of major problems by AI workers themselves. In the years since the revised edition of my book was published, what I have come to see is not only that my early pessimism was well-founded but also that some of my assessments for the future of AI were overly optimistic. In the second part of this essay I will explain why I now believe that even the cautious and guarded optimism which I once had with respect to certain isolated areas of AI research was unjustified and ultimately mistaken.

I

The early stages of AI research were characterized by overly ambitious goals, wishful rhetoric, and outlandish predictions. The goal, in general, was to equal or exceed the capacities of human beings in every area of intelligent behavior. The rhetoric turned failure after failure into partial and promising success. And the predictions had computers doing everything an intelligent human being could do within a decade or so at most. The terms on these predictions have all expired with none of the miraculous feats accomplished, and most researchers have begun to face the hard facts about the real limits of artificial intelligence.

The basic project of AI research is to produce genuine intelligence by means of a programmed digital computer. This requires in effect that human knowledge and understanding be reconstructed out of bits of isolated and meaningless data and sequences of rule-governed operations. The problems facing this approach can be put quite simply. Human knowledge and understanding do not consist of such data, rules, and operations; and nothing which does consist essentially of these things will ever duplicate any interesting range of intelligent human behavior.

Early research projects in artificial intelligence tried to meet head on the task of duplicating human mentality. Major areas of emphasis included natural language understanding, pattern recognition, and general problem solving. Problems in each of these areas were seen initially as problems of size—organizing and using a very large quantity of data. In order to understand even a small and ordinary sample of natural language, for example, a very large mass of background facts seemed to be required, and this massive collection of facts seemed in turn to require some kind of organization in terms of relevance so that not every fact required explicit consideration in every exercise of linguistic understanding. Pattern recognition research ran into similar problems. The number of possibly relevant features was immense and rules for separating those features actually relevant to recognition of a given shape or figure from all the others proved incredibly difficult to formulate. More general problem solving faced exactly the same difficulties, only several orders of magnitude larger due to the increased generality of the task.

In the first edition of *What Computers Can't Do* I argued that the problems encountered by AI workers in these research areas were not just a matter of size and would not succumb to more efficient programs and programming languages or to dramatic increases in computing speed and storage capacity. None of the available empirical evidence suggested that human beings function in the manner required by then current AI models, and much of the evidence suggested an entirely different and incompatible view of human mentality—but this view emerges only after some long-standing psychological and philosophical assumptions are discarded. Those assumptions lie at the very heart of the information processing model of the mind. Put generally, there is only one assumption—that human mental processes are essentially identical to those of a digital computer. Put more specifically, the crucial assumptions are these: (1) that mental processes are sequences of rule-governed operations and (2) that these operations are carried out on determinate bits of data (symbols) which represent features of or facts about the world (information, but only in a technical sense of that term). I can best explain why those specific assumptions are implausible by looking at the problems encountered in each area of AI research.

The main problem for programs the aim of which was to understand natural language was the need to do so either without any context to determine or disambiguate meaning or else with a context completely spelled out in terms of explicit facts, features, and rules for relating them. Even the meanings of individual terms are context- or situation-determined. Whether the word "pen" refers to a writing implement, a place for infants to play, a place in which pigs or other animals are kept, the area of a baseball field in which pitchers warm up, or a place for confining criminals is determined by the context in which the term appears within a story or conversation. It is even clearer that context determines the meaning of whole sentences. "The book is in the pen" could mean that the child's story book is in the playpen, that the pigs' enclosure is where the paperback fell out of the farmer's pocket, that the microfilm of the diary is cleverly concealed in the compartment containing the ink cartridge, and so on. We human beings don't seem to need to consider explicitly all the alternatives; and in fact it is not even clear that there could be an exhaustive list of all the alternative meanings for typical samples of natural language. We are always involved in a situation or context which seems to restrict the range of possible meanings without requiring explicit or exhaustive consideration of the range of context-free alternatives.

The obvious solution from the standpoint of AI would be to give the computer the situation. The attempt to do this in a general way has been unsuccessful and begs some important questions. The most important question begged is whether or not our command of the situation is just a matter of a number of facts which we accept, that is, a system of belief which could be made explicit. If it is, then it could at least in principle be given to a computer, and the only problems would be practical, problems of size and structure for the belief system. If our command of the situation cannot be represented as such a belief system, however, then there will be no way to get the computer into the situation or the situation into the computer so as to duplicate general human understanding. I believe that this is the real impasse which AI faces.

Influenced by philosophers such as Heidegger and Merleau-Ponty, I believe that the evidence points toward the following picture of the relation between facts and situations. Our sense of the situation we are in determines how we interpret things, what significance we place on the facts, and even what counts as facts for us at any given time. But our sense of the situation we are in is not just our belief in a set of facts, nor is it a product of independent facts or context-free features of our environment. The aspects of our surroundings which somehow give us our sense of our current situation are themselves products of a situation we were already in, so that situations grow out of situations without recourse to situation-neutral facts and features at any point. We never get into a situation from outside any situation whatsoever, nor do we do so by means of context-free data. But the computer has only such data to work with and must start completely unsituated. From the standpoint of the programmer, our natural situatedness consists of an indefinite regress of situations with no way to break in from the outside, no way to start from nothing. And this is only part of the problem for AI. Not only can the situation not be constructed out of context-free facts and features but in fact the situation as it figures in intelligent human behavior is not primarily a matter of facts and features of any kind. It is much more like an implicit and very general sense of appropriateness and seems to be triggered by global similarities to previously experienced situations rather than by any number of individual facts and features. I will try to make clear just how I think this works in the second part of this essay. Here I will simply observe that it is not surprising that digital computers, lacking access to anything very like the human situation, also lack access to anything very like human understanding.

Pattern-recognition programs encountered similarly instructive difficulties. Whether it is a matter of recognizing perceived figures and shapes or the similarity of board positions or sequences of moves in a game of chess, the context seems to guide human pattern recognition in ways that cannot be duplicated by the computer using context-free features and precise rules for relating them. Our sense of our situation seems to allow us to zero in on just those features that are relevant to the task at hand and virtually to ignore an indefinite number of further features. Moreover, a great deal of human pattern recognition seems to be based on the perception of global similarity and not to involve any feature-by-feature comparison at all.

The expert chess player sees the board in terms of fields of force rather than precise positions of each of the individual pieces, recognizes intuitively the similarity to situations encountered in previous games even though none of the individual positions of pieces and few of the objective relations among individual pieces are the same, and selects a move after explicitly examining relatively few alternatives. The computer, on the other hand, analyzes the board in terms of the position of each of the pieces and then either has recourse to heuristic rules which connect that information to precise moves or else uses brute computing force to examine every possible course of action to as great a depth as time will allow. The latter strategy has been more successful, but the moves selected by this technique are still inferior to those chosen by the human expert in spite of the fact that the computer examines thousands of times as many future positions in its selection process. I will explain exactly why this is so in the second part of this essay.

Human beings also recognize people they know or familiar surroundings without noticing, much less carefully comparing, the individual features of the persons or things recognized. Duplicating this kind of ordinary recognition has proven impossible for AI. The reason, I think, is the same as in the case of the expert chess player, but more on this later.

Programs designed to duplicate the general human ability to solve problems achieved results only by restricting the task in such a way that general human problem solving was never at issue. Programs typically solved word puzzles which were restricted so as to include only relevant information and which contained explicit cues to invoke the correct heuristic rule as needed. The human ability to identify the kind of problem faced, to sort information in terms of relevance, and to find the correct method of solution on the basis of similarity to previously solved problems—that is, full-fledged human problem solving—was simply bypassed, supplied in effect by the human "processing" of the problems to be "solved."

In the late sixties and early seventies the difficulties described above were taken seriously by workers in AI. Instead of trying to duplicate in one giant step general human understanding of the world, attention turned to producing understanding in very restricted "worlds." These artificially restricted domains were called "micro-worlds." Impressive micro-world successes included Terry Winograd's SHRDLU, Thomas Evans's Analogy

Problem Program, David Waltz's Scene Analysis Program, and Patrick Winston's program for learning concepts from examples. The micro-worlds were restricted in such a way that the problems of context-restricted relevance and context-determined meaning seemed to be manageable. The hope was that micro-world techniques could be extended to more general domains, the micro-worlds made increasingly more realistic and combined to produce eventually the everyday world, and the computer's capacity to cope with these micro-worlds thereby transformed into genuine artificial intelligence.

The subsequent failure of every attempt to generalize micro-world techniques beyond the artificially restricted domains for which they were invented has put an end to the hopes inspired by early micro-world successes and brought AI to a virtual standstill. Some researchers, including Winograd, have given up on AI entirely. The micro-world strategy failures have been instructive, however, focusing attention in the direction I had argued for more than a decade was crucial, namely, toward the nature of everyday human understanding and know-how. The problem encountered in the attempt to move from micro-worlds to any aspect of the everyday world is that micro-worlds are not worlds at all, or, from the other side, domains within the everyday world are not anything like micro-worlds. This insight emerged in the attempt to program children's story understanding. It was soon discovered that the "world" of even a single child's story, unlike a micro-world, is not a self-contained domain and cannot be treated independently of the larger everyday world onto which it opens. Everyday understanding is presupposed in every real domain, no matter how small. The everyday world is not composed of smaller independent worlds at all, is not like a building which can be built up of tiny bricks, but is rather a whole somehow present in each of its parts. Once this was realized micro-world research and its successes were recognized for what they really were, not small steps toward the programming of everyday or common-sense know-how and understanding but clever evasions of the real need to program such general competence and understanding. And the prospects for programming a digital computer to display our everyday understanding of the world were looking less bright all the time. Cognitive scientists were discovering the importance of images and prototypes in human understanding. Gradually most researchers were becoming convinced that human beings form images and compare them by means of holistic processes very different from the logical operations which computers perform on symbolic descriptions.[1]

A recent *Scientific American* article echoed my earlier assessment of AI:

> Probably the most telling criticism of current work in artificial intelligence is that it has not yet been successful in modeling what is called common sense. . . . [S]ubstantially better models of human cognition must be developed

before systems can be designed that will carry out even simplified versions of common-sense tasks. (133)

II

For the reasons discussed in the preceding section, I concluded in 1979 that AI would remain at a standstill in areas that required common-sense understanding of the everyday world, that there would be no major breakthroughs in interpreting ordinary samples of natural language, in recognizing ordinary objects or patterns in everyday contexts, or in everyday problem solving of any kind within a natural rather than artificially constrained setting. The evidence to date indicates that I was correct in my assessment of AI's prospects in these areas. However I also predicted success for AI in certain isolated tasks, cut off from the everyday world and seemingly self-contained, tasks such as medical diagnosis and spectrograph analysis. It appeared to me at the time that ordinary common sense played no role in such tasks and that the computer, with its massive data storage capacity and ability to perform large numbers of inferences almost instantaneously and with unerring accuracy, might well equal or exceed the performance of human experts. It has turned out that I was mistaken about this. In a book that we have just finished,[2] my brother, Stuart, and I attempt to explain this surprising result. Here I can give only a brief account of that explanation.

The attempt to give computers human expertise in these special domains has come to be referred to as "expert systems" research. It works as follows. Human experts in the domain are interviewed to ascertain the rules or principles which they employ. These are then programmed into the computer. The idea seems simple and uncontroversial. Human experts and computers work from the same facts with the same inference rules. Since the computer cannot forget or overlook any of the facts, cannot make any faulty inferences, and can make correct inferences much more swiftly than the human expert, the expertise of the computer should be superior. And yet in study after study the computer proves inferior to the human experts who provide its working principles. To understand how this is possible, we need to look closely at the processes by which human beings acquire expertise.

The following model of the stages of skill acquisition emerged from our study of that process among airplane pilots, chess players, automobile drivers, and adult learners of a second language. We later found that our model fit almost perfectly data which had been gathered independently on the acquisition of nursing skills.[3] The model consists of five stages of increasing skill which I will summarize briefly in terms of the chess players. For more mundane skills such as automobile driving, you may be able to check much of the model against your own past experience.

STAGE 1—NOVICE:

During this first stage of skill acquisition through instruction, the novice is taught to recognize various objective facts and features relevant to the skill and acquires rules for determining what to do based upon facts and features. Relevant elements of the situation are defined so clearly and objectively for the novice that recognition of them requires no reference to the overall situation in which they occur. Such elements are in this sense context-free. The novice's rules are also context-free in the sense that they are simply to be applied to these context-free elements regardless of anything else that may be going on in the overall situation. For example, the novice chess player is given a formula for assigning point values to pieces independent of their position and the rule, "always exchange your pieces for the opponent's if the total value of pieces captured exceeds that of pieces lost." The novice is generally not taught that there are situations in which this rule should be violated.

The novice typically lacks a coherent sense of his overall task and judges his performance primarily in terms of how well he has followed the rules he has learned. After he acquires more than just a few such rules, the exercise of this skill requires such concentration that his capacity to talk or listen to advice becomes very limited.

The mental processes of the novice are easily imitated by the digital computer. Since it can use more rules and consider more context-free elements in a given amount of time, the computer typically outperforms the novice.

STAGE 2—ADVANCED BEGINNER:

Performance reaches a barely acceptable level only after the novice has considerable experience in coping with real situations. In addition to the ability to handle more context-free facts and more sophisticated rules for dealing with them, this experience has the more important effect of enlarging the learner's conception of the world of the skill. Through practical experience in concrete situations with meaningful elements which neither instructor nor learner can define in terms of objectively recognizable context-free features, the advanced beginner learns to recognize when these elements are present. This recognition is based entirely on perceived similarity to previously experienced examples. These new features are situational rather than context-free. Rules for acting may now refer to situational as well as context-free elements. For example, the advanced chess beginner learns to recognize and avoid overextended positions and to respond to such situational aspects of board positions as a weakened king's side or a strong pawn structure even though he lacks precise objective definitional rules for their identification.

Because the advanced beginner has no context-free rules for identifying situational elements, he can communicate this ability to others only by the use of examples. Thus the capacity to identify such features, as well as the ability to use rules which refer to them, is beyond the reach of the computer. The use of concrete examples and the ability to learn context-determined features from them, easy for human beings but impossible for the computer, represent a severe limitation on computer intelligence.

STAGE 3—COMPETENCE:

As a result of increased experience, the number of recognizable elements present in concrete situations, both context-free and situational, eventually becomes overwhelming. To cope with this the competent performer learns or is taught to view the process of decision making in a hierarchical manner. By choosing a plan and examining only the relatively small number of facts and features which are most important, given the choice of plan, he can both simplify and improve his performance. A competent chess player,[4] for example, may decide, after studying his position and weighing alternatives, that he can attack his opponent's king. He would then ignore certain weaknesses in his own position and personal losses created by his attack, and the removal of pieces defending the enemy king would become salient.

The choice of a plan, although necessary, is no simple matter for the competent performer. It is not governed by an objective procedure like the context-free feature recognition of the novice. But performance at this level requires the choice of an organizing plan. And this choice radically alters the relation between the performer and his environment. For the novice and the advanced beginner, performance is entirely a matter of recognizing learned facts and features and then applying learned rules and procedures for dealing with them. Success and failure can be viewed as products of these learned elements and principles, of their adequacy or inadequacy. But the competent performer, after wrestling with the choice of a plan, feels personally responsible for and thus emotionally involved in the outcome of that choice. While he both understands his initial situation and decides upon a particular plan in a detached manner, he finds himself deeply involved in what transpires thereafter. A successful outcome will be very satisfying and leave a vivid memory of the chosen plan and the situation as organized in terms of that plan. Failure also will not be easily forgotten.

STAGE 4—PROFICIENCY:

The novice and advanced beginner simply follow rules. The competent performer makes conscious choices of goals and plans for achieving them after reflecting upon various alternatives. This actual decision making is detached and deliberative in nature, even though the competent performer may agonize over the selection because of his involvement in its outcome.

The proficient performer is usually very involved in his task and experiences it from a particular perspective as a result of recent previous events. As a result of having this perspective, certain features of the situation will stand out as salient and others will recede into the background and be ignored. As further events modify these salient features, there will be a gradual change in plans, expectations, and even which features stand out as salient or important. No detached choice or deliberation is involved in this process. It seems just to happen, presumably because the proficient performer has been in similar situations in the past, and memory of them triggers plans similar to those which worked in the past and expectations of further events similar to those which occurred previously.

The proficient performer's understanding and organizing of his task is intuitive, triggered naturally and without explicit thought by this prior experience. But he will still find himself thinking analytically about what to do. During this reasoning, elements that present themselves as salient due to the performer's intuitive understanding will be evaluated and combined by rule to yield decisions about the best way to manipulate the environment. The spell of involvement in the world of the skill is temporarily broken by this detached and rule-governed thinking. For example, the proficient chess player[5] can recognize a very large repertoire of types of positions. Recognizing almost immediately and without conscious effort the sense of a position, he sets about calculating a move that best achieves his intuitively recognized plan. He may, for example, know that he should attack, but he must deliberate about how best to do so.

STAGE 5—EXPERTISE:

The expert performer knows how to proceed without any detached deliberation about his situation or actions and without any conscious contemplation of alternatives. While deeply involved in coping with his environment, he does not see problems in a detached way, does not work at solving them, and does not worry about the future or devise plans. The expert's skill has become so much a part of him that he need be no more aware of it than he is of his own body in ordinary motor activity. In fact tools or instruments become like extensions of the expert's body. Chess grandmasters,[6] for example, when engrossed in a game, can lose entirely the awareness that they are manipulating pieces on a board and see themselves instead as involved participants in a world of opportunities, threats, strengths, weaknesses, hopes, and fears. When playing rapidly, they sidestep dangers in the same automatic way that a child, himself an expert, avoids missiles in a familiar video game. In general, experts neither solve problems nor make decisions; they simply do what works. The performance of the expert is fluid and his involvement in his task unbroken by detached deliberation or analysis.

The fluid performance of the expert is a natural extension of the skill of the proficient performer. The proficient performer, as a result of concrete experience, develops an intuitive understanding of a large number of situations. The expert recognizes an even larger number along with the associated successful tactic or decision. When a situation is recognized, the associated course of action simultaneously presents itself to the mind of the expert performer. It has been estimated that a master chess player can distinguish roughly 50,000 types of positions. We doubtless store far more typical situations in our memories than words in our vocabularies. Consequently these reference situations, unlike the situational elements learned by the advanced beginner, bear no names and defy complete verbal description.

The grandmaster chess player recognizes a vast repertoire of types of positions for which the desirable tactic or move becomes immediately obvious. Excellent chess players can play at a rate of speed at which they must depend almost entirely on intuition and hardly at all upon analysis and the comparison of alternatives, without any serious degradation in their performance. In a recent experiment International Master Julio Kaplan was required to add rapidly numbers presented to him audibly at the rate of about one number per second, while at the same time playing five-second-a-move chess against a slightly weaker, but master-level, player. Even with his analytical mind completely occupied with the addition, Kaplan more than held his own against the master in a series of games. Deprived of the time necessary to see problems or construct plans, Kaplan still produced fluid and coordinated play.

What emerges from this model of human skill acquisition is a progression from the analytic, rule-governed behavior of a detached subject who consciously breaks down his environment into recognizable elements, to the skilled behavior of an involved subject based on an accumulation of concrete experiences and the unconscious recognition of new situations as similar to remembered ones. The innate human ability to recognize whole current situations as similar to past ones facilitates our acquisition of high levels of skill and separates us dramatically from the artificially intelligent digital computer endowed only with context-free fact and feature-recognition devices and with inference-making power.

This model provided Stuart and me with an explanation of the failure of the expert systems approach which also connects it with the failure of previous work in AI. When the interviewer elicits rules and principles from the human expert, he forces him in effect to revert to a much lower skill level at which rules were actually operative in determining his actions and decisions. This is why experts frequently have a great deal of trouble "recalling" the rules they use even when pressed by the interviewer. They seem more naturally to think of their field of expertise as a huge set of special cases.[7] It is no wonder that systems based on principles abstracted from experts do not capture those experts' expertise and hence do not perform as well as the experts themselves.

In terms of skill level, the computer is stuck somewhere between the novice and advanced beginner level and, if our model of skill acquisition is accurate, has no way of advancing beyond this stage. What has obscured this fact for so long is the tremendous memory of the computer in terms of numbers of facts and features which can be stored and the tremendous number of rules and principles which it can utilize with super-human speed and accuracy. Although its skill is of a kind which would place it below the level of the advanced beginner, its computing power makes its performance vastly superior to that of a human being at the same skill level. But power of this kind alone is not sufficient to duplicate the ability, the intuitive expertise, of the human expert.

This model of human skill levels also explains the failure of AI researchers to duplicate human language understanding, pattern recognition, and problem solving. In each of these areas we are, for the most part, experts. We are expert perceivers, expert speakers, hearers, and readers of our native language, and expert problem solvers in most areas of everyday life. That does not mean that we do not make mistakes, but it does mean that our performance is entirely different in kind from that of the programmed digital computer. In each of these areas the computer is, at best, a very powerful and sophisticated beginner, competent in artificial microworlds where situational understanding and intuitive expertise have no part to play but incompetent in the real world of human expertise.

I still believe, as I did in 1965,[8] that computers may someday be intelligent. Real computer intelligence will be achieved, however, only after researchers abandon the idea of finding a symbolic representation of the everyday world and a rule-governed equivalent of common-sense knowhow and turn to something like a neural-net modeling of the brain instead. If such modeling turns out to be the direction that AI should follow, it will be aided by the massively parallel computing machines on the horizon—not because parallel machines can make millions of inferences per second but because faster, more parallel architecture can better implement the kind of pattern processing that does not use representations of rules and features at all.

Notes

1. For an account of the experiments which show how human beings actually use images and the unsuccessful attempts to understand this capacity in terms of programs which use features and rules, see Block, ed. and Block.

2. Hubert Dreyfus and Stuart Dreyfus. My brother, Stuart, has played an essential part in all of the critical study of machine intelligence in which I have been involved. It was Stuart, working then at RAND as a programmer in the new field of operations research, who was responsible for RAND's hiring me in 1964 as a consultant to study their pioneering work in what was then called Cognitive Simulation. And it is Stuart's intuitions about the nature of human skill acquisition and his working out of those intuitions which are summarized in the remainder of this essay.

3. See Benner.

4. Such a player would have a rating of approximately Class A which would rank him in the top 20% of tournament players.

5. Such players are termed masters and the roughly 400 American masters rank in the top 1% of all serious players.

6. There are about two dozen players holding this rank in the U.S. and they, as well as about four dozen slightly less strong players called International Masters, qualify as what we call experts.

7. See Feigenbaum and McCorduck 82.

8. The year of publication of my initial RAND report, "Alchemy and Artificial Intelligence."

Works Cited

Benner, Patricia. *From Novice to Expert: Excellence and Power in Clinical Nursing Practice.* Reading: Addison-Wesley, 1984.

Block, Ned. "Mental Pictures and Cognitive Science." *The Philosophical Review* 1983:499–541.

———, ed. *Imagery.* Cambridge: MIT P, 1981.

Dreyfus, Hubert. *What Computers Can't Do.* Rev. ed. New York: Harper and Row, 1979.

———, and Stuart Dreyfus. *Mind over Machine.* New York: Macmillan, 1986.

Feigenbaum, Edward, and Pamela McCorduck. *The Fifth Generation: Artificial Intelligence and Japan's Computer Challenge to the World.* Reading: Addison-Wesley, 1983.

Scientific American Oct. 1982: 133.

WHAT ARE WE THINKING ABOUT WHEN WE ARE THINKING ABOUT COMPUTERS? THINKING ABOUT ALIVENESS BY PLAYING COMPUTER GAMES

Sherry Turkle

Not all questions about artificial intelligence hinge on whether machines can pass a rigorous test for thinking or whether they can make moral decisions. More subtle questions involve what our attitudes toward intelligent-acting computers are and what impact seemingly intentional machines have on our views of ourselves. Sociologist/psychologist Sherry Turkle uses her research with children to show how old paradigms of thinking about machines as noncognitive mechanisms have failed children in their attempts to explain computing machines. She finds that children take computers to be "psychological machines." This understanding of machines will significantly affect the general population as the first generation of computer-literate children reaches adulthood. Turkle attempts to demonstrate that from this change in attitude arises a "decentralized" and "fluid" concept of living beings that forces us to rethink the very meaning of what it is to be "alive."

The genius of Jean Piaget (1960) showed us the degree to which it is the business of childhood to take the objects in our world and use how they "work" to construct theories—of space, time, number, causality, life, and mind. In the mid-twentieth century, when Piaget was formulating his theories, a child's world was full of things that could be understood in simple, mechanical ways. A bicycle could be understood in terms of its pedals and gears, a windup car in terms of its clockwork springs. Children were able to take electronic devices such as basic radios and (with some difficulty) bring them into this "mechanical" system of understanding. Since the end of the 1970s, however, with the introduction of electronic toys and games, the nature of many objects and how children understand them has changed. When children today remove the back of their computer toys to "see" how they work, they find a chip, a battery, and some wires. Sensing that trying to understand these objects "physically" will lead to a dead end, children try to use a "psychological" kind of understanding (Turkle 1984, 29–63). Children ask themselves if the games are conscious, if the games know, if they have feelings, and even if they "cheat." Earlier objects encouraged children to think in terms of a distinction between the world of psychology and the world of machines, but the computer does not. Its "opacity" encourages children to see computational objects as psychological machines.

During the last twenty years I have observed and interviewed hundreds of children as they have interacted with a wide range of computational objects, from computer programs on the screen to robots off the screen (Turkle 1984; 1995). My methods are ethnographic and clinical. In the late 1980s and early 1980s I began by observing children playing with the first generation of electronic toys and games. In the 1990s I have worked with children using new generations of computer games and software, including virtual "pets," and with children experimenting with online life on the Internet.

Among the first generation of computational objects was Merlin, which challenged children to games of tic-tac-toe. For children who had only played games with human opponents, reaction to this object was intense. For example, while Merlin followed an optimal strategy for winning tic-tac-toe most of the time, it was programmed to make a slip every once in a while. So when children discovered strategies that allowed them to win, when they tried these strategies a second time, they usually would not work. The machine gave the impression of not being "dumb enough" to let down its defenses twice. Robert, seven, playing with his friends on the beach, watched his friend Craig perform the "winning trick," but when he tried it, Merlin did not make its slip and the game ended in a draw. Robert, confused and frustrated, accused Merlin of being a "cheating machine." Children were used to machines being predictable. But this machine held surprises.

Robert threw Merlin into the sand in anger and frustration. "Cheater. I hope your brains break." He was overheard by Craig and Greg, aged six and eight, who salvaged the by now very sandy toy and took it upon themselves to set Robert straight. Craig offered the opinion that, "Merlin doesn't know if it cheats. It won't know if it breaks. It doesn't know if you break it, Robert. It's not alive." Greg adds, "It's smart enough to make the right kinds of noises. But it doesn't really know if it loses. That's how you can cheat it. It doesn't know you are cheating. And when it cheats it don't even know it's cheating." Jenny, six, interrupted with disdain: "Greg, to cheat you have to know you are cheating. Knowing is part of cheating."

In the early 1980s such scenes were not unusual. Confronted with objects that spoke, strategized, and "won," children were led to argue the moral and metaphysical status of machines on the basis of their psychologies: Did the machines know what they were doing? Did they have intentions, consciousness, and feelings? These first computers that entered children's lives were evocative objects: they became the occasion for new formulations about the human and the mechanical. For despite Jenny's objections that "knowing is part of cheating," children did come to see computational objects as exhibiting a kind of knowing. She was part of the first generation of children who were willing to invest machines with qualities of consciousness as they rethought the question of what is alive in the context of "machines that think."

During the past twenty years the objects of children's lives have come to include machines of even greater intelligence, toys and games and programs that make these first cyber-toys seem primitive in their ambitions. The answers to the classical Piagetian question of how children think about life are being renegotiated as they are posed in the context of computational objects (simulation games, robots, virtual pets) that explicitly present themselves as exemplars of "artificial life."

Although the presence of the first generation of computational objects (the games like Merlin, Simon, and Speak and Spell) disrupted the classical Piagetian story for talking about aliveness, the story children were telling about such objects in the early 1980s had its own coherency. Faced with intelligent toys, children took a new world of objects and imposed a new world order in which motion had given way to emotion and cognition as the discourse children used for talking about the aliveness of computers.

In the 1980s the computational objects that evoke evolution and "artificial life" (for example computer programs such as the games of the "Sim" series which stress decentralized and "emergent" processes) have strained that order to the breaking point. Children still try to impose strategies and categories, but they do so in the manner of theoretical *bricoleurs*, or tinkerers, making do with whatever materials are at hand, making do with whatever theory can fit a prevailing circumstance. When children confront these new objects and try to construct a theory about what is alive, we see them cycling through theories of "aliveness." Tim, thirteen, says of SimLife: "The animals that grow in the computer could be alive because anything that grows has a chance to be alive." Laurence, fifteen, agrees. "The whole point of this game," he tells me,

> is to show that you could get things that are alive in the computer. We get energy from the sun. The organisms in a computer get energy from the plug in the wall. I know that more people will agree with me when they make a SimLife where the creatures are smart enough to communicate. You are not going to feel comfortable if a creature that can talk to you goes extinct.

An eleven-year-old named Holly watches a group of robots with "on-board" computational intelligence navigate a maze. The robots use different strategies to reach their goal, and Holly is moved to comment on their "personalities" and their "cuteness." She finally comes to speculate on the robots' "aliveness" and blurts out an unexpected formulation: "It's like Pinocchio."

> First Pinocchio was just a puppet. He was not alive at all. Then he was an alive puppet. Then he was an alive boy. A real boy. But he was alive even before he was a real boy. So I think the robots are like that. They are alive like Pinocchio [the puppet], but not "real boys."

She clears her throat and sums up her thought: "They [the robots] are sort of alive."

Robbie, a ten-year-old who has been given a modem for her birthday, puts the emphasis on mobility when she considers whether the creatures she has evolved on SimLife are alive.

> I think they are a little alive in the game, but you can turn it off and you cannot "save" your game, so that all the creatures you have evolved go away. But if they could figure out how to get rid of that part of the program so that you would have to save the game and if your modem were on, then they could get out of your computer and go to America Online.

Sean, thirteen, who has never used a modem, comes up with a variant on Robbie's ideas about SimLife creatures and their Internet travel: "The [Sim] creatures could be more alive if they could get into DOS." Thus, children cycle through evolution and psychology and resurface ideas about motion in terms of the communication of bits on the Internet. In children's talk about digital "travel" via circulating disks or over modems, in their talk of viruses and networks, biology and motion are resurfacing in a new guise, now bound up in the ideas of communication and evolution. Significantly, the resurfacing of motion (Piaget's classical criterion for how a child decides whether a "traditional" object is alive) is now bound up with notions of a presumed psychology: children were most likely to assume that the creatures in Sim games have a desire to "get out" of the system and evolve in a wider computational world.

My current collection of comments about life by children who have played with the artifacts of artificial life that are available in the popular culture (small mobile robots, the games of the "Sim" series, and Tierra, a program which simulates evolutionary selection through survival of the fittest) includes the following notions: the robots are in control but not alive, would be alive if they had bodies, are alive because they have bodies, would be alive if they had feelings, are alive the way insects are alive but not the way people are alive; the Tierrans are not alive because they are just in the computer, could be alive if they got out of the computer and got onto America Online, are alive until you turn off the computer and then they're dead, are not alive because nothing in the computer is real; the Sim creatures are not alive but almost-alive, they would be alive if they spoke, they would be alive if they traveled, they're alive but not "real," they're not alive because they don't have bodies, they are alive because they can have babies, and finally, for an eleven-year-old who is relatively new to SimLife, they're not alive because these babies don't have parents. She says: "They show the creatures and the game tells you that they have mothers and fathers, but I don't believe it. It's just numbers, it's not really a mother and a father." There is a striking heterogeneity of theory here. Different children hold different theories and individual children are able to hold different theories at the same time.

In his history of artificial life, Steven Levy (1992, 6–7) suggested that one way to look at where artificial life can "fit in" to our way of thinking about life is to envisage a continuum in which Tierra, for example, would be more alive than a car but less alive than a bacterium. My observations suggest that children are not constructing hierarchies but are heading toward parallel definitions of life, which they "alternate" through rapid cycling. Multiple and alternating definitions, like thinking comfortably about one's identity in terms of multiple and alternating aspects of self, become a habit of mind.

Children speak easily about factors which encourage them to see the "stuff" of computers as the same "stuff" of which life is made. For example, the seemingly ubiquitous "transformer toys" shift from being machines to being robots to being animals (and sometimes people). Children playing with these objects are learning about the potentially fluid boundaries between mechanism and flesh.

I observe a group of seven year olds playing with a set of plastic transformer toys that can take the shape of armored tanks, robots, or people. The transformers can also be put into intermediate states so that a "robot" arm can protrude from a human form or a human leg from a mechanical tank. Two of the children are playing with the toys in intermediate states (that is, in states somewhere between being people, machines, and robots). A third child insists that this is not right. The toys, he says, should not be placed in hybrid states. "You should play them as all tank or all people." He is getting upset because the other two children are making a point of ignoring him. An eight-year-old girl comforts the upset child. "It's okay to play them when they are in-between. It's all the same stuff," she said, "just yucky computer 'cy-dough-plasm.'" This comment is the expression of a cyborg consciousness as it expresses itself among today's children: a tendency to see computer systems as "sort of" alive, to fluidly cycle through various explanatory concepts, and to willingly transgress boundaries. Most recently, the transgressions have involved relationships with "virtual pets" (the first and most popular of these were Tamagotchi) who demand of their owners to feed them, play games with them, inquire about their health and mood, and, when they are still babies, clean up their virtual "poop." Good parenting of a Tamagotchi will produce a healthy offspring; bad parenting will lead to illness, deformity, and finally, to the pet's virtual death. The Tamagotchi are only the first in a projected series of computational objects that seem destined to teach children a new lesson about the machine world: that computational objects need to be related to as another life form.

Today's adults grew up in a psychological culture that equated the idea of a unitary self with psychological health, and in a scientific culture that taught that when a discipline achieves maturity, it has a unifying theory. When they find themselves cycling through varying perspectives on themselves (as when they cycle through a sequence such as "I am my chemicals" to "I am my history" to "I am my genes") they usually become uncomfortable (Kramer 1993). People who grew up in the world of the mechanical are more comfortable with a definition of what is alive that excludes all but the biological and resist shifting definitions of aliveness. So, when they meet ideas of artificial life which put the processes of replication and evolution rather than biology at the center of what is alive (Langton 1989) they tend to be resistant, even if intrigued. They feel as though they are being asked to make a theoretical choice against biology and for computational process. Children who have grown up with computational objects don't experience that dichotomy. They turn the dichotomy into a menu and cycle through its choices. Today's children have learned a lesson from their cyborg objects. They cycle through the cy-dough-plasm into fluid and emergent conceptions of self and life.

Note

This essay is drawn from Turkle (1995).

References

Kramer, Peter. 1993. *Listening to Prozac: A Psychiatrist Explores Antidepressant Drugs and the Remaking of the Self.* New York: Viking.

Langton, Christopher. 1989. "Artificial Life," in *Artificial Life: The Proceedings of an Interdisciplinary Workshop on the Synthesis and Simulation of Living Systems,* ed. Christopher G. Langton, Santa Fe Institute Studies in the Science of Complexity, vol. 6. Redwood City, Cal.: Addison-Wesley.

Levy, Steven. 1992. *Artificial Life: The Quest for a New Frontier.* New York: Pantheon.

Piaget, Jean. 1960. *The Child's Conception of the World,* trans. Joan and Andrew Tomlinson. Totowa, N.J.: Littlefield, Adams.

Turkle, Sherry. 1984. *The Second Self: Computers and the Human Spirit.* New York: Simon and Schuster.

———. 1995. *Life on the Screen: Identity in the Age of the Internet.* New York: Simon and Schuster.

CHAPTER ELEVEN
Virtual Environments

EFFECTS OF PARTICIPATING IN VIRTUAL ENVIRONMENTS: A REVIEW OF CURRENT KNOWLEDGE

John Wilson

Researcher John Wilson looks at the current state of our knowledge about the "side effects" of using virtual reality (VR) devices. The article introduces the basics of VR, laying out what types of characteristics are generally attributed to VR systems. He explains that much of the current research has not sufficiently accounted for complicating factors when attributing side effects such as motion sickness, dizziness, and even "escapism." Wilson also recognizes some benefits offered through the use of VR but concludes that much more work must be done in order to explain better both the potential harms and benefits.

1. Introduction

As technologies develop, both in terms of their own intrinsic potential and also in terms of their more widespread use, often there comes some kind of backlash in their perception by the public and the media. This may be against the technology and its functionality—for instance when it is seen as being "oversold," or because of its effects on the lives of people, their livelihood, well-being and health. Such reactions are due in part to the sheer impact of a technology in respect of incidence (e.g. numbers of motor cars and consequent pollution/crowding) and use frequency or time (e.g. the office computer workstation and visual effects/musculoskeletal disorders). Also, the innate conservatism of people means that any new technologies may receive some kind of adverse reaction, and the media are

Reprinted from *Safety Science* 23, no. 1 (1996): 39–51, with permission from Elsevier Science.

very quick to pick up on this. However, adverse reactions can also be stimulated by genuine fears of the harmful effects of certain technologies.

Concern over virtual environments created within Virtual Reality (VR) technology, and particularly Head Mounted Displays (HMDs), is probably unique in that in different respects it parallels concerns for a number of different types of technology. To begin with there have been suggestions of harmful visual and musculoskeletal effects, paralleling some of the debate over VDUs generally, particularly with CRTs (cathode ray tubes). Secondly there is some evidence of disorientation, sickness and nausea in VR which parallel the debate on motion sickness in transport generally and also the debate that has run for some time now on simulator sickness. Thirdly there have been some concerns over behavioural change as a result of working (or playing) in virtual environments (VEs), which is similar to the debate over children and video games. Closely allied to this is a fourth concern, namely that virtual environments may prove to be addictive and/or an escape from reality for some people; this compares to debates over excessive television watching. Extending from this fourth is a fifth concern to do with ethics and morality in terms of both the types of worlds that might be built for people to play in (e.g. very violent worlds) and by extension concern about the possibly sinister motives of people who will build and promote certain virtual world experiences.

Anyone who has had any experience in some of today's, admittedly fairly crude, virtual environment systems may think that at least some of the concerns above are somewhat far fetched. If, however, the technology develops as fast and as far as most of those involved in it predict it will, particularly with extensions into more than just a visual experience, then it may be time for serious debate on all of the above issues: "here we have a primitive technology, unproven from a psychological, ergonomic or health and safety point of view, which may be causing short-term adaptations to the sensory system of the human user. Who knows? Probably nobody at the moment . . ." (Stone, 1992). Stone went on to identify disorientation and nausea during immersion, and disorientation, visual field fragmentation, after images, and visual fatigue as amongst possible after effects. More recently, the influential National Research Council in the USA has noted concerns about induced motion sickness, potential after effects including drowsiness, irritability and nausea, and equipment problems including excessive weight and poor fit of the HMDs (Durlach and Mayor, 1995). They further suggest that if these problems are not addressed, "the practical usage of these systems will be limited to emergency situations or to very short periods of time" (p. 3).

The author is part of a team at the Universities of Nottingham and Loughborough working on a long term project funded by the UK Health and Safety Executive (HSE) to look at what are described as the "health and safety effects of working in VR." The responsibilities of HSE are for the workplace with extension to certain entertainment sites such as fairgrounds, and so the research will concentrate upon such contexts but will draw upon ideas, findings and developments from the use of VR at home and elsewhere. Suggested potential side effects are direct or indirect, short or long term, and musculoskeletal, psychological or physiological in nature.

This paper opens with an overview of virtual environments and the nature of the virtual environment experience, and then summarises reported or suggested harmful effects. This is extended by looking at technical factors which might be implicated in any harmful effects for the participants. We then bring together some of the major reported research in the area, and look also at potential benefits of VR for health and safety, before looking at how research might be structured to overcome some of the many methodological problems involved.

At the outset it must be said that the author is largely neutral about the technical capabilities and any potential harmful effects of VR systems and virtual environments. They have great potential to allow some things to be done far better than at present, but will not be the universal computer interface of the future. Equally, it is unlikely that all virtual environments are (and will remain) potentially harmful by their very nature, but some aspects may have greater side effects than others and some of these side effects may be disturbing or harmful. Developers, researchers and regulators should be identifying and rectifying such problems.

2. The Nature of Virtual Environments

Currently we are seeing much media and public interest in Virtual Reality and also the development of a large variety of different types of VR systems. Some are for leisure and entertainment but increasingly for more serious applications in industry, medicine and education. From often conflicting information we must consider very carefully exactly what is meant by Virtual Reality. To begin with we must be very sure that, for all but entertainment and a few specialised simulator applications, virtual world developers are (or should) *not* be trying to create a "new reality" or to make participants think that they are in the real world. We are, though, trying to create virtual worlds such that participants can relate these to the real world and can perceive a match of experiences between virtual and real worlds. In particular we often want people to be able to transfer what has been experienced and learnt virtually to their subsequent "real" performance. It is the quality of the virtual experience and its saliency (its meaning and value) for the participant that are important; the virtual world builder must carefully provide sensory cues to match the perceptual and motor performance the participant requires for task completion—known as selective fidelity (Robinett, 1992; Zeltzer, 1992). Therefore, rather than

Virtual Reality it is better to talk of *virtual environments* created within Virtual Reality systems.

The virtual environment experience should enable participants to feel displaced to a new location, to interact with objects and the environment, and to feel that the objects they are manipulating or observing are behaving appropriately. Participants should be able to perceive some equivalence between the virtual and real environments, in terms of interactions with objects and of objects' interactions with each other.

In one sense, virtual environments have been around in different forms for many years (Steuer, 1992). Simulators—flight or driving—provide a virtual environment. So, at another level, do some video-based systems and, utilising a different human sensing system, CD music systems. Indeed, even a good book is often said to transport the engrossed reader to a new environment. Physical mock-ups used to "walkthrough" new workplaces to carry out ergonomics analyses are also VEs. What we are seeing now though are VE systems which are more affordable and interactive than traditional simulators, and which give a much more complete experience than CD or videos or mock-up models. Reading across the better accounts, it appears to be widely accepted that virtual environments have the following attributes (Wilson et al., 1996):

- environments are generated by computer;
- environments, or the participants' experience of them, are three dimensional; participants have a sense of presence in VEs;
- participants can navigate around VEs;
- behaviour of objects in VEs can match their behaviour in real life;
- participants can interact with VEs in real time.

It is the concentration on real-time interaction and presence (which together with autonomy, or sophistication of the model, are said by Zeltzer (1992) to be the three key components of a VE), rather than on pure quality of graphics, that distinguishes VEs from computer aided design and other 3D solid modeling systems.

Virtual environments in Virtual Reality are created out of different system elements: the architecture and software to produce visual and other images and to interface with input devices; interface systems comprising sensors and effectors (and also input devices); and communications systems for networking. Sensors allow the system to know where the participant is or what they are doing, and include position trackers and kinaesthetic sensors, mounted on the head, hand or body. Effectors provide information to the participant, and include a variety of visual and audio displays, and in the future force and tactile feedback. Input devices, strictly sensors, include six axis spaceball, space mouse and joystick.

Depending upon which elements of the available technology that they use, VE systems may be classed along a "scale of envelopment" from full simulators, to equipment using head mounted displays, gloves, body suits, etc. to head coupled (or BOOM) systems, to desktop systems. Desktop systems do provide a lower level of presence and, perhaps, interactivity, but they have advantages at the moment in terms of graphics quality, user comfort and convenience, suitability for existing work patterns (task switching, working with others), lengths of time the participant can be working and cost. Moreover, we do not need to be enveloped or clothed in equipment to be absorbed or immersed in what we do. However, all VE technologies are improving and converging; one job of the research community is to provide advice on appropriate VE technology for different applications.

When we build industrial VEs—perhaps to use in factory planning, plant layout, training for maintenance or product design (Cobb et al., 1995a; Wilson et al., 1995) then we are not trying to fool the user that the VE is in fact real. That is impossible with today's or tomorrow's technology and is anyway usually inappropriate. We are trying to create experiences that appear and behave credibly, consistently and coherently, and that allow participants to do something better than they could do otherwise and to relate the experience to the real world. For VEs in industry, it will be valuable to place participants in environments they cannot normally, or easily experience, to allow them to perform in ways not normally or easily possible, to enhance visualisation of and communication about a situation, and to allow exploration and different viewpoints for an environment.

3. The Case for and Against Harmful Effects of VEs

Reports of *potential* harmful or other side-effects for participants in VEs, during or post immersion, have been appearing with increasing frequency, although published scientific evidence is scarcer. The mere possibility of sickness, hallucinations or disorientation with Virtual Reality is meat and drink to the popular press (but also to more reputable publications, e.g. Arthur, 1992; The Lancet, 1991). When Greenfield (1994), for instance, asserts that "It is a medical fact that anyone emerging from a VR experience may experience disorientation, dislocation, nausea or exaggerated reflex responses . . ." and that "a driver suffering a sudden simulator sickness attack could cause carnage on the roads" (p. 38), no evidence is given. Nonetheless, respected authorities like Steve Ellis from NASA–Ames, with a long history of work with VEs reports that field use *can* be difficult, disorienting and nauseogenic, and that extended use could bring about nausea and altered visual and visuo-motor coordination, which could as a result interfere with driving. He also mentions possible social after effects and the "tiring" nature of some of the glove input devices (Ellis, 1994).

Bolas (1994) suggested that poorly tracked systems, with slow response and noise in the tracking system, cause nausea because of the mismatch between visual and proprioceptive or vestibular cues. This is often interpreted in terms of sensory conflict theory (see later), and is reported as akin to motion or simulator sickness (e.g. Regan, 1994). Mogal (1993) sees that delays in the system, giving lags of up to 250 ms mean that the "expectation of the brain and reality move out of sync" resulting in possibly significant adverse effects. Moshell et al. (1993), on the other hand, believe that although there is evidence of simulator sickness in VEs, "this is not a showstopper."

Looking more at visual functions. Piantanida (1993) identified potential optical distortions, both if there is no correction for any discrepancy between the participant's interpupilliary distance (IPD) and the optical centre distance for the HMD and because all lenses are imperfect anyway. He also reports all participants having mild esaphoria (eyes turning inwards when the eyes are dissociated) after wearing HMD's, and possible long term effects for a small number of people who already have intermittent exophoria or squint. However, it should be pointed out that close work anyway may be expected to produce some relative shifts in phoria. John Wann and colleagues in a series of experiments described in more detail later (e.g. Mon-Williams et al., 1993) have identified potential problems with stereoscopic-HMD wearing, which they ascribe as being largely to do with an accommodation/vergence dissociation (see later). Other visual function effects may be due to alignment problems with images or lenses ("stereoscopic visual strain"—Ellis, 1991).

The equipment itself, its comfort and fit, has also been cited, more as an irritation, discomfort and disincentive problem than a health and safety one (e.g. Bolas, 1994; Newquist, 1994; Sturtnan and Zeltzer, 1994). However, at least one manufacturer has commissioned a series of studies of the ergonomics of HMD's, including musculoskeletal, visual, auditory and electrical factors, along with assessment of problems of transmissable diseases (Cassells Associates, 1990); NASA–Ames at Moffatt Field also have an ongoing research programme to improve the ergonomics of HMD's.

Finally, there is a growing debate over social and ethical issues in using VEs, both in terms of the type of worlds provided for participants (e.g. violent worlds) and builders' responsibilities for this, and in terms of behavioural effects on participants, such as hallucinations, literalisation, dissociation, addiction, misplaced locus of control, or retreat from reality (see Shapiro and McDonald (1992), Stuart (1992) and Whitby (1993), and the papers by Kallman (1993), Sheridan (1993), Stone (1993) and Whitbeck (1993) in a special issue of *Presence*).

In summary then, there is much discussion of potentially harmful or disturbing side effects for VE participants, but with the exception of a very few reported studies which are discussed later there is little in the way of hard evidence.

4. Technical Limitations Relevant to Side Effects of Virtual Environments

Any examination of the effects of virtual environments on people—and particularly health and safety effects—must reflect three sets of issues to do with VEs. First, and obviously, there is the question of the different types of experience to be gained and the different physical and cognitive interfaces available with different VR systems. Although there may be some similarities, many health implications of HMDs will be different to those of desktop systems.

Secondly, in part related to the choice of technology but also to an extent independent of this, there are a large number of technical issues which impinge directly and indirectly on user experience and particularly on adverse effects. Interestingly, there is good *prima facie* reason to suppose that the more sophisticated the system the more likely there are to be some side effects. The more the participant can suspend disbelief about the manner of the VE creation, believing that whilst they are not in *the* real world that they are in some kind of coherent world, then perhaps the greater any effects of disorientation or sickness are likely to be. Stereoscopic systems may cause more problems than monoscopic systems (although giving a higher level of performance). Unless temporal lags can be almost eliminated then the faster systems may cause more problems than the slower, since the latter may frustrate rather than distress. Problems to do with spatial resolution are not easy to predict.

The third set of factors to be accounted for in health and safety views of VEs are to do with the virtual experience itself. This is related both to the quality of the VE, which is dependent upon technical factors, and also any individual differences. MI research in this area shows strong individual differences in reported, and to an extent objectively measured, side effects—whether these be musculoskeletal, physiological or psychological effects. This is related to consideration of who is more susceptible to suspending disbelief in VEs . . .

5. Current Research on Effects of Participating in Virtual Environments

Of potential problems due to the action of, and stresses on, the visual functioning of participants, perhaps the most widely discussed is that of accommodation—convergence dissociation. In everyday life, when we look at a near object our eyes turn inwards together (convergence) in order to see the object singly, and they focus (accommodate) in order to see the object clearly. Accommodation and convergence are intrinsically linked, and in everyday vision the eyes will both accommodate and converge for the same distance. In an immersive stereoscopic VR system, the eye does not look at the screen directly, but rather looks at an image of the screen produced by the headset optical system. The screen itself may be mere centimetres away from the eye, but the *image* may be positioned a metre or further from the eye. If the images presented to the two eyes differ, in order to render a stereoscopic image, then there will be a mismatch between accommodation and convergence. If the screens are, for example, imaged at a distance of one metre then the eyes should accommodate by one dioptre (this is an optical unit of focusing power, which is a reciprocal metre) irrespective of the position of the object on the screen. However, if the stereoscopic display geometrically positions an object at, say, 25 cm then the amount which the eyes need to converge in order to see the image as a single entity is inappropriate for the amount of accommodation needed. That this must happen is a fact of stereoscopic VR in its current form, and that there may be some effects on the participant is also generally accepted, for instance, in terms of headaches or eyeache, or in readaptation.

There are a number of related research issues and questions. What are the differential effects from monoscopic, biocular and binocular stereoscopic systems (perhaps 10% of people are unable to see stereoscopically)? With biocular displays (same image presented to each eye) all depth cues are non-stereoscopic, and therefore accommodation and convergence are driven to the same extent at the "image" meaning there is little or no dissociation. What is the impact of other technical variables such as resolution, contrast, and illumination? Do any potential problems disappear at fusion distances over a certain value? What inter- or intra-personal effects mediate the outcomes, including headset fit? Most important, do any significantly harmful or distressing effects result, and are they due to the accommodation—vergence link or to other artefacts of VE, perhaps temporal resolution?

The best known work in the area is from a team at Edinburgh (e.g. Mon-Williams et al., 1993), who took subjective reports and used conventional ophthalmic tests for 20 participants immersed for 10 minutes using an early generation commercially available binocular HMD. They described their results as worrying, with a change in visual function post-immersion for more than 50% of the sample which they ascribed to induced binocular stress. Amongst effects noted were marked changes in heterophoria which they explain on the grounds of the demands on the accommodation/vergence system. Subjects also reported some further effects including blurred vision, headaches and nausea; mostly these symptoms were short-lived. Subsequently a newer generation biocular system was used (Rushton et al., 1994), with a larger sample size, adjustments for IPD, independent eye focus, lesser temporal lags and higher screen resolution. Much reduced visual performance decrements and symptomatic reports were noted. The authors warn that it would be misleading to isolate a single factor but that a crucial difference is the biocular rather than binocular display. It appears that Tom Piantanida and Duane Boman at SRI in Stanford have found similar effects (Boman, 1994). Further useful information will be found in Yeh (1993).

None of the work reported to date has examined the various possible causal factors in isolation. Because of the multiplicity of technical and environment characteristics potentially involved there is no real certainty that the accommodation/convergence problem is the cause of any disturbing or potentially harmful effects. Work on our current research grant has taken a step back and examined dissociation of accommodation and convergence away from the possible other confounding technical variables (Howarth and Bradbury, 1994). The experiments ascertain whether dissociation between accommodation and convergence causes physiological stress, manifested as discomfort. This would be expected to happen as the demand on the fusional system varies, as when viewing a stereoscopic image in a VR headset. In addition, adaptation changes in the fusional control system, manifested as changes in heterophoria, would be expected. Change of demand is achieved by deliberately dissociating accommodation and convergence using a range of prisms, and assessing discomfort and heterophoria after the subjects perform a task for 15 or 30 minutes. (A prism will not affect the accommodation system but alters the direction of light passing through and hence will affect the vergence system), Preliminary findings suggest clear adaptive changes in heterophoria measured in the fusional system of the eye, similar to those reported by Mon-Williams et al. (1993).

Claire Regan and colleagues at the Defence Research Agency (DRA—previously the Army Personnel Research Establishment) have conducted a whole series of experimental studies into the side-effects of working in virtual environments, also assessing differential effects of changes in equipment fit, participant posture and activity, software environment, and use of anti-motion sickness drugs (Regan, 1994). The VR platform they used was of a generation between the two used in the Edinburgh work.

The main side effects examined were to do with sickness or nausea, disorientation and oculomotor discomfort. Effects like these are widely debated as to their significance in a VE experience, with analogy being drawn with motion or simulator sickness. Oman (1993) and Regan (1994) amongst others propose the relevance of sensory conflict theory (see Reason, 1974). In this it is recognised that sickness can occur both as a result of exogenous motion stimulation (especially at low frequencies—sea sickness, car sickness) and also because of a "sensory rearrangement" (Oman, p. 363), when the central nervous system receives sensory information on body orientation or movements which is unexpected from previous experience or current motor intentions. Other examples are sickness with new glasses, or wide-screen cinemas, and flight simulator and space sickness. Thus Regan and others' work has used or drawn from the Simulator Sickness Questionnaire (Kennedy et al., 1992, 1993).

In first experiments a high incidence (61%) of self-reported malaise after 20 minute immersions was found (Regan and Price, 1993a), but with marked reductions after subsequent immersions (Regan and Price, 1993b; Regan and Ramsey, 1994a). Attempts to reduce any side effects other than by adaptation have included use of motion sickness drugs (relatively successful—Regan and Ramsey, 1994b) and facilitating a more natural movement through the virtual environment. Regan (1994, p. 17–18) herself points up the inconclusive nature of her work to date. Adaptation such that side effects may be reduced may be possible if immersion is regular with short spacing, but results to date may only reflect adaptation to one particular VE. Also, much more work is needed to examine differences between fast and slow moving, simple and complex worlds, amongst others, and effects of different types and generations of technology. The effects of lag in the system may well not be uniform. If lag is to all intents and purposes absent, then there should be no problem; if lags are very large as on earlier generation systems then again there may be no problem because there is no suspension of disbelief; it is when lags are small as in current mid- to top-end systems (e.g. around 30–50 ms) that we may find problems. Furthermore, the DRA research shows that some people are more susceptible than others, just as for seasickness. What determines such susceptibility? Finally, Regan's use of measures of performance to assess side-effects of VEs proved disappointing. Reliance on self-reports runs the risk of criticism because of the experimenter-determined nature of the response scales, and possible reactivity in response due to repeated use; when subjects are alerted to sickness by being asked about it then responses may change over time. Therefore, there is a need to search for performance-based, non-repeated, or otherwise non-reactive methodologies.

6. Benefits for Health and Safety

It would not be appropriate to consider potentially harmful effects of virtual environments without looking at possible benefits also. At one level use of HMD Virtual Reality, with LCDs in place of CRT-based PCs and keyboards, may reduce any visual problems due to screen characteristics, any posture problems due to poor screen position, and physical workload from keying. Even desktop systems, with most interaction through the spaceball, may reduce static posture and repetitive keying problems.

In a more positive sense the operational use of virtual environments may be of value for health and safety. Examples of potential use are: ergonomics assessments of workplaces, interfaces and tasks, such as in design for assembly or in workspace layout; training of maintenance engineers, for instance to work in hazardous environments; improved teleoperation planning and control; general training for industry, including safe procedures for material movements and use of machine guards; home or road safety education: and rehearsal of error diagnosis and recovery in process plant (see Wilson et al., 1996).

Medical or therapeutic use of VEs is also of great potential benefit to health. Not only are uses proposed in surgery but also for treatment of such disorders as fear of heights, and the training of the visual system in cases of convergence insufficiency (Howarth and Winn, 1994).

7. Conclusions and Future Work

In the debate over side-effects for participants in virtual environments, it seems the following are the critical questions.

- Given the nature of virtual environments, what side effects are there for participants?
- What is the extent of differences in these effects for different individuals?
- Through what mechanisms are the different effects brought about?
- What are predisposing factors of Virtual Reality technology and virtual environments?
- To what extent will there be short- or long-term health and safety consequences?

Research into VR side effects suffers from certain problems or restrictions. If experiments are based on one type of system (and to include several is to massively increase experimental variables and complexity, as well as drain study resources) results *may* not transfer to other systems, which have greater or lesser temporal lags, larger or smaller fields of view, monocular, binocular or biocular viewing of varying quality. Use of measures such as the Simulator Sickness scales (Kennedy et al., 1993) opens up possibilities of reactivity to measurement; if we are asked several times if we feel nauseous, for instance, this may sensitise us to such feelings. A number of different subject biases and halo effects might be expected also. We need to investigate use of single measurement (as against repeated measure) experiments, with comparison to controls, and more discursive and informal methods of assessment, in order to reduce any problems of reactivity.

Our ongoing programme of laboratory experiments (e.g. Cobb et al., 1995b; Nichols et al., 1996) is focused on the above concerns as well as examination of VE side effects and susceptibility to the experience for different defined groups of participants. Other evaluations are being made of affective responses using checklists for mood, anxiety, stress/arousal or general health. Performance tests have been selected which can be shown to relate to hypothesised effects on tasks such as those involving psychomotor and memory performance (although Regan and Price (1993a) had little success in using tests of effects on balance and similar hypothesised outcomes). We are undertaking measures of electrical activity in the brain and heart rate variability during and post immersion, and trying out urine and saliva analysis also. Laboratory comparisons have been taken further to include comparison of effects between different types of experience (e.g. fast and slow worlds, ones with considerable visual flow or ones requiring participant head movements). Of all the lines of research looking at effects on visual functions, that concerned with accommodation/vergence appears most valuable and promising, especially since the impact of stereoscopic displays is likely to increase markedly.

In parallel with laboratory experiments, studies of participants in the field, in leisure or work settings, will allow some of the above to be carried out as well as providing longitudinal study of adaptation, behavioural change, and attitude change. Finally, to date most studies of VE participants have involved immersive experiences of about 10–30 minutes; uncomfortable equipment and virtual worlds which only command attention for a short period may be the reasons for this, as much as any ethical considerations. Nonetheless, studies of the effects of immersion in VEs for periods of hours and over consecutive periods of days are overdue (it is thought possible that US military or security agencies work may be doing this) and we have started to run with exposure times of up to 2 hours.

In summary, there would appear to be agreement that for today's and probably tomorrow's Virtual Reality systems and virtual environment experiences there are likely to be some side effects, possibly disturbing or harmful, for some participants. "It can be fully expected that as sickness brought about by low resolution displays, visual lags, and improper force feedback disappears because of technical improvements, sickness will be more frequent because of the improved ability to create virtual environments involving "vehicle" motions which are naturally nauseogenic" (Computer Graphics, 1992, p. 61).

On the other hand, with the present or future generations of technology there is no evidence that the consequences of any effects will be serious or long-lasting. It is the role of our current research to explore these issues and to suggest equipment and software design choices, instructions or user precautions which will minimise the harm from any side effects.

Acknowledgments

This paper was produced during work on grant no. 3 181/R53.133 from the Health and Safety Executive (project officer: Colin MacKay), and in part from work under grant GR/J57643 from the Control, Design and Production Group of the EPSRC. It was originally written for presentation at the IVth Annual Conference on Safety and Well-Being at Work, held at University of Loughborough in November 1994, and Alistair Cheyne is thanked for his help in moving the paper from conference to journal. Colleagues on the health and safety work include Rick Barnes, Susan Cobb, Nick Cope, Pat Costello, Mirabelle D'Cruz, Peter Howarth, Sarah Nichols and Amanda Ramsey. The paper in earlier drafts was read by Pierre DuPont, Richard Holmes, Peter Howarth, Claire Regan and Simon Rushton; their time and effort is greatly appreciated, but of course any remaining errors or misinterpretations are the author's own.

References

Arthur, C., 1992. Did reality move for you? New Scientist, 23rd May: 22–27.

Boman, D. K., 1994. Personal communication. SRI International, Menlo Park, CA.

Bolas, M. T., 1994. Human factors in the design of an immersive system. IEEE Computer Graphics and Applications, 14: 55–59.

Bryson, S. and Fisher, S. S., 1990. Defining, modelling and measuring system lag in virtual environments. SPIE 1256 (Stereoscopic Displays and Applications): 98–109.

Cassells Associates, 1990. Virtual Reality Simulation Product Safety Evaluation. Report to W. Industries (now Virtuality), October.

Cobb, S. V. G., D'Cruz, M. D. and Wilson, J. R., 1995a. Integrated manufacture: A role for virtual reality? International Journal of Industrial Ergonomics. 16: 411–425.

Cobb, S. V. G., Nichols, S. C. and Wilson, J. R., 1995b. Health and safety implications of virtual reality: In Search of an Experimental Methodology. Paper to be presented at FIVE Conference 1995, London.

Computer Graphics, 1992. Research directing in virtual environments: Report of an NSF invitational workshop. Computer Graphics, 26: 153–171.

Durlach, N. I. and Mayor, A. S. (Eds.), 1995. Virtual Reality: Scientific and Technological Challenges. National Academy Press, Washington, DC.

Ellis, S. R., 1991. Nature and origins of virtual environments: A bibliographical essay. Computing Systems in Engineering, 2: 321–347.

Ellis, S. R., 1994. What are virtual environments? IEEE Computer Graphics and Applications, 14: 17–21.

Encarnação, J., Göbel, M. and Rosenblum, L., 1994. European activities in virtual reality. IEEE Computer Graphics and Applications. 14: 66–74.

Greenfield, R., 1994. Simulator sickness. Computer Weekly, March 17th: 38.

Holmes, R., 1994. Personal communication. Virtuality Group (UK) Ltd.

Howarth, P. A., 1994. Virtual reality: An occupational health hazard of the future? Paper at the RCN Occupational Health Nurses Forum "Working for Health." Glasgow, UK, April.

Howarth, P. A. and Bradbury, J., 1994. An investigation into whether dissociating accommodation and convergence causes physiological stress. Report No. VIRART/94/1 11, Virtual Reality Applications Research Team, University of Nottingham.

Howarth, P. A. and Winn, B., 1994. The amelioration of ambpyopia during active arousal. The Optician, 207/5445.

Kalawsky, R., 1993. Critical aspects of visually coupled systems. In: Eamshaw, R., Gigante, M. and Jones, H. (Eds.), Virtual Reality Systems, Academic Press, London, pp. 302–312.

Kallman, E. A., 1993. Ethical evaluation: A necessary element in virtual environment research. Presence, 2 143–146.

Kennedy, R. S., Lane, N. E., Lilienthal, M. G., Berbaum, K. S. and Hettinger, U., 1992. Profile analysis of simulator sickness symptoms: Application to virtual environment systems. Presence, 1: 295–301.

Kennedy, R. S., Lane, N. E., Berbaum, K. S. and Lilienthal, M. G., 1993. A simulator sickness questionnaire: An enhanced method for quantifying simulator sickness. The International Journal of Aviation Psychology, 3: 203–220.

Mogal, 1993. Future trends in virtual reality technologies for workstations. Proceedings of Virtual Reality '94, Applications and Trends. Fraunhofer Institute, Stuttgart, February 27–36.

Mon-Williams, M., Wann, J. P. and Rushton, S., 1993. Binocular vision in a virtual world—Visual deficits following the wearing of a HMD. Ophthalmic and Physiological Optics, 13: 387–391.

Moshell, J. M., Blau, B. S., Knerr, B., Lampton, D. R. and Bliss, I. P., 1993. A research testbed for virtual environment training applications. IEEE.

Newquist, H. P., 1994. A day in the life of a VR user, Virtual Reality Special Report. Premier Issue 94, pp. 11–14.

Nichols, S. C., Cobb, S. V. G. and Wilson, J. R., 1996. Effects of participating in virtual environments: Towards an experimental methodology. To appear in Presence: Teleoperators and Virtual Environments, 5.

Oman, C. M., 1993. Sensory conflict In motion sickness: An observer theory approach. In: Ellis, S. R. (Ed.), Pictorial Communication in Virtual and Real Environments. Taylor & Francis, London, pp. 362–376.

Piantanida, T., 1993. Another look at HMD safety. Cyber Edge Journal, 3: 9–10, 12.

Piantanida, T., Bowman, D. K. and Gilk, J. 1993. Human perceptual issues and virtual reality. Virtual Reality Systems, 1(1), 43–52.

Pimentel, K. and Teixeira, K., 1993. Virtual Reality: Through the Looking Glass. McGraw-Hill, New York.

Reason, J. T., 1974. Man in Motion. Weidenfeld and Nicholson, London.

Regan, E. C., 1994. Some human factors issues in immersive Virtual Reality. APRE Report 94R027, Defence Research Agency.

Regan, E. C. and Price, K. R., 1993a. Some side-effects of immersion virtual reality. APRE Report 93R010. Defence Research Agency.

Regan, E. C. and Price, K. R., 1993b. Some side-effects of immersion virtual reality. APRE Report 93R033, Defence Research Agency.

Regan, E. C. and Ramsey, A. D., 1994a. Some side-effects of immersion virtual reality: The results of four immersions. APRE Report 94R012, Defence Research Agency.

Regan, E. C. and Ramsey, A. D., 1994b. Some side-effects of immersion virtual reality: An investigation into the effectiveness of hyoscine hydrobromide in reducing nausea incurred during immersion. APRE Report 94R025, Defence Research Agency.

Robinett, W., 1992. Synthetic experience: A proposed taxonomy. Presence, 1: 229–247.

Rushton, S., Mon-Williams, M. and Wann, J. P., 1994. Binocular vision in a biocular world: New-generation head-mounted displays avoid causing visual deficit. Displays, 15: 255–260.

Shapiro, M. A. and McDonald, D. G., 1992. I'm not a real doctor but I play one in virtual reality: Implications of virtual reality for judgements about reality. Journal of Communications, 42: 94–114.

Sheridan, T. B., 1993. My anxieties about virtual environments. Presence, 2: 141–142.

Steuer, J., 1992. Defining virtual reality: Dimensions determining telepresence. Journal of Communications, 42: 73–93.

Stone, RJ., 1992. Virtual Reality: Interactive Visualisation for British Industry. Proceedings of the ACME/SERC Symposium, Virtual Representations for Design and Manufacture, Coventry University, December, Paper KN2.

Stone, V. E., 1993. Social interaction and social development in virtual environments. Presence, 2: 153–161.

Stuart, R., 1992. Virtual reality: Directions in research and development. Interactive Learning International, 8: 95–100.

Sturman, D. J. and Zeltzer, D., 1994. A survey of glove-based input. IEEE Computer Graphics and Applications, 14: 30–39.

The Lancet, 1991. Seeing and believing: Ethics of virtual reality. The Lancet, August 3rd: 283–284.

Whitbeck, C., 1993. Virtual environments: Ethical issues and significant confusions. Presence, 2: 147–152.

Whitby, B., 1993. The virtual sky is not the limit: Ethics in virtual reality. Intelligent Tutoring Media, 4: 23–28.

Wilson, J. R., Brown, D. J., Cobb, S. V., D'Cruz, M. D. and Eastgate, R. M., 1995. Manufacturing operations in virtual environments. Presence: Teleoperators and Virtual Environments, 4: 306–317.

Wilson, J. R., Cobb, S. V. G., D'Cruz, M. D. and Eastgate, R. M., 1996. Virtual Reality for Industrial Application: Opportunities and Limitations. Nottingham University Press, Nottingham.

Yeh, Y-Y., 1993. Visual and perceptual issues in stereoscopic color displays. In: McAllister, D. F. (Ed.), Stereo Computer Graphics and Other True 3D Technologies. Princeton University Press, Princeton, NJ.

Zeltzer, D., 1992. Autonomy, interaction and presence. Presence, 1: 127–132.

THE VIRTUAL SKY IS NOT THE VIRTUAL LIMIT: ETHICS IN VIRTUAL REALITY

Blay Whitby

Blay Whitby surveys possible future uses of virtual reality (VR) tech-nologies and proceeds to lay out four types of arguments for design-ing explicit restrictions into VR environments. He suggests that moral action is possible only when genuine choices are available. However, to encourage people to act morally in virtual reality, it is necessary that consequences be attached to their actions. It is Whitby's hope that these insights will spark debate about the ethi-cal implications of VR research and development.

Virtual reality (VR) is the name applied to one of the latest trends in high technology research. In essence it is the delivery to a human or several humans of the most convincing illusion possible that they are in another reality. This reality exists only in digital electronic form in the memory of a computer or several computers. Hence it is accurately described as 'virtual.' Its reality stems from the convincing nature of the illusion, and most importantly for moral considerations, the way in which human participants can interact with it.

If one were to ask for a demonstration of VR, one would probably be asked to don a strange looking helmet. Inside this helmet would be a num-ber of small screens on which pictures are projected immediately in front of the wearer's eyes. One might also be asked to wear one or more 'data gloves' or similar devices. Like the helmet, these would be generously con-nected by wires to the associated computing machinery. The function of a data glove is to transmit, as accurately as possible, the movements of the wearer's hand. These movements are fed into the computer, where they are translated into "actions" (perhaps "virtual actions") within the VR. De-vices can also be attached to one's legs, though this is less common—users tend to 'float' in a given direction, rather than walk, in present day VR.

The experience of being connected to all this high technology would be (fairly) close to entering another world. One sees this world via the screens within the helmet. Movement of the head and or the eyes is sensed

---

Reprinted from *Intelligent Tutoring Media* 14, no. 1 (1993): 23–28, with permission from In-tellect, Ltd.

and the pictures appropriately modified enabling one to "look around" the world. One can (generally) move, pick up objects and interact with other characters within this world. These characters can be either computer-generated or other human participants, similarly connected via helmets, data gloves and so on. Within the world a large amount of activity may be possible. Because VR is highly interactive, what actually happens is determined by the user or users. On the other hand, what is possible is determined by the programmer or programmers. This is an important distinction to which we will return.

Many readers may feel that the experience of present-day VR is probably not convincing enough to carry the label "reality." Against this argument it must be noted that humans have immense powers of imagination and a willingness to suspend disbelief. In other words the simulated reality does not need to be a perfect simulation in order for users to come to believe that it is some form of reality.

In addition, the main imperfection in simulation at present comes from the difficulties inherent in presenting a sufficiently convincing computer generated image. Presenting a convincing visual input to a human being requires a computer which can handle a vast amount of information. This is both difficult and expensive with existing technology. It is now a familiar, but true, cliche to observe that the power and capability of computing machinery is increasing at a tremendous rate. In addition, a wide variety of techniques for producing more convincing VR are currently being researched. It is reasonable to expect, therefore, that in this crucial respect VR will become steadily more convincing.

Of course, this steady improvement will depend on the availability of financial support. This, in turn, depends on the existing and anticipated applications of VR. The question of what the applications might be is of central importance to any discussion of the ethical implications. While the technology remains a quaint experiment, it raises few, if any, moral problems. If it becomes generally applied, the moral implications will become much more important.

Implications: The Potential Applications of VR

Predictions of the future applications of new technologies are notorious for their inaccuracy. However there is little difficulty in making various predictions about the future of VR. In many respects VR represents a collection of developments of previous technologies, rather than complete innovation. Principal among these are simulators, interactive multimedia systems, and computer and arcade games. When a new technology, such as VR, becomes fashionable, its enthusiasts (and salesmen) may invest a great deal of energy in asserting that it is radically distinct from its technological antecedents. In the case of commercially available systems they have a clear vested interest in doing so. A more realistic approach would stress that most technological innovations, and VR is typical, are a relatively small development and improvement of pre-existing technologies. This approach may also help show the apparent novelty of the moral problems raised to be largely illusory.

One of the major antecedents of VR was work on flight simulation for combat helicopter pilots. VR retains much in common with flight simulation. In particular, it can provide a training environment in which mistakes are less permanent and costly than they would be in reality. This feature will provide a wealth of application areas for VR, quite possibly assisted, by the availability of generous funding for potential military applications. Just as pilots, submarine captains, and tank commanders are today trained in complex simulators they will in the near future be trained in VR. One particular advantage of VR over a simulator in this application is the way in which it can incorporate multiple participants, for example, in competition or in combat with each other. VR is likely to find successful applications in many forms of combat training.

The usefulness of VR in combat training is also accompanied by its usefulness in many forms of civilian training. In VR dangerous chemicals and machinery can be handled realistically without physical danger to the user or users. In many situations it is desirable to allow learners to make mistakes and yet protect them from the consequences of those mistakes. This is obviously the case with training for the management of nuclear power stations or dangerous chemical plants. What may not be so obvious might be the advantages of using VR instead of a laboratory for teaching physics and chemistry in schools. Of course, such a "virtual laboratory" will be limited in its ability to give practical familiarity with the equipment and techniques. However in many areas, the handling of radioactive and other dangerous materials being a conspicuous example, it will have clear advantages.

Even less obvious may be the usefulness of using VR to let users 'enter' a period of history. This would provide a useful way of teaching history, either in a school or a museum. The use of VR is already proving of interest to creative artists. Anne Barclay Morgan (Barclay Morgan 1992) has pointed out that VR (or cyberspace as it sometimes called in this area) is a medium which offers possibilities such as interactive paintings and sculptures and plots which can be changed by the audience.

In addition to training and the acquiring of factual information VR will provide a useful tool for education. It is, in many ways, the ultimate development of Seymour Papert's "microworlds" (Papert 1980). The attractions of being able to learn through doing, particularly in co-operation with others will soon be seen by educators.

Another major area where VR will sooner or later find successful application is in the field of entertainment. This, again, is an application area which is essentially an extension of existing technologies and practices. Just as the flight simulator can be seen as a training precursor of VR, so can the cinema, video game, and computer-game be seen as entertainment precursors of VR. Already arcade games are moving towards military VR in terms of the realism of their displays and the richness of interactions possible. As the technology improves there will be a strong market for VR in arcade and home entertainment.

The development of the entertainment market depends on the technology achieving a sufficiently low cost and this may take slightly longer than the developments discussed in the last couple of paragraphs. However, there is every good reason to believe that VR used for entertainment will become commonplace within a few years. Two routes of development are possible. Firstly, (relatively) low-tech, low-cost VR could become available for use in the home. Secondly, (relatively) high-tech, high-cost VR might be set up in population centres and hired by the minute by large numbers of users. These two routes are not mutually exclusive and may well be able to co-exist, just as at present many people both visit the cinema and own a video player.

Putting these two applications together produces the rather depressing conclusion that VR will also be used for advertising. The fact that there is an, almost literally, captive audience to which information can be delivered with convincing realism (yet with no test of truthfulness) will make VR just too good to miss for the advertiser. VR which claims to give the "experience" of driving the latest sports car (complete, no doubt, with admiring crowds who all seem to know one's name) will abound. The need for ethical, and legislative, controls on this application of VR should be obvious.

There can be little doubt that VR will become widespread in training, entertainment, and advertising applications. Probably most worries over their moral implications will be expressed in the context of entertainment, rather than the other application areas. However, there is a need for moral scrutiny in all three areas.

In the case of training, those designing the VR will probably have clearer objectives and may well, therefore, limit the possibilities open to the user accordingly. There is also likely to be some monitoring, even if it is just some sort of final examination, of the users of training VR. This monitoring provides at least some control over possible misuse and bad outcomes for the users of training VR.

In the case of advertising there is an obvious need to prevent the user of VR becoming a victim of intrusive advertising and to ensure that the advertising does not give a totally false impression of the value of the product to him. This may prove somewhat more difficult in the case of VR than in television or film because of the ability of a VR designer to tailor the advertising to the needs and desires of an individual. The present day advertiser tends to work with media that are aimed at groups of potential customers. A VR designer, by contrast, can easily take account of choices made by a user and use those choices to target more effective advertising techniques at a particular individual.

However, there are codes of practice in place for television and film and there is no obvious reason why these should not be immediately extended to cover VR. In the light of the sort of problem discussed in the last paragraph, improvements to these codes may well prove desirable. It is important to recognize that this constitutes no argument against using what already exists now.

Most public concern is likely to be voiced with respect to the use of VR in entertainment. The following section will therefore take the entertainment applications of VR as typical, though the conclusion will attempt to draw all three application areas together. It is the entertainment application area which will be most likely to be experienced by the general public. In addition, there are important ways in which the use of VR in entertainment is likely to be less tightly controlled than in training. On the other hand, it would seem that with VR as entertainment the sky is the limit.

The Ethical Implications of VR

Doubts have been voiced about the implications of the sort of freedom that can be provided by VR. In particular, there are worries about users having the freedom to commit rape and murder within VR. Before examining such worries in detail it is worth observing that this is an ethical rather than technical issue. It is technically possible to construct VR in such a way that almost every possibility of the user's imagination can be fulfilled. It is also possible for designers to place arbitrary limits on what is possible within a particular VR. They could, for example, simply set up a VR in such a way that killing, rape, and many other morally proscribed actions are impossible. They could even set up VR in which some form of punishment (virtual or real) was the consequence of attempting to commit a proscribed action within that VR. It is also worth observing that this issue needs to be resolved in the immediate future, since the existence of VR which allows killing or similar morally reprehensible acts will itself constitute a powerful argument against those who want to place some sort of restriction upon VR.

These are exciting, intriguing, but dangerous possibilities. When new technologies raise ethical problems in this way, misunderstandings are often generated. It is easy, for example, to assume that the novelty of the technology is, or perhaps ought to be, reflected in the novelty of the moral issues surrounding it. This is unlikely to be the case, as will be argued in the following sections.

A second group of misunderstandings stems from the fact that moral principles and beliefs are seen to be in a state of flux. The new possibilities opened up by technologies such as VR may heighten anxieties about this. In a philosophical overview of this area Colin Beardon (Beardon 1992) has argued that the emergence of VR is related to a contemporary crisis in philosophy. There is evidence that philosophical problems are raised by VR. In particular, VR (at least in its most hyped versions) closely resembles the philosophers' notion of "the experience machine" (Nozick 1974, Glover 1984). Beardon is correct to point out that debates about VR can aggravate cultural and philosophical splits in contemporary society, however this paper takes his conclusion that the best response to this is a pragmatic one.

It is sometimes even argued that morality itself no longer has any meaning with the rise of modern secular societies. To a certain extent it is simply the case that morality has always been in a state of flux. That is to say that there is a process of general debate on moral questions which probably rarely approaches consensus. This is not the place to attempt in any way to expand on this sort of debate. Instead it will be argued that there is an immediate need to resolve certain questions about what is morally acceptable in VR. These questions can be resolved by applying familiar principles. The doubts mentioned at the start of this section are about the impact of VR on human beings and the debate is therefore easiest to resolve when seen as a continuation of similar debates about the impact of older technologies on human beings.

A further group of misunderstandings surrounds questions as to who should take responsibility for discussing and resolving the moral questions surrounding new technology. The (usually unjustified) belief on the part of laymen that they are incapable of understanding the technology makes them reluctant to enter the debate. The (sometimes unjustified) belief on the part of technologists that moral questions are something they neither know nor care about makes them reluctant to start such debates. The position is further complicated by the fact that those designers of VR who set themselves high ethical standards *need* support, preferably from the public at large. Without this sort of support they will not be able to counter the arguments of customers or managers who demand morally dubious features in VR. A less satisfactory, but more practical alternative may be to form professional organizations and draw up codes, as has been done with many other forms of technology. However this takes time and there is a certain urgency to these matters.

Virtual Reality: The Case for Restrictions

VR is a technology which can offer significant benefits in training applications. In entertainment applications, it is probable that we could feel at least as positive about VR as we do about visual art or cinema, for example. In addition there are a number of arguments related to traditional views of the freedom of the individual. These take as central the technical claim that what happens within a VR is truly private. (At least in the case where there is only a single user). If one believes that individuals should be free to do absolutely anything which does not affect the freedom of others, then a VR would seem to be the ideal place to do such things.

It may not *always* be completely true that others' freedoms are unaffected by what one does within VR. In a multi-user competitive VR winning will involve someone else losing, for example. It is important not to confuse this issue. What one does within a single-user VR does not directly affect others and can therefore be regarded as private. (Indirect effects will be considered in the following.) In a multi-user VR, one can carry out actions which directly affect other users, firstly in a "virtual" sense. The "virtual" nature of these actions clearly reduces their moral significance, but may not completely remove it. The degree to which a "virtual" offence is morally reprehensible depends on (among other things) its believability to the user against whom it is committed. This would seem to be an area where empirical research is needed.

Not all the offences which might be committed within a VR are necessarily "virtual" in the above sense. The nature of interaction in a multi-user VR renders physical offences "virtual" in this sense, but there is a whole range of non-physical offences such as slander, libel, and verbal degradation which is just as "real" when committed within a VR. This is another area where the correct moral response is not difficult, but there is some urgency in ensuring that existing provisions are extended to cover the area of VR.

A more difficult set of moral problems is raised by the case of the single-user VR. If we are to deal with these problems, we need a clear account of the moral status of immoral behaviour within a VR, even when no other person is directly affected by that behaviour.

The first pragmatic step toward such an account must be to once again deny the claim that the technology makes any fundamental difference to the moral problems involved. The moral questions are to be resolved solely by consideration of the effects upon human beings of the technology. The complexity or novelty of the technology is of no concern, other than its tendency to obscure these effects. In considering the moral problems raised by VR, therefore, we are considering human problems only. Technological questions are merely a fog surrounding those problems.

A further step in clarification is to recall that VR has important overlaps with older technologies. Discussion of its moral implications, therefore, can draw on many existing notions. There is no need to return to fundamental moral principles in order to deal with most of the issues raised by VR.

There seem to be four main arguments for the restriction of certain types of activity within VR. Those clamouring for restrictions on VR may combine these arguments in practice. A clearer picture of their validity is likely to emerge from detailed and separate examination:

1) "THEY MIGHT DO IT FOR REAL"

This argument suggests that people who regularly perform morally reprehensible acts such as rape and murder within VR are as a consequence more likely to perform such acts in reality. This is certainly not a new departure in the discussion of ethics. In fact the counter argument to this suggestion is at least as old as the third century BC. It is based on the Aristotelian notion of catharsis (Aristotle 1968). Essentially, this counter argument claims that performing morally reprehensible acts within VR would tend to reduce the need for the user to perform such acts in reality.

The question as to which of these two arguments is correct is a purely empirical one. Unfortunately, it is not clear what sort of experiment could ever resolve the issue. A high correlation, for example, between those who perform rape and murder in VR and those who do it in reality does not establish any causal link. It may be that there is a level of motivation to perform morally reprehensible acts in some individuals which even the most effective catharsis cannot assuage.

A high correlation of this sort can therefore be interpreted in two completely different ways. On the one hand it might be seen as an indication that the use of VR had delayed the real performance of the morally reprehensible act. On this view the pressure to perform such acts might sometimes become too great for the cathartic effect of VR to work. On the other hand, the correlation might be interpreted as showing that performing events in VR often leads to performing them in reality. There is little prospect of resolving this debate in a scientific fashion.

However, it would be extremely foolish to dismiss this argument simply because we can see no way of testing its major claim. With many Western societies showing both a rise in civil violence and crime and an increase in the portrayal of such actions by entertainment media, there is at least the possibility of a causal link. There is also a possibility that VR might pose more of a problem than previous more "passive" media. This is because it involves physically "practising," in an important sense, the morally reprehensible acts which we would not wish performed in reality. It may well be the case that some of "behavioural conditioning" can therefore more readily be produced by VR than by previous technologies. If there is such a process, there should already be reliable, but secret, data emerging from the area of military training. Perhaps a "peace dividend" for psychological researchers could be in the form of unrestricted access to this data.

The difficulty of resolving the empirical questions should not cause us to ignore the problem. Morally speaking, it behoves scientists to commit a vast research effort to devising some way of answering these empirical questions. In the absence of such hard evidence, many people will simply assume that the answer to the empirical question must be in line with their personal prejudices. A more realistic response to this argument is that, not only do we not know at present, but we are not sure how to find out. The present state of knowledge, therefore, entails that this argument, in isolation, will not justify restrictions on VR.

2) "SOME THINGS ARE NOT ACCEPTABLE EVEN IN PRIVATE"

This argument rejects the traditional claims of personal freedom. According to the proponents of this argument, one simply does not have the right to perform morally reprehensible acts, even if no-one else will be affected by them. In other words, it is the sheer unpleasantness of an individual's actions which render them morally acceptable, even if they have no consequences whatsoever. Another way in which this might be interpreted is as having a moral duty to oneself.

The counter to this argument is the libertarian tradition on which most Western secular societies are based. Its classical expression is in J. S. Mill's *On Liberty:*

> The only part of the conduct of anyone, for which he is amenable to society, is that which concerns others. In the part which merely concerns himself, his independence is, of right, absolute. Over himself, over his own body and mind, the individual is sovereign. (Mill 1859 p. 14)

The widespread influence of views similar to Mill's is likely to form the basis of opposition to any restriction on VR based on this argument. It must be concluded, therefore, that this argument alone does not justify any restriction on the use of VR.

However, it is worth noting that Mill and most authorities in the libertarian tradition specifically exclude children from the claim of individual authority. This exclusion is reflected in the existing censorship provisions for media such as television and film. Even if video games have unfortunately slipped through this censorship net, there is an immediate need to extend provisions for the protection of children to the technology of VR.

3) "PEOPLE WILL PREFER THE VIRTUAL TO THE REAL"

According to one version of this argument, many people will become so entranced by VR that they will avoid the less compliant and enjoyable real world. VR will therefore become the ultimate opiate. If one believes that this will apply to a significant number of people for a significant proportion of their time, VR will be a threat to the fabric of society. Depending on just how convincing one feels the technology will eventually become, this argument gains plausibility from the possibility of spending time in a "world" where everything can be just as one wants it—rather than the way it is.

One detailed treatment of this sort of argument (Frude 1983) has been made in relation to technologies which promise less than VR. This is discussed elsewhere (Whitby 1988) and need not be repeated here. Instead it is worthwhile to continue the theme of observing that, despite the excitement and hype, VR is not the first technology to offer this possibility. In fact, in relation to this possibility, VR is simply the latest development in a tradition which goes at least as far back as prehistoric cave-painting. Escapist literature, films, plays and even unaided fantasy are all capable of distracting our attention and interest from reality. VR is a (possibly) more effective way of doing this.

Thus this argument also is unconvincing in isolation. Many new technologies, in particular television, have been cast as a threat to the fabric of society. Society, however, continues more or less successfully in spite of the amount of time which many people spend watching television. There is every good reason to believe that mature people can allocate their time between entertainment and work to the detriment of neither.

A further strong counter to this argument is seen when we consider its policy implications. If some people consistently find VR more attractive than "real reality" then can it be morally correct to act so as to deny them this alternative? Surely, the morally correct course of action is to pursue ways in which "real reality" can be made more attractive to them. If their choice is rational, then any attempt to deny them their preference represents the infliction of unnecessary suffering.

4) "THE DESIGNERS OF VR CAN SIGNAL SOCIAL APPROVAL OR DISAPPROVAL"

This argument takes note of the fact that what people generally do within a VR may come to be seen as acceptable in some sense. Thus the designers of VR have the ability to provide a degree of social approval or disapproval for the categories of actions which they allow within a VR. Recall that what is possible within a VR is determined by its designers. They have it within their power to reward morally reprehensible behaviour; to prevent morally reprehensible behaviour; or to punish it.

Many examples of the rewarding of morally reprehensible behaviour are provided by the current crop of arcade games. These require and encourage a level of simulated violence which would be unacceptable in reality. The designers of these games need to examine their consciences! The marketing success of these games, particularly among the young, is a gloomy portent of what might be expected from crude home-entertainment VR.

The designer of VR could just as easily prevent a user from engaging in morally reprehensible acts by simply not allowing murder, rapes, and the like to happen with the VR, or by automatically ejecting the user who attempted to commit such acts. Similarly, there would be no technical problem in providing for a suitable "virtual punishment" for users who attempt to commit various morally reprehensible acts within VR. The moral implications of these technical possibilities are discussed in the next section.

This argument seems much more convincing than the previous three. Even in the absence of evidence that users are more likely to commit morally reprehensible acts in practice, drop out of "real" interactions, and so on, there is no doubt that legitimacy is given to actions by one's being encouraged to perform them within VR.

This argument is undoubtedly the most persuasive case for restriction upon VR. However, people may consider that it is not entirely practical. The existence of, and demand for, extreme violence in computer and arcade games may seem to put irresistible pressure on VR designers to allow a similar frequency of killing and maiming. The survival of the pornography industry in spite of legal restriction, suggests that there will inevitably be virtual pornography, even if underground.

These practical problems are not an effective counter to this argument, since it is important to show approval and disapproval of certain activities, even if these standards are not always attained in practice. Ultimately, much depends on the attitude of VR designers. It should be clear that they carry a burden of moral responsibility and need to ensure that they set themselves the highest possible standards.

Conclusion: Ethical Virtual Reality

Irrespective of the problems (both practical and philosophical) involved there is a need for urgent action to discuss and identify the ethical issues involved with VR. The pace of development of modern technology can frequently prove too fast for a leisurely academic development of a philosophical and moral position. The proliferation of computer games which encourage extreme violence, for example, seems to have taken place in advance of widespread social debate[1].

Urgency of itself need not entail poorly thought out responses. This paper makes two, fairly simple, practical suggestions. Firstly there is the immediate need to extend the age-based censorship on media such as film and television to all forseeable interactive media, including VR. Secondly it encourages public (which might entail legislative) support of VR designers in establishing high ethical standards in their work. More might well be needed, but there are greater dangers in procrastination than in partial action.

Solving the immediate problems is, of course, a beginning rather than a conclusion to debate on the ethics of VR. That is an inevitable consequence of the nature of morality. Since morality entails unconstrained choices by human agents, the idea of a code (or any similar device) removing the need to think through the moral implications of our choices is impossible.

This observation applies equally to the idea that VR designers can simply outlaw immoral behaviour within their system. Since the users are effectively denied the choice of whether or not to behave in a moral fashion, their behaviour cannot therefore be described as moral. Ideally, therefore VR should allow users to behave in ways as wicked or as saintly as are possible in reality. Ideally again, the consequences of those behaviours should be as close as possible to reality. To constrain VR users is to deny them the chance to be moral within VR. It should be noted that this neutral position is most certainly not attained by the current crop of arcade games which allow a user to indulge in extreme violence against the person without experiencing any of its adverse consequences.

So far it may seem that there has been a concentration on the detrimental moral implications of VR. It is necessary to redress this by pointing out there are many positive moral implications of VR. VR can and with any luck will be used to train and explore positive moral interaction.

Moral philosophers have already begun to explore the use of simulated agents in a "virtual world" to test the rationality of moral theories and behaviour (Danielson 1992). This could be developed in fascinating ways through the technical possibilities of VR. In particular, VR could be used as a medium in which to explore the consequences of various types of behaviour. Theorists of behaviour could use this as an experimental technique to refine views on exactly how and when humans behave as they do. Theorists of morality could use them in a vast development of Danielson's work to explore the consequences of partial and widespread adoption of various ethical standards. Finally, and perhaps most importantly, the facility to have a reasonable simulation of another's experiences could refine the human ability to empathize. That is to say that the use of VR to give, for example, the experience of crime from the point of view of criminal, victim, legislator, and law-enforcer might give us all a technologically-based route to far greater moral sensibility.

Acknowledgments

I am indebted to Prof. Margaret Boden, Dr. Mike Sharples and Kyran Dale for their comments on an early draft of this paper, which I have freely incorporated into this version.

Note

1. This implies no criticism of those who spoke out against 'shoot-em-up' games in the early 1980's, many of whom may be readers of this journal. I know, for I was one of them!

References

ARISTOTLE (1968) The Poetics, in Lucas D. W.(ed) *Aristotle*, OUP.

BARCLAY MORGAN, A. (1991) Interactivity: From Sound to Motion to Narrative, in *Art Papers*, Vol. 15 No. 55. Sept./Oct. 1991.

BEARDON C. (1992) The Ethics of Virtual Reality, *Intelligent Tutoring Media* Vol. 3, No. 1. pp. 23–27.

DANIELSON, P. (1992) *Artificial Morality*, Routledge, London.

FRUDE, N. (1983) *The Intimate Machine*, New American Library, New York.

GLOVER, J. (1984) *What Sort of People Should There Be?*, Penguin, Harmondsworth, pp. 92–113.

MILL, J. S., (1859) *On Liberty*, reprinted in *John Stuart Mill: A Selection of His Works*, Robson J. M. (ed) (1966) Macmillan, Toronto, p. 14.

NOZICK, R. (1974) *Anarchy, State and Utopia*, Basic Books, New York, pp. 42–45.

PAPERT, S. (1980) *Mindstorms: Children, Computers, and Powerful Ideas*, Basic Books, New York.

WHITBY, B. (1988) *Artificial Intelligence: A Handbook of Professionalism*, Ellis Horwood, Chichester.

BEING AND BELIEVING: ETHICS OF VIRTUAL REALITY

The Lancet

This short editorial from the early 1990s about potential harms of virtual realities (particularly in the field of medicine) argues that there exist an inherent value and richness connected with reality that cannot exist in a wholly created environment. In this context, the editorial brings out concerns over a kind of escapism and the implications possible for some psychologically impaired individuals who may be unable to cope with the meaning of their own suffering.

Reprinted from *The Lancet* 338 (August 3, 1991): 283–84, with permission from the publisher.

Miniaturization and reduced costs brought computing power into the workplace.[1] Now a second computer revolution promises to make far more powerful and flexible machines available to help solve problems in medicine.[2] Prototype advanced medical computing systems can already monitor and advise on treatment in progress, issue warnings on potentially hazardous interventions, and even acquire "expert" diagnostic skills.[3] When used to support inexperienced or partly trained staff, advanced computers can enhance standards of medical care. A small proportion of the massive processing power of advanced computers can be set aside to make them easier to use.[4] Doctors who regard computers as time-consuming and unproductive will welcome innovative interfaces that allow vocal, written, and tactile communication. Very quickly, application of computers in medicine could be fundamentally altered.

Military and space technology, the entertainment industry, and the physical sciences contributed to the drive to make advanced computers user friendly. Initially, complex simulators presented low-definition displays through binocular headsets. Addition of position sensors introduced "motion parallax," with depth cues that created the illusion of being within a three-dimensional graphical display. The invention of a "DataGlove," whose movements could be sensed by the computer and then reconstructed in the display, enabled the observer and computer to interact with instructions given by the observer via simple hand movements such as pointing.[4] The overall effect was that the observer experienced a computer-generated artificial or virtual reality (VR), whose credibility depended largely on the agreement between the simulated imagery and the familiar sensible world.[5]

Such similarity can in turn be reduced to sheer computing power: true VR will be available when advanced computers are devoted to real-time processing of changes of visual, tactile, and auditory displays in response to the observer's instructions. Computers will then create smooth transitions of movement by high-definition three-dimensional images.[6] Such interactive systems for advanced computers will rapidly encourage clinical applications that introduce patients to VR. Development of a whole body 'DataSuit' may prompt the neurologist to seek to restore motor power, albeit illusory, to a brain-injured patient. Psychiatrists or psychologists may wish to evaluate the potential of VR therapeutically in anxiety and phobias, impulse control, and pathological grief, and in the pathogenesis of delusions and hallucinations.[7] Although the motives behind clinical VR experimentation may be praiseworthy—eg, it may replace the prescription of harmful psychotropics—the fact that experimentation may be well intended does not preclude early examination of ethical issues. Careful thought is required before VR-based care or clinical investigation is offered to patients, especially to those who are mentally ill. Underlying concerns include the capacity of VR to distort reality-testing in patients whose judgment is already impaired, the loss of freedom of choice of experience when in VR, and the dangers of medical paternalism.[8-11]

Suppose a clinician responsible for a severely physically handicapped patient wishes to allow him to "escape" from the confines of a bed or a wheelchair. Having carefully collected details from the lives of others, he offers a menu of "desirable" VR experiences to the patient. Very soon, that patient chooses to spend a bare necessity of time in the shared sensible world, preferring to see, hear, and touch the experiences provided by the advanced computer system and chosen by his clinician. Yet compare the VR-day with our own, and computer-generated realities are seen to be vastly incomplete. Our experiences are memorable because we want, even strive, to have them. Looking back we feel that each achievement contributes to our individuality and we realise that our experiences are continuously shaped by the views of others. Interpersonal modifications of choice and intention help us to test and adjust our views about the nature of shared realities. Our experience has many levels of purpose; VR provides only part of these. Continuous exposure to VR will impoverish those aspects of life that determine social development, interpersonal insight, and emotional judgment. Vulnerable patients should not be exposed to VR until the full extent of its likely impact can be reliably anticipated.

The menu of VR-experiences from which a patient might choose is limited by the capacity of the computer to generate accurate representations, by the skill of the designer, and by the preferences of the supervising clinician. Although the patient may choose from within that menu, choice is necessarily more constrained than in daily life. Restriction of choice in this way carries considerable potential for abuse. At one level VR becomes a terrifying instrument of torture, at another a powerful means of education. Fundamentally, the experiences generated are limited to those that man can design; the meanings a patient might attribute to them need not agree with those presumed by the VR designer. It would be irresponsible to introduce patients to a world that contains no more significance or deeper meaning than that which man can construct. For patients seeking to understand, as many do, the purpose of their suffering, VR is as unlikely as hallucinogenic drug use to provide access to a deeper reality in their search for meaning.

Medical paternalism might lead to premature and ill-judged clinical applications of VR. Without professional self-regulation, abuse by experimentalists and inept therapists seems only too likely. A VR machine may be developed, for clinically justifiable purposes, to treat phobias or help establish adaptive coping behaviours in response to stress. However, the control of the experiences of another carries with it the capacity (and responsibility) to influence the personal development of those exposed to this control. It is timely to examine medical responsibilities arising from the clinical application of VR and not to await reports of its ill-effects.

Failure to anticipate the ethical issues raised by VR could delay the introduction of advanced computing systems into medicine. Whereas the hazards of patient exposure to novel computer interfaces are ill-understood, advanced computers possess enormous potential to enhance the mental powers of their users. It is easy to foresee complex problems in the pathogenesis of disease or understanding of physiological regulatory systems that can be modeled by advanced computer simulations;[6] it would be a pity if the opportunity to obtain novel insights into human disease were delayed by justifiable concern arising from unresolved ethical issues in their clinical application.

Notes

1. Peled A. The next computer revolution. *Sci Am* 1987; 257: 35–42.

2. Rennels GD, Shortliffe E. Advanced computing for medicine. *Sci Am* 1987; 257: 146–53.

3. Barnett GO, Cimino JJ, Hupp JA, Hofler MD. Explain: An evolving diagnostic decision-support system. *JAMA* 1987; 258: 67–74.

4. Foley JD. Interfaces for advanced computers. *Sci Am* 1987; 257: 83–90.

5. Helsel SK, Roth JR. Virtual reality: theory, practice and promise. Westport: Meckler, 1991.

6. Friedhoff RM, Benzon W. Visualization. New York: W H Freeman, 1991: 132–200.

7. Stone RJ. Virtual reality—The serious side: Where next and how? Proceedings of VR'91, the first UK conference on virtual reality. Impacts and applications. London, June, 1991.

8. Stanley BH, Stanley M. Psychiatric patients in research: Protecting their autonomy. *Compr Psychiatry* 1981; 22: 420–27.

9. Tancredi LR, Maxfield CT. Regulation of psychiatric research: A socioethical analysis. *Int J Law Psychiatry* 1983; 6: 17–38.

10. Beecher HK. Ethics and clinical research. *N Engl J Med* 1966; 274: 1354–60.

11. Eichelmann B, Wikler D, Hartwig A. Ethics and psychiatric research: problems and justification. *Am J Psychiatry* 1984; 141: 400–05.

CHAPTER TWELVE
Networking and the Internet

REMARKS ON THE INTERNET
AND INFORMATION TECHNOLOGIES

Albert Gore, Jr.

One of the strongest political proponents of the development of the Internet has been former U.S. Senator and Vice President Al Gore. The pieces here are a series of statements he has made about the development of the Internet. In the first address, from 1994, Gore lays out an optimistic picture of a wonderful global network-to-be that includes no hint of any possible problems. Four years later, though still optimistic, he does point out technical problems found in information technologies, such as the Y2K bug. Finally, after the 1999 massacre at Columbine High School, Gore explicitly gives voice to some of the more difficult (if not more political) concerns related to Internet technologies, such as parental control of children's Internet access.

International Telecommunications Union

MONDAY, MARCH 21, 1994

I have come here, 8,000 kilometers from my home, to ask you to help create a Global Information Infrastructure. To explain why, I want to begin by reading you something that I first read in high school, 30 years ago.

> By means of electricity, the world of matter has become a great nerve, vibrating thousands of miles in a breathless point of time. The round globe is a vast . . . brain, instinct with intelligence!

This was not the observation of a physicist—or a neurologist. Instead, these visionary words were written in 1851 by Nathaniel Hawthorne, one of my country's greatest writers, who was inspired by the development of the telegraph.

Much as Jules Verne foresaw submarines and moon landings, Hawthorne foresaw what we are now poised to bring into being.

The ITU was created only 14 years later, in major part for the purpose of fostering an internationally compatible system of telegraphy.

For almost 150 years, people have aspired to fulfill Hawthorne's vision—to wrap nerves of communications around the globe, linking all human knowledge.

In this decade, at this conference, we now have at hand the technological breakthroughs and economic means to bring all the communities of the world together. We now can at last create a planetary information network that transmits messages and images with the speed of light from the largest city to the smallest village on every continent.

I am very proud to have the opportunity to address the first development conference of the ITU because President Clinton and I believe that an essential prerequisite to sustainable development, for all members of the human family, is the creation of this network of networks. To accomplish this purpose, legislators, regulators, and business people must do this: build and operate a Global Information Infrastructure. This GII will circle the globe with information superhighways on which all people can travel.

These highways—or, more accurately, networks of distributed intelligence—will allow us to share information, to connect, and to communicate as a global community. From these connections we will derive robust and sustainable economic progress, strong democracies, better solutions to global and local environmental challenges, improved health care, and—ultimately—a greater sense of shared stewardship of our small planet.

The Global Information Infrastructure will help educate our children and allow us to exchange ideas within a community and among nations. It will be a means by which families and friends will transcend the barriers of time and distance. It will make possible a global information marketplace, where consumers can buy or sell products.

I ask you, the delegates to this conference, to set an ambitious agenda that will help all governments, in their own sovereign nations and in international cooperation, to build this Global Information Infrastructure. For my country's part, I pledge our vigorous, continued participation in achieving this goal—in the development sector of the ITU, in other sectors and in plenipotentiary gatherings of the ITU, and in bilateral discussions held by our Departments of State and Commerce and our Federal Communications Commission.

The development of the GII must be a cooperative effort among governments and peoples. It cannot be dictated or built by a single country. It must be a democratic effort. And the distributed intelligence of the GII will spread participatory democracy.

To illustrate why, I'd like to use an example from computer science. In the past, all computers were huge mainframes with a single central processing unit, solving problems in sequence, one by one, each bit of information sent back and forth between the CPU and the vast field of memory surrounding it. Now, we have massively parallel computers with hundreds—or thousands—of tiny self-contained processors distributed throughout the memory field, all interconnected, and together far more powerful and more versatile than even the most sophisticated single processor, because they each solve a tiny piece of the problem simultaneously and when all the pieces are assembled, the problem is solved.

Similarly, the GII will be an assemblage of local, national, and regional networks, that are not only like parallel computers but in their most advanced state will in fact be a distributed, parallel computer. In a sense, the GII will be a metaphor for democracy itself. Representative democracy does not work with an all-powerful central government, arrogating all decisions to itself. That is why communism collapsed.

Instead, representative democracy relies on the assumption that the best way for a nation to make its political decisions is for each citizen— the human equivalent of the self-contained processor—to have the power to control his or her own life. To do that, people must have available the information they need. And be allowed to express their conclusions in free speech and in votes that are combined with those of millions of others. That's what guides the system as a whole.

The GII will not only be a metaphor for a functioning democracy, it will in fact promote the functioning of democracy by greatly enhancing the participation of citizens in decision-making. And it will greatly promote the ability of nations to cooperate with each other. I see a new Athenian Age of democracy forged in the flora the GII will create.

The GII will be the key to economic growth for national and international economies. For us in the United States, the information infrastructure already is to the U.S. economy of the 1990s what transportation infrastructure was to the economy of the mid-20th century.

The integration of computing and information networks into the economy makes U.S. manufacturing companies more productive, more competitive, and more adaptive to changing conditions and it will do the same for the economies of other nations. These same technologies are also enabling the service sectors of the U.S. economy to grow, to increase their scale and productivity and expand their range of product offerings and ability to respond to customer demands.

Approximately 60% of all U.S. workers are "knowledge workers"— people whose jobs depend on the information they generate and receive over our information infrastructure. As we create new jobs, 8 out of 10 are in information-intensive sectors of our economy. And these new jobs are well-paying jobs for financial analysts, computer programmers, and other educated workers.

The global economy also will be driven by the growth of the Information Age. Hundreds of billions of dollars can be added to world growth if we commit to the GII. I fervently hope this conference will take full advantage of this potential for economic growth, and not deny any country or community its right to participate in this growth. As the GII spreads, more and more people realize that information is a treasure that must be shared to be valuable. When two people communicate, they each can be enriched—and unlike traditional resources, the more you share, the more you have. As Thomas Jefferson said, "He who receives an idea from me, receives instruction himself without lessening mine; as he who lights his taper at mine, receives light without darkening me." . . .

The President and I have called for positive government action in the United States to extend the NIT to every classroom, library, hospital, and clinic in the U.S. by the end of the century. I want to urge that this conference include in its agenda for action the commitment to determine how every school and library in every country can be connected to the Internet, the world's largest computer network, in order to create a Global Digital Library. Each library could maintain a server containing books and journals in electronic form, along with indexes to help users find other materials. As more and more information is stored electronically, this global library would become more and more useful. It would allow millions of students, scholars and business people to find the information they need whether it be in Albania or Ecuador.

Private investment . . . competition . . . flexibility . . . open access . . . universal service. In addition to urging the delegates of this conference to adopt these principles as part of the Buenos Aires Declaration, guiding the next four years of telecommunications development, I assure you that the U.S. will be discussing in many flora, inside and outside the ITU, whether these principles might be usefully adopted by all countries.

The commitment of all nations to enforcing regulatory regimes to build the GII is vital to world development and many global social goals. But the power of the Global Information Infrastructure will be diminished if it cannot reach large segments of the world population. We have heard together Dr. Tarjanne's eloquent speech setting forth the challenges we face. As he points out, the 24 countries of the OECD have only 16 percent of the world's population, but they account for 70 percent of global telephone mainlines and 90 percent of mobile phone subscribers.

There are those who say the lack of economic development causes poor telecommunications. I believe they have it exactly backwards. A primitive telecommunications system causes poor economic development.

So we cannot be complacent about the disparity between the high and low income nations, whether in how many phones are available to people or whether they have such new technologies as high speed computer networks or videoconferencing. The United States delegation is devoted to working with each of you at this conference to address the many problems that hinder development. And there are many.

Financing is a problem in almost every country, even though telecommunications has proven itself to be an excellent investment.

Even where telecommunications has been identified as a top development priority, countries lack trained personnel and up-to-date information.

And in too many parts of the world, political unrest makes it difficult or impossible to maintain existing infrastructure, let alone lay new wire or deploy new capacity.

How can we work together to overcome these hurdles? Let me mention a few things industrialized countries can do to help. First, we can use the Global Information Infrastructure for technical collaboration between industrialized nations and developing countries. All agencies of the U.S. government are potential sources of information and knowledge that can be shared with partners across the globe. The Global Information Infrastructure can help development agencies link experts from every nation and enable them to solve common problems. For instance, the Pan American Health Organization has conducted hemisphere-wide teleconferences to present new methods to diagnose and prevent the spread of AIDS.

Second, multilateral institutions like the World Bank, can help nations finance the building of telecommunications infrastructure.

Third, the U.S. can help provide the technical know-how needed to deploy and use these new technologies. USAID and U.S. businesses have helped the U.S. Telecommunications Training Institute train more than 3500 telecommunications professionals from the developing world, including many in this room.

In the future, USI-II plans also to help business people, bankers, farmers, and others from the developing world find ways that computer networking, wireless technology, satellites, video links, and other telecommunications technology could improve their effectiveness and efficiency.

I challenge other nations, the development banks, and the UN system to create similar training opportunities. The head of our Peace Corps, Carol Bellamy, intends to use Peace Corps volunteers both to help deploy telecommunications and computer systems and to find innovative uses for them. Here in Argentina, a Peace Corps volunteer is doing just that.

To join the GII to the effort to protect and preserve the global environment, our Administration will soon propose using satellite and personal communication technology to create a global network of environmental information.

We will propose using the schools and students of the world to gather and study environmental information on a daily basis and communicate that data to the world through television.

But regulatory reform must accompany this technical assistance and financial aid for it to work. This requires top-level leadership and commitment—commitment to foster investment in telecommunications and commitment to adopt policies that ensure the rapid deployment and widespread use of the information infrastructure.

I opened by quoting Nathaniel Hawthorne, inspired by Samuel Morse's invention of the telegraph. Morse was also a famous portrait artist in the U.S.—his portrait of President James Monroe hangs today in the White House. While Morse was working on a portrait of General Lafayette in Washington, his wife, who lived about 500 kilometers away grew ill and died. But it took seven days for the news to reach him. In his grief and remorse, he began to wonder if it were possible to erase barriers of time and space, so that no one would be unable to reach a loved one in time of need. Pursuing this thought, he came to discover how to use electricity to convey messages, and so he invented the telegraph and, indirectly, the ITU.

The Global Information Infrastructure offers instant communication to the great human family. It can provide us the information we need to dramatically improve the quality of their lives. By linking clinics and hospitals together, it will ensure that doctors treating patients have access to the best possible information on diseases and treatments. By providing early warning on natural disasters like volcanic eruptions, tsunamis, or typhoons, it can save the lives of thousands of people.

By linking villages and towns, it can help people organize and work together to solve local and regional problems ranging from improving water supplies to preventing deforestation.

To promote, to protect, to preserve freedom and democracy, we must make telecommunications development an integral part of every nation's development. Each link we create strengthens the bonds of liberty and democracy around the world. By opening markets to stimulate the development of the global information infrastructure, we open lines of communication.

By opening lines of communication, we open minds. This summer, from my country, cameras will bring the World Cup Championship to well over one billion people. To those of you from the 23 visiting countries whose teams are in the Finals, I wish you luck—although I'll be rooting for the home team. The Global Information Infrastructure carries implications even more important than soccer. It has brought us images of earthquakes in California, of Boris Yeltsin on a tank in Red Square, of the effects of mortar shells in Sarajevo and Somalia, of the fall of the Berlin Wall. It has brought us images of war and peace, and tragedy and joy, in which we all can share.

There's a Dutch relief worker, Wam Kat, who has been broadcasting an electronic diary from Zagreb for more than a year and a half on the Internet, sharing his observations of life in Croatia. After reading Kat's Croatian diary, people around the world began to send money for relief efforts. The result: 25 houses have been rebuilt in a town destroyed by war. Governments didn't do this. People did. But such events are the hope of the future.

When I began proposing the GII in the U.S., I said that my hope is that the United States, born in revolution, can lead the way to this new, peaceful revolution. However, I believe we will reach our goal faster and with greater certainty if we walk down that path together. As Antonio Machado, Spanish poet, once said, "Path walker, there is no path, we create the path as we walk." Let us build a global community in which the people of neighboring countries view each other not as potential enemies, but as potential partners, as members of the same family in the vast, increasingly interconnected human family.

Let us seize this moment.

Let us work to link the people of the world.

Let us create this new path as *we walk it together.*

Vice President Gore Announces Five Challenges to Build a Global Information Infrastructure

PRESS RELEASE, OCTOBER 12, 1998

Minneapolis, MN — In a speech today before the United Nations' chief telecommunications organization, Vice President Gore challenged delegates representing over 180 nations to use our newest technologies to preserve our oldest values.

"Four years ago, I asked you to help create a global information superhighway," Vice President Gore said. "Today, I thank you for what you have done to bring about the most stunning revolution the world has known, and I challenge you to build on this unprecedented opportunity by putting these new global networks to work helping people."

"Today, we can build on our progress and use these powerful new forces of technology to advance our oldest and most cherished values: to extend knowledge and prosperity to the most isolated inner cities at home, and the most remote rural villages around the world; to bring 21st century learning and communication to places that don't even have phone service today; to share specialized medical technology that can save and improve lives; to deepen the meaning of democracy and freedom in this Internet age," he said.

The Vice President proposed five new challenges, which he characterized as a "Declaration of Interdependence."

First, he challenged the world community to improve access to technology so everyone on the planet is within walking distance of basic telecommunication services by the year 2005. For all our progress, 65% of the world's households still have no phone service.

Second, he challenged the world community to bridge language barriers by developing technologies with real-time digital translation so anyone on the planet can talk to anyone else. Such technologies could reduce the cost of doing business and increase international cooperation.

Third, he challenged the world community to create a global knowledge network of people working to improve the delivery of education, health care, agricultural resources, and sustainable development, and to ensure public safety. The Vice President challenged the education community to link together practitioners, academic experts, and not-for-profit organizations working on our most pressing social and economic needs.

Fourth, he challenged the world community to ensure that communications technology protects the free-flow of ideas and supports democracy and free speech. We must continue to work to ensure that the Global Information Infrastructure (GII) promotes the free-flow of ideas and supports democracy around the globe.

Fifth, he challenged the world community to create networks that allow every micro-entrepreneur in the world to advertise, market, and sell products directly to the world market. Such networks will enable entrepreneurs to keep more profits, provide information about world prices, develop technology as a business tool, increase the diversity of the global marketplace, and create jobs.

Additionally, the Vice President called on the world community to address the Year 2000 computer problem, which, if not addressed, could pose serious problems for commerce and communications all over the world.

"We must ensure that the international system is ready for the year 2000—because one weak link in the system will hurt us all," Vice President Gore said. "Together, we must solve this problem."

Remarks by the Vice President on the Internet

MAY 5, 1999

Thank you so much, Betty. And thank you for giving such a vivid illustration of what parents are going through in discovering the vulnerability that children have in using the Internet. And you, as someone well versed in this, know what to do. Many parents have felt even more overwhelmed than you have, and as a result of what the Internet service providers and the related companies in the industry are doing today, 95-plus percent of all Internet users will automatically get a pop-up page every time they go to the Internet that will show them in very easy steps how they can provide their children with the maximum protection. And I'm going to talk about some of the details in just a moment.

But first of all, I want to thank my colleagues here from the Senate. I say colleagues, because I am still a Member of the Senate after a fashion as President of the Senate. But I do want to thank both of them. Pat Leahy talked about the early days of the Information Superhighway. I want you to know that tonight, Senator Leahy will be awarded the prestigious John Peter Zinger Award by the University of Arizona for his leadership as the cyber Senator on Internet freedom issues. So, congratulations.

And I want to especially thank and praise my colleague Ben Nighthorse Campbell. Ben and Linda have been friends to Tipper and me for many, many years. I know him as a man of intergrity, who cares about his constituents, and cares about this country. He is a former school teacher and a former deputy sheriff, and a present Harley-Davidson rider and he cares a lot about these issues. And we talked in the aftermath of the tragedy at Columbine about some of the steps that can be taken to solve this problem. And, of course, everybody understands that an industry that steps forward and takes responsibility for its part of the problem shouldn't be seen as the one most responsible. Far from it. There are others who have not come forward.

I want to praise the Internet service providers for what you all are doing here today. I'm very, very grateful to you. And I want to—and just before this event, I had a conference call with the CEOs of most of the companies that are participating here today, and other representatives, and virtually the entire industry was represented, and virtually the entire industry is represented here today. And I'm grateful for your presence and your attendance here today.—I want to thank, especially, these companies who are part of today's commitment: America Online, AT&T, At-Home Network, Bell Atlantic, Commercial Internet Exchange, Disney Online, Excite Incorporated, Lycos Incorporated, MCI World Com, Microsoft Corporation, Network Solutions, Netscape Communications, MindSpring Enterprises Incorporated, Prodigy Communications Corporation, Yahoo Incorporated. And there are trade groups that have played a key role in this as well, and I want to thank them as a group.

I want to thank Katherine Montgomery who is present, and is co-Founder and President of the Center for Media Education. Katherine, thank you very much. And Assistant Secretary of Commerce Larry Irving—thank you for your leadership. All of the Members of Congress in both parties, who have worked with the Internet industry and who could not be present here at this event, but who deserve credit for being involved in helping to address this issue. Laurie Lipper, Director of the Children's

Partnership, is here, and thank you, Laurie. And to Betty again, thank you. And I want to acknowledge Betty's husband, David, is here, and her children Brian and Megan are here. Thank you. I'm not sure they'd want to be recognized and singled out.

I also want to acknowledge Bob Chase who is President of the NEA. Thank you, Bob. And Bob travelled with me out to the memorial service at Columbine, and we remember Dave Sanders, the teacher there, along with the students who were killed and lost their lives.

Well, ladies and gentlemen, when I was out there at that memorial service with my wife, Tipper, and others who were present, we physically embraced each of the parents and family members of those who lost their lives. I told a group the other day, without using the name of the parent involved, that one of the fathers whispered in my ear during our embrace and said, these children cannot have died in vain. We have to act. Promise me that there will be changes. And he repeated with a tone of urgency that would not be denied. Promise me. And like any of you, my response was, I promise.

And all of us have an obligation as Americans to cross party lines, to pull together public, private partnerships, to pass laws where necessary, and to change our lives in order to honor those who died at Columbine High School. And one of the very first industries to come forward in its effort to keep that promise, is the Internet industry. And there will be time to evaluate how well this works. But I want to say at the outset, I'm very impressed with what this industry is committing to do here today.

Let me emphasize again—we may never fully understand exactly what happened there, or why. And we all do understand that there are many factors involved. And we don't all agree on what to do about all the factors. I, for example, believe that guns are way too available, and I think that there should be more restrictions. I believe that there's way too much screen violence and media violence on television and in the movies and in video games. I believe that parents need to do a better job, and schools need to do a better job. The national debate that has begun will continue and, I predict, will intensify. Because we know this is real and serious. And we have to respond to it.

But among all of these many factors, one element that has been brought up and discussed is the role that the Internet has played. And thank goodness, the companies involved with the Internet, for their part, have felt the urgency and have come forward with a response that I think is going to make a big difference. And we understand that the Internet's stunning technology gives children and families access to an incredible world of information. And life, itself—most of it's great, but there are some dark corners. There are some free-fire zones and red light districts in cyberspace, from which children must be protected. How do we protect them? That's what today's announcement is all about. It's true that at Columbine, the killers used the Internet to contact messages of cruelty and hate, and to spread them. But it is also true that in the aftermath of the tragedy, the people of Jefferson County, Colorado, turned to the Internet to connect with those who had previously experienced the same kind of tragedy in Paducah, Jonesboro, Springfield, and elsewhere, and they were embraced by the empathy of the whole nation in part through e-mail. So, when it comes to the Internet, too many parents feel now they're faced with a false choice—between unplugging that computer in the family room, or spending every single moment looking over their child's shoulder to make sure they're not wandering into some dangerous, online alleyway.

We're here today because there is a third choice—a better way. As a result of intensive, ongoing talks with the Internet industry, Congressional leaders, and public citizens' groups, and others who are concerned about this, the industry is, today, creating a new Parents' Protection Page, which will appear on virtually every Internet starting point automatically by this July—two months from now. Now, that's action, and that's speed. From a single place that will pop up automatically on almost every computer screen, parents will be provided the tools to guide their children safely down the Information Superhighway. On the Parents' Protection Page, parents will find easy steps to block out inappropriate content. Parents will be told in simple language how they can filter out the good content from content which they, as parents, decide their children are not ready to handle. They, themselves, would describe it as bad content. Parents can see which websites and chat rooms their children have visited. And children will know that their parents will have access to that information. Parents will be able to set strict time limits on their children's Internet use. I predict that will be a popular feature, among these others. And parents can restrict their children's e-mail contact to keep the potential predators at bay; purveyors of pornography, and hatred, and violence, and evil. And they can make sure that personal information about their children or about their families will not fall into the wrong hands.

This new Parents' Protection Page will help ensure that children are not surfing into dangerous waters when they surf the Web. By establishing one simple place to block and monitor what children will see, the Parents' Protection Page puts control of the computer keyboard back into the hands of America's parents, where it really belongs.

In addition, this page will help parents steer their children to the very best of the Internet. It will provide links to educational sites, while offering tips for parents on how to best protect their children. Now, I want to be very clear about the fact that most sites on the Internet are engaging and educational. But parents need strong, new tools to block out the pornography, violence, and hate. A responsible parent would never let a new student driver drive down the Interstate highway without any supervision. And neither should we allow young children to roam unsupervised on the Information Superhighway. And that realization has been slow to dawn on many families. But I hope that one of the aftermaths of the tragedy at Columbine that woke up this country is to make more parents aware that they have to play an aggressive, proactive role in protecting their children on the Internet. That's one of the reasons why our Administration has worked very hard over the past several years to give parents more of the help they need.

Back in 1997, we created this Parents Guide to the Internet, in the Department of Education. And we had a series of meetings back at that time with the industry. And some of the ideas announced today, like the one-click, automatic access, actually came up, first of all, in this room, around a table here in the Roosevelt Room two years ago. This guide requires no technical knowledge. In fact, it walks parents through the basics about the Internet itself, and how to use some of the tools that, up until today, have been admittedly a little hard for some parents to gain access to. You talked about how it was kind of overwhelming, Betty. I think most parents feel that. But having it right there, staring you in the face every time you turn the computer on—that's going to make it a lot easier.

I urge all parents who would want this written guide to call 1-800-USA-LEARN, and it will be made available to you. I'm also pleased to report that our Federal Communications Commission has a Web site, FCC.GOV, that has a page called Parents, Kids, and Communications that explains the options parents have to control their children's exposure to inappropriate content, which includes not only Internet blocking and filtering tools, but also the V-chip and cable box locks for television, and a 900-number block for the telephone.

Before I close, I just want to summarize by saying that I do believe that all of these efforts will make a big difference. But let us understand that the industry having acted here, this is where a parent's responsibility begins—not where it ends. These are tools being made available. These are warning signs that have to be heeded. These are guides that have to be followed. And the primary responsibility, after we take all of the other steps that need to be taken—and I mentioned most of them here—the primary responsibility still lies with parents.

So I hope the message goes out loudly and clearly. The best protection is an involved parent, taking time to pass on the right values to children. But government and industry do have a responsibility to make it easier and simpler for parents to do so.

So, I want to again thank the Internet industry—95 percent of which is involved in this, and represented here—for taking the important steps forward that are being announced here today. Thank you all very much. . . .

LOSING OUR SOULS IN CYBERSPACE

Mark A. Kellner and Douglas Groothuis

Computer journalist Mark Kellner interviews religious ethicist Doug-las Groothuis about cyberspace and (Christian) spirituality. Their discussion raises issues including the extent to which the mode of on-line interaction itself can interfere with spiritual growth, the danger of sinful temptation in cyber-pornography, and the positive ben-efits of computer-based forms of communication. Although the discussion centers on a particular Christian viewpoint, many of the ideas and concerns that are addressed may, when generalized, apply within other religious and ethical traditions.

Introduction

Promise Keepers has a Web site, but so does Penthouse. A New Jersey pastor evangelizes a young man in Finland by E-mail exchanges, but one of the 39 Heaven's Gate suicides turns out to be a Cincinnati postal worker re-cruited online. The Internet is cause for both joy and concern. How should Christians view the Internet—as today's Roman roads that promise immense potential for spreading the gospel? Or as a Vanity Fair that must be bypassed?

Douglas Groothuis, assistant professor of religion and ethics at Den-ver Seminary, offers compelling answers and cautions in his new book, *The Soul in Cyberspace* (Baker, 1997). He talked with Mark A. Kellner, editor of *PC Portables* magazine.

Interview

In your book, you warn about the danger of Internet involvement, yet you have a Web site for your work. Are you a compromised Luddite?

I set up two extremes in the book. One extreme is a digitopian—a Bill Gates who believes that machines will only enhance the economy and society. The other is the Luddite who wants to destroy machines. While machines can dehumanize us and destabilize good patterns of life, to say the answer is to destroy the technology is wrong.

Reprinted from *Christianity Today* (September 1, 1997): 54–55, with the permission of the author, Mark A. Kellner (www.markkellner.com).

At the same time, technologies are not neutral. Machines are created by humans who bear the image of God but who also live "east of Eden." As "deposed royalty" (as Pascal put it), our technologies will bear the marks of both our greatness and our sinfulness. Christians should determine how the Internet shapes the messages it conveys, where it serves us well, where it doesn't, and how to tell the difference. We must always ask if the medium is appropriate for our Christian message. How much truth can be communicated in a chat room?

How does the Internet dehumanize us?

Through lack of personal presence. An important theological question is: How disembodied should our communication be?

The Internet distributes information widely and quickly, but in a merely electronic form, which lacks the personal presence at the heart of biblical discipleship, fellowship, and worship. When cyberspace begins to replace embodied interactions, we fail to honor the incarnational nature of Christianity. We may be "connected" to people around the world through the Internet while we neglect our spouses, neighbors, and churches. This is wrong.

You write of cyberspace's "ecological effect." What do you mean by that?

This is a concept from Neil Postman, who writes that major technological innovations don't just add something new to an environment, but change the whole environment ecologically or structurally. For instance, the printing press didn't just add more books to European culture, it transformed how people acquired knowledge, how they thought, how they viewed authority, and so on.

Similarly, cyberspace technologies are having an ecological effect on the culture as a whole. When everyone gets "wired," nothing remains the same. The sensibilities that tend to be created or reinforced by cyberspace interactions—a desire for more and more immediate information, a superficial surfing mentality, an impatience with ambiguity, and so forth—will spill over into other areas of life. One of your concerns is the way we conceive of God's Word.

I am afraid hypertext technologies which give us the ability to rearrange texts and connect with other texts almost effortlessly may corrode our sense of authorial intent, fixed meaning, and intellectual coherence. Some postmodernist thinkers revel in this. They claim that the intrusive authority of the author is being overthrown through these hypertext technologies. We are all authors and have the right to create our own meanings and truths. This kind of cyber-relativism refuses to admit any determinative and authoritative meaning—either in Scripture or anywhere else. It is really high-tech nihilism and poison to the soul.

Christians may innocently fall into this error by using Bible software in a manner that divorces Scripture from its literary genre and contextual meaning. I can run a program that gives me a host of texts on, say, "righteousness," but the program cannot present the meaning of each text in its context, nor can it give me a theology of righteousness. The ability to move around biblical texts at will and find references instantly may end up lessening our understanding of what God has communicated in the Bible. Nevertheless, if we remain rooted to God's Word as it was originally given, we may use these technologies wisely.

In what ways does the Internet challenge the Christian perspective of the person and the physical world?

Some contemporary thinkers, such as Sherry Turkle, believe that cyberspace is the perfect medium to illustrate the postmodernist view that the self is entirely constructed—that there is no given human nature and no normative self. Given the anonymity of much online communication, and the artificial environments that can be created, one can experiment with various identities, even crossing genders or assuming mythical personae in online fantasy role-playing games.

Yet, from a biblical point of view, this is deception and is unhealthy for the soul. Although Christians each express the grace of Christ individually and uniquely, there is a basic pattern of godliness laid out in Scripture and made real through the Holy Spirit. Endless experimentation with identities in cyberspace is not the way of edification or sanctification. It may well be the way of madness. We are already fragmented enough as individuals and as a culture. Cyberspace may only make this worse.

How much of a problem do you see cybersex posing for Christians?

If there's already a significant problem mostly with pornography with Christian men—as I hear from counselors and pastors—then the temptations will multiply in cyberspace because of the potential for anonymity and easier access. You're only a few points and clicks away from very hardcore pornography on the Internet. You don't have to go to the seedy side of town to buy a magazine or risk being discovered at a video store. We have to exercise a lot of self-control to avoid temptation.

I was doing research on Heaven's Gate, and I went to a newsmagazine's home page. It contained a solicitation for pornography: "Photos of women" and "Click here for a full body shot." I didn't click, but this is an example. You also receive unsolicited E-mail for pornographic photos and promiscuous chat rooms. You just have to resolve that you're not going to take the first step, and you have to be careful that your kids don't get hooked into it.

In protecting our children, are you simply saying parents should be parents, or is there more that needs to be done?

I do think there's a role for the state here to criminalize the distribution of pornography, especially to minors. It may be asking too much to ask parents to control completely what is on their end. The ultimate issue, however, is not governmental restrictions or blocking programs, but instilling our children with the proper principles and a Christian world-view so kids have a biblically informed conscience. They have to learn how to say no for themselves and say yes to what's holy and what's wholesome.

Is the church as aware and savvy about cyberspace as it needs to be?
It's not even close. I think people in the church tend to slip into three categories, all of which are unacceptable. The first is just oblivion; they don't know anything about it. The second is the digitopian temptation, seeing the Internet as an unmitigated good, a way to communicate the gospel broadly without seeing the dark side. The other extreme is the Christian Luddite. I talked with a man on a call-in radio show who said the Internet is so dangerous we should have nothing to do with it.

What are practical ways Christians can make use of the Internet— would you as a professor welcome cyberspace seminaries?
There are a variety of useful Web pages Christian and non-Christian. My wife and I have a Web page (www.gospelcom.net/ivpress/groothuis), and I use E-mail to keep in touch with people I could not otherwise easily contact. I have profitably used the Internet to research treatments for certain rare health problems.

I would, however, fear putting seminary education entirely online, because this eliminates the uniquely and irreducibly personal element of teaching and learning. The spontaneity and serendipity of the classroom cannot be replaced by any online forum or CD-ROM technology. To think otherwise is to fall for the digitopian deception that learning is no more than information acquisition. People learn best in supportive educational communities, not sitting alone before computer screens.

A RAPE IN CYBERSPACE

Julian Dibbell

Julian Dibbell's article about a "virtual rape" in a cyberplace called LambdaMOO has enjoyed a great deal of exposure in both media and academic circles. Dibbell's description raises questions about the

From *The Village Voice*, 21 December 1993, 36–42. V. V. Publishing Corporation; reprinted with permission of *The Village Voice*.

common separation between "real" and "virtual" experiences while it brings to the fore many important issues, including the creation of on-line community, virtual bodies, politics, misuse of resources, and the use of language to describe computer-mediated events. Among other things, Dibbell demonstrates that virtual communities allow for real, personal, and social experiences, and this fact alone calls forth ethical questions about virtual interactions and their effects on both virtual characters and real-life users.

. . . Call me Dr. Bombay. Some months ago—let's say about halfway between the first time you heard the words *information superhighway* and the first time you wished you never had—I found myself tripping now and then down the well-traveled information lane that leads to LambdaMOO, a very large and very busy rustic mansion built entirely of words. In the odd free moment I would type the commands that called those words onto my computer screen, dropping me with what seemed a warm electric thud inside the house's darkened coat closet, where I checked my quotidian identity, stepped into the persona and appearance of a minor character from a long-gone television sitcom, and stepped out into the glaring chatter of the crowded living room. Sometimes, when the mood struck me, I emerged as a dolphin instead.

I won't say why I chose to masquerade as Samantha Stevens's outlandish cousin, or as the dolphin, or what exactly led to my mild addiction to the semifictional digital otherworlds known around the Internet as multi-user dimensions, or MUDs. This isn't my story, after all. It's the story of a man named Mr. Bungle, and of the ghostly sexual violence he committed in the halls of LambdaMOO, and most importantly of the ways his violence and his victims challenged the 1000 and more residents of that surreal, magic-infested mansion to become, finally, the community so many of them already believed they were.

That I was myself one of those residents has little direct bearing on the story's events. I mention it only as a warning that my own perspective is perhaps too steeped in the surreality and magic of the place to serve as an entirely appropriate guide. For the Bungle Affair raises questions that—here on the brink of a future in which human life may find itself as tightly enveloped in digital environments as it is today in the architectural kind—demand a clear-eyed, sober, and unmystified consideration. It asks us to shut our ears momentarily to the techno-utopian ecstasies of West Coast cyberhippies and look without illusion upon the present possibilities for building, in the on-line spaces of this world, societies more decent and free than those mapped onto dirt and concrete and capital. It asks us to behold the new bodies awaiting us in virtual space undazzled by their phantom powers, and to get to the crucial work of sorting out the socially meaningful differences between those bodies and our physical ones. And most forthrightly it asks us to wrap our late-modern ontologies, epistemologies, sexual ethics, and common sense around the curious notion of rape by voodoo doll—and to try not to warp them beyond recognition in the process. . . .

The facts begin (as they often do) with a time and a place. The time was a Monday night in March, and the place, as I've said, was the living room—which, due to the inviting warmth of its decor, is so invariably packed with chitchatters as to be roughly synonymous among LambdaMOOers with a party. So strong, indeed, is the sense of convivial common ground invested in the living room that a cruel mind could hardly imagine a better place in which to stage a violation of LambdaMOO's communal spirit. And there was cruelty enough lurking in the appearance Mr. Bungle presented to the virtual world—he was at the time a fat, oleaginous, Bisquick-faced clown dressed in cum-stained harlequin garb and girdled with a mistletoe-and-hemlock belt whose buckle bore the quaint inscription "KISS ME UNDER THIS, BITCH!" But whether cruelty motivated his choice of crime scene is not among the established facts of the case. It is a fact only that he did choose the living room. The remaining facts tell us a bit more about the inner world of Mr. Bungle, though only perhaps that it couldn't have been a very comfortable place. They tell us that he commenced his assault entirely unprovoked, at or about 10 p.m. Pacific Standard Time. That he began by using his voodoo doll to force one of the room's occupants to sexually service him in a variety of more or less conventional ways. That this victim was legba, a Haitian trickster spirit of indeterminate gender, brown-skinned and wearing an expensive pearl gray suit, top hat, and dark glasses. That legba heaped vicious imprecations on him all the while and that he was soon ejected bodily from the room. That he hid himself away then in his private chambers somewhere on the mansion grounds and continued the attacks without interruption, since the voodoo doll worked just as well at a distance as in proximity. That he turned his attentions now to Starsinger, a rather pointedly nondescript female character, tall, stout, and brown-haired, forcing her into unwanted liaisons with other individuals present in the room, among them legba, Bakunin (the well-known radical), and Juniper (the squirrel). That his actions grew progressively violent. That he made legba eat his/her own pubic hair. That he caused Starsinger to violate herself with a piece of kitchen cutlery. That his distant laughter echoed evilly in the living room with every successive outrage. That he could not be stopped until at last someone summoned Zippy, a wise and trusted old-timer who brought with him a gun of near wizardly powers, a gun that didn't kill but enveloped its targets in a cage impermeable even to a voodoo doll's powers. That Zippy fired this gun at Mr. Bungle, thwarting the doll at last and silencing the evil, distant laughter.

These particulars, as I said, are unambiguous. But they are far from simple, for the simple reason that every set of facts in virtual reality (or VR, as the locals abbreviate it) is shadowed by a second, complicating set: the "real-life" facts. And while a certain tension invariably buzzes in the gap between the hard, prosaic RL facts and their more fluid, dreamy VR counterparts, the dissonance in the Bungle case is striking. No hideous clowns or trickster spirits appear in the RL version of the incident, no voodoo dolls or wizard guns, indeed no rape at all as any RL court of law has yet defined it. The actors in the drama were university students for the most part, and they sat rather undramatically before computer screens the entire time, their only actions a spidery flitting of fingers across standard QWERTY keyboards. No bodies touched. Whatever physical interaction occurred consisted of a mingling of electronic signals sent from sites spread out between New York City and Sydney, Australia. Those signals met in LambdaMOO, certainly, just as the hideous clown and the living room party did, but what was LambdaMOO after all? Not an enchanted mansion or anything of the sort—just a middlingly complex database, maintained for experimental purposes inside a Xerox Corporation research computer in Palo Alto and open to public access via the Internet.

To be more precise about it, LambdaMOO was a MUD. Or to be yet more precise, it was a subspecies of MUD known as a MOO, which is short for "MUD, Object-Oriented." All of which means that it was a kind of database especially designed to give users the vivid impression of moving through a physical space that in reality exists only as descriptive data filed away on a hard drive. When users dial into LambdaMOO, for instance, the program immediately presents them with a brief textual description of one of the rooms of the database's fictional mansion (the coat closet, say). If the user wants to leave this room, she can enter a command to move in a particular direction and the database will replace the original description with a new one corresponding to the room located in the direction she chose. When the new description scrolls across the user's screen it lists not only the fixed features of the room but all its contents at that moment—including things (tools, toys, weapons) and other users (each represented as a "character" over which he or she has sole control).

As far as the database program is concerned, all of these entities—rooms, things, characters—are just different subprograms that the program allows to interact according to rules very roughly mimicking the laws of the physical world. Characters may not leave a room in a given direction, for instance, unless the room subprogram contains an "exit" at that compass point. And if a character "says" or "does" something (as directed by its user-owner), then only the users whose characters are also located in that room will see the output describing the statement or action. Aside from such basic constraints, however, LambdaMOOers are allowed a broad freedom to create—they can describe their characters any way they like, they can make rooms of their own and decorate them to taste, and they can build new objects almost at will. The combination of all this busy user activity with the hard physics of the database can certainly induce a lucid illusion of presence—but when all is said and done the only thing you *really* see when you visit LambdaMOO is a kind of slow-crawling script, lines of dialogue and stage direction creeping steadily up your computer screen.

Which is all just to say that, to the extent that Mr. Bungle's assault happened in real life at all, it happened as a sort of Punch-and-Judy show, in which the puppets and the scenery were made of nothing more substantial than digital code and snippets of creative writing. . . .

[H]e entered sadistic fantasies into the "voodoo doll," a subprogram that served the not exactly kosher purpose of attributing actions to other characters that their users did not actually write. And thus a woman in Haverford, Pennsylvania, whose account on the MOO attached her to a character she called Starsinger, was given the unasked-for opportunity to read the words "As if against her will, Starsinger jabs a steak knife up her ass, causing immense joy. You hear Mr. Bungle laughing evilly in the distance." And thus the woman in Seattle who had written herself the character called legba, with a view perhaps to tasting in imagination a deity's freedom from the burdens of the gendered flesh, got to read similarly constructed sentences in which legba, messenger of the gods, lord of crossroads and communications, suffered a brand of degradation all too customarily reserved for the embodied female.

"Mostly voodoo dolls are amusing," wrote legba on the evening after Bungle's rampage, posting a public statement to the widely read in-MOO mailing list called *social-issues, a forum for debate on matters of import to the entire populace. "And mostly I tend to think that restrictive measures around here cause more trouble than they prevent. But I also think that Mr. Bungle was being a vicious, vile fuckhead, and I . . . want his sorry ass scattered from #17 to the Cinder Pile. I'm not calling for policies, trials, or better jails. I'm not sure what I'm calling for. Virtual castration, if I could manage it. Mostly, [this type of thing] doesn't happen here. Mostly, perhaps I thought it wouldn't happen to me. Mostly, I trust people to conduct themselves with some veneer of civility. Mostly, I want his ass."

Months later, the woman in Seattle would confide to me that as she wrote those words posttraumatic tears were streaming down her face—a real-life fact that should suffice to prove that the words' emotional content was no mere playacting. The precise tenor of that content, however, its mingling of murderous rage and eyeball-rolling annoyance, was a curious amalgam that neither the RL nor the VR facts alone can quite account for. Where virtual reality and its conventions would have us believe that legba and Starsinger were brutally raped in their own living room, here was the victim legba scolding Mr. Bungle for a breach of "civility." Where real life, on the other hand, insists the incident was only an episode in a free-form version of Dungeons and Dragons, confined to the realm of the symbolic and at no point threatening any player's life, limb, or material well-being, here now was the player legba issuing aggrieved and heartfelt calls for Mr. Bungle's dismemberment. Ludicrously excessive by RL's lights, woefully understated by VR's, the tone of legba's response made sense only in the buzzing, dissonant gap between them.

Which is to say it made the only kind of sense that *can* be made of MUDly phenomena. For while the *facts* attached to any event born of a MUD's strange, ethereal universe may march in straight, tandem lines separated neatly into the virtual and the real, its meaning lies always in that gap. You learn this axiom early in your life as a player, and it's of no small relevance to the Bungle case that you usually learn it between the sheets, so to speak. Netsex, tinysex, virtual sex—however you name it, in real-life reality it's nothing more than a 900-line encounter stripped of even the vestigial physicality of the voice. And yet as any but the most inhibited of newbies can tell you, it's possibly the headiest experience the very heady world of MUDs has to offer. Amid flurries of even the most cursorily described caresses, sighs, and penetrations, the glands do engage, and often as throbbingly as they would in a real-life assignation—sometimes even more so, given the combined power of anonymity and textual suggestiveness to unshackle deep-seated fantasies. . . .

And small wonder indeed that the sexual nature of Mr. Bungle's crime provoked such powerful feelings, and not just in legba (who, be it noted, was in real life a theory-savvy doctoral candidate and a longtime MOOer, but just as baffled and overwhelmed by the force of her own reaction, she later would attest, as any panting undergrad might have been). Even players who had never experienced MUD rape (the vast majority of male-presenting characters, but not as large a majority of the female-presenting as might be hoped) immediately appreciated its gravity and were moved to condemnation of the perp. legba's missive to *social-issues* followed a strongly worded one from Zippy ("Well, well," it began, "no matter what else happens on Lambda, I can always be sure that some jerk is going to reinforce my low opinion of humanity") and was itself followed by others from Moriah, Raccoon, Crawfish, and evangeline. Starsinger also let her feelings ("pissed") be known. And even Jander, the Clueless Samaritan who had responded to Bungle's cries for help and uncaged him shortly after the incident, expressed his regret once apprised of Bungle's deeds, which he allowed to be "despicable."

A sense was brewing that something needed to be done—done soon and in something like an organized fashion—about Mr. Bungle, in particular, and about MUD rape, in general. . . . [T]he answer no doubt seemed obvious to many. But it wasn't until the evening of the second day after the incident that legba, finally and rather solemnly, gave it voice:

"I am requesting that Mr. Bungle be toaded for raping Starsinger and I. I have never done this before, and have thought about it for days. He hurt us both."

That was all. Three simple sentences posted to *social. Reading them, an outsider might never guess that they were an application for a death warrant. . . . [N]ot only are the description and attributes of the toaded player erased, but the account itself goes too. The annihilation of the character, thus, is total.

And nothing less than total annihilation, it seemed, would do to settle LambdaMOO's accounts with Mr. Bungle. Within minutes of the posting of legba's appeal, SamIAm, the Australian Deleuzean, who had witnessed much of the attack from the back room of his suburban Sydney home, seconded the motion with a brief message crisply entitled "Toad the fukr." SamIAm's posting was seconded almost as quickly by that of Bakunin, covictim of Mr. Bungle and well-known radical, who in real life happened also to be married to the real-life legba. And over the course of the next 24 hours as many as 50 players made it known, on *social and in a variety of other forms and forums, that they would be pleased to see Mr. Bungle erased from the face of the MOO. And with dissent so far confined to a dozen or so antitoading hardliners, the numbers suggested that the citizenry was indeed moving towards a resolve to have Bungle's virtual head.

There was one small but stubborn obstacle in the way of this resolve, however, and that was a curious state of social affairs known in some quarters of the MOO as the New Direction. It was all very fine, you see, for the LambdaMOO rabble to get it in their heads to liquidate one of their peers, but when the time came to actually do the deed it would require the services of a nobler class of character. It would require a wizard. Master-programmers of the MOO, spelunkers of the database's deepest code-structures and custodians of its day-to-day administrative trivia, wizards are also the only players empowered to issue the toad command, a feature maintained on nearly all MUDs as a quick-and-dirty means of social control. But the wizards of LambdaMOO, after years of adjudicating all manner of interplayer disputes with little to show for it but their own weariness and the smoldering resentment of the general populace, had decided they'd had enough of the social sphere. And so, four months before the Bungle incident, the archwizard Haakon (known in RL as Pavel Curtis, Xerox researcher and LambdaMOO's principal architect) formalized this decision in a document called "LambdaMOO Takes a New Direction," which he placed in the living room for all to see. In it, Haakon announced that the wizards from that day forth were pure technicians. From then on, they would make no decisions affecting the social life of the MOO, but only implement whatever decisions the community as a whole directed them to. From then on, it was decreed, LambdaMOO would just have to grow up and solve its problems on its own.

Faced with the task of inventing its own self-governance from scratch, the LambdaMOO population had so far done what any other loose, amorphous agglomeration of individuals would have done: they'd let it slide. But now the task took on new urgency. Since getting the wizards to toad Mr. Bungle (or to toad the likes of him in the future) required a convincing case that the cry for his head came from the community at large, then the community itself would have to be defined; and if the community was to be convincingly defined, then some form of social organization, no matter how rudimentary, would have to be settled on. . . . Parliamentarian legalist types argued that unfortunately Bungle could not legitimately be toaded at all, since there were no explicit MOO rules against rape, or against just about anything else—and the sooner such rules were established, they added, and maybe even a full-blown judiciary system complete with elected officials and prisons to enforce those rules, the better. Others, with a royalist streak in them, seemed to feel that Bungle's as-yet-unpunished outrage only proved this New Direction silliness had gone on long enough, and that it was high time the wizardocracy returned to the position of swift and decisive leadership their player class was born to.

And then there were what I'll call the technolibertarians. For them, MUD rapists were of course assholes, but the presence of assholes on the system was a technical inevitability, like noise on a phone line, and best dealt with not through repressive social disciplinary mechanisms but through the timely deployment of defensive software tools. Some asshole blasting violent, graphic language at you? Don't whine to the authorities about it— hit the @gag command and the asshole's statements will be blocked from your screen (and only yours). It's simple, it's effective, and it censors no one.

But the Bungle case was rather hard on such arguments. For one thing, the extremely public nature of the living room meant that gagging would spare the victims only from witnessing their own violation, but not from having others witness it. You might want to argue that what those victims didn't directly experience couldn't hurt them, but consider how that wisdom would sound to a woman who'd been, say, fondled by strangers while passed out drunk and you have a rough idea how it might go over with a crowd of hardcore MOOers. Consider, for another thing, that many of the biologically female participants in the Bungle debate had been around long enough to grow lethally weary of the gag-and-get-over-it school of virtual-rape counseling, with its fine line between empowering victims and holding them responsible for their own suffering, and its shrugging indifference to the window of pain between the moment the rape-text starts flowing and the moment a gag shuts it off. From the outset it was clear that the technolibertarians were going to have to tiptoe through this issue with care, and for the most part they did.

Yet no position was trickier to maintain than that of the MOO's resident anarchists. Like the technolibbers, the anarchists didn't care much for punishments or policies or power elites. Like them, they hoped the MOO could be a place where people interacted fulfillingly without the need for such things. But their high hopes were complicated, in general, by a somewhat less thoroughgoing faith in technology ("Even if you can't tear down the master's house with the master's tools"—read a slogan written into one anarchist player's self-description—"it is a damned good place to start"). And at present they were additionally complicated by the fact that the most vocal anarchists in the discussion were none other than legba, Bakunin, and SamIAm, who wanted to see Mr. Bungle toaded as badly as anyone did.

Needless to say, a pro–death penalty platform is not an especially comfortable one for an anarchist to sit on, so these particular anarchists were now at great pains to sever the conceptual ties between toading and capital punishment. Toading, they insisted (almost convincingly), was much more closely analogous to banishment; it was a kind of turning of the communal back on the offending party, a collective action which, if carried out properly, was entirely consistent with anarchist models of community. And carrying it out properly meant first and foremost building a consensus around it—a messy process for which there were no easy technocratic substitutes. It was going to take plenty of good old-fashioned, jawbone-intensive grassroots organizing.

So that when the time came, at 7 p.m. PST on the evening of the third day after the occurrence in the living room, to gather in evangeline's room for her proposed real-time open conclave, Bakunin and legba were among the first to arrive. But this was hardly to be an anarchist-dominated affair, for the room was crowding rapidly with representatives of all the MOO's political stripes, and even a few wizards. . . . Peaking in number at around 30, this was one of the largest crowds that ever gathered in a single LambdaMOO chamber, and while evangeline had given her place a description that made it "infinite in expanse and fluid in form," it now seemed anything but roomy. You could almost feel the claustrophobic air of the place, dank and overheated by virtual bodies, pressing against your skin.

I know you could because I too was there, making my lone and insignificant appearance in this story. . . .

. . . [T]he discussion that raged around me was of an almost unrelieved earnestness, bent it seemed on examining every last aspect and implication of Mr. Bungle's crime. There were the central questions, of course: thumbs up or down on Bungle's virtual existence? And if down, how then to insure that his toading was not just some isolated lynching but a first step toward shaping LambdaMOO into a legitimate community? Surrounding these, however, a tangle of weighty side issues proliferated. What, some wondered, was the real-life legal status of the offense? Could Bungle's university administrators punish him for sexual harassment? Could he be prosecuted under California state laws against obscene phone calls? Little enthusiasm was shown for pursuing either of these lines of action, which testifies both to the uniqueness of the crime and to the nimbleness with which the discussants were negotiating its idiosyncracies. Many were the casual references to Bungle's deed as simply "rape," but these in no way implied that the players had lost sight of all distinctions between the virtual and physical versions, or that they believed Bungle should be dealt with in the same way a real-life criminal would. He had committed a MOO crime, and his punishment, if any, would be meted out via the MOO.

On the other hand, little patience was shown toward any attempts to downplay the seriousness of what Mr. Bungle had done. When the affable HerkieCosmo proposed, more in the way of an hypothesis than an assertion, that "perhaps it's better to release . . . violent tendencies in a virtual environment rather than in real life," he was tut-tutted so swiftly and relentlessly that he withdrew the hypothesis altogether, apologizing humbly as he did so. Not that the assembly was averse to putting matters into a more philosophical perspective. "Where does the body end and the mind begin?" young Quastro asked, amid recurring attempts to fine-tune the differences between real and virtual violence. "Is not the mind a part of the body?" "In MOO, the body IS the mind," offered HerkieCosmo gamely, and not at all implausibly, demonstrating the ease with which very knotty metaphysical conundrums come undone in VR. The not-so-aptly named Obvious seemed to agree, arriving after deep consideration of the nature of Bungle's crime at the hardly novel yet now somehow newly resonant conjecture "all reality might consist of ideas, who knows." . . .

It was almost a relief, therefore, when midway through the evening Mr. Bungle himself, the living, breathing cause of all this talk, teleported into the room. Not that it was much of a surprise. Oddly enough, in the three days since his release from Zippy's cage, Bungle had returned more than once to wander the public spaces of LambdaMOO, walking willingly into one of the fiercest storms of ill will and invective ever to rain down on a player. He'd been taking it all with a curious and mostly silent passivity, and when challenged face to virtual face by both legba and the genderless elder statescharacter PatGently to defend himself on *social*, he'd demurred, mumbling something about Christ and expiation. He was equally quiet now, and his reception was still uniformly cool. legba fixed an arctic stare on him—"no hate, no anger, no interest at all. Just . . . watching." Others were more actively unfriendly. "Asshole," spat Karl Porcupine, "creep." But the harshest of the MOO's hostility toward him had already been vented, and the attention he drew now was motivated more, it seemed, by the opportunity to probe the rapist's mind, to find out what made it tick and if possible how to get it to tick differently. In short, they wanted to know why he'd done it. So they asked him.

And Mr. Bungle thought about it. And as eddies of discussion and debate continued to swirl around him, he thought about it some more. And then he said this:

"I engaged in a bit of a psychological device that is called thought-polarization, the fact that this is not RL simply added to heighten the affect of the device. It was purely a sequence of events with no consequence on my RL existence."

They might have known. Stilted though its diction was, the gist of the answer was simple, and something many in the room had probably already surmised: Mr. Bungle was a psycho. Not, perhaps, in real life—but then in real life it's possible for reasonable people to assume, as Bungle clearly did, that what transpires between word-costumed characters within the boundaries of a make-believe world is, if not mere play, then at most some kind of emotional laboratory experiment. Inside the MOO, however, such thinking marked a person as one of two basically subcompetent types. The first was the newbie, in which case the confusion was understandable. . . . But while Mr. Bungle hadn't been around as long as most MOOers, he'd been around long enough to leave his newbie status behind, and his delusional statement therefore placed him among the second type: the sociopath.

And as there is but small percentage in arguing with a head case, the room's attention gradually abandoned Mr. Bungle and returned to the discussions that had previously occupied it. But if the debate had been edging toward ineffectuality before, Bungle's anticlimactic appearance had evidently robbed it of any forward motion whatsoever. . . . [A]t this point what seemed clear was that evangeline's meeting had died, at last, and without any practical results to mark its passing.

It was also at this point, most likely, that JoeFeedback reached his decision. JoeFeedback was a wizard, a taciturn sort of fellow who'd sat brooding on the sidelines all evening. He hadn't said a lot, but what he had said indicated that he took the crime committed against legba and Starsinger very seriously, and that he felt no particular compassion toward the character who had committed it. But on the other hand he had made it equally plain that he took the elimination of a fellow player just as seriously, and moreover that he had no desire to return to the days of wizardly fiat. It must have been difficult, therefore, to reconcile the conflicting impulses churning within him at that moment. In fact, it was probably impossible, for as much as he would have liked to make himself an instrument of LambdaMOO's collective will, he surely realized that under the present order of things he must in the final analysis either act alone or not act at all.

So JoeFeedback acted alone.

He told the lingering few players in the room that he had to go, and then he went. It was a minute or two before ten. He did it quietly and he did it privately, but all anyone had to do to know he'd done it was to type the @who command, which was normally what you typed if you wanted to know a player's present location and the time he last logged in. But if you had run a @who on Mr. Bungle not too long after JoeFeedback left evangeline's room, the database would have told you something different.

"Mr. Bungle," it would have said, "is not the name of any player."

The date, as it happened, was April Fool's Day, and it would still be April Fool's Day for another two hours. But this was no joke: Mr. Bungle was truly dead and truly gone.

They say that LambdaMOO has never been the same since Mr. Bungle's toading. They say as well that nothing's really changed. And though it skirts the fuzziest of dream-logics to say that both these statements are true, the MOO is just the sort of fuzzy, dreamlike place in which such contradictions thrive.

Certainly whatever civil society now informs LambdaMOO owes its existence to the Bungle Affair. The archwizard Haakon made sure of that. Away on business for the duration of the episode, Haakon returned to find its wreckage strewn across the tiny universe he'd set in motion. The death of a player, the trauma of several others, and the angst-ridden conscience of his colleague JoeFeedback presented themselves to his concerned and astonished attention, and he resolved to see if he couldn't learn some lesson from it all. For the better part of a day he brooded over the record of events and arguments left in *social, then he sat pondering the chaotically evolving shape of his creation, and at the day's end he descended once again into the social arena of the MOO with another history-altering proclamation.

It was probably his last, for what he now decreed was the final, missing piece of the New Direction. In a few days, Haakon announced, he would build into the database a system of petitions and ballots whereby anyone could put to popular vote any social scheme requiring wizardly powers for its implementation, with the results of the vote to be binding on the wizards. At last and for good, the awkward gap between the will of the players and the efficacy of the technicians would be closed. And though some anarchists grumbled about the irony of Haakon's dictatorially imposing universal suffrage on an unconsulted populace, in general the citizens of LambdaMOO seemed to find it hard to fault a system more purely democratic than any that could ever exist in real life. Eight months and a dozen ballot measures later, widespread participation in the new regime has produced a small arsenal of mechanisms for dealing with the types of violence that called the system into being. MOO residents now have access to a @boot command, for instance, with which to summarily eject berserker "guest" characters. And players can bring suit against one another through an ad hoc arbitration system in which mutually agreed-upon judges have at their disposition the full range of wizardly punishments up to and including the capital.

Yet the continued dependence on death as the ultimate keeper of the peace suggests that this new MOO order may not be built on the most solid of foundations. For if life on LambdaMOO began to acquire more coherence in the wake of the toading, death retained all the fuzziness of pre-Bungle days. This truth was rather dramatically borne out, not too many days after Bungle departed, by the arrival of a strange new character named Dr. Jest. There was a forceful eccentricity to the newcomer's manner, but the oddest thing about his style was its striking yet unnameable familiarity. And when he developed the annoying habit of stuffing fellow players into a jar containing a tiny simulacrum of a certain deceased rapist, the source of this familiarity became obvious:

Mr. Bungle had risen from the grave.

In itself, Bungle's reincarnation as Dr. Jest was a remarkable turn of events, but perhaps even more remarkable was the utter lack of amazement with which the LambdaMOO public took note of it. . . . [H]is punishment, ultimately, had been no more or less symbolic than his crime.

What *was* surprising, however, was that Mr. Bungle/Dr. Jest seemed to have taken the symbolism to heart. Dark themes still obsessed him— the objects he created gave off wafts of Nazi imagery and medical torture— but he no longer radiated the aggressively antisocial vibes he had before. He was a lot less unpleasant to look at (the outrageously seedy clown description had been replaced by that of a mildly creepy but actually rather natty young man, with "blue eyes . . . suggestive of conspiracy, untamed eroticism and perhaps a sense of understanding of the future"), and aside from the occasional jar-stuffing incident, he was also a lot less dangerous to be around. It was obvious he'd undergone some sort of personal transformation in the days since I'd first glimpsed him back in evangeline's crowded room—nothing radical maybe, but powerful nonetheless, and resonant enough with my own experience, I felt, that it might be more than professionally interesting to talk with him, and perhaps compare notes.

For I too was undergoing a transformation in the aftermath of that night in evangeline's, and I'm still not entirely sure what to make of it. As I pursued my runaway fascination with the discussion I had heard there, as I pored over the *social debate and got to know legba and some of the other victims and witnesses, I could feel my newbie consciousness falling away from me. Where before I'd found it hard to take virtual rape seriously, I now was finding it difficult to remember how I could ever *not* have taken it seriously. I was proud to have arrived at this perspective—it felt like an exotic sort of achievement, and it definitely made my ongoing experience of the MOO a richer one.

But it was also having some unsettling effects on the way I looked at the rest of the world. Sometimes, for instance, it was hard for me to understand why RL society classifies RL rape alongside crimes against person or property. Since rape can occur without any physical pain or damage, I found myself reasoning, then it must be classed as a crime against the mind—more intimately and deeply hurtful, to be sure, than cross burnings, wolf whistles, and virtual rape, but undeniably located on the same conceptual continuum. I did not, however, conclude as a result that rapists were protected in any fashion by the First Amendment. Quite the opposite, in fact: the more seriously I took the notion of virtual rape, the less seriously I was able to take the notion of freedom of speech, with its tidy division of the world into the symbolic and the real. . . .

. . . I can no longer convince myself that our wishful insulation of language from the realm of action has ever been anything but a valuable kludge, a philosophically damaged stopgap against oppression that would just have to do till something truer and more elegant came along.

Am I wrong to think this truer, more elegant thing can be found on LambdaMOO? Perhaps, but I continue to seek it there, sensing its presence just beneath the surface of every interaction. I have even thought, as I said, that discussing with Dr. Jest our shared experience of the workings of the MOO might help me in my search. But when that notion first occurred to me, I still felt somewhat intimidated by his lingering criminal aura, and I hemmed and hawed a good long time before finally resolving to drop him MOO-mail requesting an interview. By then it was too late. For reasons known only to himself, Dr. Jest had stopped logging in. . . .

ON SPACE, SEX, AND BEING STALKED

Pamela Gilbert

English professor Pamela Gilbert uses her personal experiences of being stalked on the Internet to explore and bring to the surface paradoxes and unique elements that have arisen through the use of the Internet. The Internet allows a kind of immediacy for the retrieval and dissemination of information. In Gilbert's case, Internet postings by her stalker affected her life both on-line and off. Illustrating how officials such as police and university administrators have difficulty applying old rules and laws to new Internet problems, Gilbert's experience has left an indelible impact that stifles her cyberspace interactions, among others.

Reprinted from *Women and Performance* 9, no. 1 (1996): 125–49, with the permission of the author and publisher.

I am completely seduced by the Net, a project of both pathos and grandeur. Those who write about it are often dazzled by the potential of performative subjectivities and virtual communities, so ripe with utopian promise.[1] Yet utopias, as Haraway (among others) has noted, are often masks for imperialist fantasy.[2] The ideal reader of hypertext is praised at the expense of real readers; the lure of an Internet community in which gender, race, and class can be discarded as irrelevant or constructed at will is offered without the recognition that the microtechnology on which the Net depends is the product of exploitation of largely third world, largely female labor, for whom the Net itself has no more personal relevance than Neptune.[3] . . . And yet . . . I love the web, the WELL, the MOOs. I myself am careless of the cautions I raise in my own theorizing. . . .

Recently, an ex-colleague whom I had dated briefly over a year ago developed psychological problems and began stalking me, particularly on the Internet. In real life, stalkers usually stalk in proximity to their victims—they want the victim to see them and know they are there—they feed on the victim's reaction. On the Net, proximity takes on a new meaning. Obviously, there are important differences between the situation of someone who is regularly within shooting range of her or his stalker and someone who is being stalked from two thousand miles away. To gloss over this would be to trivialize the sufferings of victims of constant and immediate physical threat. However, I still feel remarkably as though my personal space has been violated. This has led me to think about just what I mean when I say "personal space," and has demonstrated to me the ways that cyber "space" interacts with gender. This experience has also led to contemplation of just how women are supposed to fight back against crimes for which most legal experts cannot even provide a clear, actionable definition.

To someone who doesn't know the Net well, fighting seems to be a simple enough process. Most of the Net seems perpetually prepared to fight, or "flame," at the slightest insinuation. People who would never gratuitously insult others face-to-face are eager to do so in the aggressive environment of the Net. I, too, feel myself to be unconstrained on the Net; after all, it's only words, it's not really like, say, walking down a dark alley in a dangerous neighborhood. And yet, I actually spend most of my time in "safe" places—academic listservs which have the highest female-identified membership on the Net and usenet groups that are not particularly aggressive. . . . Although I know perfectly well that I am physically in private space and that the Net is not properly a space in which I move at all (I am stationary, and data is potentiated on my screen—to the extent that anything "moves" at all, it is data through phone lines, in linear sequence), I treat the Net like a space, nonlinear, three-dimensional, at least semipublic, in which I perform both as an individual and as a professional, with relationships and potential relationships with others.

The stalker—let's call him "Tim"—had been a colleague of mine for several years at the small state university campus in Southern California where he was a faculty member and I was a part-time lecturer. We were friendly "coffee buddies," but that was about it. After moving to the Midwest to take another job, I met up with him at the Modern Language Association (MLA) meeting in Toronto for dinner, and began a casual dating relationship that lasted for two weekends, one in February and one in August. I rapidly discovered that Tim had some very serious problems which made the relationship unworkable, including substance abuse, depression, and impotence. When I tried to talk to him about these issues, he became angry. When he wanted to get together again, I put him off; finally he insisted on an explanation, and in January 1995 I told him I no longer wanted to continue dating him. He was furious, which surprised me, given the relatively brief and casual nature of the relationship, but I tried to be cordial and overlook what I believed he would eventually see as an irrational reaction. He continued to send me angry e-mail and finally, I stopped responding entirely.

Then some odd things started to happen. He began showing up on listservs on which I was active, and in which he had little professional interest. When he started, I was surprised at how invasive his presence felt. . . . Every time I posted or responded to a post, I had the sense of being watched. Of course if I didn't respond publicly to a post that clearly appealed to my area of expertise, I knew he would be "reading" that silence as well. Still, I tried to shrug it off—it's a free Net, after all.

He upped the ante by using others on the Net to remind me of his presence. . . . A . . . disturbing manifestation occurred one night in April as I was checking my mail, sitting in my partner's apartment, advancing through the screens of mostly listserv mail with the delete key. A personal message from a grad student in New York came up on screen; she explained that she was doing research on pornography, and that Tim had seen her query and kindly given her my address, explaining that I was an expert on the topic. Later I discovered that he supposed me to be terrified that my work as a nude model some twelve years previously would be exposed; the e-mail from New York was, from his perspective, a cat-and-mouse game. However, I did not make the connection between my modeling, which I had told Tim about years earlier, and the implied threat concealed as an academic query. But I did read it as a hostile action, and understood that the hostility was somehow connected to sex. . . .

I was concerned, but finally, I concluded that, while irrational and certainly annoying, what he had done was not really harmful. However, I wondered about that as I sent a message to the grad student explaining that there had been a mistake of some sort and wishing her luck on her research. On one level, the whole incident seemed ludicrously junior-high schoolish—petty even to take notice of it. On another, he had misrepresented me professionally and lied to and used an innocent third party, again in the professional arena, for not very laudable personal aims.

Still, nothing else happened and I soon forgot about Tim entirely. Then in May 1995, I received a message from him, making no mention of earlier events, and implying that he wanted to reestablish a friendly professional correspondence. I responded frankly and cordially. We continued this occasional correspondence throughout the summer, which I spent out of the country doing research. . . . I sensed some hostility in his messages occasionally, but dismissed it as residual.

Upon my return to Wisconsin on August 22, 1995, I received a typed letter from an address I did not recognize; it had been sent in June. It was from a colleague and personal friend of Tim's, "Naomi." It explained that Tim had been hunting for nude pictures that had been taken of me between the ages of sixteen and twenty (there followed a list of items she had actually seen in his possession) and that he was planning to use them to hurt me professionally. Specifically, he had planned to send them to my colleagues and students at the beginning of the term, and/or to send them to search committees, knowing I would be on the market. He had done all of this at the same time he had been engaged in "friendly" correspondence with me.

For several minutes I simply couldn't take it in. The betrayal of confidence, the realization that I had so completely misjudged a situation, and most of all, the cold calculation and, from my perspective, utterly "motiveless malice" left me unable to think reasonably. . . . I sat down and tried to control my breathing, and to think about what the situation meant. . . . I tried to calm myself, checking in on my e-mail, forcing myself to read each message. And suddenly, there on the screen was a message from Tim. "Welcome home."

Over the next two days, I contacted authorities at my university and explained the situation to them. On their advice, I filed a report with campus security and also contacted a local women's organization that put me in touch with a wonderfully supportive lawyer who led me through the complexities of dealing with the local authorities. With the lawyer on the line, I called Tim and told him that he was to stop harassing me and not to contact me in any way. (His response was a bored "Can you call back another time? I'm busy now.") I was starting to breathe more easily; after all, if the worst he could do was mail these decade-old photos, an action which would reflect far more on him than on me and be legally actionable in the bargain—well, I had certainly survived worse things. Then I called Naomi, and found that I had bigger problems than I thought.

Tim's irrationality had grown into an obsession of epic proportions. He had been tracking my movements through finger, seeing when I logged on and making (usually erroneous) assumptions about my whereabouts and sleep patterns. . . . He had me followed by a student of his, with whom he had shared the pictures and a good deal of his planning, at the San Diego MLA. He had ordered my dissertation through ILL, and done textual analysis on it and on all my e-mail, much of which he could quote verbatim. He had researched my life, and read up on abnormal psychology for insights into "my" personality, and even taught a course on paranoia based on the results. He spent his spare time scouring porn stores and interviewing . . . , hunting down anyone who he thought could give him information about my life. Tim had described me to Naomi and several other people on his campus as a nymphomaniac with Mafia connections, possibly a Satanist, who "slept with big Hollywood lawyers." He had taken a GIF of my face, from a videotape of a public television talk program I had done for the university, and posted it on the alt.sex groups with my name, offering $200 for any information or pictures of me pertaining to the time when I was sixteen to twenty. Having gotten some pictures in an initial response, he posted those, again with my name and the years he was interested in, and more money offers.

I immediately began hunting his posts online, and found them pretty quickly. He was posting pictures of me to alt.sex.pictures and alt.binaries.erotica groups, especially teen.female. I began to surf these groups, most of which I had never read before, documenting his activities. In these newsgroups, I had the uncomfortable sense of being in "places" I would not normally go—the difference of course being that I could "go" there silently and invisibly. Having been harassed by Tim in my own "spaces" on the Net, I now found myself lurking in spaces in which he was "at home."

I didn't have to look (or lurk) long. Tim posted the pictures to multiple groups while I was online. A surge of adrenaline went through me as they appeared on the screen, and I snapped back from the keyboard as if I'd been struck. This was a contact with me—intimate, private, feeling like I had somehow been "hit" through the Net, our contemporaneous physical connection through two keyboards upon which our fingers rested simultaneously—and also public, as the files appeared and would continue to appear on screens around the world, "published" and disseminated without my consent at almost unimaginable speed. There is no exact analogy. An obscene phone call might be the closest one: it is also a kind of contact, an invasion of private space from private space, and a threat, no matter how innocuous the message, yet it lacks the public qualities of a Net attack, which can continue in that public vein whether or not the "target" participates directly. A phone can be hung up.

Nor was the threat wholly a discursive one. Most disturbingly, Tim had talked often of buying a gun, and confronting me with it in Chicago. I questioned Naomi closely about the circumstances of Tim's conversations which involved fantasies or threats of physical violence against me. . . . Naomi had said to him that "no human being" deserved what he was planning to do to me; his response was "She has ruled herself out of the human race. They shoot mad dogs, don't they?" ("That's bad," said one expert on sexual violence I talked to later. "Once they see you as not human, it justifies anything.") . . . Naomi remarked that she really didn't think Tim was violent, but noted also that his pattern was to talk about something for quite a while, plan it in detail, and then do it. He followed this pattern when he came up with the idea of offering money on the Net for information about me, and on several later occasions . . . and in June, he was just starting to talk about the gun. That was when Naomi refused to discuss it with him anymore, and, having first consulted her minister, decided to write to me. . . .

The threat of violence was sobering. Having been so utterly mistaken by him in the first place, and seeing no rational pattern in his actions, I felt incapable of predicting him. Further, whereas most victims of obsessional stalking are advised to absent themselves, since the obsession feeds on their reactions and on their presence, he was feeding his obsession on the videos and pictures, on the Internet trading of GIFs and JPEGs, on his ability to track me through finger and on listservs. Knowing he was six hours away, door to door, any noise outside made me jump. When conferences I was speaking at posted their programs on the Net, I winced. And when I got to those conferences, I never left the hotel alone. Although I tried to keep a sense of proportion, to laugh about it, living with this constant threat was both time consuming and emotionally wearing.

The complication of distance and the use of the Internet created difficulties for law enforcement officials, particularly with regard to jurisdiction. Still, police in both states took an active interest, despite occasional confusion about how to proceed. The local District Attorney called me in with a Victim Witness representative; and drafted a letter putting Tim on notice that he was under investigation. . . .

Not particularly supportive, perhaps not surprisingly, was the administration of the university where Tim had recently been tenured. Despite my six years as a lecturer there, I was told I was not a member of the campus community and therefore had "no standing" to make a complaint to them about Tim's behavior. The president told me that even though it was quite clear that Tim was obsessed with me and had been open about his hatred, it did "not reflect on him as a faculty member, but only as a private citizen." (I found this distinction between Tim's professional and personal life ironic, given that this was precisely the division he was seeking to invalidate in my life.) They said they couldn't help for fear of being sued. . . .

Meanwhile, I contacted a lawyer . . . who was an expert on stalking, and she advised me to disseminate information as widely as possible: "The more people who know the story, the safer you are," she said. Another sexual assault and harassment adviser agreed: "Use your resources, take control of the situation, be active instead of passive, and work with

your network of friends who can support you." I did so, and was heartened
by contacts from friends and acquaintances around the country, many of
whom took the initiative to track information, search cyber archives,
crawl the web, consult legal advisers, and get in touch with others who
knew me. I also took charge by calling more of the people whom Tim had
been in contact with.

The Net, a space defamiliarized by its status as a place of assault, became a locus of power again for me, as I connected with friends and supporters, gathered information, and turned my gaze (and others') back on
the watcher. Again, the only negative reaction I got was from his university: an administrator to whom Tim had shown the pictures declined
to discuss it with police, saying he "didn't remember" it and it was
"harmless boy talk." . . . As one academic put it upon hearing the story,
"Whatever happened to social censure? This is why people get mugged
in broad daylight."

As I gained perspective, I realized that Tim's behavior was essentially
an appropriation of power—as sexual harassment tends to be. The novel,
the pictures, the storytelling was all part of an effort to make me over in
an image of his choosing, to narrate my life, person, and body, and to de-
prive me of the ability to do so. . . .

Pictures of me were being used as puppets, with Tim as ventriloquist
puppet master. Describing it in those terms enabled me to see the limits
of his power. Ultimately, his power over me was a matter of perception,
and by going to the police, subjecting him to scrutiny, and forcing him out
of his own "panoptic" position, I had reappropriated a good deal of it. . . .

Ironically, I was aided by his colleagues. Since his campus had dealt
with the problem in absolute secrecy, the whole story had of course already spread across several campuses. The chair of his department cautioned me: "Right now everyone is on your side. But if you keep talking
about it, people might get the idea that you are obsessed." I was amused,
since at that point, I had largely stopped "talking about it"; it was thirty
or so other folks she needed to quiet down. But there was a darker subtext
to her statement: victims get sympathy, but only if they are willing to continue being victims, quiet and passive. The word "hysterical" was bandied
about. Tim's and my competing stories were imbricated in other, pre-
existing narratives of gender and social control. . . .

The schism between my academic professional life and modeling history was a locus of power, and had been tapped as such by Tim. Like a be-
sieged town destroying its own armory, I resolutely demolished what was
left of my privacy in that area. Still, there were private spaces within private spaces, "registers" of privacy I did not want violated, places in my
discourse I did (and do) not want to go. Perhaps these metaphors of space
(public/private) are necessary to our understanding of privacy because our
bodies, existing in spaces, each of which defines its own decorum largely

based on degree and type of publicness, are fundamental to those definitions of selfhood-among-others. (And perhaps this is why the exhibition of "private parts" in pictures or performance dislocates the usual distinctions between public and private so effectively.)

The metaphor of space—so technically inappropriate to describe the Net—seems inescapable. . . . George Landow, perhaps the most prestigious theorist of Hypertext, conceives the electronic author's most important challenge as providing (imposing?) spatial orientation for (on?) the reader: "The first [problem] . . . is how to indicate the destination of links, and the second, how to welcome the user on arrival to that destination." (1991:188–189) . . . This obsession with mapping, with being located (which is based on the potential of being lost-as if there must be a particular place to go), doesn't it smack a bit of the economy of the one, as Irigaray says, rather than the multiple, the decentered? . . .

I want, in short, to know where the bodies are buried. And I know there are bodies. And so do a lot of Netters, apparently, who drag their bodies, or versions of them, into MOOS, chat "rooms" and other pseudo-environments specifically designed for Bodies. . . . The metaphor of the Net as space masks the disassociation of Netters from their bodies, masks the fact that the bodies are elsewhere, real, material, and invested with a responsible subjectivity. Here it is clearest that gender is information, discourse rather than nature—and sexuality, offline or on it, functions linguistically. But the deployment of this potentially dematerialized information has material effects, and historically, they have been to the detriment of women. Net space, even with its highly performative inflection, is gendered in very traditional ways. We appropriate technology to our own physiques, and resolutely refuse to change our perceptions to fit the parameters of our inventions. . . .

There are differences in the perceived materiality of verbal and visual sexuality on the Net. Verbal sexuality occurs in many forms, from the assault of a specifically sexual "flame" in public or unwanted obscenity sent directly to a private "mailbox." It can also be interactive, ranging from flirtation in postings to direct, interactive verbal "intercourse" in MOOS, IRCs, or the talk function of e-mail. Such interactions may be casual or may involve long-term, committed relationships. Often they involve masquerade and transgendering; always, they involve performance, at least at the literary level of narrative voice, and thus, always, they invoke authorship, and thus, materiality, however uncertain and dispersed. The Internet at its best is interactive and consensual, although consent may be an issue precisely because of its performative nature. Has a man who has sex in a MOO with a black teenaged female character given his consent to have sex if that character actually represents a middle-aged white male? Do such questions have meaning in a MOO, in which "bodies" and therefore the ethics with which use of them is inscribed, have no real existence, except descriptive and symbolic? On the other hand, do any bodies exist which are not descriptive and symbolic? Is the MOO-body (a line of programming) merely another genre of "real" body, or is it something else entirely? Regardless, heterosexism and male dominance is impossible to enforce in e-sex, even while their values pervade the Net.

There is also "pornography," verbal or visual (and, for those with MIME capabilities, increasingly, auditory). Verbal pornography or erotica like that posted, for example, on alt.sex.stories is usually not directly interpersonal, addressed as it is both to the self and to a larger, "faceless" audience. However, the unique atmosphere of the Net can give a "coterie" flavor even to this: as Netters in a particular group comment instantaneously on each others' stories, authors incorporate each other into stories and playfully encode each others' fantasies in hidden and not-so-hidden messages to clearly identified others within the mass audience.[4] However, as recent events in Michigan—wherein one student terrorized another by using her name and description in a "snuff" fantasy on usenet—prove, such writing can also be a mode of harassment and terrorism, as real people are unwillingly made part of narratives which target them for unwanted attention. Libel laws would make it extremely difficult to publish such stories through conventional channels; on the Net, all it takes is the press of a key or click of a mouse.

Obviously, my own experience with visual pornography on the Net has not been a happy one. But even allowing for bias in myself as an observer, the distinctions between the text-based groups and the image-based groups are startlingly apparent. Women more rarely speak in the image based groups, although many of the groups appear to be all "about" women (something women on alt.feminism can appreciate). These groups are largely about looking at images of absent women with other men. The language of many posters is both sexual and economic; some posters trade GIFs with a kind of frenzy, sometimes offering money or other goods for pictures, as the man stalking me did, even though there are hundreds of pictures available for free. For these posters, the sexual charge seems often to derive not so much from the image, but from the prospect of exhibiting and exchanging the image, and the overwhelmingly largest proportion of the images center on females.

. . . On the Net, in that ecstasy of immediacy, these images acquire the mobility and all-at-onceness of capital in the electronic age. The question remains: why are these images treated as commodities, traded, valued, and so forth, when they are infinitely reproducible? If, as Irigaray argues, women-as-commodities occupy three roles (mother, virgin, prostitute), the figure of the prostitute is the ascendant one in pornography: her body represents "usage that is exchanged," and, in this case, the more she is used (desired), the more she is worth.[5] . . .

Sexuality and subjectivity are both discursively constructed, specifically through narrative. Nowhere is this more apparent than in the largely verbal, entirely discursive atmosphere of the Net, in which bodies have no materiality. Perhaps the most important difference between the two types of groups is that, by their very nature, the text-based groups imply a speaker, a writer, and a certain perspective toward the characters described in the stories. The pictures groups are most frequently images of one person posted by another, who states nothing or a few comments (often in the title). The picture appears to "speak for itself," that is, for the woman depicted in it. The act of enunciation, (posting) and the subject of that enunciation tends to disappear behind the image. As Anthony Paul Kerby (and other narrative theorists) points out, in our culture, the "other's 'body' becomes both the site of narration and the site of ascription for subjectivity. . . . Even when the speaker is absent . . . ascription to an embodied authorial origin occurs."[6] The visual image of the woman's body tends to stand as that site, both of narration and ascription, whereas in fact it is the object of narration. The image of the body-commodity obscures the absence of the material body on which it is partially based and with which it is at odds. "Proper" ascription is complicated by the woman's participation, at some level, in the process of communication—for example, in my case, my having posed for the pictures originally. The commodity, as it is consumed, does not simply separate from the material body with which it was originally associated, but appropriates its subjectivity.

I have a difficult, double relationship with those pictures—on one level, they do not represent what I feel is "me" in a significant way—they are not expressive of my desires (except, indirectly, my desire for money at the time they were taken) or my aesthetics, either as they were when the pictures were taken, or now. . . . And yet, the photos do . . . "represent" me. They are recognizable as "me" and, most importantly, are read as expressive of my subjectivity. . . .

The performances of those pictures were, for me, separated from my performance of my own subjectivity. Tim's intent was not to join, but to subsume my materiality and my subjectivity into the representations which he had, and had made.

. . . Ordinarily, a stalker who turns violent completes and defeats his process in the death of his victim. However, Tim could infinitely pursue and narrate "me" in photos and images, an object of desire and aggression. . . .

My "battle" with Tim was fought in two arenas. In the realm of the material threat, there were guns and guards to be considered. Potentially this battle would actually be fought with those guns and guards; this has not yet happened. The other level was that of space and subjectivity. Where on the Net could I safely "go," where was I being watched, being tracked, and how would that translate into the material realm?. . .

The war of words we were engaged in also used weapons of "real" power—the narratives we engaged in had effects on other people's behavior, and on our own, as we created and mobilized available stories about selfhood, otherness, gender, sex, law, violence, sanity, pornography, and academic life. I found that the Net mirrors and, in some cases, intensifies the conflicts and hierarchy, especially gendered and economic, of the world it is a part of, but it also offers new ways to disrupt those power imbalances. The Net is not "just words" (as if anything were either that or, conversely, anything else) but a space of social action, in which subjects are responsible for their utterances and performances, and in which discursive actions can mobilize material effects. Like other social spaces, it is not safe. We have to take it upon ourselves to use and to demand an ethics of care-respect, and to continue to use and demand it whether we get it or not.[7]

I am, as now are you, faced with an absence of new information, a Story without an ending. When he hired his lawyer, Tim stopped posting on the Internet. . . . I later discovered, however, that he has continued his "research." I knew then that I would probably never have the satisfaction of a real closure, never feel really secure from Tim either on the Internet or in my campus parking lot. On the Internet, our physical power is equal, depending in part on technical ability, which can be acquired. Our social power is neither equal, nor imbalanced in clearly defined or constant ways. In the parking lot, of course, the stakes are different.

Notes

1. The utopian rhetoric is particularly evident in the theoretical work which has been done on the potential of hypertext, evincing a surprising naivete on the part of literary critics who should be more sensitive to the power/knowledge relationship. . . . See for example, George P. Landow and Paul Delany, *Hypermedia and Literary Studies* (Cambridge, Mass., 1991) and George Landow, *Hypertext: The Convergence of Contemporary Literary Theory and Technology* (Baltimore, 1992).

2. Donna Haraway, "A Manifesto for Cyborgs," rpt. in *Coming to Terms: Feminism, Theory, Politics,* ed. Elizabeth Weed (New York, 1989).

3. See for example, Aihwa Ong, *Spirits of Resistance and Capitalist Discipline: Factory Women in Malaysia* (Albany, 1987); Annette Fuentes and Barbara Ehrenreich, *Women in the Global Factory* (Boston, 1983).

4. The stories, even on Usenet, thus become interactive, to say nothing of the possibilities for interactive authorship with hypertexts, especially on the web. Many posters (especially women, who seem to participate more in these groups than in the ones involving pictures) remark that they feel their desires legitimated by finding others who have found satisfying lives which fulfill these desires.

5. I want to emphasize again that this analysis refers to a particular behavior exhibited by some of the members of these groups, including Tim. This is not meant

to imply that all participants in these groups participate in this dynamic, nor that those who do, do so at all times or from a single motivation.

6. Anthony Paul Kerby, *Narrative and the Self* (Bloomington, 1991) p. 71. See also Hermans and Kempen, *The Dialogical Self: Meaning as Movement* (New York, 1993).

7. See Margaret Urban Walker, "Moral Understandings: Alternative 'Epistemology' for a Feminist Ethics," in Explor*ations in Feminist Ethics: Theory and Practice*, ed. Eve Browning Cole and Susan Coultrap-McQuin (Bloomington, 1992).

Works Cited

Fuentes, Annette and Barbara Ehrenreich. 1983. *Women in the Global Factory.* Boston: South End Press.

Irigaray, Luce. 1985. "Women on the Market." *This Sex Which Is Not One*, trans. Catherine Porter with Carolyn Burke, 170–191. Ithaca: Cornell University Press.

Hermans, Hubert J. M. and Harry J. G. Kempen. 1993. *The Dialogical Self Meaning as Movement.* New York: Academic Press.

Kerby, Anthony Paul. 1991. *Narrative and the Self.* Bloomington: Indiana University Press.

Landow, George. 1992. *Hypertext: The Convergence of Contemporary Literary Theory and Technology.* Baltimore: Johns Hopkins University Press.

Landow, George P. and Paul Delany, 1991. *Hypermedia and Literary Studies*, Cambridge, Mass.: MIT Press.

Ong, Aihwa. 1987. *Spirits of Resistance and Capitalist Discipline: Factory Women in Malaysia.* Albany: State University of New York Press.

Walker, Margaret Urban. 1992. "Moral Understandings: Alternative 'Epistemology' for a Feminist Ethics." *Explorations in Feminist Ethics: Theory and Practice*, Eve Browning Cole and Susan Coultrap-McQuin, eds., 165–175. Bloomington: Indiana University Press.

Selected Bibliography for Section Four

Journal Articles, News Stories, and Anthology Contributions

Caruso, Denise. "Critics Are Picking Apart a Professor's Study That Linked Internet Use to Loneliness and Depression." *New York Times*, 14 September 1998, 5.

Inman, Dean, et al. "VR Education and Rehabilitation." *Communications of the ACM* 40, no. 8 (1997): 53–58.

Khalil, Omar. "Artificial Decision-Making and Artificial Ethics: A Management Concern." *Journal of Business Ethics* 14, no. 4 (1996): 313–21.

Lloyd, Dan. "Frankenstein's Children: Artificial Intelligence and Human Value." *Metaphilosophy* 16, no. 4 (1985): 307–18.

Michals, Debra. "Cyber-Rape: How Virtual Is It?" *Ms* 7, no. 5 (1997): 68–72.

Mour, James. "Is Ethics Computable?" *Metaphilosophy* 26, nos. 1–2 (January–April 1995): 1–21.

Nemire, Kenneth, et al. "Human Factors Engineering of a Virtual Laboratory for Students with Physical Disabilities." *Presence* 3, no. 3 (1994): 216–26.

Thalmann, Nadia, and Daniel Thalmann. "Towards Virtual Humans in Medicine: A Prospective View." *Computerized Medical Imaging and Graphics* 18, no. 2 (1994): 98–106.

Turkle, Sherry. "Who Am We." *Wired* 4, no. 1 (1996): 148.

Zimmerli, Walther. "Human Minds, Robots, and the Technician of the Future." *Research in Philosophy and Technology* 9 (1989): 183–96.

Books

Aukstakalnis, Steve, and David Blatner. *Silicon Mirage: The Art and Science of Virtual Reality*. Peachpit Press, 1992.

Benedikt, Michael, ed. *Cyber Space: First Steps*. MIT Press, 1991.

Gelernter, David. *The Muse in the Machine*. The Free Press, 1994.

Heim, Michael. *The Metaphysics of Virtual Reality*. Oxford University Press, 1993.

———. *Virtual Realism*. Oxford University Press, 1998.

Levy, Steven. *Artificial Life: A Report from the Frontier Where Computers Meet Biology*. Vintage Books, 1992.

North, Max, et al. *Virtual Reality Therapy*. IPI Press, 1996.

Porter, David, ed. *Internet Culture*. Routledge, 1996.

Rheingold, Howard. *Virtual Reality*. Summit Books, 1991.

Shields, Rob, ed. *Cultures of Internet: Virtual Spaces, Real Histories, Living Bodies*. Sage Publications, 1996.

Slouka, Mark. *War of the Worlds: Cyberspace and the High-Tech Assault on Reality*. Basic Books, 1995.

Stoll, Clifford. *Silicon Snake Oil: Second Thoughts on the Information Highway*. Doubleday, 1995.

Turkle, Sherry. *Life on the Screen*. Simon & Schuster, 1995.

Wexelblat, Alan, ed. *Virtual Reality: Applications and Explorations*. Academic Press, 1993.

Web Resources

"Americans in the Information Age Falling Through the Net" (http://www.ntia.doc.gov/ntiahome/digitaldivide/).

Human Interaction Technologies Lab (http://www.hitl.washington.edu/).

The White House (http://www.whitehouse.gov).

Novels

Asimov, Isaac. *I, Robot*. Doubleday, 1950.
———, and Robert Silverberg. *Positronic Man*. Doubleday, 1992.
Clarke, Arthur C. *2001: A Space Odyssey*. New American Library, 1968.
Gibson, William. *Neuromancer*. Ace Books, 1995.

Films

2001: A Space Odyssey. Directed by Stanley Kubrick. MGM, 1968.
eXistenZ. Directed by David Cronenberg. Dimension Films, 1999.
The Matrix. Directed by Andy Wachowski and Larry Wachowski. Village Road-
　　show Productions, 1999.
Thirteenth Floor. Directed by Josef Rusnak. Centropolis Film Productions, 1999.
Until the End of the World. Directed by Wim Wenders. Warner Brothers, 1991.

ACM/IEEE Software Engineering Code of Ethics and Professional Practice

ACM/IEEE-CS Joint Task Force on Software Engineering Ethics and Professional Practices

Preamble

Computers have a central and growing role in commerce, industry, government, medicine, education, entertainment and society at large. Software engineers are those who contribute by direct participation or by teaching, to the analysis, specification, design, development, certification, maintenance and testing of software systems. Because of their roles in developing software systems, software engineers have significant opportunities to do good or cause harm, to enable others to do good or cause harm, or to influence others to do good or cause harm. To ensure, as much as possible, that their efforts will be used for good, software engineers must commit themselves to making software engineering a beneficial and respected profession. In accordance with that commitment, software engineers shall adhere to the following Code of Ethics and Professional Practice.

The Code contains eight Principles related to the behavior of and decisions made by professional software engineers, including practitioners, educators, managers, supervisors and policy makers, as well as trainees and students of the profession. The Principles identify the ethically responsible relationships in which individuals, groups, and organizations participate and the primary obligations within these relationships. The Clauses of each Principle are illustrations of some of the obligations included in these relationships. These obligations are founded in the software engineer's humanity, in special care owed to people affected by the work of software engineers, and the unique elements of the practice of software engineering. The Code prescribes these as obligations of anyone claiming to be or aspiring to be a software engineer.

It is not intended that the individual parts of the Code be used in isolation to justify errors of omission or commission. The list of Principles and Clauses is not exhaustive. The Clauses should not be read as separating the acceptable from the unacceptable in professional conduct in all practical situations. The Code is not a simple ethical algorithm that generates ethical decisions. In some situations standards may be in tension with each other or with standards from other sources. These situations require the software engineer to use ethical judgment to act in a manner which is most consistent with the spirit of the Code of Ethics and Professional Practice, given the circumstances.

Ethical tensions can best be addressed by thoughtful consideration of fundamental principles, rather than blind reliance on detailed regulations. These Principles should influence software engineers to consider broadly who is affected by their work; to examine if they and their colleagues are treating other human beings with due respect; to consider how the public, if reasonably well informed, would view their decisions; to analyze how the least empowered will be affected by their decisions; and to consider whether their acts would be judged worthy of the ideal professional working as a software engineer. In all these judgments concern for the health, safety and welfare of the public is primary; that is, the "Public Interest" is central to this Code.

The dynamic and demanding context of software engineering requires a code that is adaptable and relevant to new situations as they occur. However, even in this generality, the Code provides support for software engineers and managers of software engineers who need to take positive action in a specific case by documenting the ethical stance of the profession. The Code provides an ethical foundation to which individuals within teams and the team as a whole can appeal. The Code helps to define those actions that are ethically improper to request of a software engineer or teams of software engineers.

The Code is not simply for adjudicating the nature of questionable acts; it also has an important educational function. As this Code expresses the consensus of the profession on ethical issues, it is a means to educate both the public and aspiring professionals about the ethical obligations of all software engineers.

Principles

PRINCIPLE 1: PUBLIC

Software engineers shall act consistently with the public interest. In particular, software engineers shall, as appropriate:

1.01. Accept full responsibility for their own work.

1.02. Moderate the interests of the software engineer, the employer, the client and the users with the public good.

1.03. Approve software only if they have a well-founded belief that it is safe, meets specifications, passes appropriate tests, and does not diminish quality of life, diminish privacy or harm the environment. The ultimate effect of the work should be to the public good.

1.04. Disclose to appropriate persons or authorities any actual or potential danger to the user, the public, or the environment, that they reasonably believe to be associated with software or related documents.

1.05. Cooperate in efforts to address matters of grave public concern caused by software, its installation, maintenance, support or documentation.

1.06. Be fair and avoid deception in all statements, particularly public ones, concerning software or related documents, methods and tools.

1.07. Consider issues of physical disabilities, allocation of resources, economic disadvantage and other factors that can diminish access to the benefits of software.

1.08. Be encouraged to volunteer professional skills to good causes and contribute to public education concerning the discipline.

PRINCIPLE 2: CLIENT AND EMPLOYER

Software engineers shall act in a manner that is in the best interests of their client and employer, consistent with the public interest. In particular, software engineers shall, as appropriate:

2.01. Provide service in their areas of competence, being honest and forthright about any limitations of their experience and education.

2.02. Not knowingly use software that is obtained or retained either illegally or unethically.

2.03. Use the property of a client or employer only in ways properly authorized, and with the client's or employer's knowledge and consent.

2.04. Ensure that any document upon which they rely has been approved, when required, by someone authorized to approve it.

2.05. Keep private any confidential information gained in their professional work, where such confidentiality is consistent with the public interest and consistent with the law.

2.06. Identify, document, collect evidence and report to the client or the employer promptly if, in their opinion, a project is likely to fail, to prove too expensive, to violate intellectual property law, or otherwise to be problematic.

2.07. Identify, document, and report significant issues of social concern, of which they are aware, in software or related documents, to the employer or the client.

2.08. Accept no outside work detrimental to the work they perform for their primary employer.

2.09. Promote no interest adverse to their employer or client, unless a higher ethical concern is being compromised; in that case, inform the employer or another appropriate authority of the ethical concern.

PRINCIPLE 3: PRODUCT

Software engineers shall ensure that their products and related modifications meet the highest professional standards possible. In particular, software engineers shall, as appropriate:

3.01. Strive for high quality, acceptable cost and a reasonable schedule, ensuring significant tradeoffs are clear to and accepted by the employer and the client, and are available for consideration by the user and the public.

3.02. Ensure proper and achievable goals and objectives for any project on which they work or propose.

3.03. Identify, define and address ethical, economic, cultural, legal and environmental issues related to work projects.

3.04. Ensure that they are qualified for any project on which they work or propose to work by an appropriate combination of education and training, and experience.

3.05. Ensure an appropriate method is used for any project on which they work or propose to work.

3.06. Work to follow professional standards, when available, that are most appropriate for the task at hand, departing from these only when ethically or technically justified.

3.07. Strive to fully understand the specifications for software on which they work.

3.08. Ensure that specifications for software on which they work have been well documented, satisfy the users' requirements and have the appropriate approvals.

3.09. Ensure realistic quantitative estimates of cost, scheduling, personnel, quality and outcomes on any project on which they work or propose to work and provide an uncertainty assessment of these estimates.

3.10. Ensure adequate testing, debugging, and review of software and related documents on which they work.

3.11. Ensure adequate documentation, including significant problems discovered and solutions adopted, for any project on which they work.

3.12. Work to develop software and related documents that respect the privacy of those who will be affected by that software.

3.13. Be careful to use only accurate data derived by ethical and lawful means, and use it only in ways properly authorized.

3.14. Maintain the integrity of data, being sensitive to outdated or flawed occurrences.

3.15. Treat all forms of software maintenance with the same professionalism as new development.

PRINCIPLE 4: JUDGMENT

Software engineers shall maintain integrity and independence in their professional judgment. In particular, software engineers shall, as appropriate:

4.01. Temper all technical judgments by the need to support and maintain human values.

4.02. Only endorse documents either prepared under their supervision or within their areas of competence and with which they are in agreement.

4.03. Maintain professional objectivity with respect to any software or related documents they are asked to evaluate.

4.04. Not engage in deceptive financial practices such as bribery, double billing, or other improper financial practices.

4.05. Disclose to all concerned parties those conflicts of interest that cannot reasonably be avoided or escaped.

4.06. Refuse to participate, as members or advisors, in a private, governmental or professional body concerned with software related issues, in which they, their employers or their clients have undisclosed potential conflicts of interest.

PRINCIPLE 5: MANAGEMENT

Software engineering managers and leaders shall subscribe to and promote an ethical approach to the management of software development and maintenance. In particular, those managing or leading software engineers shall, as appropriate:

5.01. Ensure good management for any project on which they work, including effective procedures for promotion of quality and reduction of risk.

5.02. Ensure that software engineers are informed of standards before being held to them.

5.03. Ensure that software engineers know the employer's policies and procedures for protecting passwords, files and information that is confidential to the employer or confidential to others.

5.04. Assign work only after taking into account appropriate contributions of education and experience tempered with a desire to further that education and experience.

5.05. Ensure realistic quantitative estimates of cost, scheduling, personnel, quality and outcomes on any project on which they work or propose to work, and provide an uncertainty assessment of these estimates.

5.06. Attract potential software engineers only by full and accurate description of the conditions of employment.

5.07. Offer fair and just remuneration.

5.08. Not unjustly prevent someone from taking a position for which that person is suitably qualified.

5.09. Ensure that there is a fair agreement concerning ownership of any software, processes, research, writing, or other intellectual property to which a software engineer has contributed.

5.10. Provide for due process in hearing charges of violation of an employer's policy or of this Code.

5.11. Not ask a software engineer to do anything inconsistent with this Code.

5.12. Not punish anyone for expressing ethical concerns about a project.

PRINCIPLE 6: PROFESSION

Software engineers shall advance the integrity and reputation of the profession consistent with the public interest. In particular, software engineers shall, as appropriate:

6.01. Help develop an organizational environment favorable to acting ethically.

6.02. Promote public knowledge of software engineering.

6.03. Extend software engineering knowledge by appropriate participation in professional organizations, meetings and publications.

6.04. Support, as members of a profession, other software engineers striving to follow this Code.

6.05. Not promote their own interest at the expense of the profession, client or employer.

6.06. Obey all laws governing their work, unless, in exceptional circumstances, such compliance is inconsistent with the public interest.

6.07. Be accurate in stating the characteristics of software on which they work, avoiding not only false claims but also claims that might reasonably be supposed to be speculative, vacuous, deceptive, misleading, or doubtful.

6.08. Take responsibility for detecting, correcting, and reporting errors in software and associated documents on which they work.

6.09. Ensure that clients, employers, and supervisors know of the software engineer's commitment to this Code of ethics, and the subsequent ramifications of such commitment.

6.10. Avoid associations with businesses and organizations which are in conflict with this code.

6.11. Recognize that violations of this Code are inconsistent with being a professional software engineer.

6.12. Express concerns to the people involved when significant violations of this Code are detected unless this is impossible, counter-productive, or dangerous.

6.13. Report significant violations of this Code to appropriate authorities when it is clear that consultation with people involved in these significant violations is impossible, counter-productive or dangerous.

PRINCIPLE 7: COLLEAGUES

Software engineers shall be fair to and supportive of their colleagues. In particular, software engineers shall, as appropriate:

7.01. Encourage colleagues to adhere to this Code.

7.02. Assist colleagues in professional development.

7.03. Credit fully the work of others and refrain from taking undue credit.

7.04. Review the work of others in an objective, candid, and properly-documented way.

7.05. Give a fair hearing to the opinions, concerns, or complaints of a colleague.

7.06. Assist colleagues in being fully aware of current standard work practices including policies and procedures for protecting passwords, files and other confidential information, and security measures in general.

7.07. Not unfairly intervene in the career of any colleague; however, concern for the employer, the client or public interest may compel software engineers, in good faith, to question the competence of a colleague.

7.08. In situations outside of their own areas of competence, call upon the opinions of other professionals who have competence in that area.

PRINCIPLE 8: SELF

Software engineers shall participate in lifelong learning regarding the practice of their profession and shall promote an ethical approach to the practice of the profession. In particular, software engineers shall continually endeavor to:

8.01. Further their knowledge of developments in the analysis, specification, design, development, maintenance and testing of software and related documents, together with the management of the development process.

8.02. Improve their ability to create safe, reliable, and useful quality software at reasonable cost and within a reasonable time.

8.03. Improve their ability to produce accurate, informative, and well-written documentation.

8.04. Improve their understanding of the software and related documents on which they work and of the environment in which they will be used.

8.05. Improve their knowledge of relevant standards and the law governing the software and related documents on which they work.

8.06. Improve their knowledge of this Code, its interpretation, and its application to their work.

8.07. Not give unfair treatment to anyone because of any irrelevant prejudices.

8.08. Not influence others to undertake any action that involves a breach of this Code.

8.09. Recognize that personal violations of this Code are inconsistent with being a professional software engineer.

This Code was developed by the ACM/IEEE-CS joint task force on Software Engineering Ethics and Professional Practices (SEEPP):

Executive Committee: Donald Gotterbarn (Chair), Keith Miller and Simon Rogerson;

Members: Steve Barber, Peter Barnes, Ilene Burnstein, Michael Davis, Amr El-Kadi, N. Ben Fairweather, Milton Fulghum, N. Jayaram, Tom Jewett, Mark Kanko, Ernie Kallman, Duncan Langford, Joyce Currie Little, Ed Mechler, Manuel J. Norman, Douglas Phillips, Peter Ron Prinzivalli, Patrick Sullivan, John Weckert, Vivian Weil, S. Weisband and Laurie Honour Werth.

Codes of Ethics of Selected Foreign Professional Societies

COMPUTER SOCIETY OF INDIA (CSI)

Code of Ethics

Approved by Executive Committee in its Meeting on 8th May, 1993, amended effective 1st July, 1998.

Code of Ethics for CSI Members (All Categories)

1. A member of the Computer Society of India (CSI) shall:

- Organise the resources available to him and optimise these in attaining the objectives of his organisation.
- Not misuse his authority or office for personal gains.
- Comply with the Indian laws relating to the management of his organisation and operate within the spirit of these laws.
- Conduct his affairs so as to uphold, project and further the image and reputation of the CSI.
- Maintain integrity in research and publications.

2. As regard his ORGANISATION, CSI member should:

- Act with integrity in carrying out the lawful policy and instructions of his organisation and uphold its image and reputation.

Reprinted with permission of CSI.

- Plan, establish and review objectives and tasks for himself and his subordinates which are compatible with the Codes of Practice of other professionals in the enterprise, and direct all available effort towards the success of the enterprise rather than of himself.
- Fully respect the confidentiality of information which comes to him in the course of his duties, and not use confidential information for personal gains or in a manner which may be detrimental to his organisation or his clients.
- Not snoop around in other people's computer files.
- In his contacts and dealings with other people, demonstrate his personal integrity and humanity and when called to give an opinion in his professional capacity, shall, to the best of his ability, give an opinion that is objective and reliable.

3. As regards the EMPLOYEES, CSI member should:

- Set an example to his subordinates through his own work and performance, through his leadership and by taking account of the needs and problems of his subordinates.
- Develop people under him to become qualified for higher duties.
- Pay proper regard to the safety and well-being of the personnel for whom he is responsible.
- Share his experience with fellow professionals.

4. As regards the CLIENTS, CSI member should:

- Ensure that the terms of all contracts and terms of business be stated clearly and unambiguously.
- Not use the computer to harm other people or to bear false witness.
- Be objective and impartial when giving independent advice.

5. As regards the COMMUNITY, CSI member should:

- Make the most effective use of all natural resources employed.
- Be ready to give professional assistance in community affairs.
- Not appropriate other people's intellectual output.
- Always use a computer in ways that ensure consideration and respect for fellow humans.

ASSOCIAZIONE ITALIANA PER L'INFORMATICA ED IL CALCOLO AUTOMATICO

Professional Code of Conduct for AICA Members

English translation provided November 1993

"I, ... (First and second Name), member of AICA, affirms of being, particularly in such a capacity, pledged to carry out his professional duties—as an employee or as an entrepreneur—with deep professional honesty and aware that this implies:

1. A constant personal engagement in keeping updated on the developments of informatics in the fields that are more directly connected to his activity.
2. To make full use of all his competence in carrying out his duties, at least up to the level that he declared to have when he accepted them, and not to declare to have a higher level of competence than the one he effectively has.
3. To maintain the most complete secrecy on the data and news concerning his employer or clients.
4. To have conscience of the possible social impact of his work.
5. Impartiality in the decisions he will take or suggest and to be frank in declaring his possible actual interests in the choices of solutions of problems he is dealing with.
6. To be conscious of the responsibility he has in consequence of the most technical aspects of his activity—beginning with those of analysis and programming—because they are unfamiliar to other people, and because they can cause severe negative consequences if improperly used.
7. To avoid using non understandable languages when proposing solutions of problems identified or submitted to his attention, keeping constantly aware that such use may even unwillingly, hide substantial aspects.

He pledges also to renounce to his own economic interest, or to the economic interest of his employer, when acting on behalf or in name of the Society (AICA)."

JAPAN INFORMATION SERVICE INDUSTRY ASSOCIATION (JISA)

Code of Ethics and Professional Conduct

English translation provided in November, 1993

Aiming at high and reliable position in the Japanese industry, every member of the Japan Information Service Industry Association (JISA) has committed itself to abide by the following code.

1. General Declaration

Every member company should realize the mission of the information service industry and fulfill its social responsibility not only to the region it belongs to, but also to society as a whole.

2. Business Conduct

Every member company should understand that its prosperity could be inseparably linked to its clients and make every effort to win their confidence of partnership by:

1. entering into a contract with clear and exact terms and implementing them faithfully.
2. strictly adhering to the client's need to keep its project, its strategies, and any other related information confidential.
3. and constantly providing the clients with quality service.

3. Internal Imperatives

1. Member companies should not make trouble to other member companies by acting against the rules of competition.

---

2. Member companies should not hire an employee away from another member company in order to gain confidential information and/or win away a contract.
3. Member companies should strictly abide by the law and any contacts entered into regarding intellectual property rights.
4. Member companies should participate in the association's activities as often as possible in order to exchange technology and experience, and raise the level of the whole industry.
5. Member companies should make every effort to provide a satisfactory work environment for their employees, as well as provide them with good and safe working conditions.
6. Member companies should try to develop their employees' technological faculties, to help them cultivate themselves and to teach them to have pride in their work and professional conduct.

NEW ZEALAND COMPUTER SOCIETY

Code of Ethics and Professional Conduct

The Code of Ethics set out hereunder is issued under the provisions of clause 24 of the Constitution of the New Zealand Computer Society Incorporated and is binding on all Fellows, Advanced Members and Associates of the Society.

Preamble

Members, while pursuing the profession of information processing (the design, construction and operation of information processing systems) will use their special knowledge and skill for the benefit of the public, will serve employers and clients with integrity and loyalty, subject to an overriding responsibility to the public interest, and will strive to enhance the competence and prestige of the profession.

In Relation to the Public

The member . . .

P1. shall have a proper regard for the confidentiality of personal data and shall not use professional skills to infringe the rights of others.
P2. shall express an opinion on a professional subject only when it is based on honest belief and knowledge.
P3. shall declare any personal financial interest in making any statement, criticism or argument concerning information processing.
P4. shall not advertise goods or professional services in a misleading manner.

In Relation to Employers and Clients

The member . . .

E1. shall not disclose or use any confidential information obtained in the course of professional duties without the consent of the person or parties concerned, unless required by law to do so.
E2. shall declare to clients or employers any business connection, interest or application which might influence professional judgement or impair the disinterested quality of advice or service offered to such a client or employer.
E3. shall not recommend or supply goods or services to employer or clients without first disclosing any financial interest in them.
E4. shall exercise professional skills with competence, care and attention.
E5. shall not invite or solicit applications for employment from an employee of a client without that client's prior consent (For this purpose a public advertisement is not considered to be an invitation to any particular person).
E6. in undertaking to provide services other than as an employee, shall state clearly to the client before giving the services, the terms of service and the basis or amount of charges.
E7. shall not accept professional work for personal benefit without due regard for the interest of any existing client or employer.

In Relation to the Society

The member . . .

S1. shall not bring the Society into disrepute.

S2. shall not, without sufficient authority, represent that views expressed constitute the views of the Society.

In Relation to Others

The member . . .

O1. shall not set out to injure the professional reputation or practice of another person, and will conduct professional competition in a manner consistent with this.
O2. shall not infringe the rights of property of others by selling or using any property obtained or developed by the member during engagement or employment or otherwise.

SINGAPORE COMPUTER SOCIETY (SCS)

Professional Code of Conduct

General Principles

1. SCS members will act at all times with integrity.
2. SCS members will accept full responsibility for their work.
3. SCS members will always aim to increase their competence.
4. SCS members will act with professionalism to enhance the prestige of the profession and the Society.

Professional Ideas

1. SCS MEMBERS WILL ACT AT ALL TIMES WITH INTEGRITY

- SCS members will not lay claim to a level of competence that they do not possess.

Reprinted with permission of SCS.

- SCS members will act with complete discretion when entrusted with confidential information.
- SCS members will be impartial when giving advice and will disclose any relevant personal interests.
- SCS members will give credit for work done by others where credit is due.

2. SCS MEMBERS WILL ACCEPT FULL RESPONSIBILITY FOR THEIR WORK

- SCS members will carry out their assignments in a professional manner.
- SCS members will adhere to their employer's or client's standards and guidelines.
- SCS members will indicate to their employers or clients the consequences to be expected if their professional judgement is overruled.

3. SCS MEMBERS WILL ALWAYS AIM TO INCREASE THEIR COMPETENCE

- SCS members will continue to upgrade their knowledge and skills, and be aware of relevant development in the technology they are involved in.
- SCS members will provide opportunity and encouragement for professional development and advancement to fellow professionals and aspirants to the profession.
- SCS members will extend public knowledge, understanding and appreciation of information technology and to oppose false or deceptive statements related to information technology of which they are aware.

4. SCS MEMBERS WILL ACT WITH PROFESSIONALISM TO ENHANCE THE PRESTIGE OF THE PROFESSION AND THE SOCIETY

- SCS members will uphold and improve the professional standards of the Society through participation in their formulation, establishment and enforcement.
- SCS members will not seek personal advantage to the detriment of the Society.
- SCS members will not speak on behalf of the Society without proper authority.
- SCS members will not slander the professional reputation of any other person.
- SCS members will use their special knowledge and skill for the advancement of human welfare.

THE COMPUTER SOCIETY OF ZIMBABWE

Code of Professional Conduct for Registered Consultants

A practising Information Processing consultant who is registered with the Computer Society of Zimbabwe is required to adhere to the under mentioned rules in addition to those enunciated for corporate members of the Society.

1. Serve the best interest of the client at all times.
2. Obtain business and promote the practice in a manner which is ethical, dignified in presentation, accurate and not misleading in content.
3. Refrain from practising during a period when the consultant's judgement is or might be impaired through any cause.
4. Disclose to a client any personal or financial interests, or other significant circumstance, which might influence the work for that client in any way not stated in the terms of reference, before a contract between the client and the consultant is agreed, and in particular:
    i) any directorship or controlling interest in any business in competition with the client;
    ii) any interest or involvement with goods or services recommended or supplied to the client by the consultant;
    iii) any personal relationship with persons in the client's employ; and/or
    iv) the existence but not the name of any other current client of the consultant or the consultancy with competing interests.
5. Negotiate agreements and charge for consulting services only in an ethical and professional manner.
6. Agree to remain with and to continue to provide professional advice to a client who has fulfilled the clients' side of the contractual obligations, until such time as the client agrees to terminate the work.
7. Refrain from offering employment to the client's staff without the client's prior permission or from inviting an employee of a client to consider alternative employment.
8. Respect the confidentiality of client information and not to disclose or cause to be disclosed or use to the consultant's own advantage any such information without the client's prior permission.
9. Accept assignments only where there is a reasonable and informed expectation of successfully meeting requirements, and attempt at all

times to keep all parties concerned (e.g. co-workers, management, clients and users) properly informed on the progress and status of the tasks involved. (*This clause applies to ALL Corporate members.*)

10. Express an opinion on a subject within his/her competence only when it is founded on adequate knowledge and honest conviction and will properly qualify himself/herself when expressing an opinion outside of his/her competence. (*This clause applies to ALL Corporate members.*)

MONTGOMERY COUNTY PUBLIC SCHOOL SYSTEM

Appropriate Usage Agreements

The following Appropriate Usage Agreements were developed by a committee within the Montgomery County Public School System, in Virginia, for use by students at various grade levels.

Using the Internet at [Name of School] Grades 2–5

If I read these pages carefully, and [after] my mother or father signs the second sheet, I may be allowed to use a computer at [Name of School] to look at the Internet and send messages to people around the world. But I also know that if I do not use the Internet in the right way, my teacher or Principal may need to punish me. In fact, I may not be allowed to use the Internet again at school.

I will read the rules for using the Internet that are given below and will ask an adult at my school if I do not understand what any of them mean.

- I will be polite to other people when writing to them (or talking with them) while I am on the Internet. I will not use curse words or any language that my teacher or parent would not want me to use in my classroom.
- I will never give my name, my home address, any personal information about me or my family, or my telephone number to anyone I write to or talk with on the Internet. I know that almost anyone I contact is a stranger to me, and that I don't share personal information with strangers no matter how nice they seem to be.

Reprinted by permission of the Montgomery County Public School System, Christiansburg, VA.

- I know that my teacher and my Principal want me to use the Internet to learn more about the subjects I am studying in my classroom. I will not use the Internet for any other reason. For example, I will not search for a comic book site when I am supposed to be looking for something in science.
- Because the people I write to or talk with on the Internet cannot see me, they will not know what I look like or even how old I am. When I am on the Internet, I promise never to tell people that I am someone else. And I will never send them personal information, such as a picture or my name, by using an envelop and stamp.
- I understand that sometimes I may see a site on the Internet that has pictures or words that my teacher or parents would not want me to see. I will not try to find those sites and, if I come across one of them by accident, I will leave it as soon as I can. For example, suppose I am searching for a type of animal and find a picture that only adults should see. I quickly use my forward or backward keys to take me to another site. I will not continue to look at the site with the bad picture and will not show it to others around me. I also will not print it out or save the picture.
- I agree that I cannot use the words or pictures I see on an Internet site without giving credit to the person who owns the site. For example, I will not copy information from the Internet and hand it in to my teacher as my own work.
- I may be given a password—a special word that only I know. I may have to use this password to sign onto a computer or to send mail over the Internet. I know that I must never tell a friend what that password is. My password should be known only by me. And I know that I should never use a password for myself if that password belongs to someone else. For example, John asks me to loan him my password so he can send someone an e-mail message. John cannot remember what password he was given. I would not loan my password to him and would never ask to use his.

STUDENT'S AGREEMENT (FOR STUDENTS IN THE SECOND GRADE OR ABOVE)

I have read the information that is written above. If I did not understand the meaning of part of it, I asked an adult to explain it to me. I agree to follow these rules at all times when I use the Internet at school.

_____
Signature

_____
Date

PARENT OR GUARDIAN

My son or daughter, who has signed above, understands the rules that he or she is to follow in using the Internet at school. I have talked to him or her to make sure that those rules are understood. I realize that teachers and other school officials will try their best to provide only educationally-sound material from the Internet to my child and that, should objectionable pictures or information appear by accident, they will take immediate action to correct that situation. I give my permission to Montgomery County Public Schools for my son or daughter to use the Internet while on school property.

———————————————
Signature

———————————————
Date

Acceptable Use Policy for Internet Access Grades 6–12

With the permission of your parent or guardian, [Name of School] offers you an opportunity to use the Internet at school. We expect you to use the Internet while in our building only for educational purposes approved by [Name of School]. This use is a privilege, not a right, and we may discipline you or take away your right to use the Internet at school if you misuse this privilege. You are responsible for your own actions while you are on the Internet at [Name of School] and are also accountable for any online activities that occur by others because you have allowed them to use your account.

As a student, you should read the following regulations and then sign this form to show that you understand your responsibilities in using the Internet at this school.

While using the Internet from school properties,

- While online, I will not use language which may be offensive to other users. I will treat others with respect. The written and verbal messages I send while on the Internet will not contain profanity, obscene comments, sexually explicit material, nor expressions of bigotry, racism, and hate.
- I will not place unlawful information on the Internet, nor will I use the Internet illegally in any way that violates federal, state, or local laws or statutes. I will never falsify my identity while using the Internet.
- I will not use the Internet for non-school related activities.
- I will not send chain letters nor any pyramid scheme either to a list of people or to an individual, nor will I send any other type of

communication that might cause a congestion of the Internet or interfere with the work of others.

- I will not use the Internet to buy or sell, or to attempt to buy or sell, any service or product.
- I will not change any computer file that does not belong to me.
- I will not use copyrighted materials from the Internet without permission of the author. I will cite the source where appropriate.
- I will never knowingly give my password to others, nor will I use another person's password.
- I will never use the Internet to send or obtain pornographic or inappropriate material or files.
- Except for the usual information contained in the headers of my electronic mail, I will never give out personal information such as name, address, phone number, or gender.
- I will never knowingly circumvent, or try to circumvent, security measures on either Montgomery County Public Schools' computers or on computers at any remote site.
- I will never attempt to gain unlawful access to another person's or organization's resources, programs, or data.
- I will not make, or attempt to make, any malicious attempt to harm or destroy data of another user on the Internet, including the uploading, downloading, or creation of computer viruses.

STUDENT'S AGREEMENT

I have read the Acceptable Use Policy for Internet Access, as written above, and understand fully and agree to follow the principles and guidelines it contains.

_____
Signature

_____
Date

PARENT'S AGREEMENT

As the parent or guardian of this student, I have read the Acceptable Use Policy for Internet Access as written above. I understand that Internet access at school for students of Montgomery County Public Schools is provided for educational purposes only. I understand that employees of the school system will make every reasonable effort to restrict access to all controversial material on the Internet, but I will not hold them responsible for materials my son or daughter acquires or sees as a result of the use of the Internet from school facilities. I give my permission to [Name of School] to allow the student above to use the Internet on computers at the school.

_____

Signature

_____

Date

CARNEGIE-MELLON UNIVERSITY

Computing and Information Resources Code of Ethics

The ethical principles which apply to everyday community life also apply to computing. Every member of Carnegie Mellon has two basic rights: privacy and a fair share of resources. It is unethical for any other person to violate these rights.

Privacy

- On shared computer systems every user is assigned an ID. Nobody else should use an ID without explicit permission from the owner.
- All files belong to somebody. They should be assumed to be private and confidential unless the owner has explicitly made them available to others.
- Messages sent to other users should always identify the sender.
- Network traffic should be considered private.
- Obscenities should not be sent by computer.
- Records relating to the use of computing and information resources are confidential.

Resources

- Nobody should deliberately attempt to degrade or disrupt system performance or to interfere with the work of others.
- Loopholes in computer systems or knowledge of a special password should not be used to alter computer systems, obtain extra resources, or take resources from another person.
- Computing equipment owned by departments or individuals should be used only with the owner's permission.
- University resources are provided for university purposes. Any use of computing for commercial purposes or personal financial gain must be authorized in advance. Many of the agreements that the university has specifically forbid this activity.
- Computing and information resources are community resources. Theft, mutilation, and abuse of these resources violate the nature and spirit of community and intellectual inquiry.

System Administration

- On rare occasions, computing staff may access others' files, but only when strictly necessary for the maintenance of a system.
- If a loophole is found in the security of any computer system, it should be reported to the system administrator and not used for personal gain or to disrupt the work of others.
- The distribution of programs and databases is controlled by the laws of copyright, licensing agreements, and trade secret laws. These must be observed.

This code of ethics lays down general guidelines for the use of computing and information resources. Failure to observe the code may lead to disciplinary action. Offenses that involve academic dishonesty will be considered particularly serious.

U.S. GOVERNMENT COMPUTER SYSTEM SECURITY STATEMENT

Use of this or any other DoD interest computer system constitutes a consent to monitoring at all times.

This is a DoD interest computer system. All DoD interest computer systems and related equipment are intended for the communication, transmission, processing, and storage of official U.S. Government or other authorized information only. All DoD interest computer systems are subject to monitoring at all times to ensure proper functioning of equipment and systems including security devices and systems, to prevent unauthorized use and violations of statutes and security regulations, to deter criminal activity, and for other similar purposes. Any user of a DoD interest computer system should be aware that any information placed in the system is subject to monitoring and is not subject to any expectation of privacy.

If monitoring of this or any other DoD interest computer system reveals possible evidence of violation of criminal statutes, this evidence and any other related information, including identification information about the user, may be provided to law enforcement officials. If monitoring of this or any other DoD interest computer systems reveals violations of security regulations or unauthorized use, employees who violate security regulations or make unauthorized use of DoD interest computer systems are subject to appropriate disciplinary action.

CYBERTOWN.COM

Rules and Terms for Chatting in Cybertown (1997)

Introduction

Cybertown is set in a future where people are not discriminated against on the basis of personal beliefs, sex, age or race and a future where people are not attacked for these things. The intention of Le Café is to provide an oasis for rationality, pleasant discourse and harmony rather than tirades and insults against those who disagree with your views. There are plenty of places on the old EarthNet you can go if you want to vent your spleen or degrade yourself by trying to degrade another. This is not one of them. Not to stifle your communication, but let's make this a *fun* place

---

to hang out. There was enough misery and conflict on pre-21st century Earth. After all, this is why many of us left Earth in the first place!

The *public* (as opposed to the private) chat rooms are *NOT* sex-chat rooms. There are at least four reasons for this:

1. Le Café is part of a family-oriented town that includes young children among its visitors
2. It would violate our Charter with our Earth service providers to allow sexually-explicit chat here
3. It's not fair to those who come here for pleasant chat with friends
4. There are plenty of places you can go on the Net if you feel compelled to publicly indulge in sexually-explicit chat

NOTE: THESE RULES APPLY TO THE PUBLIC ROOMS—what you do in the private rooms is your own business—what you do in the public rooms becomes everybody's business and the appropriate actions may be taken.

Terms and Conditions for Using These Rooms

1. You agree to refrain from using the Cybertown chat rooms for the following activities:
    a. Making statements that are grossly offensive including blatant expressions of bigotry, racism, hatred, or profanity
    b. Indulging in abusive, defamatory or harrassing behavior or insults or personal attacks or threats of harm to anyone or promoting physical harm or injury against any group or individual
    c. Promoting or providing instructional information about illegal activities. You also may not indulge in activities that infringe upon anyone else's copyright(s). Specifically, you cannot advocate illegal conduct or participate in illegal or fraudulent schemes. You can't use our chat rooms to distribute unauthorized copies of copyrighted material, including photos, artwork, text, recordings, designs or computer programs
    d. Engaging in sexually-explicit chat or nicknames that would generally be considered offensive in a public place
    e. Indulging in racial, ethnic, sexual, or religious slurs, disruptive behavior of any kind including statements that incite others to violate the rules, or making lewd comments
    f. Attempting to post or use of computer programs that contain destructive features, such as viruses, worms, Trojan horses, bots scripts and so on
    g. Excessive shouting (use of all caps) or flooding (continuous posting of repetitive text) in the chat areas

    h. Impersonation of or false representation of yourself as a Cybertown Sysop, staff member or Community Leader is prohibited

    i. We encourage communication between our community members but posting or transmitting of unauthorized or unsolicited advertising, promotional materials, or any other forms of solicitation to other users, in these chat rooms, except in those areas that may be designated for such a purpose are not allowed

When in doubt about appropriate behavior here, remember that Cybertown is an electronic world, but the people here are real. So, just as when you join any gathering of people, we ask that you treat others with respect and with care.

2. Neither Cybertown nor its access providers are responsible for the content of these chat rooms. That responsibility lies solely with the people using the rooms since they are the ones creating the content. The opinions and views expressed in these chat rooms do not necessarily reflect those of Cybertown or its access providers.

3. Due to legal requirements neither the owners of Cybertown nor its access providers monitor these chat rooms, but the community itself, in the interests of fostering positive community spirit, has decided what it will and won't accept in these rooms. By popular demand, obscenity filters have been added to the main rooms.

4. Chatters can be held legally liable for the contents of their speech, and may be held legally accountable if their speech includes, for example, defamatory comments.

5. You agree to indemnify and hold harmless Cybertown and its access providers for any loss, liability, claim, damage, and expenses (including reasonable attorney fees) arising from or in connection with the contents of your speech and your use of these chat rooms.

What Can You Do If Someone Is Violating the Rules for Using These Rooms?

Right now the software provides the following protections for you:

1. You can choose any user(s) to ignore and thus not see their communication or

2. You can refuse private messages or

3. You can instantly create a private room into which they cannot enter or

4. You can contact a Community Leader who is responsible for maintaining order (see list on next page) and they will gag the offender.

Tell them what the problem is, what room you're in, what day and time and if a person was bothering you, what his/her name is and any other details you feel are important.

If you are a kid or a teenager and someone asks to meet you, make a note of his name and IP address and make sure you tell your parents.

APPENDIX D
Further Resources
in Computer Ethics

Books (Monographs and Anthologies)

Baase, Sarah. *A Gift of Fire: Social, Legal, and Ethical Issues in Computing.* Prentice Hall, 1997.

Berleur, Jacques, and Klaus Brunnstein, eds. *Ethics of Computing—Codes, Spaces for Discussion and Law.* Chapman & Hall, 1996.

Brown, Geoffrey. *Information Game: Ethical Issues in a Microchip World.* Prometheus Books, 1990.

Bynum, Terrell Ward, and James Moor, eds. *Digital Phoenix.* Blackwell, 1998.

Dejoie, Roy, George Fowler, and David Paradice. *Ethical Issues in Information Systems.* Boyd & Fraser, 1991.

Edgar, Stacey L. *Morality and Machines: Perspectives on Computer Ethics.* Jones & Bartlett, 1996.

Ermann, M. David, Mary B. Williams, and Claudio Gutierrez, eds. *Computer, Ethics, and Society.* 2d ed. Oxford University Press, 1997.

Forester, Tom, and Perry Morrison. *Computer Ethics: Cautionary Tales and Ethical Dilemmas in Computer.* 2d ed. MIT Press, 1996.

Garson, G. David. *Computer Technology and Social Issues.* Idea Group, 1995.

Johnson, Deborah. *Computer Ethics.* 2d ed. Prentice Hall, 1994.

———, and Helen Nissenbaum, eds. *Computer, Ethics, and Social Values.* Prentice Hall, 1995.

Kizza, Joseph Migga. *Social and Ethical Effects of the Computer Revolution.* McFarland & Company, 1996.

———, D. Gries, and F. B. Schneider, eds. *Ethical and Social Issues in the Information Age.* Springer Verlag, 1997.

Kling, Rob, ed. *Computerization and Controversy: Value Conflicts and Social Choices.* Academic Press, 1995.

Koocher, Gerald P. *Ethics in Cyberspace.* Lawrence Erlbaum, 1996.

Langford, Duncan. *Practical Computer Ethics.* Books Britain, 1995.

Spinello, Richard. *Ethical Aspects of Information Technology.* Prentice Hall, 1997.

———. *Case Studies in Information and Computer Ethics.* Prentice Hall, 1997.

Stichler, Richard N., and Robert Hauptman, eds. *Ethics, Information and Technology: Readings.* McFarland, 1998.

Weckert, John, and Douglas Adeney. *Computer and Information Ethics.* Greenwood Press, 1997.

Journals

American Philosophical Association Newsletter on Philosophy and Computers
Communications of the ACM
Computers and Society
Computers in Human Behavior
Ethics and Information Technology
Journal of Business Ethics
Inter@active Week
Metaphilosophy
Philosophy and Computers
Science and Engineering Ethics

Web Resources (Subject to Frequent Change)

Australian Institute of Computer Ethics (AICE): *http://www.aice.swin.edu.au/*
Bibliography on Computer Ethics (Virginia Tech). *http://courses.cs.vt.edu/~cs3604/ lib/Bibliography/Biblio.acm.html*
Computer and Information Ethics Resources on the WWW (Univ. of British Columbia): *http://www.ethics.ubc.ca/resources/computer/*
Computer Ethics Institute (The Brookings Institute): http://www.brook.edu/its/cei/ cei_hp.htm#FIN_INKIND_SUP
Computer Ethics Resources (University of Texas): *http://www.cs.utexas.edu/users/ ethics/comp_main.html*
Electronic Frontier Foundation: *http://www.eff.net/*
Ethics on the World Wide Web (California State University, Fullerton): *http: //commfaculty.fullerton.edu/lester/ethics/computer.html*
Information Systems Ethics (ISWorld Net): *http://www.siu.edu/departments/ coba/mgmt/iswnet/isethics/*